J. A Graft, Cincinnati Company

J. A. Graft & co.'s Legal Directory

lawyers, merchants and all business men, containing a synopsis of the collection laws.

J. A Graft, Cincinnati Company

J. A. Graft & co.'s Legal Directory
lawyers, merchants and all business men, containing a synopsis of the collection laws.

ISBN/EAN: 9783337815837

Printed in Europe, USA, Canada, Australia, Japan

Cover: Foto ©Andreas Hilbeck / pixelio.de

More available books at **www.hansebooks.com**

ELEVENTH YEAR—JANUARY, 1886.

J. A. GRAFT & CO.'S

LEGAL DIRECTORY

1886

For Lawyers, Merchants and all Business Men,

CONTAINING

A SYNOPSIS OF THE COLLECTION LAWS OF EACH STATE, TERRITORY AND CANADA, ALSO FORMS ADAPTED TO THE LAWS OF EACH STATE.

The Address of One of the Leading and Most Reliable Attorneys in Over Five Thousand Cities and Towns in the United States, Canada and Europe.

ALSO, THE POPULATION OF THE DIFFERENT CITIES AND TOWNS IN THE UNITED STATES AND CANADA.

COMPILED AND PUBLISHED BY

J. A. GRAFT & CO.

No. 319 BROADWAY,
NEW YORK.

NOS. 73, 74 & 75 JOHNSTON BUILDING,
CINCINNATI.

PREFACE.

Mercantile Associations have become of such great importance to, and an absolute necessity of, the business community, for the proper protection of its financial interest, that we do not consider it necessary to enlarge on their usefulness. This is an Association of Attorneys for mutual aid in the collection of claims and the transaction of legal business. Its organization was begun in 1875, and its present enviable position as one of the best MERCANTILE AGENCIES is owing mainly to the promptness and fidelity with which its numerous correspondents have discharged their duties to one another, and to its extensive mercantile clientage.

The annual volume of the LEGAL DIRECTORY is presented to the public, greatly enlarged and improved, containing many new features. It will be found to be a reliable guide for Attorneys and all Business Men in transacting legal business, collection of claims, etc., by furnishing a list of reliable and trustworthy Attorneys, to whom all legal business, collections, etc., may be intrusted, and assured prompt attention. In addition to our list of reliable Attorneys, we also furnish a complete digest of the Collection Laws, etc., of each State, Territory and Canada, compiled especially for us by our correspondents; also, the Population of each City and Town; this information has been carefully obtained and compiled, and will be found to be very useful.

For the use of members of the Association desiring to transact secret business by telegraph, such as obtaining reports, etc., we have given a system of CIPHER TELEGRAPH.

We call especial attention to the fact that we are the only firm in the United States publishing a full list of English Lawyers, and we are prepared to attend to any legal business anywhere in Great Britain and Ireland.

The list of Attorneys is compiled from correspondence with Banks or Bankers and the leading business men throughout the country, and can be relied upon as being accurate in every particular.

We shall consider it a personal favor if those discovering any errors, etc., in the Directory, will notify us of them, so that we can make corrections for our future editions. Any further information desired by our patrons, which we can furnish, will be cheerfully given.

We shall continue the quarterly issue of the Directory.

J. A. GRAFT & CO.

TELEGRAPH CODE

—OF—

J. A. GRAFT & CO.'S

LEGAL DIRECTORY, REPORTING AND COLLECTION AGENCY.

Give the name of the person or firm and then add the words in the key that will express the desired question or answer.

AMOUNT KEY.

Ash	$ 25	Spruce	$1,300	Danger	$ 9,000	Nymph	$ 70,000
Box	50	Walnut	1,400	Dark	10,000	Ocean	75,000
Board	100	Willow	1,500	Day	15,000	Patriot	80,000
Cherry	200	Watch	1,600	Editor	20,000	Quack	85,000
Cedar	300	Artic	1,700	Expose	25,000	Ruby	90,000
Chestnut	400	Brown	1,800	Field	30,000	Sky	95,000
Ebony	500	Bed	1,900	Gem	35,000	Tiger	100,000
Elm	600	Barn	2,000	Hawk	40,000	Union	150,000
Hickory	700	Bear	3,000	Invalid	45,000	Venus	200,000
Larch	800	Capitol	4,000	Jail	50,000	Wild	250,000
Maple	900	Cannon	5,000	King	55,000	Xenia	300,000
Plank	1,000	Canoe	6,000	Legal	60,000	Yatch	400,000
Park	1,100	Cave	7,000	Mask	65,000	Zone	500,000
Rosewood	1,200	Daisy	8,000				

QUESTIONS.

Ajar—Are there any mortgages on real estate?
Basket—Any liens on stock or other personal?
Blonde—Send us full detailed report by return mail.
Corn—Is his credit good at home?
Duke—What is he supposed to be worth?
Elk—Value of personal property and stock.
Fort—Is he in any financial trouble?
Fish—Are his habits and character good?
Globe—Has he ever failed, or compromised or asked an extension?
Honest—Cash value of his real estate.
Inn—Does he pay promptly?
Jig—Answer by telegraph at our expense.
Kill—Is his indebtedness heavy?
Lion—Does he own any real estate?
Moon—Is real estate in his own name?

ANSWERS.

Bell—Supposed to be worth $ (use amount key).
Brig—Meets all debts promptly.
Coin—Has failed.
Cork—Slow pay generally.
Copper—Asking an extension.
Dock—Character and habits good.
Doom—Claims can not be collected.
Drum—Real estate is mortgaged for $.
Excel—Chattel mortgage on stock for $.
Elf—Credit not good at home
Knob—Is offering to compromise.
Lash—Very little in debt.
Lay—Has compromised.
Lynx—Real estate is not mortgaged.
May—Heavily in debt.
Moss—Not in any financial trouble.
Modoc—Has assigned and failed.
Muff—Is fully insured.
Mill—Temporarily embarrassed.
Fertile—Has judgments against him.
Fork—Real estate in wife's name worth $
Gay—Never failed or compromised.
Gain—Business capacity, character, etc., bad.
Gall—Unworthy of credit.
Index—Suits are pending against him.
Icy—Selling at a sacrifice.
Idol—Doing a safe business.
Jaw—Claims can be collected by suit.
Kind—Indebtedness supposed to be $.
Novel—Real estate in wife's name.
Navy—Loosing money.
Nail—Credit good at home.
Oak—Stock and personal property worth $
Oar—Real estate valued at $.
Pecan—Not considered good for that amount.
Rebus—Is not insured.
Scoff—Considered good for that amount,
Title—Stock and personal not mortgaged.

TIME KEY.

Arab, 30 days; **Bay**, 60 days; **Cubit**, 90 days; **Duty**, 4 months; **Echo**, 6 months **Foe**, 1 year.

EXAMPLE—To Conely, Maybury & Lucking, Attorneys, Detroit, Mich:

J. P. Durham & Co., Dry Goods, Detroit: Fort—Globe—Basket—Elk—Inn—Jig.

Reads thus: J. P. Durham & Co., Dry Goods, Detroit: Is he in any financial trouble? Has he ever failed or compromised? Any liens on stock or other personal? Value of personal property and stock? Does he pay promptly? Answer by telegraph at our expense.

REPLY: Moss—Gay—Title—Oak—Day—Brig.

Reads thus: Not in any financial trouble; never failed or compromised; stock and personal not mortgaged; stock and personal worth $15,000; meets all debts promptly.

Rates of Collection.

On all sums not exceeding $100.............................								10 per cent.
" " "	exceeding $100,	not exc'g	$500,	on excess	over	$100,	8	"
" " "	"	500, "	" 1,000,	"	"	" 100,	6	"
" " "	"	1,000 "	" 2,000,	"	"	" 100,	5	"
" " "	"	2,000 "	" 3,000,	"	"	" 200,	4	"
" " "	"	3,000..............		"	"	" 300,	2½	"

Where defense in a suit is made, or an important opinion is given, the fees will be the same as the Attorneys usually charge their local clients for like services.

A charge of $2.00 is the lowest collection fee in any case.

No charge, however, unless collection is made.

No suit to be brought by Attorneys, unless ordered so to do, and costs advanced by subscriber, and when claims are put in judgment for future attention, the Attorney's fees must be agreed upon between the client and the Attorney.

Attorneys receiving claims direct from other Attorneys of this Agency may, upon collection, retain two-thirds of the collection fee, one-third being due the Attorney from whom claim was received, and to whom proceeds and fees should be remitted at once.

Claims settled by clients subject to the above rates.

Charges of examination of records at the usual rates for such service. All collections subject to aboverates. Except in the state of Mississippi, where rates are fixed by Bar Associations.

NOTICE.

Parties corresponding with Attorneys named in the Directory should *always* sign themselves "Subscribers to J. A. Graft & Co.'s Legal Directory." Should any Attorney fail to give prompt attention to correspondence, collections, or business intrusted to his care, we will be thankful to patrons of the Directory to notify us promptly in any such case.

INDEX.

APPENDIX—Attorneys' Cards.

LAWS OF ALABAMA

RELATIVE TO THE

COLLECTION OF DEBTS, Etc.

Prepared expressly for J. A. Graft & Co.'s Legal Directory.

ASSIGNMENTS.—1. Assignments, verbal or written, of any property, made in trust for the use of the person making the same, are void as to existing or subsequent creditors.

2. All conveyances, verbal or written, of any property made with intent to hinder, delay or defraud creditors, purchasers or other persons, or judgments suffered with like intent, are void as to the persons hindered or delayed.

3. Every deed, mortgage, *assignment*, or deed of trust made to secure a pre-existing debt is fraudulent and void as to the creditors of the grantor, when any creditor provided for thereby is required to make any release, or to do any other act impairing his existing rights before participating in or receiving the securities therein provided for him.

4. A debtor in failing circumstances may prefer one or more of his creditors in the payment of their demands, when it is done *bona fide*, and the sale of property for such purposes is for an adequate consideration; but when a *general* assignment is made no such preference can be given.

ACTIONS UPON ACCOUNTS.—Whenever action is brought on an account, if the plaintiff file with the complaint an *itemized statement of the articles constituting the account* and the charges made therefor, verified by an affidavit, made before an officer *authorized by the laws of this State* to take affidavits, that the account is true and correct, due and unpaid (state when it was due,) on the trial of said cause the account so verified shall be received in evidence, as if the same was proved by the deposition of the witness, unless within the time allowed by law for pleading, the defendant shall appear and file an affidavit, *denying*, to the best of his knowledge, information and belief, the correctness of the account, or that he is liable for the amount due therein.

(Affidavits under this law, when made out of the State of Alabama, should be made before a Commissioner for Alabama only).

ATTACHMENTS AT LAW.—Attachments may issue,

1. To enforce the collection of a debt, whether it be due or not, at the time the attachment is taken out.

2. For any monied demand, the amount of which can be certainly ascertained.

3. To recover damages for the breach of contract when the damages are not certain or liquidated.

4. When the action sounds in damages merely.

No attachment must issue unless the plaintiff (his agent or attorney for him) execute bond in double the amount claimed to be due, with surety payable to defendant, with condition that plaintiff will prosecute his attachment to effect, and pay the defendant all such costs and damages as he may sustain by the wrongful or vexatious suing out of the attachment.

The plaintiff, his agent or attorney, must also make affidavit of the existence of one of the following grounds of attachment, to-wit: That the defendant resides out of the State; that defendant absconds; that defendant secretes himself so that the ordinary process of law can not be served on him; that the defendant is about to remove out of the State; that the defendant is about to remove his property out of the State, so that plaintiff will probably lose his debt, or will have to sue for it in another State; that the defendant is about fraudulently to dispose of his property; that the defendant has fraudulently disposed of his property; or that the defendant has money, property or effects liable to satisfy his debts which he fraudulently withholds.

Defendant can not deny the grounds of attachment in the attachment suit, but may bring suit at any time on the attachment bond for wrongfully suing out the attachment, after the attachment has issued, and within time prescribed by statute of limitations.

COLLECTIONS. ACTIONS.—All civil actions commenced by summons and complaint, a copy of which must be served on the defendant. When the summons is served twenty days before the return term thereof the cause must stand for trial at the first term of said court

EXEMPTIONS.—1. Personal property of any *resident* of this State to the value of one thousand dollars, to be selected by such resident, is exempt from sale under legal process or any *debt contracted*.

2. The homestead of every *resident* of this State, not exceeding one hundred and sixty acres of land, to be selected by the owner thereof, and not in any city, town or village, and not exceeding two thousand dollars in value, and the appurtenances thereon owned and *occupied* by such resident; or, in lieu thereof, any lot with the appurtenances, in a city, town or village, not exceeding in value two thousand dollars, owned and occupied by such resident. If the same can not be allotted, then two thousand dollars of the value thereof shall be exempt from levy and sale for the collection of *debts contracted*.

As to executions on judgments founded on torts there is no exemption.

GENERAL ASSIGNMENTS.–1 General assignments do not absolve debtors from their liabilities.

2. Every *general assignment* made by a debtor, by which a preference or priority of payment is given to one or more creditors, shall be an enure to the benefit of *all* the creditors equally.

INSOLVENT LAWS.—There are no insolvent laws in this State by which debtors can be relieved of their debts. No imprisonment for debt in this State.

Two terms of the Circuit Court in each county annually.

INTEREST.—The legal rate of interest is 8 per cent., whether by contract or otherwise. In suits on usurious contracts, the principal only is collectable, and if upon the trial it is made to appear that the contract was intentionally usurious, the defendant recovers full cost.

JUDGMENTS AND EXECUTIONS.—Execution issues within fifteen days after the adjournment of the court at which judgment was rendered, and is a lien on the real and personal property of defendant, within the county in which it is received by the Sheriff, and only from the time it is so received, which lien continues as long as the execution is regularly issued and delivered to the sheriff, without the lapse of an entire term.

LIMITANION OF ACTIONS—CIVIL.—1. Actions upon a judgment or decree of any court of the State, of the United States, or any State or Territory of the United States, must be brought within twenty years.

2. Actions founded upon any contract or writing under seal; actions for the recovery of land, tenements or the possession thereof; motions and other actions against Sheriffs or other public officers, for non-feasance, misfeasance, or malfeasance in office, must be brought within ten years.

3. Actions for trespass to real or personal property; actions for the detention or conversion of personal property; actions founded on a promise in writing not under seal; actions for recovery of money on loan or stated account; motions and other actions against attorneys-at-law, for failing to pay over money of their clients, or for neglect or omission of duty; and all other actions arising from a simple contract or specialty, must be *brought within* six years.

4. Actions to recover money due by open or unliquidated account must be brought within three years from the date of the last item of said account, or within three years from the time when, by usage or custom, the said account shall be due.

ALABAMA FORMS.

[Form 1—AFFIDAVIT FOR PROVING OPEN ACCOUNT.]

Before me (name and style of officer), personally appears ——, who being duly sworn on oath, says that the foregoing account is just and true, correct and unpaid.
Sworn to and Subscribed before me, —— date. (*Signature of Affiant.*)
(*Officer's signature.*)

[Form 2—ACKNOWLEDGMENT OF DEED].

STATE OF ——, } ss,
County of ——, }

I, (name and style of officer) hereby certify that —— and ——, his wife, who are known to me, acknowledged before me this day that, being informed of the contents of the foregoing conveyance, they executed the same, voluntarily, on the day the same bears date.

Given under my hand this —— day of ——, A, D. 18—.

(*Signature and title of officer.*)

[Form 3—DEED].

STATE OF ——, } ss.
County of ——, }

I ——, of ——, in consideration of ——, paid in hand by —— of ——; receipt whereof is hereby acknowledged, do grant, bargain, sell and convey to ——. (Here insert full description of property.)

To have and to hold the above granted real estate to said ——, and his heirs in fee simple forever. And I do covenant that the same are free of all encumbrance, and that I will warrant and defend title herein conveyed, against lawful claims of all persons whatever.

In Testimony Whereof, I have set my hand and seal, this —— day of ——, 18—. [L. S.]

Attested by two witnesses, or acknowledged as in form. See title Acknowledgment, and see title Deeds.

[Form 4—INSTRUCTIONS AND FORMS FOR TAKING DEPOSITIONS].

No particular form of notice is required. Any proper writing, signed by counsel, requiring notice of time and place of taking. This applies to the practice generally in use, in relation to notice, counsel using their own phraseology to inform the other side of any desired fact.

CAPTION.

Deposition of ——, a witness sworn and examined under and by virtue of a commission issued out of the —— Court for —— County, State of Alabama, in a certain cause therein depending, wherein —— is plaintiff, and —— defendant. And the said ——, the witness named in said commission, being first duly sworn to speak the truth, the whole truth, and nothing but the truth, doth depose and say as follows:

To the first interrogatory he saith:

To the second interrogatory he saith;

To the first cross-interrogatory he saith:

When finished witness signs and certificate of Commissioner is added.

CERTIFICATE TO DEPOSITIONS.

I, the Commissionhr named in said Commission, hereby certify that I caused to come before me, at, ——, the witness, ——; that he was duly sworn and examined, and that his evidence was taken down, as near as may be, in his own language; that it was read over to him and subscribed by him in my presence; that I have personal knowledge of the identy of said witness (or proof of his identity has been made), and that he is the person named in said interrogatories and commission annexed, and that I am not of counsel or kin to any of the parties to the cause, or in any manner interested in the result of the same. As witness my hand and seal, this —— day of ——, A. D., 188—.

——————, Commissioner.

Deposition is then sealed with three seals, and Commissioner writes his name on each of these seals. Not only forms, but printed instructions accompany all commissions issued from the Courts of Alabama.

[Form 5—WILLS].

THE STATE OF——, } ss.
County of——,

I ——, of the County of ——, and State of ——, being of a sound and disposing mind and memory, do make, publish, and declare this my last Will and Testament.

Clause 1. I will and bequeath, &c. Clause 2. I will and bequeath, &c.

In Testimony Whereof, I have hereunto set my hand and affixed my seal, on this the —— day of ——, A. D., 188—.

Signed, sealed, published and delivered, as last Will and Testament, in presence of } ——. [L. S.]

—— ——
—— —— } Two witnesses required.

[Form 6—PROBATE OF WILL].

THE STATE OF——, } ss.
County of——,

I ——, (name and style of officer), hereby certify that ——, one of the subscribing witnesses to the foregoing last Will and Testament of ——, and who is known to me, appeared before me this day, and being duly sworn, stated, on oath, that ——, the testator, signed, sealed and published the foregoing as his last Will and Testament, in his presence and in the presence of ——, the other subscribing witness, on the day the same bears date, that he and the other subscribing witness attested the same, as witnesses, in the presence of each other and in the presence of the testator, ——; and that the said —— aforesaid was at said time of a sound and disposing mind and memory.

Given Under My Hand, This —— day of ——, 188—. *(Signature of Officer.)*

LAWS OF ARIZONA TERRITORY

RELATIVE TO THE

COLLECTION OF DEBTS, Etc.

Prepared expressly for J. A. Graft & Co.'s Legal Directory, by John J. Hawkins, of the Prescott Bar.

Laws relative to arrest on civil process, attachments, executions, exemption of real and personal property, homesteads, garnishment, interest, judgments and limitations of actions, are similar to those of California, except that the law does not provide for any declaration of homestead. The character of homestead is acquired by actual residence.

NO INSOLVENT LAWS IN ARIZONA.

CHATTEL MORTGAGES—May be given on all property and furniture in hotels and public boarding houses, when given to secure purchase price; on saw mill, grist mill and steamboat machinery, tools and machinery used by machinists, foundrymen and other mechanics; steam boilers, steam engines, locomotives, engines and rolling stock of railroads, printing presses, instruments and chests of surgeons, physicians and dentists, libraries of all persons, machinery and apparatus for mining purposes, growing crops, grain in store and field, teams, implements and stock on farm, provided the mortgage be executed and recorded in the manner prescribed by the act; and declares that no chattel mortgage shall be valid (except between the parties thereto) unless the same shall have been made, executed and recorded in conformity to the provisions of the act; provided, however, that if the mortgagee receives and retains actual possession of the property mortgaged, he may omit the recording of his mortgage.

MORTGAGES—On real estate must be executed and recorded like deeds, and the remedy for enforcing them is by civil action.

After sale, under decree of foreclosure, the mortgagee has six months to redeem, by paying amount of bid and 18 per cent. thereon, and such taxes as may have been paid by the purchaser.

Satisfaction may be entered in the margin of the record book, and signed and acknowledged by the mortgagee in presence of the recorder, or it may be by a separate instrument executed and recorded in the same manner as the mortgage.—Comp. Laws, 1877, §§ 2281-3.

Refusal or neglect to execute and acknowledge a certificate of discharge of a mortgage, after performance of the conditions thereof for seven days, and after being requested, and after tender of his reasonable charges, makes the mortgagee liable to the mortgagor for one hundred dollars, and for actual damages occasioned by such refusal or neglect. (*See Chattel Mortgages.*

NOTES AND BILLS—Are negotiable obligations, collectible by and in the name of the holder. Three days' grace are allowed, except on sight drafts, and any one of the holidays specified in the statute coming within said three days' grace shall be counted as one of such days. The days specified are the 1st of January, the 4th of July, the 25th of December, commonly called Christmas, and the first day of the week, commonly called Sunday, and no presentment for payment of any note or bill or other negotiable instrument shall be made on either of said days.

[For Legal Forms adapted to the Laws of Arizona, see Forms at end of California, published in this work.]

LAWS OF ARKANSAS

RELATIVE TO THE

COLLECTION OF DEBTS, Etc.

Prepared expressly for J. A. Graft & Co.'s Legal Directory, by Coleman and Yancey, Attorneys at Law, Batesville, Ark.

ACTIONS.—Suits in the Circuit Court are commenced by filing a complaint, signed by the party or his attorney, verified by affidavit in Justice Court; no written pleadings are necessary—the account or note sued on must be filed. The defendent is required to answer in the Circuit Court, on the day which the case is set for trial. In Common Law actions, where the summons has been served ten days in the county where the action is brought, or in an adjoining county, or twenty days elsewhere in the State, or sixty days out of the State. In justice Court the answer must be filed on the day on which the case is set for trial. If the summons has been served five days previous thereto, where the amount in controversy does not exceed fifty dollars; or where the amount in controversy exceeds fifty dollars, where the summons has been served ten days previous thereto. Gnatt's Digest, Sections 3726 and 4582.

APPEALS.—Appeals can be taken from a judgment of a Justice of the Peace within thirty days from the rendering of the judgment. Appeals from the Circuit Court may be taken at any time within three years from the rendering of judgment. Appeals from the Probate Court to the Circuit Court may be taken at any time within one year from the rendition of the judgment, and from the County Court to the Circuit Court at the term at which judgment is rendered, or at the next regular term. Gnatt's Digest. Sections 3819, 3821, 1066 and 705 and Acts 1874-5, Page 268.

ASSIGNMENTS.—Assignments for the benefit of creditors, are authorized, before the assignee can do anything towards the execution of the assignment, he must, in the office of the Probate Clerk, file a complete inventory and discription of the property, and execute a bond to the State, in double the value of the property assigned, conditioned to faithfully perform the trust, dispose of property to the best advantage, and pay the proceeds to the creditors named in the assignment, and perform his duties faithfully as required by law.

CHATTLE MORTGAGES.—Chattle Mortgages become liens from time of filing—if not recorded, the lien expires in twelve months, unless the mortgagee or his agent shall, thirty days before the expiration of the year, file an affidavit, showing the interest the mortgagee has in the property, and the amount yet due on same.—Acts 1877, Page 80.

CLAIMS AGAINST ESTATES.—Claims must be presented within two years from the grant of letters of administration; if not so presented, are barred. Claims are paid in the following order: First, funeral expenses; Second, expenses of last sickness, wages of servants, and demands for medicines and medical attendance during last sickness; Third, judgments rendered against the deceased in his life-time, and which are liens on the lands of the deceased, if he died possessed of any, otherwise to be regarded as debts due by contract.

DEPOSITIONS.—Depositions used in the following cases: First, where the witness does not reside in the county where the action is pending or in an adjoining county, or is absent from the State, or is in the Military service; second, where the witness is unable from infirmity to attend court; third, where the witness resides thirty or more miles from the Court where the action is pending; fourth, where the witness is a State Officer, a Practicing Attorney, or doctor, keeper or guard of the penitentiary, or Judge or Clerk of a Court. Depositions are out or in the State upon notice or commission and interrogations. The notice must be signed by the party giving it or his attorney, addressed to the party on whom it is to be served, and specify the time and place of taking the deposition, and the action or proceeding in which it is to be used. Notice may be served as a summons. One day's notice must be given for each thirty miles to be traveled, and one day for preparation where the distance is less than one hundred miles, and two days where it is more.

EVIDENCE.—Husband and wife for or against each other persons, convicted of any capital or infamous crime without the consent of both parties to the suit, and infants under ten years old cannot testify. Gnatt's Digest, Section 2482.

Affidavits may be read to verify a pleading, to prove the service of a summons, notice, or other process; to obtain a provisional remedy, a stay of proceedings, a warning order, or in support of a motion. Gnatt's Digest, Section 2536.

Witnesses are not excluded on account of interest.Either or both parties may testify in a suit.—Constitution 1874, Sec. 2.

No imprisonment for debt except in cases of fraud.—Constitution of 1874, Article II, Section 16.

EXEMPTION.—The personal property of any resident of this State, who is not married or the head of a family, to be selected by such resident, not exceeding in value the sum of two hundred dollars, in addition to his or her wearing apparel, shall be exempt from seizure on attachment or sale on execution, or other process from any court, issued for the collection of any debt by contract. Provided that no property shall be exempt from execution for debts contracted for the purchase money therefor, while on the hands of the vender.

The personal property of any resident of this State, who is married or the head of a family, to be selected by such resident, not exceeding in value the sum of five hundred dollars, in addition to his or her wearing apparel, and that of his or her family, shall be exempt from seizure on attachments, or sale on execution, or other process from any court, on debt by contract.

The homestead of any resident of this State, who is married or the head of a family, shall not be subject to the lien of any judgment or decree of any court, or to sale under execution, or other process thereon, except such as may be rendered for the purchase money, or for specific liens, laborers, or mechanics' liens, for improving the same, or for taxes, or against administrators, guardians, receivers, attorneys, for moneys collected by them, and other trustees of an express trust, for moneys due from them in their fiduciary capacity. The homestead outside of any city, town, or village, owned and occupied as a residence, shall consist of not exceeding one hundred and sixty acres of land, with improvements thereon, to be selected by the owner. Provided the same shall not exceed the sum of twenty-five hundred dollars, and in no event shall the homestead be reduced to less than eighty acres, without regard to value.

The homestead in any town, city or village, owned and occupied as a residence, shall consist of not exceeding one acre of land, with the improvements thereon, to be selected by the owner, provided the same shall not exceed in value the sum of twenty-five hundred dollars, and in no event shall such homestead be reduced to less than one-quarter of an acre of land, without regard to value.

If the owner of a homestead die, leaving a widow, but no children, and said widow has no separate homestead in her own right, the same shall be exempt, and the rents and profits shall vest on her during her natural life. Provided that if the owner leaves children, one or more, said child or children shall share with said widow, and be entitled to one-half of the rents and profits till each of them arrive at twenty-one years of age, each child's rights to cease at twenty-one years of age, and the shares to go to the younger children, and then all to go to the widow, and provided that said widow or children may reside on said homestead or not. And in case of the death of the widow all of said homestead shall be vested in the minor children of the testator or intestate.—Constitution 1874, Article IX, Sections 1, 2, 3, 4, 5, 6.

INTEREST.—All contracts for a greater interest than ten per centum per annum as to principal and interest shall be void, and the General Assembly shall prohibit the same by law; but when no rate of interest shall be agreed upon, the rate shall be six per cent. per annum.—Article XIX, Section 13, Constitution.

LIMITATION.—All actions of debt founded on contract or liability, not in writing; all actions of account and the like, founded on any contract, express or implied; all actions for injuring goods or chattels must be brought within three years from the time the cause of action accrued. Actions on promissory notes and other instruments must be commenced in five years after the cause of action accrued. Actions on judgments and decrees must be brought within ten years after right of action accrued. A right of action which has been barred may be revived by part payment or a new promise in writing. Limitation of actions for the recovery of real estate, seven years, saving in favor of married women, infants, and insane persons, two years after these disabilities are removed, and this clause applies to all periods of limitation of actions.—Gnatt's Digest, title limitation.

MARRIED WOMEN.—The real and personal property of any *femme covert* in this State, acquired either before or after marriage, whether by gift, grant, inheritance, devise, or otherwise, shall, so long as she may choose, be and remain her separate estate and property, and may be devised, bequeathed and conveyed by her the same as if she was a *femme sole*, and the same shall not be subject to the debts of her husband.—Constitution, Article IX, Section 7.

The widow is entitled, absolutely entitled, to one-third of the personal property of which her husband has seized, and one-third of the realty during her life. If the husband dies leaving no children, she is entitled to one-half interest in the lands for her life, and one-half of the personalty absolutely.—Gnatt's Digest, chapter 44.

MORTGAGFS.—Mortgages must be acknowledged same as deeds—no lien by reason of title filed for record; but good between the parties. Sales of chattels render on credit of three months—really on credit of not less than three nor more than six months. Property, except for the purchase money, must bring two-thirds of its appraised value; or, if it does not, personalty cannot again be offered in less than sixty days and in one year.

NOTES AND BILLS OF EXCHANGE—Are not changed by the code, and are governed, as heretofore, by the law merchant.

PRACTICE.—Common law forms of actions are abolished, and a code of practice adopted similar to the Kentucky code of practice.

PROOF OF CLAIMS.—In suits on accounts, the affidavit of the plaintiff that the account is just and correct, is sufficient to establish the same, unless the defendant, under oath, shall deny the correctness of the account, either in whole or in part, in which case the plaintiff shall be held such part of his account as is denied by other evidence.—Gnatt's Digest, section 2,537.

Non-resident plaintiffs must, in all cases, give bond for security of costs.

Sealed and Unsealed Instruments.—All distinctions between abolished by Constitution, schedule, section one (1).

Redemption.—Real estate or any interest therein, when sold under execution or decree, may be redeemed by the debtor from the purchaser or his vendees, within twelve months after the sale, by paying to the Clerk of the Court where the execution issued, the purchase money with fifteen per cent. per annum. The Sheriff gives the purchaser a certificate of sale, but the purchaser is not entitled to a conveyance or possession of the premises until the time for redeeming has expired.—Gnatt's Digest, section 2,696.

The following are the grounds of attachment: First. In an action for the recovery of money where the action is against:

1. A defendant, or several defendants, who, or some one of whom is a foreign corporation or a non-resident of the State, or
2. Who has been absent therefrom four months, or
3. Has departed the State, with intent to defraud his creditors, or
4. Has left the county of his residence to avoid the service of a summons, or
5. So conceals himself that a summons can not be served on him, or
6. Is about to remove, or has removed his property, or a material part thereof, out of this State, not leaving enough therein to satisfy the plaintiff's claim, or the claim of said defendant's creditors, or
7. Has sold, conveyed, or otherwise disposed of his property, or suffered, or permitted it to be sold with the fraudulent intent to hinder, cheat, or delay his creditors, or
8. Is about to sell, convey, or otherwise dispose of his property with such intent.—Civil Code, pages 75 and 76. sections 1–8.

ARKANSAS FORMS.

[Form 1.--AFFIDAVIT—To Account].

—— the plaintiff in the above entitled cause deposes and says that the annexed and foregoing account against —— is just and correct, and that no part of the same has been paid, except as credited thereon, and that there is still due and unpaid the sum of —— dollars.

Subscribed and sworn to before me this —— day of —— 18—.

[*Signature.*]

[Form 1a—CLAIM AGAINST ESTATE—Deceased Persons].

State of Arkansas, }
County of——, } ss.

I, —— do solemnly swear that nothing has been paid or delivered toward the satisfaction of the above demand, except what is credited thereon, and that the sum of —— dollars above demanded is justly due. [*Signature.*]

[Form 2—WARRANTY DEED].

WITH RELINQUISHMENT OF DOWER.

Know all Men by these Presents: That we —— and —— his wife for and in consideration of the sum of —— dollars, paid by ——, do hereby grant, bargain and sell unto the said ——, and unto —h— heirs and assigns forever, the following lands lying in the County of —— and State of Arkansas, to-wit: —— and we do hereby covenant with said —— that we will warrant the title to such lands against all claims whatever.

To have and to hold the same unto the said —— and unto —h— heirs and assigns forever, with all appurtenances thereto belonging. ——

And I, ——, wife of the said ——, for and in consideration of the said sum of money, do hereby release and relinquish unto the said —— all my right of dower in and to the said lands.

Witness our hands and seals on this ——day of ——, 188—.

[SEAL.]
[SEAL.]

ACKNOWLEDGMENT.

STATE OF ARKANSAS, }
County of——, } ss.

Be it Remembered, That on this day came before the undersigned, a —— within and for the County aforesaid, duly commissioned, and acting —— to me well known as the grantor in the foregoing Deed, and stated that he had execuetd the same for the consideration and purposes therein mentioned and set forth.

And on the same day also voluntarily appeared before me the said —— wife of the said ——, to me well known, and, in the absence of her said husband, declared that she had of her own free will, signed and sealed the relinquishment of Dower in the foregoing Deed, for the purposes therein contained and set forth, without compulsion or undue influence of her said husband.

Witness, My hand and seal as such —— on the —— day of ——, 188—

[*Signature.*]

CERTIFICATE OF RECORD.

STATE OF ARKANSAS, }
County of——, } ss.

I, ——, County Clerk and Ex-Officio Recorder for the County aforesaid, do hereby certify that the annexed and foregoing instrument of writing was filed for Record in my office on the —— day of ——, A. D. 188—, at —— o'clock —— M., and the same is now duly recorded, with the acknowledgments and certificates thereon, in "Record Book ——," page ——

In Witness Whereof, I have hereunto set my hand and affixed the seal of said Court, this —— day of ——, 188— [*Signature.*]

County Clerk and Ex-Officio Recorder.

[Form 3--AFFIDAVIT—For Attachment].

—— plaintiff states that the claim in this action against the defendant —— is for money due (here state nature of the claim) and that it is a just claim; that he ought, as he believes, to recover thereon —— dollars; and that said defendant has departed from this State with the intent to defraud his creditors (or state any other grounds.)

Sworn to before me this the —— day of ——, 188—

[Form 4 -OF BOND TO OBTAIN ATTACHMENT].

[Style of Case.]

We undertake that the plaintiff —— shall pay to the defendant —— (or defendants mentioning them) all damages which he may sustain by reason of this action if the order therefor is wrongfully obtained.

Attest,
—— *Clerk.*

[Form 5.—BOND OF DEFENDANT TO OBTAIN.]

DISCHARGE OF ATTACHMENT.

We undertake and are bound to the plaintiff —— in the sum of —— dollars, that the defendant shall perform the judgment of the Court in this action.

[Form 6.—FOR TAKING DEPOSITIONS.]

(Caption)

The deposition of ——, etc., taken on the —— day of ——, 18—, at the —— office, in the city or town of ——, County of ——, State of ——, and to be read as evidence in behalf of plaintiff (defendant) an action between ——, plaintiff, and ——, defendant, pending in the —— Court.

CERTIFICATE OF OFFICER.

STATE OF ARKANSAS, } ss.
County of——, }

I, ——, Notary Public for —— County, do hereby certify that the foregoing depositions of —— etc., were taken before me, and were read to and subscribed by them in my presence at the time and place, and the action mentioned in the caption, the said —— etc., having been first sworn by me that the evidence they should give in the action should be the truth, the whole truth, and nothing but the truth, and their statements reduced to writing, by me in their presence (*or by them in my presence*), the plaintiff alone being at the examination (*or the defendant, or both the plaintiff and defendant either in person or by attorney, or both,*)

Given under my hand, etc.

[Form 7.—NOTICES TO TAKE DEPOSITION.]

(Style of Case.)

To——

You are hereby notified that Depositions of witnesses to be read in evidence in the above entitled case on the part of the plaintiff, will be taken at the office of——, in the County of ——, State of Arkansas, on the —— day of ——, 18—, between the hour of 8 o'clock A. M. and 6 o'clock P. M., and that the taking of said depositions if not completed on that day, will be continued from day to day at the same place, and between the same hours, until completed.

[Form 9.--DEED OF TRUST.]

Know all Men by these Presents: That ——, for and in consideration of the sum of One Dollar to ——, in hand paid, and the premises hereinafter set forth, do hereby grant, bargain and sell unto —— and unto —— heirs and assigns forever, the following property: —— To hold the same in trust for ——.

This sale is on condition that whereas, ——, justly indebted unto said —— in the sum of ——Dollars, evidenced by ——,

Now, if —— shall pay said moneys at the times and in the manner aforesaid, then the above conveyance shall be null and void, else to remain in full force. And in case of non-payment, then the said grantee-- or —— assignee-- shall have power to sell such property at public sale, to the highest bidder for cash, at ——, in the —— of——, County of ——, and State of Arkansas, public notice of the time and place said sale having been first given —— days, by advertising in some newspaper published in said County, at which sale the said grantee-- or the creditor-- aforesaid for whose benefit this Deed is made, may bid and purchase as any third person might do, —— hereby warrant the title to said property against all claims, and authorize the said grantee— or to convey said property to any one purchasing at said sale, and to convey an absolute title thereto, and recitals of his Deed of Conveyance shall be taken as prima facie truth. And the proceeds of said sale shall be applied first, to payment of all costs and expenses attending said sale; second, to the payment of said debt and interest, and the remainder, if any, shall be paid to said grantor. And if at any time the Trustee to whom the conveyance is made shall be incapacitated from sickness, absence, death, or any other cause from carrying out the objects of this Trust, then said —— shall have a right to appoint a Trustee in his place by endorsement of such appointment on this Deed, which substituted Trustee shall have the same powers in every respect as are conceded to the grantee--in this Deed; and the endorsement aforesaid shall be prima facie evidence of the fact that a necessity has arisen for the appointment of such substituted Trustee under the provisions of this Deed.

Witness, —— hand— and seal-- on this —— day of ——, 188--. [SEAL.]
[SEAL.]

For form of Acknowledgment and Certificate of Record see form 2, Warranty Deed.

[Form 10--OPENING AND CLOSING FORM OF A WILL.]

Know all Men by these Presents, That I, —— of —— in the County of ——, State of ——, being of sound health. (or bad health) and of sound and disposing mind and memory, do make and publish this, my last will and testament, hereby revoking all former wills by me at any time heretofore made. (Here follows the body of the will.)

In Testimony Whereof, I hereunto set my hand and seal and publish and declare this to be my last will and testament, in the presence of the witnesses named below, this —— day of —— in the year 18--. Witnesses ——. [*Signature.*]

WITNESSES' ATTEST.

Signed, sealed, published and declared by said —— as for his last will and testament in the presence of us, who, in his presence and in the presence of each other, and at his request, have subscribed our names as witnesses thereto.

Witnesses ——. Attest.

[*Two witnesses required*]

LAWS OF CALIFORNIA

RELATIVE TO THE

COLLECTION OF DEBTS, Etc.

Prepared expressly for J. A. Graft & Co.'s Legal Directory, by Wm. H. H. Hart, Attorney and Counsellor-at-Law, San Francisco, Cal.

Actions—Commenced by filing complaint. Court always in session (legal holidays and non-judicial days excepted). Summons may issue by order of plaintiff at any time within one year after filing complaint. In the Superior Courts the defendant must answer within ten days after service, if served in same county. If served elsewhere, thirty days. Attachment may issue with summons, or any time thereafter, upon contracts, express or implied, if payable in the State and not secured; or if security is worthless or not responsible. Bonds must be given in the ordinary way in such cases, in the higher courts not less than $200, nor more than the amount claimed; in justices' courts not less than $100, nor more than the amount claimed.

Arrests.—A debtor may be arrested in the following cases: First, in an action for the recovery of money or damages on a cause of action arising upon a contract, express or implied, when the defendant is about to depart from the State with intent to defraud his creditors; second, in an action for a fine or penalty, or for money or property embezzled, or fraudulently misapplied or converted to his own use, by a public officer, or an officer of a corporation, or an attorney, factor, broker, agent or clerk, in the course of his employment as such, or by any other person in a judiciary capacity; or for misconduct or neglect in office or in a professional employment, or for a willful violation of duty; third, in an action to recover the possession of personal property unjustly detained, when the property or any part thereof has been concealed, removed or disposed of to persons, its being found or taken by the sheriff; fourth, when the defendant has been guilty of a fraud, in contracting a debt or incurring the obligations for which the action is brought, or in concealing or disposing of the property for the taking, detention, conversion of which the action was brought; fifth, when the defendant has removed or disposed of property, or is about to do so with intent to defraud his creditors. No female debtor or defendant can be arrested on civil process.

Assignments.—An insolvent debtor may execute an assignment to one or more assignees, in trust, for the satisfaction of all his creditors, as follows: By petition in writing, subscribed by the assignor, or his agent thereunto authorized by writing. It must be acknowledged, or proved and certified in the mode prescribed by law for recording transfer of real property and recorded according to law, assignee not to be regarded as a purchaser for value; within twenty days after assignment assignor must make and file a true inventory with the County Recorder, and annex thereto an affidavit that the same is true to the best of his knowledge and belief; assignee, within thirty days after assignment, must enter into a bond to the people of this State, in amount to be fixed by Judge, with sufficient sureties, and file same in office of County Recorder; assignee may be required to account after six months from date of assignment; property exempt and life insurance of assignor do not pass to assignee; assignee not held liable for acts done in good faith, because assignment is afterwards adjudged void; when assignment has once been executed and recorded it can not be afterwards cancelled or modified by the parties thereto, without the consent of every creditor effected thereby.

ATTACHMENTS—May issue at the time of issuing summons, or at any time afterward, in the following cases: First, upon a contract, express or implied, for the direct payment of money, when the contract is made payable in this State and is not recovered by any mortgage or lien, real or personal property, or any pledge of personal property, or if originally so secured such security has, without any act of the plaintiff, or the person to whom the security was given become valuless; second, upon a contract, express or implied, against a defendant not residing in the State.

BONDS FOR COSTS—Only required of non-residents, not exceeding $300.

COURTS.—Supreme Court always in session. Has originally an appellate jurisdiction power to issue writs of *mandamus*, *certiorari*, prohibition, *habeas corpus*, etc. Appellate jurisdiction in equity cases (except such as arise in justices' courts), in cases at law involving title or possession of realty or legality of tax, impost, assessment, toll, municipal fine, or where demand, exclusive of interest or value of property amounts to $300. In cases of forcible entry and detainer, insolvency, to prevent or abate nuisance, and in probate matters as provided by law, in special proceedings, criminal procedure in courts of record, on questions of law alone.

EXECUTIONS.—No stay; issues immediately after judgment; only delayed by appeal when bond is given.

EXEMPTIONS.—Office furniture in value $200. Necessary household and kitchen furniture, wearing apparel, beds and bedding, provisions for family use for ninety days; three cows and their calves; four hogs with their pigs, and food for one month; farming utensils, two horses, oxen or mules; all seed, grain and vegetable seed; tools and implements of a mechanic or artisan; instruments and chest of a surgeon, physician, surveyer or dentist, with their professional libraries; libraries of professional men and their instruments and office furniture; the cabin or dwelling of a miner to the value of $500, with all mining implements, two horses, mules or oxen, if necessary to be used with windlass, etc.; also his claim, not exceeding in value $1,000; two horses, mules or oxen, wagon, etc., by which teamster earns his living; one horse for physician or minister; poultry in value $25; thirty days' earnings of debtor preceding levy, if necessary to support family; if claim is for necessaries only one-half of wages is exempt; shares in homestead association, if incorporated under the laws of this State; all musical instruments, wearing apparel of master, officer or seaman, life insurance, annuities and lodge beneficiaries; homestead, not exceeding in value $5,000, except for purchase money.

INTEREST.—The legal rate is 7 per cent. after debt becomes due and until entre of judgment, but parties may agree upon any rate of interest whatever, simple or compound; a judgment bears interest from the entry, at the rate of 7 per cent. per annum.

INSOLVENCY.—Every insolvent debtor, upon compliance with the law may be discharged from his debts and liabilities, upon either a voluntary or involuntary petition to the Superior Court; the voluntary petition of debtor owing debts exceeding $300; may apply in the county where he has resided for six months next preceeding the filing of his petition; must state place of residence, his inability to pay his debts in full, his willingness to surrender all his estate and effects for the benefit of his creditors, and his desire to obtain his discharge from his debts and liabilities, and shall annex thereunto a schedule and inventory and valuation, the filing of which shall be an act of insolvency and thereupon such petitioner shall be adjudged an insolvent debtor. Petition, schedule and inventory must be verified by debtor on filing same; court shall make an order declaring the petitioner insolvent and direct Sheriff to take possession of the estate and keep same until assignee is appointed;

the clerk shall immediately publish a copy of said order, etc. In adjudication of involuntary insolvency may be made on the petition of five or more creditors, residents of this State, whose demands accrued in this State, and amount in the aggregate to not less than $500, and must be verified by at least three petitioners, in substance about the same as United States bankruptcy; same must be accompanied by a bond with two sureties, in at least $500. Upon filing Court shall issue order that debtor show cause, etc.

Two or more persons who are partners may be adjudged insolvent, on petition of such partners or one of them, or on petition of five or more creditors of such partnership; also applies to corporations. Debtor may apply for discharge at any time after three months from application, etc.

JUSTICES' COURTS.—Jurisdiction in actions on contract for recovery of money not exceeding $300, damages for injury to person, injury or detention of personal property, injury to realty, when question of title is not raised, amount not exceeding $300; for fines, penalties, when no issue is raised as to legality of tax, impost, assessment, toll or municipal fine; to enter judgment by confession, exclusive of interest, not exceeding $300. They have concurrent jurisdiction with the Superior Court within their townships, in actions for forcible entry and detainer when rental value of property does not exceed $25 per month, and damages claimed at $200; to enforce and foreclose liens on personal property when amount of liens or value of property does not amount to $300.

MARRIED WOMEN.—No dower. May become sole traders and liable on all their contracts. All property owned by her before marriage, and that acquired afterwards by gift, bequest, devise or descent, with rents, issues and profits, is her separate property. At death of wife, all property goes to husband; at death of husband, wife takes half, balance to children.

PROTEST.—Foreign paper protested by law. Merchant, local or inland bills may be presented by holder, and he may give notice in writing of non-payment.

STATUES OF LIMITATION.—Actions for recovery of possession of realty on judgment or decree of any court of record in the United States, or for mesne profits of real estate, *five years*. On written obligations executed within the State, *four years*. Liability created by statue, other than penalty or forfeiture, trespass to real property, for detention or injury to, or recovery of, personal property, for relief on ground of fraud (after discovery), *three years*. On obligations not written, or those executed without the State or against officer, for official acts or omissions, to recover damage for death caused by wrongful act or negligence of another, *two years*. Action upon a statue for a penalty or forfeiture of bond, in criminal actions, for libel, slander, battery, false imprisonment, or seduction, against a city or corporation for damage by a mob, *one year*. Actions against an officer *de facto;* to recover property seized, or damages done by officer by seizure, and to recover stock sold for delinquent assessment, *six months*. Actions not specified, *four years*. No limitation to recover deposits with any bank, banker, trust company, saving and loan societies. Absence of defendant from State deducted. Revivor; new promise in writing.

SUPERIOR COURT—Held in each county, and at least one Judge for each county; always in session; original jurisdiction in equity cases and concurrent with Supreme Court involving questions of realty, taxes, imposts, assessments, toll, municipal fines and demands to the amount of $300, forcible entry and detainer, insolvency, to prevent and abate nuisances and probate matters; also divorce proceedings, not otherwise provided for; in all criminal cases amounting to felony and misdemeanors, nor otherwise provided for, naturalization, etc. Appellate jurisdiction in cases arising in justices' and other inferior courts, as prescribed by law, power to issue writs of injunctions, etc. Process extends to all parts of the State. Actions to quiet title, enforce liens against, or possession of realty, must be brought in county where land is situated.

TAXES—Due fourth Monday of October, delinquent last Monday in December. Advertised first Monday in February; sale not less than twenty-one days nor more than twenty-eight days thereafter. One year to redeem; penalty, 50 per cent.

CALIFORNIA FORMS.

A conveyance by a married woman has no validity until acknowledged. (C. C., Sec. 1186).

The following forms are used:

[Form I--GENERAL FORM OF ACKNOWLEDGMENTS].

STATE OF ——, } ss.
County of—. }

On this — day of —, in the year —, before me, (name and quality of officer), personally appeared —, know to me (or proved to me on the oath of —), to be the person whose name is subscribed to the within instrument, and acknowledged to me that he (or they) executed the same.

[SEAL] (C. C. § 1189). *(Signature and title of officer).*

If the deed be executed by a corporation, after the words "known to me," etc., insert "to be the President (or Secretary) of the corporation that executed the within instrument. (C. C., § 1190).

OF A MARRIED WOMAN.

STATE OF ——, } ss.
County of—. }

On this — day of —, in the year —, before me, (name and quality of officer), personally appeared ——, known to me (or proved to me on the oath of——) to be the person whose name is subscribed to the within instrument, described as a married woman; and upon an examination without the hearing of her husband, I made her acquainted with the contents of the instrument, and thereupon she acknowledged to me that she executed the same, and that she does not wish to retract such execution.

[SEAL]. (C. C., § 1191). *(Signature and title of officer).*

By subscribing witness, see form 1.

By an attorney in fact, same as the general form, but after the word "instrument" insert "as the attorney in fact of —— and acknowledged that he subscribed the name of —— thereto as principal, and his own name as attorney in fact." (C. C., § 1192).

Acknowledgments must be authenticated by the signature, followed by the name or title of office, and the official seal affixed, if the officer has by law an official seal. The seal may be made by an impression on the paper, or on wax or other substance attached. (C. C., § § 1193, 1628).

[Form 1a—PROOF BY SUBSCRIBING WITNESS].

STATE OF CALIFORNIA, } ss.
County of —, }

On this — day of —, in the year one thousand eight hundred and —, before me ——, a ——, personally appeared ——, known to me to be the person whose name is subscribed to the within instrument as a subscribing witness thereto, and that said ——, being by me sworn, on oath testified and proved to me that ——, the person whose name is subscribed to said instrument as a party, is the person described in it, and that the said —— executed the same, and that he, the said——, subscribed his name thereto as a witness.

In Witness Whereof, I have hereunto set my hand and —— the day and year in this certificate first above written.

[SEAL]. *(Signature and title.)*

[Form 2—CLAIM AGAINST ESTATE].

In the Superior Court of the — County of —, State of California. In the matter of the estate of —, deceased. Creditor's claim, $—. —, 188—. Letters —, deceased, having been granted to —, the undersigned, — creditor-- of said deceased, present— — claim against the estate of said deceased, with the necessary vouchers, to said —— for approval as follows, to-wit: Estate of ——, deceased, To ——, Dr.

[Form 2a—FOR ITEMS OF ACCOUNT].

STATE OF——, } ss.
County of——, }

——, whose foregoing claim is herewith presented to the (executor or administrator) of said deceased, being duly sworn, says that the amount thereof, to-wit, the sum of —— dollars, is justly due to said claimant ; that no payments have been made thereon which are not credited, and that there are no offsets to the same, to the knowledge of said——. *(Signature of Affiant).*

Subscribed and Sworn to before me, this —— day of ——, A D., 188—

(Signature and title of Officer).

[Form 3—ARTICLES OF INCORPORATION].

Know all Men by these Presents: That we, the undersigned, do hereby organize and form a corporation, under and by virtue of the laws of the State of California, to be known as and named the (giving proposed name). That the purpose for which said corporation is formed by us is (giving purposes and objects in full). That the place where the principal business of said corporation is to be transacted is the City of——, in the State of California, and the term for which said corporation is to exist is —— years. That the number of directors of said corporation is to be five, and the names and residences of the directors who are appointed for the first year are as follows: ——, residing at ——; ——, residing at ——; ——, residing at ——; ——, residing at——; and——,residing at ——. That the capital stock of said corporation is —— dollars, divided into —— shares. That the amount of the capital stock of said corporation actually subscribed is —— dollars, and by the following persons, to-wit: ——, —— dollars; ——, —— dollars; ——, —— dollars, etc.

In Witness Whereof, We have hereunto set our hands, this —— day of ——, A. D., 188—.

(Signature).
(Acknowledged like conveyance of real property). *(Signature).*
(Signature).
(Signature).
(Signature).

[Form 4—DEEDS].

I, ——, grant to ——, all that real property situated in —— County, State of California, described as follows: (insert description; or, if the property has a descriptive name, that is sufficient, as "Ravenswood.")

Witness my hand, this —— day of ——, A, D. 18—.

[SEAL]. (C. C., § 1092), *Signature).*

[Form 5—INSTRUCTIONS FOR TAKING DEPOSITIONS].

1. If the time and place of executing the commission are not named therein, the Commissioner may subpœna the witness to appear before him at such time and place as he may appoint.

2. At the hearing, the Commissioner will administer the oath to the witness; and the Commissioner, witness, or some impartial person, must then reduce the answers of the witness in interrogatories to writing, as near as may be in the language of the witness.

3. When the examination is closed, the depositions should be made up in this form:

THE HEADING OR CAPTION.

Deposition of ——, a witness, sworn and examined under and by virtue of a commission issued out of the —— Court, in and for the County of ——, in the State of California, in a certain cause therein pending between ——, plaintiff, and ——, defendant.

——, of the City of ——, State of ——, being duly sworn to speak the truth, the whole truth, and nothing but the truth, deposes and says as follows:

1. To the first interrogatory he answers——.
2. To the second interrogatory he answers——.
3. To the third cross-interrogatory he answers——, etc.

When the deposition is finished, it must be subscribed by the witness, and certified by Commissioner, as follows:

STATE OF——, } ss. CERTIFICATE.
County of——, }

I, ——, the Commissioner named in said commission, do hereby certify that the witness, ——, above named, appeared before me, and, after being duly sworn, his evidence was duly taken down and thereafter read over and corrected by him, after which he subscribed the same in my presence, on the —— day of ——, A. D., 188—, at my office in the City of ——, in said County and State aforesaid; and that I have personal knowledge of the identity of said witness, (or if unacquainted with the witness, "that proof has been made before me of the personal identity of said witness.")

In Witness Whereof, I have hereunto set my hand and official seal, this —— day of ——, A. D., 188—. ——, *Commissioner.* [SEAL].

4. The Commissioner will attach together and fold the commission, interrogatories, answers, or any document deposed to or identified by the witness, in a packet, and securely seal the same. He will then write his name across the seal, and direct the packet thus: —— *vs.* ——. To ——, Esq., Clerk of the —— Court for —— County, California.

5. The package may be sent by mail or other usual channel of conveyance.

[Form 5a—FORMS FOR DEPOSITIONS].

STATE OF CALIFORNIA, County of——. } IN THE —— COURT.

——, *vs.* ——, } AFFIDAVIT FOR EXAMINATION OF WITNESS.

——, being duly sworn, deposes and says, that he is the —— in the above entitled cause, and that the summons has been served on —— the defendant— therein, —— that —— necessary and material witness— on the part of the ——, that said witness ——

(Signature of Affiant).

Subscribed and Sworn to, before me, this —— day of ——, A. D., 18—.

(Signature and title of officer.)

——, *vs.* ——. } NOTICE OF EXAMINATION OF WITNESS.

STATE OF CALIFORNIA, County of——. } SS.

SIR:—You will please take notice that the deposition of ——, witness on behalf of the —— in the above entitled cause, to be used upon the trial thereof, will be taken before ——, at ——, in the County of ——, on the —— day of ——, at the hour of ——, in the —— noon of that day, and if not concluded on that day, the taking will be continued from day to day, and from time to time successively until closed. And you will further take notice, that the above is a copy of the affidavit showing that the case is one mentioned in section 2021 of the Code of Civil procedure.

Yours, etc.,

To ——, *Attorney for* ——. ——, *Attorney for* ——.

[Form 6—FORM FOR LAST WILL AND TESTAMENT].

In the Name of God, Amen: I, ——, of ——, County of ——, State of ——, of the age of —— years, and being of sound and disposing mind and memory, and not acting under duress, menace, fraud or undue influence of any person whatever, do make, publish, and declare this my last will and testament, in manner following, that is to say:

First, ——.

Secondly, ——.

Lastly, I hereby nominate and appoint —— the executor of this, my last will and testament [without bond if so desired], and hereby revoke all former wills by me made.

In Witness Whereof, I have hereunto set my hand and seal, this —— day of——, in the year of our Lord, one thousand eight hundred and ——.

(Signature). [SEAL].

The foregoing instrument, consisting of —— page— besides this, was at the date thereof, by the said ——, signed and sealed, and published as, and declared to be —— last will and testament, in presence of us, who, at —— request, and in —— presence, and in the presence of each other, have subscribed our names as witnesses thereto.

——, *Residing at* ——.

——, *Residing at* ——.

LAWS OF COLORADO

RELATIVE TO THE

COLLECTION OF DEBTS, Etc.

Revised expressly for J. A. Graft & Co's Legal Directory,

ATTACHMENT.—Lies in actions on contract; against a non-resident, foreign corporation, when the debtor leaves the State and remains absent four (4) months, the debt having been due four months; when the debtor is about to leave the State, with the intent to defraud his creditors, or has or is about to dispose of his property with like intent; when the debt is incurred for an article, or thing which should have been paid on delivery, or performance, and on past due accounts.

BILLS AND NOTES.—Are assignable by statue so as to vest the assignee with all rights of his assignor.

Diligence must be used against maker to hold endorser. All written contracts are assignable.

Chattel mortgages must be in due form, acknowledged and recorded where the property or most of it is at time of mortgage. The Justice or Notary taking acknowledgment must keep a record of the date, parties and a list of the chattels.

It is a criminal offence to sell or convey chattels under mortgage without consent of mortgagee or notice to purchaser. Actual notice or knowledge of a mortgage is same as record.

Conveyances of land must be in common law form; acknowledgment and recording same as Illinois.

Husband and wife need not join, each conveys separately, except homestead, when they must join.

ESTATES OF DECEASED PERSONS.—Claims must be presented within a year from letters. Real and personal property descends one-half to widow, one-half to children. The widow takes whole estate when there are no children.

EXEMPTIONS.—Homestead of $2,000 and specific exemptions of personal property, which might amount to two or three thousand more, to the head of family.

No imprisonment for debt, except for fraud or wilful deceit.

INTEREST.—Legal rate 10 per cent., but parties may agree in writing on any per cent.

Judgments of Courts of Records, are liens on real estate after a transcript is accorded in recorders office, of proper county, for six years.

JURISDICTION.—Justices up to $300, County Courts to $2,000, District Courts unlimited.

LIMITATION.—On all contracts, six years.

MARRIED WOMEN.—Hold, enjoy and convey all property as if sole, and may sue and be sued as *femme sole*.

PRACTICE, CODE.—Wills must be in writing, witnessed by at least two disinterested persons.

WITNESSES.—All persons are competent. Interests effects credibility only.

MINING LAW.—Is a very important branch here, but a mere synopsis is apt to mislead. Better consult a local lawyer in all cases.

1775329

COLORADO FORMS.

[Form 1--ACKNOWLEDGMENT].

STATE OF ————, } ss.
County of—, }

I ——, a ——, within and for the County and State aforesaid, do hereby certify that ——, who is personally known to me to be the person who subscribed the above and foregoing instrument in writing, and acknowledged that he signed, sealed and delivered the same as his free and voluntary act, for the uses and purposes therein set forth.

Given Under My Hand, and —— seal, this — day —188—.

(*Signature and title of Officer*).

Form 2,—BOND FOR COSTS].

————, }
vs. } —— Court.
————. }

I do hereby enter myself security for costs in this case, and acknowledge myself bound to pay or cause to be paid all costs which may accrue in this action, either to the opposite party or to any of the officers of this Court, pursuant to the laws of this State.

Dated, this — day of ——, 188--. (Signed). ————,

[Form 3--DEPOSITIONS].

STATE OF————, } In the District Court of the —— Judicial District of the State of Colorado, within and for the County of — aforesaid
County of——. } — the — Term, A. D., 188--.

————, Plaintiff,
vs.
— ——, Defendant.

To the above named ——, or — h-- Attorney:

Take Notice, That on the — day of ——. A. D., 188--, the —— will sue out from the Clerk's office of the said Court a *dedimus protestatum* or commission pursuant to the statute, to take the deposition-- of ——, residing in the — of ——, in the County of ——, in the State of ——, to be read in evidence on the part of the ——, upon the trial of the above entitled cause. The said *dedimus protestatum* or commission to be directed to ——, Esquire, of the — of ——, in said County and State. The interrogatories to be propounded to the said —— in this behalf, on the part of the ——, are hereunto subjoined; and you can file cross interrogatories and join in such commission, if you shall see fit so to do.

Dated at ——, this — day of —, 188--. ——, Attorney for ——.

STATE OF ————, } In the District Court of the —— Judicial District of the State of Colorado, within and for the County of ——, aforesaid, —, the —— Term, A. D., 188--.
Coudty of——. }

————. Plaintiff,
vs.
————, Defendant.

Interrogatories to be propounded to ——, witness — to be produced, sworn and examined in this behalf, on the part of the ——, by virtue of the commission or *dedimus potestatum* to be issued in pursuance of the foregoing notice.

First Interrogatory: What is your name, age, occupation and place of residence?

Second Interrogatory: Do you know the parties, plaintiff and defendant in this cause, or either of them? If yea, how long have you known them, and each of them, respectively?

Third Interrogatory:

CERTIFICATE.

STATE OF ————, } ss.
County of ——, }

I ——, a —— Commissioner, appointed by the annexed commission, do hereby certify that the above and foregoing deposition was taken before me and by me, (or by ——, a disinterested person in my presence and under my direction), reduced to writing; that the said (—— witness), was by me first duly sworn to testify the truth, the whole truth, and nothing but the truth in suit now pending in the —— Court, in and for the County of ——, in the State of ——, wherein —— is plaintiff, and —— is defendant, and that after said deposition had been all taken, it was carefully read over by me to said witness, and then by him subscribed as his deposition in my presence.

Witness My Hand, and official seal, this — day of ——, 188—

(*Signature and title of officer*.

All formalities may be waived by stipulation and on oral questions. Must be addressed to Court where to be used; not testimonial.

LAWS OF CONNECTICUT.

RELATIVE TO THE

COLLECTION OF DEBTS, Etc.

Prepared expressly for J. A. Graft & Co.'s Legal Directory, by Geo. G. Sill, Attorney at Law, Hartford, Conn.

ASSIGNMENTS AND INSOLVENCY.—(Gen. Stat., p. 378).—If a debt, exceeding one hundred dollars, is sued for, and no sufficient property can be found to attach, the creditor can apply to the Court of probate to appoint a trustee in insolvency of the debtor's estate. A citation then issues, and a hearing is had. If the petition is granted, the trustee takes all the debtor's estate, not exempt from execution, and voluntary conveyances, and attachments on mesne process or incomplete levies of execution, commenced within sixty days previous, are dissolved. The debtor receives an allowance from his estate for the support of his family, and, if he pays seventy per cent. of all claims proved, obtains a full discharge. Commissioners are appointed, in each case, to pass upon claims presented, with an appeal to the Superior Court. Three to six months are allowed for proving claims. Proving claim, and accepting dividend, does not operate as a discharge of the debtor. Preferential assignments are not allowed, but assignments in insolvency can be voluntarily made by any one to a trustee of his own selection; subject to the substitution of another by the Court of Probate, if deemed proper. The estate is settled in substantially the same way as in involuntary proceedings.

All debts due any laborer or mechanic, for personal wages for labor performed, within three months, are preferred, to the amount of one hundred dollars; also the costs of incomplete levies of executions and attachments, which are dissolved by insolvency proceedings.

ATTACHMENT—Is served by attaching goods or lands of defendant, or, if none be found, by attaching the person, when liable. Non-resident plaintiff must furnish bond for costs.

Goods concealed in hands of agents, or debts due to the defendant, are reached by foreign attachment, which takes the place of garnishment. No assignment of future earnings will prevent their attachment when earned, unless made to secure a *bona fide* debt, due at the date of such assignment, the amount of which shall be stated therein, as nearly as possible, nor unless the term for which they are assigned, shall be definitely limited in the assignment, nor unless recorded, before such attachment, in the town clerk's office in the town where the assignor resides, or if he reside without the State, in the town where the employer reside, and a copy left with the employer. (Public Acts, 1878, p. 263.

EXECUTIONS—Issue on the return of final judgment, and are returnable within sixty days. No execution issued in an action, founded on contract merely, can be levied on the body of the debtor, except for breach of promise of marriage, misconduct, or neglect in office or professional employment, or breach of trust. Real estate levied on must be appraised by three indifferent persons. Stay of execution, only on appeal, or in special causes, at discretion of court.

EXEMPTIONS.—Necessary apparel, beds and bedding, household furniture, arms, implements of debtor's trade, one oyster boat, worth not over two hundred dollars, one cow, of a value not exceeding one hundred and fifty dollars, ten sheep, of same value, two swine, poultry, not exceeding twenty-five dollars in value, twenty-five bushel of charcoal, two tons of coal, two hundred pounds of flour, two cords of wood, two tons of hay, two hundred pounds of beef, five bushels of potatoes or turnips, two hundred pounds of fish, ten bushels of corn or rye, twenty pounds of wool or flax, one stove, the horse, buggy, harness, saddle, and bridle of a practicing physician (provided the value of the horse does not exceed two hundred dollars) the library of any person to the value of five hundred dollars, one sewing machine, burial lots, and one pew in church, so much of any debt which has accrued by reason of the personal services or labor of the debtor, having a family, which he is liable to support, as shall not exceed twenty-five dollars, and all pension moneys and allowances from benefit societies, shall be exempted from foreign attachment and execution; provided that in all suits for house rents, or provisions, only ten dollars shall be exempted, and no exemption shall be allowed upon debts for personal board; also wages of a minor, to the amount of ten dollars, are exempt, though no exemption is allowed in suit for personal board, or necessaries furnished the minor.

INTEREST.—The rate is six per cent. in the absence of any agreement to the contrary.

MORTGAGES—Of real estate are executed, acknowledged, and recorded in the same manner as deeds, and are foreclosed by bill in equity. The equity of redemption exists for a limited time, fixed by the court, depending upon the value of the equity. Chattel mortages, to be good against third party, where the mortgagor retains possession, must be executed, acknowledged, and recorded, as mortgages of land, and can only be made of the following described personal property, with or without the real estate, in which the same is situated or used, namely: Machinery, engines or implements, situated and used in any manufacturing or mechanical establishment, machinery, engines, implements, cases, types, cuts, or plates, situated and used in any printing, publishing, or engraving establishment, household furniture in a dwelling house, used by the owner therein in housekeeping, hay and tobacco, in leaf, in any building. Piano, organ, melodeon, and any musical instruments used by an orchestra or band. (Public Acts, 1881, p. 79.)

Hotel keepers may mortgage the furniture, fixtures, and other personal chattels contained and used in the hotels occupied by them, or employed in connection therewith. Chattel mortgages are foreclosed by sale under order of court.

NOTES AND BILLS.—Promissory notes, for the payment of money only, payable to any person, or his order, or to bearer, are negotiable. (Gen. Stat., p. 343.)

Negotiable demand notes are deemed over-due and dishonored after four months. When third day of grace falls upon a holiday or Sunday, presentation for payment should be made on the next preceding secular or business day.

Judgment notes (so-called) are not allowed. No particular form of note is recommended.

CONNECTICUT FORMS.

[Form 1.—ACKNOWLEDGMENT.]

STATE OF CONNECTICUT, } ss.
County of —— }

Personally appeared ——, the signer and sealer of the foregoing instrument, and acknowledged the same to be his free act and deed, before me.

In Testimony Whereof I have hereunto set my hand and affixed my official seal, at , in said County, this —— day of ——, A. D. 18—.

[L. S.] ——————

Commissioner for the State of Connecticut.

[Form 2.—ASSIGNMENT IN INSOLVENCY.]

STATE OF CONNECTICUT, } ss.
County of —— }

Know all Men by these Presents, That —— of —— the —— of —— and State of Connecticut, in consideration of the sum of one dollar to —— in hand paid by ——, of ——, in said State, and in further consideration of the uses and trusts hereinafter conferred upon and assumed by said ——, do hereby give, grant, sell, convey, transfer and assign to said —— all — real and personal estate, debts, demands, claims, and choses in action of every kind whatsoever, and wheresoever the same may be situated, except what property is by law exempt from execution, and excepting also the sum of one hundred dollars in cash.

To have and to hold the same to h— the said —— in trust for the purposes following, viz: to be held, managed and disposed of for the benefit of all —— creditors in proportion to their respective claims: and pursuant to the provisions of the statutes of said State, in such case made and provided.

In Witness whereof — have hereunto set — hand and — seal this — day of —, A. D. 18—.

Signed, sealed, and delivered in the presence of } [L. S.] [L. S.]

STATE OF CONNECTICUT, } ss. A. D. 18.
County of —— }

Personally Appeared ——, signer— and sealer— of the foregoing instrument, and acknowledged the same to be —— free act and deed before me.

——, *Justice of the Peace.*
——, *Commissioner of the Superior Court.*

[Form 3.—WARRANTEE DEED.]

To all People to whom these Presents shall come: Greeting: Know ye, that ——, of the Town of ——, County of ——, and State of Connecticut, for the consideration of —— dollars, received to —— full satisfaction of ——. Do give, grant, bargain, sell, and confirm unto the said ——.

To Have and to Hold The above granted premises, with the appurtenances thereof, unto ——, the said grantee, —— heirs and assigns forever, —— and their own proper use and behoof. And also ——, the said grantor— do— for —— sell —— heirs, executors and administrators, covenant with the said grantee, —— heirs and assigns, that at and until the unsealing of these presents —— well seized of the premises as a good indefeasible estate, in fee simple, and have good right to bargain and sell the same in manner and form as is above written; and that the same is free from all incumbrances whatsoever ——. (For conditions for Mortgage Deed, insert form 3*a* from 1 to 2).

And Furthermore, ——the said grantor— do— by these presents bind —— sel—— and —— heirs forever to warrant and defend the above granted and bargained premises to —— the said grantee, —— heirs and assigns against all claims and demands whatsoever ——.

In Witness Whereof — have hereunto set — hand and seal this — day of — in the year of our Lord one thousand eight hundred and —.

Signed and delivered in presence of } [L. S.] [L. S.]

[Form 3*a*.—CONDITIONS FOR MORTGAGE DEED.]

(1) *The Condition of this Deed is such*, That whereas the said grantor —— justly indebted to the said grantee in the sum of —— dollars, as evidenced by —— promissory note— of even date herewith, payable to the said grantee or order ——.

Now Therefore, If said note— shall be well and truly paid according to —— tenor, then this deed shall be void; otherwise to remain in full force and effect. (2)

(ACKNOWLEDGMENT.)

STATE OF CONNECTICUT, } ss. A. D. 18—.
County of —— }

Personally appeared ——, signer and sealer of the foregoing instrument, and acknowledged the same to be —— free act and deed, before me.

——, *Notary Public*,
Justice of the Peace, or
Commissioner of the Superior Court. } *as the case may be.*

[Form 4.—DEPOSITIONS.]

[CAPTION.]

——
vs.
—— STATE OF CONNECTICUT, } ss.
COUNTY OF ——. }

——, of ——, County of——, State, of——, being first duly cautioned and sworn, deposed and said, as follows: (Here state testimony).

Every witness must sign his own deposition. "Exhibits" should be annexed and signed by witness and magistrate.

[Form 4a.—CERTIFICATE TO DEPOSITION.]

STATE OF ——)
COUNTY OF——} ss. the —— day of ——, A. D., 188—.
TOWN OF ——)

Then personally appeared the above named ——, signer of the foregoing deposition, and after having been duly cautioned to speak the whole truth, and carefully examined, did subscribe the same and make oath before me that the same contains the truth, the whole truth, and nothing but the truth.

The foregoing deposition is taken pursuant to the annexed notice at the request of the —— to be read on the trial of an action pending before the —— Court, within and for the County of ——, and State of Connecticut, in which action —— plaintiff and —— defendant—.

The cause of taking this deposition is that the said deponent lives more than twenty miles from the place of trial, and out of the State of Connecticut.

The adverse party was notified to be present at the taking of this deposition, and was present thereat.

Subscribed, taken and sworn to before me. *(Signature and title.)*

[INSTRUCTIONS.]

The Commissioner must caution the witnesses to speak the whole truth, shall carefully examine them and have them subscribe to the deposition and make oath to it before such authority, who shall attest the same and certify that the adverse party or his agent was present, (if so) or that he was notified; and shall also certify the reason of taking such deposition; shall seal it up and direct it as follows: ——*vs.* ——. To the Hon. —— Court, for ——County, Connecticut. The deposition of ——, to be used in said cause, taken and sealed up and directed by me; (*Signature and title*) where it is to be used, and deliver it, if desired, to the party at whose request it was taken.

Persons in interest may not write, draw up, or dictate the deposition.

Depositions to be read on the trial of any civil action may be taken in any foreign State or country without the limits of the United States, pursuant to the provisions of law, before the following described officers of the United States, viz: Foreign Ministers, Secretaries of Legation, Consuls and Vice-Consuls; and a certificate from the Secretary of State of the United States shall be sufficient evidence to prove the official character of the person taking the deposition,

Whenever a party in a civil action shall be notified to appear at the taking of any deposition, the party thus notified may, if he see cause, take depositions at the same time and place designated in said notice, to be used in the same cause, without any further notice to the opposite party; and the notice thus given shall be deemed sufficient notice to both parties that depositions will then and there be taken by them.

When a deposition is taken in the absence of the adverse party, or his agent or attorney, the party taking such deposition shall lodge it with the Clerk of the Court to which it is addressed, on the first day of the session of said Court, for the inspection of the adverse party, unless before that time he has delivered the same, or a copy thereof, to said adverse party. But the Court may, in its discretion, direct that said deposition be lodged with the Clerk at some subsequent time, instead of the time aforesaid. And if this rule be not complied with, such deposition shall not be read in evidence.

[Form 5.—MORTGAGE OF PERSONAL PROPERTY.]

Know all Men by these Presents, That ——, of —— in the County of —— and State of Connecticut, for the consideration of —— dollars, received to —— full satisfaction of ——, do hereby bargain, sell, transfer and convey unto the said —— the following articles of property: (Here describe property).

To Have and to Hold the same To —— the said ——, executor—, administrator—, and assign— forever, to —— and —— own proper use and behoof: And, —— the said —— for —— sel—, heirs, executor— and administrator—, covenant and agree with the said —— to warrant and defend the said goods to —— the said —— against all persons whatever.

The Condition of this Deed is such, That whereas the said grantor —— justly indebted to the said grantee in the sum of —— dollars as evidenced by —— promissory note - of even date herewith, payable to the said grantee or order, —— with interest ——.

Now Therefore, If said note— shall be well and truly paid according to its tenor, then this deed shall be void, otherwise to remain in full force and effect.

In Witness whereof, —— have hereunto set —— hand and seal this —— day of ——, in the year of our Lord one thousand eight hundred and ——.

Signed, sealed and delivered, in presence of } [L. S.]
—————— } [L. S.]

STATE OF CONNECTICUT, } ss. A. D. 18—
County of —— }

Personally appeared ——, signer— and sealer of the foregoing instrument, and acknowledged the same to be —— free act and deed, before me.

——, *Justice of the Peace.*

LAWS OF DAKOTA TERRITORY

RELATIVE TO THE

COLLECTION OF DEBTS, Etc.

Prepared expressly for J. A. Graft & Co.'s Legal Directory.

ASSIGNMENT AND INSOLVENCY.—Insolvent debtor may in good faith make assignment in trust for benefit of creditors, which may provide for any subsisting liability of the assignor, whether absolute or contingent. Such assignment is subject to provisions of the code relative to trusts and fraudulent transfers. Any debtor may make assignment without consent of creditors and be thereby discharged from all his debts and liabilities by strictly complying with the provisions of statute.

ATTACHMENTS.—Process issues at the time of the commencement of the action, or at any time prior to rendition of judgment in actions on contract for the recovery of money only, or in an action for the wrongful conversion of personal property, against a corporation created by or under the laws of any other Territory, State, Government, or Country, or

Against a defendant who is not a resident of this Territory, or

Against a defendant who has absconded or concealed himself; or whenever any person or corporation is about to remove any of his or its property from this Territory, or has assigned, disposed of, secreted, or is about to assign, dispose of, or secrete any of his or its property with intent to defraud creditors, as hereinafter mentioned.

Attachment law amended in 1883, further provides:

That whenever any debtor residing in this Territory is about to remove from the County where he resides with the intention of permanently changing his or her place of residence, it shall be lawful for his or her creditors to demand of such debtor security for such debts, and in case of failure or neglect to secure the same, such creditor shall have the right of attachment against the property of such delinquent debtor under the provisions of law regulating attachment proceedings. Plaintiff must make affidavit setting forth one or more of the grounds for the issuing of attachment, and furnish bonds in not less than $250 for the protection of the defendant to cover costs and damages caused by a wrongful suing out of said attachment.

In Justices' Courts the bonds must be not less than fifty dollars nor more than three hundred dollars.

EXECUTIONS.—Executions issue, of course, at any time within five years after rendition of judgment; after five years, leave of court must be obtained, unless an execution issued within the five years has been returned unsatisfied, in which event another execution can be issued without leave of Court.

Lands levied upon need not be appraised. The officer serving the execution is required to notify the debtor (if the head of a family) of his right to claim a homestead, and it is made his duty, in case a homestead has not already been designated, to cause a homestead to be marked out, and recorded, commencing at some designated corner of the dwelling house, and set aside 160 acres if in the country, and not exceeding one acre if within a town plat, each of which is without regard to value, and no judgment against the homestead is of any validity, except for purchase money of the same, or mechanics' liens for improvements to the same, and taxes on the homestead. Executions are returnable within sixty days when issued from Clerk of Court, and thirty days when issued out of Justices' Courts.

Real estate sold under execution or other process as provided by law, may be redeemed within one year from day of sale; purchaser entitled to value of monthly rents from time of purchase, when not redeemed when debtor retains possession.

EXEMPTIONS—Exempt from execution or other mien process, fifteen hundred dollars of personal property, and in addition, the propeity absolutely exempt, as follows:

1. All family pictures.
2. A pew, or other sitting in any house of worship.
3. A lot or lots in any burial grounds.
4. The family Bible and all school books used by the family, and all other books used as a part of the family library not exceeding in value one hundred dollars.
5. All wearing apparel of the debtor and his family.
6. The provisions necessary for the debtor and his family for one years' supply, either provided or growing, or both, and fuel necessary for one year.

INTEREST.—The legal rate of interest is 7 per cent. Parties may contract for a higher rate, not to exceed 12 per cent. A person taking, receiving, retaining, or contracting for any higher rate of interest than 12 per cent., shall forfeit all the interest so taken, received, or contracted for.

Interest on open accounts commences from the date of the last item charged in a regular account, either debit or credit, except in the Black Hills counties, to wit: Lawrence, Pennington, Center, Mandan, and Forsyth, wherein it shall be lawful to take, receive, retain, and contract for any rate agreed upon between the parties. Interest is payable on all judgments recovered in the courts of this Territory at the rate of 7 per cent. per annum.

Mortgages of real property must be in writing, with the formalities required in case of grants of real property. Wife need not join, except in mortgage or conveyance of homestead. If containing power of sale, may be foreclosed by advertisement without intervention of court. Mortgagee has right of possession during the year of redemption after sale, but liable for rents, damages, and waste in case he does not redeem. Chattle mortgages are void as against creditors and subsequent purchasers in good faith, unless filed in office of Register of Deeds in the county of the residence of the mortgagor.

NOTES AND BILLS OF EXCHANGE.—Three days of grace allowed on all bills of exchange or sight drafts (unless grace is waived), whether foreign or domestic, and on all promissory notes, bills of exchange and drafts, on the face of which time is specified, and notes on demand for payment of same. Acceptances must be in writing by the drawee, or an acceptor for honor. To hold endorser, the instrument must be presented on the day of maturity, and notice of dishonor given. Damages are allowed in favor of holder for value on bills of exchange, drawn or negotiated within the Territory and protested for non-acceptance or non-payment. Apparent maturity of a non-interest-bearing sight or demand note is ten days after date, in addition to the time required for transmission; on interest-bearing notes, one year from date.

DAKOTA FORMS.

[FORM 1—ACKNOWLEDGMENT BY HUSBAND AND WIFE].

STATE OF ——, }
County of —— } SS.

Be it Remembered, That on this——day of——, A. D., 18—, before me (here insert name and title of Officer), within and for the County of ——, personally appeared ——, and ——, his wife, well known to me to be the persons who are described in, and who executed the within instrument, and duly acknowledged to me that they executed the same freely, and the said ——, wife of said——, and whose name is subscribed to the within instrument, upon an examination without the hearing of her said husband, being by me made acquainted with the contents of the said instrument, acknowledged to me that she executed the same freely, and that she did not wish to retract such execution.

[L. S.] *(Signature and title of officer.)*

[FORM 2—INSTRUCTIONS FOR TAKING DEPOSITIONS].

CAPTION.

Depositions of witnesses taken before me (name and title of officer), within and for the County of ——, in the State of ——, on the —— day of——, in the year ——, pursuant to the annexed notice, in an action pending in the (name the Court), wherein —— is plaintiff and —— is defendant; and for said plaintiff (or defendant, as the case may be).

(Here state whether plaintiff or defendant were present or represented by counsel).

——, of the County of ——, of lawful age, being first duly sworn (or affirmed) by me, as hereinafter certified, deposes and says: (Here insert the interrogatories and testimony).

If more than one witness, the next deposition may be commenced immediately below the preceeding, as follows:

Also ——, of the County of, etc.

Close the depositions in form as follows:

CERTIFICATE.

I, ——, (name and title of officer) do hereby certify that the above named (naming all the witnesses who have testified), was by me first duly sworn (or affirmed) to testify the truth, the whole truth, and nothing but the truth, in the above entitled cause, and that the foregoing depositions, by them respectively subscribed, were reduced to writing by me (or if by any other person, name him, and say, by ——, who is not interested in said action, in my presence), and were respectively subscribed by said witnesses in my presence, and were taken at the time and place in the annexed notice specified; that I am not counsel, attorney or relative of either party, or interested in the event of said action; (if there be adjournments, add) and said depositions were commenced at the time and place, in said notice specified, and continued by adjournment from day to day, at the same place, and between the same hours, as in the notice specified, and for the reasons above stated.

In Testimony Whereof, I have hereunto set my hand and affixed my official seal, this —— day of ——, A. D., eighteen hundred and ——.

[SEAL.] *(Signature and title of officer.)*

Then securely pack and seal the Depositions, and mail them, addressed to the Clerk of the Court in which the action is pending, and indorsed as follows: ——, vs. ——, Depositions in said action on behalf of the ——, taken, sealed up, addressed and transmitted by me.

(Signature and title.)

LAWS OF DELAWARE.

RELATIVE TO THE

COLLECTION OF DEBTS, Etc.

Prepared expressly for J. A. Graft & Co.'s Legal Directory,

UNITED STATES CIRCUIT COURT.—Terms at Wilmington on 3rd Tuesdays in June and October.

UNITED STATES DISTRICT COURT.—Terms at Wilmington on 2nd Tuesdays in January, April, June and September.

COURT OF ERRORS AND APPEALS.—At Dover. Terms, 2nd Tuesdays in January and June.

COURT OF CHANCERY.—Terms: *New Castle County,* at Wilmington, 3d Monday in February and 1st Monday in September.

Kent County, at Dover, 1st Tuesday after the 4th Monday in March, and on the 4th Monday in September.

Sussex County, at Georgetown, 2d Monday in March, and 3rd Monday in September.

ORPHANS' COURT.—Terms are the same as in the Court of Chancery.

SUPERIOR COURT.—Regular terms: *Sussex County,* on the 2d Monday in April and October.

Kent County, 4th Monday in April and October.

New Castle County, on the 3rd Monday after the commencement of the April term in Kent County, and on the 4th Monday in November.

The U. S. Circuit Court has jurisdiction in all civil cases where the damages claimed amount to $500, and the plaintiff is a citizen of another State.

The Superior Court has general jurisdiction of all civil cases.

Justices of the peace have jurisdiction within their respective counties, where the amount demanded does not exceed $100, exclusive of interest. Stay of execution for six months shall be granted to a person pleading his freehold, if found sufficient to secure the debt, and for nine months upon giving sufficient security. The defendant may appeal to the Superior Court at any time within fifteen days, by giving security to prosecute the appeal. No appeal is allowed unless the judgment before the justice of the peace exceeds five dollars, or in case of a trial before referees, unless the amount exceeds $15.

PRACTICE to a great extent is under the common law, with some statutory modifications. The full name and residence of the party sending a claim should always accompany the account. In case of a partnership, the full names and residence of each member of the firm should be furnished. In case of a corporation the correct title should be given, and also under the laws of what State the company was incorporated. Officers are not compelled to issue or execute process until their fees are paid, in the case of non-residents, and they may be ruled to give security for costs.

In all actions in the Superior Court upon bills, notes, bonds, or other instruments of writing for the payment of money, or for the recovery of book accounts, or foreign judgments, and in all actions of *scire facias*, recognizances in the Orphans' Court and Court of Chancery, judgments, or mortgages, judgment by default shall be entered upon motion by the plaintiff, or his attorney, on the last day of the regular term to which the original process is returnable, notwithstanding appearance by the defendant; unless the defendant, or if there be more than one, one or more of them, shall have previously filed in the cause an affidavit that he, or they, have a legal defense to the whole or part of such cause of action, and setting forth the nature and character of the same. But no judgment shall be entered unless the plaintiff shall, on or before the first day of the term to which the original process shall be returnable, file in the office of the Prothonotary a copy of the instrument of writing, book entries, or claims, or in case of a *scire facias*, a certified abstract or transcript of the judgment, mortgage, or recognizance, and in case of a foreign judgment, a copy of said judgment, certified to under the Act of Congress, passed May 26, 1790, with an affidavit stating the sum demanded, and that he, or they, verily believe that the same is justly and truly due. Stay of execution for six months on all such judgments shall be granted, upon security being given for the debt, interest, and costs.

AFFIDAVITS.—In case of a suit by a corporation, the affidavit shall be by the cashier or treasurer. Affidavits taken out of the State shall be before any judge of any court of record, the mayor or chief magistrate of any city or borough, a commissioner of deeds for the State, or any consul or vice-consul of the United States, such affidavit being certified under the hand and official seal, or seal of court, city, or borough as the case may be, of the person taking the same.

ACTIONS.—Suits may be commenced by capias, or summons, or, when the defendant is a non-resident, by process of foreign attachment.

ARRESTS.—Non-resident plaintiff cannot arrest non-resident defendant, on *mesne* process, for any debt contracted without the State. No writ of *capias ad satisfaciendum* can be issued until a writ of *fi fa* on the judgment shall have been issued, and a return thereon that the defendant has not sufficient property within the county to pay the debt, interest, and costs, or an affidavit to the same effect, alleging fraud, shall have been made. The party arrested upon an affidavit of fraud may have a hearing before any judge in vacation, upon the specifications. No writ of *capias ad respondendum* can be issued against a citizen of this State, except upon an affidavit, made by the plaintiff and filed in the Prothonotary's office, that the defendant has absconded or is about to abscond from the place of his usual abode, or that the defendant is justly indebted to the plaintiff in a sum exceeding fifty dollars, and that he verily believes the said defendant has secreted, conveyed away, assigned, settled, or disposed of property of the value of more than $100, with intent to defraud his creditors. The supposed fraudulant transaction must be specified and set forth in the affidavit.

Exception is made in case of actions for libel, slander, or injury to person or property, accompanied by violence, upon affidavit of the cause of action being filed with the praecipe.

ATTACHMENTS.—A writ of domestic attachment may be issued, after a return to a summons, or *capias* issued and delivered to the sheriff or coroner ten days before the return thereof, showing that the defendant cannot be found, and proof satisfactory to the Court of the cause of action, or upon affidavit, filed with the Prothonotary, that the defendant is justly indebted to the plaintiff in a sum exceeding fifty dollars, and has absconded from the place of his usual abode, or gone out of the State, with intent to defraud his creditors or to elude process, as is believed. The proceeds of sales of property attached are divided among all creditors. A writ of foreign attachment may be issued against any non-resident after a return as above, or an affidavit "that the defendant resides out of the State, and is justly indebted to the plaintiff in a sum exceeding fifty dollars."

The plaintiff is entitled to the full benefit of his diligence and discovery. The property of foreign corporations may be attached. All attachments may be dissolved by entering special bail. The goods and chattels, rights and credits of a defendant may be attached. The garnishee shall answer or plead as the plaintiff shall elect.

JUDGMENTS.—Of courts of record are a lien upon real estate, from the date of entering, for twenty years, after which they will be presumed to be paid.

Judgments obtained before justice of the peace may be made a lien on land, by filing a transcript in the Superior Court, after a return of *nulla bona*, or when the defendant has pleaded his freehold. Judgments obtained in other States must be sued on as other debts.

EXECUTION may issue from a court of record to any county, as soon as judgment is obtained, except in case of a stay. Real estate cannot be levied upon until personal property is exhausted. Personal property is bound from the time the writ is placed in the sheriff's hands, if actually levied upon within 60 days thereafter. The lien of such levy is good for three years, as against subsequent executions. Property sold on execution or mortgage cannot be redeemed.

Landlords' claim for rent, not exceeding one year, has preference, in case of the sale of goods of tenant under execution process.

LIMITATIONS.—All actions of account, *assumpsit*, case, trespass, replevin, detinue, or debt not founded on specialty or record, must be brought within three years from the accruing of the right of action, and in case of bills of exchange, promissory notes, or acknowledgments.

Actual seizin within 20 years is necessary to maintain an action for the recovery of lands, tenements, hereditaments. Right of equity barred after 20 years.

INTEREST.—The legal rate of interest is six per cent.; the penalty for usury is the forfeiture of the whole sum lent.

EXEMPTIONS.—Family bibles, school books, and family library, family pictures, seat or pew in church, lot in burial ground, all wearing apparel of debtor and family, and in addition to the above the tools, implements, and fixtures, necessary to carry on trade or business, not exceeding in value $75. Head of family, in addition to the above, other personal property that may be chosen by the debtor, not exceeding $200. Wages are exempt from execution attachment in New Castle County.

Testimony.—Interest excludes, but a party to the suit may be examined by the adverse party, as if on cross examination.

Claims against Deceased Persons are paid in the following order:

1. Funeral expenses.
2. Bills for medical attendance, medicines, nursing during and necessaries for last illness.
3. Wages of servants.
4. Rent not exceeding one year.
5. Judgments.
6. Mortgages, recognizances, and other obligations of record.
7. Obligations and contracts under seal.
8. Contracts, under hand, for payment of money or delivery of goods.
9. Other demands.

All claims incurred during the life-time of the deceased must be probated, and the affidavit must set forth "that nothing has been paid or delivered towards satisfaction of said debt, except what is mentioned, and that the sum demanded is justly and truly due." One year allowed to settle the estate from the date of letters.

Married Woman.—The real and personal property of a married woman, which she has at the time of her marriage, or which she shall acquire from any person other than her husband, shall be her sole and separate property, and is not liable for the debts of her husband. She is entitled to wages for personal labor, and may sue in her own name for the same. She may make contracts in respect to her own property, and prosecute and defend suits in regard to it. She may give a bond or warrant of attorney, and dispose of her property, real and personal, by will, without the consent of her husband.

Corporations.—There is a general incorporation act.

Wills.—Any person of twenty-one years and upwards, of sound and disposing mind, may make a will. Wills must be in writing, signed by the testator, or if he be unable to write, by some person at his request, and be attested by two or more witnesses in the testator's presence.

Deeds.—But one witness is necessary to deeds; a scroll answers for a seal. If a deed is not recorded within one year after sealing and delivery, it will not avail against a *bona fide* purchaser, creditor, or mortgagee, without notice.

Acknowledgments out of the State may be taken before any consul-general, consul or commercial agent of the United States, before any judge of a district or circuit court of the United States, or the chancellor or any judge of a court of record, or the mayor or chief officer of any city or borough, and certified under the hand of such chancellor, judge, mayor, or officer, and the seal of his office, city, or borough; or in open court certified under the hand of the clerk and the seal of the court; or before a commissioner of deeds appointed by the Governor.

DELAWARE FORMS.

[Form 1.—ACKNOWLEDGMENT BY CORPORATION.]

STATE OF ——, } ss.
—— County. }

Be it remembered that on this —— day of ——, A. D. ——, personally came before me (name and title) ——, president of (corporate title) a corporation of the State of Delaware, party to the foregoing indenture, known to me personally (or proved on the oath of the witness) to be such, and acknowledged the said indenture to be his own act and deed, and the act and deed of his company; that the signature of the president is his own proper handwriting, that the seal affixed is the common or corporate seal of the said company; and that his act of sealing, executing and delivering said indenture was duly authorized by said company.

Given under my hand and official seal, the day and year aforesaid.

(*Name and title*).

[Form 2.—ACKNOWLEDGMENT OF DEED FOR HUSBAND AND WIFE.]

STATE OF DELAWARE, } ss.
County of —— }

Be it remembered, that on this —— day of ——, in the year of our Lord, eighteen, etc., personally came before me (name and title), —— and ——, his wife, parties to this indenture, known to me personally to be such, and severally acknowledged this indenture to be their deed.

And the said —— being at the same time privately examined by me, apart from her said husband, acknowledged that she executed the said indenture willingly, without compulsion, or threats, or fears of her husband's displeasure.

Given under my hand and seal of office, the day and year aforesaid.

(*Name and title*).

[Form 3.—DEPOSITIONS.]

[CAPTION.]

Depositions of witness produced, sworn (or affirmed) and examined on the —— day of ——, in the year of our Lord one thousand eight hundred and ——, to ——, in the —— of ——, in ——, County, and State of ——, by virtue of a commission issued out of ——, of the State of Delaware, in and for —— County, to —— directed, for the examination of witnesses in a cause therein depending between ——, plaintiff, and ——, defendant, on the part and behalf of ——, the ——.

Note.—If a clerk has been employed, add, "The clerk by me employed in taking, writing, transcribing, and engrossing the said depositions having first duly taken the oath assigned to the said commission according to the tenor thereof."

[COMMENCEMENT OF DEPOSITION OF EACH WITNESS.]

——, of ——, in the —— of ——, aged —— years, —— a witness produced, sworn (or affirmed), and examined on the part and behalf of the ——, deposeth and saith as follows:

To the first interrogatory in chief, he answers and says: ——

(*Signature.*)

[CONCLUSION.]

Sworn to and subscribed before me, the —— day of —— A. D. 188—.

——, *Commissioner.*

[PROOF OF EXHIBIT INDORSED.]

—— —— plaintiff }
vs. } 188—
—— defendant. }

At the execution of a commission in this cause, this paper writing was produced and shown to —— a witness, sworn and examined, and by him deposed to at the time of his examination in behalf of ——. ——, *Commissioner.*

[CERTIFICATE AT CLOSE.]

To —— I, —— commissioner named in the foregoing writ do certify that in pursuance of the authority therein contained, I caused the several witnesses whose depositions appear in the schedule thereto annexed to be examined on oath or affirmation upon the interrogatories annexed, and that I caused such examinations to be reduced to writing as the same in such schedule appear. ——, *Commissioner.*

[RETURN INDORSED ON COMMISSION.]

The execution of this commission appears in a certain schedule annexed.

——, *Commissioner.*

[INDORSE ENVELOPE THUS]:

—— }
vs. } To ——, (Name the Court).
—— }

To (Name the presiding Judge, whose name is given in the commission).

LAWS OF THE DISTRICT OF COLUMBIA

RELATIVE TO THE

COLLECTION OF DEBTS, Etc.

Prepared expressly for J. A. Graft & Co.'s Legal Directory, by Milton C. Banard, Attorney at Law, Washington, D. C.

ACTIONS.—Under fifty dollars Justices of the Peace have exclusive jurisdiction, from fifty to one hundred dollars, concurrent jurisdiction with the Supreme Court, above one hundred dollars, suits must be brought in the Supreme Court. Costs must be paid in advance, ten dollars deposited with the clerk, and the marshal paid for services of process, subpœnas, etc., when served. No arrest for debt.

ASSIGNMENTS—May be made under the common law, and creditors preferred. There is no insolvent or bankrupt law in force.

ATTACHMENTS—Can only be issued when defendant, (1) is a non-resident, (2) evades service of process by concealment or absence, (3) has removed or is about to remove property from the D. C., to defeat just demands. This must be shown by affidavit of the plaintiff, and one or more witnesses, and plaintiff must give bond, approved by the clerk, for all damages for wrongful suing out of the attachment.

Goods properly attached can not be discharged, unless defendant gives approved bond to pay final judgment.

BILLS OF SALE, OR CHATTEL MORTGAGES—Must be acknowledged and recorded within twenty days, or they are void. They are void, as to creditors, when given upon a stock in trade, and use and possession retained.

EXEMPTION—Wearing apparel, household furniture, to three hundred dollars in value, implements of trade, to the value of two hundred dollars; stock in trade, to the value of two hundred dollars; libraries to the value of three hundred dollars; one horse and harness, and cart, wagon or dray, farming utensils, family pictures and library, to value of four hundred dollars; one cow, one swine, six sheep, and earnings, not exceeding one hundred dollars per month. These are only to head of a family.

INTEREST.—Where rate is not specified, six (6) per cent. is legal rate, but any rate, not exceeding ten (10) per cent., when stipulated for in writing, is lawful. The penalty for usury is only loss of *all* interest, which interest may be recovered by suit brought within one year after payment.

INSOLVENTS.—There is no insolvent or bankrupt law in force in this District.

JUDGMENT.—Before a Magistrate good for three years, before Supreme Court for twelve years. Can not be entered upon judgment bond or separate papers. Judgment of the Supreme Court of the District of Columbia may be renewed for twelve years by writ of *scire facias*.

LIMITATION—On simple contracts, book debts or accounts, three years. Specialties under seal, twelve years. Deeds of trust twenty years. No exceptions in favor of non-residents.

MARRIED WOMEN.—Rights of married women to all property, real or personal, acquired from any other source than husband, are same as if they were *femme sole*, and they can be sued, and sue, in respect to them, separately.

MECHANIC'S LIENS—Note of may be filed by the contractor, sub-contractor, material man, journeyman or laborer, respectively, any time after the commencement or within three months after the completion of building or repairs; and when filed, is a lien upon the building erected or repaired, and the lot of ground on which it stands, and takes precedence of all other liens or incumbrances recorded or attached, subsequent to the commencement of the work done.

MORTGAGES—Are seldom used. Deeds of trust with power of sale on default, prevail on chattel and real estate securities.

NOTES AND BILLS.—Law merchants is in force in regard to drafts, notes, and bills of exchange. One action may be brought against all persons liable, jointly or severally.

RECORDING OF DEED, ETC.—All deeds, deeds of trust, mortgages, and all other instruments of writing entitled to be recorded in the office of the Recorder of Deeds, take effect from the date of record, except as modified by the Mechanic's Lien Law.

REDEMPTION.—There is no provision of law for the redemption from judicial sales, or those made under deeds of trust.

Terms of Court.—First Tuesday of every month, except August, for return of process and judgments by default. Trial terms commence fourth Monday of January, second Monday of May, and third Monday of October.

Set-Off.—Mutual debts may be set-off in all actions.

Stay of Executions.—When no appeal is taken, execution issues forthwith on judgments of the Supreme Court. Magistrates judgments may be stayed, upon a proper bond, for one month, when the sum does not exceed twenty dollars; two months from twenty to forty dollars; four months from forty to seventy-five dollars, and six months from seventy-five to one hundred dollars.

Salaries of persons employed by the United States, or the District of Columbia, can not be attached.

DISTRICT OF COLUMBIA FORMS.

[FORM 1—ACKNOWLEDGMENT OF HUSBAND AND WIFE].

District of Columbia, to-wit :

I, ——, a —— in and for the District aforesaid, do hereby certify, that —— part — to a certain deed bearing date on the —— day of ——, A. D., 188—, and hereunto annexed, personally appeared before me, in the District aforesaid, the said —— being personally well known to me to be the person who executed the said Deed, and acknowledged the same to be —— act and deed, and the said —— being by me examined privily and apart from —— husband, and having the Deed aforesaid fully explained to ——, acknowledged the same to be —— act and deed, and declared that—— had willingly signed, sealed, and delivered the same, and that —— wished not to retract it.

Given under my hand and —— seal this —— day of ——, A. D., 188—.

[SEAL].

[FORM 2—AFFIDAVIT].

In the Supreme Court of the District of Columbia.

State of —— } SS. {No.——
County of —— } {At Law.

Before me, a Notary Public, duly commissioned and authorized to administer oaths, personally appeared —— (plaintiff or agent or attorney of plaintiff) and made oath that the cause of action against defendant— in this suit is —— (the promissory note described in the annexed declaration) and that the sum claimed by the plaintiff to-wit, $ —— with interest, as set forth in the declaration, is justly due the plaintiff— from the defendant—, exclusively of all set-offs and just grounds of defense.

Sworn to and subscribed before me, the —— day of —— 188—.

[SEAL]. ———— ————

[FORM 7—AFFIDAVIT].

District of Columbia, to-wit :

This day, appeared —— and made oath on the Holy Evangels of Almighty God, that the annexed account as stated is just and true ; and that —— not received any part of the money stated to be due, or any security or satisfaction for same, (except what is credited).

TEST :

$——

[FORM 14—DEED OF TRUST].

This Indenture, Made this —— day of ——, in the year of our Lord one thousand eight hundred and ——, by and between —— of the first part, and —— of the second part :

Whereas, —— justly indebted unto —— in the full sum of —— for which amount —— and being desirous to secure the punctual payment of said note-- when, and as the same shall —— become due and payable, with all interest and costs due and accruing thereon, as well as any renewals or extensions, therefore execute these presents :

Now, Therefore this Indenture Witnesseth, That the said part— of the first part, for and in consideration of the premises aforesaid, and further, the sum of one dollar, in lawful money of the United States, paid to —— by said part— of the second part, ha— granted, bargained, sold, allienel, enfeoffed, released, and conveyed, and do —— by these presents grant, bargain, sell, allien, enfeoff, release, and convey unto the said part— of the second part, and the survivor of them, his heirs and assigns, the following described Real Estate, situated in the —— of ——, District of Columbia, to-wit:

(Here describe the property).

together with all the easements, hereditaments, and appurtenances to the same belonging, or in anywise appertaining, and all the estate, right, title, interest and claim whatsoever, whether in law or in equity, of the said part— of the first part, of, in, to or out of the said piece— or parcel— of land and premises.

To Have and to Hold the said piece or parcel of land and premises, with the appurtenances unto and to the use of the said parties of the second part, the survivor of them, or his heirs and assigns.

In and upon the Trusts Nevertheless, Hereinafter mentioned and declared, that is, in trust to permit the said —— heirs or assigns, to use and occupy the said described premises, and the rents, issues and profits thereof, to take, have, and apply to and for —— and their sole use and benefit, until default be made in the payment of said —— or any installment of interest due thereon, or any proper cost, charge, commission, half-commission or expense in and about the same.

And upon the full payment of all of said —— and any extensions or renewals thereof, and the interest thereon, and all other proper costs, charges, commissions, half-commissions, and expenses incurred by means of these trusts, at any time before the sale hereinafter provided for, to release and reconvey the said described premises unto the said —— heirs or assigns, at —— or their cost.

And upon this further trust, (here insert all the conditions; power of sale, etc., etc. See precedent in Massachusetts forms, published herein).

In Testimony Whereof, the said part— of the first part ha— hereunto set —— hand and seal on the day and year first hereinbefore written.

Signed, sealed and delivered in presence of: [SEAL]. [SEAL].

[FORM 10—DEED].

This Indenture, Made this —— day of ——, in the year of our Lord one thousand eight hundred and eighty— by and between —— of the first part, and —— of the second part:

Witnesseth, That the said part— of the first part, for and in consideration of the sum of —— dollars, in lawful money of the United States, to —— in hand paid by the said part— of the second part, at and before the sealing and delivery of these presents, the receipt whereof is hereby acknowledged, ha— granted, bargained, sold, allienel, enfeoffed, released, and conveyed and —— by these presents, grant, bargain, sell, allien, enfeoff, release, and convey unto the said part— of the second part, —— heirs and assigns forever, the following described real estate, situate (here describe the property).

Together with all the improvements, ways, easements, rights, privileges, appurtenances and hereditaments to the same belonging, or in anywise appertaining, and all the remainders, reversions, rents, issues and profits thereof; and all the estate, right, title, interest, claim, and demand whatsoever, either at law or in equity, of the said part— of the first part, of, in, to, or out of the said — piece or parcel — of land and premises.

To Have and to Hold the said piece or parcel of land and premises, with the appurtenances, unto the said part— of the second part, —— heirs and assigns, to —— sole use, benefit and behoof forever.

And the said —— for —— heirs, executors and administrators, —— hereby covenant, promise, and agree, to and with the said part of the said part— of the second part, —— heirs and assigns that —— the said part— of the first part, and —— heirs, shall and will warrant and forever defend the said piece— or parcel— of land and premises and appurtenances, unto the said part— of the second part, —— heirs and assigns, from and against the claims of all persons claiming or to claim the same, or any part thereof, by, from, under or through ——.

And further, that ——, the said part— of the first part and —— heirs shall and will, at any and at all times hereafter, upon the request and at the cost of the said part— of the second part, —— heirs or assigns, make and execute all such other Deed or Deeds or other assurance in law for the more certain and effectual conveyance of the said piece— or parcel— of land and premises and appurtenances, unto the said part— of the second part, —— heirs or assigns, as the said part— of the second part, —— heirs or assigns, or —— counsel learned in the law, shall advise, devise or require.

In Testimony Whereof the said part— of the first part ha— hereunto set —— hand — and seal—, on the day and year first hereinbefore written

Signed, sealed, and delivered in the presence of [SEAL.] [SEAL.]

——

Form 11.—NOTICE TO TAKE DEPOSITIONS—DE BENE ESSE.

IN THE SUPREME COURT OF THE DISTRICT OF COLUMBIA.

——— *vs.* ——— } At Law No.——

To———:

Take Notice that on ——, the —— day of ——, 188—, at —— o'clock — M., the deposition—, *de bene esse*, of ——, of the —— of —— County of ——, in the State of ——, will be taken on behalf of the —— herein, before who is —— at —— in the —— of —— County of —— in the State of ——, at which time and place you are entitled to be present and cross-examine said witness—; the said witness— residing at ——, more than one hundred miles from the place where the trial of this action is to be had.

Dated Washington, D. C., this —— day of ——, 188—.

[*Signature and title.*]

The officer before whom depositions are taken should seal them and direct to "Clerk of the Supreme Court of the District of Columbia," endorse on envelope, title and number of the cause, and write on the back of envelope, "Sealed up and mailed by me, the —— day of ——, 188—," and sign.

Certificate of officer may be in form following No. 13.

[Form 13.—CERTIFICATE TO DEPOSITIONS—DE BENE ESSE.]

IN THE SUPREME COURT OF THE DISTRICT OF COLUMBIA.

——— *vs.* ——— } At Law No.——

I Hereby Certify that on the —— day of —— A. D. 188—, at ——, personally appeared before me, pursuant to the notice hereto annexed, at — — o'clock —— M., ——, the witness— named in said notice, and —— appeared as counsel for the plaintiff—, and —— as counsel for the defendant; and the said ——, being by me first duly cautioned, and sworn to testify the whole truth, and being carefully examined, deposed and said, as appears by the deposition hereto annexed; and I further certify that the said deposition was then and there reduced to writing by me (or in witnesses' presence), and was, after it had been reduced to writing, subscribed by the witness ——.

And I Further Certify that the reason why said deposition was taken was that the said witness— reside— at ——, more than one hundred miles from Washington, D. C., the place where this cause is to be tried, (or other reason, if any).

I Further Certify that the fee for taking the said deposition—, ——, has been paid to me by ——, and that the same is just and reasonable.

In Testimony Whereof, I have hereunto set my hand and official seal at ——, in the County of —, and State of ——, this —— day of ——, A. D. 188—.

[*Signature and title.*]

(See also Forms at end of Laws of Maryland).

LAWS OF FLORIDA

RELATIVE TO THE

COLLECTIN OF DEBTS, Etc.

Prepared expressly for J. A. Graft & Co.'s Legal Directory, by M. C. Jordan, Attorney and Counsellor-at-Law, Jacksonville, Fla.

ARRESTS.—No arrest or imprisonment for debt. Money or goods obtained by false or fraudulant pretenses is a violation of the criminal laws of the State, and punishable only as such.

ASSIGNMENTS.—May be made with or without preference.

ATTACHMENTS.—Will be issued where affidavit shows that sum demanded is due, and that affiant has reason to believe that debtor is about to fraudulently part with his property, or will fraudulently part with his property before judgment can be recovered, or is actually removing, or about to remove out of the State, or that debtor is a non-resident, or has absconded, or is concealing or secreting himself or his property, or is about removing his property into another circuit, where the debt is over

$100, or is about removing his property into another county, where the sum is $100 or less, or that debt was contracted under false or fraudulent representations, when amount is $100 or less. Attachments will also be issued upon debts of over $100, when same will become due within nine months, where the debtor is actually removing his property from the State, or is fraudulently disposing or secreting the same to avoid payment of his just debts. Where sum is $100 or less, and will be due within three months, attachment will be issued on any of the above-mentioned grounds. Garnishments may issue before or after judgment and execution, upon affidavit showing that debtor will not have, or has not, visible property subject to levy. Bond in double the sum sued for, with two sureties, is required in all cases before attachment will be issued, where the sum is more than $100. Only one surety necessary where it is $100 or less.

Claims and accounts for collection should be itemized, and when sent by a co-partnership firm, should be occompanied with the full names of individual members. In case of suit to enforce payment of the amount over $100, ten dollars should be remitted to cover court costs, etc. Where amount is $100 or less, five dollars will be sufficient. Accounts or claims need not be sworn to before notary or Florida commissioner, except when against estates of deceased persons. If disputed, they only need be proved or established by testimony of witnesses in open court, or by deposition taken after notice to adverse party. One unimpeached witness is sufficient to prove an account or claim.

Executions—Are liens only on personal property from the time they are received by the sheriff or constable. They can be issued at any time after ten days, and within three years from rendition of judgments, after that time upon *scire facias* proceedings reviving judgment. There is no redemption of property sold under execution, and, technically, there is no stay of execution.

Exemptions.—Personal property, $1000; realty, 160 acres, with improvements, if outside corporate limits of town or city; if within, half an acre, with improvements, not to exceed the place of business and residence of the head of a family. Upon his death it descends to his heirs, subject to none of his liabilities. The insurance on his life also passes to the beneficiaries named in policy in the same manner. Exemptions are personal privileges, and may be waived by absolute or defeasible conveyances. Exemptions of realty do not apply against purchase money, or labor, or improvements thereon. Money due for personal labor or services to the head of a family is also exempt.

Insolvency.—No insolvency laws, except as to estates of decedents, in which case claims will be settled in the following order: Expenses of administration, funeral and attendance of physician or surgeon, after which all other claims will be settled *pro rata*.

Interest.—No usury laws. Legal interest, eight per cent., unless otherwise expressed in the contract.

Limitations.—Statutable penalties or forfeiture, and libel, slander, assault, battery, or false imprisonment, two years; statutable liabilities, except penalties and forfeiture, trespass to realty; actions involving the recovery of or damage to personal property, and for relief on ground of fraud (to run from discovery), three years; book accounts, four years; promissory notes or other written contracts not under seal, five years; realty, seven years; judgments and contracts, under seal, twenty years; all actions not above specified, four years. Limitation does not run during absence of debtor from State. If cause of action accrued in another State, and is barred by its statute, it is also barred here. Disability not available unless it existed when cause of action accrued. No special limitation on claims or accounts filed with assignee, if defendant is out of the State. A debt can be revived only by new and distinct promise. Claims against decedents are barred in two years after expiration of notice for presentation is given by executor or administrator, except where disabilities exist, in which case two years are allowed after removal of disability. Executors or administrators can not be made to pay debts of deceased until six months after granting letters testamentary or of administration, and no legacy or distribution to heirs can be required until expiration of same period, and then only upon bond or security, if required, to refund a due proportion thereof if necessary, to pay debts or demands, presented within the two years abovementioned.

MORTGAGES, DEEDS, ETC.—All bills of sale or other instruments of writing, made to secure payment of money, are deemed mortgages. Mortgages are only liens, and the possession of the mortgagor can only be defeated by foreclosure and sale of property. Chattel mortgages are void as against third parties, unless property mortgaged is delivered to mortgagee, or the mortgage recorded, within twenty days after its execution. Deeds and mortgages should be executed in presence of two witnesses, and acknowledged before any officer authorized by the laws of the State where executed to take acknowledgments. If acknowledged before officer not having an official seal, there should be attached a certificate, under seal, from a clerk of a Court of Record, or of the Secretary of the State, that the officer taking the acknowledgment was, at the date thereof, the person he is therein represented, that his signature is genuine, and that the instrument is executed and acknowledged according to law. Wife may join husband and relinquish dower right in same deed, or execute a separate deed. Her acknowledgment should state that she executed the deed freely and voluntarily, and without any compulsion, constraint, apprehension or fear of or from her husband. A scrawl, with the word "seal" written thereon, is good in law. Deeds of real property, unless recorded within six months, are void as against a subsequent purchaser.

JUDGMENTS—Are liens upon real estate only of debtor in county where same is obtained or recorded. Judgments of Justice's Courts are not liens until recorded in County Clerk's office, when they become judgments of equal dignity with those of Courts of Record. This must be done within four years after rendition, or new suits must be brought. Judgments of other States are of no force, except as evidence for new suit. There is no law of this State permitting attorneys' fees to be taxed in judgments. They may be taxed in the foreclosure of mortgages, when they contain such a promise or agreement.

MARRIED WOMEN—May have separate estate and property, but neither are liable for the debts of her husband nor for her own debts, unless she specially charge her property for the payment of the same. She may become liable, and her property also for her debts, when she does business as a free trader by permission of the Circuit Court of the county wherein such business is conducted.

PROMISSORY NOTES, BILLS OF EXCHANGE, and other negotiable paper governed by the law merchant.

FLORIDA FORMS.

Form 1—RELINQUISHMENT OF DOWER, WIFE.

STATE OF ——— } SS.
County of ——— }

I, (title of officer), do hereby certify unto all whom it may concern that ———, to me well known as the wife of ———, and as one of the persons described in, and who execute the foregoing deed of conveyance, ———, did this day to me, on a private examination made separately and apart from her said husband, acknowledged and declared that she executed the same and made herself a party thereto, for the purpose of renouncing and relinquishing all and every right of dower in and to the lands in said conveyance described, and that the same was done by her freely and voluntarily, and without any constraint, apprehension or fear of or from her said husband, the said ———.

In Testimony Whereof, I have hereunto set my hand and affixed my official seal, this — day of ———, 18—.

[L. S.] [*Signature and title of officer*].

[Form 2.—FORM OF CAPTION TO DEPOSITION].

Deposition of witnesses, produced, sworn and examined on the —— day of —— A. D., 18—, at the County of ——, in the State of ——, by virtue of the annexed commission issued out of the Clerk's office of the Court of the —— in the County of ——, State of Florida, to us directed, for the examination of the said witnesses, in a cause there pending between ——, plaintiff, and ——, defendant, on the part of the plaintiff or defendant, as the case may be, being duly sworn, deposeth and answereth as follows, namely :

(Give names of witnesses).

1. To the first interrogatory, the witness saith that, etc., and so on, to each successive interrogatory until the whole are answered. The witness must then sign the deposition, and the commissioners attest the signature by the following jurat :

Sworn to and subscribed before us, the —— day of ——, 18—.

——, } *Commissioners.*
——,

If there are any cross-interrogatories, the commissioners should proceed with them, inserting the answers immediately following the answers of the direct interrogatories, in the form following :

The said witness answers and deposes to the cross-interrogatories as follows, namely :

"1. To the first cross-interrogatory he answers and says," etc., and the answers to the cross-interrogatories should be signed by the witness and attested by the commissioners, in the same manner as directed for the direct interrogatories.

At least two commissioners must join in the execution of the commission.

4. When the examination is concluded, the commission, interrogatories and answers must be inclosed in an envelope—the commissioners must write their names across the seals of the envelopes, and having indorsed thereon the title of the cause, thus :

—— *vs.* ——, third judicial circuit of Florida, in Circuit Court, ——County.

Direct the packet to ——, Clerk Circuit Court, of —— County, Florida.

5 Packages containing the commission, etc., may be returned to the Clerk of the Court by a party in the cause, or other person, or by mail.

Note.—The customary abbreviations, or initials of office, or of the Christian names of the commissioners, postmasters, magistrates, clerks, attorneys and witnesses are admissable.

LAWS OF GEORGIA

RELATIVE TO THE

COLLECTION OF DEBTS, Etc.

Prepared expressly for J. A. Graft & Co.'s Legal Directory, by Dean and Ewing, Attorneys and Counsellors at Law, Rome, Ga.

Arrest for Debt.—Imprisonment for debt prohibited by the Constitution of Georgia.

Assignments.—The following acts by debtors are declared to be fraudulent in law against creditors, and as to them null and void:

1st. Every assignment or transfer by a debtor, insolvent at the time, of real or personal property, or choses in action of any description where any trust or benefit is reserved to the assignor or any person for him.

2d. Every conveyance of real or personal estate, by writing or otherwise, and every bond, suit, judgment and execution, or contract of any description, had or made with intention to delay or defraud creditors and such intention known to the party taking. A *bona fide* transaction, on a valuable consideration and without notice or grounds for reasonable suspicion, shall be valid.

3d. Every voluntary deed or conveyance, not for a valuable consideration, made by a debtor insolvent at the time; but a debtor may prefer one creditor to another, and, to that end, he may, *bona fide*, give a lien by mortgage or other legal means, or he may sell in payment of the debt. or he may transfer negotiable papers as collateral security. The surplus in such cases not being reserved for his own benefit or that of any other favored creditor to the exclusion of other creditors.

"In all cases of voluntary assignments by insolvent debtors for the benefit of creditors, the assignment must be accompanied by a sworn statement of assetts of the insolvent person, firm or corporation."

ATTACHMENTS.—Attachments for debt may issue:

1st. When the debtor resides out of the State.

2d. When he is actually removing, or about to remove without the limits of the county.

3d. When he absconds.

4th. When he conceals himself.

5th. When he resists a legal arrest.

6th. When he is causing his property to be removed beyond the limits of the State.

7th. When the debt is created by the purchase of property, upon such debt becoming due, when the debtor who created such debt is in the possession of the property for the purchase of which the debt was created—or when said property is in the possession of any one holding the same for the benefit of said debtor, or in fraud against the creditor, and judgment on such attachments shall take rank from the date of the *levy of the attachment.*

8th. Whenever a debtor shall sell, or convey, or conceal his property liable for the payment of his debts, for the purpose of avoiding the payment of the same, or shall threaten or prepare to do so.

9th. Whenever any person shall make a fraudulant lien on his property.

Before attachment can issue, it must appear by the affidavit of the creditor, his agent, or attorney at law, or in fact, that some one of the grounds above enumerated exists, and the amount of the debt claimed to be due must also be sworn to. If affidavit is made by the attorney or agent, he may swear the amount claimed is due to the best of his knowledge and belief, but the grounds for attachment must be sworn to positively. Bond with security in at least double the amount of the debts sworn to, must accompany the affidavit.

In cases where attachment can not issue, the creditor can not seize the property of the debtor until after judgment, except in equity by a receiver or by garnishment.

CONDITIONAL SALE OF PERSONAL PROPERTY.—Whenever personal property is sold and delivered with the condition affixed to the sale that the title thereto is to remain in the vendor until the purchase price therefor shall have been paid, in order for the reservation of title to be valid against *third persons*, the written contract of such conditional sale shall be executed, attested, and recorded in the same manner as is provided by existing laws for the execution and attestation of mortgages on personal property.

EVIDENCE.—Parties in interest are competent as witnesses in all civil suits except where one of the parties to the original contract is dead.

GARNISHMENT.—In all cases where attachment may issue, in all cases where suit is pending, in all cases where a judgment has been obtained, the plaintiff is entitled to process of garnishment, by which the party garnished is required to return, under oath, what he is indebted to the debtor, what property, money or effects of the defendant he has in his hands at the date of the service of the summons of garnishment, and also what property, money or effects may come into his or her hands at any time from the date of said service to the date of the answer. And said garnishee shall also answer what he or she owes the defendant at the date of the service, and also what he or she may become indebted to the defendant at any time between the date of the service of the summons and the answer thereto. Before summons of garnishment can issue, there must be affidavit made to the amount due and the grounds for the garnishment, and bond given similar to cases of attachment.

The daily, weekly or monthly wages of journeymen, mechanics, and day laborers are not subject to the process of garnishment.

Homestead Exemptions—Against all contracts subsequent to the 25th of July, 1868, and prior to the 5th day of December, 1877. Each head of a family, or guardian or trustee of a family of minor children, is entitled to a homestead of realty to the value of two thousand dollars in specie, and personal property to the value of one thousand dollars in specie, both to be valued at the time they are set apart.

Against all contracts subsequent to the 5th of December, 1877, each head of a family, or guardian, or trustee of a family of minor children, or every aged or infirm person, or person having the care and support of dependent females of any age, who is not the head of a family—is entitled to a homestead exempt from levy and sale by any process whatever (*except for taxes, for the purchase money of same, for labor done thereon, for material furnished therefor, or for the removal of incumbrances thereon*); these exceptions apply also in case stated above, of realty, or personalty, or both, to the value in the aggregate of sixteen hundred dollars—or, the debtor who is the head of a family, may, at his option claim as his homestead fifty acres of land and five additional acres for each of his or her children under the age of sixteen years, or in lieu of the above real estate in a town, or city, or village, not exceeding five hundred dollars in value, together with a farm horse or mule, one cow and calf, ten head of hogs, fifty dollars worth of provisions and five dollars additional for each child. Fifty bushels of corn, one thousand pounds of fodder, one one-horse wagon, one table and a set of chairs sufficient for the use of the family, one loom, one spinning wheel, two pair cards and one hundred pounds of lint, cotton, common tools of trade of himself and wife, equipments and arms of a militia soldier and trooper's horse, ordinary cooking utensils and table crockery, wearing apparel of himself and family, family Bible, religious works and school books, family portraits. The library of a professional man in actual practice, or business, not exceeding three hundred dollars in value and be selected by himself, one family sewing machine. This last exemption is good, whether the debtor is the head of a family or not, against every debt except the purchase money.

Any debtor may, except as to wearing apparel and $300 worth of household and kitchen furniture and provisions, waive or renounce his right to the benefit of the exemptions provided for by the constitution and laws of Georgia, by a waiver, either general or specific, in writing, simply stating that he does so waive or renounce such right, which waiver may be stated in the contract of indebtedness, or contemporaneously therewith, or subsequently thereto, in a separate paper.

The exemption after the death or subsequent marriage of the wife remains for the support of the minor children of the debtor during their minority.

Interest.—The legal rate of interest is 7 per cent., unless a higher rate is specified in writing, when as high as 8 per cent. is lawful.

Judgments.—In the Superior Courts judgments can be obtained at the first, or appearance term, upon suits on contracts for rent, if no defense is sustained.

In all other judgments can be obtained at the second, or trial term, if no defense is sustained.

In the Justices' Courts, which have jurisdiction in all civel cases where the principal sum claimed does not exceed $100, judgments can be obtained at the first, or appearance term, if no defense is sustained.

The judgments of all the courts in this State are, from their date, liens upon all property of the debtor, real and personal, not specially exempted.

Executions may issue at any time after judgment is signed and filed, and is returnable to the next term after being issued.

Execution may be stayed for sixty days if the judgment is over $30, and for forty days if the judgment is for $30 or less, by giving bond and security within four days after the adjournment of the court at which the judgment is rendered.

LIMITATIONS OF ACTIONS.—For open accounts, four years; notes, etc., six years; sealed instruments, twenty years. Judgments to be kept open and retain their lien must have execution issued thereon within seven years, or they become dormant.

Execution must be levied, or have some entry thereon by the Sheriff or other proper officer every seven years, or the judgment becomes dormant. Dormant judgments may be revived within three years. A promise to renew or revive the debt barred by the statute of limitations must be in the handwriting of the debtor, and signed by him or some one authorized by him.

All debts contracted prior to June 1, 1865, are barred if not sued on prior to the 1st of January, 1870. All suits or proceedings by or in behalf of any cestinque trust for the recovery of any realty sold as the property of such cestinque trust by the order of the Chancellor where the said cestinque trust was not represented by a guardian *ad litem*, must be commenced within three years from the removal of the legal disability of said cestinque trust to sue.

All proceedings to set aside judgments or decrees of the court must be made within three years from the rendering of such judgment or decree.

MARRIED WOMEN.—All property of the wife in possession at the time of marriage, or afterwards acquired by her, is her separate property, and not liable for the payment of any debt, default or contract of her husband.

A married woman may sue or be sued in any of the courts of this State in the following cases:

1st. When the action concerns her separate property.

2nd. When the action is between herself and husband.

3rd. When she is living separate and apart from her husband.

In no case is she required to prosecute or defend by a guardian or next friend.

MORTGAGES.—Do not pass title are simply security for debt, may be foreclosed either in compliance with statutory provisions or by bill in equity. A mortgage in this State must clearly indicate the creation of lien, specify the debt to secure which it is given and the property upon which it is to take effect. If executed in this State it must be executed in the presence of and attested by or proved before a Notary Public or Justice of the Peace or Clerk of the Superior Court, and in case of real property by one other witness, and recorded within thirty days from its date. If the mortgage is executed out of this State it must be attested by a Commissioner of Deeds for the State of Georgia, or a Consul or Vice-Consul of the United States, (the certificate of these officers under their Seals being evidence of the fact) or by a Judge of a Court of Record in the State where executed, with a certificate of the Clerk, under the seal of such Court, of the genuineness of the signature of such Judge. Or, if subsequently to its execution the deed or mortgage is acknowledged in the presence of either of the above named officers that fact certified on the deed or mortgage by such officer shall entitle it to be recorded.

WIDOWS' RIGHT OF DOWER.—The wife has a right to an estate for life in one-third of the lands, according to valuation, including the dwelling-house (which is not to be valued unless in a town or city), of which the husband was seized and possessed at the time of his death, or to which the husband obtained title in right of his wife.

No lien created by the husband in his life time, though assented to by the wife, shall in any manner iterfere with her right to dower.

GEORGIA FORMS.

[Form 1.—ACKNOWLEDGMENT.]

STATE OF GEORGIA, }
—— County, } SS.

I (name and style of officer), hereby certify that ——, who is personally known to me, acknowledged before me, this day, that, knowing the contents of the foregoing instrument, he executed the same voluntarily on the day the same bears date.

Witness my hand this ——day of—— , 188—. [*Officer's Signature*].

[Form 2.—AFFIDAVIT IN ATTACHMENT.]

STATE OF GEORGIA, }
—— County, } SS.

Before me the subscriber, a ——, in and for said County, ——, personally —— and on oath, says that —— is indebted to him in the sum of —— dollars, and that the said ——(here state the grounds of attachment). [See Laws, title, Attachment].

[*Affiant's Signature*].

Sworn to before ——this —— day of ——, 18—
[*Officer's Signature*].

Form 3.—BOND IN ATTACHMENT].

STATE OF GEORGIA, }
—— County, } SS.

We, ——, principal, and ——, security, acknowledge ourselves bound unto —— in the sum of —— dollars, subject to the following conditions:

That the said ——, principal, is seeking an attachment against the said ——, which is now about to be sued out, returnable to the —— term of the ——Court of the County aforesaid: Now, if the said —— shall pay all damages that the said —— may sustain, and also all costs that may be incurred by him in consequence of suing out such attachment, in the event that the said —— shall fail to recover in said case, then this bond to be void This —— day of ——, 188—,

EXECUTED IN PRESENCE OF } —— (L. S.)
[*Officer's Signature*]. } —— (L. S.)

[Form 4.—ATTACHMENT WRIT].

STATE OF GEORGIA, }
—— County, } SS.

To all and singular, the Sheriffs and Constables of said State:

You are hereby commanded to attach and seize so much of the property of —— as will make the sum of —— dollars, and all costs, and also to serve such summons and garnishment as may be placed in your hands, and that you make return of this attachment, with your actings and doings entered thereon, to the —— term of the —— Court of said County, to which Court this attachment is hereby made returnable. Hereof fail not.

Witness my hand and seal, this the —— day of ——, 18—.

—— (L. S.)

Form 5.—CAPTION AND CERTIFICATE TO DEPOSITIONS].

STATE OF GEORGIA, }
—— County, } SS. (Code, § 3883).

By virtue of a commission to us directed by the Honorable the —— Court of ——, Georgia, in the case of —— *versus* ——, the undersigned Commissioners have caused ——, the witness in said commission named to come before us, who, being duly sworn true answers to make to the annexed interrogatories, deposes and says:

To the first interrogatory he answers ——.
To the second interrogatory he answers ——.
To the first cross-interrogatory he answers ——.
To the second cross-interrogatory he answers ——. [*Witness' signature.*]
Answered, subscribed, and sworn to before us, this —— day of ——, 18—.

—— COM.
—— COM.

INSTRUCTIONS.

The interrogatories, answers and commission should then be sealed up in an envelope with the names of the Commissioners written across the seal and directed to the officer of the Court whence the commission issued. The package can be sent by mail or intrusted to the party or some private hand. In the former case the postmaster receiving it from the Commissioner must certify to the fact thus: "Received this package from ——, one of the Commissioners, this —— day of ——, 188—. ——, postmaster at ——; and the postmaster delivering it to the Court must certify to its reception by due course of mail. This certificate may be as follows: "Received this package by due course of mail, and the same has since remained in my possession, unopened and unaltered. This —— day of ——, 188—. ——, postmaster at ——. The person receiving and delivering the package in Court must make affidavit as set out in the above certificate, in open Court, an entry of which is made upon the package as follows: "Received in open Court from ——, postmaster at ——, upon the usual oath, with leave to open. This —— day of ——, 18—. ——, Clerk." The package then becomes an office paper, to be used by either party, under the direction of the Court.

DEPOSITIONS—WHEN COMMISSION WAIVED.

(Instructions for forms 6 and 6*a*).

Where any party to a suit in any Court of this State shall desire to examine a witness by written interrogatories, and the opposite party or his attorney shall in writing waive commission, the answers of the witness may be taken by virtue of such agreement which shall operate in lieu of a commission, and the persons acting as Commissioners shall be authorized to administer the usual oath to the witness.

A caption in substance as follows shall be sufficient:

[Form 6.—CAPTION.]

STATE OF GEORGIA,
—— County. } ss.

By virtue of an agreement between the parties or counsel in the case of —— *versus* ——, pending in the —— Court of —— County, the undersigned acting as Commissioners, have caused ——, a witness in said case to come before us, who being duly sworn true answers to make to the annexed interrogatories, deposes and answers as follows:

To the first interrogatory he answers ——.
To the second interrogatory he answers ——.
To the first cross-interrogatory he answers ——.
To the second cross-interrogatory he answers ——.

[*Witness' Signature.*]

Answered, subscribed and sworn to, before us, this —— day of ——, 18—.

——, COM.
——, COM.

[Form 6*a*.—CERTIFICATE TO DEPOSITION.]

——
vs. } IN THE —— COURT OF ——COUNTY, GEORGIA.
——

Depositions of —— and —— witness (or witnesses) for the plaintiff (or defendant), in the above stated case, taken upon notice, beginning on the —— day of ——, 18—, at —— in the presence of ——, (plaintiff and defendant or their attorneys, or both), the witness (or witnesses) being first duly sworn, deposed as follows: (Here stating each question, both direct and cross, with the answer delivered by the witness immediately after it, and concluding as follows:) The foregoing depositions were taken before me as stated in the caption and the answer reduced to writing by me (or by the witness in my presence), and I certify that I am not interested in the cause, nor of kin or counsel to either of the parties.

(Code, § 3895). ——, COM.

LAWS OF IDAHO TERRITORY

RELATIVE TO THE

COLLECTION OF DEBTS, Etc.

Prepared expressly for J. A. Graft & Co.'s Legal Directory.

ASSIGNMENTS AND INSOLVENCY.—An insolvent debtor may be discharged of his debts by executing an assignment of all his property, real and personal, which, with a sworn inventory of property, and schedule of creditors, must be filed in the District Court. At a creditors' meeting, held after thirty days' notice given, one or more assignee, not exceeding three, are appointed, and claims proved. Court will set aside property exempt, and issue order for sale of insolvent's propery. Any creditor may oppose proceedings on the ground of fraud, and, if the allegation be proven, the debtor shall be forever deprived of the benefit of the insolvent laws.

ATTACHMENTS.—Attachment process may issue in actions on contracts for the direct payment of money, where no mortgage or pledge had been given, or where such security, if given, has been rendered nugatory by act of defendant. Plaintiff must furnish bond, with two sufficient sureties. Garnishment process may issue in aid of attachment or execution, and the garnishee must make answer under oath. Defendant, in a civil action for recovery of money or damages, under a contract, expressed or implied, may be arrested, when about to depart from the Territory, with intent to defraud, or when the debt or obligation was fraudulently contracted.

CHATTEL MORTGAGES—May be given upon all kinds of personal property. To be valid against subsequent incumbrancers, or purchasers in good faith for a valuable consideration, the mortgage must show the residence and the profession, trade, or occupation of the mortgagor and mortgagee, and the mortgagor must make affidavit thereto, that the mortgage is made in good faith, and without any design to hinder, delay or defraud creditors. When so made, they must be recorded in the county recorder's office, of the county where the mortgagor resides, and also in the county where the property is located. One day is allowed for every twenty miles of the distance necessarily traveled in going to recorder's office. Unless otherwise stipulated, property will remain in the possession of the mortgagor. Chattel mortgages must be foreclosed by action, and property sold, unless it is provided in the mortgage that the mortgagee may take possession of the property (upon failure to pay), and, after notice, as specified in mortgage, sell the property and pay the claim, paying over the balance to debtor.

EXECUTIONS—Issue at any time within five years after judgment. The only stay is by appeal, with secured bond. Six months allowed for redemption.

EXEMPTION.—Homestead, not exceeding five thousand dollars, if duly acknowledged and recorded; office furniture and library, one hundred dollars; necessary household and kitchen furniture, and provisions for family for three months; certain farm animals, &c., with food for three months; tools and implements of husbandry up to two hundred dollars; libraries of professional men, and team used by a laborer or teamster, are also exempt.

INTEREST.—Ten per cent. is the legal rate, where there is no express contract, fixing a different rate. Parties may agree in writing for any rate not exceeding one and one-half per cent. per month, but any judgment rendered upon such contract bears only ten per cent. per annum. Penalty for greater rate than above specified, is three times the amount so paid, and the party receiving a greater sum subjects himself to pay a fine of three hundred dollars, or six months imprisonment, or both. (6th Sess., p. 72.)

Interest does not commence to run on open accounts until a balance is struck and agreed to, or a settlement is had.

MORTGAGES—Are executed and acknowledged in the same manner as deeds. They are not usually accompanied by a bond. They need not be signed by the wife of a married man, unless the property to be mortgaged is her separate property, or is the homestead. Mortgages are not conveyances, whatever their terms, so as to enable the owner of the mortgage to recover possession of the real property without a foreclosure and sale.

Mortgages are discharged by a satisfaction piece, duly proved, acknowledged, and recorded; or by entry of satisfaction on the margin of the record, witnessed by the recorder. The manner of foreclosure is prescribed by statute, it being by action in the District Court, and a personal decree obtained in same action against the mortgagor for any deficiency from the debt, and costs arising on sale of the mortgaged premises, an attorney's fee is allowed if stipulated for in the mortgage. The decree is for a strict foreclosure, under the decisions of the courts of the Territory. There is no redemption.

A mortgage is a mere security for the payment of money.

NOTES AND BILLS OF EXCHANGE.—No grace on sight drafts. Damages for protested bills; domestic, fifteen per cent.; foreign, thirty per cent.

IDAHO FORMS.

[Form 1.—CERTIFICATE OF ACKNOWLEDGMENT].

STATE OF ——, } SS.
County of ——

On this —— day of ——, A. D., 18—, before me, ——, Commissioner for the Territory of Idaho, personally appeared ——, personally known to me to be the person described in, and who executed the foregoing instrument, and who acknowleged to me that he executed the same freely and voluntarily, for the purposes therein mentioned.

In Witness Whereof, I have hereunto set my hand and official seal, the day and year aforesaid.

[L. S.] *(Signature and title of officer).*

(If taken before officer not a Commissioner, change title in form to suit).

[Form 2.—INSTRUCTIONS FOR TAKING DEPOSITION].

If taken out of the Territory, must be taken upon commission issued from the Court where the suit is pending, under the seal of said Court or upon an order of the Judge of such Court. It must be issued to the person agreed upon by the parties, or if they do not agree, to any Judge or Justice of the Peace, or Commissioner appointed by the Governor of the Territory, selected by the officer granting the commission. They must be taken upon interrogatories, direct and cross, prepared and settled; or, if the parties agree, it may be taken without written interrogatories. The officer taking the deposition must administer an oath to the witness, and certify the deposition to the Court, and inclose the same in a sealed envelope, directed to the Clerk of the Court from which the commission issued, or to such other person as may be agreed upon, and forwarded by mail or other usual channel of conveyance.

(For sufficient legal form of Caption and Certificate, see Forms of other States, published herein).

LAWS OF ILLINOIS.

RELATIVE TO THE

COLLECTION OF DEBTS Etc.

Revised expressly for J. A. Graft & Co.'s Legal Directory, by Herbert B. Johnson, Attorney and Counsellor at Law, Chicago, Ills.

ACTIONS.—Real actions must be brought in Courts of Records where land is situated. Non-residents of State required to file bonds for costs before writ issues. Forms of actions are those of common law, viz., assumpsit, debt, covenant, etc. Action must be brought in county where defendant or one of them, resides, or may be found.

ARRESTS.—*Capias ad respondendum* will issue on bond, and affidavit of plaintiff that debt was fraudulently contracted, or that defendant is about to remove, conceal or assign his effects with intent to hinder or defraud his creditors.

ASSIGNMENT.—No preference of creditors. Three months allowed for creditors to file claims. Assignee under control of County Courts, and is required to file bond on assuming trust. Final settlement to be made within one year from expiration of three months.

ATTACHMENT—Issues upon bond, and affidavit stating one of usual statutory grounds, viz.: non-residence, about to leave State and remove property, about to conceal, assign or dispose of property to hinder creditor. Having so concealed, assigned or disposed of property within two years last past. Debt fraudulently contracted, fraud being evidenced by writing signed by debtor, his agent or attorney, etc.

BILLS OF SALE AND CHATTEL MORTGAGES.—Of no effect as to third parties, unless mortgagee takes possession, or instrument reserves possession in mortgagor, and acknowledgment is entered upon docket of justice in town or city where mortgagor resides, and recorded in office of Recorder of the County. When so executed is good until principal debt is due, provided same matures within two years. Possession must be taken immediately upon maturity of debt.

COSTS.—Bond for costs required of non-residents.

CORPORATIONS—Organized under general laws. Stockholders liable to the amount of unpaid stock. Original holder and assignee liable to amount of such stock (unpaid).

COURTS.—Jurisdiction of Justice. $200; County Court, $1,000. Appellate jurisdiction from Justice. Terms: County Court, twice a year in most counties; Circuit Court (general jurisdiction, two to four terms; in Chicago, monthly; also, Superior Court of Cook County, jurisdiction, etc., same as Circuit Court.

DEEDS—Without the State may be acknowledged before officers usually authorized to take acknowledgments, viz.: Justices, Notarys Public, Judges, Mayors, Clerks of Court, etc. In case of Justices of Peace a certificate of their official character, from the proper clerk, must be attached.

EXECUTION.—Issues on judgment of a Justice after twenty days. In county record may issue immediately upon judgment, and is a lien upon personal property after coming into the hands of an officer.

EXEMPTIONS.—Homestead of the value of $1,000; continues after death of householder for benefit of family. Proceeds of sale exempt for one year; also, insurance money, from loss of homestead. Debtors without family allowed exemption of $100, personal property, besides wearing apparel,etc. Head of a family,value of $300 of personalty. Wages of head of family to amount of $50 exempt. No exemptions upon claims of laborer or domestic.

GARNISHMENT.—Creditor may garnishee money due any debtor, or money or property, in hands of another. Garnishee process will issue in attachment against person owing debtor, or having money or property of debtor belonging to him; but in all other cases process can only issue after judgment, and return on execution "no property found."

INTEREST.—Legal rate six per cent. Contract in writing as high as eight per cent. Usury forfeits entire interest.

JUDGMENT—Of a Court of Record is a lien on real estate for seven years, if execution is issued within one year. A transcript of judgment from justice becomes a lien on real estate when filed in a Court of Record.

LIMITATION.—Action on unwritten contracts, express or implied, five years; actions on written contracts, ten years; foreclosure of mortgages and trust deeds, ten years from the date action accrues; to recover lands, twenty years.

MARRIED WOMEN.—Rights the same as of single women, except that she cannot become member of a partnership without her husband's consent. Husband and wife both chargeable with debts contracted in maintenance of a family. Wife may be sued jointly or severally for same.

NOTES AND BILLS.—Fraud in execution avoids in hands of innocent holder, fraud in consideration will not. To charge indorser due dilligence must be exercised, and suit brought at first term of court having jurisdiction, unless the maker is insolvent, or a non-resident, or has left the State, a guarantor is held regardless of any attempt to recover from the maker. Total or partial failure of consideration,is good defence, except in hands of innocent holders for value before maturity.

PROOF OF CLAIMS.—Party claiming under contract for payment of money, who files, with his declaration, an affidavit, stating nature and amount due after allowing set-offs, etc., is entitled to judgment, as by default, unless defendant files affidavit that he verily believes he has a good defence to demand, or a part of it, etc.

On default affidavit is *prima facie* proof of amount due.

REDEMPTION.—Lands sold on execution or foreclosure may be redeemed by debtor or mortgagor within one year, and by judgment creditor from previous judgment, after twelve and within fifteen months; from tax sale, within two years.

STATUTE OF FRAUDS.—Usual provisions of the statute. Conveyances of any interest in lands or lease, for a term greater than one year, must be in writing. To charge person for the debt of another, his agreement must be in writing, signed by himself or authorized agent.

ILLINOIS FORMS.

[Form 1.—AFFIDAVIT.]

The following form of affidavit may be used:

STATE OF ——,
County of—— } ss.

(John Doe) of ——, in the County and State aforesaid, being duly sworn, on oath says, that he is a member of the firm of (Doe & Roe), composed of (Richard Roe) and this deponent; that (Henry Higgins and James Brown), composing the firm of (Higgins & Brown), of Chicago, in the State of Illinois, are justly indebted to said firm of (Doe & Roe) in the sum of —— dollars and —— cents, for goods, wares and merchandise sold and delivered by the said (Doe & Roe) to the said (Higgins & Brown) (or upon promissory note describing it), which said sum of money is now due to the said (Doe & Roe) from the said (Higgins & Brown), after allowing to the said (Higgins & Brown) all just credits, deductions and set-offs. And that the said (Doe & Roe) are about to bring suit against the said (Higgins & Brown) in the —— Court of —— County, to recover said sum. (John Doe.)

The foregoing affidavit was subscribed and sworn to by the said ——, before me on this —— day of ——, A. D., 18—. And I certify that I am duly authorized by the laws of the State of —— to administer oaths.

[*Signature, official title and seal.*

[Form 2.—ACKNOWLEDGMENT OF DEEDS.]

"This [name of instrument] was acknowledged before me by [name of grantor]; [when the acknowledgment is by a resident], entered by me this —— day of —— 188—. Witness my hand and —— seal. [*Name of officer.*

[SEAL.]

[Form 3.—SECURITY FOR COSTS.]

Non-resident plaintiffs are required to give security for costs, Such security may be substantially in the following form:

A. B.
vs. } (Title of Court.)
C. D.

I, (E. F,) do enter myself security for costs which may accrue in the above cause. Dated this —— day of ——, A. D. 18—.

[Signed] —— ——.

[Underwood, 313.]

[Form 4.—WARRANTY DEED.]

"The grantor [here insert the name or names and place of residence of] for and in consideration of [here insert consideration] in hand paid, convey and warrants to [here insert the grantee's name or names] the following described real estate: [here insert description], situated in the County of ——, in the State of Illinois. Dated this —— day of ——, A. D. 188—.

A. B.
[SEAL.]

"The grantor [here insert grantor's name and place of residence] for the consideration of [here insert consideration], convey and quit claim to [here insert grantee's name or names] in the following described real estate [here insert description [situated in the County of ——, in the State of Illinois. Dated this —— day of ——, A. D. 188—.

A. B.
[SEAL.]

[Form 5.—CERTIFICATE OF ACKNOWLEDGMENT.]

STATE OF——————, }
County of——————. }

I, [here give name of officer and his official title] do hereby certify that [name of grantor, and if acknowledged by wife, her name, and add "his wife"] personally known to me to be the same person whose name is [or are] subscribed to the foregoing instrument, appeared before me this day in person and acknowledged that he [she or they] signed, sealed and delivered the said instrument as his [her or their] free and voluntary act, for the uses and purposes therein set forth. [If conveyance releases homestead right add] "including the release and waiver of the right of homestead." Given under my hand and [private or official, as the case may be] seal this [day of the month], day of [month], A. D. [year.] [*Signature of officer.*]

[SEAL.]

[Form 6.—FOR TAKING, CERTIFYING AND RETURNING DEPOSITIONS.]

[CAPTION.]

The deposition of ——, of the County of ——, State of ——, a witness of lawful age produced, sworn and examined on his oath (or affirmation) on the —— day of ——, A. D. 188—, at the (office or house) of ——, in the (town or city) of ——, in the County of —— and State of ——, by me, ——, a commissioner duly appointed by a *dedimus potestatum*, or commission issued out of the Clerk's office of the —— Court of —— Coun in the State of Illinois, bearing test in the name of ——, Clerk of said Court, with the seal of said Court affixed thereto, and to me directed as such commissioner for the examination of the said ——, a witness in a certain suit and matter in controversy now pending and undetermined in the said —— Court of —— County wherein —— is plaintiff, and —— is defendant, in behalf of the said ——, as w upon the cross-interrogatories of the said —— as on the interrogatories of the said ——, which were attached to or enclosed in the said commission, and upon no e others.

The said —— being by me first duly sworn (or affirmed) as a witness in the said cause previous to the commencement of his examination, to testify the truth, as well on the part of the plaintiff as the defendant. In relation to the matters in controversy between the said plaintiff and defendant, so far as he should be interrogated, testified and deposed as follows:

Interrogatory first, (Here insert first interrogatory.)
Answer to first interrogatory, (Here insert answer.)

Form 7.—COMMISSIONER'S CERTIFICATE.]

I, ——, of the County of ——, and State of ——, a commissioner duly appointed to take the deposition of the said ——, whose name is subscribed to the foregoing deposition, do hereby certify that previous to the commencement of the examination of the said —— as a witness in the suit between the said ——, plaintiff, and the said ——, defendant, he was duly sworn by me, as such commissioner, to testify the truth in relation to the matters in controversy between the said ——, plaintiff, and ——, defendant, so far as he should be interrogated concerning the same: that the deposition was taken at my office, in the city of ——, in the County of ——, and State of —— on the —— day of ——, A. D. 188—, and that after said deposition was taken by me as aforesaid, the interrogatories and answers thereto as written down, were read over to said witness, and that thereupon the same was signed and sworn to by the said witness, ——, the oath being administered by me as such commissioner, at the place and on the day and year last aforesaid.

(Signed) *Commissioner.*

[Form 8.—MORTGAGES OF REAL ESTATE.]

"The mortgagor (name) mortgages and warrants to (name) to secure the payment of (here nature and amount of indebtedness, showing when due, rate of interest, and whether secured by note or otherwise) the following real estate (here insert description) situated in the County of ——, in the State of Illinois.

"Dated this —— day of ——, A. D. 188—.

"[A. B.] [L. S.]"

LAWS OF INDIANA

RELATIVE TO THE

COLLECTION OF DEBTS, Etc.

Revised expressly for J. A. Graft & Co.'s Legal Directory.

ACTION.—There is in this State but one form of civil action, and no distinction in pleading and practice between actions at law and suits in equity.

ASSIGNMENTS.—Any debtor in embarrassed or failing circumstances, may make a general assignment of all his property in trust for the benefit of all his *bona fide* creditors, which must be by deed of indenture acknowledged and recorded in the Recorder's office of county where the debtor resides, within ten days after its execution. The indenture must contain a full description of the real estate assigned, and be accompanied by a schedule containing an enumeration and description of all personal property.

The indenture is not operative until filed for record, when it takes precedence to executions, attachments, etc., not theretofore levied.

The assignor is allowed the benefit of the $600 exemption as against debts upon contract, but no exemption from claims founded in tort.

ATTACHMENTS.—The plaintiff at the time of filing his complaint, or at any time afterwards, may have an attachment against the property of the defendant, in the case and in the manner hereafter stated:

1st, Where the defendant, or one of several defendants, is a foreign corporation or a non-resident of the state. 2nd, Where the defendant, or one of several defendants, is secretly leaving, or has left the State, with intent to defraud his creditors; or 3d, So conceals himself that a summons can not be served upon him; or 4th, Is removing, or about to remove, his property, subject to execution, or a material part thereof, out of the State, not leaving enough to satisfy the plaintiff's claim; or 5th and 6th, Has sold, conveyed, or is about to sell and convey, or otherwise dispose of his property, subject to execution, or has suffered or permitted it to be sold, with the fraudulent intent to cheat hinder, or delay his creditors. Under the 2nd, 4th, 5th and 6th clauses attachment can be had in debts to become due.

DECEDENTS' ESTATES, ETC.—Letters of administration shall be granted in their order: 1, To the husband or wife. 2, To the next of kin. 3, To the largest creditor residing in the State; and 4, If no person thus entitled shall apply within thirty days after death of intestate, the Clerk of Court shall appoint a competent inhabitant of the county.

After inventory and appraisement of decedent's personal estate, the widow may select and take articles to the value of $500, or that amount in cash, and receipt to executor or administrator for the same.

If the entire estate of the decedent does not exceed in value $500, the widow, on petition filed, may take the same, discharged of all debts of decedent, except mortgages of realty and expenses of funeral and last sickness.

Claims against estates of decedents are classed as follows: 1, Expenses of administration. 2, Expenses of last sickness and funeral. 3, Judgments which are liens upon the decedent's real estate, and mortgages of real and personal property existing in his lifetime. 4, General debts. 5, To legatees. 6, To distributees. There shall be no preference as to claims of the same class. (R. S. 1876, Vol II, p. 534.)

The surviving partner or partners have the right to settle and close up the partnership affairs. Such surviving partner or partners shall give bonds, and, within sixty days after such death, shall file a complete inventory of all the partnership assets and liabilities. (R. S. 1876, Vol I, p. 641.)

Depositions—May be taken before any Judge, Justice of the Peace, Notary Public, Mayor or Recorder of a city, Clerk of a court of record, or Commissioner appointed for the purpose. The officer taking the deposition can not decide legal questions. Objections may be raised either at the time of taking the deposition, and noted by the officer, or in court at the time of trial. (See forms following.)

Dower—is abolished. Widow takes, as heir and in fee simple, one-third of real estate, except when real estate exceeds $10,000, one-fourth, and when it exceeds $20,000, one-fifth, *as against creditors only*; otherwise one-third. She takes one-third of personal property. If but one child or descendant, widow takes one-half. She may elect to take under the will or the law. If she marry a second time, having children by former husband, she can not, during such coverture, alienate real estate received by former marriage, and if she dies during such coverture, real estate goes to children by previous marriage.

Divorces—May be granted for the following causes and no others: 1, Adultery, except as hereinafter provided. 2, Impotency, existing at time of marriage. 3, Abandonment for two years. 4, Cruel and inhuman treatment of either party by the other. 5, Habitual drunkenness by either party, or failure of husband to make reasonable provision for his family. 6, Failure of husband to make reasonable provision for his family for a period of two years. 7, Conviction, subsequent to the marriage, of either party of an infamous crime.

The care of minor children, and the granting of alimony, are within the discretion of court. (R. S. 1876, Vol. II, p. 324.)

Examination of Party to Suit, etc.—Either party to a suit may, upon five day's notice, compel the opposite party to attend before any officer authorized to take depositions, and be examined as to all matters in controversy in suit, which examination shall be reduced to writing and may be used in evidence.

Exemption.—Upon filing the necessary affidavit and schedule, any *resident householder* may exempt property to be selected by him to the amount of $600 as against claims founded on contract made since May 31st, 1879, and to the amount of $300 on claims contracted before that date. No exemption as against judgments founded on tort. Married women, whether householders or not, may, if resident of the State, claim $600 exempt in like manner as householder. To all employees one month's wages are exempt.

Quere. Can an exemption be claimed as against judgment for the costs of the opposite party? U. S. Dist. Court for Dist. of Indiana, *in re Owen*, 6th Bissel, 432: Gresham, J., holds that judgment for the cost of the opposite party is not "a judgment founded on contract," and can not be scheduled against under the exemption laws.

Garnishment.—If, at time an order of attachment issues, or before or afterwards, the plaintiff, or other person in his behalf, shall file an affidavit that he has good reason to believe that any person (naming him) has property of defendant, of any description, in his possession or under his control, which the officer can not attach, or that such person is indebted to defendant, a writ of garnishment shall issue against such person, and he shall be accountable to the plaintiff for the amount of money, property or credits so under his control, or due the defendant from him, from the time of service of summons in garnishment. But all employes are entitled to one month's wages free from garnishment.

Interest—May be charged at 6 per cent. on money due and payment withheld or delayed on accounts stated. 8 per cent. may be charged on written agreement, and may be taken in advance. Where no rate specified, it is 6 per cent. All judgments bear 6 per cent. Usury forfeits excess above 6 per cent.

JUSTICES OF THE PEACE—Have jurisdiction in civil actions, attachments, replevin, etc., to $200.

JUDGMENT LIEN—Holds for ten years after the rendition of judgment or the last execution, upon real estate in county where rendered; so, too, of transcript of judgment of Justice of the Peace, where transcript is filed in Clerk's office in any county in State. Judgment may be revived within twenty years after rendition. Execution lien on real and personal property in county from time of issuing.

LIMITATIONS.—Actions must be brought within six years after the cause has accrued on accounts, and contracts not in writing for use, rents, and profit of real property, for injury to property, damages for any detention thereof, and recovering possession of personal property, and for relief against frauds. Actions for injuries to person, or character, and for a penalty given by statutes, must be commenced within two (2) years, against a public officer within five (5) years, but against the officer, or his representative, for money collected, and not turned over, any time within six (6) years. For the recovery of real property, sold on execution debt, or his heirs, or any person claiming under him, by title acquired after date of judgment, within ten (10) years after the same. Upon promissory notes, bills of exchange, and other written contracts, for the payment of money hereafter executed, *within ten years*. Provided, that all such contracts as have been heretofore executed, may be enforced under this act, within such time only as they have to run, before being barred under the existing law, limiting the commencement of actions, and not afterward. Upon contracts in writing, other than those for the payment of money, on jndgments of courts of records, and for the recovery of the possesession of real estate, within twenty years.

MARRIED WOMEN, RIGHTS OF.—All property she owns at time of marriage, or acquires during coverture, remains her own separate property, and can not be sold for husband's debts. May sell her separate personal property same as if she were *sole*. May carry on business on her sole account, and have profits of such business; husband shall not be liable for debts on account of such business. May make contract in reference to her personal, and the management of her real property, and her separate estate shall be liable therefor on judicial process. Husband must join in conveyance of her lands. She is bound by her covenants of title in conveyance of her real estate. May not incumber her separate property, acquired by descent, devise or gift, as security for any one. Is bound by her contracts, except as surety, but can not make any executory contract concerning her separate real estate, nor convey or encumber it without her husband joining with her, or where he has abandoned her, by permission of court.

She may charge her husband's real estate or personal property for her support, where he has abandoned her, by decree of court.

MORTGAGES.—Must be recorded in county where land is situated within 45 days in order to preserve priority.

CHATTEL MORTGAGES—must be recorded in county where mortgagor resides within ten days after execution to be good as to third parties.

NOTES AND BILLS.—Bills of exchange and promissory notes, payable in bank within the State, are governed by the law merchant. Three days grace allowed on all commercial paper payable within the State, except when third day is holiday, then paper matures on second day. All notes and bills should contain the clause: "Without relief from valuation or appraisement law."

PROOF OF CLAIMS.—The full name of each of the claimants should be sent with the claim. An itemized bill of particulars, the correctness of which is sworn to by the claimant, or some one in his behalf, is sufficient proof, in case of default by the defendant, but not otherwise.

REDEMPTION.—Real estate sold on execution or decree, may be redeemed within one year from date of sale, by payment of amount for which it sold, with 8 per cent. thereon from date of sale.

STAY OF EXECUTION—May be had by giving one or more sufficient freehold sureties; in higher courts, on judgments not exceeding $6, 30 days; over $6 and not exceeding $12, 90 days; over $12 and not exceeding $20, 90 days; over $20 and not exceeding $40, 120 days; over $40 and not exceeding $100, 150 days; over $100, 180 days. In Justices' courts, if over $40 and under $75, 150 days; over $75, 180 days; smaller amounts same as higher courts.

INDIANA FORMS.

[Form 1.—AFFDAVIT TO ACCOUNT].

STATE OF INDIANA, }
—— County. }

Before me (state name of officer), a (state official title), of said County and State came ——, who being by me duly sworn, says that the annexed account in favor of —— against ——, is correct; that no payments have been made thereon except the credits thereon given; that there are no set-offs against the same to his knowledge; that the balance shown in said statement of account, to-wit: —— Dollars, is now justly due and owing to said ——, all of which he verily believes.

(*Signature and title of officer*).

Subscribed and sworn to before me, on the —— day of —— 18—.
[SEAL]. *Signature.*

[Form 2.—ACKNOWLEDGMENT].

STATE OF INDIANA, } SS.
—— County. }

Before me, (name), a (official capacity), in and for said County, this —— day of —— 18—, personally appeared the within named —— and acknowledged the execution of the annexed Deed:

Witness, my hand and —— seal. *Signature.*

[Form 3.—AFFIDAVIT IN ATTACHMENT].

——
vs. } Before —— Justice of the Peace, —— the plaintiff says that the claim
—— } in this action against the defendant, is for (state nature of claim, whether note or account), and that the claim is just, and that he believes he ought to recover —— dollars, and —— cents, and the said (state ground of attachment).

Signature. [SEAL].

Sworn to and subscribed before me this —— day of ——, 18—.

——*Justice.* [SEAL].

[Form 4.—BOND IN ATTACHMENT].

——
vs. } Before —— Justice of the Peace, we undertake that the plaintiff shall
—— } duly prosecute these proceedings and pay the defendant all damages which he may sustain, if these proceedings are wrongful and oppressive.

Signature. [SEAL].
Signature. [SEAL].

Taken by me, this —— day of —— 188—.

—— Justice. [SEAL].

Form 5.—PROMISSORY NOTE].

$—— ——, 1881.

—— days after date, —— promise to pay to the order of ——, —— dollars, payable at ——, for value received, without any relief whatever from valuation or appraisement laws, with interest at eight per cent. per annum after maturity, and until paid, with —— per cent. attorney's fee. *Signature.*
Signature.

[Form 6.—BILL OF EXCHANGE OR DRAFT].

$—— ——, Ind., ——, 18—.

——pay to the order of ——, —— dollars, payable at ——, without any relief whatever from valuation or appraisement laws, for value received, with interest at ten per cent. per annum after maturity, and until paid, and —— per cent. attorney's fees; and charge to

To —— }
—— } *Signature.*

(Form 7.—CHATTEL MORTGAGE].

Know all Men by these Presents, That —— of —— County, in the State of Indiana, party of the first part, ha— this day bargained and sold, and do hereby bargain and sell unto ——, of Indiana, party of the second part, for the sum of ——dollars, in hand paid, receipt whereof is hereby acknowledged, the following described property, to-wit: ——

The Condition of this Bill of Sale is, (Here insert conditions about the debt, etc.), without relief from valuation or appraisement laws, with attorney's fees. Now, if the said party of the first part shall well and truly pay said notes at maturity, with all the interest thereon, then this instrument shall be void, otherwise to remain in full force. (Here insert other conditions as to possession, etc., as the case may be).

Witness, —— hand— and seal— this ——day of —— 188—.

[SEAL].
[SEAL].

STATE OF INDIANA, } ss. (ACKNOWLEDGMENT).
County of — }

Before me, the undersigned, a — in and for said County and State, this — day of — 188—, personally appeared — to me well known, and acknowledged the execution of the foregoing instrument as — free act and deed.

Witness, My hand and official seal. *Signature.*

[Form 8.—AFFIDAVIT TO CLAIM—vs. Estates of deceased persons].

STATE OF INDIANA, } ss.
—County. }

Before the Clerk of the Circuit Court of said County and State came —, who being by me duly sworn, says that the annexed — in favor of —, against the estate of — deceased, is correct; that no payments have been made thereon except the credits thereon given; that there are no set-offs against the same to his knowledge; that the balance shown in said —, to-wit: — dollars, is now justly due and owing to —, all of which he verily believes.

Signature.

Subscribed and Sworn to before me, on the — day of —, 18—. *Clerk.*

[Form 9.—WARRANTY DEED].

This Indenture Witnesseth, That —, of — County, in the State of Indiana, convey and warrant to —, of — County, in the State of Indiana, for the sum of — dollars, the following real estate, in — County, in the State of Indiana, to-wit: [Here insert description].

In testimony whereof, the said — ha— hereunto set — hand and seal—, this — day of —, 18—.

Signature. [SEAL], *Signature.* [SEAL].
Signature. [SEAL]. *Signature.* [SEAL].

STATE OF INDIANA, } ss.
— County. }

Before me, — a — in and for said County, this — day of — 18—, personally appeared the within named — and acknowledged the execution of the annexed Deed.

Witness, My hand and — Seal.

Signature.

[Form 10.—DEPOSITIONS].

—
vs. } IN THE (FORM OF NOTICE).
—

The — hereby notified that on the — day of — 188—, between the hours of — o'clock A. M., and — o'clock P. M., before — or some other person authorized to take Depositions, at — in the — of — County of — and State of — the — will proceed to take depositions to be read in evidence on the trial of the above entitled cause, and will continue taking the same from day to day thereafter, between the same hours, until the whole be taken.

Dated —188—. — Attorney for —

We acknowledge service of foregoing notice the — day of —, 188—.

— Attorneys for —.

[Form 11.—INSTRUCTIONS FOR TAKING DEPOSITIONS FOR INDIANA].

(CAPTION).

Depositions of — witness[es] in a certain action now pending in the — Court — of the State of Indiana, wherein — is plaintiff, and — is defendant, taken before me, pursuant to the annexed Notice and Commission, at the time and place in my certificate hereinafter named, to be used as evidence on the part of — in said action. The said — of lawful age, being first duly sworn, deposeth as follows:

QUESTION BY —(Insert questions and answers, and add the following Certificate).

[Form 12.—CERTIFICATE].

STATE OF —, } ss.
— County. }

I —- in and for said County, do hereby Certify that — the above named deponent[s] was (were) by me first sworn to tell the truth, the whole truth, and nothing but the truth, in the case now pending in the — of the State of Indiana, wherein — is plaintiff, and — is defendant; that the foregoing deposition(s) was (were) all written by me (or by —, a disinterested person in my presence and under my direction), and that said deponent (or deponents severally) subscribed his (or their respective) deposition(s) after the same had been carefully read over to him (or them) by me; that the — (adverse party) was (or was not) present, (either) in person (or by attorney) at the taking of said deposition(s); that all said deposition(s) was (or were) taken at — in the — of — County of — and State of — on the — day(s) of —, 18—, between the hours of — o'clock A. M. and — o'clock P. M. of said day (or days), agreeably in all respects to the annexed notice (and commission).

[L. S.] *In Witness Whereof*, I hereunto subscribe my name, and affix my (official) seal, this — day of — A. D., eighteen hundred and —

Signature.

(INSTRUCTIONS).

Leading questions should not be asked. Examine the instructions below.

Exhibits should be attached by wafer or otherwise, to the question or answer, or some other part of the deposition. The notice (and commission) if any, should be attached to the deposition, Each witness must sign his deposition.

A commission is not necessary, if the deposition is to be taken in this State. If the commission contains the name of the officer, his official certificate will be sufficient, but if it do not, and the officer have no official seal, the certificate and seal of a Clerk of a Court of Record of the County will be necessary. Depositions may be taken before any Judge, Justice of the Peace, Notary Public, Mayor or Recorder of a City, Clerk of a Court of Record, or Commissioner, either within or without this State. The officer must seal up the deposition, and direct the same to the Clerk of the Court in which the action is pending, endorsing on the envelope the names of the parties, and of the witnesses whose depositions are enclosed. The officer should tax the cost, and state which party pays them.

[Form 12.—OPENING AND CLOSING FORM OF WILLS].

In the name of the benevolent Father of all, I, A. B., of (state place of residence), do make and publish this my last will and testament.

ITEM 1.—I give and devise and bequeath, etc.

In testimony whereof I have hereunto set my hand and seal, this —— day of ——, 18—. A. B.

WITNESSES' ATTEST.

Signed and acknowledged by said A. B., as his last will and testament, in our presence, and signed by us in his presence and in the presence of each other.

C. D.
E. F.

(Two witnesses are necessary.)

LAWS OF IOWA

RELATIVE TO THE

COLLECTION OF DEBTS, Etc.

Prepared expressly for J. A. Graft & Co.'s Legal Directory.

ACCOUNTS.—In suits on account, the items of the account must be set out in a bill of particulars; and in case of failure, so to do the petition, is subject to demurrer for this defect. But when set out as above required, and duly verified, if the defendant fails to appear, or appearing fails to controvert the items, or any portion thereof, by pleading duly verified; then the account, or such portion thereof as is not controverted, is taken to be true.

ASSIGNMENTS.—No general assignment for the benefit of creditors, is valid in this State, unless for the benefit of all creditors in proportion to their respective claims. The above is not construed to prohibit a debtor, who is at the time, unable to pay all his debts, from paying or giving mortgages to secure to any one creditor all his claim, even though doing so, may leave nothing for the payment of others.

Assignments should be acknowledged and recorded like conveyances of real estate, and should have attached to them an inventory of all the property of the assignor, together with a list of his creditors, and the amount of their respective claims. The assignee, must, within twenty days, on pain of removal, file a similar inventory and valuation with the Clerk of the District or Circuit Court, and, then and there, file a bond for the faithful performance of the trust in double the amount of his inventory and valuation. He is also required to publish for six weeks, notice of the assignment, and to mail to all creditors known to him, notice to present their claims within three months. Provisions are made for the death, inability, or refusal to act of the assignee.

ATTACHMENTS. Property not exempt from execution, may be attached on any of the following grounds: First, that the defendant is a foreign corporation, or acting as such; or, second, that he is a non-resident of the State; or, third, that he is about to remove his property out of the State, without leaving sufficient remaining for the payment of his debts; or, fourth, that he has disposed of his property, in whole, or in part, with intent to defraud his creditors; or, fifth, that the defendant is about to dispose of his property, with intent to defraud his creditors; or, sixth, that he has absconded so, that the ordinary process cannot be served upon him; or, seventh, that he is about to remove permanently out of the county, and has property therein, not exempt from execution; and that he refuses to pay or secure the plaintiff; or, eighth, that he is about to remove permanently out of the State, and refuses to pay or secure the debt due the plaintiff; or, ninth, that he is about to remove his property, or a part thereof, out of the county, with intent to defraud his creditors; or, tenth, that he is about to convert his property, or a part thereof into money, for the purpose of placing it beyond the reach of his creditors; or, eleventh, that he has property or rights in action, which he conceals; or, twelfth, that the debt is due for property obtained under false pretences.

An attachment may issue before the debt is due, when nothing but time is wanting to fix an absolute indebtedness, on any of the fourth, fifth, or twelfth grounds above given; or that the defendant is about to remove from the State, and refuses to make any arrangements for securing the payment of the debt when it falls due, and which contemplated removal, was not known to the plaintiff at the time the debt was contracted.

CLAIMS, PROOF OF—See account.

COST BOND—If the defendant before answering, make and file an affidavit, that he has a good defense in whole or in part the plaintiff, if he be a non-resident of the State, or a private or foreign corporation, will be required to give bond for the payment of all costs.

COLLECTIONS.—Attorney fees on written contracts, made since July 4th, 1880, containing an agreement to pay an attorney's fee, shall be allowed and taxed as part of the cost, as follows:

For the first $200 or fraction thereof, ten per cent. of the amount found due. For the excess of $200, up to $500, five per cent. For the excess of $500, up to $1,000, three per cent. For all in excess of $1,000, one per cent.; provided that the plaintiff shall be entitled to recover not to exceed one-half of the above collection fee, in case payment is made after commencement of suit, and before return day.

EVIDENCE.—Common law rules of evidence, relating to competency of witnesses materially altered. Interest in the result of the action, does not disqualify any one from being a witness. Neither husband nor wife can be a witness one against the other, except in an action one against the other, but they may in all cases be witnesses for each other. Confidential communications made to attorneys, physicians, ministers, etc., can not be disclosed.

EXECUTIONS.—Executions are issuable, immediately upon the rendition of judgment, and at any time before the judgment is barred. In Justices' Court, execution must be returned within thirty days, and in a Court of Record, within seventy days. Execution may be stayed where the amount is less than one hundred dollars for three months, and where the amount is over one hundred dollars for six months, provided the defendant, within ten days of the rendition of judgment, give a bond with one or more sufficient freehold sureties, for the payment of the judgment, interest and costs.

EXEMPTIONS.—Homestead of 40 acres in country, and half an acre if within a town *plat*, with buildings without regard to value. Personal property exempt includes tools, instruments, library, necessary team, &c., of mechanic, farmer, teacher or professional man; wearing apparel, household and kitchen furniture, $200; certain farm animals and necessary food for six months. Earnings of debtor within 90 days of levy are exempt. Foregoing relates only to residents, being the head of a family; unmarried persons and non-residents being only entitled to retain their own clothing and trunks. Where debtor is a printer, the printing press and types, furniture and material up to $1,200 are exempt.

GARNISHMENT.—See attachment.

INSOLVENT LAWS.—See assignments.

INTEREST.—The legal rate of interest is six per cent., but parties may contract for any rate not exceeding ten per cent. In cases on contract providing for more than ten per cent., the court will render judgment for the amount of ten cents on the hundred by the year, in favor of the State of Iowa, for the use of the school fund of the county, where the action is pending, and in no case shall the plaintiff have judgment for more than the principal sum. Accounts bear interest after six months from the date of the last item.

JUDGMENTS.—Judgments in the District and Circuit Courts may be obtained at first term after suit commences, if undefended, and they are a lien upon all real property of the defendant, from the rendition of the judgment, in the county where the same is rendered, and in any other in the State from the time of filing a transcript of the judgment in the office of the Clerk of that county.

Judgments in Justices' Court are a lien upon the real property of the defendant, from and after the filing of a transcript of the judgment in the office of the Clerk of the District and Circuit Courts of the county, in which they are rendered, from whence transcripts may be sent to other counties in the State, the same as if rendered in the District or Circuit Court. No judgment is a lien upon personal property, until said property is actually levied upon under execution.

LIMITATIONS OF ACTIONS.—Actions founded on injuries to the person, or reputation must be brought within two years. Actions to enforce a mechanic's lien within two years from filing the statement in the Clerk's office. Those against any officer where the liability arises out of any official act, within three years; those founded on unwritten contracts or injuries to property, or for fraud and all other actions not otherwise provided for in this respect, within five years; those founded on written contracts or judgments of any court, other than a court of record, and those brought for the recovery of real estate, within ten years; those founded on judgment of a court of record of this or any other State, or of the United States, within twenty years.

MARRIED WOMEN.—A married woman has the same control over and right to her real and personal property of every kind, however acquired, as her husband has over his. Expenses of the family and education of the children are chargeable upon the property of both.

IOWA FORMS.

[Form 1.—ACKNOWLEDGMENT.]

STATE OF ——, } ss.
—— County. }

Be it remembered, that on this —— day of ——, 188—, before the undersigned ——, a —— in and for said County, personally appeared —— to me personally known to be the identical person whose name —— affixed to the foregoing instrument as grantor and acknowledged the same to be —— voluntary act and deed.

Witness my hand and —— seal the day and year last above written.

[SEAL.]

Signature.
[*Title of office.*]

[Form 2.—DEPOSITIONS.]

[CAPTION.]

Depositions of witnesses produced, sworn and examined at ——, in the County of ——, and State of — , before me, ——, (stating name and style of office of the officer), ——, in pursuance of the annexed commission to me directed in an action now pending in the —— Court of the State of Iowa in and for —— County, wherein —— is plaintiff, and —— defendant, on behalf of the (plaintiff or defendant). A. B., of lawful age, being produced, sworn and examined, on behalf of (plaintiff or defendant), deposed as follows:

The witness should be sworn before being examined, and after signing he should again be sworn to the statements therein made, and the usual jurat of the officer attached, to-wit:

Subscribed and sworn to by said ——, before me and in my presence, this —— day of ——, 188—.

After the depositions of all the witnesses are closed the following certificate should be added:

STATE OF ——, } ss.
—— County }

I, ——, (name of commission and official style), ——, within and for —— County, State of ——, do hereby certify that in pursuance of the annexed commission, I caused to come before me at my office in ——, in said County and State, A. B. C. D., &c., (names of all the witnesses), on the —— day of ——, 188—, who were then and there by me sworn and examined on the interrogatories and cross-interrogatories to said commission annexed, and their answers reduced to writing, and after being read over to said witnesses, the same were subscribed and sworn to by them respectively in my presence, and their depositions are now herewith returned, and I further certify that neither of the parties, nor the agent or attorney of either was present during said examination.

Witness my hand and official seal this —— day of ——, 18—.

[*Signature and title of officer.*]

[FOR QUIT CLAIM DEED.]

For the consideration of —— dollars I hereby quit claim to —— all my interest in the following tract of land: (Describing it.)

[FOR DEED IN FEE SIMPLE, WITHOUT WARRANTY.]

For the consideration of —— dollars I hereby convey to —— the following tract of land: (Describing it.)

[FOR A DEED WITH WARRANTY.]

The same as the last preceding form, adding: "And I warrant the title against all persons whomsoever."

For Form of Acknowledgment, see Form 1.

LAWS OF KANSAS.

RELATIVE TO THE

COLLECTION OF DEBTS, Etc.

Prepared expressly for J. A. Graft & Co.'s Legal Directory, by E. N. O. Clough, Attorney and Counsellor at Law, Leavenworth, Kas.

ASSIGNMENTS AND INSOLVENCY.—Assignment must be for all creditors alike; deed of assignment must be executed and recorded like conveyances of real property; sworn inventory must be filed within thirty days from date of assignment, unless court grants further time. Appraisers are appointed by District Court, and receive three dollars per day each for their services. Sworn appraisement must be filed by appraisers within five days from date of their appointment. Assignee is required to give bond in double the amount of the appraisement, said bond to be approved by the Court or Judge or Clerk thereof, in vacation, and recorded by clerk of said court. Assignee shall exhibit on oath a statement of accounts, with proper vouchers, to District Court, at its first regular term after the end of one year from execution of assignment, and yearly thereafter until assigned estate is settled.

If assignee fail to comply with provisions herein contained, he may, on motion of creditor or creditors, be cited by the court to appear, and on failure to do so may be discharged as such assignee, but no such citation shall be issued till after one year from date of assignment.

Assignee shall appoint a day within six months of assignment, for the adjustment of accounts, at county seat of county where inventory is filed, and shall give notice of such time and place by publication in some public newspaper, three months previous thereto. The assignee is, in all respects, subject to order of court, and his accounts are passed upon by a commissioner before his discharge.

ATTACHMENT.—The creditor in a civil action for the recovery of money may, at or after the commencement thereof, have an attachment against the property of the debtor, where the debtor, or one of several debtors, is a foreign corporation, or non-resident of the State, (but no attachment shall be granted on the ground or grounds in this clause stated, for any claim other than a demand arising upon contract, judgment or decree, unless the cause of action arose wholly within the limits of this State, which fact must be established on the trial), or where the debtor, or one of several debtors, has absconded with intent to defraud his creditors or has left the county of his residence to avoid the service of summons; or so conceals himself that a summons can not be served upon him; or is about to remove his property, or a part thereof, out of the jurisdiction of the court, with intent to defraud his creditors, or is about to convert his property, or a part thereof, into money, for the purpose of placing it beyond the reach of his creditors; or has property or rights in action which he conceals, or has assigned, removed or disposed of, or is about to dispose of, his property, or a part thereof, with the intent to defraud, hinder or delay his creditors; or fraudulently contracted the debt; or fraudulently incurred the liability or obligation for which suit is about to be or has been brought; or when the damages for which the action is brought are for the injuries arising from the commission of some felony or misdemeanor, or the seduction of some female; or when the debtor has failed to pay for any article or thing delivered for which, by contract, he was bound to pay on delivery.

An undertaking is required in attachment in double the amount sued for, conditioned that the plaintiff shall pay the defendant all damages he may sustain by reason of the attachment, if the order be wrongfully obtained, but no undertaking shall be required when the party or parties defendant are all non-residents of the state or a foreign corporation. The undertaking in District Court to be approved by the Clerk; in Justices' Courts, by the Justice.

ACCOUNTS.—Proved in ordinary manner.

COURTS.—District Courts hold from two to three terms annually in nearly every county, and have original jurisdiction in cases at law and in equity. Probate Courts hold regular terms in each county on the first Monday in January, April, July, and October. Special or adjourned terms may be held, as business may require, and said Courts are always open for business.

Jurisdiction of District Court unlimited. Justices' jurisdiction in civil actions, for the recovery of money, $300; to recover specific personal property, $100.

COSTS—BOND FOR.—In District Court *every* plaintiff must give security for costs, or deposit $15 in lieu thereof, or make affidavit that, by reason of his poverty, he is unable to do so.

In Justices' Court every *non-resident* plaintiff *must* give security for costs at beginning of suit, or deposit the probable amout of said costs, and all plaintiffs *may* be required to, in the discretion of the Justice.

EXEMPTION.—Every person residing in this state, and being the head of a family, shall have exempt from seizure and sale upon any attachment, execution, or other process issued from any court in this State, the following articles of personal property:

Family library, pictures and musical instruments; a pew in place of public worship, and a lot in any burial ground; wearing apparel of debtor and family; all household furniture used by debtor and his family, including sewing machine, looms and other implements of industry not exceeding $500 in value; two cows, ten hogs, one yoke of oxen, and one horse or mule, or in lieu thereof, one span of horses or mules; twenty sheep and wool from same; either in raw material or manufactured; food for support of stock mentioned, for one year, either provided or growing, or both; one wagon, cart, or dray, two plows, one drag, harness and tackle for teams, not exceeding in value $300; necessary tools and implements of any mechanic, and, in addition thereto, stock in trade, not exceeding $400 in value; the library, implements and office furniture of any professional man; earnings for personal services, for three months prior to issuing execution, when made to appear by affidavit that same is for the maintenance of his family.

Any person who is not the head of a family, and who resides in this State, shall have the following property only exempt:

The wearing apparel of the debtor; a pew in a place of public worship, and a lot in any burial ground; necessary tools and instruments of any mechanic, miner or other person, used for the purpose of carrying on his trade or business, and, in addition thereto, stock in trade, not exceeding in value $400; library, implements and office furniture of any professional man; earnings for personal services for three months prior to issuing execution, when made to appear that such earnings are necessary for the maintenance of a family supported wholly or partly by his labor.

Also a homestead of 160 acres of farming land, or one acre within an incorporated town or city, with buildings thereon, unlimited in value. A lien may be created on homestead by husband and wife, both joining in the mortgage.

GARNISHMENT.—When the plaintiff, his agent or attorney, shall make oath in writing that any person or corporation has property of the defendant, or is indebted to him, a garnishment summons may issue to such person or corporation, and a copy of order of attachment, with notice that he appear and answer. When suit is brought before a Justice of the Peace, and either of above-named persons shall make affidavit, in substance the same as one above referred to in District Court, the Justice of the Peace shall issue such summons, either at the commencement of suit or afterwards.

INTEREST.—Legal rate seven per cent., but twelve per cent. may be stipulated for by contract. A charge above twelve per cent. occasions forfeiture only, there being no penalty for usury. Judgments draw the legal rate from date of rendition, but where judgment is obtained on a promissory note or other contract, in which a greater rate was agreed upon, such judgment shall be drawn at the contract rate.

LIMITATION OF ACTIONS.—Actions concerning real property must be brought within two, five, or fifteen years, according to the reason of bringing same; on official bonds and contracts in writing, within five years; contracts not in writing, three years; trespass, detinue, replevin, and for relief on the ground of fraud, two years. Revivor: part payment or written acknowledgment or promise.

KANSAS FORMS.

[Form 1.—AFFIDAVIT TO PROVE AN ACCOUNT.]

STATE OF KANSAS, } ss.
—— County. }

Before me, the Probate Judge (or Notary Public, as it may be), in and for said County, personally came ——, and being by me first duly sworn, upon his oath says that the account hereto annexed is just, true and correct, and that to the best of his knowledge and belief, he has given credit to said estate for all payments and off-sets to which it is entitled, and that the balance of —— dollars claimed is justly due.

(*Signature.*

Subscribed and sworn to before me this —— day of ——, A. D. 188—.

Signature Probate Judge.

[Form 2.—BOND FOR COSTS.]

STATE OF KANSAS, } ss.
—— County. }

IN THE DISTRICT COURT IN AND FOR SAID COUNTY.

Whereas —— plaintiff—, is about to bring a civil action in the District Court of ——County, Kansas, against ——, now therefore —— the plaintiff— as principal and ——, as surety hereby agree that the said plaintiff— will pay all costs that may accrue in said action, in case he shall be adjudged to pay them; or in case the same cannot be collected from the defendant—, if judgment be obtained against said defendant—, that the plaintiff— will pay the costs made by himself.

(*Signature.*)

Witness —— hands this —— day of —— A. D. 188—.

(*Signature.*)

[Form 3.—ACKNOWLEDGMENT.]

STATE OF KANSAS, } ss.
—— County. }

Be it remembered, That on this —— day of ——, A. D. 188—, before me, a —— in and for said County and State, appeared —— to me personally known to be the same person— who executed the foregoing instrument, and duly acknowledged the execution of the same.

In Testimony Whereof, I have hereunto subscribed my name and affixed my official seal on the day and year above written. (*Signature.*)

[Form 4a.—NOTICE TO TAKE DEPOSITIONS.]

—— COURT, COUNTY OF —— STATE OF KANSAS.

——————, *Plaintiff,*
vs.
——————, *Defendant.*

The above named —— will take notice, that on —— the — day —— A. D. 188—, the —— above named, will take the DEPOSITIONS of sundry WITNESSES, to be used as evidence on the trial of the above entitled cause, at —— in the County of ——, in the State of · · between the hours of eight o'clock A. M. and six o'clock P. M., of said day, and that the taking of the same will be adjourned from day to day, between the same hours, until said depositions are completed.

The taking of said depositions to commence at —— o'clock — M. of each day.

Signature.
Attorney for ——

Waiver of all objections to the official character of the officer hereby entered, and the service of the above notice is hereby acknowledged this —— day of ——, A. D. 188—.

Signature.
Attorney for ——

[Form 45.—FOR DEPOSITIONS.]

(CAPTION,)

"Depositions of sundry witnesses taken before me (here insert the name of the magistrate and his official character, as Justice of the Peace, Notary Public, etc.,) within and for the County of ——, in the —— of ——, on the —— day of ——, in the year ——, between the hours of — A. M., and — P. M., at —— in said County, pursuant to the annexed notice, (or agreement, as the case may be), to be read in evidence on behalf of the (plaintiff or defendant, as the case may be), in the said action. A. B , of lawful age, being by me first duly examined, cautioned and solemnly sworn to testify the truth, the whole truth, and nothing but the truth, (or affirmed) deposeth and saith that" (here write the deposition), and so on with all the witnesses.

The deposition may be taken by stating the facts in narrative form, or in reply to questions first written down.

The depositions may be taken before any Judge, Justice or Chancellor of any Court of Record, a Justice of the Peace, Notary Public, Mayor, or Chief Magistrate of any city or town corporate; or a Commissioner appointed by the Governor of the State of Kansas to take depositions—such officer not to be attorney or relative of either party, nor otherwise interested in the even of the suit.

If there are adjournments, they should be noted by the Magistrate, or other officer, from day to day, at the close of the day and legal reasons therefor given.

Objections should be entered to witnesses supposed to be interested, and to questions supposed to be illegal. This entry is made on behalf of the party raising the objection, simply by a short note made by the magistrate or officer taking the deposition.

Each witness must sign his own deposition.

The notice must be attached to the depositions and enclosed with them.

INSTRUCTIONS.

The depositions should be commenced on the day named, and some portion of a deposition taken on each successive day, Sundays excepted, adjournments being from Saturday to Monday; Sundays and national holidays not being regarded. A legal reason for every adjournment should appear in the officer's certificate.

When depositions are taken under agreement, the above instructions will be followed, except where they are modified by the agreement. In such case the agreement will be followed. It should be attached to the depositions, if sent, and referred to in the caption, as the notice is when taken under a notice.

If taken by interrogatories and cross-interrogatories, under agreement or otherwise, each interrogatory and cross-interrogatory must be put to each witness and answered so far as he can answer it, and the answer written down. The deposition must show that each interrogatory and cross-interrogatory was thus put and answered.

The fees for taking depositions should be taxed, and a memorandum made by whom they were paid. Close the depositions with a certificate in the form following, viz:

CERTIFICATE TO DEPOSITION.

"I, A. A., (naming the official character of the magistrate according to the fact), do hereby certify that (naming all the witnesses who have testified), were by me first severally sworn (or affirmed) to testify the truth, the whole truth, and nothing but the truth, and that the depositions by th. m respectively subscribed as above set forth, were reduced to writing by myself (or if by any other person, name him and say, 'by ——, who is not interested in the suit, in my presence, and') in the presence of the witnesses respectively, and were respectively subscribed by the said witness in my presence, and were taken at the time and place in the annexed notice (or agreement specified; that I am not Council, Attorney, or relative of either party, or otherwise interested in the event of this suit, if there be adjournment, add) and commenced at the time in the notice specified, and continued by adjournments from day to day, as above stated. Signed A. B."

INSTRUCTIONS CONTINUED.

If the depositions are taken before the Mayor, Notary Public, or Commissioner, appointed aforesaid, they must be certified under his official seal. If before any of the other officers above named, a certificate must be annexed, under the seal of the Court of the County, or the great seal of the State, that the officer by whom the depositions were taken was, at the time of taking the same, such officer as he represents himself to be in his certificate. This should be attached to the Magistrate's certificate.

This proof of official character is omitted when waived by agreement of parties at the foot of notice. This agreement does not waive the taking them at the time and place named in the notice.

FURTHER INSTRUCTIONS.

The whole should be sealed up by the Magistrate, the title of the suit endorsed on the outside, the name of the officer taking the same, and "Depositions on behalf" (the party taking the same) and addressed to the "Clerk of the —— Court at ——, Kansas," or, "—— Justice of the Peace at ——," as the case may be. The officer before whom the depositions are taken should endorse across the back of the envelope "These depositions sealed up by me," and sign his name officially thereto.

[Form 5.—AFFIDAVIT FOR ORDER OF ATTACHMENT.]

——, *Plaintiff.*
vs.
——, *Defendant.*
} IN THE DISTRICT COURT OF SALINE COUNTY, KANSAS.

The said plaintiff, ——, makes oath that the claim in this action is on a promissory note executed by said defendant to said plaintiff, and dated April 1, 1880, whereby said defendant promised to pay to said plaintiff the sum of $500 in one year after date (or other nature of the claim) that said claim is just, and that he ought, as he believes, to recover thereon —— dollars and —— cents. He also makes oath that said —— has assigned and disposed of his property with intent to hinder, delay and defraud his creditors (or in lieu of this state the ground relied upon for the attachment.)

Subscribed and sworn to before me, ——, this —— day of ——, A. D. 188—.

——, *Notary Public.*

[Form 6.—UNDERTAKING FOR ATTACHMENT.]

TITLE.

Whereas, said plaintiff has commenced a civil action against said defendant in said Court to recover the sum of $——, and has applied to the clerk of said Court by filing the necessary affidavit, for an Order of Attachment, to be issued in said action against the said defendant.

Now, therefore, we, ——, and ——, hereby undertake to the said defendant in the penal sum of $—— that the plaintiff shall pay to the said defendant all damages which the said defendant may sustain by reason of said Attachment if the order be wrongfully obtained.

Witness our hands, this —— day of ——, A. D. 18—.

Signature.

The above Undertaking and sureties thereto approved this —— day of ——, 18—.

——, *Clerk of said Court.*

[Form 7.—CHATTEL MORTGAGE.)

The undersigned, of ——, County of ——, State of ——, in consideration of the sum of —— dollars, and interest, the receipt of which is hereby acknowledged, and for the purpose of securing the payment of the same to ——, according to the condition of a promissory note, bearing date April ——, 18—, do hereby sell and mortgage unto said ——, and his assigns, the following described property, now in my possession, in the Town, County and State aforesaid, and free from all encumbrances, to-wit: (Description.)

Provided, that if the undersigned shall pay the said debt, then this mortgage shall be void. And it is hereby agreed, that if default be made in the payment of said debt, or any part thereof, or if any attempt be made to remove or dispose of said property, or if, at any time, said —— shall deem the debt unsafe or insecure, he is hereby authorized, his heirs or assigns, or his authorized agent, to enter upon the premises where the said property may be, and remove and sell the same, at public or private sale, and out of the proceeds retain the amount then owing on said debt, with expenses attending the same, rendering to the undersigned the surplus, after the whole of said debt shall have been paid, with charges aforesaid.

Witness my hand and seal this —— day of ——, 18—.

Signature.

(Form 8—CHARACTER OF INCORPORATION),

The subscribers, having associated themselves for the purpose of engaging in the business of manufacturing flour, and being desirous to be incorporated under the laws of the State of Kansas, do declare the following to be the objects, articles and conditions of their said association, agreeably to which they desire to be incorporated.

FIRST.—The name of the corporation shall be The Salina Flouring Mills.

SECOND.—The purpose for which formed is the manufacturing of flour from grain purchased therefore, and the selling of the same.

THIRD.—The place where the business of the corporation is to be transacted in Salina, Kansas.

FOURTH.—The term for which said corporation shall exist is ninety-nine years.

FIFTH.—The number of directors is five, and the names and residences of those appointed for the first year are as follows: (Insert names and place of residence).

SIXTH.—The amount of the capital stock is one hundred thousand dollars, divided into one hundred shares of one thousand dollars each.

Witness our hands this —— day of ——. A. D. 18—.

(To be signed by five or more incorporators, three at least being citizens of this State, and acknowledged by them before an officer authorized to take acknowledgments of deeds).

[Form 9—WARRANTY DEED].

This Indenture, made this —— day of ——, in the year of our Lord One Thousand Eight Hundred and ——, between ——, of ——, in the County of ——, and State of ——, of the first part, and ——, of the second part;

Witnesseth, That the said part—of the first part, in consideration of the sum of —— dollars to —— duly paid, ha — sold, and by these presents do — give, grant, bargain and sell to the said part — of the second part, —— heirs and assigns, all that tract or parcel of land situated in the County of ——, and State of ——, and described as follows, to-wit: [Description].

with the appurtenances, and all the estate, title and interest of the said part—of the first part therein. And the said —— do — hereby covenant and agree that at the delivery hereof, —— the lawful owner — of the premises above granted, and seized of a good and indefeasible estate of inheritance therein, free and clear of all incumbrances, and that —— will *warrant and defend* in the quiet and peaceable possession of the said part — of the second part, —— heirs and assigns *forever*, against all persons lawfully claiming the same,

In Witness Whereof, The said part — of the first part ha — hereunto set —— hand — and seal — the day and year above written.

Signed, sealed and delivered in the presence of

{ —————— { —————— [seal].
{ —————— { —————— [Seal]

ACKNOWLEDGMENT:

STATE OF KANSAS, }
——County, } ss.

Be it Remembered, That on this —— day of ——, A. D. 18—, before me, a —— in and for said County and State, appeared ——, to me personally known to be the same person — who executed the foregoing instrument, and duly acknowledged the execution of the same.

In Testimony Whereof, I have hereunto subscribed my name and affixed my official seal on the day and year above written.

——

DECLARATION OF ATTESTING WITNESSES.

NOTE.—No particular form is required as the declaration of attesting witnesses, The following will be sufficient:

(ATTEST OF WITTNESSES TO A WILL).

Subscribed and declared by the above-named A. B. as and for his last will and testament, in the presence of us, who have hereunto subscribed our names as witnesses thereto, in his presence and in the presence of each other C. D.
E. F.

[Form 10—AFFIDAVIT FOR SUIT BY POOR PERSON].

STATE OF KANSAS, }
——County. } ss.

IN THE DISTRICT COURT FOR SAID COUNTY.

I do solemnly swear that the cause of action set forth in the petition hereto preffixed is just, and I do further swear that by reason of my poverty I am unable to give security for costs.

LAWS OF KENTUCKY

RELATIVE TO THE

COLLECTION OF DEBTS, Etc.

Prepared expressly for J. A. Graft & Co.'s Legal Directory, by J. F. & C. H. Fisk, Attorneys and Counselors-at-Law, Covington, Ky.

Attachment.—The plaintiff may have an attachment against the property of the defendant, or of a garnishee in an action of the recovery of money. When the suit is against:

1. A defendant who is a foreign corporation, or a non-resident of the State.
2. Who has been absent therefrom four months, or
3. Who has departed therefrom with the intent to defraud his creditors, or
4. Has left the county of his residence to avoid the service of a summons, or
5. So conceals himself that a summons can not be served upon him, or
6. Is about to remove, or has removed his property, or a material part thereof, out of this State, not leaving enough therein to satisfy the plaintiff's claims, or the claims of defendant's creditors, or
7. Has sold, conveyed, or otherwise disposed of his property, or suffered or permitted it to be sold, with the fraudulent intent to cheat, hinder, or delay his creditors, or
8. Is about to sell, convey, or otherwise dispose of his property, with such intent. But an attachment shall not be granted on the ground that the defendant is a foreign corporation, or a non-resident of this State, for any claim other than a debt or demand, arising upon a contract, expressed or implied, or a judgment or award.

In order to get an attachment the plaintiff must make affidavit, showing:

1. The nature of the plaintiff's claim.
2. That it is just.
3. The sum which the affiant believes that the plaintiff ought to recover, and
4. The existence of any one of the grounds above enumerated.

No attachment will issue until bond and security is given in double the amount claimed.

An attachment and garnishment will be given against a party who has no property in this State, subject to execution, or not enought thereof to satisfy plaintiff's demand, and when the collection of the demand will be endangered by delay in obtaining judgment, or return of property found. Also, in an action to recover possession of personal property which has been ordered delivered to the plaintiff and which, or part of which, has been removed or concealed so that order of delivery can not be executed by the sheriff. (Civil Code, title 8, ch. 3.)

Action—Is commenced in this State by filing in a petition, constituting the plaintiff's cause of action, and causing a summons to be issued, or a warning order to be made thereon.

Non-residents must give bond for costs in every case.

Exemptions.—The following property is exempt from execution, attachment before debt is due, attachment or distress against a *bona-fide* housekeeper, with a family, in this State, and on all liabilities created after May 1st, 1870, the libraries of preachers, the professional libraries of lawyers, physicians, and surgeons, and their instruments to the amount of five hundred dollars;

and one horse with cart or dray, for laboring man. The wages not to exceed fifty dollars, of all persons who work for wages, not to apply to debts contracted for food, raiment, house rent for family, tools, not to exceed fifty dollars in value, of a mechanic, who is a *bona-fide* housekeeper, with family. (Gen. Stat., ch. 38, art. XIII, Secs. 6-9.)

Of any mechanic *actually engaged* in the prosecution of his mechanical business, material, manufactured articles, and articles in process of manufacture not exceeding $200 in value.

So much land, including the dwelling house and appurtenances owned by the debtor, as shall not exceed in value one thousand dollars; also one sewing machine, one two-horse wagon, or ox cart, one set of gear, washing apparatus, not exceeding fifty dollars in value; carpeting for one room, all the school books, a prayer book, hymn book, one bureau, one wardrobe, one washstand, one clock, six cups and saucers, six plates, six knives and forks.

As against debts contracted *before* June 1, 1884, the following exemptions are allowed in addition to above: Two work beasts, or one and yoke of oxen, two cows and calves, five sheep, wearing apparel, and the usual household and kitchen furniture, of about the value of one hundred dollars.

As against debts contracted on or after June 1, 1884, the following exemptions are allowed:

Two work beasts, or one work beast and one yoke of oxen, or in lieu of each work beast or yoke of oxen, if not on hand, $75 worth of other personal property; two plows and gear, or, in lieu of each, if not on hand, $7.50 worth of other personal property; one wagon and set of gear, or cart or dray, or if not on hand, $50 worth of other personal property; two axes, three hoes, one spade, one shovel; two cows and calf, or if not on hand, $25 worth of other personal property in lieu of each cow or cow and calf; beds, bedding and furniture for each, sufficient for family use; one loom and spinning wheel and pair of cards; all the spun yarn and manufactured cloth manufactured by the family, necessary for family use; carpeting for all family rooms in use; one cooking stove and all cooking utensils; all the table-ware and cutlery on hand for family use; one table; all books, not exceeding $50 in value; two saddles and their appendages; two bridles; six chairs, or so many as shall not exceed $8 in value; all the poultry on hand; ten head of sheep, or, if not on hand, personal property not exceeding $2.50 for each sheep; all wearing apparel; provisions for family for one year, or, if not on hand, growing crop or other personal property not exceeding $50 in value for each member of the family; food suitable for the live stock, or, if not on hand, $70 worth of other personal property; washing apparatus not exceeding in value $50; one bureau; one wardrobe; one washstand; one gun not exceeding $50 in value; one sewing machine; and all family portraits and pictures. (Acts 1883-4, Vol, I, p. 76.)

GARNISHMENT. When an execution has been returned, "no property found," the plaintiff may bring suit in equity, for a discovery of the defendant under oath of all legal and equitable interest chosen in action, money and all other property to which he is entitled, and for subjecting the same to the satisfaction of the judgment. And in such actions persons indebted to the pefendant in the execution, or holding money or property in which he has an interest, or holding evidences, or securities for same, may also be made defendants. (Civil Code, section 439.)

In such an action the plaintiff may have attachment against defendant without bond. (*Ibid* 441.)

The court may compel the surrender of the money or property, and, if refused, the court can commit them to jail. (*Ibid* 443.)

INSOLVENCY AND ASSIGNMENTS.—Deeds of assignment are treated as all other deeds. (Gen. Stat., p. 250.)

The assignee is named by debtor, he must give bond, approved by the County Court, and take an oath to perform his duties.

The assignee is under the control of the Court of Equity, and settlements are made in this court. (Civil Code, section 737.)

Notice to prove claims is given by publication in newspapers. A creditor can sue assignee on claims rejected by him. The inventory must be sworn to by him.

By statute, if preference is given by deed, transfer or mortgage to a creditor, in contemplation of insolvency, a Court of Equity will set the same aside, if suit be brought by another creditor within six months, and the same will operate as a general assignment for the benefit of creditors. (Gen. Stat., art. II, ch. 44.)

A defendant in a civil action can be arrested, and held to bail, when there is an affidavit of the plaintiff showing:

1. The nature of the plaintiff's claim.
2. That it is just.
3. The amount or value which the affiant believes that the plaintiff ought to recover.

4. That the affiant believes, either in that the defendant is about to depart from this State, and with intent to defraud his creditors, has concealed, or removed, from this State, his property or so much thereof, that the process of the court, after judgment, can not be executed, or that the defendant has moneys, or securities for money, or evidences of debt in the possession of himself, or of others, for his use, and is about

to depart from this State, without leaving property enough therein sufficient to satisfy plaintiff's claim. To do this, bond and security must be given. The defendant, in default of bail, is committed to jail, where he must remain until he pays the debt, or takes the insolvent dedtor's oath. (Civil Code, title 8, ch. 1.)

There is a statute law, giving mechanics and material men a lien, from the commencement of the work, upon the improvements and the interest of the employer in the land, for work done and material furnished. But the lien is dissolved unless the claimant, within sixty days from time he ceases to labor or furnish materials, files notice in County Clerk's office setting forth his lien and describing property to be covered thereby.

Sub-contractors and laborers may acquire a lien on same, to the extent of the amount due the principal contractor, and unpaid at the time of giving notice, by giving the employer written notice of their claim, and they look to the land and improvements for compensation.

The limitation for suit on mechanic's lien is twelve months from the filing of notice in clerk's office. (Gen. Stat., ch. 70, and acts 1881.)

Interest.—The legal rate of interest in this State is six per cent., and no contract may be made at any greater rate. (See act of March 14th, 1878, in force April 1st, 1878.)

The penalty for usury is forfeiture of all interest in excess of the legal rate. Six per cent. is allowed upon judgments rendered, and judgments upon written contracts bear the same rate of interest provided for in the contract, not exceeding the legal rate, as fixed by the above law. Interest, at the legal rate, may be recovered upon open accounts, by proper pleading of the maturity of debt, and the default of the defendant. Prior to the adoption of the law quoted above, it was allowable to cotnract for a rate not exceeding eight per cent. per annum.

It is the duty of the clerk to issue executions on judgments from the Justice's and County Court in five days, from Circuit Court in ten days, from Louisville Chancery Court in fifteen days, to be returnable on a rule day, not under thirty, or over ninety days.

An execution may be stayed by giving the proper bond. (Gen. Stat., ch. 38. art. XI.)

A judgment does not constitute a lien on the property of the defendant. Writ of *fieri facias* binds estate of defendant from the time it is delivered to proper officer to execute. (Gen. Stat., ch. 38.)

As to claims against the estate of deceased persons, no more proof is required of non-residents than of residents. An executor or administrator can not be a non-resident, and if after they become non-residents, they may be removed. No suit can be brought against the personal representative within six months after qualification. Before payment is made by a representative, demand must be made of him, accompanied by affidavit of claimant or agent that the claim is just, and has never, to his knowledge, been paid, and that there is no off-set or discount against the same, or any usury embraced therein. If any payment has been made, or there is any off-set or discount against the demand, or any usury embraced therein, the affidavit must fully state the payment, off-set, discount or usury; claims not *prima facie*, must be proved. No action can be brought or recovery had until after such affidavit and demand. (Gen. Stat., ch. 39, art. II.)

If the personal estate is insolvent, suit may be brought by a creditor, to sell the real estate, and settle the accounts of the personal representative. (Civil Code, sec. 428.)

Actions upon contracts in writing, official bond, or upon judgment of any court, must be brought in fifteen years.

Actions upon contracts, expressed or implied, not in writing, for trespass upon real or personal property, on bills of exchange, drafts, or upon promissory notes, placed upon the footing of bills of exchange, or upon accounts between merchants and their agents, or for relief, on the ground of fraud, must be brought within five years.

An action upon a merchant's account for goods, sold and delivered, or any article charged in such store account, shall be commenced within two years, from the date of January next succeeding the respective dates of the delivery of the articles charged. (Gen. Stat. ch. 71.)

Non-residents and corporations must, in all cases, give security for cost.

Interest does not disqualify a party from testifying.

KENTUCKY FORMS.

[Form 1.—CERTIFICATE WHEN DEED IS ACKNOWLEDGED IN A FOREIGN STATE.]

STATE OF ———, } SCT.
County of ———, }

I, ———, do certify that this instrument of writing from ———, and ———, his wife, was this day produced to me by the parties, and acknowledged and delivered by ———, and ———, his wife, parties thereto, to be their act and deed, and the contents and effect of the instrument being explained to the said ——— by me, separately and apart from her husband, she thereupon declared that she did freely and voluntarily execute and deliver the same to be her act and deed, and consented that the same might be recorded.

Given under my hand and seal of office, this —— day of ——, 188—.

(*Signature and title of officer.*

(*Note.*—Deeds acknowledged out of the State of Kentucky are only valid when acknowledged before the following named officers, viz: a Clerk of a Court or deputy; Mayor of a city, Commissioner of deeds, Judge of a Court or a Notary Public; all with seal.)

[Form 2.—AFFIDAVIT FOR PROOF OF DEBT ON WRITTEN CONTRACT OR ACCOUNTS.]

STATE OF ———, } SCT.
County of — — }

In the matter of the (account or note) due ——— from the estate of ———, deceased, or assigned (as the case may be). This day came ———, who being first duly sworn, says that ——— a ——— (if a corporation, that he is president or secretary, adding on blank line below under the laws of what State it is organized), (account or note) hereto attached against the estate of said ——— for ——— dollars, is a just demand, and has never to h— knowledge or belief, been paid; and that there is no off-set or discount against the same, or any usury therein.

And this affiant further says that the account herein claimed is due for the (articles or services) mentioned therein, and that the same were (sold and delivered, or rendered) by said claimant to the said ———, at —— special instance and request, and that —— promised to pay the sums therein charged.

Subscribed and sworn to before me by ———, this —— day of ——, 188—.

(*Signature and title of officer.*)

[Form 3.—AFFIDAVIT TO PROVE CLAIM *vs.* AN ESTATE.]

STATE OF ———, } SCT.
County of ——. }

In the matter of the account due ———, from the estate of ———, deceased or assigned (as case may be) this day came ———, a witness for said claimant, who being first sworn deposes and says that —he has examined the account hereto attached, which is for —— dollars, and that —he knows that the articles or services mentioned in said account —— (sold and delivered or rendered) by the said claimant to the said ———, and that he has no interest in the same ———.

(*Affiant's signature.*

Subscribed and sworn to before me by ———, this —— day of ——, 188—.

(*Signature and title of officer.*)

[Form 4.—INSTRUCTIONS AND FORMS FOR TAKING DEPOSITIONS.]

The interrogatories should be copied into the first deposition; but after that it will be sufficient to say in the other depositions that the witness, in answer to the first interrogatory, says, etc., and so on of the others.

The attested copies of the interrogatories should be annexed to and returned with the depositions.

The officer should be particularly careful to see that the printed interrogatories "by the Clerk" are answered.

CAPTION.

The depositions of ——— and ———, taken on behalf of the plaintiff in an action pending in the ——— Chancery Court, wherein ——— is plaintiff, and ——— is defendant. The said (name of witness) having been first duly sworn deposes as follows:

(Here follows the deposition, which after having been read to the witness be subscribed by him.)

CERTIFICATE—THIS MAY BE VARIED TO SUIT.

THE STATE OF ——
County of ——. } SS.

I, ——, a Notary Public in and for the County and State aforesaid, do certify that the above and foregoing depositions of —— and —— were taken before me at my office in the —— of ——. County of ——, and State of ——, on the —— day of ——, 188—, upon the interrogatories hereunto annexed, that the said witnesses were each duly sworn according to law before giving their testimony, that the testimony of each of said witnesses was written by me (or if either of the witnesses wrote his own testimony, state the fact, and that it was so written in the presence of the officer), read to and subscribed by him in my presence. I further certify that in the taking of said deposition neither party was present in person, nor represented by agent or attorney (or if both or either party attended, state the fact.)

——, *Notary Public.* [SEAL.]

When the depositions are completed, seal them up in an envelope and direct to the Clerk of the proper Court, with an indorsement signed by the officer showing them to be depositions, and the style of the case in which they are taken, and either delivered by him to the Clerk, or mailed by him in person, care being taken to see that the postage is prepaid.

LAWS OF LOUISIANA

RELATIVE TO THE

COLLECTION OF DEBTS, Etc.

Prepared expressly for J. A. Graft & Co.'s Legal Directory.

ARREST.—Is allowed, but only the *person* of the debtor is secured. The debtor can be discharged, on giving bond that he will not leave the State for three months. Should he depart his bondsman is liable for the judgment. This is the only practical value of the writ, which only issues when the debtor is about to leave the State, "without leaving in it sufficient property to satisfy the judgment, which the creditor expects to obtain in the suit he intends to bring against him." A non-resident of the State cannot be arrested unless it appear that he has absconded from his residence.

Creditor must give bond to secure issuance of the writ.

ASSIGNMENTS.—See Insolvency.

ATTACHMENT.—Issues on creditors making affidavit to facts alleged, and giving bond. Whenever, (1) the debtor resides out of the State; (2) has, or is about permanently to leave it; (3) conceals himself in order to avoid service of citation; when he has mortgaged, assigned or disposed of, or is about to mortgage, assign or dispose of his property, rights or credits, or some part thereof, with intent to defraud his creditors, or give an undue preference to some of them; when he has converted, or is about to convert his property into money or evidences of debt, with intent to place his property beyond the reach of his creditors. Whenever the debtor is about to remove his property out of the State before the debt becomes due, non-resident creditors are entitled to the writ to enforce their claims same as resident creditors.

EXEMPTIONS.—Homesteads, or the homestead owned by the debtor and occupied by him, consisting of lands, buildings, etc., whether rural or urban, of every head of a family or person having a mother or father, a person or persons dependent on him or her for support; also one work horse, or wagon, or cart, one yoke of oxen, two cows and calves, twenty-five head of hogs, or one thousand pounds of bacon, or its equivalent in pork, whether these exempted objects be attached to a homestead or not, and on a farm the necessary quantity of corn and fodder for the current year, and the necessary farming implements to the value of $2,000; the limit is $2,000. The property exempt cannot exceed that amount in value. The wife, owning that much in her own right, and being in the active enjoyment of it, prevents the husband from claiming a homestead.

A Sheriff or constable cannot seize the linen and clothes belonging to the debtor or his wife, nor his bed, bedding or bedstead, nor those of his family, nor his arms and military accoutrements, nor the tools and instruments, and books and sewing machines, necessary for the exercise of his or her calling, trade or profession, by which he or she makes a living; nor shall he, in any case, seize the rights of personal servitude, of use and habitation, of usufruct to the estate of a minor child, nor the income of dotal property, nor money due for the salary of an officer, laborers' wages, nor the cooking stove and utensils, nor the plates, dishes, knives and forks and spoons, nor the dining table and dining chairs, nor washtubs, nor smoothing-irons and ironing furnaces, nor family portraits belonging to the debtor, nor the musical instruments played on or practiced on by any member of the family.

The widow, in necessitous circumstances, has a right to $1,000.

GARNISHMENT.—Issues whenever a third person has property of debtor in his possession; it follows the writ.

INSOLVENCY.—May be voluntary or involuntary. In order for debtor to obtain discharge a majority of his creditors, in number and amount, must agree. Any person may make a surrender, if done *bona fide*. A petition to the Judge of his domicile, stating the cause which necessitated it, asking a meeting of his creditors, upon which an order is granted which stays all further proceedings against debtor. Attached to petition must be a schedule, signed and sworn to, giving a full statement of his (the debtor's) affairs, the losses sustained, names, residences and amounts due each creditor, and property of every kind, with a fair value. Absent creditors are usually represented by counsel appointed by the Court, till they secure counsel for themselves.

INTEREST.—Legal rate is five per cent., a greater rate up to eight per cent. may be agreed on. All debts bear interest at five per cent. from date they become due.

LIMITATIONS.—PRESCRIPTIONS.—Open accounts are prescribed in three years; closed acknowledged accounts in ten years; notes, in five.

LIENS AND PRIVILEGES.—When on real estate, must be recorded in the parish (county) where the property is situated.

Liens and privileges are many, under our jurisprudence. Those of principal interest are:

1. Salary of overseer on crop for current year.
2. Supplies or money furnished to raise the crop, or carry on the plantation, rests on crops or proceeds.
3. The workman, for the price of his labor on the thing he has made or repaired.
4. Landlords.
5. The pledges.
6. Depositors, on price of thing deposited.
7. Money laid out to preserve the thing.
8. Vendors.
9. Innkeeper's. on effects of traveler.
10. Carrier's charges.
11. Architects, workmen, etc,, on buildings.
12. Furnisher of materials used in construction of the building.

PROVISIONAL SEIZURE.—Issues when creditor sues on a title, importing a confession of judgment; when lessor sues for rent; when seamen asks for it against a vessel on which he is employed, in order that it may not leave port till his claim be paid; when property is abandoned, or the owner is unknown or absent; and against property pledged; plantation or farm laborers may have the writ against the crop, or any other property on which they have a privilege, on making affidavit that it is about to be removed from the "place." No bond.

SEQUESTRATION—Issues on creditors making affidavit to truth of facts alleged, and giving bond, when creditors fear that pending a petition in insolvency for a stay of proceedings, the debtor may place the whole, or part of his property beyond their reach. Whenever the creditor has a lien or privilege on the property; whenever a creditor, by special mortgage apprehends that the property will be removed out of the State before he can have the benefit of his mortgage.

(Note: Sequestration, of course, issue in other instances; those given relate to collections.)

LOUISIANA FORMS.

[Form 1—DEED].

WITH OR WITHOUT MORTGAGE, RENUNCIATION OF WIFE'S CLAIMS, ETC.

STATE OF LOUISIANA, }
Parish of——. }

Be it known, That on the day of the date hereof, and in presence of the witnesses hereinafter named and undersigned, before me ——, a Notary Public in and for said Parish of ——, state of Louisiana, aforesaid, duly commissioned and sworn, personally came and appeared ——, resident of the Parish (or County) of —— State of ——, who declared that, for the consideration, and upon the terms and consideration hereinafter expressed, he hath bargained and sold, and doth, by these presents, grant, bargain, sell, convey, assign and set over, with all legal warranties, unto and in favor of ——, resident in the Parish (or County) of——, state of ——, here present, (or, if represented by power of attorney, so state), purchasing and accepting and acknowledging due possession thereof the following described real estate, to-wit: A certain tract or parcel of land, situated (Describe property in full).

To Have and to Hold, The property thus described and conveyed unto the said purchaser, his heirs and assigns, forever warranted and defended against the lawful claims and demands of every person whomsoever and against all encumbrances.

This sale and conveyance is made and accepted for and in consideration of the sum and price of $ ——(if the sale is for cash in the whole, say), cash in hand paid by said purchaser to said vendor, who hereby acknowledges due receipt thereof.

(If the sale be on time, with mortgage and vendor's lien, say) paid and to be paid as follows, to-wit: $——, cash, the receipt whereof is acknowledged, and the balance in —— and —— years from the date hereof. For the unpaid portion of which purchase price said purchaser has made and executed his —— promissory notes of even date herewith, drawn to the order of said vendor (or it may be drawn to his own order and by him endorsed). each for the sum of $ ——, and due respectively in —— and —— years from the date hereof, and bearing eight per cent. per annum interest from date (or maturity) until paid, which notes, having paraphed the same —— "*Ne Varietur*," in order to identify the same herewith I have delivered unto said vendor, who hereby acknowledges due receipt thereof.

And Now, In order to secure the final and punctual payment of said notes, in principal and interest, and of attorneys' fees, in case of suit to enforce the payment of any portion thereof, which fees are hereby fixed at five per cent., on any amount so in suit, ——, the said vendor retains and the said purchaser grants on the property hereinbefore conveyed a special mortgage with vendor's lien in favor of said vendor or of any future holder of said notes, or of either of them, to the extent of any unpaid portion of said price, interest, costs and fees as aforesaid. The said property so to remain mortgaged and hypothecated untill the full and final payment of said indebtedness.

(A clause may here be inserted, providing that the purchaser shall keep said property insured for benefit of vendor).

By the certificate of the State, Parish and City tax-collectors, hereunto annexed, it appears that all the taxes due to date on said property have been paid.

By the certificate of the Recorder of Mortgages it appears that there are no mortgages of record bearing upon said property.

(The foregoing clause can be waived by consent of parties, in which case the waiver should be inserted).

The foregoing act was then read to said parties and by them approved.

Thus done and passed at my office in the City (or Parish) of ——, State of Louisiana, in presence of Messrs. ——, and ——, competant witnesses, who sign as such with said parties, and we, the said Notary on this the —— day of ——, in the year of our Lord, one thousand eight hundred and eighty ——.

——, *First Witness* ——, *Vendor's Signature.*
——, *Second Witness.* ——, *Purchaser's Signature.*
[SEAL]. ——, *Notary's Signature.*

[No seal or scroll of private individuals is required].

[Form 2—INSTRUCTIONS AND FORMS FOR DEPOSITIONS].

CAPTION.

Depositions of witnesses, produced, sworn and examined on the days hereinafter mentioned, at [name the office and place], under and by virtue of the annexed commission, issued out of the Honorable the —— Court, in and for —— to take Depositions in a certain cause pending and at issue in said Court, between ——, plaintiff, and ——, defendant, and numbered —— on the docket of said Honorable Court.

——, residing in——, being first duly sworn on the Holy Bible, [or Holy Evangelists; or if the witness affirms let it be so stated], on this the day —— day of ——, 188—, doth depose and say as follows, to-wit:

First: To the first interrogatory he said: [Give the answer of witness as dictated by him to each direct and cross-interrogatory]. Let the answer be written down by the officer in presence of the witness, or by the witness himself, on sheets fastened at the upper ends, and conclude with the signature of the witness and the jurat of the officer. Should the answers of the witness be committed to writing by a Clerk, mention should be made thereof. Let the Depositions conclude with the following:

CERTIFICATE.

I, ——, the undersigned [give capacity of officer], do hereby certify that I caused [insert the names of all the witnesses], witnesses hereinbefore named and examined, to appear before me at the times and places above designated, and after publicly and solemnly swearing [or affirming] each, separately, to tell the truth, the whole truth, and nothing but the truth, in answer to the annexed direct and cross-interrogatories, I then and there proceeded to examine each witness separately, by propounding to him the said direct and cross-interrogatories, and reducing in my presence and in presence of the witness his answers thereto in writing, with my own hand, [if such is the case; if not, state facts fully], and then caused each witness to sign his deposition in my presence, as already stated.

In Testimony Whereof I have hereunto set my hand and seal, [if he has one] on this the —— day of ——, A. D., 188—.

(SEAL). *Signature of officer, with quality).*

The officer must then seal the package, indorse the fact with the title, number and Court upon it, and male it to the Clerk of the Court from which the commission issued.

LAWS OF MAINE

RELATIVE TO THE

COLLECTION OF DEBTS, Etc.

Prepared expressly for J. A. Graft & Co.'s Legal Directory, by John C. Cobb, Attorney-at-Law, 31½ Exchange Street, Portland, Me.

ASSIGNMENTS AND INSOLVENCY.—An insolvent law provides a system of insolvency, voluntary and involuntary, where debts are not less than three hundred dollars, with assignee elected, subject to approval of the court, who dispose of property, pay expenses, and divide the assets. The insolvent may be discharged from his debts contracted and due, and owing to parties in this State, and from all debts to parties out of the State, when creditor proves his claim and becomes a party to the insolvency proceedings; but debts due to parties out of the State and not contracted here, and when creditors do not become parties to the insolvency proceedings, are not discharged, and are not effected by such proceedings, so far as remedies are concerned. Fraudulent conveyances and preferences are declared void. Penalties are provided for misconduct of insolvent assignee and messenger. Debts contracted by fraud, and breach of trust, are not affected by discharge, which may be annulled within two years, for cause. Proceedings are in the Probate Court, with appeals, in certain cases, to the Supreme

Judicial Court, which has full equity power in all matters arising under the law. If debts are less than three hundred dollars the debtor may make a general disclosure, and be discharged from arrest.

An assignment law, for benefit of creditors, is still on the statute books; but the Court has held that an assignment under it, by one who is insolvent, is void, since the enactment of the insolvent law.

ATTACHMENT—Of any personal property not exempt, and of any interest in real estate, is, as a matter of course, and continues thirty days after judgment. Personal property may be appraised, and sold on the writ (unless a bond is given), and proceeds held. It is essential to an attachment of real estate, that the plaintiff's claim be specified, particularly in the declaration. Where property is attached in a suit, against one joint owner, any other may have it appraised, and give bond, and receive it. Incumbered chattels may be attached by paying incumbrances. Stock in corporations is attached, by leaving a copy of writ, with notice of attachment, with clerk, cashier, or treasurer. Corporate property and franchises of toll corporations, may be attached and levied on. No attachment can be made until debt is payable. (R. S.. ch. 81, secs. 21–59.)

CHATTEL MORTGAGES.—If the mortgagor remains in possession, to be valid against third parties, must be recorded in town clerk's office, where mortgagor resides; or, if out of the State, where they are made; or, if of a corporation, where its place of business is. No renewal is required. They are foreclosed by written notice served on the mortgagor by the mortgagee (or published, if he is out of the State, and recorded in the same place as the mortgage, and is completed in sixty days after the record. (R. S., ch. 91, secs. 1–8.)

Under these provisions it is usual for the mortgagor to retain possession. Notes are also given for property, stipulating that it shall remain the property of the payee until the note is paid, and are subject to the same regulations as to record, and foreclosure as mortgages. (R. S., ch. 111, sec. 5; 1872, ch. 71.)

EXECUTION—May be issued any time after twenty-four hours from rendition of judgment, and are returnable in three months. Will run against the body, where judgment is for more than ten dollars, unless debtor is a married woman, may be renewed at any time within three years, or judgment may be sued within twenty years. No stay is allowed, except by the court for special cause, and for one year against absent defendants. Real estate may be levied upon by sale or appraisal, and may be redeemed within one year.

Personal property is levied upon by sale.

EXEMPTIONS.—The following *personal property* is exempt from attachment and levy: wearing apparel, fifty dollars worth of household furniture, necessary for family; one bedstead, bed and bedding for each two members, family portraits, bibles, school books in actual use; copy of State Statutes, library worth one hundred and fifty dollars, pew in use, one cooking, and all iron warming stoves, charcoal, twelve cords wood at home for use; five tons of anthracite, and fifty bushels of bituminous coal, ten dollars worth of lumber, wood, or bark; all produce till harvested; one barrel flour, thirty bushels af corn, grain, and potatoes; half an acre of flax, and manufactures therefrom for use; tools of trade; sewing machine, worth one hundred dollars; one pair of working cattle, or one pair of horses or mules, worth three hundred dollars, and hay to keep them through the winter; one harness, worth twenty dollars, for each horse or mule; a horse sled, or ox sled, two swine, one cow, and a heifer under three years of age, or two cows, if no oxen, horse, or mule; ten sheep, with their wool and lambs, until one year old, hay sufficient to keep them through the winter; fifty-dollars worth of domestic fowl, one plow, one cart, or truck wagon, one harrow, one yoke, with bows, ring and staple, two chains, one ox sled, one mowing machine, one boat of two tons, employed in fishing, and owned exclusively by an inhabitant of the State, life insurance policies, except excess of annual cash premiums, for two years above one hundred and fifty dollars. *Real Estate.*—Lot of land and buildings, worth five hundred dollars, if owner files required certificate in registry of deeds, is exempt as a homestead, from all attachments, except for liens of mechanics and material men, also one cemetery lot. (R. S., ch. 81, secs. 59–63; Laws of 1874, ch. 155; Laws of 1879, ch. 99.)

INTEREST.—The legal rate of interest is six per cent., but the parties may agree in writing for any rate of interest. Judgments bear interest at the rate of six per cent. On open accounts current, interest would commence when the party, to whom the balance is due, makes demand of payment. No usury laws.

MORTGAGES ON REAL ESTATE—Are deeds poll, with condition of defeasance, executed and recorded in the same manner as deeds. Notes are usually given for the debt; bonds are sometimes used. They are foreclosed in three years, or in a less time—not less than one year—if so stipulated in the mortgage. Absolute deed, with bond back, constitute a mortgage. Foreclosure by taking possession is:

1. By judgment and possession taken.
2. Entry by written consent of mortgagor.
3. Entry peaceably, if not opposed, with two witnesses, who make a sworn certificate of the fact. Abstract of writ and return, written consent, and certificate to be recorded in same place as mortgage, within thirty days after entry. Possession must be retained. Foreclosure, without taking possession, is:

1. By three weeks notice in a newspaper, describing land, stating that condition is broken, and claiming foreclosed.
2. By service of same on mortgagor, to be recorded within thirty days after last publication or service. Time runs from possession taken, first publication, and service of notice. Bills in equity lies for discharge of mortgage satisfied, and to redeem mortgage after tender, or demand for account and refusal, or neglect of mortgagee to furnish it. Writ of entry may be had for recovery of estate from mortgage in possession, after mortgage is satisfied. Mortgages are discharged by an entry in the margin of the record, signed by the mortgagee personally, or by an attorney-at-law, authorized in writing, or by a deed of release. (R. S., ch. 90.)

No statute exists in regard to power of sale mortgages, but they are in use, and recognized by the court.

NOTES AND BILLS OF EXCHANGE.—Three days grace is allowed on all bills of exchange, and promissory notes not on demand, which are payable within this State. Promissory notes for the payment of money, to order or bearer, are negotiable. Demand and notice are necessary to bind indorsers. The maker and indorser can not be sued in one action. Damages on domestic bills, three to nine per cent.; no statute in relation to damages on foreign bills protested. Legal holidays are Sundays, day of public fast, or thanksgiving, fixed by Governor and Council, January 1st, February 22d, July 4th, December 25, and Memorial day.

MAINE FORMS.

[Form 1—ACKNOWLEDGMENT].

STATE OF ———, } ss.
County of ———, }

On this ——— day of ——— A. D. 188—, personally appeared before me the above named ——— and acknowledged the above instrument to be his free act and deed for the purpose therein mentioned.

In Testimony Whereof, I have hereunto set my hand and affixed my official seal the day and year last first above written.

[L. S.] *Signature and title of officer.*

Form 2—DEPOSITIONS].

STATE OF ———, } ss.
County of ———, }

On this ——— day of ——— 188 —, personally appeared before me a ———(name and title of officer) the within named deponent, and having first been sworn to testify the truth, the whole truth, and nothing but the truth, relating to the cause for which his deposition was taken, gave and subscribed the foregoing deposition in answer to the direct and cross-interrogatories attached, which was reduced to writing by me. This deposition was taken at the request of ——— , and to be used in an action of ——— now pending between him and ———, and to be tried in the Supreme Judicial Court next to be held at ——— within and for the County of ———on the ——— of ——— 188—.

In Testimony Whereof I have hereunto set my hand and affixed my official seal the day and year first above written. [SEAL], *Signature and Title of Officer.*

LAWS OF MARYLAND.

RELATIVE TO THE

COLLECTION OF DEBTS, Etc.

Prepared expressly for J. A. Graft & Co.'s Legal Directory, by Winfield M. Simpson, Attorney and Counsellor-at-Law, Baltimore, Md.

ATTACHMENTS—Can be obtained against the effects of a non-resident or an absconding debtor, and where a debtor is disposing of, concealing or removing his property from the State with intent to defraud his creditors; also in cases where the debt was fraudulently contracted.

ARREST.—Imprisonment for debt prohibited by the Constitution.

ASSIGNMENTS.—A debtor can make an assignment for the benefit of creditors, but no preference is permitted.

CHATTEL MORTGAGES AND BILLS OF SALE—Must be recorded within twenty days.

EXEMPTIONS.—Wearing apparel, mechanical text-books and books of professional men, tools of mechanics, and all tools or other mechanical instruments or appliances moved or worked by the hand or foot necessary to the practice of any trade or profession, and used in the practice thereof, and other property to be selected by the debtor to the value of $100. No homestead.

INSOLVENCY.—A debtor can obtain his discharge by petition, setting forth his inability to pay his indebtedness, and conveying to trustee appointed by the Court for that purpose, all his property, real, personal and mixed, the exemptions allowed by law excepted; provided he has not at any time disposed of his property, or any part thereof, to delay or defraud his creditors, and any creditor or creditors, the aggregate of whose claims against a debtor amount to at least $250, can, by petition, have such debtor declared insolvent, if he has committed any act of insolvency specified in the statute, namely: departing from or remaining absent from this State with the intent to defraud his creditors; concealing himself to avoid service of process; fraudulently to conceal or remove any of his property, or to transfer the same with the intent to hinder or defraud his creditors; or by giving unlawful preferences; when insolvent, to confess or allow judgment to be entered against him by any connivance, or fraudulently to stop or suspend payment of his negotiable paper, and failing to resume payment thereof within twenty days, provided such proceedings are instituted within sixty days after the act of insolvency is committed. No discharge under the insolvent law can affect the rights of a non-resident creditor, unless he voluntarily becomes a party to the proceedings.

INTEREST.—Legal, six per cent; usury forfeits excess.

JUSTICE OF THE PEACE.—Jurisdiction, $100.

LIMITATION OF ACTIONS.—Open accounts and simple contracts, three years; sealed instruments and judgments, twelve years. Revivor: Judgments by *scire facias;* other debts by any promise or acknowledgment, written or verbal.

MARRIED WOMEN.—The property of wife is not liable for the debts of husband nor subject to his control; husband, however, must join in deed conveying or transferring the same, but she, by will, can dispose of it, as if she were a *feme sole.*

MARYLAND FORMS.

[Form 1.—BILL OF SALE.]

I, ——, of ——, in consideration of —— dollars, paid me by ——, do hereby bargain and sell to the said —— the following property (here describe the property).

Witness my hand and seal this —— day of ——, in the year ——. [SEAL.]

[Form 2.—ACKNOWLEDGMENT AND AFFIDAVIT.]

STATE OF MARYLAND, }
—— County. } SS.

I hereby certify that on this —— day of ——, in the year —— before me (insert the style of the officer taking the acknowledgment) personally appeared —— the above named bargainor and acknowledged the foregoing bill of sale to be his act, and at the same time also appeared before me ——, the above named bargainee, and made oath that the consideration mentioned in the foregoing bill of sale is true and *bona fide* as therein set forth.

(Add a Jurat, and Test: same as 2a.)

[Form 2*a*.—PROOF OF ACKNOWLEDGMENT BY HUSBAND AND WIFE.]

STATE OF MARYLAND, }
—— County. } SS.

I hereby certify that on this —— day of ——, A. D. 188—, before me, (here insert name and title of official) personally appeared —— and ——, his wife, and did each acknowledge the aforesaid deed (or other instrument) to be their respective act.

In Testimony Whereof, I have hereunto subscribed my name and affixed my official seal the day and year above written.

[SEAL.] (*Signature and title.*)

[Form 3.—DEED OF TRUST.]

This deed made this —— day of ——, in the year ——, by me, ——, witnesseth, that whereas (here insert the consideration for making the deed) I, the said ——, do grant unto ——, as trustee, the following property, (here describe the property) in trust for the following purposes: (here insert the purposes of the Trust, and any covenant that may be agreed upon.)

Test: A. B. [SEAL.]

[Form 3*a*.—FORM OF DEED CONVEYING REAL ESTATE IN FEE SIMPLE.]

This deed made this —— day of ——, in the year ——, by (here insert the name of the grantor) witnesseth, that in consideration of (here insert consideration) I, the said ——, do grant unto (here insert the name of grantee) all that (here describe the property.)

Witness my hand and seal. [SEAL.]

Test: A. B.

[Form 4.—DEPOSITIONS.]

INSTRUCTIONS.

Before proceeding to act, you will take the oath headed, "Commissioner's oath," before a person authorized to administer an oath, and get this person to write at the foot thereof, in effect as follows: "The above oath was administered by me this —— day of ——, in the year ——, to —— and ——, the Commissioners within named;" and sign his name and title.

The Commissioners may appoint a Clerk, and if so, one of the Commissioners shall administer to him the oath headed on the commission, "Clerk's oath," and certify as follows: "The preceding oath was administered to ——, appointed Clerk by me, before proceeding to execute this commission," which shall be signed by one of the acting Commissioners. One of the Commissioners will administer to the witness to whom they are about to examine, an oath or affirmation, in the established form of the place, "To make true answers to all such questions as shall be asked upon the interrogatories annexed to the commission, without favor or affectation to either party, and therein speak the truth, the whole truth, and nothing but the truth."

The caption may be as follows:

CAPTION.

"At the execution of the annexed commission, issued out of the Circuit Court for —— County, directed to us and empowering us to examine witnesses in the cause pending in said Court, between ——, plaintiff, and ——, defendant, we —— and ——, Commissioners therein named having met on the first day of ——, in the year ——, at 10 o'clock, in the city (or town) of ——, and taken before ——, a Justice of the Peace for the said County of ——, duly commissioned and qualified, the oath annexed to the said commission, did proceed to take the following depositions, to-wit:

——, a witness of lawful age, produced on the part of the plaintiffs, being duly sworn and examined on the interrogatories herewith returned, deposes and says:

"To the first interrogatory, that ——,

"Answer," (Write down answer, and when done, add the following certificate): "There being no other witnesses to be examined, the Commissioners closed the said commission, and herewith return the same under their hands and seals, this —— day of ——, in the year ——.

[SEAL.] [Signed], ——.
[SEAL.] [Signed], ——.

[Form 5.—MORTGAGE OF REAL ESTATE.]

This mortgage, made this —— day of ——, in the year ——, by me, ——, witnesseth that, in consideration of the sum of —— dollars, now due from me to the said ——, I, the said ——, do grant unto the said ——, (here describe the property) provided that if I, the said ——, shall pay, on or before the —— day of ——, in the year ——, to the said ——, the sum of —— dollars, with interest thereon, from ——, then this mortgage shall be void.

Witness my hand and seal.

Test: A. B. [SEAL.]

[Form 6.—CHATTEL MORTGAGE.]

I, ——, of —— County, Maryland, being now indebted to ——, of —— County, in the sum of —— dollars, with interest from ——, in consideration thereof, do hereby bargain and sell to the said ——, the following property (here describe the property) provided that if the said —— shall pay to the said —— the sum of —— dollars, with interest thereon, on or before the —— day of ——, then these presents shall be void.

Witness my hand, this —— day of ——, 18—. [SEAL.]

ACKNOWLEDGMENT TO CHATTEL MORTGAGE.

STATE OF MARYLAND, }
City of —— } SS.

I hereby certify that on this —— day of ——, in the year ——, before the subscriber (here insert the official style of the person taking the acknowledgment) personally appeared ——, the mortgagor named in the above mortgage, and acknowledged the same to be his act, and at the same time also appeared ——, the above named mortgagee, and made oath that the consideration expressed in the above mortgage is true, and *bona fide*, as therein expressed.

Witness my hand and seal this —— day of ——, 188—. [SEAL.]

LAWS OF MASSACHUSETTS

RELATIVE TO THE

COLLECTIN OF DEBTS, Etc.

Prepared expressly for J. A. Graft & Co.'s Legal Directory, by E. P. & H. A. Bartholomew, Attorneys and Counsellors at Law, Springfield, Mass.

ACKNOWLEDGMENTS.—Deeds must be acknowledged by grantors or one of them, or by the attorney executing the same, and in the State before a Justice of the Peace or Notary Public; in any other part of the United States before a Justice, Notary, Magistrate, or commissioner appointed for the purpose by the Governor of the State. In any foreign country before such Justice, Notary, Magistrate, or commissioner, or before a Minister, Consul, or Consular offices of the United States accredited to such country.

ADMINISTRATION—. Shall be granted; First: To the widow of deceased, or next of kin, or both as the Court deems fit; Second: To the husband of deceased, being competent and willing, if feasible and proper; Third: All said persons being incompetent, unsuitable, renouncing the suit, or neglecting without good cause, for 30 days after decease of the intestate, to one or more of principal creditors; Fourth: Such creditors being unwilling, or incompetent, to whom the court deems fit; Fifth: There being no widow, husband or next of kin, in the commonwealth, to a public administration, in preference to creditors.

ALIENS—. May purchase, hold and convey real and personal estate.

APPEAL—. May be taken from Inferior Courts to the Superior Court, if claimed within 24 hours after judgement entered, parties appealing must give bond to prosecute appeal. Appeal lies from Superior Court to Supreme Court on questions of law only, from Courts of insolvency to the Superior Court; From Probate Courts to Supreme Courts, when claimed within thirty days, from act complained of.

ARREST FOR DEBT.—On mesne process in action of contract may be made if the plaintiff, or some one in his behalf, make affidavit, and prove to the satisfaction of some magistrate, that he has good cause of action, and he expects to recover the sum of $20, exclusive of costs that he has reason to believe that the defendant has property to the amount of $20, or more, not exempt from being taken on execution, and that he has reason to believe that the defendant intends to leave the State, or instead of second and third that the defendant is an attorney-at law, and the debt sought to be recovered is money collected by the defendant for the plaintiff, and not paid over in a reasonable time.

No person can be arrested on an execution, except for costs, or action of tort, unless the original debt amounted to $20 or more, and then only after a hearing before a magistrate.

No woman can be arrested on mense process, in action of contract, but she may be cited before the Court of Insolvency, as judgment debtor, and if it be shown that she has property not exempt from attachment, she will be compelled to surrender the sum for the creditors' benefit.

ATTACHMENT.—Real and personal estate may be attached on the or iginal suit, to attach real estate, the debt or damage must be not less-than $20, attachment may be dissolved by bond.

BILLS AND NOTES.—Grace of 3 days is allowed on all negotiable paper, payable at sight, or future time, certain, within the commonwealth. No grace on paper payable on demand, or checks drawn on a bank.

CHATTEL MORTGAGES.—Must be recorded within fifteen days, to be valid, except as to the parties, in the Clerk's office of the city or town where the mortgagor resides, and also of the city or town where is his principal place of business. The mortgagor living out of the commonwealth,the mortgage must be recorded in the town or city where the property is. No seal or acknowledgment necessary.

CORPORATIONS.—May be established, except for selling intoxicating liquors, and banking under the general laws. Unless stockholders have paid the full value of their shares they are liable for debt contracted before the original capital is paid in.

COURTS.—The District, Municipal, Police Courts, and Trial Justices have original and exclusive jurisdiction when the debt does not exceed $100, and concurrent with the Superior Court, up to $300.

The Superior Court has jurisdiction, where the amount claimed, exceeds $100.

Supreme Court has original, and exclusive jurisdiction of petitions for divorce and concurrent jurisdiction with the Superior Court, of petition for partition; writs of entry for foreclosure of mortgag and actions where the damage on property claimed exceeds in amount of value, $4,000, in Suffolk, and $1,000 in other counties. The Probate Court has jurisdiction of the probate of wills; granting administration; the appointment of guardians; the adoption of children and the change of names. The Probate Court is also the Court of Insolvency, and is a Court of Record.

CREDITORS BILL.—The Supreme Judicial Court has jurisdiction in equity to reach and apply in payment of a debt, any property, right, tile, or interest, legal or equitable, of a debtor within this State, which cannot be come at to be attached or taken on execution in a suit at law against such debtor. Also any property, right, title or interest, real or personal, of a debtor liable to be attached or taken on execution in a suit at law against him, and fraudulently conveyed by him, with intent to defeat, delay or defraud his creditors, or purchased or directly or indirectly paid for by him, the record or other title to which is returned in the vendor, or is conveyed to a third person with intent to defeat, delay or defraud the creditors of the debtor.

DEPOSITIONS.—Pending action, the Court will issue commission to take depositions of witnesses out of the State, and such deposition has the same validity as if taken within the State. Depositions of United States soldier may be taken before a United States Army Officer above the rank of Lieuenant of United States Sailors', before any paymaster, surgeon, or officer in command of his vessel.

ESTATES OF PERSONS DECEASED.—Are subject to payment of debts of the deceased, and may be taken on execution against the executor. Personal estate must be exhausted before recourse can be had to the real estate. If more claims are presented than the estate can pay, it must be rendered insolvent.

EXECUTIONS.—Cannot issue within 24 hours after judgment, and are returnable within 60 days after date, and must issue within one year after judgment. If returned to Court unsatisfied, an alias may be had.

EXEMPTION FROM ATTACHMENTS AND EXECUTION.—Homestead to the value of $800, if claim is made and recorded. Homestead furniture exceeding $300, fuel not exceeding $20, library not exceeding $50; one sewing machine; necessary wearing apparel; pew in church; one cow, six sheep, one swine and two tons of hay; tools and fixtures necessary for carrying on his business, not exceeding $100; material and stock designed and procured by him and necessary for carrying on his business or trade and intended to be used or wrought therein not exceeding $100; boats and fishing tackle used by the owner, to the value of $100; provisions not exceeding $50; uniform of officer and soldier; a right of burial and tomb, while in use as such; shares in certain co-operative association not exceeding $20.

INSOLVENT LAW.—Any inhabitant of the State, owing debts to an amount of $200, contracted as such inhabitant, may apply by petition to the Judge of Insolvency [who also is Judge of Probate], in the county where he resides, setting forth his inability to pay his debts, and his willingness to surrender all of his property (not by law exempt) to his creditors. A warrant thereupon issues to a messenger (who is deputy sheriff), who takes possession of the insolvent assets. The insolvent furnishes, on oath, and within five days after the warrant is issued, a list of all his creditors and assets. The creditors are notified at the first meeting, at which meeting the creditors can vote for assignee, who is chosen by a majority in value, provided the number is more than five and less than ten. All debts must be proven by oath of the creditor, or his agent or attorney, if he does not reside in the State, and must be presented for allowance at one of the meetings of the insolvent. All parties to the insolvency proceedings may be examined on oath, if requested by the Judge. Appeals are allowed to the Superior Court to any person aggrieved. Appeals must be entered with the Register, and entered at the next term of the Superior Court. Insolvency dissolves all attachments less than four months old.

THE PREFERRED CLAIMS ON—1. Debts due to the United States, or the State of Massachusetts, or any county, city, or town therein.

2. Wages due operators, clerks, or servants, not exceeding $100 for labor performed within one year of first publication of notice, or when suit has been commenced for the sum within one year from performance, and is pending or has terminated within one year from said publication.

3. Debts due physicians for medical attendance on debtor or family rendered within six months prior to commencement of proceedings in insolvency, not exceeding $50.

4. Debts due any person who by laws of the United States, or this State, is entitled to preference.

5. Legal fees, costs and expenses of suit and for custody of property if attachment was made of insolvent's property.

The assignee exhibits his account at the third meeting, and the Judge thereon orders dividends. If the insolvent estate pays 50 per cent., or if a majority in number and value of his creditors give their assent in writing within six months from the first proceedings, the insolvent is entitled to his discharge. Any fraud prevents his discharge and any fraudulent concealment of any part of his estate, or removal of it out of the State, is punished by imprisonment in the State's prison. Claims due the parties out of the State, and not proved against the insolvent's estate, are not discharged.

Creditors may petition debtors into insolvency.

Debtor can make no preference of his creditors that would be binding against insolvency.

The assignee gives no bond, unless requested to do so by the Judge.

Also, by act of 1884, debtor may at any time after filing of petition and schedules in insolvency, file a proposal for composition with creditors, stating amount of dividend, which shall be payable only in money, and time of payment, with written consent of majority in number and value of creditors; if for payment of not less than fifty per cent., to general creditors; if less than fifty per cent., three-quarters in number and value of such creditors; and the Court shall, if the composition appears duly assented to, consistent with justice and for the interest of creditors, order the composition confirmed: and upon deposit of all payments, vouchers, and securities within time limited by Court therefor, shall grant to debtor a discharge from his debts.

INTEREST.—Legal rate, six per cent. No usury law. Any interest allowed by contract.

JUDGMENT—Does not constitute a lien on defendant's property unless an attachment was made on the original writ; property not exempt may be seized on the execution taken out on any judgment. Foreign judgments are proved by certified copies. Six per cent. interest is allowed on all judgments. On default, judgment entered on last day of term.

LIEN.—Any person who furnishes labor or material for constructing or repairing any building, may have a lien on the same, or on the owner's interest in the land, on which the same is situated, if claimed duly within 30 days from time labor ceases; but when the material is not furnished the owner, on his own order, notice in unity must be given him, of the claim of lien, when the materials are furnished, suit to enforce said lien must be commenced within 60 days. Besides the common law liens, there is a lien on vessels for labor on, and material used, in building or repairing them, to be claimed duly within 4 days after vessel leaves port. Boarding house keepers have lien on baggage, and effects of guests, except mariners. There is a lien on horses and other domestic animals for boarding, pasturing, etc., the same.

LIMITATION OF ACTIONS.—Real actions, action by payee or his administrator's on a witnessed note, personal actions not elsewhere limited and Judgments of a Court of Record, must be brought within 20 years.

Actions of contract, formed on any contract not under seal, express or implied, except judgments. Actions for arrears of rent, on leases not sealed. Actions of replevin, and all others, for taking, detaining or injuring chattels. All actions of tort except as follows, 6 years. Actions against sheriff's for deputys' default, 4 years.

Actions for assault and battery, false imprisonment,slander and libel and for the conversion of personal property brought against executors administrators, guardians', trustees, sheriffs' deputy sheriffs', constables, assignees in insolvency, 2 years. Actions and suits for penalties brought in behalf of plaintiff, 1 year.

This limitation does not run against a person under disability at time this cause of action accrued on account of minority, insanity, or absence from State.

Acknowledgment or new promise, to take debt out of operation of statutes of limitation, must be in writing signed by the party chargeable.

MARRIED WOMEN.—All property, either real or personal, of a married woman, whether acquired before or after marriage, in any way, except by gift of husband, other than apparel and ornaments etc., to the value of not more than $2000, not fraudulent as to creditors, is her separate estate, and may be used as she sees fit, and is not subject to the control of her husband or liable for his debts. She has the same rights, and subject to the same liability, as she would if sole, except she cannot convey to, nor contract with her husband, nor impair his rights as tenant by this courtesy without his written consent. A married woman doing business on her separate account must file a certificate with the City or Town Clerk where she does business, setting forth her name, the name of her husband, the nature of her business, and the place where it is to be done, otherwise her property will be liable for her husband's debts, The husband may file such certificate, and if no such certificate is filed the husband is liable upon all contracts made in such business. Her contracts concerning her property,business or labor, are not binding on her husband, and his property is not held therefore, if certificate as above is duly filed.

MORTGAGES AND DEEDS OF TRUST.—Mortgages are in form like warranty deeds, with clause of defeasance. All mortgages are now made with power of sale clause, and may be foreclosed after entry of mortgage for breech of condition, and a certificate of the same rendered within 30 days: or by suit of law; or by sale under the power of sale after proper notice. Trust Deeds are not in general use.

REDEMPTION.—Lands taken on execution may be redeemed by debtor, within 1 year after levy. Mortgaged personal property within sixty days after notice of foreclosure. By owner or mortgagee of real estate sold for non payment of taxes within two years from sale.

REPLEVIN.--Possession of specific chattels unlawfully taken or detained from the rightful owner can be obtained by this writ only. It lies for goods worth above $20, and chattle distraint. Jewelry and clothing on the person cannot be replevied. Plaintiff must furnish official bond.

STATUTE OF LANDS.—No action can be brought in the following cases, unless the promise or agreement on which such action is granted is evidenced by writing signed by the person to be charged therewith or some one thereto lawfully authorized by him:

1. To charge an executor, administrator, or assignee under an insolvent law of this State, upon a special promise to answer damages out of his own estate. 2. To charge a person on a special promise to answer for the debt, default, or misdoings of another. 3. When an agreement made upon consideration of marriage, or not to be performed within one year from the making thereof. 4. When a contract for the sale of lands, tenements, or hereditaments, or any interests in, or concerning them. But the consideration of the contract need not be in writing. 5. Upon a promise of a discharged insolvent debtor, to revive the debt. 6. Upon a representation, or assurance concerning the character, conduct, credit, ability, trade, or dealings of a person. Upon a contract for the sale of goods and wares, merchandise, for $50 or more, unless the purchaser receive a part of the goods, or offer some pay in earnest, or part payment.

Every contract written, or oral for the sale or the transfer of stock and bonds is void, unless the contracting party is the owner, or is by him authorized to sell the same.

STAY OF EXECUTION.—No especial stay laws.

TAXES.—Assessed on real estate are a lien for two years after they are committed to the collector. If not paid, collector may sell.

TRUSTEE PROCESS.—Most personal actions may be commenced by trustee process, and any person or corporation may be summoned as trustee of the defendant.

WITNESS.—Testimony of parties in interest admissable.

MASSACHUSETTS FORMS.

[Form 1—CHATTEL MORTGAGE].

Know all men by these Presents, that —— in consideration of —— paid by—— the receipt whereof is hereby acknowledged, do hereby grant, sell, transfer and deliver unto the said —— the following goods and chattels, namely: (Description of goods).

To have and to hold all and singular the said goods and chattels to the said —— and —— executors, administrators, and assigns, to their own use and behoof forever.

And —— hereby covenant with the grantee that —— the lawful owner of the said goods and chattels; that they are free from all incumbrances, —— that —— have good right to sell the same as aforesaid; and that —— will *warrant and defend* the same against the lawful claims and demands of all persons ——.

Provided nevertheless that if the grantor, or —— executors, administrators, or assigns, shall pay unto the grantee, or —— executors, administrators or assigns the sum of —— in —— from this date, with interest —— at the rate of —— per cent per ——, and until such payment shall keep the said goods and chattels insured against fire in a sum not less than —— dollars for the benefit of the grantee and —— executors, administrators, and assigns, at such insurance office as they shall approve; shall not waste or destroy the same, nor suffer them or any part thereof to be attached on the mesne process, and shall not, except with the consent in writing of the grantee or —— representatives, attempt to sell or to remove from —— the same or any part thereof, —then this deed, as also —— note of even date herewith, signed by the said —— whereby —— promise to pay to the grantee or order the said sum and interest at the times aforesaid, shall —— be void.

But upon any default in the performance or observance of the foregoing condition, the grantee or —— executors, administrators, or assigns, may *sell* the said goods and chattels by public auction, first giving —— day's notice, in writing of the time and place of sale to the grantor or —— representatives. And out of the money arising from such sale, the grantee or —— representatives shall be entitled to retain all sums then secured by this mortgage, whether then or thereafter payable, including all costs, charges and expenses incurred or sustained by —— them in relation to the said property, or to discharge any claims or liens of third persons affecting the same, rendering the surplus, if any, to the grantor or —— executors, administrators, or assigns.

And it is agreed that the grantee or —— executors, administrators, or assigns, or any person or persons in their behalf, may purchase at any sale made as aforesaid; and that until default in the performance of the condition of this deed, the grantor and —— executors, administrators, and assigns, may retain possession of the above mortgaged property and may use and enjoy the same.

In witness whereof —— the said —— hereunto set —— hand and seal this —— day of —— in the year one thousand eight hundred and ——
Signed, sealed, and delivered in presence of

[*Signature*].

The mortgage should be acknowledged and recorded. See Form 5a.

[Form 2—AGREEMENT OF ASSOCIATION].

TO FORM A CORPORATION.

We whose names are hereto subscribed, do, by this Agreement, associate ourselves with the intention to constitute a Corporation according to the provisions of the two hundred and twenty-fourth chapter of the Acts of the General Court of the Commonwealth of Massachusetts passed in the year eighteen hundred and seventy, approved May ninth in said year, and the Acts in amendment thereof and in addition thereto.

The name by which the Corporation shall be known is ——

The purpose for which the Corporation is constituted is ——

The place within which the Corporation is established or located is the —— of within said Commonwealth.

The amount of its Capital Stock is —— dollars

The par value of its shares is —— dollars.

The number of its shares is ——

In witness whereof, we have hereunto set our hands this —— day of —— in the year eighteen hundred and eighty.

[Form 3—NOTICE OF FIRST MEETING.]

To ——

You are hereby notified that the first meeting of the subscribers to an agreement to associate themselves with the intention to constitute a Corporation to be known by the name of —— dated —— for the purpose of organizing said Corporation by the adoption of by-laws and election of officers ——. —— and the transaction of such other business as may properly come before the meeting, will be held on —— the —— day of —— at —— o'clock, —— M., at ——

—— *one of the subscribers to said agreement.*

——. 188

ss. ——, 188

I certify that I have served the foregoing notice upon each of the subscribers by —— seven days at least before the day fixed for the first meeting. [*Signature*].

ss. ——, 188

Subscribed and sworn to,
Before me, Justice of the Peace.

[Form 4—CERTIFICATE OF ORGANIZATION].

We, —— President, —— Treasurer, —— and —— being a majority of the directors of —— in compliance with the requirements of the eleventh section of chapter two hundred and twenty-four of the Acts of the year eighteen hundred and seventy, do hereby certify, that the following is a true copy of the agreement of association to constitute said Corporation, with the names of the subscribers thereto.

"We, whose names are hereto subscribed, do by this agreement, associate ourselves with the intention to constitute a Corporation according to the provisions of the two hundred and twenty-fourth chapter of the Acts of the General court of the Commonwealth of Massachusetts, passed in the year eighteen hundred and seventy, approved May ninth in said year, and the Acts in amendment thereof and in addition thereto.

The name by which the Corporation shall be known is ——

The purpose for which the Corporation is constituted is ——

The place within which the Corporation is established or located is the —— of —— within said Commonwealth. The amount of its Capital Stock is —— dollars. The par value of its shares is —— dollars. The number of its shares is ——

In witness whereof, we have hereunto set our hands, this —— day of —— in the year eighteen hundred and eighty ——

That the first meeting of the subscribers to said agreement was held on the —— day of —— in the year eighteen hundred and eighty ——

In witness whereof, we have hereto signed our names, this —— day of —— in the year eighteen hundred and eighty ——

COMMONWEALTH OF MASSACHUSETTS. } ss.

Then personally appeared the above named —— and severally made oath that the foregoing certificate by them subscribed, is true to the best of their knowledge and belief.

Before me,

In making the foregoing certificate, care should be taken—

1. To insert the full and exact name of the corporation, as adopted in the articles of agreement, in the proper places, without abbreviation or change.

2. To give an exact copy of the articles of agreement, with the names of all the subscribers thereto as they are subscribed, and not by substituting initials for full names.

3. In filling the blanks for date on the *first* page to insert the date of the agreement of association. The place for the date of this certificate is on the second page.

4. In case there have been adjournments of the first meeting, to add a statement of that fact after filling in the blanks on the second page with the date of the first meeting. The expressions, "And by adjournment on the —— day of —— in said year," or "And by successive adjournments on the —— day of —— and on the —— day of ——, both in said year," are sufficient for the purpose.

[Form 5—WARRANTY DEED.]

Know all men by these presents, that —— of —— in consideration of ——, paid by —— of ——, the receipt whereof is hereby acknowledged, do hereby give, grant, bargain, sell, and convey unto the said —— [Description].

To have and to hold the granted premises, with all the privileges and appurtenances thereto belonging, to the said —— and — heirs and assigns, to their own use and behoof forever.

And — do hereby, for —— and — heirs, executors, and administrators, covenant with the said grantee and — heirs and assigns that —— lawfully seized in fee-simple of the granted premises, that they are free from all incumbrances —— that — have good right to sell and convey the same as aforesaid; and that — will and — heirs, executors, and administrators, shall *warrant and defend* the same to the said grantee and — heirs and assigns forever against the lawful claims and demands of all persons ——

And for the consideration aforesaid —— do hereby release unto the said grantee and —— heirs and assigns all right of or to both *dower and homestead* in the granted premises.

In witness whereof — the said —— hereunto set — hand and seal this — day of — in the year one thousand eight hundred and ——

Signed, sealed and delivered in presence of }

[*Signature*].

[Form 5a—ACKNOWLEDGMENTS].

COMMONWEALTH OF MASSACHUSETTS, Suffolk. } ss.

Boston, March 1, 1881. Then personally appeared the above named —— and —— and (severally) acknowledged the foregoing instrument to be h —free act and deed.

Before me ——, *Justice of the Peace* [*if within the State; if without, some proper officer*].

[Form 6—DEPOSITIONS].

COMMONWEALTH OF MASSACHUSETTS, Suffolk. } ss.

To any Commissioner appointed by the Governor of said Commonwealth of Massachusetts, or to any Justice of the Peace, Notary Public, or other officer legally empowered to take Depositions, or Affidavits in ——

Greeting;

Assured of your prudence and fidelity, *We do by these presents* appoint and empower you to take the deposition of —— to be used in a suit now pending in our Superior Court, between —— as Plaintiff , and —— as Defendant ; and on certain days, to be by you appointed to cause the Deponent to come before you; and h carefully examine on oath or affirmation in answer to several interrogatories hereunto annexed; and reduce the examination, or cause the same to be reduced, to writing in your presence; and after such deposition shall thus be reduced to writing, it shall be carefully read to or by the deponent, and shall then be subscribed by h

You shall permit neither party to attend at the taking of the deposition, either himself or by any attorney or agent, nor to communicate by interrogatories or suggestions with the Deponent whilst giving h deposition in answer to the interrogatories annexed to his commission. And you shall take such deposition in a place separate and apart from all other persons, and permit no person to be present during such examination, except the Deponent and yourself, and such disinterested person [if any] as you may see fit to appoint as a clerk, to assist you in reducing the deposition to writing. And you shall put the several interrogatories and cross-interrogatories to the Deponent in their order, and take the answer of the Deponent to each, fully and clearly before proceeding to the next, and not read to the Deponent, nor permit the Deponent to read, a succeeding interrogatory, until the answer to the preceeding has been fully taken down.

Of this our writ, with your doings by warrant of the same, you will make return under seal into our said Court with all convenient expedition.

Witness the Honorable ——Chief Justice of our said court, and the seal thereof, at our City of Boston, on this — day of — in the year of our Lord one thousand eight hundred and eighty.

——, Clerk,

STATE OF, ——. } SS.

Pursuant to the foregoing Commission I caused the said ——, to come before me on the — day of ——, A. D. 188 , and having sworn the said —— to testify the whole truth, and nothing but the truth, relating to the cause for which the deposition is taken, I examined the said —— and reduced his testimony to writing. Neither of said parties was present by himself, or by any agent or an attorney, nor did either of them communicate in any manner with the Deponent, whilst giving his deposition; and I took said deposition separate and apart from all other persons, no person being present except myself ——; and in taking the depositions I put the interrogatories and cross-interrogatories to the Deponent as directed in the foregoing Commission, and in all respects fully and exactly complied with the directions in said Commission in taking the same. And after the said deposition was taken, I carefully read the same to the said ——, and he subscribed it in my presence. ——

[Form 7—INSOLVENCY].

COMMONWEALTH OF MASSACHUSETTS, Suffolk } SS.

COURT OF INSOLVENCY.

In the case of —— Insolvent Debtor —— I, —— of —— Do Swear, That said, —— by —— whom proceedings in Insolvency have been instituted, at and before the date of such proceedings, was and still is —— justly and truly indebted to me in the sum ——dollars, for which sum, or any part thereof, I have not, nor has any other person to my use, to my knowledge or belief, received any security or satisfaction whatever, beyond what has been disposed of agreeably to law.

And I do Further Swear, That the said claim was not procured by me for the purpose of influencing the proceedings in this case.

And I do Further Swear, That I have not —— directly or indirectly, made or entered into any bargain, arrangement, or agreement, express or implied, to sell, transfer or dispose of, my claim, or any part of my claim, against said debtor, nor have, directly or indirectly, received or taken, or made or entered into any bargain, arrangement, or agreement, express or implied, to take or receive, directly or indirectly, any money, property, or consideration whatsoever to myself, or to any person or persons, to my use or benefit, under or with any understanding or agreement, express or, implied, whereby my vote for asignee , or my assent to the debtor's discharge is or shall be in any way affected, influenced, or controlled, or whereby the proceedings in this case are or shall be affected, influenced or controlled.

[*Signature*].

Suffolk, ss- 188

Then personally appeared the above named —— and made solemn oath that the foregoing declaration, by him subscribed, is true.

Before me,

Justice of the Peace.

[Form 8—TRUST DEED].

Provided nevertheless, that if ——, or —— heirs, executors, administrators, or assigns shall pay unto the grantee , or —— executors, administrators, or assigns, the sum of —— in — years from this date, with interest semi-annually at the rate of —— per cent. per annum, and until such payment shall pay all taxes and assessment on the granted premises; shall keep the buildings thereon insured against fire in a sum not less than —— dollars, for the benefit of the grantee , and shall not commit or suffer any strip or waste of the granted premises, or any breach of any covenant herein contained, then this deed, as also,——note of even date herewith, signed by——, whereby —— promise to pay to the grantee or order the said sum and interest at the times aforesaid, shall be void.

But upon any default in the performance or observance of the foregoing condition, the grantee , or —— executors, administrators, or assigns, may *sell* the granted premises, or such portion thereof as may remain subject to this mortgage in case of any partial release hereof, together with all improvements that may be thereon, at public auction in said —— first publishing a notice of the time and place of sale once each week for three successive weeks in some one newspaper published in said —— and may convey the same by proper deed or deeds to the purchaser or purchasers absolutely and in fee simple; and such sale shall forever bar —— and all persons claiming under —— from all rights and interest in the granted premises, whether at law or in equity. And out of money arising from such sale the grantee or —— representatives shall be entitled to retain all sums then secured by this deed, whether then or thereafter payable, including all costs, charges, and expenses incurred or sustained, by them by reason of any default in the performance or observance of the said condition, rendering the surplus, if any, to —— or —— heirs, or assigns; and —— hereby, for —— and —— heirs and assigns, covenant with the grantee and —— heirs, executors, administrators, and assigns that, in case a sale shall be made under the foregoing power, —— or they will upon request execute, acknowledge, and deliver to the purchaser or purchasers a deed or deeds of release confirming such sale.

And it is agreed that the grantee , or —— executors, administrators, or assigns, or any person or persons in their behalf, may purchase at any sale made as aforesaid and that no other purchaser shall be answerable for the application of the purchased money; and that, until default in the performance of the condition of this deed —— and ——heirs and assigns may hold and enjoy the granted premises and receive the rents and profits thereof.

—— the receipt whereof is hereby acknowledged, do hereby give, grant, bargain, sell and convey unto the said ——

To have and to hold the granted premises, with all the privileges and appurtenances thereto belonging to the said—— and —— heirs and assigns, to their own use and behoof forever.

[Form 9—FORMAL OPENING AND CLOSING OF A WILL].

OPENING.

Be it remembered that I, ——, of ——, being of sound mind and memory, but knowing the uncertainty of this life, do make this my last will and testament. After the payment of my just debts and funeral charges, I Bequeath and devise as follows:

CLOSING.

In testimony whereof I hereunto set my hand and—— in the presence of three witnesses, declare this to be my last will. This —— day of ——, in the year one thousand eight hundred and ——

Signed].

FORM OF DECLARATION TO BE GIVEN BY ATTESTING WITNESSES.

On this, —— day of —— A. D., 188—, —— of —— signed the foregoing instrument in our presence, declaring it to be —— last will. And, as witnesses thereof, we three do now at —— request, in —— presence, and in the presence of each other, hereto subscribe our names.

LAWS OF MICHIGAN.

RELATIVE TO THE

COLLECTION OF DEBTS, Etc.

Prepared expressly for J. A. Graft & Co's Legal Directory.

AFFIDAVITS.—An affidavit to be used in this State, taken in any other State, may be sworn to before a commissioner for Michigan, or it may be taken before any Notary or Justice of the Peace, authorized by the laws of his own State to administer oaths, and the genuineness of his signature, and the fact that he was such Notary or Justice at the date of the jurat, must be certified to by the Clerk of a Court of Record of the county, under his official seal.

ARRESTS.—No arrest or imprisonment for debt, except where defendant has collected money as public officer, or in professional employment, and failed to turn it over. May arrest in civil actions for torts. No female can be arrested in any civil action.

ASSIGNMENTS.—May be made for benefit of all creditors. Must be without preference, and of all the debtor's property. Regulated by statute of 1879, and amendment of 1881. Creditors must prove debts within ninety days after notice from assignee.

ATTACHMENTS—May be issued, if affidavit made by plaintiff or agent, that affiant has good reason to believe, and does believe, that debtor has absconded, or is about to abscond from the State; or is concealed herein, to the injury of his creditors; or that he has assigned, disposed of, or concealed any of his property, or is about to do so, with intent to defraud his creditors; or that he has fraudulently contracted the debt, or that defendant is not a resident of this State, and has not resided therein for three months immediately preceding the time of making the affidavit, or that defendant is a foreign corporation.

BILLS OF EXCHANGE AND PROMISSORY NOTES.—The drawer, maker, endorser, and guarantor of the payment of a note or bill may be sued in one action as though they were all joint contractors. No person can be charged as acceptor of a bill of exchange, unless his acceptance is in writing, signed by himself or his lawful agent. Guarantee of payment or collection is negotiable, and passes to holder of note by assignment of the note merely, whether endorsed on the note itself or on a separate paper.

CHATTEL MORTGAGES—Must be filed in office of township, or city clerk, where mortgagor resides, if he resides within the State; if without the State, then where property is situated. If not filed, and possession is not taken immediately by the mortgagee, then the mortgage is void, as against creditors, and subsequent purchasers, and mortgagees in good faith. Such filing ceases to be notice after one year, unless within thirty days before the expiration of the year, the mortgage is renewed by affidavit.

COURTS.—JUSTICE'S COURTS.—Jurisdiction in actions of contract to $300, tort $100. No jurisdiction in actions for slander, libel, malicious prosecution, or in real actions.

CIRCUIT COURTS—In each county—General jurisdiction of almost all actions, and appellate jurisdiction over Justice and Probate Courts.

DEEDS AND MORTGAGES—If executed in any other State or Territory, they may be acknowledged before a commissioner for Michigan; may be executed according to the laws of the State where executed; if not acknowledged before a commissioner for Michigan, a certificate of a Clerk of a Court of Record in the county must be attached, certifying, under his seal, that the person taking the acknowledgment is such officer as is represented, that clerk believes his signature to be genuine, and that the instrument is executed according to laws of that State or Territory. They must be recorded in Register's office of county where land lies, in order to be effectual as against subsequent purchasers, and mortgagees in good faith.

DEPOSITIONS.—When taken in any other State or Territory, to be used in Michigan, are taken under a commission, issued out of the Michigan Court, and on the back of the commission are printed full instructions for taking and returning the evidence.

Depositions in Michigan, to be used in other States, may be taken according to the laws and practice of the foreign State. We have a statute providing for the subpœnaing of witnesses in such cases.

DOWER.—The widow has the use, during her natural life, of one-third part of all lands whereof her husband was seized of an estate of inheritance at any time during coverture.

EVIDENCE.—Parties are competent witnesses in any court, in any case, with a few exceptions.

EXECUTIONS.—In Justice's Court executions may issue five days after judgment, returnable in sixty days. Executions may issue in Circuit Court at once after judgment, returnable in not less than twenty nor more than ninety days from the date of issue. Justice Court judgments may be stayed, by giving good security, for four months, if sum is not over fifty dollars; if over fifty dollars, for six months.

EXEMPTIONS—REAL ESTATE.—To every householder a homestead, not exceeding forty acres in the country, or a house and lot in any city or village, not exceeding in either case fifteen hundred dollars in value. If such homestead is worth more than fifteen hundred dollars and can be divided, the debtor may select a portion of it worth that amount, and the remainder is subject to levy or execution. If worth more than fifteen hundred dollars and indivisible, it may be appraised by six jurors, and the debtor must pay the surplus over and above fifteen hundred dollars or the amount due on execution or decree, or else in sixty days the whole property may be sold and the excess over fifteen hundred dollars applied upon the debt. A mortgage or other conveyance of a homestead, if the owner is married, is void unless signed by his wife, except where given to secure all or a portion of the purchase price of the same.

1. Personal property.
2. Spinning wheels, looms, and stoves in dwellings.
3. A seat, pew, or slip in any church.
4. Cemeteries, tombs, and places of burial.
5. All wearing apparel and arms required by law.
6. Library and school books not exceeding one hundred and fifty dollars, and all family pictures.
7. To each householder 10 sheep with their fleeces, 2 cows, 5 swine, provisions and fuel for six months.
8. Household goods, furniture, and utensils not exceeding two hundred and fifty dollars.
9. The tools, implements, materials, stock, apparatus, teams, vehicle, horses, or other things to enable the person to carry on the business in which he is wholly or principally engaged, not exceeding in value two hundred and fifty dollars. A sufficient quantity of hay, grain, feed, and roots, whether growing or otherwise, for properly keeping said animals six months.
10. One sewing machine for each family.

GARNISHMENT.—Writ may issue on filing affidavit that affiant has good reason to believe, and does believe, that any person has property, etc., or money belonging to defendant, or is indebted to him; and that affiant is justly apprehensive of loss of debt, unless writ issue.

GRACE.—The customary three days allowed on all bills of exchange payable at sight or at a future day certain, within this State, and on all negotiable promissory notes, unless payable on a day certain or on demand. Bank checks and drafts are payable on presentation without grace.

INTEREST.—The legal rate is seven per cent. per annum. Parties may contract in writing for any rate not higher than ten.

JUDGMENTS—Not liens in this State, until levy is actually made by execution. May be obtained where there is no defense in Circuit Courts, in from twenty-five to sixty days, depending on the time of service, with reference to sessions of court, and the like; in Justice Courts, may be obtained in a few days.

LIMITATIONS—On accounts and notes actions must be brought within six years from maturity, or last payment. Sealed instruments and judgments, ten years. A revivor may be by a part payment, or promise in writing.

MARRIED WOMEN—May take hold, convey, demise, bequeath, or incumber real and personal property, and may contract in reference thereto, the same as if she were *femme sole*. She can not personally become surety for another's undertaking, but may charge her property to secure another's undertaking.

MORTGAGES.—See deeds and mortgages, and chattel mortgages.

PRACTICE.—Common law, with some few statutory modifications.

PROBATE COURTS.—Jurisdiction over estates of deceased persons, and infants, lunatics, etc.

PROOF OF CLAIMS.—*Prima facie* proof may be made of open accounts, and accounts stated, and of the individuals composing a partnership, by attaching affidavit of the same to the process, by which suit is commenced. This will be overcome, however, if the defendant denies the same by affidavit, at the time of putting in his pleas. As to the verification of proof, see affidavit.

REDEMPTION—Of real estate, sold on execution, may be made by the debtor at any time within a year after the sale or payment of judgment, interest, and costs; by any other creditor, at any time within fifteen months.

SUPREME COURTS.—Appellate jurisdiction generally, and original jurisdiction in cases of mandamus, quo warranto, and prohibitions.

SET-OFFS—Allowed of cross demands, where both are liquidated, or capable of being ascertained by calculation.

STAY OF EXECUTIONS.—See executions.

TAXES—Assessed the second Monday of May; Review days, the third Monday of May, and next two days. Become a lien on real estate first Monday of December. Sales of realty for delinquent taxes, first Monday of next October. One year thereafter is allowed for redemption. Tax deed is *prima facie* evidence of regularity of all proceedings back of it, but this may be rebutted.

City taxes depend on charter provisions.

WILLS.—Every person of full age and sound mind who is the owner of real or personal property may dispose of the same by will. Nuncupative wills excepted. All wills made in this state, in order to effectually pass property, shall be in writing by the testator, or by some person in his presence and by his express direction, and attested and subscribed in the presence of the testator or by two or more competent witnesses. Wills duly approved and allowed in other states of the Union, or in foreign countries according to their laws, may be filed and recorded in the Probate Courts of this State.

MICHIGAN FORMS.

[Form 1—ACKNOWLEDGMENTS FOR DEEDS AND MORTGAGES.]

STATE OF MICHIGAN, }
County of——, }

On this —— day of ——, in the year one thousand eight hundred and ——, before me, [the name of the officer who takes the acknowledgment], a [Notary Public, Justice of the Peace, or official title], in and for said County, personally appeared —— (names of the grantors), to me known to be the same persons, described in, and who executed the within instrument, who —— acknowledged the same to be their free act and deed.

——, Notary Public [or official title], —— County, Michigan.

ACKNOWLEDGMENT OF DEED OUT OF THE STATE.

Deeds acknowledged out of the State, unless before a Commissioner appointed by the Governor of this State for that purpose, shall have attached thereto a certificate of the Clerk of a Court of Record of the County or district, or of the secretary of State of the State where acknowledged, under the seal of his office, that the officer taking the acknowledgment was, at the time, such officer as he is represented to be, and that he believes the signature of such officer to such certificate of acknowledgment to be genuine, and that the deeds is executed and acknowledged according to the laws of such State, Territory or district. [C. L. page 1343, § 4212].

[Form 2—INSTRUCTIONS FOR TAKING DEPOSITIONS.]

The person — to whom such commission shall be directed, or any one of them, unless otherwise expressly directed therein, shall execute the same as follows:

1., They, or any of them, shall publicly administer an oath to the witness named in the commission, that the answers given by them to the interrogatories proposed to them shall be the truth, the whole truth, and nothing but the truth.

2, The examination of each witness shall be reduced to writing, subscribed by witness and certified by Commissioners.

All exhibits produced shall be annexed to the deposition to which they relate, and shall be subscribed by the witness proving the same, and shall be certified by the Commissioners. [This section must be understood to refer to such papers as can be produced upon the examination]. If the paper referred to be a record not subject to the control of the party or the Commissioners, it will be sufficient to annex a copy, and the original may be produced, on the trial, separate from the commission.

4., The Commissioners shall sign each sheet of the depositions.

☞ The above instructions should be strictly pursued throughout.

The commission may be executed by any one of the commissioners, without the others,

FORM OF OATH.

"You do solemnly swear that the answers given by you to the interrogatories proposed to you shall be the truth, the whole truth and nothing but the truth—so help you God"

FORM OF AFFIRMATION.

"You do solemnly and sincerely affirm, that the answers given by you to the interrogatories proposed to you, shall be the truth, the whole truth, and nothing but the truth. This you do under the pains and penalties of perjury."

And in all cases certify the mode of administering the oath.

FORM OF CAPTION.

Deposition of ——, of ——, in the State of ——, a witness, produced, sworn and examined, on the, ——day of ——, A. D., 188—, at ——, in the said State of ——, by virtue of a commission issued out of the Circuit Court and for the County of——, in the State of Michigan, on the —— day of ——, A. D., 188—, and directed to us [or me], or either of us, Commissioners for the examination of ——, witness in a cause depending all in said Court, between ——, plaintiff, and——, defendant, on the part of said ——. Having read said commission, and the instructions thereto annexed, and having administered an oath to said witness, that the answers given by him to the interrogatories proposed to him, should be the truth, the whole truth, and nothing but the truth, I (or we) proceed to the examination as follows, viz:

——, of ——, in the State of ——, aged —— and upwards, a witness, produced, sworn and examined on the part of the —— in said cause, deposeth as follows, viz:

1., To the first interrogatory, this deponent —— that he ——.

2., To the second interrogatory, this deponent saith, ——.

Under this head and in this manner you will proceed with the examination of the witness on the interrogatories [and cross-interrogatories if any], taking down the answer to each. You will yourselves ask such questions arising on the interrogatories, as you deem necessary in order to elicit the whole truth. If their be one or more interrogatories to which the witness cannot depose, knowing nothing of the matters therein contained, let the answer be as follows:

"To the —— interrogatory this deponent saith that he knows nothing and can depose nothing to the matters therein contained." The witness must subscribe his name to the deposition, when engrossed, and on the margin of each sheet the Commissioners will also write their names. At the bottom of the deposition, after it is signed by the witness, Commissioners will add their certificate, in substance as follows:

CERTIFICATE.

STATE OF ——, } ss.
County of —— }

On the —— day of ——, A. D., 188—, at the ——, in said County and State, personally appeared before us ——, one of the witnesses above named, and after having taken the oath, prescribed in the instructions annexed to the commission mentioned in the caption to the above deposition, which oath was administered by ——, and taken by such witness with uplifted hand (or by whatever other mode), declared that the foregoing deposition, by him subscribed, contains the truth, the whole truth, and nothing but the truth; said witness residing without the State of Michigan. The deposition was reduced to writing by ——, one of the Commissioners, (or by a "disinterested person," in our presence, or "by the witness himself.")

——,
——, } *Commissioners.*
——,

If any exhibits are offered and proved, add to the foregoing certificate as follows, to-wit: "The paper writing hereto attached and marked as exhibit ——, was produced and proved before us by the witness ——, as by reference to his examination may appear."

When you have gone through with the witness, and his deposition is engrossed and subscribed by him, you will annex the interrogatories to the commission with tape, the tie of which you will seal, and write and subscribe on the back of the commission the following return:

"The execution of the foregoing commission appears in certain schedules hereunto annexed."

——,
——, } *Commissioners*
——,

When the whole is completed and tacked together, as above directed, inclose it in a letter or package, seal it, and direct as follows, viz:

To —— Esquire, Clerk of the Circuit Court for the County of ——, Michigan,

The within deposition of ——, to be read in a cause pending before the Circuit Court for the County of ——, was taken, sealed up and transmited by

——,
——, } *Commissioners.*
——,

LAWS OF MINNESOTA

RELATIVE TO THE

COLLECTION OF DEBTS, Etc.

Prepared expressly for J. A. Graft & Co.'s Legal Directory, by Richardson & Day. Attorneys and Counsellors at Law, Austin, Mower Co., Minn.

Acknowledgments.—Deeds must be signed, sealed, and acknowledged by the grantor, and attested by two witnesses. A scroll or device answers for a seal. Within the State acknowledgments may be made before any Judge or Clerk of a court of record, Justice of the Peace, Notary Public, Register of Deeds, Court Commissioner, or County Auditor. Without the State, but within the United States, by Judges or Clerks of courts of record, Justices of the Peace (whose certificate must be authenticated with certificate of Clerk of Court) and Notaries Public, also by Commissioners in any of the States or Territories of the United States, duly appointed and commissioned by the Governor of this State. In foreign countries, before any Notary Public, Minister, Consul, or other diplomatic or commercial agent of the United States there accredited and resident.

Assignments must be in writing, subscribed by debtor or debtors and acknowledged. Debtor must file inventory of all property within ten days after filing assignment. Assignee must give bond with two or more sureties to be approved by Judge of District Court in double the amount of property inventoried. Claim must be verified by oath of the party, except claims of the United States or State of Minnesota. Debts are paid in the following order after paying costs and charges of assignment: First, debts due the United States and the State of Minnesota, and all taxes levied and unpaid, to be paid in full; Second, debts owing for wages of servants, laborers, and mechanics, and clerks for labor and service performed by them within three months next preceding the date of assignment, which are paid in full to the exclusion of all other indebtedness, if there be sufficient wherewith to pay the same in full. If not, they shall be paid pro rata.

If an insolvent debtor confesses judgment, makes a conveyance, does any act for the purpose of preferring any creditor, or omits to do any act for the purpose of preventing any creditor from obtaining a preference, or does not within ten days after a levy upon his property, make an assignment for the benefit of all his creditors, or institute proceedings to obtain a release of execution against him, then, or at any time within sixty days, any two creditors having claims aggregating $200 may petition the Court for the appointment of a receiver for all of the debtor's property except such as is exempt by law.

Upon the appointment of an assignee or receiver, all levies upon the debtor's property shall be withdrawn, unless the assignee or receiver deems best to have such levies remain, but such levies shall be for the benefit of all the creditors. When the complaint upon which judgment is based was filed more than twenty days before judgment rendered, such judgment shall be preferred.

Costs of actions commenced, in which attachments or liens are made, that are subsequently set aside by an assignment, are payable by the assignee or receiver from the first money coming into his hands.

Any debtor who confesses or suffers judgment to be rendered against him for the purpose of preferring any creditor, may be fined not to exceed $500, and, in case he fail to pay the fine, may be imprisoned not to exceed six months.

Conveyances and payments made by an insolvent debtor within four months of insolvency, in contemplation of insolvency, to parties having reasonable cause to believe the debtor to be insolvent, are void, and may be recorded by the assignee or receiver. All suits shall be brought in the name of the assignee or receiver. Appeals from orders of assignees or receivers disallowing claims may be made to the District Court. The assignee must, within ten days after disallowing a claim, notify the creditors. Assignees and receivers may be removed upon a petition of two-thirds of the creditors. No creditor is entitled to share in the distribution of the estate, unless he shall first file a release of his claim in the District Court, upon which judgment is entered, discharging the debtor from all claims or debts held by the creditor filing such release; but if a creditor does not file his claim and release the same is not barred. Judgment can be taken and enforced against future acquired property.

The assignee or receiver shall publish notice of his appointment, and shall mail notice to each creditor, and the creditors shall file their claims within twenty days after notice.

The assignee or receiver shall distribute the estate in the following order:

1st. Cost of proceeding. 2d. Debts due the United States. 3d. Debts due the State of Minnesota. 4th. Taxes and assessments. 5th. Clerks, servants, and laborers, for labor performed within three months, in full, not exceeding $50 to each. The balance shall be distributed pro rata between the creditors.

APPEAL.—From Justice's Court when judgment, or in replevin, when the value of the property exceeds fifteen dollars.

From District to Supreme Court, which is the court of last resort.

ARREST.—(See Supplementary Proceedings.) Not allowed for debt.

ATTACHMENTS may issue from Justice's Court upon filing bond in double the value of the property, and affidavit of plaintiff or some person in his behalf that he has good reason to believe: 1st, that defendant is a non-resident corporation; 2nd, that defendant is not a resident of this State, and has not resided therein for three months preceding the time of making the affidavit; 3rd, that defendant has absconded or is about to abscond from the State; 4th, that defendant has removed or is about to remove his property out of the State with intent to defraud his creditors; 5th, that defendant resides in any other county and more than 100 miles from the residence of the Justice; 6th, that defendant contracted the debt under fraudulent representations; 7th, that defendant so conceals himself that the summons can not be served upon him; 8th, that defendant has, or is about to, fraudulently convey or dispose of his property so as to hinder, delay, and defraud his creditors. In attachments in District Courts plaintiff's affidavit must state facts, and can not be made on information and belief, as in Justices' Courts. Bond of $100 is not allowed in this State in Justice's Court, and not less than $250 in District Court required.

BILLS OF EXCHANGE.—On all bills of exchange, payable at sight, or at a future day certain, and on all negotiable promissory notes, orders, and drafts payable at a future day certain, within this State, in which there is no express stipulation to the contrary, grace is allowed according to the custom of merchants. No grace on demand paper. Damages five per cent. on domestic, and ten per cent. on foreign paper protested. Notes obtained by fraudulent representation without negligence on part of maker void; question of negligence one of fact for jury.

Bills of exchange, promissory notes, drafts, and contracts due, payable or to be executed on Sunday, Thanksgiving, Good Friday, Christmas, New Years, February 22d, and July 4, are payable or performable upon the business day next preceding said days.

COSTS.—In District Court, allowed to prevailing party: to plaintiff, upon judgment in his favor for $100 or more, in an action for the recovery of money only, when no issue of law or fact is joined, $5; when issue is joined, $10; to defendant, on dismissal, $5; when judgment is in his favor, on merits, $10. The resident plaintiffs must give security for costs.

COURTS.—*Terms and Jurisdiction.*—District Courts, holding one or two terms a year in each organized county, (three in Ramsey and Hennepin counties), have original jurisdiction in all civil actions involving over $100; in all actions where a Justice has not jurisdiction, without regard to amount; and in all equitable actions and proceedings, and may issue process in term time or vacation throughout the State, returnable to the proper county. A Probate Court with usual powers is established in each organized county, and holds term on the first Monday of each month. Justice's jurisdiction, $100.

Supreme Court sits at Saint Paul on the first Tuesday of April and October.

EXECUTIONS may issue from District Courts at any time within ten years after judgment, and to any county where a transcript has been docketed.

Executions are returnable in sixty days, but may be renewed for sixty days at a time for any length of time, upon the request of judgment creditor or his attorney. Personalty is first levied on, and is sold on ten days' notice; real estate after six weeks publication. In Justices' Courts execution may issue ten days after entry of judgment, returnable in thirty days, and renewable from time to time for periods of thirty days. In courts of record six months stay is granted on defendant filing bond with two free-hold sureties, approved by the court, conditioned to pay amount of judgment with costs, and interest at the rate of ten per cent. per annum. Stay in Justices' Courts may be had in the same manner, where judgment is under $10, one month; $10 to $25, two months; $25 to $50, three months; $50 to $75, four months; over $75, six months. Real estate sold on execution is subject to redemption for one year from date of sale.

No execution against the person.

DEPOSITION may be taken within the State, orally or upon interrogation, upon notice.

Without the State commission issues to take the testimony of the witness, or same may be taken orally, upon notice.

DIVORCE.—Action must be brought in county where plaintiff resides, if a resident.

Plaintiff must have been a resident for one year immediately preceding commencement of action.

Granted for adultery, impotency, cruel and inhuman treatment. Sentence to imprisonment in State's prison, willful desertion for three years; habitual drunkenness for one year. The Court may order alimony, change custody of children, and protect party from injury.

ESTATES OF DECEDENTS.—Personal: widow is allowed her wearing apparel, and that of her husband; household furniture not exceeding $500 in value; remainder is distributed in same proportion as real estate.

Real estate: after assignment of dower and homestead to widow (see Married Women), remainder descends equally to the children of the deceased, and to the issue of any deceased child, *per stirpes*. If no child, or issue of deceased child, to decedent's father. If no father, one-third to decedent's mother; balance equally to sisters and brothers; other provisions for additional cases.

EXEMPTIONS.—Surviving husband or wife holds homestead free from debts of deceased for life of survivor. Homestead of eighty acres in country; half an acre if in city, town, or village not incorporated, and of less than 5,000 inhabitants, and one lot if in larger cities, towns, or villages, with dwelling house thereon, without regard to value. Wearing apparel, books, pictures, and furniture, up to $500; three cows, ten swine, twenty sheep, and wool from the same, a yoke of oxen and a horse, or, in lieu thereof, a span of horses or mules; necessary food for stock for one year; wagon, plows, and farming utensils up to $300; one year's seed grain not exceeding 150 bushels in all, and provisions for family for one year. The tools and instruments of a miner, mechanic, or other person, and stock in trade up to $400; library and instruments of a professional man; $20 wages of laboring man or woman, for services rendered within ninety days preceding the issue of process. Also, where the debtor is a printer, publisher, or editor of a newspaper, all the presses, stones, type, cases, and other tools and implements, not exceeding $2,000, and stock in trade up to $400.

INTEREST.—Seven per cent. is the legal rate of interest upon every legal indebtedness, including judgments and accounts. Since July 1, 1879, the highest rate of interest allowed to be taken by special contract is ten per cent. The penalty for usury is forfeiture of the entire amount of the note or other instrument, and of all interest.

JUDGMENTS.—If no defense is made, judgments can be obtained at the expiration of twenty days, and upon being docketed in the office of the clerk of the court, they become liens upon all real estate of the debtor in the county where docketed, owned by him at that time or afterward acquired, for ten years after date of docketing, and can be enforced during that time by execution against the real or personal property of judgment debtor.

LIENS.—Statute gives lien for work and labor performed by mechanic on any building, boat, or vessel, and for materials furnished for the erection, alteration, or repairing of any building, boat, or vessel, and the real estate on which any building is situated, not to exceed eighty acres in the country, or one half acre in a village or town, or one lot in any platted city of more than 5,000 inhabitants; also gives to servants and clerks a lien on personal property, not to exceed $200 in amount, for work performed within six months next preceding filing of lien.

LIMITATIONS TO SUITS.—On contracts, express or implied, six years; on judgments or to foreclose mortgage, ten years; real actions, twenty years. Revivor: Part payment or new promise in writing.

MARRIED WOMEN.—All property acquired by wife before or after marriage remains her separate estate, neither controlled by or liable for the debts of her husband. Married women are held on their contracts and bound by them the same as if unmarried: except, a married woman can not sell her real estate, or make any conveyance of land other than a mortgage for the purchase money or a lease for three years or less, without her husband joins in the conveyance. Estates in dower and by the curtesy are abolished, and the surviving wife or husband is entitled to the homestead for life free from debts of the deceased, and to one equal undivided one-third of all other lands of which the deceased was seized during coverture, subject to payment of lawful debts of the deceased, but free from any testamentary or other disposition.

MORTGAGES on real estate must be recorded, and are foreclosed by action or publication. A year is allowed for redemption. Chattel mortgages are void as against creditors and subsequent mortgagees and purchasers in good faith, unless acknowledged and filed with the Town or City Clerk, both where property is situated and where mortgagor resides. They are then valid, but cease to be notice after two years from date of filing. Interest of mortgagor subject to sale on execution, and purchaser is substituted in place of mortgagor, and acquires rights of redemption.

SUITS.—There is only one form of action, and all civil actions must be prosecuted in the name of the real party in interest, except suits by administrators, etc. Full name of plaintiff must be furnished. Process to commence suit in the District Court must be served on the debtor twenty days before judgment can be taken by default, except action for divorce, when summons must be served at least thirty days before defendant will be in default. A deposit of $3 with Clerk of Court for costs in all civil actions hereafter begun is required before entry of action on docket (Hennepin and Ramsey county excepted). Process in Justices' Courts must be served not less than six nor more than twenty days before return day.

TAXES.—Taxes become due and payable Dec. 1; personal property tax delinquent March 1; real property tax delinquent June 1; penalty of 5 per cent. attached on personal property March 1, and on real property of 10 per cent. after June 1. County Treasurer to levy distress on goods and chattels and sell the same at public vendue for personal property tax, and real estate is sold for tax on third Monday in September each year, and is subject to two years redemption. Tax judgments draw interest at the rate of one and one-half per cent. per month from date of sale.

WITNESS.—Not incompetent by reason of interest in event of the action, nor by reason of having been convicted of crime.

Party to action or interested in result can not give evidence of or concerning conversations with or admissions of a deceased or insane party or person relative to matters at issue between the parties.

A husband or wife can not be witnesses for or against each other without the other's consent, nor can either without such consent be examined as to any communication made by one to the other during marriage; but this does not apply to a civil action by one against the other, nor to proceedings for crime committed by one against the other.

Privileged communications may not be testified to without the consent of the person making them.

MINNESOTA FORMS.

[Form 1—CHATTLE MORTGAGE.]

Know all Men by these Presents, That——, of the town of——, County of ——, State of Minnesota, party of the first part, being justly indebted to ——, party of the second part, in the sum of —— dollars, which is hereby confessed and acknowledged, has, for the purpose of securing the payment of said debt, granted, bargained, sold and mortgaged, and by these presents does grant, bargain, sell and mortgage unto the said part of the second part, his heirs and assigns, all that certain personal property described as follows, to-wit: (Describe property).

All the said property being now in the possession of said first party, in the town of ——, County of ——, and State first aforesaid, and free from all incumbrances.

To Have and to Hold, All and singular, the personal property aforesaid, forever; provided always, and these presents are upon this express condition, that if the said party of the first part shall pay, or cause to be paid, unto the said party of the second part, his heirs and assigns, the sum of —— dollars, according to the conditions of ——, then these presents to be void and of no effect. But if default shall be made in payment of said sum of money or the interest thereof, at the time the same shall become due, or if any attempt shall be made to remove, dispose of, or injure said property or any part thereof, by said party of the first part, or any other person, or if said party of the first part, does not take proper care of said property, then, thereupon and thereafter, it shall be lawful, and the said first party hereby authorizes the said second party, his heirs and asigns, or his authorized agent, to take said property, wherever the same may be found, and remove and sell and dispose of the same and all equity of redemption, at public auction, according to the statute in such case made and provided, —— retaining such sum as shall pay the amount due, and an attorney's fee of ten dollars, and such other expenses as may have been incurred, returning the surplus money, if any there may be, to the said party of the first part, his heirs or assigns. And as long as the conditions of this mortgage are fulfilled the said first party to remain in peaceful possession of said property, and in consideration thereof agrees to keep said property in as good condition as it now is, at said first party's cost and expense——.

In witness whereof, The said party of the first part ha —hereunto set —— hand —— and seal—, this —— day of, A. D. 188—.

in presence of
———— ————
———————— } —— [SEAL].
—— [SEAL].

ACKNOWLEDGMENT.

STATE OF MINNESOTA, }
County of ——. }

Personally Appeared Before me this —— day of ——, A. D. 188 —, ——, to me known as the person described in, and who executed the foregoing mortgage, and acknowledged that —— executed the same freely and voluntarily for the uses and purposes therein expressed.

[*Signature*].

[Form 2—FORM AND INSTRUCTIONS FOR TAKING DEPOSITIONS].

The examination may, if so stated in the notice, be adjourned from day to day, at the time or place specified in the notice or order, or within one hour thereafter, the examination shall commence; witnesses shall be sworn before testifying, to testify the whole truth and nothing but the truth, relative to the cause; the testimony shall be written by the officers and the proceedings adjourned from day to day until closed.

Either party may appear in person, or by agent or attorney, and take part in the examination; the testimony, when completed, shall be carefully read over to the witness, and he may add thereto or qualify the same. The witness shall sign upon each piece of paper on which any portion of his testimony is written, and at the end of the deposition also; and the officer shall add jurat as follows:

"Subscribed and sworn to before me, this —— day of, ——, A. D., 188—.
——— [SEAL]."

CAPTION.

The name of the State, County, Court, and title of Cause, as found in the notice or order, should be given at the head of the deposition, and the testimony preceded by the following.

"Testimony of ——, of ——, in the county of——, State of ——, taken before ——, a ——, by virtue of the notice (or order) hereto attached, as stated in the return thereto." If there are interrogatories, they need not be copied, but before each answer should be put the following:

"To the first interrogatory the witness deposes and says:" "To the second interrogatory the witness, etc."

CERTIFICATE.

The certificate should be in the following form, and should be under the hand and official seal of the officer taking the deposition, if he have any.

STATE OF ——, }
County of——. }

Be it Known That I took the annexed depositions pursuant to the annexed notice (or order); that I was then and there a ——, that I exercised the power of that office in taking such depositions; that by virtue thereof I was then and there authorized to administer an oath: that each witness before testifying was duly sworn to testify the whole truth and nothing but the truth, relative to the cause specified in the annexed notice (or order); that the testimony of each witness was correctly read over to him by me before he signed the same; that the examination was conducted on behalf of the plaintiff — by ——, that the examination was conducted on behalf of the defendant — by ——.

Witness my hand and seal, this —— day of ——, 18 —

[*Signature and title of officer*].

FURTHER INSTRUCTIONS.

The papers should be formed into one package, fastened securely, in the following order: notice (or order), interrogatories and cross-interrogatories, deposition, exhibits (if any), and certificate. A minute of the fees of magistrate and witness, and by whom paid, should be added.

The package should be enclosed in an envelope and addressed to the Justice of the Peace, Judge of the Probate Court, or, if the cause be pending in any other Court, to the Clerk thereof, as the case may be. Across the end of the envelope the officer should endorse, "Deposition in the case of —— *vs.* ——," The package must be sent by mail to the Court where the cause is pending and opened by the proper officer after which it is subject to inspection by either party. (Ch. 73, § § 33, 37).

[Form 3.—MORTGAGE DEED.]

This Indenture, Made this —— day of —— in the year of our Lord one thousand eight hundred and —— between ——, part— of the first part, and ——, part— of the second part, *Witnesseth*, that the said part— of the first part, for and in consideration of the sum of —— dollars, to —— in hand paid by the said part— of the second part, the receipt whereof is hereby acknowledged do by these presents, grant, bargain, sell and convey, to the said part— of the second part, —— heirs and assigns forever, all —— tract or parcel of land, lying and being in the County of ——, and State of Minnesota, described as follows, to-wit: (Here describe property).

To Have and to Hold the Same, Together with all the hereditaments and appurtenances thereunto belonging or in anywise appertaining, unto the said part— of the second part, ——, heirs and assigns forever. And the said ——, part— of the first part, do covenant with the said part— of the second part, heirs and assigns, as follows: First, that he —— lawfully seized of said premises; Second, that he ha— good right to convey the same; Third, that the same are free from all encumbrances; ——Fourth, that the said part— of the second part, —— heirs and assigns, shall, quietly enjoy and possess the same; and that the said part— of the first part will warrant and defend the title to the same against all lawful claims.

Provided Nevertheless. That if the said ——, part— of the first part, —— heirs, executors or administrators, shall well and truly pay or cause to be paid to the said part— of the second part, heirs, executors, administrators or assigns, the sum of —— dollars, and interest according to the condition of ——
bearing even date herewith, then this deed shall be null and void, otherwise to be and remain in full force and effect. But if default shall be made in the payment of said sum of money, or interest, or any part thereof, at the time and in the manner hereinbefore specified for the payment thereof, the said part— of the first part in such case do hereby authorize and empower the said part— of the second part, —— heirs, executors, administrators or assigns, to sell the said hereby granted premises at public auction, and convey the same to the purchaser in fee simple, agreeably to the statute in such case, made and provided, and out of the moneys arising from such sale to retain the principal and interest which shall then be due on the said —— together with all costs and charges, and also the sum of —— dollars as attorney's fees, and pay the overplus if any, to the said part— of the first part, —— heirs, administrators or assigns.

And the said —— do further covenant and agree to and with the said part— of the second part, —— heirs, executors administrators and assigns, to pay said sum of money above specified, at the time and in the manner above mentioned, together with all costs and expenses, if any there shall be, and also in case of the foreclosure of this mortgage, the sum of —— dollars, as attorney's fees, in addition to all sums and costs allowed in that behalf by law, which said sum is hereby acknowledged and declared to be a part of the debt hereby secured, and which shall be assessed and payable as part of said debt, and that he will pay all taxes and assessments of every nature that may be assessed on said premises, or any part thereof, previous to the day appointed by law for the sale of lands for Town, City, or County Taxes.

In Testimony Whereof, The said part— of the first part ha— hereunto set —— hand and affixed —— seal the day and year first above written.

Signed, sealed and delivered in presence of }

——————— } ——, [SEAL.]
——————— } ——, [SEAL.]

ACKNOWLEDGMENT.

STATE OF —— } ss
County of ——. }

I, ——, within and for said County, do hereby certify that on this —— day of —— A. D., 18—, personally came before me, ——, to me well known to be the same person— described in and who executed the foregoing instrument, and —— acknowledged that he executed the same freely and voluntarily for the purposes and uses therein expressed.

[Form 4.—QUIT CLAIM DEED.]

This Indenture, Made this —— day of ——, in the year of our Lord one thousand eight hundred and ——, between ——, part— of the first part, and ——, part— of the second part:

Witnesseth, That the said part— of the first part, in consideration of the sum of —— dollars to —— in hand paid by the said part— of the second part, the receipt whereof is hereby acknowledged, do—, by these presents, grant, bargain, sell, release, and quit claim, unto the said part— of the second part, —— heirs and assigns, forever, ——, all the following tract— or parcel— of land lying and being in the County of ——, and state of Minnesota, described as follows, to-wit: (Describe property.)

Together with all and singular, the hereditaments and appurtenances thereunto belonging, or in anywise appertaining. So that neither —— nor any other person claiming by, from or under —— (or either of us) shall have or claim any right, title, interest in or to the same or any part thereof.

In Testimony Whereof, the said part— of the first part hereunto set —— hand— and seal—, the day and year first above written.

Signed, sealed and delivered in presence of
———— } Witnesses. ——, [SEAL.]
———— ——, [SEAL.]

ACKNOWLEDGMENT—FOR QUIT CLAIM DEED.

STATE OF ——, } ss.
County of ——. }

I, (name and official character), within and for said County, do hereby certify that on the —— day of ——, A. D. 18—, personally came before me ——, to me known to be the same person— described in and who executed the foregoing instrument, and —— acknowledged that —— executed the same freely and voluntarily.

Signature.

[Form 5.—WARRANTY DEED.]

This Indenture, Made this —— day of ——, in the year of our Lord one thousand eight hundred and eighty —, between ——, of the County of ——, and State of Minnesota, part— of the first part, and ——, part— of the second part: *Witnesseth*, That the said part— of the first part, for and in consideration of the sum of —— dollars, to —— in hand paid by the said part— of the second part, the receipt whereof is hereby acknowledged, ha— granted, bargained, sold and conveyed, and by these presents do— grant, bargain, sell, and convey unto the said part — of the second part, —— heirs and assigns, forever, all— the following described tract—, piece— or parcel— of land, situate in the County of ——, and state of Minnesota, and known and described as follows, to-wit: (Here describe property.)

To Have and to Hold the same, together with all and singular, the hereditaments and appurtenances thereunto belonging, or in anywise appertaining, unto the said part— of the second part, —— heirs and assigns forever. And the said ——, part— of the first part, do— covenant with the said part— of the second part, —— heirs and assigns, as follows: First, that —— lawfully seized of said premises; second, that —— good right to convey the same; third, that the same are free from all encumbrances: ——; fourth, that the said part— of the second part, —— heirs and assigns, shall quietly enjoy and possess the same; and fifth, that the said part— of the first part will warrant and defend the title to the same against all lawful claims.

In Testimony Whereof, the said part— of the first part ha— hereunto set —— hand and seal, the day and year first above written.

Signed, sealed and delivered in presence of
———— } ——, [SEAL.]
———— ——, [SEAL.]
——, [SEAL.]
——, [SEAL.]

STATE OF ——, } ss.
County of ——. }

Be it Known, That on this —— day of ——, A. D. 188—, before me personally came ——, to me personally known to be the identical person— described in and who executed the foregoing instrument, and duly acknowledged that —— executed the same for the purposes and uses therein expressed.

(Signature and title of officer.)

ACKNOWLEDGMENT BY AGENT FOR CORPORATION.

STATE OF ——, }
County of ——, } ss.

Be it Known, that on this —— day of ——, A. D. 188—, before me personally came ——(agent's name), to me well known to be the identical person— described in, and who executed the foregoing instrument, for and in behalf of —— (corporate name), and duly acknowledged that —— he — executed the same freely and voluntarily, as such agent, for the uses and purposes therein expressed, and as the act of said —— (corporate name). (*Signature and title of officer.*)

LAWS OF MISSISSIPPI

RELATIVE TO THE

COLLECTION OF DEBTS, Etc.

Revised expressly for J. A. Graft & Co.'s Legal Directory, by W. C. Forsee, Attorney and Counsellor-at-Law, Meridian, Mississippi.

ACTIONS.—Common law as to substance. Forms immaterial. Fictions and much technicality abolished. Law suits commence by declaration and summons issued thereon; equity by bill and summons. Security for costs demandable of non-residents and insolvents. Security for costs demandable from non-residents; but any resident of the state may commence or prosecute any action in form of paupers, by filing an affidavit of his inability to pay or secure costs.

AFFIDAVITS.—Made before Judge, Court of Records, Clerk of said Courts, Supervisors, Justices of Peace, Notary Public, or Master, or Commissioner in Chancery, or Commissioner of the State in other States.

ALIENS.—Resident, or non-resident, may acquire and hold real estate; dispose of it, or transmit by descent.

APPEALS—From Justices to Circuit Court to be taken in five days; *certorari* in six months. From Circuit and Chancery to Supreme, in two years.

ARREST—For debt, abolished.

ASSIGNMENTS—Must be in writing, signed by party making, and recorded.

ATTACHMENTS—Issue for all debts, damages growing out of breach of any contract, and claim founded on State penal laws. Creditor, agent, or attorney, files affidavit of amount and character of claim, and charging one or more of following grounds: 1. That defendant is foreign corporation, or a non-resident of this State. 2. That he has removed, or is about to remove himself, or his property, out of the State. 3. That he so absconds, or conceals himself that he cannot be served with summons. 4. That he contracted the debt or incurred the obligation, in conducting the business of a ship, steamboat, or other water craft, in some of the navigable waters of this State. 5. That he has property, or rights in action which he conceals and unjustly refuses to apply to the payment of his debts. 6. That he has assigned, or disposed of, or is about to assign or dispose of, his property, or rights in action, or some part thereof, with intent to defraud his creditors. 7. That he has converted, or is about to convert his property into money, or evidences of of debt, with intent to place it beyond the reach of his creditors. 8. That he fraudulently contracted the debt, or incurred the obligation for which suit has been, or is about to be brought.

Before writ issues, bond, with security in double the amount of debt claimed, must be executed, conditioned to pay all such damages as defendant shall sustain by the wrongful suing out of the attachment, and costs. Non-residents may attach. Attachments, triable at first term, may issue for debts due, or not due. Writ may be levied on lands, tenements, money, goods, chattels, and debts of defendant, wherever found. Upon suggestion, a garnishment clause may be added to writ.

Defendant may contest grounds, as a preliminary and separate issue. If successful, may recover actual damages for wrongful issuance of writ. Plaintiff can not defeat recovery of damages by dismissing suit. Successful contest of grounds abates suit and dissolves attachment.

CHATTEL MORTGAGES—May be executed as other mortgages and trust deeds. Delivery of possession unnecessary. Rules as to acknowledgment and record, apply. On removal of mortgaged property to another county, mortgagee may be protected against purchasers and incumbrancers by recording in latter county in twelve months after removal. Mortgages and deeds of trust allowed to be made on growing crops, and crops to be grown in fifteen months.

CLAIMS AGAINST DECEASED PERSONS—Registered in Chancery Clerk's office in one year after administrator's first notice, otherwise barred. Before registered, claims must be proved and allowed by clerk. Bonds, bills and notes must be exhibited, with creditor's oath attached, that no part of the money thereby secured is paid, except as credited, and that no security, or satisfaction has been given for same. Short copies of judgments and decrees, certified by seal of clerk of proper court, and that there is no entry of satisfaction, must be filed, with similar affidavit, when claim is a judgment, or decree. Insolvent estates to be so declared; notice for four weeks published; claim barred then, unless presented in six months.

DEEDS.—Husband and wife, independant of each other, and need not join, except conveyances of homestead. Estates may be created to commence *in future.* Every estate a fee, unless specially limited, or intention of limitation clearly appears. Conveyance, or devises permissable to succession of donees then living, not exceeding two, and to heirs of body of remainder none, and, in default, to right heirs of donor. Rule in Shelly's case; dower, courtesy and tenancy by entirety abolished. Acknowledgment and proof of deeds, and other written contracts, required to be recorded, made in United States, but out of Miss., taken before any Justice of U. S. Supreme, or Judge of U. S. Dist.; or Judge or Justices of Supreme, or Superior Court of any State or Territory, or Justice of Peace, whose official character shall be certified under s al of a Court of Record in his county, or by Miss. Commissioners residing in such State or Territory, or by Notary Public, or by Clerk of a Court of Record, having seal of office, in any State or Territory of the Union. Unacknowledged instruments, proven as above by one or more witnesses. Acknowledgments must be in this form, substantially: "State of——, county of—— } Personally appeared before me, (state the sort of office.) the within named, A. B., who acknowledged that he signed and delivered the foregoing instrument, on the day and year therein mentioned. Given under my hand, this—— day of——, A. D. (Sign),"

EVIDENCE.—Interest or relationship no disqualification, except no one can establish his own claim for or against estate of deceased person which originated during life time of decedent, or which he has transferred since the death.

EXECUTIONS—Must be issued and delivered by clerk to sheriff, within twenty days of adjournment of Court. After first executions may be taken out in seven years after the last issued. In justice's courts five days must elapse after judgment before execution issues. Equitable and undivided interests, bank notes, bills, are evidences of debt circulating as money and stocks, vendible under execution at law or equity. Executions, where there is no judgment lien, bind the property actually levied on from the time of levy.

EXEMPTIONS.—None, where purchase money, in whole or part, forms debt on which judgment is founded, nor for non-payment of taxes or assessments, nor for materials furnished, nor labor done, nor where debt is for labor performed, nor upon forfeited recognizance or bail bond. Subject to these exceptions, there is exempt a homestead to every citizen, male or female, being a householder and having a family, not exceeding $2,000 in value, nor, if farm in county 160 acres in extent. Also to each head of family, or housekeeper, 2 horses or mules, or 1 yoke oxen, 2 cows and calves, 5 head stock hogs, 5 sheep, 150 bushels corn, 300 bundles fodder, 10 bushels wheat or rice, 200 pounds meat, 1 cart or wagon, not worth more than $100, 1 sewing machine, household and kitchen furniture, not to exceed $100 in value, crops, while growing. To persons in towns, villages, and cities, not to exceed $250 in value of such personal property as they select. Also $100 of a laborer's wages, tools of mechanic, agricultural implements of farmer for two laborers, implements of a laborer necessary, books of students, wearing apparel, libraries of attorneys, physicians and ministers, and instruments of surgeons and dentists, not to exceed $250 in value; arms and accoutrements of militiamen, globes, books and maps of teachers of schools, academies and colleges, life insurance policy, not exceeding $10,000. In case no widow, husband or children survive, at death exempt property liable to creditors. Debtor may sell or remove exempt property from State.

GARNISHMENT—May issue on a law judgment, or equity decree, and only before judgment as incident to attachment. Numerous issues, on suggestions of plaintiff, that person named as garnishee owes defendant, or has custody of his property, or knows who does owe or hold property for him. Garnishee must answer under oath as to truth of suggestion, which answer may be traversed and trial had.

INSOLVENT LAWS.—None in Mississippi.

INTEREST.—Legal rate, 6 per cent. Parties may contract for 10 per cent. Whole interest forfeited in cases of usury.

JUDGMENTS.—May be had at first term in Justices, Circuit and Chancery Courts, when there is personal service and no pleadings filed. Without personal service, or when plea is filed, no judgment can be had at first term, except in Justices Courts, and in *quo warranto* attachment and replevin suits in Circuit Court. All judgments may be enrolled on judgment roll in Circuit Clerk's office, and, when enrolled, are liens upon property of defendant in such county from enrollment, except Circuit Court judgments, which bind from rendition. Judgments must be enrolled within twenty days after rendition, to take effect.

JUSTICES' JURISDICTION.—Justices have jurisdiction in all matters of law where only $150, or less, is involved.

LIENS.—Common law liens are administered; also agricultural and mechanics' liens exist by statute.

LIMITATIONS.—Verbal contracts, three years; actions on penalty and torts, one year; domestic judgments, seven years; foreign judgments, seven years, unless against person then resid nt in this State, when three years; executors and administrators, within four years after qualification; all other personal actions, six years, and real actions ten years.

MARRIED WOMEN.—Absolutely emancipated.

NOTES AND BILLS.—Every promise in writing to pay a sum of money, or acknowledging the same to be due, is a promissory note. May be assigned in writing; and assignee may sue on in his own name. Defendant allowed benefit of all defences existing previous to notice to him of assignment. Rule does not apply to paper payable to bearer, or payable in another State, or country. Notes not protestable; domestic and foreign bills protestable.

PROOF OF CLAIMS.—Account sued on may be sworn to, stating to its correctness, and that it is due from the party against whom it is charged; such affidavit entitles to judgment at trial term without further proof, unless defendant makes counter affidavit. Defendant may l kewise prove set-off. Don't apply to accounts against decedents, and suits against executors and administrators.

RECORDING.—Deeds, conveying estates of freehold, or inheritance, or term of years, covenants, or agreements made in consideration of marriage, deeds of marriage settlement, wherein lands, money, or other personalty shall be seated; all deeds of trust and mortgages whatsoever, title bonds, and other written contracts in relation to lands, must be recorded in Chancery Clerk's office of county where property is situated; otherwise voidable by subsequent *bona fide* purchaser, or any creditor. The deed, or writing, must be acknowledged, attested or proven, before recorded. Record constructive notice from date of filing. Actual possession and occupancy by grantee equivalent to record.

SERVICES.—Summons must be served five days before return day. Publication on non-residents, four weeks in newspapers, and sent to address of non-resident.

WILLS.—Madé by persons twenty-one years old. Witnessed by two persons, if not written wholly and subscribed by hand of testator. Nuncupative wills allowed soldiers and marines, and persons in their last sickness, under certain circumstances.

[For Legal Forms adapted to the Laws of this State see Missouri forms.]

LAWS OF MISSOURI

RELATIVE TO THE

COLLECTION OF DEBTS, Etc.

Prepared expressly for J. A. Graft & Co.'s Legal Directory, by Mills and Flitcraft, Attorneys and Counsellors at Law, St. Louis, Missouri.

ACTIONS—WHERE BROUGHT.—Suits instituted by summons shall be brought: First, when the defendant is a resident of the State, either in the county within which the defendant resides, or in the county which the plaintiff resides, and the defendant may be found; Second, when there are several defendants, and they reside in different counties, the suit may be brought in any such county; Third, when there are several defendants, some residents and others non-residents of the State, suit may be brought in any county in which any defendant resides; Fourth, when all of the defendants are non-residents of the State, suit may be brought in any county. [Rev. Stat. Sec. 3,481].

Suits by attachments shall be brought in the county where property may be found. [Rev. Stat. Sec. 3,482].

ASSIGNMENTS.—Assignments must be for th creditors of the assignor, and are made by deed acl corded. The assignor makes affidavit as to the nat estate, and bond is required, to be approved by tl double the value of the estate assigned. The assign ventory, and sworn appraisers appraise the value. after the assignment the assignee is required to appo for the hearing and allowance or demands, and n notice, by advertisement, and by lettter to all know day named, and for two consecutive days thereafter, at the place appointed from 9 a. m. to 5 p. m. Cr present claims, shall be precluded from any benefit the hearing on any demand presented at the time m good cause shown, to such time as is deemed right creditor, who shall fail to lay his claim before said term, on account of sickness, absence from the State, may at any time before the declaration of the fina prove up his claim, and the same may be allowed, dividends paid thereon, as in the case of other allo Stat. Sec. 373).

The assignee shall require such evidence and no of such demands, as is required to establish demand acter in the Circuit Court, in suits between the orig contract. (Rev. Stat. Sec. 375).

Appeals from descisions of assignee to Circuit C

ATTACHMENTS.—Plaintiff in any civil action ma against the property of the defendant, or of any one ants, in any one or more of the following cases: 1. ant is not a resident of the State. 2. Where the de tion, whose chief office or place of business is o Where the defendant conceals himself, so that the the law cannot be served upon him. 4. Where the sconded, or absented himself from his usual place of so that the ordinary process of the law cannot be se Where the defendent is about to remove his prope this State, with the intent to defraud, hinder or dela Where the defendant is about to remove out of thi tent to change his domicile. 7. Where the defend conveyed or assigned his property or effects so as to creditors. 8. Where the defendant has fraudulentl ed or disposed of his property or effects so as to hind tors. 9. Where the defendant is about, fraudulent sign his property or effects, so as to hinder or delay Where the defendant is about, fraudulently, to con pose of his property or effects, so as to hinder or dela Where the cause of action accrued out of this State, has absconded, or secretly removed his property State. 12. Where the damages for which the actio injuries arising from the commission of some felony for the seduction of any female. 13. Where the pay the price or value of any article or thing delive tract, he was bound to pay upon the delivery. 14. W for was fraudulently contracted, on the part of the Sec. 398].

Attachments for debts not yet due, may issue mentioned, except the first four, but judgment is no maturity of demand. Plaintiff, or some one for him that the plaintiff has a just demand against the defe amount which the affiant believes the plaintiff oug allowing all just credits and set-offs is ——— dollars, and that he has good reason to believe, and does believe in the existence of one or more of the above causes of attachment. Bond in double amount of suit is required, to be approved by the Clerk; sureties to be resident householders of the county. All property and debts may be levied on. Attachments may be sued out after suit has been pending.

BILLS AND NOTES.— Acceptance must be in writing, signed by the acceptor or his lawful agent. If acceptance on a paper other than the bill, it shall not bind the acceptor, except in favor of a person to whom such acceptance shall have been shown, and who, upon the faith thereof, shall have received the bill for a valuable consideration. Notes payable to order of bearer, and expressed to be for value received, are negotiable as inland bills of exchange.

PROTEST AND DAMAGES.—Damages allowed after protest of bill: 1. If the bill shall have been drawn on any person within this State, at the rate of four per centum on the principal sum specified in the bill. 2. If the bill shall have been drawn on any person, at any place out of this State, but within the limited States, or the Territories thereof, at the rate of ten per centum on the principal sum specified in the bill. 3. If the bill shall have been drawn on any person, at any port or place without the United States and their Territories, at the rate of twenty per centum on the principal sum specified in the bill. [Rev. Stat. Sec. 539].

HOLIDAYS—DAYS OF GRACE—January 1, February 22, July 4, any general States election day, any thanksgiving day appointed by the Governor of this State, or by the President of the United States, and December 25, are public holidays, and when any such holidays fall upon Sunday, the Monday next following shall be considered such holiday. For all purposes of presentment of mercantile paper and protesting "such holidays shall be treated and considered the same as the first day of the week, commonly called Sunday, and all bills of exchange, bonds, promissory notes, or other mercantile paper falling due on any such holidays, shall be considered as falling due on the next succeeding day, unless such succeeding day be a holiday or Sunday. In such case it shall be considered as falling due the day previous. [Rev. Stat. Sec. 552.].

COSTS SECURITY FOR.—Non-residents must furnish security for costs on bringing actions in this State, by giving the written undertaking of some resident who shall acknowledge, himself to be bound for all costs which may accrue or by depositing with the clerk a sum of money sufficient to pay all costs, subject to be increased by order of Court. The ordinary deposit required in the Circuit Court is $25.00, and before a Justice of the Peace $10.00, in the United States Circuit Court $25.00.

COURTS—JURISDICTION.—United States Circuit Court. Terms: St. Louis, third Mondays in March and September; Jefferson City, third Mondays, April and November; Kansas City, third Mondays in May and October. United States District Court, Eastern District, St Louis, Terms: first Mondays in May and November, Western District, Jefferson City, first Mondays in March and September; Kansas City, third, Mondays in May and October. State Circuit Courts have general jurisdiction except over probate matters, and cases exclusively cognizable before Justices of the Peace. Probate Courts have jurisdiction over administrations, probate of wills, and settlements of estates of minors, and persons of unsound mind. Appeals lie to Circuit Court. Justices of the Peace have original jurisdiction of all civil actions founded upon contract or cost or bond required by statute, when the sum demanded, exclusive of interest and costs, does not exceed one hundred and fifty dollars. In counties and cities having over fifty thousand inhabitants, jurisdiction in above cases extends to actions for recovery of two hundred and fifty dollars.

Deeds—May be acknowledged or proved. If acknowledged or proved within this State, they must be before some Judge, Justice or Clerk thereof, Notary Public or some Justice of the Peace of the county in which the real estate conveyed or affected, is situated. If acknowledged, or proved, without this State, and within the United States, by any Notary Public, or by any Court of the United States, or of any State or Territory having a seal, or the Clerk or any such Court, or any commissioner appointed by the Governor of this State to take the acknowledgment of deeds. If acknowledged or proved without the United States, by any Court of any State, Kingdom or Empire, having a seal, or the mayor or chief officer of any city or town, having an official seal, or by any minister, or consular officer of the United States, or Notary Public, having a seal.

Certificate:

State of ——, County of ——, } *ss.* Be it remembered, that on this —— day of —— A. D., 18—, before me, the undersigned, [style of officer, county and State], duly commissioned and qualified, came ————, who is personally known to me to be the same person whose name is subscribed to the foregoing instrument of writing as a party thereto, and he acknowledged the same to be his act and deed for the purposes mentioned. In witness whereof, I do hereto set my hand and affix my official seal, the day and year last above mentioned. [Signature and title].

Certificate of husband and wife, proceed as before, inserting names of husband and wife, and before the witnessing clause, add "and she, the said ——, wife of said ——, acknowledged upon an examination, separate and apart from her said husband, that she executed said instrument and relinquished her dower, on the real estate therein conveyed, freely, and without compulsion or undue influence on the part of her said husband."

Depositions.—Upon proper notice and interrogatories filed in any Court of Record where suit is pending in the State, commissions, with the interrogatories annexed, will be issued by such Court to take the depositions of witnesses residing out of this State. Depositions may be taken out of this State without commission by any officer appointed by authority of the laws of this State. to take depositions without this State. Depositions, if taken within this State, may be taken by some Judge, Justice, Justice of the Peace, Notary Public, Mayor or chief officer of a town having a seal of office. Depositions may be taken without this State by some officer out of this State appointed by authority of the laws of this State to take depositions, or by some consul, or commercial or diplomatic representative of the United States having a seal of office, or by some Judge, Justice of the Peace, or other judical officer, or by some Notary Public, within the government where the witness may be found. (§ 2133).

Exemptions.—Of one not the head of the family: 1. The wearing apparel of all persons. 2. The necessary tools and impliments of trade of any mechanic, whilst carrying on his trade.

When owned by the head of a family: 1. Ten head of choice hogs, ten head of choice sheep, and the product thereof in wool, yarn or cloth, two cows and calves, two plows, one axe, one hoe and one set of plow gears, and all necessary farm implements for the use of one man. 2. Working animals of the value of one hundred and fifty dollars. 3. The spinning wheels and cards, one loom, an apparatus necessary for manufacturing cloth in a private family. 4. All the spun yarn, thread and cloth manufactured for family use. 5. Any quantity of hemp, flax and wool, not exceeding twenty-five pounds each. 6. All wearing apparel of the family, four beds with the usual bedding, and such other household and kitchen furniture, not exceeding the value of one hundred dollars, as may be necessary for the family, agreeably to an inventory thereof, to be returned on oath, with the execution, by the officer whose duty it may be to levy the same. 7. The necessary tools and implements of trade of any mechanic, while carrying on his trade. 8. Any and all arms and military equipments, required by law to be kept. 9. All such provisions as may be on hand for family use, not exceeding one hundred dollars in value. 10. The bibles and other books used in a family, lettered grave stone and one pew in a house of worship. 11. All lawyers, physicians, ministers of the gospel, and teachers in the actual prosecution of their calling, shall have the privilege of selecting such books as shall be necessary to their profession, in the place of other property herein allowed at their option; and doctors of medicine, in lieu of other property exempt from execution, may be allowed to select their medicines. In lieu of the first and second subdivisions, a head of a family may select other property of the value of three hundred dollars.

Husband and Wife.—Husband not liable for debts of wife contracted before marriage, except to the extent of property acquired from wife. Wife's property not subject to husband's debts, unless by writing she shall permit him to use the same as his own.

Homesteads.—In the country shall not exceed one hundred and sixty acres of land, or exceed the total value of $1,500, in incorporated towns and cities of less than ten thousand inhabitants, homesteads shall not include more than five acres of ground, or exceed the total value of $1,500. In towns of ten thousand and less than forty thousand, not more than thirty square rods and $1,500 value. In cities exceeding forty thousand inhabitants not more than eighteen square rods and $3,000 value.

Interest.—Lawful rate six per cent., but parties may agree in writing for the payment of not exceeding ten per centum. Interest on judgments at the rate of six per cent., but judgments on contracts bearing more than six per cent. shall bear the same interest borne by such contracts. Penalty for usury is the forfeiture of all interest to the common school fund, and the defendant may recover his costs. Interest may be compounded by contract, but not oftener than once a year. Accounts do not bear interest until demand of payment is made.

Judgments— Of courts of record, are liens on the real estate of person against whom they are rendered, situate in the county for which the court is held, and continue for three years, subject to be revived for ten years. Judgments are not a lien on personal property until after levy. Transcripts of judgments before Justices of the Peace may be filed in the Circuit Court, and thereby become liens on real estate.

Limitations.—Actions for recovery on real estate shall be commenced within ten years, except military bounty lands, which shall be within two years. Personal actions, upon written instruments for payment of money or property, or covenants in deeds, or actions for relief, within ten years; upon contracts, expressed or implied; upon liabilities under statute, other than a penalty or forfeiture; upon actions of trespass on real estate for taking, detaining and injuring goods, and for the recovery of the specific personal property, within five years, except that in cases of fraud, the cause of action is deemed not to have accrued until the discovery by the aggrieved party, at any time within ten years of the facts constituting the fraud; within three years actions must be brought against sheriffs, coroners or other officers, upon a liability incurred by the doing of an act in official capacity, or the omission of official duty, and upon penalties and forfeitures, where the action is given to the party aggrieved, or to such party and the State. Acknowledgment of indebtedness must be in writing after statute has once elasped. Limitation on accounts current run from the last item on the adverse side.

SERVICE OF PROCESS.—In Circuit Courts, fifteen day's service before the first day of the next term, is required. Suits may be entered before Justices of the Peace at any time and summons shall be served at least ten days before the day of appearance therein mentioned. Service may be made by leaving copy of summons at usual place of abode with some person of family, above the age of fifteen years.

MISSOURI FORMS.

[Form 1.—ACKNOWLEDGMENT.]

(Begin in all Cases by a Caption specifying the State and Place where the acknowledgment is taken.)

IN THE CASE OF NATURAL PERSONS ACTING IN THEIR OWN RIGHT:—On this —— day of——, 18—, before me personally appeared A. B., (or A. B. and C. D.,) to me known to be the person (or persons) described in and who executed the foregoing instrument, and acknowledged that he (or they) executed the same as his (or their) free act and deed.

IN THE CASE OF NATURAL PERSONS ACTING BY ATTORNEY:—On this —— day of——, 18—, personally appeared A. B. to me, personally known to be the person who executed the foregoing instrument in behalf of C D., and acknowledged that he executed the same, as the free act and deed of said C. D.

IN THE CASE OF CORPORATIONS OR JOINT STOCK ASSOCIATIONS:—On this —— day of ——, 18—, before me appeared A. B., to me personally known, who, being by me duly sworn (or affirmed), did say that he is the President (or other officer or agent of the corporation or association) of (describing the corporation or association), and that the seal affixed to said instrument is the corporate seal of said corporation (or association), and that said instrument was signed and sealed in behalf of said corporation (or association), by authority of its Board of Directors (or Trustees), and said A. B. acknowledges said instrument to be the free act and deed of said corporation (or association).

In case the corporation or association has no corporate seal, omit the words "the seal affixed to said instrument is the corporate seal of said corporation (or association), and that," and add at the end of the affidavit clause the words "and that said corporation (or association) has no corporate seal."

[Form 1*a*.—ACKNOWLEDGMENT BY TRUSTEE OF A MARRIED WOMAN AND THE HUSBAND.]

STATE OF ——, }
County of ——. } SS.

Be it Remembered, That on this —— day of ——, A. D. 18—, before the undersigned, a (title of officer), within and for the County of ——, personally came ——, Trustee of ——, wife of ——, and ——, husband of said ——, who are personally known to me to be the same persons whose names are subscribed to the foregoing instrument of writing, as parties thereto, and they acknowledge the same to be their act and deed for the purposes therein mentioned. And the said —— being by me first made acquainted with the contents of said instrument, upon an examination separate and apart from —— husband—, acknowledged that —— executed the same, to be her act and deed for the purposes therein named, freely and without fear, compulsion or undue influence of —— said husband.

In Testimony Whereof, I have hereunto set my hand and affixed my official seal, at my office, in ——, the day and year first above written.

[SEAL.] *(Signature and title.)*

[Form 1*b*.—AFFIDAVIT AND ACKNOWLEDGMENT TO CHATTEL MORTGAGE.]

STATE OF ——, }
County of ——, } SS.

——, being duly sworn, on —— oath says that ——, the legal and absolute owner of the personal property above described, and that the same is free from all claims and liens whatsoever. *(Signature of affiant.)*

Subscribed and sworn to before me, }
this —— day of ——, A. D. 18—. } SS. *(Signature of officer.)*

[SEAL.]

STATE OF ——, } ss.
City of ——. }

Be it Remembered, That on this —— day of ——, A. D. 18—, before the undersigned, a ——, within and for the City of ——, and State of ——, personally came ——, who — personally known to me to be the same person whose name — subscribed to the foregoing instrument of writing, as part — thereto, and acknowledged the same to be —— voluntary act and deed for the uses and purposes therein mentioned.

[SEAL.]

In Testimony Whereof, I have hereunto set my hand and affixed my official seal, at my office, in ——, the day and year first above written.. .. ..

(*Signature and title of officer.*)

NOTE.—If the acknowledgment be taken by a Notary Public, the certificate must state the dates of his being duly qualified and of the expiration of his term of office. The blank space above the signature is provided for this statement. The following formula is ample: "I was qualified ——, 18—, and my term expires ——, 18—."

Form 1c.—SINGLE ACKNOWLEDGMENT.]

STATE OF ——, } ss.
County of ——. }

Be it Remembered, That on this —— day of ——, A. D. 18—, before the undersigned, a —— within and for the County of ——, aforesaid, personally came ——, who is personally known to me to be the same person whose name is subscribed to the foregoing instrument of writing, as a party thereto, and —— acknowledged the same to be —— act and deed for the purposes therein mentioned. And the said —— further declared —— to be single and unmarried.

In Testimony Whereof, I have hereunto set my hand and affixed my official seal, at my office, in ——, in said County, the day and year first above written.

(*Signature and title.*)

[Form 2.—WARRANTY DEED.]

This Deed, Made and entered into this —— day of ——, eighteen hundred and eighty—, by and between —— of ——, part— of the first part, and —— of ——, part— of the second part, witnesseth, that the said part— of the first part, for and in consideration of —— dollars, to —— paid by the said part— of the second part, the receipt of which is hereby acknowledged, do by these presents grant, bargain and sell, convey and confirm unto the said part— of the second part, the following described tract— or parcel— of land, situated in the County of ——, in the State of ——to-wit: (Here describe property.)

To Have and to Hold The same, together with all rights, immunities, privileges and appurtenances to the same belonging, unto the said part— of the second part, and to —— heirs and assigns forever: the said —— hereby covenanting that —— heirs, executors and administrators, shall and will warrant and defend the title to the premises unto the said part— of the second part, and to —— heirs and assigns forever, against the claims of all persons whomsoever.

In Witness Whereof The said part— of the first part ha— hereunto set —— hand and seal, the day and year first above written. —— [SEAL.]

For acknowledgment, see Form 1, above.

[Form 3.—FORMS AND INSTRUCTIONS FOR TAKING DEPOSITIONS.]

[R. S., 1879, Ch. 26.]

NOTICE.

——, Plaintiff,
vs.
——, Defendant. } In the ——, Court of ——. County of ——, State of Missouri.

To the above named ——:

You are hereby notified that depositions of witnesses to be read in evidence in the above entitled cause, on the part of the ——, will be taken at —— ——, in the County of —— and State of ——, on the —— day of ——, 18—, between the hours of eight o'clock in the forenoon and six o'clock in the afternoon of that day; and that the taking of said depositions, if not completed on that day, will be continued from day to day, at the same place and between the same hours, until completed.

Service of the above notice is hereby acknowledged, and issue of dedimus, and all exceptions as to time, waived.
—— 18——.
——
—— } ——.
——.
——.

CAPTION.

———, Plaintiff, *vs.* ———, Defendant. } In —— Court, —— County of ——, State of ——, No.—

Deposition – of witness— produced, sworn and examined on the —— day of ——, in the year of our Lord, 18—, between the hours of —— o'clock in the forenoon and —— o'clock in the afternoon of that day, at ——, in the County of —— and State of ——, before me, (name and title of officer), in a certain cause now pending in the —— Court, ——, in the County of ——, in the State of ——, between ——, plaintiff—, and ——, defendant—, on the part of the ——.

Present, ——, Esq., on behalf of the plaintiff--, and ——, Esq., on behalf of the defendant—.

——, of lawful age, being produced, sworn and examined on the part of the ——, deposeth and saith ——.

CERTIFICATE TO DEPOSITIONS.

STATE OF ——, County of ——. } SS.

I, ——, do hereby certify that in pursuance of the annexed ——, came before me at ——, in the County and State last aforesaid, ——, who w— by me —— to testify the whole truth of —— knowledge touching the matter in controversy aforesaid; that —— w— examined and —— examination was reduced to writing and subscribed by ——, in my presence, on the day, between the hours and at the place in that behalf first aforesaid, and —— said deposition —— now herewith returned, and I hereby certify that the said —— are residents of ——. (And I further certify that I was duly qualified as a Notary Public on the —— day of ——, 18—, and my term expires ——, 18—.)

In Testimony Whereof, I have hereunto set my hand*——, at ——, in the County [L. S.] and State aforesaid, this —— day of ——, 18—.

(*Signature of officer.*)

*"And official seal," if taken before an officer having an official seal.

[Fees and postage $——, paid by ——.]

INSTRUCTIONS FOR TAKING DEPOSITIONS.

Every deposition must be reduced to writing in presence of the officer before whom it is taken, and signed by the witness. If any paper or exhibit is produced and proved or referred to by the witness, it ought to be described in his deposition, or marked and referred to by the deponent in such manner that it may be identified when the deposition is read; and all such papers and exhibits must be attached to and returned with the deposition.

The officer will annex, at the foot of the deposition of each witness, the following certificate:

"Subscribed and sworn to before me, on the day, at the place, and within the hours first aforesaid."

[If the officer taking the deposition have an official seal, it must be affixed to each certificate.

(*Name and title of officer.*)

Then proceed with other depositions (if any) in the same form, annexing a like certificate to each. When all the witnesses who appear have been sworn and examined and their depositions reduced to writing, subscribed and certified, as above, the officer will attach to the depositions all papers and exhibits proved or referred to in the examination, and the commission and notice, with the following certificate endorsed thereon or attached thereto.

If the officer know the residence of the witnesses, he will include the following in his certificate: "And I further certify that the said (insert the names of witnesses), are residents of the County of ——, in the State of ——. Given at ——, in the County of ——, and State of ——, this —— day of ——, 18.

[If the officer taking the deposition have an official seal, it must be affixed to each certificate.]

[*Name and title of officer.*)

The return should be accompanied by a certificate of the official character of the officer taking the depositions, attested by the seal of the State of his residence, or by the seal of some Court of record within said State which may be as follows:

"I hereby certify that (state the name), on (here insert, in words at length, the date at which the depositions are taken and certified) in the year of our Lord 18—, was and now is (here state the style of the officer), within and for the ——, State of ——, duly commissioned and acting as such, and that full faith and credit are due to his acts as such."

[SEAL.] *In Testimony Whereof*, I (here state name of officer and style of office) have hereunto subscribed my name and affixed the seal of office, this —— day of ——, 18—.

(*Signature and title of officer.*)

The depositions, papers and exhibits, commission, notice and certificates, should be enclosed in a strong envelope, securely sealed, and direct the same to the Clerk of the —— Court of the County of ——, Missouri, noting on the envelope the style of the cause, and contents, thus:

——————, Plaintiff,
vs.
——————, Defendant, } Depositions for (state whether for defendant or plaintiff.)

If the package is transmitted by mail, see that the proper post-office address is given thereon.

The depositions must be begun on the day mentioned in the notice. If they can not be completed on that day, the taking of them may be adjourned to the succeeding day only, and for no longer time, unless upon agreement, and at the same place, and between the same hours. The person taking them should, in such case, make the following entry, closing the business for that day:

"Not being able to complete the taking of said depositions, by reason that (here insert the reason) I adjourned the further taking of the same till to-morrow, (or to such time as may be agreed upon) then to be continued at the same place and between the same hours mentioned in the annexed notice."

If the officer taking the deposition have an official seal, it must be affixed to each certificate. *(Name and title of officer.)*

On the succeeding day, let the person taking the deposition commence as follows:

Pursuant to adjournment, as above stated, on the —— day of ——, 18—, between the hours of —— in the forenoon, and —— in the afternoon, at the ——, I continued the taking of said depositions, as follows, viz: —— in continuation of his deposition, commenced yesterday, on his oath, further says, etc.

The provisions of the Act approved March 25th, 1875, requires that "every certificate made by any Notary Public to which his seal is attached, shall, in addition to the ordinary recital, contain a statement of the date of his being duly qualified, and of the date of the expiration of his term of office.

☞ The foregoing directions must be strictly observed, or the depositions will be unavailing.

[Form 4.—AFFIDAVIT TO ACCOUNT.]

[General Form.]

STATE OF ——,
County of ——. } SS.

Be it Remembered, That on this —— day of ——, A. D. 18—, before me, ——, a Notary Public within and for said —— and State, appeared ——, who being by me duly sworn, deposes and says, that he is ——, of the firm of ——, which is composed of ——, doing business in —— and State aforesaid. That ——, of ——, State of ——, owes and is justly indebted to said —— in the full sum of —— dollars, ——, for goods, wares and merchandise, sold and delivered to —— at —— special instance and request; that the annexed statement, marked "Exhibit A," by the Notary, is a just, true and strictly correct account of said indebtedness, showing items, dates and prices; that said demand remains due and unpaid, and has not been settled or paid by said ——, or by any other person; that there are no just credits, off-sets or counter-claims against said demand, either in law or in equity; and that said sum is now due exclusive of any payment, set-off or usurious interest; and that lawful interest is due thereon from ——.

(Signature of affiant.)

[SEAL.] Sworn to and subscribed before me the day and year first aforesaid.
Witness my hand and Notarial Seal. ——, Notary Public.

FORM OF AFFIDAVIT TO CLAIM AGAINST AN ESTATE.

STATE OF ——,
County of ——. } SS.

——, the above named claimant, being duly sworn, on his oath says, that to the best of his knowledge and belief, he has given credit to the estate of ——, deceased, for all payments and off-setts to which it is entitled, and that the balance claimed is justly due.

Sworn to, etc. (as in general form.) *(Signature of claimant.)*

FORM OF RETURN OF SERVICE.

STATE OF ——,
County of ——. } SS.

——, of lawful age, being duly sworn, on his oath says, that on the —— day of ——, 18—, in the County of ——, aforesaid, he served the above notice on ——, administrator of the estate of ——, deceased, by delivering to him, in person, a true copy of said notice and demand.

(Signature of person serving notice.)

[SEAL.] Sworn to and subscribed before me, this —— day of ——, A. D. 18—.

(Signature and title of officer.)

FORM OF WAIVER OF NOTICE.

I hereby waive the service of notice on the within (or foregoing) demand, this —— day of ——, 18—. ———, administrator of ———, deceased.

[Form 5—OPENING AND CLOSING OF WILLS].

In the name of God, Amen: I, (name of testator), of ———, County of ———, State of ———, being of sound mind and memory, do hereby make, publish and declare this my last will and testament, (hereby revoking any and all wills by me heretofore made):

1., It is my wish that all my lawful debts and funeral expenses shall be paid out of my estate, &c. 2., I give, devise and bequeath, &c,

(*Wife and all children of testator must be named.*)

In testimony whereof I do hereunto set my hand and affix my seal the —— of ——, A. D., 18 —

———. [SEAL].

ATTESTING CLAUSE FOR WITNESSES.

Signed, sealed, published and declared by the said, ——— as and for his last will and testament, in our presence and in the presence of each other, this, —— day of —— 18 —; in testimony whereof we do, in his presence, and in presence of each other, and at his request, sign our names hereto as witnesses.

C. D.
E. F.

NOTE.—If C. D. signed testator's name, add, "I. C. D. having signed said testator's name to said will at his request."

[Form 6—WARRANTY DEED].

This Deed, made and entered into this——day of——eighteen hundred and——by and between ——— of ——— party of the first part, and ——— of ——— part —— of the second part, WITNESSETH that the said part———of the first part, for and in consideration of ——— Dollars, to —— paid by the said part———of the second part, the receipt of which is hereby acknowledged, do by these presents GRANT, BARGAIN AND SELL, CONVEY AND CONFIRM unto the said part———of the second part, the following described tract or parcel of land, situated in the County of ——— in the State of ——— to wit:

To have and to Hold the same, together with all rights, immunities, privileges and appurtenances to the same belonging, unto the said part—— of the second part, and to —— heirs and assigns, forever; the said ——— hereby covenanting that —— heirs, executors and administrators, shall and will WARRANT AND DEFEND the title to the premises unto the siad part——of the second part, and to —— heirs and assigns forever, against the lawful claims of all persons whomsoever.

In Witness Whereof; the said part——of the first part ha — hereunto set —— hand and seal the day and year first above written.

WITNESS: ——————— ———————[SEAL.]——

——————————— ——————————————

——————————— ——————— ——[SEAL.]

LAWS OF MONTANA TERRITORY

RELATIVE TO THE

COLLECTION OF DEBTS, Etc.

Prepared expressly for J. A. Graft & Co.'s Legal Directory.

ASSIGNMENTS AND INSOLVENCY.—There is no general law permitting an assignment by an insolvent, except when he has been arrested in an action, when he may assign his property to receive his discharge.

ATTACHMENTS.—All property not exempt from execution may be attached, by filing sufficient bonds in double the amount claimed, if it be less than one thousand dollars; if more than ten thousand dollars, then in that amount; and an affidavit, showing that defendant is indebted to plaintiff upon a contract, express or implied, for the payment of money, gold dust, or other property, then due, which is not secured by a mortgage lien, or pledge upon real or personal property; or, if so secured, that the security has become insufficient by the act of the defendant, or other means. Attachments may also be had before demand is due, if defendant is leaving, or about to leave the Territory, with all his or her property, moneys, or other effects, which might be subjected to the payment of the debt, for the purpose of defrauding his creditors; or that defendant is disposing of, or about to dispose of, his property subject to execution, for the purpose of defrauding his creditors, which must appear by affidavit.

The Sheriff is directed in the writ to attach sufficient property to cover the demand of plaintiff. Credits, or other personal property in the possession, or under the control of another, are attached by the Sheriff serving upon such person a copy of the writ, and a notice that such credits, other property, or debts, as the case may be, are attached, etc. (See Code of Civil Procedure, ch. 4, title VII, adopted February 16, 1877.)

CHATTEL MORTGAGES.—A chattel mortgage is not good against the rights of third parties, unless possession is given to mortgagee, or the mortgage is acknowledged and recorded, expressly providing that the mortgagor may retain possession. Such mortgage must be recorded in the county where mortgagor resided when the same was made, and is good for one year from date of record. A person selling mortgaged chattels during the continuance of the lien, forfeits to the purchaser twice the value thereof, and by act February 11, 1876, is guilty of misdemeanor, and may, on conviction, be fined not less than fifty dollars, nor more than five hundred dollars.

EXECUTIONS—Issue at any time within five years, and to any county, and are made returnable in not less than ten, nor more than sixty days. Personal property is first levied on, and is sold after five days' notice. There is no stay law. Six months are allowed for redemption of real property sold under execution.

EXEMPTION.—Homestead, not exceeding one hundred and sixty acres in country; half an acre, if within a town plat, city or village, and in each case limited to $2,500. Usual personal schedule, and to farmer, implements, stock, seeds, etc., $800; tools, teams, and libraries of professional and business men, and mechanics; dwelling of miner, $500; his tools and machinery, $500; wages of laborer for thirty days preceding the levy, where necessary for the support of the family, are also exempt. Only married persons, or the heads of families can claim the exemption under the homestead claim.

INTEREST.—Parties may stipulate for any rate of interest. When no contract is made as to interest, the legal rate, ten per cent. per annum, governs after debt is due. There is no usury law. (Cod. Stat., title bills of exchange and promissory notes.)

MORTGAGES.—Mortgages on real estate must be executed and recorded like deeds. The foreclosure of a mortgage is a civil action, provided for in Code of Civil Procedure, 1877, p. 135. The mortgagor has six months in which to redeem after sale. Satisfaction may be made by entry in margin of record, or by separate instrument, duly executed. Failure to enter satisfaction for one week after request subjects the delinquent to forfeiture of one hundred dollars to mortgagee, besides other damages.

NOTES AND BILLS OF EXCHANGE.—Foreign and inland bills of exchange and promissory notes are negotiable, and commercial paper is subject to the law merchant, as to protest, grace, etc.

MONTANA FORMS.

(Form 1—CERTIFICATE OF ACKNOWLEDGMENT).

STATE OF ——, } ss.
County of ——. }

On this —— day of ——, A, D., 18—, before me —— , a Commissioner for the Territory of Montana, duly commissioned and qualified according to the laws of said Territory, in and for said County, personally appeared ——, personally known to me to be the person described in, and who executed the foregoing instrument, and who acknowledged to me that he executed the same freely and voluntarily, for the purpose therein mentioned.

In Witness Whereof, I have hereunto set my hand and affixed my official seal, this —— day of ——, A. D., 188 –.

(L. S.) *(Signature and title of Officer).*

(*Note:* When acknowledgment is taken by officer other than a Commissioner, then insert title of such officer in certificate).

Form 2—INSTRUCTIONS FOR TAKING DEPOSITIONS].

Depositions of a witness out of the Territory may be taken at any time after service of summons or appearance of defendant, by giving adverse party or his attorney, five day's previous notice, accompanied with a copy of interrogatories, and suing out of the Clerk's office a commission under seal, to be directed to any —— Commission, or to any Judge, Justice of the Peace, Clerk of a Court of Record, or Notary Public of the City or County where the witness resides, authorizing and requiring him to cause such witness to come before him at such time and place as he may designate and appoint, and faithfully to take his or her deposition upon all such interrogations as may be enclosed or attached to such commission, both on the part of the plaintiff and defendant, and to certify the same when taken, together with the said commission and interrogations, into the Court in which such cause may be depending, with the least possible delay. If issued to any Country without the United States, it may be directed to a Minister, Ambassador, Consul, Vice-Consul, or Consulor Agent of the United States in such country, or to a person agreed upon by the parties.

(For sufficient legal-forms of Caption and certificate, see Forms at end of Laws of Arkansas, published in this work).

LAWS OF NEBRASKA

RELATIVE TO THE

COLLECTION OF DEBTS, Etc.

Prepared expressly for J. A. Graft & Co.'s Legal Directory.

ACKNOWLEDGMENTS.—May be executed and acknowledged before a commissioner, appointed by the governor of this State for that purpose, or before any officer appointed according to the laws of the State or Territory wherein the deed or other instrument in writing is executed and acknowledged.

ARREST AND IMPRISONMENT FOR DEBT ON CIVIL PROCESS.—Civil arrests can be made before or after judgment, on filing an affidavit, showing the nature and justice of the demand, with the amount thereof, and also the existence of one of the following causes; 1st. Converting property to defraud creditors. 2d. Assigning, removing or disposing of property to defraud creditors. 3d. Concealing property or rights of action. 4th. Fraudulently contracting the debt. 5th. Removing property out of jurisdiction of court to defraud creditors. The affidavit must contain a statement of facts justifying belief. A bond in double the amonnt of the demand must be given, conditioned for the payment of all damages.

ATTACHMENTS.—In all cases of attachment, an affidavit must be filed before the order of attachment issues, and a bond must be filed in double the amount of the debt, excepting when the debtor is a non-resident of the State. The body of the debtor may be attached for the reasons, and in the manner above set forth.

BILLS OF EXCHANGE AND PROMISSORY NOTES.—All negotiable instruments are entitled to three days' grace. Bonds and promissory notes and bills of exchange for any sum of money certain, made payable to any person or order, or to any person or assigns, are only negotiable by indorsement. Any such instruments, made payable to a person or bearer, are negotiable by delivery merely. To entitle an indorser of a negotiable instrument to maintain an action against any prior indorser, he must first use due diligence to obtain the money of the maker, drawer or obligor. Demand of payment on the third day of grace, and notice of non-payment or non-acceptance, are adjudged due diligence, unless other conditions are expressed in the indorsement.

COMMENCEMENT OF SUIT.—Process of summons, replevin and attachment, issued by justices of the peace, must be made returnable not less than three, nor more than twelve days from its date. Process issued by County Judge must be made returnable on the first Monday of the month following the date of its issuance, if ten full days intervene between day of service and the first Monday, otherwise it must be made returnable on the first Monday of the month next succeeding. An action in the District Court is commenced by petition. The return day of the summons is the second Monday after the day of its date. When service of the summons is made personally on the debtor, he shall answer or demur before the third Monday. Ordinarily a cause can be brought to issue the fifth Monday after the filing of the petition.

CONSIGNMENTS.—If the consignee appropriates the consigned goods to his own use, it is an embezzlement, and if the goods be over $35 in value, the act is punishable as a felony, by imprisonment in the penitentiary for from one to seven years. The indictment must be found within three years. The consignor may also have the consignee arrested in a civil action.

CONTRACTS OF MARRIED WOMEN.—The property, real and personal, which any woman in this State may own at the time of her marriage, and any real or personal property which shall come to her by descent, devise, bequest or gift of any person, except her husband (excepting marriage settlements), shall remain her sole and separate property, notwithstanding her marriage, and not be subject to the disposal of her husband, or liable for his debts. She may bargain and sell, and enter into contracts with reference to any of her separate property, in the same manner, to the same extent, and with like effect as a married man, in relation to his real and personal property. In dealing with married women, it must be explicitly stated, or understood between the parties, that her separate estate will be bound, else the husband only can be held. She may sue and be sued, the same as if unmarried, and carry on any trade or business, or perform labor on her sole or separate account, and her earnings are not subject to the husband's debts or control.

ESTATES OF DECEASED PERSONS.—Claims must be presented for allowance usually within one year. Time may be extended for special reasons, not exceeding three years in all. Administrators and executors liable to be cited to settle accounts, at any time, for special reasons shown. Widow entitled to personal property of estate amounting to $250, to be selected by her, and further allowance of $200 in money, besides one year's support of family. All claims (except in suits on foreclosure of mortgage on real estate), must be filed and allowed in County Court. The County Court is the Probate Court in this State, and is composed of one Judge. License to sell real estate to pay debts must be obtained from District Court. Widow is entitled to one-third real estate of deceased husband, as at common law, for use during natural life, unless legally barred. She may forfeit dower by simply joining husband in deed of conveyance, or accepting jointure of life estate before marriage. Wife being non-resident does not effect her right to dower in husband's lands in this State. Widow may occupy dwelling of deceased husband one year, and have reasonable sustenance free. Common law tenant by courtesy obtains, unless there are living issue of wife by former husband, in which event property of wife descends to them.

EXEMPTIONS.—A homestead consisting of any quantity of land, not exceeding one hundred and sixty acres, and the dwelling house thereon, and its appurtenances, to be selected by the owner thereof, and not included in any incorporated city or village; or, instead thereof, at the option of the owner, a quantity of contiguous land, not exceeding one-half an acre, with buildings thereon, and appurtenances, all not over $2,000 in value, being within an incorporated town, city or village; or in lieu of the above, a lot or parcel of contiguous land, not exceeding twenty acres, being within the limits of an incorporated town, city or village, the said parcel or lot of land not being laid off into streets, blocks and lots, owned and occupied by any resident of the State, being the head of a family, shall not be subject to attachment, levy or sale, upon execution or other process issuing out of any court in this State, so long as the same shall be occupied by the debtor as a homestead, provided, however, that such farm lands, lots, etc., do not exceed in value $2,000. All heads of families who have neither lands, town lots, nor houses subject to exemption as a homestead, under the laws of this State, shall have, exempt from forced sale on execution, the sum of $500 in personal property. No property hereinafter mentioned shall be liable to attachment, execution of sale, or any final process, issued from any court of this State, against any person being a resident of this State, and the head of a family. The family bible; family pictures, school books and library for the use of the family; all necessary wearing apparel of the debtor and his family; all beds, bedsteads and bedding necessary for the use of such family; all stoves and appendages put up or kept for the use of the debtor's family, not to exceed four; all cooking utensils, and all other household furniture not herein enumerated, to be selected by the debtor, not exceeding in value $100; one cow, three hogs, and all pigs under six months old; and if the debtor be at the time actually engaged in the business of agriculture, in addition to the above, one yoke of oxen, or a pair of horses in lieu thereof, ten sheep, and the wool therefrom, either in the raw material or manufactured into yarn or cloth; the necessary food for the stock mentioned in this section for the period of three months; one wagon, cart or dray, two plows and one drag; the necessary gearing for the team herein exempted, and other farming implements not exceeding $50 in value; the provisions for the debtor and his family necessary for six months support, either provided or growing, or both, and fuel necessary for six months; the tools and instruments of any mechanic, miner or other person, used and kept for the purpose of carrying on his trade or business; the library and implements of any professional man. Unmarried child residing on homestead, is allowed it exempt if parents both dead. The widow or widower, together or either one without the other, and with or without a child living with them, or if all children are dead, are entitled to homestead. That is, a widow or widower is deemed head of a family even without child.

INTEREST.—Seven per cent. is the legal rate, or any rate not exceeding ten per cent., on express written contracts. If more is exacted, the contract remains good as to principal, but all the interest is forfeited.

JUDGMENT, EXECUTION, AND STAY OF EXECUTION.—Judgment may be obtained at the first term after the issues are formed, unless, for good cause shown, the action is continued by order of the court. In justices' courts judgment may be obtained usually within four days where no defense is put in, or continuance granted upon showing; but no action can be continued in the first instance beyond thirty days. Execution for the enforcement of judgment may issue at any time. Executions on all judgments rendered by justices of the peace may be stayed as follows: On judgments of $5 and under, for the period of sixty days; on judgments over $5 and not exceeding $50, for ninety days; over $50 and not exceeding $100, for six months. On all judgments and decrees of District Court, except in cases brought upon appeal or error, a stay of nine months, when damages exceed $100, may be taken. In all cases of stay of execution an undertaking with sureties must be entered into by the party desiring the stay, conditional for the payment of the judgment costs, and interest at seven per cent., excepting in cases of foreclosure of mortgages on real estate, and orders for a specific performance where the title to real estate is concerned, in which case no undertaking is required. Application for stay of foreclosure must be made in twenty days from decree.

JURISDICTION OF COURTS.—Justice's courts have original jurisdiction in actions for debt when the amount claimed does not exceed $200; county courts above $100 and up to $1000, and the County Court also has Justice's jurisdiction. District courts have original jurisdiction in all matters exceeding $200, and concurrent jurisdiction with justice's and county courts where the debt is over $25, and not exceeding $1000.

LIMITATION OF ACTIONS.—Actions to recover the title to, or an interest in, real estate and foreclosure of mortgage, must be commenced within ten years from the time the cause of action accrued. Actions for forcible entry and detainer must be commenced in one year after the cause of action accrued; within five years upon any agreement, contract or promise in writing, or foreign judgment; within four years upon contracts not in writing, accounts and liabilities created by statute, other than forfeiture of penalty. Actions on official bonds, undertakings in attachment, replevin and injunction, can only be brought within ten years. All causes of action which have become barred by the law of any State or Territory of the United States shall be deemed barred by the law of this State. If a party entitled to bring an action be, at the time the cause of action accrued, under twenty-one years, old, a married woman, insane or imprisoned, such person shall be entitled to bring such action within the times limited after such disability shall have been removed. When a cause of action accrues against a person, if such person be out of the State, or shall have absconded or conceals himself, or if, after a cause of action accrues, such person shall depart from the State, or abscond or conceal himself, the time of his absence or concealment shall be deducted from the period of limitation.

NEBRASKA FORMS.

(Form 1—WARRANTY DEED).

Know All Men by these Presents: That —— of the County of ——, and State of ——, for and in consideration of the sum of —— dollars, in hand paid, do hereby grant, bargain, sell, convey, and confirm unto —— of the County of ——, and State of —— the following described real estate, situated in ——, in —— County, and State of —— to-wit: —— and — do hereby covenant with the said —— and —— heirs and assigns, that —— lawfully seized of said premises; that they are free from incumbrance, that —— ha — good right and lawful authority to sell the same; and —— do hereby covenant to warrant and defend the title to said premises against the lawful claims of all persons whomsoever.

And the said —— hereby relinquishes all —— in and to the above described premises,

Signed this —— day of —— A. D., 18 — *Signature.*

IN PRESENCE OF

[Form 1a—ACKNOWLEDGMENT].

THE STATE OF NEBRASKA, } ss.
—— County. }

On this —— day of —— A. D., 18—, before me —— a (*title of officer*) duly —— and qualified for and residing in said County, personally came —— to me known to be the identical person — described in and who executed the foregoing conveyance as grantor — and acknowledged, the said instrument to be —— voluntary act and deed.

Witness my hand and —— the day and year last above written.

Signature.

[Form 2—CHATTEL MORTGAGE].

This Indenture, Made this —— day of —— A. D., 188 —, between —— of —— County, Nebraska, party of the first part, and ——of the same place, party of the second part:

WHEREAS, the said party of the first part is justly indebted to the said party of the second part, in the sum of —— dollars, on —— certain promissory note — of even date herewith, due ——, signed by ——, and payable to the order of ——

NOW THIS INDENTURE WITNESSETH, that the said party of the first part, for the better securing of the note — above described, according to the true intent and meaning thereof, and also for and in consideration of the sum of $1, to —— in hand paid by the said party of the second part at or before delivery of these presents, the receipt whereof is hereby acknowledged, ha — granted, bargained, sold, conveyed, and confirmed and by these presents do — grant, bargain, sell, convey, and confirm unto the said party of the second part, and to —— heirs and assigns forever, all the following described goods, chattels, and fixtures, etc., that is to say: ——

TO HAVE AND TO HOLD all and singular the said property, goods, chattels, fixtures, etc., unto the said party of the second part, and —— executors, administrators, and assigns, to —— and —— use forever. And —— the said mortgagor — do — solemnly declare and represent unto the said mortgagee — that —— lawfully possesed of the said goods and chattels, as of —— own property, that the same are free and clear of all incumbrance, for the purpose of obtaining the above money.

PROVIDED NEVERTHELESS, That if the said mortgagor —, —— executors, or administrators shall well and truly pay unto the said mortgagee —, —— executors, administrators, or assigns, the sum of —— dollars, then this mortgage, as also —— certain promissory note —, bearing even date herewith, signed by the said mortgagor —, whereby —— promise— to pay the said mortgage— — the said sum at the time aforesaid, shall both be void; otherwise, shall remain in full force and virtue.

(Here insert any other conditions).

In Witness Whereof, The said mortgagor — ha — hereunto set —— hand, this —— day of —— A. D., 188—

Signed, sealed and delivered in presence of } *Signature.*
Signature. } *Signature.*

[The instrument must be acknowledged and recorded same as a deed, unless the mortgagee take possession of the mortgaged chattels].

Form 3—BOND FOR COST.

STATE OF NEBRASKA, } ss.
—— County }

IN THE DISTRICT COURT.

We hereby acknowledge ourselves —— security for costs in the within cause.

Signature.

[*Indorse on back of petition*].

[Form 4—NOTICE TO TAKE DEPOSITIONS.

—— COURT, COUNTY OF —— STATE OF NEBRASKA. ——— *Plaintiff*, } vs. ——— *Defendant.* }

To the aboved named —— (defendant or plaintiff) you are hereby notified that said —— (plaintiff or defendant) will take the testimony of —— at —— Nebraska, at the office of —— a duly authorized Justice of the Peace, commencing at the hour of ten o'clock in the forenoon on the —— day of ——188 —, with power to adjourn from day to day until all such testimony shall have been taken.

Signature.

(Form 4*a*—INSTRUCTIONS FOR TAKING DEPOSTIONS).

[BEGIN WITH THE FOLLOWING CAPTION].

"Depositions of sundry witnesses taken before me [here insert the name of the magistrate and his official character, as Justice of the Peace, Notary Public etc.,] within and for the County of ——, in the State of ——, on the——day of——, in the year ——, between the hours of — A. M., and — P, M, at —— in said County, pursuant to the annexed notice, [or agreement, as the case may be,] to be read in evidence on behalf of the [plaintiff or defendant as the case may be] in an action pending in ——, [naming the Court] in which —— plaintiff and —— defendant."

A. B., of lawful age, being by me first duly examined, cautioned and solemnly sworn [or affirmed] deposeth and saith as follows, viz: [here write the deposition] and so on with all the witnesses.

The Deposition may be taken by stating the facts in reply to questions first written down, or in the narrative form.

In Nebraska they may be taken before a Judge or Clerk of the Supreme or District Court, Probate Judge or before a Justice of the Peace, Notary Public, Mayor, or Chief Magistrate of any city or town corporate, Master Commissioner or person empowered by a special commision; out of Nebraska, by a Judge, Justice, or Chancellor of any Court of Record, a Justice of the Peace, Notary Public, Mayor, or Chief Magistrate of any city or town corporate, Commissioner appointed by the Governor of Nebraska to take depositions, or any person authorized by a special commission.

If there are adjournments, they should be noted by the Magistrate, or other officer taking the depositions, from day to day, at the close of the day, with the reasons therefor,

Objections should be entered to witnesses supposed to be interested, and to questions supposed to be illegal. This entry is made on behalf of the party raising the objection, simply by a short note made by the magistrate or officer taking the deposition.

Each witness must sign his own deposition.

The notice must be attached to the depositions and enclosed with them.

The depositions must be commenced on the day named, and some portion of a deposition taken on each successive day, Sundays excepted, adjournments being from Saturday to Monday; Sundays and National holidays not being regarded.

When depositions are taken under an agreement, the above instructions will be followed, except where they are are modified by the agreement. In such case the agreement will be followed. It should be attached to the depositions if sent, and refered to in the caption, as the notice is when taken under a notice.

If taken by interrogatories and cross-interrogatories, under agreement or otherwise, every interrogatory and cross-interrogatory must be put to each witness, and answered so far as he can answer it. and the answer be written down. The deposition must show that each interrogatory and cross-interrogatory was thus put and answered.

The fees for taking the depositions should be taken, and a memorandum made by whom they were paid. Close the depositions with a Certificate in the form following, viz:

"I. A. B., (naming the official character of the magistrate according to the fact, do hereby certify that [naming all the witnesses who have testified] where by me first severally sworn [or affirmed] to testify the truth, the whole truth, and nothing but the truth, and that the depositions by them respectively subscribed as above set forth, were reduced to writing by myself, [or if by any other person, name him and say, by ——, who is not interrested in the suit, in my presence, and] in the presence of the witnesses respectively, and were respectively subscribed by the said witnesses in my presence, and were taken at the time and place in the annexed notice [or agreement] specified; that I am not counsel, attorney or relative of either party, or otherwise interested in the event of this suit;[if there be adjournments, add] and said depositions were commenced at the time in said notice specified, and continued by adjournments from day to day as above stated

[Signed]. In testimony whereof, etc. "A. B."

Depositions taken before any authorized officer having an official seal must be certified by him under such seal and his official signature. If the officer have no official seal, the deposition [if not taken in this State,] must be certified and signed by such officer, and further authenticated by parol proof adduced in Court, or by the official certificate and seal of any Secretary or other officer of state keeping the great seal thereof, or *of the clerk or prothonotary of any court, having a seal*, attesting that such Judicial or other officer was, at the time of taking the same, authorized to do so, (as being one of the officers above mentioned), This certificate should be attached to the certificate of the officer taking the deposition.

This proof of offici l character is omitted when waived by agreement of parties by endorsement on notice; but this agreement does not waive the taking at the specified time and place.

The whole should be sealed up by the officer taking the same, and the envelope address to the Clerk of the Court in which the action is pending, and endorsed as follows;

"A. B. against C. D. [giving the title of the cause]. Depositions in said action on behalf of the ——[plaintiff or defendant, as the case may be]. These depositions taken, sealed up, indorsed, addressed, and transmitted by me.

L. S. *Notary Public.*

[Form 5—MORTGAGE DEED,

Know all Men by these Presents, That —— of —— County, State of ——, in consideration of the sum of —— dollars, in hand paid, do hereby sell and convey unto —— of —— County, and State of —— the following described premises situated in —— County, and State of —— to-wit: —

The intention being to convey hereby an absolute title in fee simple, including all the rights of homestead, to have and to hold the premises above described, with all the appurtenances thereunto belonging, unto the said —— and to —— heirs and assigns forever; provided always and these presents are upon the express condition that if the said —— heirs, executors, or administrators, shall pay or cause to be paid the said —— heirs, executors, administrators, or assigns, the sum of —— dollars, on the —— day of —— 188—, with interest thereon —— according to the tenor and effect of the —— promissory note of said —— bearing even date with these presents, then these presents to be void, otherwise to be and remain in full force.

Signed the —— day of —— A. D. 188 —

IN PRESENCE OF } *Signature.* *Signature.*

[Must be acknowledged and recorded like deeds].

[Form 6—QUIT CLAIM DEED].

Know all Men by these Presents, That——of the County of ——, and State of —— for the consideration of —— dollars, hereby Quit Claim to —— of the County of —— State of ——, the following described real estate, situated in ——, in the County of —— and State of —— to-wit:

In Witness Whereof, —— have set — hand this —— day of —— 188 —

IN PRESENCE OF } *Signature.* *Signature.*

LAWS OF NEVADA

RELATIVE TO THE

COLLECTION OF DEBTS, Etc.

Prepared expressly for J. A. Graft & Co.'s Legal Directory,

ASSIGNMENTS AND INSOLVENCY.—Insolvent debtors may be discharged from their debts by complying with provisions of insolvent laws. An assignment of insolvent debtor, not in compliance with insolvent laws, is void as to creditors.

ATTACHMENTS.—Writ of attachment may be issued with summons, or at any time afterwards on affidavit and bond. In an action upon a contract for the direct payment of money, made, or by the terms thereof payable, in this State, which is not secured by mortgage, lien, or pledge, upon real or personal property, situated, or being in the State, if so secured, when such security has been rendered nugatory by the act of the defendant; or in an action upon a contract against a defendant not residing in this State.

Garnishee process may be had in aid of attachment. A fraudulent or absconding debtor, or one who conceals his property, or removes or disposes of it, with intent to defraud his creditors, may be arrested on affidavit of the fact made, surety in not less than $500 being given by the plaintiff.

CHATTEL MORTGAGES.—No mortgage of personal property shall be valid, unless possession be delivered to and retained by the mortgagee; provided, that growing crops may be mortgaged by the execution, acknowledgment, and recording of a mortgage instrument, without such possession. Chattel mortgages are foreclosed by action at any time after the debt secured becomes due, and before it is barred by the statute of limitations. There is no statutory provisions in regard to chattel mortgages, except as to growing crops. Where the mortgagor of stock in trade remains in possession, the transaction is only binding as between himself and the mortgagee, and is void as to creditors.

EXECUTIONS.—STAY OF EXECUTION; JUDGMENTS.—The laws of Nevada on these points are similar to those of California, except that when redemption is made of real estate, eighteen per cent. must be paid, in addition to purchase money.

EXEMPTIONS.—Homestead, $5,000. Personal and mining property, tools, implements, etc., exempt, same as in California.

INTEREST.—The legal rate is ten per cent. per annum, but parties may contract in writing for the payment of any other rate. After a judgment on such a contract, only the original claim shall draw interest.

MORTGAGES.—A mortgage of real property, whatever its terms, shall not be deemed a conveyance, so as to enable the owner of the mortgage to recover possession of the real property, without a foreclosure and sale. (Stat. 1869.)

But one form of action for the recovery of any debt, or enforcement of any right secured by lien or mortgage upon property, real or personal, which is by action for foreclosure. Judgment is for amount found due, with a decree or order of sale of incumbered property, and for the application of the proceeds to the payment of the debt; balance remaining due, if any, is docketed against the defendant personally liable. It is only necessary that the mortgagee should join in discharge. The discharge may be made either upon the margin of the record of the mortgage, or by satisfaction piece, duly acknowledged and recorded. Before any satisfaction or discharge of a mortgage can be made, the law exacts an oath by the mortgagee, or agent of mortgagee, to be made before the Recorder having custody of the record of the mortgage, that all State and county taxes, assessed and levied upon the moneys or debt secured by the mortgage, have been paid. This oath can only be made before the County Recorder having the custody of the record of the mortgage, to be discharged.

NOTES AND BILLS OF EXCHANGE.—Protest and notice will hold the indorser, and the general statute of limitation, six years, is the limitation of the right of action.

Fifteen per cent. damages are allowed on domestic, and twenty per cent. on foreign bills protested. Grace is not allowed on sight drafts.

[For Legal forms adapted to the Laws of Nevada, see Forms at end of Laws of California, published in this work].

LAWS OF NEW HAMPSHIRE

RELATIVE TO THE

COLLECTION OF DEBTS, Etc.

Prepared expressly for J. A. Graft & Co.'s Legal Directory, by N. H. Wilson, Attorney and Counsellor-at-Law, Manchester, N. H.

ACTIONS.—Original forms of process are, writs of attachments, capias summons, replevin, and trustee process, or foreign attachment. In actions brought by non-residents, some responsible resident is required to indorse the writ. The attorney bringing the suit may be, and usually is, the endorser.

If either party resides in this State, transitory actions should be brought in the county in which one of the party resides.

AFFIDAVITS—May be made before any officer authorized to take depositions.

ARRESTS.—No woman, Sheriff, or voter, on election day, is liable to arrest on civil process. No person is liable to arrest on real action, or action of ejectment, or on action founded on contract, unless the debt exceeds thirteen dollars and thirty-three cents, and then only by its appearing by affidavit, on the back of the writ, or execution signed by the plaintiff, or some one for him, that the defendant is, in his belief, justly indebted to him in a sum exceeding thirteen dollars and thirty-three cents, and that he conceals his property, or is about to leave the State, to avoid payment of his debts.

ASSIGNMENTS—Of future earnings valid against creditors, when given for just debt, due from assignor to assignee. A copy thereof, duly accepted in writing on the back, being filed with the clerk of the town where the assignor lives.

EVIDENCE.—Testimony of parties in interests admissible.

EXEMPTIONS —There is exempt from attachment, and from liability, to be taken on execution:

1. Necessary wearing apparel of the debtor and his family.
2. Comfortable beds, bedsteads, and bedding necessary for the debtor, his wife, and children.
3. Household furniture, to the value of one hundred dollars.

4. One cooking stove, and the necessary furniture belonging to the same.

5. One sewing machine, kept for the use of the debtor or his family.

6. Provisions and fuel, to the value of fifty dollars.

7. Uniform, arms, and equipments, of every officer and private in the militia.

8. Bibles, school books, and library, used by debtor, or his family, to value of two hundred dollars.

9. Tools of his occupation, to the value of one hundred dollars.

10. One hog, and one pig, and the pork of same when slaughtered.

11. Six sheep, and fleeces of same.

12. One cow, a yoke of oxen, or a horse when required, for farming or teaming purposes, or other actual use, and four tons of hay.

13. Domestic fowl to the value of fifty dollars.

The debtor's right to one pew in any meeting house, and one lot in any cemetery.

Homestead of householder, five hundred dollars.

INTEREST.—Six per cent. Contracts for greater rate not void, but legal rate only recoverable. Penalty for receiving over six per cent., forfeiture of three times the excess of such.

LIMITATIONS.—Actions for the recovery of real estate, upon notes secured by mortgage, and upon judgments, recognizances, and contracts, under seal, must be brought within twenty years after right of action accrues. Actions for trespass to person, and slander, within two years. All other personal actions, within six years after cause of action accrues.

A debt is revived by a new promise.

MARRIED WOMEN—Holding separate estate, or doing business in their own name, may sue, and be sued, in relation thereto, as if sole.

Are not liable for debts of husband. Are not bound by any undertaking by them for their husbands, or in their behalf.

STAY OF EXECUTION—Is not made in any case, except by special order of court.

There are no insolvent laws in use in this State.

Assignments for benefit of creditors, binding only upon mutual consent of all parties interested.

SERVICE—Of writs in all cases fourteen days, before return day.

TRUSTEE PROCESS—May be used to reach money, goods, rights, and credits of the defendant in the hands of another, except in actions of replevin, trespass to the person, defamation, or malicious prosecution.

Twenty dollars of defendant's earnings are exempt from trustee process, unless the claim is for necessaries.

Non-resident trustees may be charged upon deposition of their agent.

NEW HAMPSHIRE FORMS.

[Form 1.—ASSOCIATION TO FORM A CORPORATION.]

UNDER LAWS OF NEW HAMPSHIRE.

STATE OF ——, }
County of ——. } ss.

Be it Known, That by virtue of the provisions contained in chapter one hundred and fifty-two of the General Laws of New Hampshire; we, ——, of, etc., ——, being of lawful age, do hereby associate ourselves together as a Corporation, with our associates and successors, to be known as the —— Company; the principal office and place of business of said companys to be at ——, in said County ——. The object for which this Corporation is established, is to (here state business.)

The capital stock of said Corporation shall be (state amount, which must not be less than $1,000 or more than $1,000,000), and shall be divided into —— shares of —— dollars each.

The first meeting of this Corporation shall be held at ——, in ——, on the —— day of —— next, at —— o'clock in the ——noon, without further notice.

Witness our Hands, at ——, in said County, this —— day of —— , A. D. 18—.

——. [SEAL.]
——. [SEAL.]

This agreement to be recorded in the office of the Clerk of the town in which the principal business is to be carried on, and in that of the Secretary of State. (G. L., Ch. 152, § 1).

Form 2.—ACKNOWLEDGMENT FOR WARRANTY DEED.]

STATE OF ——, }
County of ——. } ss.

—— personally appeared and acknowledged the foregoing instrument to be —— voluntary act and deed. Before me, ——, 18—.

(Signature and title of officer.)

[Form 3.—NOTICE TO TAKE DEPOSITIONS.]

STATE OF ——, }
County of ——. } ss.

To ——:

You are hereby notified that one or more depositions will be taken before ——, a Justice of the Peace in and for the County of ——, at —— , in the County of ——, on the —— day of ——, 18 —, at —— of the clock in the ——noon; to be used in a plea ——, to be heard and tried at the Supreme Court, to be holden at ——, in and for the County of ——, on the —— Tuesday of ——, 18—. In which plea you are —— and ——, of ——, in said County of ——.

Dated at ——, the —— day of ——, A. D. 18—.

——, Justice of the Peace.

[Form 4.—CERTIFICATE TO DEPOSITIONS.]

—— County, } ss.

Personally appeared before me, the subscriber, a Justice of the Peace for said County, the within named —— at ——, in said County, on the —— day of ——, 18—, and made solemn oath that the within deposition, by him subscribed, contains the truth, the whole truth, and nothing but the truth, relative to the cause for which it was taken. The said deposition is taken at the request of ——, to be used at the Supreme Court to be held at ——, in and for said County of ——, on the —— Tuesday of —— next, 18—. In a plea wherein —— of —— is plaintiff, —— and said —— is defendant; and the taking of the same was begun at —— of the clock in the —— noon, and said first mentioned day, and continued till the whole were completed. That said —— being duly notified, was present, and did not object. The deponent living more than ten miles from the place of trial, is the cause of this caption. Before me,

——, Justice of the Peace.

Justice's fees. - - - - - - -
Deponent's fees - - - - - - -
Notification. - - - - - - -
Service of do. - - - - - - -
Subpœna. - - - - - - -
Service.

$

Taxed —— the ——, 18—. By ——, Justice of the Peace.

[Form 5.—AFFIDAVIT FOR CHATTEL MORTGAGE.]

We severally swear that the foregoing mortgage is made for the purpose of securing the debt specified in the condition thereof, and for no other purpose whatever; and that said debt was not created for the purpose of enabling the mortgagor to execute said mortgage, but is a just debt, honestly due and owing from the mortgagor to the mortgagee. (*Affiant's Signature.*)

STATE OF ——, } ss.
County of ——. }

On this —— day of ——, A. D. 18—, the above named —— and —— personally appearing, took and subscribed the above oath. Before me,

(*Signature and title of officer.*)

[Form 6.—WILLS.]

The commencement may be very brief, as follows:

Be it Known, That I, —— , of etc., do make this my last Will and Testament.

* * * * *

Witness my Hand and seal this —— day of ——, A. D. 18—. ——

Signed and sealed by the above named —— as his last Will and Testament, and by us in his presence, and at his request subscribed as witnesses. —— . [L. S.]

C ——. D ——.
E ——, F ——.
G ——. H ——.

Ordinarily Wills are probated in common form; that is, upon the testimony of one of the subscribing witnesses. On petition, they may be probated in solemn form. (G. L., Ch. 194).

LAWS OF NEW JERSEY

RELATIVE TO THE

COLLECTION OF DEBTS, Etc.

Prepared expressly for J. A. Graft & Co's Legal Directory by John W. Taylor, Attorney and Counsellor-at-Law, Newark, New Jersey.

Assignments for the Benefit of Creditors.—Preferences in such cases are void; the assignment must be for the equal benefit of all the creditors. Those creditors accepting the benefit of the assignment, must take their rateable shares of the proceeds, in full satisfaction of their claims. Those, however, not choosing to prove their claims, may enforce them against any after acquired property of the debtor.

Attachment.—Upon affidavit by the creditor, his agent or attorney, of the amount of his debt, and that the debtor is a non-resident, or has absconded from his creditors, the rights, credits, moneys, goods, chattels, and real estate of the debtor may be seized. Any other creditor, upon affidavit of the amount of his debt, and application to the court, will be allowed to share *pro rata* in the proceeds of the attached property.

Deeds and Mortgages.—A deed must be lodged for record within fifteen days after the date of its execution, or it will be void against a subsequent judgment creditor, or *bona fide* purchaser or mortgagee for a valuable consideration, not having notice of such prior deed.

A mortgage will be void against a subsequent judgment creditor or *bona fide* purchaser, or mortgagee for a valuable consideration, not having notice thereof, unless such mortgage shall be lodged for record at or before the time of entering such subsequent judgment, or of recording such subsequent deed or mortgage.

Exemption from Sale on Execution.—Goods and chattels of every kind, not exceeding in value (exclusive of wearing apparel) $200, and all wearing apparel, the property of any debtor having a family residing in this State, are exempt from seizure by execution, or any civil process whatever.

IMPRISONMENT FOR DEBT.—This is abolished, except in cases where there is fraud in the contract, or where the debtor removes, transfers, or conceals his property with intent to defraud his creditors.

INTEREST.—The legal rate is six per cent. In cases of usury, the creditor recovers only the actual amount loaned, without interest or costs.

LIMITATIONS.—Actions for the recovery of real estate must be brought within twenty years; actions on contracts under seal, within sixteen years after the cause of action accrues; actions on oral contracts or contracts not under seal, within six years from the time when the cause of action accrues; actions of trespass, and for torts generally, within six years.

MARRIED WOMEN.—A married woman may, in the same manner as though single, take and hold real and personal property. She is entitled to the exclusive control of all earnings or profits acquired by her in any trade or occupation carried on separately from her husband; and may bind herself by contract, in the same manner, and to the same extent, as though unmarried; which contract may be enforced by or against her, in her own name. She is not permitted, however, to become an accommodation indorser, guarantor, or surety.

She may execute valid conveyances of real estate, in certain cases, without joining her husband; as where he is an idiot, a lunatic, of unsound mind, or imprisoned on conviction of crime, or where she is living in a state of separation from him, under the final judgment or decree of any Court.

A married woman may also, as effectually as if single, dispose of her property by will, although she cannot deprive her husband of his estate by the courtesy.

NEW JERSEY FORMS.

[Form 1.—ACKNOWLEDGMENT BY HUSBAND AND WIFE.]

STATE OF ——, }
County of——, }

Be it Remembered, That on this —— day of ——, in the year one thousand eight hundred and ——, before me, ——, personally appeared ——, who, I am satisfied, —— the grantor in the within Indenture named; and I having first made known to —— the contents thereof, —— did —— acknowledge that —— signed, sealed and delivered the same as —— voluntary act and deed for the uses and purposes therein expressed.

And the said —— being by me privately examined, separate and apart from —— said husband, did further —— acknowledge that —— signed, sealed and delivered the same as —— voluntary act and deed, freely, and without any fear, threats or compulsion of or from —— said husband ——. *(Signature and title of officer.)*

[SEAL].

[Form 2.—FORMS AND INSTRUCTIONS FOR TAKING DEPOSITIONS.]

OATH OF COMMISSIONER.

STATE OF ——, } ss.
County ——. }

Be it Remembered, That on this —— day of ——, in the year of our Lord one thousand eight hundred and ——, at ——, in the County of —— and State of ——, before me ——, who am a ——, and lawfully authorized to administer oaths and affirmations in the State and County aforesaid, personally appeared ——, residing in ——, the commissioner in the within commission named, who being by me duly sworn, on —— oath do say that —— will faithfully, fairly and impartially execute the said commission. *(Commissioner's signature.)*

Sworn and Subscribed before me the —— day and year above written.

[SEAL.] *(Signature and title of officer.)*

CAPTION.

Be it Remembered, That on this —— day of ——, in the year of our Lord ——, at ——, in the —— of ——, in the County of —— and State of ——, being the time and place appointed by us for taking the examination of the witnesses named in the commission to which this schedule is annexed, we —— and ——, the commissioners therein named, having first taken the oath required of us in this behalf, faithfully, fairly and impartially to execute the said commission before ——, who is a ——, lawfully authorized to administer oaths and affirmations in said County and State, proceeded to examine such of the witnesses aforesaid as could be met with, upon the interrogatories annexed to the said commission as therein directed, and caused such examination to be taken down in writing, and signed by the witnesses respectively, and signed the same ourselves, as hereinafter follows:

——, one of the said witnesses, appearing before us, and being by us duly sworn (or "and alleging himself to be conscientiously scrupulous of taking an oath, and being thereupon duly affirmed by us, and having solemnly, sincerely and truly declared and affirmed") that the answers he should give to the said interrogatories should be the truth, the whole truth, and nothing but the truth. To the first interrogatory he says: (Here state the testimony). To the second interrogatory, he says: (Here state the testimony).

CERTIFICATE.

STATE OF ——, } ss.
County of ——, }

——, the commissioner within named, do hereby certify and return to the —— Court of —— that —— have duly executed the within commission in manner and form as is therein and thereby commanded; and that the execution thereof will fully appear by the schedule to the said commission and the accompanying interrogatories annexed.

Given under —— hand and seal, this —— day of ——, A. D. 18—.

[SEAL] (*Signature and title of officer.*)

[Form 8.—PROOF OF ACCOUNT.]

——, }
vs. } In ——.
——, }

STATE OF ——, } ss.
County of ——. }

——, being duly sworn according to law, on his oath says, that the copy of account hereto annexed, is a true copy of the book of account of original entries of the plaintiff— in this cause, so far as they relate to the plaintiffs demand therein, together with the statement of all the credits or allowances to which the defendant —— entitled; that the defendant— —— not entitled to any credits or allowances except those appearing on said statement; and that the sum of money or balance claimed by the plaintiff— is justly due and owing to ——.

(*Signature of affiant.*)

Sworn and Subscribed, this —— day of ——, A. D. 18—, before me, at ——

(*Signature and title of officer.*)

LAWS OF TERRITORY OF NEW MEXICO

RELATIVE TO THE

COLLECTION OF DEBTS, Etc.

Prepared expressly for J. A. Graft & Co.'s Legal Directory.

ASSIGNMENTS.—No statutory provisions thereon in this Territory.

COLLECTIONS.—Accounts sent to this Territory, verified by the affidavit of the creditor, are securable as proof of the indebtedness, unless denied by the defendant, under oath, in which event the claim would have to be proven by proper testimony.

EXEMPTIONS.—Homestead, to the value of $1,000, to the head of a family, and certain articles of personal property, recited in the statute, amounting to about $200.

INSOLVENCY.—No statute on the subject.

INTEREST.—Legal rate in this Territory is six per cent., but there is no usury law in the Territory, and parties may agree in writing on any amount.

LIMITATIONS.—Actions upon judgments must be brought within fifteen years.

Upon open accounts, unwritten contracts, within four years.

Upon bonds, promissory notes, etc., within six years.

NOTES AND BILLS.—No days of grace allowed.

PRACTICE.—Strict common law.

[For Legal Forms adapted to Laws of New Mexico, see Forms at end of Laws of Missouri].

LAWS OF NEW YORK.

RELATIVE TO THE

COLLECTION OF DEBTS, Etc.

Prepared expressly for J. A. Graft & Co's Legal Directory, by James S. Garlock, Attorney and Counsellor-at-Law, Rochester, New York.

ASSIGNMENTS.—Act of 1877 provides that a debtor may, by an instrument in writing, convey or assign his property, real and personal, to an assignee for the benefit of his creditors. The debtor shall, within twenty days after date of assignment, make, and deliver to the County Judge, of the county where the assignment is recorded, an inventory or schedule, showing his name, occupation, residence, and place of business, also name and place of residence of the assignee, also an account of all the debtor's creditors, the sum owing to each, with the true consideration thereof, etc. Also a true inventory of such debtor's estate, at date of the assignment, the incumbrances thereon, and all vouchers and securities relating thereto, the nominal and the actual value thereof, all of which shall be verified by the debtor's affidavit. The act does not prohibit preferences, and the debtor may prefer creditors, as he chooses.

The assignee shall give a bond for faithful performance of his duties.

The assignee may be cited by a creditor to account after one year.

COLLECTIONS.—An action for collection of a debt must be commenced by summons.

An attachment may issue with, or subsequent to the summons, when the action is brought to recover a sum of money only as damages, for one or more of the following causes:

1. Breach of contract, express or implied, other than a contract to marry.

2. Wrongful conversion of personal property.

3. Any other injury to personal property, in consequence of negligence, fraud, or other wrongful act.

The warrant of attachment is issued upon showing by the plaintiff, by affidavit, to the satisfaction of the Judge granting the same.

1. That a cause of action exists for one of the causes above specified, and if the action is to recover damages for breach of a contract, the affidavit must show that the plaintiff is entitled to recover a sum stated therein, over and above all counter claims known to him. Also that the defendant is a foreign corporation, or not a resident of the State, or if a natural person, and a resident of the State, that he has departed therefrom, with intent to defraud his creditors, or to avoid the service of a summon, or keeps himself concealed therein, with the like intent, or that he, or it has removed, or is about to remove property, from the State, with intent to defraud his or its creditors, or has assigned, disposed of, or secreted, or is about to assign, dispose of, or secrete property, with the like intent.

The attachment holds the property until execution is issued on the judgment.

Personal property is sold on execution, after six days' posting notice of sale.

On sale of real estate on execution, the judgment debtor has one year to redeem, by paying the amount for which the property was sold, and interest thereon at ten per centum per year, subsequent judgment creditors, or mortgagees, may redeem within fifteen months after such sale.

EXEMPTIONS.—The following personal property, when owned by a householder, is exempt from levy and sale on execution:

1. All spinning wheels, weaving looms, and stoves, put up, or kept for use in a dwelling house, and one sewing machine, with its appurtenances.

2. The family bible, family pictures, and school books, used by, or in the family, and other books, not exceeding in value fifty dollars, kept and used as part of the family library.

3. A seat or pew, occupied by the judgment debtor, or the family, in a place of public worship.

4. Ten sheep, with their fleeces, and the yarn or cloth manufactured therefrom; one cow, two swine; the necessary food for those animals; all necessary meat, fish, flour, and vegetables, actually provided for family use, and necessary fuel, oil, and candles, for the use of the family for sixty days.

5. Also certain specified household furniture, dishes, etc.

6. The tools and implements of a mechanic, necessary to the carrying on of his trade.

7. In addition to the above, the necessary household furniture, working tools and team, professional instruments, furniture and library, not exceeding in value two hundred and fifty dollars, when owned by a person being a householder, except for purchase money of one or more of said articles, and except for the wages of a domestic.

Where the judgment debtor is a woman she is entitled to the same exemptions as in case of a householder. A burial lot, not exceeding one-fourth of an acre. There is a homestead exemption of a lot of land with one or more buildings thereon, not exceeding one thousand dollars in value, owned and occupied as a residence, by a householder having a family; after a conveyance, or notice has been recorded, showing such intention to hold said lot as a homestead, etc.

INTERESTS.—The legal rate is six per cent. (Laws 1879, ch. 538.)

A person paying a greater rate may recover the excess in an action brought within one year. All bonds, notes, conveyances, contracts, or securities whatsoever, (except bottomry bonds) and all deposits of goods whereby there shall be reserved, or taken, or agreed to be reserved or taken, a greater rate of interest, are absolutely void, even in the hands of innocent third parties; but no corporation can plead the defense of usury, usury is a misdemeanor, punishable with a fine of $1,000, or six months imprisonment, or both. (Laws 1837, ch. 430.)

State banks have been placed on the same footing as national banks, as regards usury, and are thereby exempt from the extreme penalties above mentioned. (Laws 1870, ch. 163; sec. 64 N. Y., 212.)

INSOLVENT DEBTORS.—An insolvent debtor may be discharged from his debts under the insolvent laws of this State, upon presenting a petition to the county court of the county where such insolvent resides, showing the amount, etc., of debts owing by him, and having annexed thereto a consent by one or more of his creditors, owing debts against such insolvent, not less in amount than two-thirds of all his debts, owing to creditors residing in the United States, consenting to such discharge, etc.

LIMITATIONS.—*Within twenty years* an action on a sealed instrument, is barred by the statute of limitations after lapse of twenty years after cause of action accrued. *Within six years,* upon a contract, obligation, or liability, expressed or implied; an action to recover a chattel; an action to recover upon a liability created by statute, except a penalty or forfeiture; an action to recover damages for an injury to property, or a personal injury; an action to procure a judgment other than for a sum of money, on the ground of fraud, etc.; an action to establish a will, etc.; an action upon a judgment or decree rendered in a court, not of record, etc. *Within three years,* an action against a Sheriff, Coroner, Constable, or other officer, for non-payment of money collected upon an execution, or upon any other liability incurred by him, by doing an act in his official capacity, or by the omission of an official duty, except an escape; an action upon a statute for a penalty or forfeiture; an action against an executor, administrator, or receiver, or against the trustee of an insolvent debtor, etc.; an action to recover damages for a personal injury, resulting from negligence. *Within two years,* an action to recover damages for libel, slander, assault, battery, or false imprisonment; an action upon a statute for a forfeiture, or penalty to the people of the State. *Within one year,* an action against a Sheriff or Coroner, upon a liability incurred by him, by doing an act in his official capacity, or by the omission of an official duty, etc., an action for an escape of a prisoner, etc.

NEW YORK FORMS.

[Form 1—ACKNOWLEDGMENT BY ONE OR MORE GRANTORS].

[BY HUSBAND AND WIFE]. See Laws, title deeds.

STATE OF ——, }
County of ——. } SS.

Be it Remembered, That on this —— day of ——, A. D., eighteen hundred and ——, before me, the undersigned, a ——, within and for the County of —— and State aforesaid, personally came, —— and ——— who —— personally known to me to be the same person — whose name —— subscribed to the foregoing instrument of writing, as part — thereto, and —— acknowledged the same to be —— act and deed for the purposes therein mentioned.

[SEAL]. *In Witness Whereof*, I have hereunto set my hand and affixed my official seal, this the —— day of ——, , 18 —.

Signature and title of officer.

[Form 1b—AFFIDAVIT AND ACKNOWLEDGMENT TO CHATTEL MORTGAGE].

STATE OF ——, }
County of —— } SS.

——, being duly sworn, on —— oath says, that —— the legal and absolute owner of the personal property above described, and that the same is free from all claims and liens whatsoever.

(*Signature of affiant*).

Subscribed and sworn to before me, }
this —— day of ——, A. D., 18 —. } SS.

(*Signature of officer*).

[SEAL].

STATE OF —— ——, }
City of ——. } SS.

Be it Remembered, That on this —— day of ——, A. D., 18 —, before the undersigned, a ——, within and for the City of —— and State of ——, personally came ——, who — personally known to me to be the same person whose name — subscribed to the foregoing instrument of writing, as part — thereto, and acknowledged the same to be —— voluntary act and deed for the uses and purposes therein mentioned.

[SEAL].

In Testimony Whereof, I have hereunto set my hand and affixed my official seal, at my office, in ——, the day and year first above written

Signature and title of officer.

[Form 2—FORMS AND INSTRUCTIONS FOR TAKING DEPOSITIONS].

INSTRUCTIONS FOR TAKING DEPOSITIONS.

Depositions taken without the State for use within the State, are granted upon affidavit, in a proper case, and upon notice to the adverse party, if he has appeared in the action. The names of the witnesses are inserted in the commission, and the interrogatories [settled by consent of the parties or by order of the Judge] are annexed to the commission. The commission may issue to any competent person or persons, generally to attorneys. Where an issue of fact joined in an action is pending in the Supreme Court, a Superior City Court the Marine Court of New York City, or a County Court, the parties may, by written stipulation, or upon the direction [discretionary] of the Court or Judge, obtain the issuance of a commission without written interrogatories, and the deposition be taken upon oral questions, or partly upon oral questions and written interrogatories, or that an open commission issue. In either of last named cases written notice of the time and place of examination must be given to attorney of adverse party, at least five judical days before deposition is taken, and one judicial day in addition for each fifty miles, by usual route of travel, between residence of such attorney and place of taking deposition. Either party may on the examination produce such witnesses as he deems proper, whose testimony is taken upon oral questions. In either of last named cases the applicant cannot be examined in his own behalf, except upon consent of the parties, [L. 1879, Ch. 542, page 611]; nor can either of those methods be applied when the adverse party is an infant, or the committee of a lunatic, idiot, or habitual drunkard: or where the testimony is to be taken elsewhere than in the United States or Canada. [C. of C. P., § 887, *et seq.*]

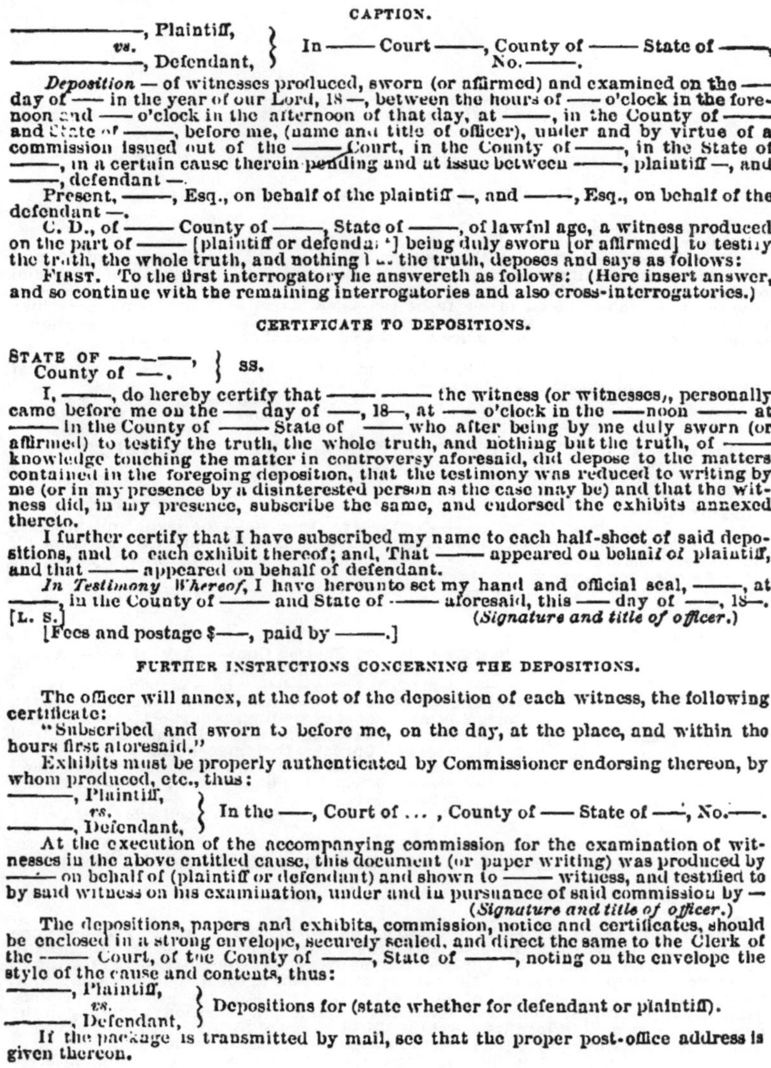

CAPTION.

———, Plaintiff,
vs.
———, Defendant, } In —— Court ——, County of —— State of ——, No. ——.

Deposition — of witnesses produced, sworn (or affirmed) and examined on the —— day of —— in the year of our Lord, 18 —, between the hours of —— o'clock in the fore-noon and —— o'clock in the afternoon of that day, at ——, in the County of —— and State of ——, before me, (name and title of officer), under and by virtue of a commission issued out of the —— Court, in the County of ——, in the State of ——, in a certain cause therein pending and at issue between ——, plaintiff —, and ——, defendant —.

Present, ——, Esq., on behalf of the plaintiff —, and ——, Esq., on behalf of the defendant —.

C. D., of —— County of ——, State of ——, of lawful age, a witness produced on the part of —— [plaintiff or defendant] being duly sworn [or affirmed] to testify the truth, the whole truth, and nothing but the truth, deposes and says as follows:

FIRST. To the first interrogatory he answereth as follows: (Here insert answer, and so continue with the remaining interrogatories and also cross-interrogatories.)

CERTIFICATE TO DEPOSITIONS.

STATE OF ———,
County of —. } ss.

I, ——, do hereby certify that —— —— the witness (or witnesses), personally came before me on the —— day of ——, 18—, at —— o'clock in the ——noon —— at —— in the County of —— State of —— who after being by me duly sworn (or affirmed) to testify the truth, the whole truth, and nothing but the truth, of —— knowledge touching the matter in controversy aforesaid, did depose to the matters contained in the foregoing deposition, that the testimony was reduced to writing by me (or in my presence by a disinterested person as the case may be) and that the witness did, in my presence, subscribe the same, and endorsed the exhibits annexed thereto.

I further certify that I have subscribed my name to each half-sheet of said depositions, and to each exhibit thereof; and, That —— appeared on behalf of plaintiff, and that —— appeared on behalf of defendant.

In Testimony Whereof, I have hereunto set my hand and official seal, ——, at ——, in the County of —— and State of —— aforesaid, this —— day of ——, 18—.

[L. S.] *(Signature and title of officer.)*

[Fees and postage $——, paid by ——.]

FURTHER INSTRUCTIONS CONCERNING THE DEPOSITIONS.

The officer will annex, at the foot of the deposition of each witness, the following certificate:

"Subscribed and sworn to before me, on the day, at the place, and within the hours first aforesaid."

Exhibits must be properly authenticated by Commissioner endorsing thereon, by whom produced, etc., thus:

——, Plaintiff,
vs.
——, Defendant, } In the ——, Court of ... , County of —— State of ——, No.——.

At the execution of the accompanying commission for the examination of witnesses in the above entitled cause, this document (or paper writing) was produced by —— on behalf of (plaintiff or defendant) and shown to —— witness, and testified to by said witness on his examination, under and in pursuance of said commission by —

(Signature and title of officer.)

The depositions, papers and exhibits, commission, notice and certificates, should be enclosed in a strong envelope, securely sealed, and direct the same to the Clerk of the —— Court, of the County of ——, State of ——, noting on the envelope the style of the cause and contents, thus:

——, Plaintiff,
vs.
——, Defendant, } Depositions for (state whether for defendant or plaintiff).

If the package is transmitted by mail, see that the proper post-office address is given thereon.

Form 3.—AFFIDAVIT TO ACCOUNT.]

[General Form.]

STATE OF ——, } ss.
County of —. }

Be it Remembered, That on this — day of —, A. D. 18—, before me — a — (title of officer) within and for said —— and State, appeared ——, who being by me duly sworn, deposes and says, that he is ——, of the firm of ——, which is composed of ——

doing business in —— and State aforesaid. That —— of —— State of ——, owes and is justly indebted to said —— in the full sum of — dollars, ——, for goods, wares and merchandise sold and delivered to — at — special instance and request; that the annexed statement, marked "Exhibit A" by the ——, is a just, true and strictly correct account of said indebtedness, showing items, dates and prices; that said demand remains due and unpaid, and has not been settled or paid by said ——, or by any other person; that there are no just credits, off-sets or counter-claims against said demand, either in law or in equity; and that said sum is now due exclusive of any payment, set-off or usurious interest; and that lawful interest is due thereon from —. (*Signature of affiant.*

[SEAL.] Sworn to and subscribed before me the day and year first aforesaid.
Witness my hand and Official Seal.

(*Signature and title of officer.*)

LAWS OF NORTH CAROLINA

RELATIVE TO THE

COLLECTION OF DEBTS, Etc.

Prepared expressly for J. A. Graft & Co.'s Legal Directory.

ASSIGNMENTS.—An insolvent party may assign his estate for the benefit of creditors, and prefer one to another; but his *debts* are only discharged upon payment in full, or upon compromise.

Petition and assignment only discharge from liability to arrest.

ATTACHMENT.—The property of foreign corporations, and of non-resident, or absconding or concealing defendants, may be attached. The attachment may be granted at the time of issuing the summons, or at any time thereafter. Personal service of summons must be made, or publication thereof commenced, within thirty days after obtaining a warrant of attachment.

ARREST AND BAIL.—A defendant may be arrested at the commencement of a civil action, when it appear by affidavit, or otherwise satisfactorily to the Court, that the defendant is a non-resident, or about to remove from this State, or the action is for the recovery of damages, on an action not arising out of contract, where the action is for injury to person or character, or for wrongfully taking, detaining, or converting property.

2. Where the action is for a fine or penalty; or for money received, or for property embezzled; or fraudulently misapplied by a public officer, or by an attorney, or an officer or agent of a corporation, or banking association, in the course of his employment as such; or by any factor agent, broker, or other person in a fiduciary capacity, or for any misconduct in official or professional employment.

3. Where the action is to recover possession of personal property, unjustly detained; where the same has been concealed, removed, or disposed of, with intent to prevent recovery, or deprive plaintiff of the benefit of it.

4. Where defendant has been guilty of a fraud in the transaction.

5. Where the defendant has removed or disposed of his property, or is about to do so, with intent to defraud his creditors.

FEMALES may not be arrested, except for wilful injury to person, character, or property.

EXECUTION—From a Justice's Court, may issue immediately, if not stayed, and is returnable in sixty days. From Superior Court, returnable at succeeding term.

EXEMPTIONS FROM EXECUTION.—Every resident of this State may hold personal property, to the amount of $500, and real property to the amount of $1,000, exempt from the execution of any court, but subject to such taxes, as may be lawfully exacted. The homestead may be voluntarily subjected to laborers' liens, or other debts, and is liable for unpaid purchase money, unless released. The debtor's title to it is in fee simple.

FORECLOSURE OF REGISTERED MORTGAGES—Is allowed, when proper power of sale is therein given.

JURISDICTION.—Justice's of the Peace have exclusive original jurisdiction of all matters arising out of contract, where the amount demanded, exclusive of interest, does not exceed $200. Also of actions for the possession of personalty, where the value thereof does not exceed $50.

LIMITATIONS.—*Within ten years*, an action upon a judgment or decree of any Court of U. S., or State, or territory; upon a sealed instrument, against the principal thereto, (three years being the limit against the surety,) after maturity, or last partial payment; for foreclosure of a mortgage or deed in trust for creditor with power of sale, of realty, where the mortgagor or grantor has been in possession within ten years after forfeiture, or power of sale become absolute, or last payment made on same; and for redemption of mortgage, after right of action accrued.

Within seven years, on a judgment of a Justice of the Peace; and by a creditor of a deceased person against his personal representative, but if claimed, is rejected, then within six months after such rejection.

Within six years, on the official bond of any public officer; against an executor, administrator, or guardian on his official bond; and for injury to any incorporeal heriditament.

Within three years, upon a contract, express or implied, except such as are above mentioned, and upon a liability created by statute, other than a penalty or forfeiture, unless other time be therein prescribed; for trespass upon real property; and for taking, detaining, converting or injuring goods or chattels, including actions for specific recovery; and for criminal conversation, or other injury to person, or rights of another, not arising out of contract and against sureties of executors, administrators and guardians or the official bonds of their principals; against bail; for fees due Clerk, Sheriff or other officer: and for relief on ground of fraud, counting only after the discovery of the fraud.

Within one year, against officers for trespass; upon statute for penalty or forfeiture; for libel, assault, battery or false imprisonment; against an officer for an escape; or by a creditor of a deceased person after notice served in writing to present his claim.

Within six months, for slander. Any other relief to which a party may think entitled must be sued for in ten years.

MORTGAGE OF PERSONAL PROPERTY.—Allowed by statute to secure debts of $300 or less. Such mortgages upon produce unplanted are held valid, and so generally given now that separate books are provided for their registration.

MARRIED WOMEN—Own and control their estates as before marriage, but cannot convey without their husband. They have also a dower interest in all real estate owned or acquired by the husband during the coverture.

STAY OF EXECUTION.—On giving sufficient security, the party against whom judgment is rendered, may stay execution, as follows: On less than $25.00 for one month; $25.00 to $50.00 three months; $50.00 to

$100.00 four months; above $100.00 six months. Execution may then issue against both principal and surety for the debt with interest accrued and costs.

WITNESS.—Any party may be a witness on either side without regard to personal interest, save as to transactions with persons since deceased.

NORTH CAROLINA FORMS.

[Form 1.—CERTIFICATE OF ACKNOWLEDGMENT FOR HUSBAND AND WIFE.]

STATE OF ——, }
County of ——. } SS.

Before Me (Insert name and title of officer), this day personally appeared ——, and his wife, ——, parties named in the foregoing deed, and the said deed being also produced, and exhibited before me, the same ——, and his wife, ——, acknowledged the execution thereof, as their act and deed, for the purposes therein expressed, and the said ——, being by me privately examined, separate and apart from her said husband, touching her voluntary execution of the same, doth state that she signed the same freely and voluntarily, and without fear or compulsion of her said husband, or any other person whatsoever, and doth still voluntarily assent thereto.

In Witness Whereof, I have set my hand and affixed my official seal, this —— day of ——, 18—. (*Signature and title of officer.*)

[L. S.]

Form 2.—INSTRUCTIONS AND FORMS FOR DEPOSITIONS.]

STATE OF ——, }
County of ——. } SS.

Pursuant to the annexed commission, directing the undersigned commissioner to take the deposition of —— (and other, as the case may be), a witness (or witnesses), for the plaintiff, (or defendant), to be read in evidence in a suit now pending in the Superior Court of —— County, wherein —— is plaintiff, and —— is defendant, at my office, No. ——, —— street in city of ——, and State of ——, on the —— day of ——, at 9 o'clock A. M., the plaintiff and defendant being present, (or not present, as the case may be), in person (or represented by counsel, I proceeded to examine the said ——, who being by me first duly sworn, deposes as follows:

First question. (Write out the question and answer)

The deposition should be read to the witness, and signed by him, and then countersigned by the commissioner.

CERTIFICATE.

I, —— the commissioner named in the annexed commission, do hereby certify that the evidence of the witness ——, was taken down under oath, and subscribed by him in my presence, on the —— day of ——, 18—, at my office, No. ——, —— street, city of ——, County of ——, and State of ——; and that I have personal knowledge of said witness (or that proof of his identity has been made before me); and I further certify that both (or neither, or only one) of the said parties were present (or were represented by counsel) at the taking of said deposition.

Witness My Hand and seal, this —— day of ——, 18—. ——, [SEAL.]
Commissioner.

Place the deposition in an envelope, seal carefully with wax, and direct to Clerk of the Court issuing the deposition, first enclosing a memorandum as follows:

——, }
vs. } Superior Court, —— County, North Carolina.
——, }

Deposition of ——, taken by order of Court in the above entitled action, by ——, Commissioner. (Signed), ——, [SEAL.]
Commissioner.

Also enclose the notice given by the party taking the deposition, of the time and place for taking the deposition.

If for any reason the deposition can not be taken or entered on the first day set, the commissioner should adjourn to a certain hour on the next day; and so *die ad diem*, until the deposition can be taken.

LAWS OF OHIO

RELATIVE TO THE

COLLECTION OF DEBTS, Etc.

Prepared expressly for J. A. Graft & Co.'s Legal Directory.

ACKNOWLEDGMENTS—May be taken by any Judge or Clerk of a Court of Record, Justice of the Peace, Notary Public, Commissioner for Ohio, Mayor, or other presiding officer of an incorporated city or town. When executed, acknowledged and proved out of this State, in accordance with the laws of the place where executed, they will be as valid as if executed in this State. Husband must join in conveyance of wife's property. Two witnesses are required to attest signatures in all matters affecting real estate. Instruments of conveyance between husband and wife must be signed, sealed and acknowledged by husband and wife and attested by two witnesses. Officer taking acknowledgment must certify that he examined the wife separate and apart from her husband, and made known to her the contents of the instrument, that she voluntarily signed, sealed and acknowledged the same, and that she is still satisfied therewith as her act and deed.

AFFIDAVITS—May be made in or out of this State, before any person authorized to take depositions, and must be authenticated in the same way as depositions, except that in affidavits verifying pleadings, the certificate of the officer, signed officially by him, shall be evidence that the affidavit was duly made, that the name of the officer was written by himself, and that he was such officer.

ASSIGNMENTS.—An insolvent debtor may make an assignment in trust for the benefit of creditors. Assignee must, within ten days after delivery of assignment to him, produce the original assignment, or copy thereof, in the Probate Court, file same and enter into a bond in such sum and with such sureties as court shall approve. Notice of appointment, for three successive weeks, in a newspaper of general circulation, shall be given after bond entered into, and creditor shall, within six months after publication of notice, present claim with affidavit that said claim is just and lawful, the consideration thereof, and what, if any, set-offs or counter-claims exist thereto; what collateral or personal security, if any, the claimant holds for same, or that he has no security whatever. Any surety or person jointly liable with assignor is allowed to present and prove his claim on which he is bound. Suit must be brought on rejected claims within thirty days. Assignment made in contemplation of insolvency, with intent to prefer one or more creditors, inures to the benefit of all creditors. Assignment made with intent to hinder, delay or defraud creditors, shall be declared void at the suit of any creditor, and such assignment, after having been declared void, or a preferred assignment, is cause for the appointment of trustee. No assignment shall be construed to include property exempt, unless the exemption is expressly waived. Preferred claims are: Taxes of every description assessed against assignor, and wages for all labor performed by any one in the assignor's service within one year preceding the assignment, not exceeding $300.

ATTACHMENT.—In a civil action for the recovery of money the plaintiff may at, or after the commencement thereof, have an attachment against the property of the defendant, upon the grounds herein stated:

1. When the defendant, or one of several defendants, is a foreign corporation, or a non-resident of this State.

2. Has absconded, with intent to defraud his creditors.

3. Has left the county of his residence, to avoid the service of a summons.

4. So conceals himself that a summons can not be served upon him.

5. Is about to remove his property, or a part thereof, out of the jurisdiction of the court with the intent to defraud his creditors.

6. Is about to convert his property, or a part thereof, into money, for the purpose of placing it beyond the reach of his creditors.

7. Has property, or rights in action, which he conceals.

8. Has assigned, removed, disposed of, or is about to dispose of, his property, or a part thereof, with intent to defraud his creditors.

9. Has fraudulently, or criminally, contracted the debt, or incurred the obligation, for which suit is about to be, or has been brought.

But an attachment shall not be granted on the ground that the defendant is a foreign corporation, or a non-resident of this State, for any claim other than a debt or demand, arising upon contract judgment, or decree, or for causing death by a negligent or wrongful act.

The clerk of the court in which action is brought, will issue the attachment, when there is filed in his office an affidavit, showing:

1. The nature of the plaintiff's claim.

2. That it is just.

3. The amount which affiant believes the plaintiff ought to recover.

4. Some one of the above mentioned grounds.

Where the defendant is a foreign corporation, or a non-resident, the order of attachment is issued without an undertaking, but in all other cases it shall not issue until an undertaking in double the plaintiff's claim, to be approved by the clerk, is executed, conditioned for the payment of all damages to defendant, in case said attachment is wrongfully issued. An attachment may issue before debt is due, where the debtor has sold, conveyed, or otherwise disposed of his property, with intent to cheat or defraud his creditors, or hinder or delay them in the collection of their debts, or is about to make such sale, or is about to remove his property, with fraudulent intent. Where the officer can not get possession of the property sought to be attached, he may leave with the person alleged, by affidavit, to be in possession of the same, a copy of the order of attachment, and a notice to appear and answer, touching such property.

Courts. *Terms and Jurisdiction.* Justice's Courts have exclusive original jurisdiction of any sum not exceeding $100, and concurrent jurisdiction with the Court of Common Pleas of any sum from $100 to $300. Superior Courts of Cincinnati, Cleveland and Dayton, have the same general jurisdiction in actions for debt that is exercised by the Courts of Common Pleas. Common Pleas Courts have original jurisdiction where the amount in controversy exceeds $100.

Depositions—May be used only in the following cases:

1. When the witness does not reside in, or is absent from, the county where the action or proceeding is pending; or by change of venue, is sent for trial.

2. When the witness is dead, or from age, infirmity, or imprisonment, is unable to attend court.

3. When the testimony is required upon a motion, or where the oral examination of the witness is not required.

Either party may commence taking testimony by deposition at any time after service upon the defendant.

Depositions taken in this State, to be used therein, must be taken before an officer deriving his authority from the State, and they may be taken out of this State before a Judge, Justice, or Chancellor, of any

Court of Record, a Justice of the Peace, Notary Public, Mayor, or Chief Magistrate, of any municipal corporation, a commissioner, appointed by the governor, or any person authorized by a special commission from this State. Such officer must not be an attorney, or relative of either party, or otherwise interested in the event of the action.

Written notice of the intention to take a deposition must be given to the adverse party, specifying the action, name of court, time and place it will be taken, and, if a party to the suit is to testify, it must so state, or his testimony can not be used. Time must be given, so as to allow adverse party sufficient time, exclusive of Sundays, day of service, and one day's preparation, to go to place of taking same, by ordinary and usual modes of conveyance. Examinations, if so stated in notice, may be adjourned from day to day. The deposition so taken must be sealed in an envelope, endorsed with the title of the cause, and the name of the officer before whom it was taken, and it must be transmitted to the clerk of the court where action is pending, and remain under seal, until opened by the clerk by order of the court, or at the request of a party, or his attorney.

The officer must annex to the deposition, under his official seal, a certificate, showing:

1. That the witness was sworn to testify the truth, the whole truth, and nothing but the truth.

2. That the deposition was reduced to writing by some proper person, naming him.

3. That the deposition was written, and subscribed, in the presence of the officer certifying thereto.

4. That the deposition was taken at the time and place specified in the notice.

Executions—Issue from the Court of Common Pleas to any county. Execution against the person will only issue when the Judge of one of the Superior Courts is satisfied of the existence of cause—such as concealment of property by the debtor—or where debtor was arrested before judgment and not discharged under the law. Lands levied on must be appraised by three disinterested freeholders, and can not be sold for less than two-thirds of such appraisement. Executions are stayed before Justices, by entering into a bond to adverse party within ten days after rendition of judgment, on judgments for $5 and under, sixty days; $5 and under $20, ninety days; $20 and under $50, one hundred and fifty days; $50 and upward, two hundred and forty days. No stay on judgment in favor of any person for wages due for manual labor performed.

Exemptions—Every person who has a family, and every widow, may hold the following property exempt from execution, attachment or sale for any debt, damages, fine or amercement:

1. The wearing apparel of such person or family, beds, bedsteads and bedding necessary for the same, one cooking stove and pipe, one stove and pipe used for warming the dwelling, and fuel for sixty days, actually provided, and designed for the use of such person or family.

2. One cow, or if the debtor owns none, household furniture to be selected by such debtor not exceeding $35 in value; two swine or the pork therefrom, or if the debtor owns no swine, household furniture to be selected by such debtor not exceeding $15 in value; six sheep, their wool and the cloth or other articles manufactured therefrom, or in lieu thereof household furniture, to be selected by the debtor, not exceeding $15, and food for such animals for sixty days.

3. Bibles, hymn books, psalm books, testaments and school books used in the family, and all family pictures.

4. Provisions actually provided and designed for the use of such person or family not exceeding $50 in value, and other articles of household or kitchen furniture necessary for such person or family, not exceeding $50 in value.

5. One sewing machine, one knitting machine, and all the tools and implements of the debtor necessary for carrying on his or her trade or business, whether mechanical or agricultural, not exceeding $100 in value.

6. The personal earnings of the debtor and of his or her minor child or children for three months, when it is made to appear by affidavit that such earnings are necessary for such person or family.

7. All articles, specimens and cabinets of natural history or science, except such as are intended for show or exhibition for money or pecuniary gain.

8. Every drayman, who is the head of a family, in addition to the above exemptions, shall hold one horse, harness and dray exempt from execution. Every agriculturist who is the head of a family, in addition to the exemptions specified in paragraphs one to seven inclusive, shall hold exempt from execution one horse or one yoke of cattle with the necessary gearing for the same, one wagon; and every practitioner of medicine, the head of a family, in addition to the exemptions specified in paragraphs one to seven inclusive, shall hold exempt one horse, one saddle and bridle, snd also books, medicines and instruments pertaining to his profession not exceeding $100 in value.

Every unmarried woman may hold the following property exempt from execution, attachment or sale:

1. Wearing apparel not exceeding $100.
2. One sewing machine.
3. One knitting machine.
4. A bible, hymn book, psalm book and any other books not exceeding in value $25.

Any beneficiary fund, not exceeding $5,000, set apart, appropriated or paid by any benevolent association or society according to its rules and regulations to the family of any deceased member, or to any member of such family, shall not be liable to be taken by any process or proceedings, legal or equitable, to pay any debt of such deceased member.

The regalia, insignia of office, journals of proceedings, account books and the private work belonging to any benevolent society in this State, shall be exempt, etc.

All property used by any municipal corporation or fire company for the purpose of extinguishing fire shall be exempt, but the owner may create liens thereon by mortgage, etc. Any resident being the head of a family and not the owner of a homestead, can hold other personal property to be selected by him, and not appraised at over $500, in addition to the chattel property specified above. No exemption runs against claim for labor amounting to less than $100. The above exemption may be claimed by any one who has a family, and by every widow, against whom an action is prosecuted in this State, whether such debtor is or is nct a resident of this State.

Homestead—Husband and wife living together, a widow or widower living together with an unmarried daughter or unmarried minor son, may hold exempt from sale on judgment or order a family homestead not exceeding $1,000 in value; the wife may make demand if the husband refuse, but neither can make such demand if the other has a homestead.

Interest.—The legal rate is six per cent. Parties may contract in writing for eight per cent. No penalty is attached for the violation of the law. If a contract is made for a higher rate than eight per cent., the contract as to interest is void, and the recovery is limited to the principal sum and six per cent. Interest is computed upon judgments and decrees at the rate specified in the instrument upon which said judgment or decree is rendered. Interest is not recoverable on open running accounts, when there are no circumstances from which an agreement to allow interest can be inferred, and there has been no vexatious delay of payment. Open accounts draw interest after statement is made and account rendered. Interest from and after maturity may be allowed on items of wages or salary, payable monthly.

JUDGMENTS—Are a lien on real property of defendant within the county, which lien continues for five years. If execution be not levied within one year from the rendition of the judgment, said judgment shall not operate to the prejudice of any other *bona fide* judgment creditor.

LIMITATION OF SUITS—Upon contracts not in writing, express or implied, six years; specialty or any agreement in writing, fifteen years; real actions, twenty-one years. An action may be taken out of the statute by part payment, acknowledgment, or promise *in writing*.

MARRIED WOMEN—Retain all their separate property, real and personal, owned at marriage or acquired thereafter, with all the rents, incomes and profits thereof. Wife can contract for the improvement, repair and cultivation of her real estate, and may lease the same for not exceeding three years. A married woman engaged in business may sue and be sued alone, and her separate property is liable for any judgment rendered against her. The husband must unite in all deeds and mortgages of the wife's separate real estate. A widow is entitled to dower in all real estate owned by her husband during her coverture. A married woman's separate property cannot be charged with her general engagements unless by a contract valid in law to bind the same, or such facts as make it between the parties just and equitable.

A debt incurred by a married woman for her benefit or that of her separate estate, and upon its credit, and the giving of a note therefor, are facts from which a court of equity may imply and enforce a charge against such property.

MORTGAGES—Must be executed as deeds, and the first mortgage recorded has the preference. Are foreclosed by suit in the Court of Common Pleas, and there is no redemption of lands sold under foreclosure. Chattel mortgages, or a true copy thereof, must be deposited with the Clerk of the township where the mortgagor resides, and are void unless re-filed within thirty days of the expiration of one year from their execution, and annually thereafter.

NOTES AND BILLS OF EXCHANGE.—All bonds, notes and bills payable at a day certain after date, or after sight, are entitled to three days of grace in the time of payment. When the third day of grace is the first day of the week, the demand shall be made on the next preceding business day. The first day of January, the 4th day of July, the 25th of December, and any day appointed or recommended by the Governor of Ohio, or the President of the United States, as a day of Fast or Thanksgiving, is treated and considered as the first day of the week. When the 1st day of January, 4th day of July, or the 25th day of December shall be the first day of the week, the succeeding Monday is also treated and considered as the first day of the week. When made payable to order or bearer, they are negotiable by indorsement thereon, and vest the title thereof in indorsee.

SUITS.—There is but one form of action, known as a civil action, which must be prosecuted in the name of the real party in interest, except as to administrators, trustees, etc. In certain cases service may be made by publication.

TAXES—Are due on December 20th of each year, but the party charged may at his option pay one-half then and the remainder on or before June 20th following. Lands delinquent for three semi-annual instalments are sold by the County Treasurer. Owner can redeem within two years by paying amount for which the land was sold, all subsequent taxes and interest, and a penalty of fifteen per cent. if redeemed within one year, and twenty-five per cent. if within two years.

OHIO FORMS.

FORM FOR PROOF OF ACCOUNT FOR SUIT IN OHIO.

STATE OF ——,
County of ——, } ss.
City of ——,

——, of lawful age, being duly ——, says that he is (of firm, state name, and names of all members), —— claimant; that the annexed account against —— is just, true and correct, and is a true transcript thereof from the books of original entry of the said ——; that it is for goods sold and delivered —— by the said —— to the said —— at —— request, at the dates and for the prices therein specified; that there is due thereupon, from said —— to said ——, the sum of —— dollars, besides interest from and after ——, no part of which has been paid, and that there is no just or legal off-set, credit or counterclaim against said sum of —— to deponent's knowledge and belief.

....

Sworn to and subscribed before me —— a (official title as Commissioner, Notary or Justice of the Peace, if J. P. his official character should be certified) this the day of ——, A. D. 18—, at ——

{ Official Seal. } WITNESS my hand and official seal, on the day and year, and at ——

——————

AFFIDAVIT IN PROOF OF CLAIM AGAINST INSOLVENT DEBTOR IN OHIO.

(Ohio Rev. Stat., Sec. 6354.)

THE STATE OF ——,
County of ——, } ss.

BEFORE ME personally appeared ——, who being duly sworn, says that he is (a member of the firm of ——, composed of ——) —— the owner— of the claim hereto attached; that said claim is just and lawful; that the consideration therefor is (state it, viz: goods sold and delivered, &c.) —— that there is now due and unpaid on said claim the sum of $—— with interest thereon at the rate of —— per cent. per annum from the —— day of ——, 18—; that there are no set-offs nor counter claims whatever against the same, and that said owner— ha— no security whatever for the same, (or, if he has collateral or personal security, state it.)

Affiant ———.

Sworn to before me, and signed in my presence, this —— day of ——, A. D. 18—.

[SEAL.] A. B. (Commissioner for Ohio, or N. P.) ——

AFFIDAVIT TO CLAIM AGAINST DECEDENT'S ESTATE IN OHIO.

(Revised Stat. Ohio, Sec. 6092.)

STATE OF ———,
County of ——, }
City of ——.

A. B., being first duly sworn, says that —— the above annexed claim against the estate of ——, deceased, is true and correct as stated, that it is justly due and unpaid, that there is due to —— from the said estate —— thereon, the sum of ($—) —— dollars; that no payments have been made thereon, and that there are no set-offs against the same, to the knowledge of deponent.

....

Sworn to and subscribed before me, this —— day of ——, 18—.

[SEAL.] (C. D. Commissioner for Ohio, or N. P.)

OHIO DEED. MORTGAGE SAME EXCEPT PROVISO OR DEFEASANCE.

(Ohio Revised Stat., Sec. 4106, &c.)

Know all Men by these Presents:

That A. B. and C. D., his wife, of ——, in consideration of —— dollars, to —— paid by E. F., of ——, the receipt whereof is hereby acknowledged, do hereby grant, bargain, sell and convey to the said ——, heirs and assigns forever. ———— (Here describe property), and all the estate, title and interest of the said ——, either in law or in equity, of, in, and to the said premises: Together with all the privileges and appurtenances to the same belonging: To have and to hold the same to the only proper use of the said —— heirs and assigns forever, and the said —— for ——, heirs, executors and administrators, do hereby covenant with the said —— heirs and assigns, that —— the true and lawful owner of the said premises, and ha— full power to convey the same; and that the title so conveyed is clear, free and unincumbered: and further, that —— will warrant and defend the same against all claim or claims of all persons whatsoever.

In Witness Whereof, the said A. B. and C. D., his wife, who —— hereby release —— right and expectancy of dower in the said premises, ha— hereunto set —— hand and seal——, this —— day of ——, in the year of our Lord, one thousand eight hundred and ——

Signed, sealed, acknowledged and delivered in presence of us

....[SEAL.]

....[SEAL.]

(Two witnesses.)

[Form 1.—ACKNOWLEDGMENT.]

STATE OF OHIO,
—— County. } ss.

Be it Remembered, That on this —— day of ——, A. D. 18—, before me, the subscriber, (a Notary Public or Justice of the Peace) personally came —— and —— his wife, who acknowledged the signing and sealing of the foregoing instrument to be their voluntary act and deed, for the uses and purposes therein expressed.*

And the said —— wife of the said —— being examined by me, separate and apart from her said husband, and the contents of said instrument made known and explained to her by me, did declare that she did voluntarily sign, seal, and acknowledge the same, and that she was still satisfied therewith, as her free act and deed, for the uses and purposes therein mentioned.†

† This clause is omitted where acknowledgment is by an unmarried person.

In Witness Whereof, I have hereunto set my hand and affixed my official (Notarial) seal, on the day and year last above written. J. A. K. N. P. or J. P.

* The above form down to the asterisk, answers for a single or many unmarried persons.

[Form 2.—AFFIDAVIT TO ACCOUNT.]

STATE OF OHIO,
County of ——. } ss.

—— being duly sworn, says the foregoing is a true and correct copy of his account against the estate of ——, deceased, as copied from his (or their) books of original entry, and is due and unpaid, and that he holds no collateral or other security therefor, nor are there any credits thereon (except as therein stated.)

Sworn to and signed by —— before me this —— day of —— A. D. 18—.

J. A. K. *N. P. or J. P.*

[Form 3.—ARTICLES OF AGREEMENT.]

This Article of Agreement entered into this —— day of —— A. D. 18—, by and between —— of the first part, and —— of the second part, witnesseth:

(Here state the thing agreed upon, with conditions, etc.)

Witness our hands and seals this, etc.)

[Form 5.—FORM OF ARTICLES OF ASSOCIATION FOR FORMING A CORPORATION.]

We, the undersigned, hereby associate ourselves together for the purpose of forming a corporation under the laws of the State of Ohio.

1. The name of this association shall be the ——
2. This association shall be located in ——, Ohio.
3. It is formed for the purpose of —— (here state object.)
4. (Here state capital, number of shares, etc.)

In witness, we have hereunto set our hands and seals, this —— day of ——, 18—.

(Form 7—INSTUCTIONS FOR TAKING DEPOSITIONS).

(CAPTION).

" Depositions of witnesses taken in a cause pending in a Court of (here name the Court in which the suit is pending) wherein —— is plaintiff, and —— defendant, and for said plaintiff [or defendant, as the case may be], in pursuance of the notice hereto attached." [Here state which of the parties was present].

"A. B., of the County of ——, of lawful age, being first duly sworn [or affirmed] by me, as hereinafter certified, deposes and says." (Here insert the depositions, either by stating the facts in a narrative form or in the form of answers to questions first written down).

If more than one witness, the next deposition may be commenced immediately below the preceeding, as follows:

" Also C. D., of ——, of lawful age, being," etc , (same as in first deposition).

At the end of the whole, the certificate of the officer must be annexed, and may be as follows:

CERTIFICATE TO DEPOSITIONS.

"I. E. F. (naming the official character of the officer), do hereby certify that the above named [naming all the witnesses] were by me first duly sworn (or affirmed) to testify the truth, the whole truth, and nothing but the truth, in the above entitled cause, and that the foregoing depositons by them respectively subscribed were reduced to writing by me and subscribed by the said witnesses in my presence [or if by any other person, here insert his name, and state that he was a disinterested person, and they were written in the presence of the officer), and were taken at time and place in the inclosed notice specified. In testimony whereof, I have hereunto set my hand (if the officer have a seal add) and official seal this —— day of ——, A. D., 188 —,"

Signature.

[Sign, stating official character].

If adjournments, instead of the words " and were taken at the time and place in the inclosed notice specified," insert " and were commenced at the time and place in the notice specified, and continued by adjournment from day to day, at the same place, and between the same hours, as in the notice specified, and for the reasons above stated."

The sealed package containing the deposition should be addressed to " The Clerk of the Court of (naming the Court in which the suit is pending), at ——, Ohio." Across the seals write: " Depositions in the case of A. B. *vs* C. D. taken, sealed up addressed, and transmitted by me." [Signed, with official character. The address should be " To —— the Clerk of the —— Court of ——, County ——, Ohio.

LAWS OF OREGON

RELATIVE TO THE

COLLECTION OF DEBTS, Etc.

Prepared expressly for J. A. Graft & Co.'s Legal Directory, by S. R. Hammer, Attorney and Counselor-at-Law, Salem, Oregon.

ACTIONS.—Actions must be brought in the name of the real party in interest, upon notes and accounts, within six years; upon instruments under seal, judgments and for the recovery of land, ten years, except in case of infants; femme coverts, prisoners or insane, in which case the time may be extended five years—but not more than one after such disability is removed.

ATTACHMENT—May be had by plaintiff any time after summons issues, for debt upon contract made or payable within the State, not secured, upon giving bond in the amount sued for, surety justifying in double the amount.

ARREST.—The defendant may be arrested in case he is about to leave the State, or in secreting his property with intent to defraud his creditors, or the contract was fraudulent. No female can be arrested for debt.

ASSIGNMENT.—May be made by debtors, for benefit of all creditors, which discharges attachments. Creditors have then three months in which to prove their debt.

COURTS.—Separate supreme court of three judges, and five circuit courts, with one judge each, all elective, and hold their offices for six years. One county judge in each county, elected every four years, and a justice of the peace in each voting precinct, elected for two years.

Justices' courts have jurisdiction of $250, but execution therefrom, cannot reach land. Transcript of judgment may be filed with the clerk of county, and become lien upon land, and may be executed as a judgment of circuit court. County courts have jurisdiction of $500.

Disbursements, but no costs, are allowed in justices' courts. If plaintiff fails to recover $50 in circuit or county court, the defendant recovers costs and disbursments; otherwise, plaintiff recovers them.

DEEDS.—Should be executed out of the State, according to the laws of the place where executed, and acknowledged before a Notary Public, Justice of the Peace or Judge, whose official character and signature must be certified to by a clerk of court of record, under seal. Such clerk must also certify, that it is executed and acknowledged, according to the laws of such place.

EXEMPT FROM EXECUTION.—Books, pictures, musical instruments to the value of $75; wearing apparel, $100; each member of the family, $50; tools, implements, library, one yoke of oxen or one pair of horses, vehicle or harness, necessary to carry on his trade or profession; also food to support such team, if any, for sixty days; owned by a house holder, and in actual use; ten sheep, with one year's fleece, or the yarn or cloth manufactured therefrom; two cows and five swine; household goods to the amount of $300; provisions for animals for three months, and such as is necessary for the support of the family for six months; and one months wages if necessary for the support of family, and a homstead of value of $2,000, by acts of 1882.

INTEREST.—The legal rate is eight per cent. Parties may agree upon ten per cent. per annum.

MARRIED WOMEN—May sue and be sued as sole; own and hold separate property, and may sell the same. Her property is liable for expense and education of family; is entitled to her wages.

PARTIES.—Jointly liable or promissory notes, or other obligations or undertakings, may be sued jointly or severally.

PLEADINGS.—May be verified by the attorney or agent, if the party be out of the county, or the action be on a promissory note or other instrument of writing, and such attorney or agent has possession thereof.

TIME TO ANSWER.—Defendants in County and Circuit Courts have ten days to answer. In Justice's Courts the time is filed by the court, not less than six, nor more than seventy days.

OREGON FORMS.

[Form 1—ACKNOWLEDGMENT].

(Where Husband and Wife join in Conveyance).

STATE OF OREGON, }
County of ——. } ss.

This certifies that on the —— day of ——, A. D., 18 —, personally came before me, a —— in and for said County, the within-named —— and ——, his wife, to me known to be the identical person — described in, and who executed the within instrument and acknowledged to me that —— executed the same for the uses and purposes therein named. And the said ——, on examination separate and apart from her said husband, acknowledged to me that she executed the same freely, and without fear or compulsion from any one.

Witness my hand —— this —— day of ——, A. D., 18—. ——.

NOTE.—For unmarried man or woman, that part relating to wife and separate examination can be omitted. The words "freely, and without fear or compulsion from, *any one*," are important where wife joins.

[Certificate of Clerk of Court to genuineness of signature, and to authority of officer taking.)

(Form 1a—ACKNOWLEDGMENT),

STATE OF —— }
County of—.. } ss.

I, ——, Clerk —— in and for said County and State (being a Court of Record), do hereby certify that —— the person subscribing the annexed certificate of acknowledgment, and before whom said acknowledgment was made, was, at the date thereof, a —— in and for said County and State, duly qualified; that by virtue of his said office he is authorized to take acknowledgments and administer oaths. I further certify that I am acquainted with the handwriting of the said ——, and believe the signature of the said ——, subscribed to the said certificate, is his genuine signature, and that the within and foregoing —— is executed and acknowledged according to the laws of the State of ——.

In Witness Whereof, I have hereunto set my hand and affixed my official seal, this the —— day of ——, A. D., 18 —.

——.

[Form 2—AFFIDAVIT].

STATE OF OREGON, }
—— County. } ss,

I. A. B., do solemnly swear that the foregoing claim is justly due me from the estate of C. D., late of said County, deceased; That no payments have been made thereupon except as above stated; and that there are no just counter claims to the same to my knowledge.

Subscribed and Sworn to before me this —— day of —— A. D., 188 —

Signature.

(Form 3—AGREEMENT).

It is agreed between A. B. of ——, and C. D. of ——, in the State of Oregon, as follows:

The said A. B. is to etc.
The said C. D. is to etc.
The consideration of this agreement is as expressed above, and the reciprocal covenants of the parties.

In Witness Whereof, we do hereto set our hands and seals the —— day of —— A. D. 18—.

A. B. [Seal.]
C. D, [Seal].

[Form 4—ASSIGNMENT.]

I. A. B. of —— County, Oregon, engaged in the business of ——, having become embarrassed, and believing my assetts insufficient to pay all my just debts in the ordinary course of business under proceedings at law, and desiring to secure a just and equal distribution of my property among all my creditors alike, and reposing confidence as I do in C. D. of ——, in said State, do hereby bargain, sell, convey assign and set over to said C. D. all my property, real, personal and mixed, in trust for the uses mentioned in the act of the Legislative Assembly, entitled, "An Act to secure creditors a just division of the estates of debtors who convey to assignees for the benefit of creditors," approved October 18, 1878.

E. F. } *Witnesses*
G. H. } A. B. [Seal.]

[Form 5—AFFIDAVIT FOR ATTACHMENT].

In the —— Court for the State of Oregon, for the County of ——,

—— *Plaintiff*, }
vs, }
—— *Defendant*, }

STATE OF OREGON, } ss.
County of —— }

I, ——, being duly sworn, say, that ——; that the aboved-named defendant is indebted to ——, the above-named plaintiff, in the sum of —— dollars, over and above all legal set-offs and counterclaims; That said indebtedness arises out of the following facts, viz:(State same as in short complaint); that the defendant ——; that the payment of said indebtedness has not been secured by any mortgage, lien or pledge upon real or personal property; that the foregoing sum of —— dollars, for which this attachment is asked, is an actual *bona fide*, existing debt, due and owing from said defendant to said plaintiff; and that this attachment is not sought, nor this action prosecuted, to hinder, delay or defraud any creditor or creditors of said defendants.

Subscribed and sworn, to etc.

[Form 6.—ARTICLES OF ASSOCIATION.]

Know all Men by these Presents, That we A. B., C. D. and E. F., of —— do hereby incorporate ourselves under the General Laws of Oregon relating to Private Incorporations:

FIRST. The name of such Corporation shall be —— and its duration shall be perpetual (or if limited state for what time.)

SECOND. The enterprise, business, pursuit, or occupation of said Corporation is and shall be, etc. (make this full and particular to avoid *ultra vires*.)

THIRD. The principal office and place of business of said Corporation shall be at ——

FOURTH. The amount of Capital Stock of such Corporation shall be —— dollars.

FIFTH. Said capital shall be divided into —— shares of —— dollars each. (If the Corporation is formed for the purpose of navigating any stream or other water, or building any railway, road, canal or bridge, the termini must be stated particularly.)

Witness our hands and seals, etc.
(Acknowledged same as a deed.)

[Form 7.—DEED.]

(For form of Acknowledgments, see title "Acknowledgments" and Form 1.)

In consideration of —— dollars to me paid, I, A. B., hereby grant, bargain, sell and convey (and covenant to warrant and defend) unto C. D. and to his heirs and assigns (insert description) situate in —— County, State of Oregon.

Witness my hand and seal the —— day of ——, A. D. 18— A. B. [SEAL.]

Witnesses: }
E. F. }
G. F. }

[Form 8.—NOTICE TO TAKE DEPOSITIONS.]

(TITLE OF CAUSE.)

——, to A. B., said (defendant or plaintiff) and ——, his attorneys, you are respectfully notified that on the —— day of ——, 18—, at ——, in the County of ——, and State of ——, at the hour of —— o'clock — M., the (plaintiff or defendant) will take the depositions of ——, and ——before A. A., (describing the officer) to be used upon the trial of said action (or suit) when and where you can appear and cross-examine, if you so desire.

Signature.

Form 8a.—FORM OF CAPTION TO DEPOSITION.]

(TITLE OF CAUSE.)

Depositions of —— and —— and ——, witnesses in behalf of plaintiff (or defendant) in the above entitled action (or suit) taken before me, a ——, etc., at etc.——, on the ——, etc., pursuant to notice hereto annexed (or agreement of parties annexed) C. D. appearing as attorney for the plaintiff, and E. F. as attorney for defendant, (or no appearance being made for defendant), to-wit: John Doe, being first duly sworn, testified in answer to interrogatories as follows:

Form 8b —CERTIFICATE TO DEPOSITION.]

STATE OF ——, }
County of ——. } ss.

I, A. B., a (describe his official station) in and for said County, do hereby certify that on the —— day of ——, A. D. 18 –, at my office in —— in said County and State, between the hours of —— and —— of each day, the foregoing depositions of —— and —— were taken before me pursuant to the notice (or agreement) hereto annexed, appearance for the parties being made as stated in the Caption to such depositions; that such depositions were reduced to writing by me; that after being completed, each deposition was read to or by the witness making the same, and subscribed by him. That before proceeding to take such depositions, each of said witnesses was sworn by me to tell the truth, the whole truth, and nothing but the truth in relation to the matters in controversy in said action (or suit).

Witness, etc.

INSTRUCTIONS.

When depositions are completed they must be sealed up in an envelope, directed to the Clerk of the Court or Justice of the Peace where action is pending, and forwarded by mail or other usual mode of conveyance, Title of cause and names of witnesses should be marked on one end of the envelope.

LAWS OF PENNSYLVANIA

RELATIVE TO THE

COLLECTION OF DEBTS, Etc.

Prepared expressly for J. A. Graft & Co.'s Legal Directory.

ACKNOWLEDGMENTS, AFFIDAVITS, ETC.—Out of this State, can be taken by a Commissioner for Pennsylvania, or a Notary Public, under his official seal. Also by any officer so authorized by the laws of the State, wherein the acknowledgment is taken, but he must attach to his certificate of acknowledgment, a certificate from the Prothonotary, or other proper officer of a Court of Record of the county, under the seal of said Court, showing the official character and authority of the officer taking such acknowledgment.

ACTIONS.—On a contract may be begun by a summons, made returnable to the next term of Court. The summons must issue before, but can be served on the return day. After the return of the writ, and ten days after service thereof, if the defendant has not appeared, judgment can be taken against him in default. (Return day's judgments, in default, etc., are regulated by rule of the various Courts throughout this commonwealth.)

A summons from a justice is returnable on a day named therein, not more than eight nor less than five days from the date of the writ, and it must be served at least four days before the day of hearing. If the defendant does not appear, judgment can be taken against him in default. Both plaintiff and defendant can appeal, or *certiorari* within *twenty days* after judgment, but a non-resident plaintiff, before doing so, can be required to give security for costs.

ARREST.—Imprisonment for debt has been abolished, excepting in proceeding, as for contempt, to enforce civil remedies, actions for fines or penalties, etc. When the defendant has been arrested, and after he has suffered an imprisonment for at least *sixty days*, he can be discharged from further imprisonment by the Court of Common Pleas, under the "Insolvent Laws," but such a discharge does not release him from the debt.

ASSIGNMENT.—A debtor can make an assignment of all or any portion of his estate for the benefit of all his creditors, but any preference will make it void.

The assignee must file an inventory and appraisment, verified by affidavit, within *thirty days*, and immediately thereafter give bond in double its amount, and he must file his account within one year. The claims of miners, mechanics, and a few others, are preferred to the amount of $200, but all other claims are paid pro rata. The debtor is not discharged from his debts, by the assignment, but remains liable for an unpaid balance.

A debtor may prefer his creditor, however, by confessing a judgment to him, or by assigning to him specific property as security for, or in full payment of his indebtedness, before making an assignment.

ATTACHMENT.—Can issue, upon proof by affidavit, that the defendant is indebted to the plaintiff, in a sum certain, over and above all set-offs, and has assigned, disposed of, removed or secreted, or is about to assign, dispose of, remove or secrete any of his property, with intent to defraud his creditors; or that the defendant is about to remove from the county, any of his property with a like fraudulent intent, or that he has rights in action, money, stocks, or evidences of indebtedness which he fraudulently conceals; or that he fraudulently contracted the debt for which such claim is made. Provided the plaintiff gives bond in double the amount of his claim, to prosecute the suit with effect.

The attachment can be dissolved, by defendant giving bond in double the amount of plaintiff's claim.

Bills of sale are good between the parties making them, but will not hold as against creditors, unless an actual delivery has been made, and possession retained by purchase.

CHATTEL MORTGAGES—Do not exist in this Commonwealth.

DOMESTIC ATTACHMENT.—Can issue against an absconding debtor. A trustee is appointed, and the debtor's effect taken in charge by him, sold, etc., and the proceeds distributed pro rata among the creditors.

EXEMPTION.—The law exempts from levy and sale upon execution, or distress for rent, the wearing apparel of defendant and his family, the bibles, school books and sewing machines in use in his family, and any other property, real or personal, which he may claim as exempt, to the value of $300. The exemption must be claimed by the defendant, and being a personal right merely, it can be waived by him if he does not wish to take advantage of it.

FOREIGN ATTACHMENT.—A non-resident debtor, who, is not within the county at the time the writ issues, can be attached by his real and personal property, but the defendant, by appearing and giving sufficient bond, can have the attachment dissolved. Foreign attachment can be brought by a non-resident plaintiff also.

INSOLVENT.—None other than treated of under arrest.

Interest.—The legal rate is six per cent. Usurious interest cannot be collected, and if paid, may be recovered back, provided suit is brought therefor within six months. Most of the savings banks are, by special statutes, authorized to loan money at higher rates of interest, but by act of 1878, all banking companies are prohibited from taking more than six per cent. Commission merchants and agents may contract with parties outside the State, for seven per cent. It is not usury for a borrower to contract to pay the taxes upon the money lent, nor to pay a reasonable attorney's fee, in case suit is brought for its collection. Interest is due upon every debt from the time it becomes due and payable. The rate is the same on all debts, whether secured by judgment or not.

Judgment.—Is good for twenty years, but is a lien on real estate, only for five years from its date. Its lien may be continued indefinitely, however, by reviving it every five years. It is not a lien on after-acquired real estate until revived.

Limitation.—Actions on contracts, and on all instruments not under seal, must be begun within six years from the time when right of action accrues. The presumption of payment against instruments under seal arises after twenty years, but this presumption can be overcome by proof of non-payment. Actions for the recovery of real estate must be brought within twenty-one years, except in the case of persons under some legal disability, who can bring their action within thirty years after the right of entry has accrued.

A debt barred by the statute may be revived, by an acknowledgment of it, coupled with a promise to pay, by the debtor, and the promise to pay will be implied, if the acknowledgment of the debt is plain and unambiguous.

Married Women.—Any property owned by a woman at the time of her marriage, or which may accrue to her during her coverture, is her separate property, and is not liable for her husband's debts. He must join with her, in conveying or encumbering her separate real estate. He has his right of "courtesy" in her estate, and she her right of "dower" in his estate, and therefor both must join in the deed of conveyance of either's estate, and the wife must be examined, separate and apart from her husband, and her acknowledgment taken.

Although in general, a married woman cannot make a contract, she can charge her separate estate, for debts contracted by her for necessaries, which have been furnished to her, for the support of herself and family.

Every married woman can secure to herself, her separate earnings, by petitioning the Court of Common Pleas.

Whenever any husband, from drunkeness, profligacy, or any other cause, shall neglect or refuse to provide for his wife, or shall desert her, she shall have all the rights and privileges of a *femme sole* trader, *i. e.*, she can make contracts, engage in business, etc., independent of her husband, and can sue and be sued, without joining him in the action, and her property of whatever kind, and howsoever acquired, shall be subject to her free and absolute disposal.

Negotiable Paper.—In general, notes, checks, and bills of exchange are negotiable, and pass by endorsement, and in the hands of an innocent holder for value, who purchased the same be for maturity, they are clear of all *equities*. Over due notes are not negotiable, and a purchaser takes subject to all *equities* and defenses. Three days of grace are allowed on all negotiable paper, except sight drafts and checks, but if the third day of grace falls on Sunday, or a legal holiday, such paper becomes due on the secular day next preceeding it. The holder of negotiable paper can sue the maker, or the indorser, or indorsers, or either, or all of them at the same time, as he pleases, but the satisfaction of one judgment will satisfy all.

PROOF OF CLAIMS.—Book accounts are prov d by producing the book of original entries, and notes, checks, etc., by proving the signature or indorsement.

A judgment obtained in any other State is conclusive evidence of debt when sued upon, if it is proved by a copy of the record, duly certified, and if the record shows that the defendant was served or appeared.

REPLEVIN.—Is the method by which one person seeks to recover possession of his goods and chattels, which are held by another, but before this writ will issue, the plaintiff must give bond to prosecute his suit with effect.

TROVER AND CONVERSION.—Is brought to recover damages for the wrongful conversion of the goods and chattels of another.

STAY OF EXECUTION.—In general, when a judgment is recovered on a contract, the defendant, by giving security for the debt, or if he be a freeholder, without giving security, is entitled to the following stay of execution, to wit.:

1. On a judgment not exceeding $200, a stay for six months.
2. On a judgment in excess of $200, and not exceeding $500, a stay for six months.
3. On a judgment in excess of $500, a stay for one year. And when the judgment is given by a Justice of the Peace, defendant is entitled to the following stay of execution, to wit:

1. On a judgment in excess of $5.33, and not exceeding $20.00, a stay for three months.
2. On a judgment in excess of $20.00, and not exceeding $60.00, a stay for six months.
3. On a judgment in excess of $60.00, a stay for nine months.

PENNSYLVANIA FORMS.

(Form 1—CERTIFICATE OF ACKNOWLEDGMENT BY HUSBAND AND WIFE

STATE OF PENNSYLVANIA, }
County of —— } ss.

Be it Remembered, that on the —— day of —— A. D., 188 — before me, (here insert name and title of official) duly commissioned in and for said County, came —— and ——, his wife, and acknowledged the foregoing indenture to be there act and deed, and desired the same to be recorded as such. She, the said ——, being of lawful age, and by me examined separate and apart from her said husband, and the contents of said deed being first fully made known to her did thereupon declare that she did voluntarily and of her own free will and accord, sign and seal, and as her act and deed deliver the same without any coercion or compulsion of her said husband.

Witness my hand and seal, the day and year aforesaid.

[SEAL.] *[Signature and title]*.

[Form 1*a*—PROOF BY SUBSCRIBING WITNESS.]

STATE OF PENNSYLVANIA, }
County of —— } ss.

Be it Remembered, that on the —— day of —— A. D., 188 — before me, [here insert name and title of official] duly commissioned in and for said County, personally appeared——one of the subscribing witnesses to the execution of the above indenture, who being duly sworn [or affirmed] according to law, doth depose and say that he did see ——, the grantor above named, sign and seal, and as his act and deed, deliver the above indenture deed or conveyance], for the use and purposes therein mentioned, and that he did also see —— subscribe his name thereunto as the other witness of such sealing and delivery, and that the name of this deponent thereunto set and subscribed as a witness is of this deponent's own proper hand writing.

Sworn [or affirmed] to and subscribed before me the day and year aforesaid.

Witness my hand and official seal.

(SEAL) *[Signature and title.]* *[Signature of Witnesses]*.

——:o:——

A deed thus duly acknowledged or proved may be offered in evidence without further proof. And a deed *must* be acknowledged or proved before it can be recorded. The record of an unacknowledged deed is a mere unauthorized copy, and has no effect whatever.

(Form 2—GENERAL ASSIGNMENT).

This Indenture, Made the —— day of —— Anno Domini one thousand eight hundred and —— between —— of —— in the County of —— and State of Pennsylvania, of the first part, and —— of the same place, of the other part:

Whereas, the said —— is indebted unto divers persons in different sums of money and is at present unable to discharge his just debts, and is willing to assign all his property for the benefit of his creditors.

Now this Indenture witnesseth, that the said —— for and in consideration of the said debts, and also in consideration of the sum of one dollar, to him in hand paid by the said —— the receipt whereof is hereby acknowledged, ha— granted, assigned, bargained and sold, aliened, released and confirmed, and by these presents do —— grant, assign, bargain and sell, alien, release and confirm, unto the said —— his heirs, executors, administrators and assigns, all (here describe the lands) and also all the goods, chattels and effects, and property of every kind, real, personal and mixed of the said —— (except, however, so much as may be exempt from execution).

To Have and to Hold, the same and every part and parcel thereof unto the said ——, his heirs, executors, administrators and assigns, forever: IN TRUST, nevertheless, and to the only uses, intents, and purposes following, that is to say, after paying and discharging the expenses incident to this trust; then he the said —— shall, as soon as convenient, sell and dispose of all the lands, utensils, goods and chattels of him the said ——, and collect and recover all the outstanding claims and debts due to him, the said —— and with the moneys arising therefrom, after deducting his the said —— reasonable costs and charges, shall and do pay the creditors of the said —— their respective just demands in full, if there shall be sufficient assets to satisfy the whole; and if there shall not be sufficient assets to satisfy all the just demands of the creditors in full, then *pro rata* according to the amount of their respective demands without preference as between individuals.

Lastly, should any surplus remain after the payment of the several debts aforesaid, to return the said surplus to the said ——, his heirs, executors, administrators and assigns, and the said —— do hereby nominate and appoint the said —— his true and lawful attorney irrevocable, to ask, demand, sue for, levy, recover and receive, all sum and sums of money to be due and owing, and on receipt thereof in whole or in part, to give aquitances, or other sufficient discharges in the law; to make compromises, or other arrangements that he may deem beneficial to this TRUST, ratifying and confirming hereby, and holding for firm and effectual all and whatsoever he shall lawfully do therein.

In Witness Whereof, the said parties have hereunto set their hands and seals the —— day and year first above written.

Sealed and delivered in the presence of us {

[The above should be acknowledged in the same manner as other deeds. See Deeds].

[Form 3—PROMISSORY NOTE WITH POWER TO CONFESS JUDGMENT].

$ —— —————— PENN., 188 —

—— months after date, —— promise to pay to —— or —— assigns, the sum of —— dollars without defalcation for value received: And—— hereby authorized any attorney of any Court of Record, in Pennsylvania, or any other State, to appear for —— and after one or more declarations filed as of the last, next, or any subsequent term, to confess judgment against —— for the said sum, with release of errors, etc; and —— hereby also waive all stay of execution from and after the maturity of the above note. And —— for —— and —— legal representatives, hereby waive and relinquish unto the said——and——legal representatives, all benefit that may accrue to —— by virtue of any and every law made or to be made, to exempt any of —— property or estate from levy and sale under execution, or any part of the proceeds arising from the sale thereof from the payment of the said moneys or any part thereof.

In witness whereof, ——have hereunto set —— hand and seal the day and year aforesaid.

WITNESS. [SEAL].

[Form 4—AFFIDAVIT TO ACCOUNT].

STATE OF PENNSYLVANIA, } ss.
County of —— }

Before me, the subscriber, ——. a Notary Public [or Commissioner] for the Commonwealth of Pennsylvania] duly commissioned and authorized to administer oaths, affirmations, etc., personally appeared —— of the firm of ——, [or book-keeper for —- as the case may be] who being by me sworn in due form of law, did depose and say that the annexed account against —— is correctly copied from the books of original entry of ——, that the charges were made in said books at or about the time of their respective dates; that the goods for which said charges were made were sold and delivered as charged; that the charges are correct, and the account just and true as stated; that there is now due and owing thereon the sum of —— dollars, with interest thereon from the —— day of —— A. D. 188 —, that no part of said principal sum or interest has ever been paid, or in any manner settled, and that there are no deductions or off-sets of any kind, except such as are therein specified and credited.

[*Signature of affiant*].

Sworn to and subscribed before me, this —— day of —— A. D. 188 —

In Witness Whereof, I have hereto set my hand and official seal, the day and year aforesaid. (*Signature of officer, official title and seal*).

[Form 5—CAPTION TO DEPOSITION].

"Depositions of witnesses produced, sworn [or affirmed], and examined, on the —— day of —— in the year of our Lord one thousand eight hundred and eighty — at the office of —— No. — street, in the city of —— and State of —— under and by virtue of a commission issued out of the Court of Common Please for —— County [as the case may be] to —— directed, for the examination of witnesses in a certain cause depending in said Court, wherein —— is plaintiff, and —— is defendant."

[INSTRUCTION.]

The Commissioner will examine the witnesses separately after administering to each of them an oath or affirmation [in the usual form, or in such form as shall be binding on his conscience] that the answers he will give to the interrogatories and cross-interrogatories (if any) shall be the truth, the whole truth, and nothing but the truth.

The Commissioner will then draw up in writing, the answers of the witnesses to the interrogatories in the following form:

"A. B. (insert residence and occupation), aged —— years and upwards, being duly sworn (or affirmed) and examined on the part of the plaintiff (or defendant) doth depose and say, as follows: 1. To the first interrogatory, he says, etc., (insert the answer). 2. To the second interrogatory he says, etc., (and so through the interrogatories, until all have been answered). If their are cross-interrogatories, the deposition will proceed thus: 1. To the first cross-interrogatory, he saith, etc., [and so on throughout]. Every interrogatory and cross-interrogatory, and each branch and clause thereof, must be answered, if the witness merely declare "that he has no knowledge of the matter inquired of." The witness must sign the deposition, or make his mark, if he cannot write, and the Commissioner will certify opposite the signature or mark, as follows:

Form—*Continued.*

"Examination taken, reduced to writing, and by the witness subscribed and sworn (or affirmed) to, this —— day of —— A. D. 188—, before me, —— *Commissioner.*

(INSTRUCTIONS).

And the Commissioner will also sign his name to each page of testimony. If, in the examination, any paper, exhibit, or document be produced, or referred to, it must be marked by some letter or figure, and further identified by the Commissioner in the following manner: "At the execution of a commission to take testimony, between —— plaintiff, and —— defendant, this paper was produced and deposed unto by —— (here give the witness' name) at the time of his examination, to which the Commissioner and witness will sign their names.

[INTERPRETER.]

If an interpreter should be employed, he must be sworn [or affirmed] that he "will truly and faithfully interprete the oath and interrogatories to —— a witness now to be examined, out of the English language into the — language; and will truly and faithfully interpret an answer of the said witness thereto out of the —— language into the English language." The deposition must also be signed by the interpreter, and the fact certified by the Commissioner.

The Commissioner will indorse his return on the commission thus: "The execution of this commission appears in certain schedules hereto annexed." The fees of the Commissioner should also be indorsed. The depositions and exhibits must be bound up with the commission, some tape passing through and connecting the whole, and securely inclosed in a packet, sealed with the Commissioner's seal, with his name written across, or by the side of the seal. The name of the case must be indorsed on the envelope, and it must be addressed to the Court from which the commission issued. Unless otherwise instructed, it should be returned by mail with the following additional indorsement, (*Form*) "Deposited in the post-office at —— this —— day of —— A, D, 188 —, by me," and this should be signed by the commissioner. No person is allowed to be present during the examination but the Commissioner and the witness, and such disinterested person as the Commissioner may (if he think fit) appoint as clerk. (6 Barr. 449). The instructions should be literally followed, as a slight variance may vitiate the execution of the commission. (See Troubat & Haley's Practice, § 597 *et seq.*)

LAWS OF RHODE ISLAND

RELATIVE TO THE

COLLECTION OF DEBTS, Etc.

Prepared expressly for J. A. Graft & Co.'s Legal Directory.

Assignments and Insolvency.—There is no general insolvent law. Assignments for equal benefit of all creditors are allowed; all preferences are void. Any debtor whose property, real or personal, is attached, may dissolve the attachment by a general assignment for the equal benefit of his creditors.

Three or more creditors, representing, collectively, one-fourth in amount of all claims against any debtor, may, within sixty days of any attachment of his property, or any transfer by him of property, in the way of preference, secure the setting aside of such assignment and transfer, and the appointment of a receiver, to convert the debtor's property and assets into money, and distribute equally among all creditors. Such proceedings do not entitle the debtor to a discharge, which is only obtained by actual release from each creditor.

Attachments.—Attachment process will issue on creditor making affidavit as to his claim, and that debtor is a corporation established out of the State, or has left the State, and is not expected to return in season to be served with process, returnable to the next term of such court, or has committed fraud in contracting the debt on which suit is brought, or in the concealment or disposition of his property, or since contracting the debt on which suit is brought, has been the owner of property, or in the receipt of an income, which he has refused, or neglected, to apply toward the payment of said debt, though requested by the creditor so to do. Personal property of the debtor (unless secured by bill of exchange or negotiable promissory note) in the hands of any person, partnership, or corporation, is subject to garnishment.

Chattel Mortgages—May, like mortgages of real estate, be foreclosed (or redeemed) within twenty years. Record is necessary, in office of clerk of town where mortgagor resides unless possession is taken of the property by the mortgagee. (Gen. Stats., ch. 165, sec. 9.)

No mortgage is good against purchaser, or attaching creditor, unless recorded, or the mortgagee is in possession, or can prove actual notice.

Foreclosure is usually by sale, under powers in the mortgage, but may be effected by possession, for sixty days after breach of condition.

EXECUTIONS—Are returnable at the next term of court after they issue, and can only be stayed by order of the court. There is no redemption of property sold under execution. In default of goods and chattels on which to levy, execution may issue against the body of the debtor, in cases where fraud is alleged.

EXEMPTIONS.—The necessary wearing apparel of a debtor and his family; his necessary working tools, not exceeding $200 in value; his household furniture and family stores, if a housekeeper, not exceeding $300 in value; the bibles, school, and other books in use in his family; one cow, and one and a half tons of hay, of a housekeeper; one hog and one pig, and the pork of same, of a housekeeper; arms, equipments, etc., of a militia man; one pew in church; a burial lot; mariner's wages, until after the termination of the voyage in which same have been earned; debts secured by bills of exchange on negotiable promissory notes; and ten dollars due as the wages of labor, are exempt from attachment and execution. (Gen. Stat., ch. 198.)

INTEREST.—The legal rate of interest is six per cent., but any rate of interest agreed upon between the parties may be taken. Rates on judgments, notes or open accounts, etc., is six per cent., unless a different rate be stipulated by the parties. Interest begins to run on accounts from the expiration of stipulated term of credit, or at a time fixed by usage of trade.

MORTGAGES.—Real estate mortgages are to be executed in the same manner as other deeds, and recorded in the town clerk's office of the town wherein the estate is situated.

Personal or chattel mortgages are to be executed in like manner, and recorded in the town clerk's office, of the town where the mortgagor resides, unless the mortgagee takes and holds possession of the property.

Foreclosure is usually enforced by sale, under power in the mortgage, which enables the mortgagee to sell after ten or twenty days' notice, given by advertisement in public newspaper, twenty days after default.

In the absence of such power, the mortgagee may foreclose in equity, usually within a year, and at small expense, or he may obtain possession of real estate by suit at law in six to nine months, in which case the mortgagor, his heirs, executors, administrators, or assigns, may redeem within three years. Possession of real estate may also be taken by the mortgagee, by peaceable and open entry, in presence of two witnesses, whose certificate thereof is to be recorded, the mortgagor having the right to redeem within three years.

A mortgage of personal property is foreclosed, unless the mortgagor redeem, within sixty days after breach of condition. (Gen. Stat., ch. 165.)

Mortgages are discharged by entry of satisfaction on the face of the record, or upon the mortgage, by the mortagee, or by separate deed of release. (Gen. Stat., ch. 165.)

Mortgages are almost always given to secure promissory note of mortgagor to mortgagee's order described in the mortgage. They are never accompanied by bonds.

NOTES AND BILLS OF EXCHANGE—Are governed by rules and usages of commercial law. The usual three days' grace is allowed (see Syn.'74, p. 242) except on bills drawn at sight, due and payable in this State, which are payable on presentation. (Gen. Stats., ch. 129, sec. 6.)

If the third day of grace be Sunday, or a legal holiday, payment must be made on the day preceeding.

LEGAL HOLIDAYS.—The 4th of July, December 25th, February 22d (if coming on Sunday the day following), May 30, (if Sunday, the day preceeding), and such day as Thanksgiving or solemn fast, as may be appointed by the Governor, General Assembly, the President, or Congress. (Ib., sec. 7.)

Indorsers of commercial paper, are holden on notice from Notary Public in accordance with the usages of merchants, in no way do the statutes of the State regulate it.

RHODE ISLAND FORMS.

[Form 1.—ACKNOWLEDGMENT BY HUSBAND AND WIFE.]

STATE OF ———, } ss.
County of ——. }

Be it Remembered, That on this —— day of ——, A. D. 18—, before me (name and title of officer), personally appeared ———, and ———, his wife: and the said ——— acknowledged the foregoing instrument, by him signed, to be his free and voluntary act and deed; and the said ———, being by me examined privily and apart from her said husband, and having said instrument shown and explained to her by me, acknowledges the same to be her voluntary act, and that she does not wish to retract the same.

In Witness Whereof, I have set my hand and affixed my official seal at ———, the day and year above written.

[L. S.] *(Signature and title of officer)*

[Form 2.—INSTRUCTIONS AND FORMS FOR TAKING DEPOSITIONS.]

A Commissioner or Magistrate, authorized to take depositions, will issue a notification to the adverse party, stating the time and place appointed, and the names of witnesses to be examined, which must be served by a sheriff, or by any impartial and disinterested person, who must make oath to his return. The depositions when taken will be returned under seal to the Court in which the suit is pending, with a certificate, stating the contents and naming the case, indorsed by the Magistrate, over his signature.

FORM OF CAPTION TO DEPOSITION.

STATE OF ———, } ss.
County ——. }

Be it Remembered, That in ———, County of ——, State of ———, on the —— day of —— personally appeared before me at ———, who, being by me first sworn to testify the whole truth, and nothing but the truth, gave the foregoing deposition, which was by me reduced to writing in his presence (or by him reduced to writing in my presence), and by him signed in my presence.

Taken ——— (by virtue of annexed commission at the request of ———, as case may be.) to be used in the trial of an action pending in the ——— Court ——— to be holden in ——— within and for the County of —...., in the State of Rhode Island, on the —— in ———.

The adverse party was duly notified, as appears by return of the notification hereto annexed, and was present [or was not present.]

I further state that I am not attorney or of counsel for either of said parties, nor interested in the result of said suit.

In Witness Whereof, I have hereunto subscribed my name and affixed my official seal this —— day of ——, A. D. eighteen hundred and ——.

[L. S.] [*Signature and title of officer.*]

LAWS OF SOUTH CAROLINA

RELATIVE TO THE

COLLECTION OF DEBTS, Etc.

Prepared expressly for J. A. Graft & Co.'s Legal Directory, by Smythe & Lee, Attorneys and Counsellors at Law, Charleston, S. C.

ASSIGNMENTS.—There are two kinds of assignments for the benefit of creditors: voluntary assignment, and assignment under process. Where a debtor assigns his property for the benefit of his creditors, it is permissable for them to name an agent, or agents, corresponding in number with that of the assignees, to act with them. Within ten days after the assignment, the assignees must call the creditors together. Upon their refusal, or neglect so to do, their estate becomes forfeited, and the creditors have a right to meet and appoint their agent. Before the meeting of the creditors, the assignees can make no sale, or transfer, affecting the assigned estate; but, if the creditors refuse, or neglect to name an agent, the assignees have power to act alone. Two and a half per cent. upon money paid out, and five per cent. upon money received, is the compensation to which the assignees are entitled. They should report to the creditors once every three months. A debtor, reserving nothing to himself from the assignment of his property, can make what preferences he may choose.

A surrender of all his estate entitles a debtor, under arrest or confinement, to his release from such arrest, or confinement. No debtor, who is not a party to these proceedings, is affected by them.

ATTACHMENTS.—Amended code, chapter iv., sec. 250: In an action arising for the recovery of money or for the recovery of property, whether real or personal, and damages for the wrongful conversion and detention of personal property, or in an action for the recovery of damages for injury done to either person or property, against a corporation created by or under the laws of any other State, Government, or country, or against a defendant who is not a resident of this State, or against a defendant who has absconded, or concealed himself, or whenever any person or corporation is about to remove any of his, or its property from this State, or has assigned, disposed of, or secreted, or is about to assign, dispose of, or secrete any of his, or its property, with intent to defraud creditors, (as hereinafter mentioned,) the plaintiff, at the time of issuing the summons, or at any time afterwards, may have the property of such defendant, or corporation, attached, (in the manner hereinafter prescribed,) as a security for the satisfaction of such judgment as the plaintiff may recover; and for the purpose of this section, an action shall be deemed commenced when the summons is issued. Provided, however, that personal service of such summons shall be made, or publication thereof commenced within thirty days.

EXEMPTIONS.—Amendment to Art. II., Sec. 32 of Constitution of 1868: "The General Assembly shall enact such laws as will exempt from attachment and sale, under any means or final process issued from any court, a homestead in lands, whether held in fee or any lesser estate, not to exceed in value one thousand dollars; and every head of a family residing in this State, whether entitled to a homestead exemption in lands or not, personal property not to exceed in value the sum of five hundred dollars. But "no property shall be exempt from attachment, levy, or sale for taxes, or for payment of obligations contracted for the purchase of said homestead, or the erection of improvements thereon."

The homestead right cannot be waived nor alienated; nor can the homestead be sold for any other purpose than the purchase of another homestead.

Claims Against Estates.—As soon as he shall have qualified, the executor, or administrator, must advertise for claims against his intestate's estate which claims must be proved by an affidavit, stating the nature and amount of the debt, and that no part of such debt has been discharged. If the executor, or administrator, entertains a doubt of the debt, the claimant may be compelled to bring suit upon it. The ordinary courts have jurisdiction over such suits, but they cannot be brought within nine months from the death of the deceased. If the administrator neglects to pay, or account, he is liable to suit upon his bond—a bond in double the value of the personal estate being requisite in the case of an administrator. No bond is required of an executor. Administrators must render an annual account before the Probate Court. If they fail so to do, a decree in that court can be had against them. The real estate of the deceased is liable to be levied upon under judgments against the administrator, or executor.

By one month's publication in a county newspaper of their intention to apply for a discharge, administrators and executors can obtain such discharge, after which they are not liable to suit. Claims against an estate must be verified before a trial justice, or notary public, if within the State, and if without, before a Commissioner for South Carolina.

There is no difference between creditors resident and non-resident. Non-resident creditors may qualify as executors, and may be appointed as administrators, upon giving security.

Interest.—Legal rate, seven per cent., but parties can contract in writing up to ten per cent. Usury forfeits all interest.

Insolvents.—To obtain his release from arrest in any civil action in this State, an insolvent must file a petition to the Court of Common Please for that county in which he is confined, setting forth the reason for his confinement, together with a full statement of his real and personal estate. The prisoner will then be brought before the Court, who will likewise direct his creditors to be summoned to appear at some fixed day after the lapse of three months, to show cause, if any, against the discharge of the prisoner. The summons must be by public notice, published for three months in the county newspaper, or, if there be no county paper, then in some paper circulated in the county.

On the appointed day an examination is made touching the facts alleged in the petition, and the prisoner is himself examined concerning them and the disposition he has made of his property, on oath, prescribed by statute, being administered to him. If the prisoner takes the prescribed oath, and the court is satisfied with the truth thereof, it is empowered to give up to the prisoner so much of his bedding, wearing apparel, working tools, and arms for muster, as shall be deemed suitable to his former station and condition in life; and, if he be the head of a family, there shall be reserved to him a homestead and such articles as are exempt from attachment, levy and sale, under the homestead act, subject to these reservations; the court shall order so much of his lands, goods and effects contained in his account, as may be necessary to satisfy the debts with which he is charged, the fees of his jail-keeper, the costs of his prosecution, and all other costs involved in prosecuting and obtaining his discharge, to be assigned to the creditor, or creditors at whose suit such petitioner stands charged, or to such other person or persons as the court shall direct.

PROOF OF CLAIMS.—Proof of claims are alike in form and character, whether held within or without the State. The defendant to suit upon a money demand must admit or deny the claim in a categorical answer; and if he denies it he must prove it. The mode of proving an open account is by producing the books of entry, by establishing the sale and delivery of the goods, or by the admission of the parties charged.

Proof of hand-writing establishes a written instrument. The testimony of witnesses, unable through infirmity to attend, or residing without the county, or more than one hundred miles from the court house, may be taken by commission. Before the defendant begins his defense, the plaintiff, if not resident, may be compelled to give security for costs.

In suit on open account, if an itemized copy of the same be served with the complaint, and the defendant does not answer, then no further proof is necessary, and judgment may be had by default. Such itemized account must, however, be sworn to before a Notary in *this* State, or Commissioner of Deeds for *this* State in any other State. The oath is, "that no part of the same has been paid by discount or otherwise, and that the account is right and true."

SUPPLEMENTARY PROCEEDINGS.—If an execution against a judgment debtor is returned unsatisfied, or, if before execution is returned, it is stated upon affidavit that the debtor has property with which he refuses to satisfy the judgment, he may be required by the judge to appear and answer concerning the same. The debtor may be examined, and other witnesses called by either party. If it appear, through affidavit, that the defendant is about to conceal himself, or to leave the State, the Sheriff may compel his attendance; and, if the judge is satisfied upon examination that there is danger of his so concealing himself, or leaving the State, he may be required to give bond, with surities, for his attendance upon the examination, and for the safe keeping of his property while the proceedings are pending. He may be committed to prison, upon his failure to give such bond.

The judge may order any property of the judgment debtor, whether in his own hands, or in those of another person, except such property as is exempt from levy and sale, and what the debtor earns for his personal service, at any time within sixty days pending the order, to be paid on the judgment.

SOUTH CAROLINA FORMS.

[Form 1.—SHORT STATUTORY FORM OF DEED.]

WITH WARRANTY CLAUSE.

THE STATE OF SOUTH CAROLINA,

Know All Men by these Presents, that I, B. B., of —— in the State aforesaid, have bargained, sold and released, and by these presents do grant, bargain, sell and release unto C. D., all that— [here describe premises] together with all and singular the rights, members, hereditaments and appurtenances to the said premises belonging, or in any wise incident or appertaining; to have and to hold all and singular the premises above mentioned, unto the said C. D., his heirs and assigns forever. And I do hereby bind myself, my heirs, executors and administrators, to warrant and forever defend all and singular, the said premises unto the said C. D., his heirs and assigns, against myself and my heirs, and against any person whomsoever, lawfully claiming or to claim the same, or any part thereof.

Witness my hand and seal this —— day of ——, in the year of our Lord ——, and in the —— year of the Independence of the United States of America.

Witness: ———— } ———— [L. S.]
———— }

[Form 2.—CERTIFICATE OF PROOF BY SUBSCRIBING WITNESS.]

STATE OF ———— }
County of ——— }

Personally appeared before me A. B. and made oath that he saw C. B. sign, seal and deliver the within conveyance, for the uses and purposes therein mentioned, and that he, with H. M. in the presence of each other, witnessed the due execution thereof.

[Signed] A. B.

Sworn to before me this —— day of ——, A. D. ——

[SEAL.] (*Signature and title of officer.*)

Form 3.—RENUNCIATION OF DOWER.]

STATE OF ———— }
County of ——— }

I, F. G., (here insert name and title in full of officer) do hereby certify unto all whom it may concern, that E. B., wife of the within named A. B., did this day appear before me, and upon being privately and separately examined by me, did declare that she does freely, voluntarily, and without any compulsion, dread or fear, of any person or persons whomsoever, renounce, release and forever relinquish unto the within named C. D., his heirs and assigns, all her interest and estate, and also all her right and claim of dower, of, in or two, all or singular, the premises within mentioned and released.

Given under my hand and seal this —— day of ——, Anno Domini ——

[L. S.] F. G. [Signed] E. B.

LAWS OF TENNESSEE

RELATIVE TO THE

COLLECTION OF DEBTS, Etc.

Prepared expressly for J. A. Graft & Co.'s Legal Directory, by Eben T. Fleming, Attorney and Counselor at Law, Nashville, Tenn.

ACCOUNTS.—An account from another county or State, with the affidavit of the plaintiff to its correctness, and the certificate of a Commissioner for Tennessee, or that of a Justice annexed thereto, with the Clerk's certificate as to official character of Justice, is conclusive against the party sought to be charged unless denied under oath. An account from another county may also be verified by affidavit before a Notary Public. Accounts against the estates of deceased persons are proven in the same manner as those against the living. (See Form 1.)

ACKNOWLEDGMENTS.—To authenticate an instrument for registration, its execution shall be acknowledged by the maker, or proved by two subscribing witnesses.

If the person executing the instrument resides, or is within the State, the acknowledgment shall be made before the Clerk or Deputy Clerk of the County Court. If without the State, but within the Union or its Territories, before any Court of Record or its Clerk, a Commissioner for Tennessee, or Notary Public of such State or Territory. If without the Union and Territories, before a Commissioner for Tennessee appointed in the country where the acknowledgment is made, or Notary Public of such country, or consul, minister or ambassador of the United States in such country.

If the acknowledgment is made before a Notary Commissioner of the State, or a consul, minister or ambassador, he shall make the certificate under his seal. If before a Judge, he shall make the certificate under his hand, and thereupon the Clerk of his Court under his seal of office, if there be a seal, or under his private seal, if there be none, as to the official character of the Judge; or the official character of the Judge may be certified by the Governor of the State or Territory, under the great seal of the State or Territory. If before a Clerk of a Court of Record of another State of the Union, and certified by him under his seal of office, the Judge, Chief Justice or presiding Magistrate of the Court shall certify to the official character of the Clerk. (See Forms 2*a* and 2*b*.)

ASSIGNMENTS.—Must be general and for the benefit of all creditors, and registered. No transfer to settle a pre-existing debt is valid unless made more than three months before assignment. (No statutory form.)

CHATTEL MORTGAGES.—Must be registered, in order to be valid against creditors or purchasers for value, without notice.

DEEDS.—Must be written or printed, signed by the grantor, and, if made within this State, acknowledged before two attesting witnesses. or before the Clerk or Deputy Clerk of the County Court, or before a Notary Public. Deeds from other States are proven before a Commissioner for Tennessee, a Notary Public, Judge of Court of Record, and Clerk of such Court, with certificate of Judge as to official character of Clerk. Registration, without proper probate, is invalid. (See Form 2.)

DEPOSITIONS.—Must be written by the deponent, or by the officer taking them, or by some one acting by mutual consent. They must be enveloped, sealed, with the Commissioner's name written across the seal, and directed to the Clerk of the Court where the cause is pending, with the title of the cause endorsed thereon, and may be sent by mail or private conveyance, or by express, in which latter case the Commissioner shall so certify. Depositions may be taken by any Judge, Notary Public, Justice of the Peace, Mayor, Clerk of Court, Commissioner for Tennessee, or any person properly commissioned or appointed by the Court or Clerk, on notice, by consent, or by order of Court. If taken where suit is pending, five days' notice is required. Of witness distant over fifty and under one hundred miles, ten days; one hundred to two hundred and fifty miles, fifteen days; two hundred and fifty to five hundred miles, thirty days. No statutory form of notice. (For caption and certificate, see Form 3.)

EXEMPTIONS.—Homestead, to the value of one thousand dollars, is exempt in favor of heads of families; also a specified amount of furniture and household articles. Wages of mechanics or laborers, to the sum of thirty dollars, is exempt.

INTEREST.—Legal rate is six per cent. per annum. Usurious interest may be recovered by action.

JUDGMENTS.—If not revived. will be barred in ten years. May be obtained on a transcript of a judgment from another State.

WILLS.—Wills of realty must be written during life of testator and signed by him, or by some one for him by his direction, and subscribed in his presence by at least two disinterested witnesses. Wills of personalty are valid, if signed by the testator, without witnesses.

Probate of wills from other States must be proven here according to our laws, and certified as prescribed by Congress. The certified copy of a will so made and recorded in the County where the land lies, shall be evidence and passes title. Witnesses should certify above their signatures that the testator acknowledged the will in their presence, and that they signed their names thereto in the presence of the testator.

TENNESSEE FORMS.

[Form 1.—AFFIDAVIT TO PROVE ACCOUNT.]

STATE OF TENNESSEE, }
——— County, }

Before me (J. P., Notary Public or Clerk), in and for the County and State aforesaid, personally appeared ——— who being duly sworn, made oath that the annexed account exhibiting the sum of ——— dollars against ——— is just and true as stated. That he or she has not received any part of the money stated to be due, or any security or satisfaction for the same, and that all just credits have been given.

Sworn to and subscribed before me, this —— day of ——, 18—. [*Signature.*]

NOTE.—This form is also used for accounts against estates of decedents.

[Form 2.—DEED.]

For, and in consideration of the sum of ——— dollars, to me in hand paid, the receipt whereof I do hereby acknowledge, I, ———, have this day bargained and sold, and by these presents do transfer and convey unto ———, his heirs and assigns, a certain tract or parcel of land as follows: (Here give description.) To have and to hold the said tract or parcel of land, with the appurtenances, estate, title and interest thereto belonging, to the said ———, his heirs and assigns forever. And I do covenant with the said ———, that I am lawfully seized and possessed of said land; have a good right to convey it; and that the same is unencumbered. And I do further covenant and bind myself, my heirs, and representatives, to warrant and forever defend the title to said land, to the said ———, his heirs and assigns, against the lawful claims of all persons whomsoever.

Witness my hand this —— day of ——, 18—.

[Form 2*a*.—ACKNOWLEDGMENT.]

STATE OF TENNESSEE, } ss.
——— County, }

Personally appeared before me ———, Clerk (or Deputy Clerk) of the County Court of said County (or Notary Public in and for said County), the within named ———, the bargainor, with whom I am personally acquainted, and who acknowledged that he executed the within instrument for the purposes therein contained.

Witness my hand, at office, (or witness my hand and official seal) this —— day of ——, 18—.

If the wife joins in the deed, after the word "contained" add the following: "And ———, wife of the said ———, having appeared before me privately and apart from her husband, the said ———, acknowledged the execution of the said deed to have been done by her freely, voluntarily, and understandingly, without compulsion or constraint from her said husband, and for the purposes therein expressed."

[Form 2b.—ACKNOWLEDGMENT.]

Before Clerk of County Court by witnesses:
STATE OF TENNESSEE, } ss.
—— County. }

Personally appeared before me — Clerk of — or deputy Clerk — of the County Court of — County aforesaid, — and —, subscribing witnesses to the within deed, who being first sworn, deposed and said that they are acquainted with — the bargainor, (or as the case may be) and that he acknowledged the same, in their presence, to be his act and deed upon the day it bears date (stating the time or period by witnesses).

Witness my hand at office, this — day of —, 18—. (*Signature.*)

NOTE.—The above Form must be varied to suit various modes of proof by witnesses, dependent upon the state of each case, as where a witness may not reside in the State, and the other witness may. The signature of the non-resident witness may be proven by another. Code 2066.

[Form 3.—DEPOSITIONS.]

The caption and certificate prescribed is as follows:

[A. B. vs. C. D.] In the — Court —— County State of —— Depositions of — and —— witness for (plaintiff or defendant) at— in the above case, taken upon notice (or interrogatories) on the — day of —, 18—, at — in the presence of the plaintiff and defendant (as the case may be). The said witness —— aged — being duly sworn, deposed as follows:

The closing certificate is as follows:

The foregoing depositions were taken before me, as stated in the caption, and reduced to writing by me (or by the witnesses in my presence). And I certify that I am not interested in the cause, nor of kin or counsel to either of the parties, and that I sealed them up and delivered them (or put them in the post-office, or delivered to express), without being out of my possession, or altered after they were taken. Given under my hand the — day of —, 18—.

[Form 4.—CHATTEL MORTGAGE.]

I hereby convey to A. B., the following property (describe the property), to be void upon condition that I pay, etc.

[Form 5.—MORTGAGE.]

I hereby convey to A. B. the following land, (describing it) to be void upon condition that I pay, etc.

[Form 6.—DEED OF TRUST.]

For the purpose of securing to A. B. a note of this date, due at twelve months, with interest from date, (or as the case may be), I hereby convey to C. D., in trust, the following property, (describing it); and if the note is not paid at maturity, I hereby authorize C. D. to sell the property herein conveyed (stating the manner, place of sale, notice, etc.,) to execute a deed to the purchaser, to pay off the amount herein secured, with interest and cost, and to hold the remainder subject to my order.

LAWS OF TEXAS

RELATIVE TO THE

COLLECTION OF DEBTS, Etc.

Prep red expressly for J. A. Graft & Co.'s Legal Directory, by Breneman & Bergström, Attorneys at Law, San Antonio, Tex.

ASSIGNMENTS.—Assignments by any insolvent debtor; or in contemplation of insolvency, must provide for a distribution of all his estate, other than that exempt by law from execution, among all his creditors, in proportion to their respective claims, and however expressed shall be so construed, and shall be acknowledged, certified and recorded, as are other conveyances of property.

He shall annex an inventory containing following statement:

1. A full account of all creditors.
2. Residence of each creditor, or if not known, fact stated.
3. Sum owing each creditor, and nature of debt.
4. True cause, and consideration of each debt, and where it arose.
5. Statement of any security for any debt.
6. A full and true inventory of all the debtor's estate, and all vouchers and securities, and value thereof.
7. An affidavit made by the debtor shall be annexed, that the same is in all respects just and true.

A debtor may make an assignment for such of his creditors only as will accept their *pro rata* of the assignor's property in full payment of their claims, provided that the debtor shall not be released unless the creditor realizes 33⅓% of his claim. Assignee shall, within thirty days, give notice of his appointment in newspaper, and give personal notice, or notice by mail, to each creditor. The creditors who consent in writing, within four months after publication, alone receive or take benefit; provided, any creditor who had no notice, may make known assent at any time, and provided, that the receipt of any portion of his claim, shall be conclusive evidence of assent of any creditor.

Assignee shall at once record assignment, and make bond, with good securities. Every consenting creditor shall, within six months from first publication of notice, file with the assignee a distinct statement of his claim, supported by affidavit, that the statement is true, that the debt is just, and that there are no credits or off-sets, that should be allowed against the claim, except as shown by the statement, and no creditor takes benefit who fails to do this. Any creditor not consenting, may garnishee assignee for any balance in his hands, after paying creditors who consent. All property conveyed by assignor previous to, and in contemplation of the assignment, with intent to defeat, delay, or defraud creditors, or give preference, shall pass to the assignee. Every lien given by owner upon goods exposed to sale, in regular course of business, contemplating a continuance, and control of business, and possession of goods by owner, shall be deemed fraudulent and void.

ATTACHMENTS.—Judges and clerks of the District and County Courts, and Justices of the Peace, may issue writs of original attachment, upon the plaintiff, his agent or attorney, making affidavit:

1. That defendant is justly indebted to plaintiff, and the amount, and
2. That defendant is not a resident of the State, or is a foreign corporation, or acting as such; or

3. That he is about to remove permanently out of the State, and has refused to pay or secure the debt due the plaintiff; or

4. That he secretes himself so that the ordinary process of law can not be served upon him; or

5. That he has secreted his property, for the purpose of defrauding his creditors; or

6. That he is about to secrete his property for the purpose of defrauding his creditors; or

7. That he is about to remove his property out of the State, without leaving sufficient remaining to pay his debts; or

8. That he is about to remove his property, or a part thereof, out of the county where the suit is brought, with intent to defraud his creditors; or

9. That he has disposed of his property, in whole or in part, with intent to defraud his creditors; or

10. That he is about to dispose of his property, with intent to defraud his creditors; or

11. That he is about to convert his property, or a part thereof, into money, for the purpose of placing it beyond the reach of his creditors; or

12. That the debt is due for property, obtained under false pretences.

The affidavit shall further state:

1. That the attachment is not sued out for the purpose of injuring or harrassing the defendant; and

2. That the plaintiff will probably lose his debt unless such attachment issues.

Suit must be first brought. May be sued out on debt not due, but final judgment not rendered until debt is due. Plaintiff required to give bond in double amount of debt. Any person claiming property may give claimant's bond, make affidavit, and try the right of property.

Exemptions.—Property reserved to every family from forced sale. The homestead of the family. The homestead shall consist of two hundred acres of land in the country, which may be in one or more parcels, with the improvements; in a city, town or village, of a lot or lots, not to exceed in value five thousand dollars, at the time of their designation, as the homestead, without reference to the value of any improvements, provided it is used for the purpose of a home, or the place of business for the head of a family.

All household and kitchen furniture; any lots in a cemetery for sepulchre; all implements of husbandry; all tools, apparatus, and books of any profession or trade; the family library, and all family portraits and pictures; five milch cows and calves; two yoke of work oxen, with necessary yokes and chains; two horses and one wagon, one carriage or buggy; one gun; twenty hogs; twenty head of sheep; all saddles, bridles, and harness necessary for the use of the family; all provisions and forage on hand for home consumption, and all current wages for personal services. Exempt to persons not constiuents of a family: A lot or lots in a cemetery, held for the purpose of sepulchre, all wearing apparel; all tools, apparatus, and books, belonging to any trade or profession; one horse, saddle and bridle; current wages for personal services. Exemption of homestead does not apply.

Where the debt is due:

1. For purchase money.
2. For taxes.
3. For improvements, but must be contracted for in writing, and executed and acknowledged by husband and wife, and acknowledgment of wife taken privately and apart from her husband.

JUDGMENT LIENS.—Any judgment, an abstract of which has been recorded and indexed in the County Court Clerk's office, from the date of such record and index, operates a lien upon all real estate then owned, or afterwards required, by the defendant in the county.

Such abstract shall show:

1. The names of plaintiff and defendant.
2. The number of the suit.
3. The date of the judgment.
4. The amount for which it was rendered, and the amount still due from the same.
5. The rate of interest, if any is specified, in the judgment.

RIGHTS OF MARRIED PERSONS.—All property owned or claimed by the husband before marriage, and that acquired afterwards, by gift, devise, or descent, as also the increase of all lands thus acquired, shall be his separate property. All property of the wife, owned or claimed by her before marriage, and that acquired afterwards, by gift, devise, or descent, as also the increase of all lands thus acquired, shall be the separate property of the wife; but the husband has sole management of it. All property acquired by either during marriage, except as above, is common property, and is disposed of by the husband only. The wife may contract debts for necessaries for herself and children, and for the benefit of her separate property, but she can not make any other contract, by which she or her separate property will be liable. Separate property of husband, where no wife survives, descends to his children, or, if no children, to his next of kin; if the wife and children survive, the wife takes one-third of the personal estate, and an estate for life in one-third of the land. The separate estate of the wife descends in like manner. Each party to the community is seized of one undivided half of the property comprising the mass.

Upon the dissolution of the marriage relation by death, all the common property goes to the survivor, if the deceased have no child or children; but if the deceased have a child or children, the survivor shall be entitled to one-half of said property, and the other half shall pass to the child or children of the deceased.

A married woman can not contract as a partner in business nor embark her separate means in trade.

INTEREST.—Legal rate, eight per cent per annum. By written contract conventional interest may be agreed upon, not to exceed twelve per cent. per annum. Usurious contracts are void for the interest, and the principal only can be collected. Usury must be specially pleaded under oath.

LIMITATION OF ACTIONS.—*Two years*, open accounts, except between merchants, their agents and factors; *four years*, notes and other written instruments, foreign judgments, and open accounts between merchant and merchant, their factors and agents; *ten years*, record judgments.

TEXAS FORMS.

(Form 1—AFFIDAVIT TO PROVE AN ACCOUNT).

THE STATE OF ——, }
County of ——, }

Before me, ——, a Notary Public, in and for said County of ——, duly commissioned and qualified, on this day personally appeared ——, who being duly sworn, on oath says ——; that the foregoing and annexed account in favor of ——, and against ——, showing an amount due of $ —, † is, within the knowledge of affiant, just and true and unpaid, that the said sum of $ —— is now due and owing to ——, and that all just and lawful off-sets, credits and payments have been allowed.

(*Affiant's signature.*)

Sworn To and Subscribed Before Me, To certify which, I hereunto sign my name and affix my seal of office, this the —— day of ——, A. D., 188 —.

——, (*title.*)

(Form 5—ADDITIONS FOR AFFIDAVIT TO CLAIM AGAINST AN ESTATE).

Follow form No 1 to † , and proceed as follows: "is just, and that all legal off-sets, payments and credits known to affiant have been allowed." "Sworn to," etc., as in form 1.

If other than owner makes affidavit, add after *allowed* "and that affiant is cognizant of the facts contained in this affidavit."

(Form 2—ACKNOWLEDGMENT),

THE STATE OF ——, }
County of ——. }

Before me, ——, a Notary Public, in and for the County of ——, on this day personally appeared ——, known to me to be the person — whose name —— subscribed to the foregoing instrument, and —— acknowledged to me that —— executed the same for the purposes and consideration therein expressed.

Given Under My Hand, and seal of office, at ——, this —— day of ——, A. D., 188 —.

——, (*title*).

Form 3—ACKNOWLEDGMENT OF MARRIED WOMEN.

THE STATE OF ——, }
County of ——. }

Before me, ——, a Notary Public, in and for the County of —— on this day personally appeared ——, wife of ——, known to me to be the person whose name is subscribed to the foregoing instrument, and having been examined by me privily and apart from her husband, and having the same fully explained to her, she, the said ——, acknowledged such instrument to be her act and deed, and declared that she had willingly signed the same for the purposes and consideration therein expressed and that she did not wish to retract it.

Given Under My Hand, and seal of office, at ——, this —— day of ——, A. D., 188 —.

——, (*title*).

Form 4—PROOF BY SUBSCRIBING WITNESS.

THE STATE OF ——, }
County of ——. }

Before me, ——, a Notary Public, in and for said County of ——, on this day personally appeared ——, known to me to be the person whose name is subscribed as a witness to the foregoing instrument of writing, and after being duly sworn by me, stated on oath that ——, the grantor — or person — who executed such instrument of writing, —— acknowledged in his presence that —— had executed the same for the purposes and consideration therein expressed, and that he, the said —— together with ——, had signed the same as witnesses at the request of said grantor—.

Given Under My Hand and seal of office, at ——, this —— day of —— A. D., 188 —.

——, (*title.*)

(Form 6—BOND AND AFFIDAVIT FOR ATTACHMENT).

——, Plaintiff, }
No, ——. *vs.* } SUIT PENDING IN THE —— COURT, OF THE STATE OF
——, Defendant. } TEXAS IN AND FOR THE COUNTY OF ——.

Know all Men by these Presents, That we, the undersigned ——, principal, and —— and ——, as sureties, do hereby acknowledge ourselves bound to pay to —— the sum of —— dollars, conditioned that the above bound ——, plaintiff— in attachment against the said ——, defendant—, will prosecute —— said suit to effect, and that —— will pay all such damages and costs as shall be adjudged against —— for wrongfully sueing out such attachment.

Witness our Hands, this —— day of ——, 18—.

——.
——.
——.

Approved: ——.

AFFIDAVIT FOR ATTACHMENT.

Before me, The undersigned authority, this day, personally appeared ——, plaintiff in the above entitled and numbered cause, who, being by me duly sworn, deposes and says that ——, the defendant —— justly indebted to —— in the sum of —— dollars, due and payable on the —— day of —— A. D., 18—, with interest on said sum, from the —— day of —— A. D., 18—, at the rate of —— per cent. per annum to this date; that the said ——, and that this attachment is not sued out for the purpose of injuring or harrassing, the defendant and that the plaintiff— will probably lose —— debt unless such attachment is issued.

Sworn to and Subscribed before me, This —— day of ——, 18—.

[*Signature of Officer*]. [*Signature of Affiant*].

[Form 8—BOND FOR COSTS].

THE STATE OF TEXAS,
County of ——
——, Plaintiff,
No. ——. *vs.*
——, Defendant.

SUIT PENDING IN —— COURT OF —— COUNTY, —— TERM, A. D. 18—.

Know all Men, That we, ——, and —— as sureties, do hereby acknowledge ourselves bound to pay to —— the sum of —— dollars.

Conditioned, That ——, plaintiff in the above entitled suit, will pay all costs that may be adjudged against —— in said suit, during the pendancy or at the final determination thereof.

Witness, our hands and scrolls for seals, this —— day of ——, A. D., 18—.

——. [SEAL].
——. [SEAL].

Approved: ——.
——. *Clerk* —— *Court*, —— *County*,

[Form 9—NOTICE OF FILING INTERROGATORIES].

——, Plaintiff,
No. ——. *vs.*
——, Defendant

SUIT PENDING IN THE DISTRICT COURT OF THE STATE OF TEXAS, IN AND FOR THE COUNTY OF ——.

To the —— in the above styled cause or ——, Attorney of Record:

Sir: You will take notice that five days after the service hereof, I shall apply to the Clerk of the above named Court for a commission to take the depositions of —— who resides in ——, in answer to the interrogatories hereto attached, to be read in evidence in behalf of the —— on the trial of said cause.

——.
——.

[Form 10—COMMISSION TO TAKE DEPOSITION OF NON-RESIDENT].

The State of Texas, To the Clerk of a Court of Record, Commissioners of Deeds for the State of Texas, or any Notary Public in and for the County of ——, State of ——

Greeting:

We hereby Authorize and Require you, Or either of you, to summon ——, a resident of your —— to come before you forthwith, and that you then and there carefully and fully examine him upon his oath, first to be taken before you, touching the annexed interrogatories:

1. That you reduce his answers so taken to writing, in proper form, and cause the same to be subscribed and sworn to by said witness.
2. That you certify under your hand and seal of office, that said answers were sworn to and subscribed before you.
3. That you seal up in an envelope the answers so taken, together with the annexed interrogatories, and this commission, with your name across the seal.
4. That you endorse on the envelope the names of the parties to this suit, and the name of said witness,
5. That you direct the package to the "Clerk of the —— Court of —— County, ——Texas.
6. That if said package is sent by mail, the postmaster or his deputy, shall indorse thereon that he received it from your hands, and sign his name thereto; or, if you intrust it to private conveyance as provided by the statute, you will apprise the person receiving it that it must be delivered to the Clerk of this Court, by himself in person; which evidence, so taken as above, is to be used on the trial of a suit now pending in the —— Court of —— County, in said State of Texas, wherein ——, plaintiff —, and —— defendant.

Herein fail not, but make due return of this writ,

Witness, ——, Clerk of —— Court for the County of —— and his seal of office, at ——, this —— day of ——, A. D., 18—.

——, *Clerk of the* —— *Court of* —— *County.*

[Form 10*a*—INSTRUCTIONS AND FORMS FOR DEPOSITIONS].

STATE OF ——, } ss.
County of ——.

—— *Plaintiff*,
vs, } No. ——, in —— Court.
—— *Defendant*,

By authority of the commission directed to me and interrogatories accompanying the same, which are hereto attached, from the Clerk of the —— Court of —— County, State of ——, in the case of —— *vs.* ——, now pending in said Court, I caused to come before me, at my office, at —— County, State of —— aforesaid, the witness therein named, a resident of —— County, State of ——, who being by me duly sworn to speak the truth, the whole truth, and nothing but the truth, in answer to the several interrogatories and cross-interrogatories in said case propounded to him, proceeded to answer the same as follows:

In answer to first interrogatory: [Answer].

Each Witness must sign his Deposition.

[CONCLUSION OF DEPOSITION].

Which answers I caused to be reduced to writing, and they were sworn to and subscribed before me at my office, in the County of ——, State of —— aforesaid, on this —— day of —— ——, 18—, by the said ——. In witness of which I have hereto set my hand and official seal.

(L. S.) [*Official title.*]

The officer will then attach the answers to the commission and interrogatories, and place them in an envelope, which the officer must seal up and write his name across the seal. He will further indorse on the envelope the names of the parties to the suit, and the name of the witness who has given his deposition, as "—— *vs.* ——," "Deposition of ——." He will then direct the envelope to the Clerk of the Court from which the commission issued, as "To the Clerk of —— Court of —— County, State of ——." He will then himself deliver the package to the postmaster, or his deputy, if sent by mail, who will indorse thereon:—

"Received the within deposition from the hands of ——, the officer who took the same ——, *Postmaster.*

[Form 11.—GENERAL WARRANTY DEED.]

STATE OF TEXAS, }
County of ——, }

Know All Men by these Presents: That ——, part—— of the first part, in consideration of ——, have granted, bargained and sold, and do hereby grant, bargain, sell, alien, convey and confirm unto the said ——, part —— of the second part, —— heirs and assigns forever: (Here describe property).

To Have and to Hold, all and singular the above described and conveyed premises and property, with all the rights, privileges, hereditaments and appurtenances thereunto belonging, or in anywise appertaining unto the said ——, part —— of the second part, —— heirs or assigns, forever; and ——, the said part—— of the first part, do hereby bind —— heirs, executors and administrators unto the said part—— of the second part, —— heirs and assigns, the —— well seized of all and singular the said property and premises; that —— ha— good right and lawful authority to make this sale, and conveyance of the same; that said property and premises are free and clear of all and every encumbrance, and that unto the said part— of the second part, —— heirs and assigns, —— and —— heirs, executors and administrators will forever WARRANT AND DEFEND the same against all adverse lawful claim or claims whatsoever.

In Testimony Whereof, —— do hereunto affix —— hand and seal, using scroll for seal, this —— day of ——, A. D. one thousand eight hundred and eighty ——.

Witnesses at request of grantor: ——, [Scroll.]
——, [Scroll.]

ACKNOWLEDGMENT.

THE STATE OF TEXAS, }
County of ——. }

Before Me, ——, in and for the County of ——, on this day personally appeared ——, known to me (or proved to me on oath of ——) to be the person whose name is subscribed to the foregoing instrument, and acknowledged to me that —— he executed the same for the purposes and consideration therein expressed.

Given under my hand and seal of office, this —— day of ——, A. D. 18—.

——, (*title.*)

WIFE'S ACKNOWLEDGMENT.

THE STATE OF TEXAS, }
County of ——. }

Before Me, ——, in and for the County of ——, on this day personally appeared ——, wife of ——, known to me to be the person whose name is subscribed to the foregoing attached instrument, and having been examined by me privily and apart from her husband and having the same fully explained to her, she, th said ——, acknowledged the said instrument to be her act and deed, and declared to me that she had willingly signed the same for the purposes and consideration therein expressed, and that she did not wish to retract it.

Given under my hand and seal of office, at ——, this —— day of ——, A. D. 18—.

(*Signature and title.*)

[Form 12.—APPLICATION AND AFFIDAVIT FOR WRIT OF GARNISHMENT.]

THE STATE OF TEXAS, }
County of — }
———— } IN —— COURT, —— COUNTY, TEXAS.
No.—— *vs.* }
————

Now Comes ——, plaintiff— in the above entitled cause, and making application for a writ of garnishment in said cause on oath says: That the sum of —— dollars, claimed in this suit of and from defendant— is just, due and unpaid, and that the defendant— ha— not, within the knowledge of plaintiff—, property in —— possession within the State subject to execution sufficient to satisfy said debt; and further says that he has reason to believe, and does believe, that ——, who resides in —— County, Texas, —— indebted to said defendant—, or has in —— hands effects belonging to said defendant—, and that the writ of garnishment applied for is not sued out to injure either the said defendant or the garnishee ——.

Wherefore —— pray that a Writ of Garnishment may issue against said ——.

(*Signature of Affiant.*)

Sworn to and subscribed before me this —— day of ——, A. D. 18—.

Clerk —— *Court* —— *County.*

[Form 13.—BOND FOR GARNISHMENT.]

Know all Men by these Presents, That ——, as principal, and —— and —— as sureties, are held and firmly bound to pay ——, defendant in the above entitled cause, the sum of —— dollars, conditioned that the above named plaintiff— will prosecute —— suit with effect, and pay all damages and costs that may be adjudged against —— for wrongfully suing out the Writ of Garnishment issued in this cause.

Witness our hands and scrolls for seals, this, the —— day of —— A. D. 18—.

[SEAL.]
[SEAL.]
[SEAL.]

Approved: ——
——

[Form 14.—DEED OF TRUST.]

THE STATE OF TEXAS, }
County of —— }

This Indenture Witnesseth: Whereas, ——, of the County of ——, State of ——, being justly indebted to ——, of the County of ——, State of ——, in the sum of ——, due by virtue of (here insert conditions of deed), the payment of which, —— with interest as above expressed ——, desirous of securing and assuring at maturity.

In Consideration Whereof, and for and in consideration of the sum of —— dollars, to —— in hand paid by ——, the receipt whereof is hereby acknowledged, —— and by these presents do grant, bargain, sell and convey, to the said —— all certain (describe property,)

To Have and to Hold the said above described property, together with all singular the rights, privileges and appurtenances to the same belonging, or in any way appertaining unto the said —— and to —— assigns forever in trust. That in case —— or —— heirs or representatives do pay to the said ——, or —— assigns, the aforesaid —— and interest at or —— the maturity thereof, then the estate and trust hereby created becomes void ——. But in case of default of such payment of the whole of said —— and interest, or upon default of the payment of either of said —— whenever any one shall become due, the whole debt and all and each and every one of said notes shall be due —— and the said —— shall at any time thereafter, at the request of ——, at public auction, to the highest bidder, for cash, at the Court house door, in the County of —— sell, between the hours of 10 A.M. and 2 P. M., the aforesaid ——, after giving by publication in one of the newspapers printed in ——, —— days notice of the time, terms, and place of sale, and when sold to the purchaser or purchasers thereof make good and sufficient title therefor, in —— capacity as trustee; and should —— fail, refuse or neglect to act, as such trustee, then the said —— shall have the power, and such power is hereby conferred upon —— to appoint a substitute trustee, in writing, under —— hond and seal, and such substitute trustee thereupon shall have the same powers and be subject to the same duties as herein conferred upon or required of the said —— to sell the aforesaid property at public auction, for cash, as aforesaid, and when sold, in his capacity as such substitute trustee, to make good and sufficient title therefor to the purchasers thereof. The proceeds of sale shall be applied by the trustee selling. First, to the payment of all costs and charges, such as the execution of this trust, and —— per cent. for selling; and secondly, in the liquidation and the residue, if any, to be paid over to ——, heirs or legal representatives.

In Witness Whereof —, the said ——, hereto subscribe— —— name and affix —— seal, (using scroll therefor) this —— day of ——, A. D. 18—.

In Presence of ——, we accept the foregoing trust.

——, Trustee. ——, [SEAL.]
——, Trustee. ——, [SEAL.]

LAWS OF UTAH TERRITORY
RELATIVE TO THE
COLLECTION OF DEBTS, Etc.

Prepared expressly for J. A. Graft & Co.'s Legal Directory, by U. J. Wenner, Attorney and Counsellor-at-Law, Salt Lake City, Utah.

ASSIGNMENTS.—No statute providing for assignments by debtor, but are made under the common law.

ACTIONS.—In District Court commenced by filing complaint and issuing summons thereon. If summons served in the county where suit is begun, time to answer or demur, ten days; if served without the county, but in the district, twenty days; in all other cases, forty days. Actions may be brought in, or out of term. In Justice's Courts the defendant must appear and answer the complaint within five days, if the summons is served in the city or precinct in which the action is brought; within ten days, if served out of the precinct or city, but in the county in which the action is brought; and within twenty days if served elsewhere. Jurisdiction of Justice's Courts in any sum less than $300. No Jurisdiction to try title to real estate.

ATTACHMENTS—May be issued at time of service of summons, or at any time thereafter, upon any contract for payment of money not secured by mortgage, lien, or pledge; upon real or personal property, if the defendant is a non-resident, or evades service, or is disposing of his property with intent to defraud his creditors.

BONDS FOR COSTS—May be required of non-resident plaintiff on notice of thirty days, by defendants, and if not given within that time, cause can be dismissed on motion. No bond required, as of course.

BILLS—NOTES.—No special statute. General law merchant controls. No Grace.

COURTS.—1st. Justice Court has jurisdiction in any sum less than $300. Appeal in all cases allowed by bond and two approved sureties, to Distrist Court. 2d. Probate Court has jurisdiction in all estate settlement and guardianship; and in divorce, by a special act of Congress. Appeal to District Court. 3d. District Courts—jurisdiction unlimited; three districts in Territory; Judges appointed by the President. 4th. Supreme Court—composed of three District Judges,—two sessions each year. Appeals from District Courts and original writs.

DEEDS OF TRUST—And mortgages with power of sale, are in common use in this Territory, the preference being in favor of trust deeds, under which sales can be made without foreclosure in court.

ESTATES OF DECEDENTS.—Claims must be filed within ten months after publication of notice of granting letters to administrator. Estate not exceeding $1,500 in value, goes to widow and children absolutely. Preference is given to claims in the following order:

1. Funeral Expenses.
2. Expense of last sickness.
3. All debts which were liens on the property of the decedent at the time of his death.
4. All other demands against the estate.

EXEMPTIONS.

1. Chairs, tables, desks and books to the value of $200.
2. Necessary household, table and kitchen furniture to the value of $300. Also one sewing machine, pictures and portraits, provisions for three months, two cows with their sucking calves, and two hogs and all sucking pigs.
3. Farming utensils and implements of a farmer not exceeding in value $300—Also 2 oxen or 2 horses or 2 mules and their harness

and their food for 60 days; also one cart or wagon; also seed vegetables, etc., actually reserved for planting within six months, not exceeding in value $200.

4. Tools of a mechanic or artisan not exceeding in value $500; the notarial seal and records of a notary public; the instruments and chests of a surgeon, physician, surveyor and dentist, with their professional libraries, and the law professional libraries, and office furniture of attorneys, counsellors and judges, and the libraries of ministers of the gospel.

5. Cabin or dwelling of a miner not exceeding in value $500; also his sluices, tools, etc., not exceeding in value $200.

6. Two oxen, two horses, or two mules, and their harness, and a cart or wagon, dray or truck, by the use of which a cartman, drayman, truckman, huckster, peddler, hackman, teamster, or other laborer habitually earns his living; and one horse with vehicle and harness, or other equipments used by a physician, surgeon, or minister of the gospel, with hay and grain for said horses sufficient for three months.

7. One-half the earnings rendered at any time within 60 days, preceding execution; fire engines, hooks, ladders, etc., arms, ammunition, uniform, equipments, etc.; homestead to head of family, to value of $1,000, and $250 for each member of the family. No exemption to non-residents, or as against an article on a suit for the purchase price.

Executions.—Executions may issue at any time within five years after entry of judgment. Stay in discretion of court. Redemption from foreclosure sale, six months, with sixty days from last redemption.

Interest.—Legal rate, 10 per cent. per annum, but parties may contract at any rate. No usury law.

Incorporations.—Mining, or other companies organized under laws of other State, or Territory, and doing business in Utah, must file with Secretary of Territory, and with Probate Judge of the county wherein their principal office in this Territory is situated, certified copies of their articles and certificate of incorporation, and of their by-laws: also, within sixty days after commencing business in this Territory, must file a designation of some person resident in the county, upon whom process of court may be served. Failure so to file, will deprive any corporation of the benefits of the statute limiting commencement of civil actions.

Limitation.—Open accounts and contracts not in writing, two years; in writing, four years; judgments, five years; in relation to land, seven years. Revivor, new promise in writing, signed by the party to be charged therewith. Suspended during absence from the Territory.

Married Women.—Dower abolished. All property owned by either spouse before marriage, and that acquired afterwards by gift, bequest, device, descent or purchase, together with the rents, issues and profits thereof, is the separate property of the spouse so owning or acquiring it, and can be controlled the same by such spouse as though unmarried.

Mortgage.—Mortgage of real estate, whatever its terms, shall not be deemed a conveyance so as to enable the owner of the mortgage to obtain possession of the property without a foreclosure and sale. But one form of action for the recovery of any debt, or the enforcement of any right secured by mortgage upon real estate, viz: by foreclosure and sale. Judgment may be rendered for amount found due, and the incumbered property subjected to sale, with a right to docket a personal judgment for the balance found due against the mortgagor.

Protest.—Law Merchant governs.

Redemption.—On sale of real property by execution, six months: and, if made by another creditor as redemptioner, sixty days additional to the judgment debtor.

Sales.—All sales of personal property are void as to creditors; unless accompanied by delivery and actual change of possession. Possessory right to mining locations are conveyed as by quit claim deed to real estate. Chattel mortgage allowed.

Taxes.—Due July 1st, annually; delinquent, October 31st. Land sold at public auction, and redeemable within two years from sale. .

Witness.—Party in interest may. Husband and wife can not, in civil cases, be a witness for the other.

[For Utah Legal Forms, see California Forms.]

LAWS OF VERMONT

RELATIVE TO THE

COLLECTION OF DEBTS, Etc.

Revised to Nov. 15, 1881, expressly for J. A. Graft & Co.'s Legal Directory, by Edward B. Sawyer, Attorney and Counsellor at Law, Hyde Park, Vermont.

ACTIONS.—The forms of actions are those prescribed by statute and common law.

ARREST.—In all actions, in form *ex delicto*, the defendant is subject to arrest. A bill is now pending before the legislature to require the plaintiff in all actions in form *ex delicto*, to file with the authority issuing the writ an affidavit stating nature and amount of claim, and that the action is commenced in "good faith" as to its merits, before body arrested.

In all actions, in form *ex contractu*, the defendant is not subject to arrest, except upon the affidavit of the creditor, his agent or attorney, "that he has good reason to believe, and does believe, that the debtor is about to abscond or remove from the State, and has money or other property, secreted about his person, or elsewhere, to an amount exceeding twenty dollars, or sufficient to satisfy the demand upon which he is to be arrested," or in case a party refuses to pay over money which he has in his hands in a fiduciary capacity.

A person not a citizen of the United States, or of this State may be arrested in any action.

ATTACHMENT.—Defendant's property, both real and personal, is liable to attachment on *mesne* process in all forms of action, and may be held to respond to final judgment and execution.

CHATTEL MORTGAGES.—May be made of all personal property. To be valid, the property must be delivered to and retained by the mortgagee, or the mortgage must be recorded in the Town Clerk's office, of the town in which the mortgagor resides, at the time of his making the same, or if he resides out of this State, in the town in which the property is situated, and no property so mortgaged shall be removed from this State, except by consent of the parties to such mortgage, or their assigns.

There must be attached to and recorded with the mortgage an affidavit, signed and sworn to by the mortgagor and mortgagee, stating that the debt secured is a just one, and honestly owing and that the mortgage is given to secure the same.

CORPORATIONS—May be formed by special charter, or by the general laws of the State.

DEEDS—Must be signed and sealed by makers in the presence of two subscribing witnesses, and acknowledged before a Judge, Justice of the Peace, Notary Public, or Master in Chancery, and the person before whom a deed is acknowledged, must add his certificate of the same.

When a wife joins in a deed it is not necessary for her to have a separate examination.

The homestead is not conveyed unless the wife joins with her husband.

The husband must join with the wife to convey her land.

The record of deeds must be made in the Town Clerk's office, of the town in which the property is situated.

A deed made out of the state may be acknowledged according to the laws of Vermont or of the State where executed.

DEPOSITIONS—May be taken before a Judge, Justice of the Peace, Notary Public, or Master in Chancery, and reasonable notice must be given.

The authority taking the same must certify that it was taken to be used in the cause, stating the title and where pending, and the reason for taking it. It must then be sealed up by such authority, and a certificate of the fact written on the sealed package. Great strictness in following the statute requirements is exacted by the courts.

EXECUTIONS—Must be served in sixty days, by levy upon personal property, if any can be found, but if not, then upon real property.

Three disinterested free-holders appraise real estate, and set out, by metes and bounds, enough to satisfy the execution.

The amount of the levy may be paid at any time within six months, otherwise the title becomes absolute in the creditor.

EXEMPTIONS,—The following is exempt from attachment or execution: Homestead of $500, and the rents or products of the same; such suitable apparel, bedding, tools, arms and articles of household furniture as may be necessary for upholding of life, tool chests of mechanics, one sewing machine kept for use, one cow, the best swine, or the meat of one swine, sheep not exceeding in number ten, and one year's product of said sheep in wool, yarn or cloth, forage sufficient for keeping not exceeding ten sheep and one cow through one winter, ten cords of fire-wood, or five tons of coal, twenty bushels of potatoes, such military arms and accoutrements as the debtor is required, by law, to furnish, and also the pistols, side arms and equipments personally used by any soldiers in the service of the United States, and kept by him or his heirs as mementoes of his service, all growing crops, ten bushels of grain, one barrel of flour, three swarms of bees and hives together with their produce in honey, two hundred pounds of sugar, and all lettered grave stones, the bibles and other books used in a family, one pew or slip in a meeting house, or place of religious worship, live poultry not exceeding in amount or value the sum of ten dollars, the professional books and instruments of physicians and the professional books of clergymen and attorneys at law to the value of $200, and also one yoke of oxen or steers, as debtor may select, two horses kept and used for team work and such as the debtor may select in lieu of oxen or steers, but not exceeding in value the sum of $200, with sufficient forage for the keeping of the same through the winter, also one two horse wagon with whiffletrees and neckyoke, or one ox cart as the debtor may choose, one sled or set of traverse sleds either for horses or oxen as the debtor may select, two harnesses, two halters, two chains, one plow and one ox yoke, which with the oxen or steers or horses which the debtor may select for team work, shall not exceed in value $250.00.

INSOLVENCY.—Courts of Insolvency are Courts of record, and the Judge and Register of each Probate District are, ex-officio, Judge and Register of the Insolvent Court of their respective districts. An inhabitant of this State owing debts exceeding the amount of $300, contracted while such inhabitant, may be judged an insolvent upon his own petition, or a person residing in this State and owing debts to an amount exceeding $300, and who commits an act of insolvency, may be judged an insolvent on the petition of any of his creditors whose claims provable exceed $250, but the petition of such creditor must be filed within ninety days after the act of insolvency.

The acts of insolvency set forth are similar to the acts of bankruptcy, as defined in the late bankrupt laws of the United States.

The insolvent's estate is managed by one or more assignees elected by the creditors, but when no choice is made by the creditors, the Judge appoints.

The adjudication of insolvency sets aside all fraudulent preferences and conveyances which take place within four months before the filing of the petition, and dissolves all attachments upon *mesne* process or execution when the property levied upon has not been sold, if levied upon within sixty days prior to the filing of the petition.

The act does not apply to railroad and banking corporations.

Debts due and payable from the debtor at the time of filing the petition, may be proved and allowed at any meeting of the creditors, and debts not payable until a future day may be proved and allowed as if presently payable, with a discount of interest, when no interest, is payable by the contract.

The act provides for the granting of a discharge to the debtor, from all debts existing at the date of the filing of the petition, and also that the debtor shall be absolutely discharged from all debts proved against his estate and from all debts provable and founded on any contract made by him, while an inhabitant of this State, if made within this State, or to be performed within the same or due to any person resident therein at the time of the filing of the petition for adjudication. The discharge does not effect a fiduciary debt. A discharge is not granted unless the assets equal thirty per cent. of the debts, or the consent of a majority in number and amount of the creditors is filed.

The property in this State of the debtor, by him acquired, subsequently to the time of filing of the petition, shall not be subject to attachment by trustee process or otherwise, in any suit to recover a debt which may have been so provable and due to any person or persons not resident in this State at the time of such filing, or founded on any contract existing at the time of said filing, and made, or to be performed out of the limits of this State. Our law is very similar to the Massachusetts law, and decisions of the courts of Massachusetts, which are much more numerous than in this State, are good precedents in our courts.

INTEREST.—Six per cent. Usurious excess is not collectible, and may be recovered back, though paid voluntarily.

LIMITATION.—No acknowledgment will prevent the operation of the statute, unless in writing and signed by the party thereby affected.

Absence from the state of debtor will prevent the operation of the statute during such time, if the debtor has no known property within the State, which might be attached by the common process of law.

Actions for slanderous words and libels, two years. Actions for assault and battery and false imprisonment, three years.

In all actions on debt upon contract, not under seal, excepting debt on judgment all actions of debt for rent, actions of account, assumpsit or on the case founded on contract, expressed or implied, actions of tresspass upon land, actions of replevin or other actions for taking, detaining or injuring goods or chattels, and all other actions on the case, except for slanderous words and libel, six years.

Debt or *scire facias* upon judgment, and debt on specialties, and actions of covenant, eight years.

Attested promissory notes, fourteen years.

MARRIED WOMEN.—A married woman, carrying on business in her own name, may sue and be sued, in all matters connected with such business, in the same manner as if she were unmarried, and execution may issue against her, and be levied on her sole and separate goods, chattels and estate.

Any married woman, whose husband shall desert her, or from any cause neglect to provide for his family, may in her own name, make contracts for her own labor, and the labor of her minor children, and in her own name, sue for and recover her own and their wages.

NOTARIES.—Appointed by Judges of County Court for two years, and have jurisdiction of State.

NOTES AND BILLS.—Entitled to three days of grace.

PRACTICE.—Common law.

SET-OFF.—Existing at the time of bringing a suit, may be pleaded to any action arising on contract.

WILLS.—Every person of full age (women at eighteen, and men at twenty-one), and of sound mind, may devise and dispose of real and personal estate.

Three attesting witnesses are necessary, who shall sign as such at the request and in the presence of the testator, and in the presence of each other, and a will must be in writing.

FORM OF COLLATERAL NOTE.

PROVIDING FOR ADDITIONAL COLLATERAL OR EXCHANGE OF COLLATERAL, WITH POWER OF SALE AND AUTHORITY TO HOLDER TO PURCHASE.

—— ——————188—.

$————

—— after date —— promise to pay to the order of ——, (where payable) ——, Dollars, for value received, negotiable and payable without defalcation or discount, at the ——, with interest at the rate of —— PER CENT. PER ANNUM, after maturity; having deposited with —— collateral security,

[Here describe the collateral securities pledged].

Which —— hereby authorize said —— assigns or legal representatives ——, to sell with or without notice, at —— in the County of ——, State of —— or at public or private sale, at the option of said —— assigns or legal representatives, in case of the non-performance of this promise, and at such sale said —— may become the purchaser of the whole or any portion of said property, applying the proceeds to the payment of this Note, including interests and accounting to —— for the surplus, if any. In case of deficiency —— promise to pay to said ——, assigns or legal representatives, the amount thereof forthwith, after such sale, with interest as above specified. The present Cash Market value of the above collateral security is —— Dollars, and it is understood and agreed: should there be any depreciation in the value of said security prior to the maturity of this Note, such an amount of additional security shall be furnished by —— as will be satisfactory to said ——, assigns or legal representatives, and should such additional security not be furnished within twenty-four hours after demand on —— so to do, then and in that event said ——, assigns or legal representatives, may proceed at once to sell as above specified, the collateral securities herein named; and it is hereby agreed and understood, that if recourse is had to the collaterals, any excess of collateral upon this Note shall be applicable to any other Note or Claim held by said ——, assigns or legal representatives, against ——, and in case of exchange of, or addition to, the collaterals above named, the provisions of this Note shall extend to such new or additional collaterals.

——————.

Witness: —————— ——————.

[For Legal Forms adapted to the Laws of this State, see Forms at end of Laws of Massachusetts and of Virginia.

LAWS OF VIRGINIA

RELATIVE TO THE

COLLECTION OF DEBTS, Etc.

Prepared expressly for J. A. Graft & Co.'s Legal Directory.

ACTIONS.—As at common law. In equity by bill or petition.

ADMINISTRATION.—1. Where there is no will, administration shall be granted to the distributees who apply therefore; preferring first the husband or wife, and then such of the others entitled to distribution, as the court shall see fit. If no application in thirty days from death of intestate, administration may be granted to one or more of creditors, or to any other person. Bond, with security, in penalty equal at least to full value of personal estate.

2. Has no control over real estate.

3. When assets, after payment of funeral expenses, charges of administration: Claims for physician's fees in last sickness, of $50, and druggist's accounts for articles furnished during same period, of $50, are not sufficient to satisfy all demands, they shall be applied:

1. Debts due United States.

2. Taxes and levies assessed upon decedent previous to his death.

3. Debts due as personal representative, trustee for persons under disabilities, guardian or committee, where the qualification was in this State, in which debts shall be included a debt for money received by a husband acting as such fiduciary, in right of wife.

4. All other demands ratably (except voluntary obligations.)

5. Voluntary obligations.

ARRESTS.—No imprisonment for debt. But upon affidavit of plaintiff to any Judge or Justice, that he has cause of action, and probable cause for believing that defendant is about to quit the State, unless he be forthwith apprehended, defendant may be held to bail. If defendant gives bond, with security, that he will answer such interrogatories as may be filed in four months after judgment, decree, or order, and make such conveyance and delivery as is required, or perform and satisfy such judgment, decree, or order, he may be discharged.

Bond, with security, required of plaintiff before *capias* is sued out.

ASSIGNMENTS.—Assignees may sue in their own names, and all evidences of debt may be assigned by indorsement. Any person, insolvent or not, may make conveyance for benefit of creditors, preferring one or more.

ATTACHMENTS.—Besides tenants liable for rent:

1. Non-residents having estate, or sued with parties who reside within the State.

2. And defendants removing, intending to remove, or who have removed, their effects out of the State, so that judgment or decree would be unavailing, may be proceeded against by attachment, or affidavit of the facts.

Against class 1, attachment may issue, in action at law, for debt, or damages for breach of contract, or in equity upon any such claim, or in a suit for specific performance, where a certain sum is claimed.

Against class 2, in any action at law to recover specific personal property, or money upon any claim, or damages for any wrong, that is, including torts.

Against tenants and debtors, removing effects, etc., any Justice of the Peace may issue attachment, whether the claim be due or not; otherwise the writ must be obtained from the Clerk of the Court. A non-resident may attach the estate, within this State, of another non-resident. Bond, with security, required, usually double the amount claimed, when property taken possession of by officer.

COURTS.—JUSTICES OF THE PEACE.—Jurisdiction in civil cases to $100, with right of appeal in ten days, upon appellant giving bond for payment of judgment, and all costs and damages, if it is affirmed, where matter in controversy, exclusive of interest, is of a greater amount or value than $10; or where the constitutionality or validity of an ordinance or by-law of a corporation is involved.

Before trial, if amount in controversy exceeds the value of $20, Justice, upon application of defendant, shall remove cause to the court of the county, or corporation.

COUNTY COURTS.—Jurisdiction, criminal, as to misdemeanors, with right of accused in capital cases to elect, to be tried by Circuit Court. Probate of wills. Settlement of fiduciary accounts. Opening roads. Establishing landings, ferries, etc,

CIRCUIT COURTS.—Jurisdiction, chancery and common law cases in all sums over $20.

SUPREME COURT OF APPEALS.—Five Judges. Apellate jurisdiction in all criminal cases, and in civil suits where matter in controversy exceeds $500 in value. Petition for an appeal from or writ of error or *supersedeas* to any final judgment, decree, or order must be presented within one year after such judgment, etc.

DEEDS.—The word "grant," in every deed conveying lands shall, unless an exception be made therein, be construed to include all the estate, right, title, and interest whatever, both at law and in equity, of the grantor in or to such lands. Must be in writing, signed, sealed, acknowledged, or proven. Acknowledgments before Justice, a Commissioner in Chancery of a Court of Record, or Notary Public, within the United States.

DOWER.—Widow is endowered of one-third of real estate.

EXEMPTIONS.—The family bible, family pictures, school books, and library, not exceeding in value $100; a seat or pew in church; a lot in burial ground; all necessary wearing apparel of the debtor and family; all beds, bedsteads, and bedding necessary for use of family; all stoves and appendages, not to exceed three; one cow, one horse, six chairs, one table, and other specified articles of household and kitchen furniture, and certain provisions, mechanics' tools, not to exceed in value $100; where debtor actually engaged in agriculture, one yoke of oxen, or a pair of horses or mules, can be claimed by householder, or head of family.

HOMESTEAD.—In real or personal property, not to exceed $2,000. Debtor may waive it in bond, note, or other writing. If householder or head of family, die without claiming it, right survives to widow and infant children. It can not be claimed in certain specified cases:

1. For purchase price of property.
2. For services rendered by a laborer or mechanic.
3. For liabilities incurred by any public officer, or officer of a court, or any fiduciary, or attorney-at-law, for money collected.
4. For lawful claim for any taxes, levies, or assessments, accruing after 1st day of January, 1866.

5. For rent hereafter accruing.

6. For the legal or taxable fees of any public officer, or officer of a court.

7. Where debtor has waived it.

INTEREST.—The legal rate is six per cent. If a greater rate is charged the lender forfeits all interest.

LIMITATIONS.—On sealed instruments twenty years. Notes, contracts in writing, not sealed, and contracts not in writing, etc., five years. Retail store accounts, two years. Wholesale store accounts, and between merchant and merchant, their factories or servants settling accounts concerning trade, where action of account would be five years from cessation of dealing between the parties.

WIDOW.—Where there is no will as to personal estate. If no issue, entitled absolutely to such of personal estate in surplus (after payment of debts) as shall be acquired by intestate in virtue of his marriage with her, and remain in kind at his death. She shall also be entitled, if intestate leave issue by former marriage to one-third; if no such issue, to one-half of the residue of such surplus.

WILLS— Must be in writing, signed by testator, or some one for him, in his presence, and by his direction; and, unless wholly written by the testator, must be attested by two competent witnesses, subscribing their names to the same in the presence of the testator. Every person of sound mind and twenty-one years of age, may make a will and dispose of their estate, and persons of eighteen and upwards, may dispose of personalty by will. Married women may make wills in the exercise of a power, or as to their separate estate.

WOMEN MARRIED.—1. The real and personal property of any female who may hereafter marry, and which she shall own at the time of her marriage and the rents, issues, and profits thereof, and any property, real or personal, acquired by a married woman, as a separate and sole trader, shall not be subject to the disposal of her husband, nor be liable for his debts and shall be, and continue her separate and sole property; and any such married woman shall have power to contract in relation thereto, or for the disposal thereof, and may sue. and be sued, as if she were a *femme sole*; provided, that her husband shall join in any contract in reference to her real or personal property, other than such as she may acquire as sole trader; and shall be joined with her in any action by or against her; and provided, further, that nothing herein contained shall deprive her of the power to create, without the concurrence of her husband, a charge upon such sole and separate estate as she would be empowered to charge without the concurrence of her husband, if this act had not been passed.

2. All real and personal estate hereafter acquired by any woman, whether by gift, grant, purchase, inheritance, devise, or bequest, shall be, and continue her sole and separate estate, subject to the provisions and limitations of the preceeding section, although the marriage may have been solemnized previous to the passage of this act; and she may devise and bequeath the same as if she were unmarried; and it shall not be liable to the debts and liabiliaies of her husband; provided, that nothing contained in this act shall be construed to deprive the husband of courtesy in the wife's real estate, nor the wife of dower in her husband's estate; and, provided, further, that the sole and separate estate created by any gift, grant, devise, or bequest, shall be held according to the terms and powers, and be subject to the provisions and limitations thereof, and to the provisions and limitations of this act, so far as they are in conflict therewith; provided, that nothing herein contained shall be construed as to modify or alter section seven, of chapter one hundred

and twenty-three, of the code of eighteen hundred and seventy-three, except as hereinafter provided, that is to say, where the wife is a minor, having an estate in the hands of a guardian, it shall not be lawful for said guardian to pay, or turn over her estate before she attains the age of twenty-one years, notwithstanding her marriage.

VIRGINIA FORMS.

[Form 1*a*.—ACKNOWLEDGMENT.]

STATE OF VIRGINIA, —— of ——, to-wit:
I, ——, for the —— aforesaid, in the State of Virginia, do certify that ——, whose name —— signed to the within writing, bearing date on the —— day of ——, 18—, ha— acknowledged the same before me in —— aforesaid. Given under my hand this —— day of ——, 18—. (*Signature.*)
Note.—To be acknowledged before a Justice or a Notary Public.

[Form 1*b*.—ACKNOWLEDGMENT BY WIFE.]

STATE OF VIRGINIA, —— of ——, to-wit:
——, for the —— of ——, in the State of Virginia, do certify that ——, the wife of ——, whose names are signed to the within writing, bearing date on the —— day of ——, 18—, personally appeared before ——, in the —— aforesaid, and being examined by —— privily and apart from her husband, and having the writing aforesaid fully explained to her, she, the said ——, acknowledged the said writing to be her act, and declared that she had willingly executed the same, and does not wish to retract it. Given under —— hand—, this —— day of ——, 18—.
Note.—Before two Justices and one Notary Public. (*Signature.*)

[Form 2.—NOTICE TO TAKE DEPOSITIONS.]

To ——:
You will please take notice that —— shall proceed, on the —— day of ——, A. D. 18—, between the hours of —— o'clock A. M., and —— o'clock P. M., at ——, to take the depositions of ——, to be read in evidence on the trial of a suit now pending in the —— Court for the —— of —— in the State of ——, in which —— plaintiff, and —— defendant; and if from any cause the taking of said depositions shall not be commenced, or being commenced shall not be completed, on that day, the same will be continued from day to day, or from time to time until completed.

(*Signature.*)

[Form 3—DEPOSITIONS.]

——
vs. } In the —— Court of the ——.
——

The depositions of —— and others, taken before me ——, a Notary Public, for the State of ——, pursuant to notice hereto annexed, at the office of ——, in the State of ——, on the —— day of ——, 18—, between the hours of 6 A. M. and 6 P. M., to be read as evidence on behalf of ——, in a certain cause now pending in the —— Court of ——, wherein —— is plaintiff, and —— is defendant.
Present: ——, Counsel for plaintiff; ——, Counsel for defendant,
——, (the witness) being duly sworn on the Holy Evangelist of Almighty God, deposeth and saith as follows:
1st Question: By Counsel for Plaintiff: —— ? Answer: ——.
2nd Question: By Counsel for Plaintiff: —— ? Answer: ——.
When the depositions are completed, the following certificate is annexed.

[Form 4.—CERTIFICATE TO DEPOSITION.]

STATE OF ——, } ss.
County of——. }

——, a —— for the —— of ——, in the State of ——, (or the person named in the commission hereto annexed) do hereby certify that the foregoing depositions were duly taken, reduced to writing and signed by the witness—, respectively, before me, at the place— and the time— therein mentioned, pursuant to the annexed notice and commission. In witness whereof, I have hereunto set my hand and affixed my official seal, (if any) at —— aforesaid this —— day of —— 18—. (*Signature.*)
N. B. If the person taking the depositions (not being a Justice of the Peace), have no official seal, the genuineness of his signature must be authenticated by some officer of the State or County under his official seal.

[Form 5.—DEED OF RELEASE.]

This Deed, made this —— day of ——, in the year one thousand eight hundred and ——, between —— of the —— of the first part, and —— of the —— of the second part, and —— of the —— of the third part: Whereas, the said ——, in order to secure to the said —— the payment of the sum of ——, did, by —— deed, bearing date on the —— day of ——, 18—, recorded in the office of the Clerk of ——, convey to the said ——, heirs and assigns, certain —— estate described in the said deed, as follows: (Here describe property); and the said sum of money —— having been fully paid to the said ——, he the said —— ha— requested that the estate conveyed by the said deed of trust to the said —— in the said property hereinbefore mentioned and described, be now released to —— the said ——. This deed, therefore, witnesseth: That for and in consideration of the premises, as well as of the sum of five dollars, the said ——, with the consent of the said ——, signified by —— signing and sealing this deed, do —— release to the said —— all —— claim upon the said property.

Witness the following signatures and seals:

—— [L. S.]
—— [L. S.]
—— [L. S.]

[Form 7.—DEED OF BARGAIN AND SALE.]

This Deed, made this —— day ——, in the year one thousand eight hundred and ——, between —— of the first part, and —— of the second part; Witnesseth, that in consideration of the sum of —— dollars, the said —— do— grant unto the said ——, with general warranty, all (here describe property.)

The said —— covenant— that —— ha— the right to convey the said land to the grantee; that —— ha— done no act to encumber the said land; that the grantee shall have quiet possession of the said land, free from all encumbrances, and that —— part— of the first part, will execute such further assurance of the said land as may be requisite.

Witness the following signature —— seal ——.

——. [SEAL.]
——. [SEAL.]
——. [SEAL.]
——. [SEAL.]

[Form 8.—INJUNCTION BOND.]

Know all Men by these Presents, That we —— are held and firmly bound unto the Commonwealth of Virginia in the sum of —— dollars, to the payment whereof, well and truly to be made to the said Commonwealth of Virginia, we bind ourselves and each of us, our and each of our heirs, executors and administrators, jointly and severally, firmly by these presents. Sealed with our seals, and dated this —— day of —— one thousand eight hundred and ——.

The conditions of the above obligations are such, That whereas the above bound ——, on —— bill in Chancery against ——, addressed to the Judge of ——, has obtained from —— an injunction to enjoin and restrain—— —— until the future order of the said Court; and whereas it is provided, by the order of the said Judge awarding the said injunction, that the plaintiff shall not have the benefit thereof until ——, or some one of —— shall enter into a bond, with good security, in the Clerk's office of the said Court, payable to the Commonwealth of Virginia, in the penalty of —— dollars, and conditioned to pay all such costs as may be awarded against the plaintiff—, and all such damages as shall be incurred in case the said injunction be dissolved: Now, therefore, if the said —— shall pay all such costs as may be awarded against ——, and all such damages as shall be incurred in case the injunction be dissolved, then this obligation to be void, or else to remain in full force and virtue.

Executed in presence of ——.

[SEAL.]
[SEAL.]
[SEAL.]

[Form 9.—DEED OF TRUST.]

This Deed made this —— day of —— in the year 18—, between ——, of the —— part— of the first part, and —— of the ——, part— of the second part, Witnesseth: That the said part— of the first part do— grant unto the said part— of the second part the following property, to-wit: (Here describe property.)

In Trust, To secure to —— of the —— the payment of the sum of ——.

In the event that default shall be made in the payment of either of the above mentioned —— as they become due and payable, then the Trustees, or either of them, on being required so to do by ——, executors, administrators, or assigns, shall sell the property hereby conveyed. And it is covenanted and agreed between the parties aforesaid, that in case of a sale, the same shall be made after first advertising the time, place, and terms thereof, for —— days in some newspaper published in the City of Richmond, and upon the following terms, to-wit: For cash as to so much of the proceeds as may be necessapy to defray the expenses of executing this trust, the fees for drawing and recording this deed, if then unpaid, and to discharge the amount of money then payable upon the said ——, and if at the time of such sale any of the said —— shall not have become due and payable, and the purchase money be sufficient, such part or parts of the said purchase money as will be sufficient to pay off and discharge such remaining —— shall be made payable at such time or times as the said remaining —— will become due; the payment of which part or parts shall be properly secured; and in case the net proceeds of sale shall be insufficient to pay off all of the said —— in full, then the same shall be applied towards the payment of the said —— in the order of their maturity, intending hereby to create a priority in favor of each of said —— over any other —— which may become due and payable subsequent thereto; and if their be any residue of said purchase money, the same shall be made payable at such time, and secured in such manner as the said part— of the first part —— executors, administrators or assigns, shall prescribe and direct, or in case of —— failure to give such direction, at such time and in such manner as the said Trustees, or either of them, shall think fit. The said part— of the first part covenant— to pay all taxes, assessments, dues and charges upon the said property hereby conveyed, so long as —— or —— heirs or assigns shall hold the same, and hereby waive— the benefit of —— homestead exemption as to the debt— secured by this deed.

If no default shall be made in the payment of the above mentioned debt, then, upon the request of the part— of the first part, a good and sufficient deed of release shall be executed to —— at —— own proper costs and charges.

Witness the following signature— and seal—. [SEAL.] [SEAL.]

LAWS OF WASHINGTON TERRITORY

RELATIVE TO THE

COLLECTION OF DEBTS, Etc.

Prepared expressly for J. A. Graft & Co.'s Legal Directory.

ACKNOWLEDGMENT.—Acknowledgments may be taken before a Judge of the Supreme Court, a Judge of the Probate Court, a Justice of the Peace, a County Auditor, a Clerk of the District, or Supreme Court, or a Notary Public, duly qualified according to law. Acknowledgments to deeds of conveyance of real estate taken in other States, or Territories, of the United States, may be taken before any person authorized by law to take acknowledgments. Unless taken before a Commissioner of Deeds for this Territory, or a Clerk of a Court of Record, the certificate of the Clerk of a Court of Record must be attached to the acknowledgment, showing that the officer officiating was at the time duly qualified to act as such.

ASSIGNMENTS.—All creditors are alike in this Territory, there being no preferences to any class. A debtor cannot get a release from his debts by the consent of a majority of his creditors. When the assignment embraces all the debtor's property upon petition to District Court, in absence of fraud, he will be discharged from all his debts.

COLLECTIONS.—All accounts transmitted for collection should be made out in detail, and verified by the oath of the claimant. All accounts bear interest after due, whether presented or not. Accounts against the estates of deceased persons must be accompanied by the affidavit of the claimant to the effect that the amount claimed is correct, and that no part of the same has been paid.

CHATTEL MORTGAGES.—A chattel mortgage must be accompanied by the affidavit of the mortgagor that it is made in good faith, without design to hinder, delay, or defraud creditors, and acknowledged and recorded in the County Auditor's office.

EXEMPTIONS.—All real and personal property of the wife for husband's debts. Her property is liable for her own debts contracted before marriage, but not for debts of her husband.

To the head of a family a homestead, not exceeding in value $1,000, while occupied by himself or family.

Homestead may be mortgaged, but, to be valid, must be signed by wife.

Wearing apparel of every person, and family libraries, family pictures and keepsakes.

To each householder necessary household goods, not exceeding in value one hundred and fifty dollars; two cows and calves, five hogs, two stands of bees, twenty-five domestic fowls, and provisions and food for such householder and family for six months.

To a farmer, one span of horses, or two yoke of oxen and one wagon, and farming utensils in use on the farm not exceeding in value two hundred dollars.

To a mechanic, tools used to carry on his trade, and material not to exceed in value five hundred dollars.

The libraries of physicians, attorneys, clergymen, and other professional men, not to exceed in value five hundred dollars.

To a physician, one horse and buggy, used in practice, and medicines and instruments, not exceeding in value two hundred dollars.

All firearms kept for the use of any person, or family.

To a teamster and drayman, engaged for the support of himself or family, a span of horses and one wagon, or dray.

To any person, a canoe, or small boat, with rigging, not exceeding in the aggregate the sum of fifty dollars.

To a person engaged on lighting, for the support of himself or family, one or more lighters, barges, or scows, and rigging, not exceeding in value two hundred and fifty dollars.

No property is exempt, however, from execution issued from a judgment for the purchase price, or taxes levied thereon.

INTEREST.—The legal rate of interest is ten per cent., but parties may contract in writing for any rate.

JUDGMENTS.—Judgments bear the legal rate of interest from the date of their rendition; if upon a written contract, to draw the same rate of interest specified in such written contract.

In order that a judgment may be a lien upon the real estate of the judgment debtor, a transcript of the judgment must be filed in the office of the County Auditor of the county in which the land is situated.

LIMITATIONS.—The following actions must be commenced within three years:

Upon a contract, or liability, express or implied, which does not arise out of a written instrument.

An action for taking, detaining, or injuring personal property, including an action for the specific recovery thereof.

An action for relief upon the ground of fraud.

An action for waste, or trespass upon real property.

An action upon a statute for a penalty or forfeiture.

The following actions must be commenced within six years from the time the cause of action occurs:

An action upon a contract, in writing, or liability arising out of a writen agreement.

An action for rents and profits of real estate.

An action upon a judgment of any court.

In an action upon an open account, to recover balance, the cause of action shall be deemed to have accrued from the date of the last item proved.

An action must be commenced within three years against a Sheriff, Coroner, or Constable, upon a liability incurred in his official capacity, including the non payment of money collected upon an execution.

An action for the recovery of real estate must be commenced within ten years.

An action must be commenced within two years for libel, slander, assault, assault and battery, and false imprisonment.

Within one year an action against a Sheriff, or other officer, for the escape of a prisoner arrested on civil process.

MARRIED WOMEN.—A married woman may sue and be sued without joining her husband, when the action concerns her separate property. All property of the wife owned by her before marriage, the profits of her own labor, and the property acquired afterwards by gift, bequest, devise, or descent, with the rents, issues, and profits thereof, is her separate property.

WILLS.—In all cases where it is provided by the last will and testament of the deceased that the estate shall be settled in a manner provided in such last will and testament, and that letters testamentary shall not be required, it shall not be necessary to take out letters testamentary, or of administration, except to admit to such will in the manner required by existing laws; and after the probate of such will, all such estates may be managed without the intervention of the Probate Court, if said last will so provides. And, provided further, if the party named in the will fail to execute the trust faithfully, then, upon the petition of any creditor of such estate, or any of the heirs, or of any person on behalf of any minor heirs, it shall be the duty of the Probate Court where such estate is situated to cite such persons having the management of such estate to appear before such Court; and, if it appear that such trust is not faithfully discharged, then letters testamentary, or of administration, shall be required in such cases, and all other matters and proceedings shall be had and required as are now required in the administration of estates.

WASHINGTON TERRITORY FORMS.

[Form 1—DEED AND ACKNOWLEDGMENT].

This Indenture, Made this —— day of ——, in the year of our Lord, one thousand eight hundred and ——, between ——, the part— of the first part, and ——, the part— of the second part, Witnesseth, that the said part— of the first part, for and in consideration of the sum of —— dollars, gold Coin of the United States, to —— in hand paid, by the said part— of the second part, the receipt whereof is hereby acknowledged, and do— by these presents grant, bargain, sell, convey and confirm unto the said part— of the second part, and to —— heirs, and assigns, the following described tract or parcel of land, situate, lying and being in the County of —— and Territory of Washington, and particularly bounded and described as follows, to-wit: [Here describe property].

Together with all and singular the tenements, hereditaments and appurtenances thereunto belonging, or in anywise appertaining.

To Have and to Hold The said premises, with the appurtenances unto the said part— of the second part, and to — heirs and assigns forever. And the said part— of the first part for —— heirs, executors and administrators, do— covenant and agree to and with the said part— of the second part, —— heirs and assigns, that the said premises in the quiet and peaceable possession of the said part— of the second part-—, heirs and assigns, against the said part— of the first part, and against all and every person or persons whomsoever, lawfully claiming or to claim the same by, through or under the said part— of the first part, shall and will warrant, and by these presents forever defend.

In Witness Whereof, The said part— of the first part ha— hereunto set —— hand — and seal ——, the day and year first above written.

Signed, sealed and delivered in presence of
——————
——————

—— [SEAL].
—— [SEAL].

[ACKNOWLEDGMENT].

TERRITORY OF WASHINGTON, } ss.
County of —— }

On this —— day of —— in the year of Our Lord one thousand eight hundred and ——, before me, a Notary Public, in and for the Territory of Washington, personally appeared the within named ——; whose name —— subscribed to the foregoing instrument as part— thereto, personally known to me to be the individual— described in, and who executed the within deed, and acknowledged that —— executed the same freely and voluntarily, for the uses and purposes therein mentioned.

And the said ——, wife of the said ——, being of full age, and having been by me examined separate and apart from her said husband, and the contents of the within deed having been by me fully made known unto her, acknowledged that she did voluntarily, of her own free will, and without fear of, or coercion from her said husband, execute the same.

In Testimony Whereof, I have hereunto set my hand and affixed my official seal, the day and year first above written. ——, *Notary Public.*

[Form 2—CHATTEL MORTGAGE].

WITH AFFIDAVIT AND ACKNOWLEDGMENT.

This Mortgage, made the —— day of —— in the year A. D. eighteen hundred and —— by ——, of the —— County of ——, Territory of ——, by occupation ——. Mortgagor to ——, of the —— County of —— Territory of ——, by occupation —— —— mortgagee . *Witnesseth:*

That said mortgagor— mortgaged— to the said Mortgagee— all that certain personal property situated and described as follows, to-wit: (Here describe property). As security for the payment to ——, the said mortgagee— of ——. —— dollars, —— of the United States of America, on —— day of ——, in the year, A. D. eighteen hundred and ——, with interest thereon at the rate of —— per cent. per ——, according to the terms and conditions of — certain promissory note— bearing —— date —— and payable to the order of ——.

In Testimony Whereof, —— the mortgagor — herein named ha— hereunto set — hand and seal the day and date first above written.

Signed and executed in the presence of,
——————
—————— [SEAL].

AFFIDAVIT.

TERRITORY OF WASHINGTON, } ss.
County of ——— }

——, the mortgagor — in the foregoing mortgage named, being duly sworn, doth depose and say that the aforesaid mortgage is made in good faith, and without any design to hinder, delay or defraud creditors. [*Signature*].

Subscribed and sworn to before me this —— day of ——, A. D. 188—.
——, *Notary Public.*

ACKNOWLEDGMENT.

TERRITORY OF WASHINGTON, } ss.
County of ——— }

On this — day of A. D. 188 —, before me —— personally came ——, to me known to be the individual described in, and who executed the within instrument and acknowledged that —— signed and sealed the same as —— free and voluntary act and deed, for the uses and purposes therein mentioned.

Witness my hand and official seal, the day and year in this certificate first above written. ——, *Notary Public.*

[Form 3—CAPTION AND CERTIFICATE TO DEPOSITION].

[For full instruction, etc., see Laws, Title, Depositions].

CAPTION.

The depositions of —— taken on the —— day of —— 18 —, at the, —— office, in the city or town of ——, County of —— State or Territory of —— and to be read as evidence in behalf of plaintiff [defendant] in an action between —— plaintiff, and —— defendant, pending in the —— Conrt of ——.

When the deposition is completed, it shall be carefully read to the witness and subscribed by him, and certified by the officer substantially as follows: ——

CERTIFICATE.

TERRITORY OF WASHINGTON, } ss.
County of ———, }

I —— (state title of officer taking testimony), in and for said County, —— do hereby certify that the above deposition— was (or were) taken before me and reduced to writing by myself (or witness, as the case may be), at ——, in said County, —— on the —— day of, ——, A. D., 188 —, at —— o.clock, in pursuance of notice hereunto annexed, that the above named witness—, before examination, was [or were] sworn, [or affirmed] to testify the truth, the whole truth, and nothing but the truth; and that the said deposition was carefully read to [or by] said witness—, and then subscribed by him [or them]. [*Signature and title of officer.*]

Dated at ——, the —— day of —— 188 ——.

The deposition must then be inclosed in a sealed envelope title of the [cause and name of Court should be indorsed on envelope or wrapper] and mailed, or delivered to the Clerk of the Court in which the action is pending.

LAWS OF WEST VIRGINIA

RELATIVE TO THE

COLLECTION OF DEBTS, Etc.

Prepared expressly for J. A. Graft & Co.'s Legal Directory, by James B. Menager, Attorney and Counsellor at Law, Point Pleasant, W. Va.

ARREST.—An order for the arrest of a defendant in a civil action, may issue upon the affidavit of the plaintiff, or some credible person showing the nature and justice of the plaintiff's claim, the amount thereof, and the existence of some one of the following grounds for the arrest of the defendant:

1. That the defendant has removed or is about to remove any of his property out of the State, with intent to defraud his creditors; or

That he has converted or is about to convert his property or any part thereof into money or securities with like intent; or

That he has assigned, disposed of, or removed his property, or any part thereof, or is about to do so with like intent; or

That he has property, or rights of action, which he fraudulently conceals; or

That he fraudulently contracted the debt, or incurred the liability for which the action or suit is brought; or

That he is about to leave the State, and reside permanently in another State or county without paying the debt, or liability for which the action or suit is brought. But such order shall not issue until the plaintiff, or some person for him shall deliver to the clerk of the Court in which such action is pending, or to the Justice, if it be before a Justice, a bond, in penalty double the amount sworn to, with one or more sureties to effect, that the plaintiff will pay the defendant all damages he may sustain by reason of the arrest, should it thereafter appear that the order was wrongfully obtained.

The defendant may be discharged by giving bond and security, that he will answer such interrogatories as may be filed within four months after judgment, claim or order, and make the required conveyance or delivery, or perform and satisfy such claim or order.

ASSIGNMENTS.—Any bond, note, accounts or writing not negotiable may be assigned and an action thereupon may be maintained by the assignee in his own name, without the addition of "assignee;" but he shall allow all just discounts, not only against himself, but against the assignor, before the defendant had notice of the assignment. In every such action the plaintiff may write claims payable to him individually, with those payable to him as such assigned.

Assignments for the benefit of creditors may be made by deed, acknowledged as other deeds, and recorded in the clerk's office of the county wherein the property is situated. Any person named by the debtor may be assignee.

ATTACHMENTS.—When an action or suit is about to be, or is instituted for the recovery of any claim or debt arising out of contract, or to recover damages for any wrong, the plaintiff, at the commencement of the action, or at any time thereafter, and before judgment may have an order of attachment against the property of the defendant by filing his affidavit, or that of some credible person, stating the nature of the plaintiff's claim and the amount at the best, which the plaintiff is justly entitled to recover, and that the affiant believes that some one of the following grounds exist for such attachment: That the defendant, or one of the defendants is a foreign corporation, or is a non-resident of the state, or that he has left or is about to leave the state with intent to defraud his creditors; or that he so conceals himself, that a summons can not be served upon him; or that he is removing, or is about to remove his property, or a material part thereof, out of the state, with intent to defraud his creditors; or that he is converting, or is about to convert his property, or a material part thereof, into money or securities, with like intent; or that he has assigned or disposed of his property, or a material part thereof, or is about to do so, with like intent; or that he has property, or rights of action, which he conceals; or that he fraudulently contracted the debt or incurred the liability, for which the action or suit is brought. Upon the creditor, giving bond in penalty double the amount of his claim, the officer to whom the order of attachment is directed, is required to take the attached property into possession.

Effects or money due the defendant in the hands of a third party, can be garnisheed.

Bills of Exchange and Promissory Notes.—All promissory notes or checks payable in this state, at a particular bank, or at a particular office thereof, for discount and deposit, or the place of business of a savings institution, or savings bank, and every inland bill of exchange, payable in this state, shall be deemed negotiable.

Three days of grace are allowed, except on bills of exchange payable at sight, on which there shall be no grace. Upon a bill drawn within, and payable without the State, and within the United States, the holder can recover, in addition to what else the party liable for the principal is bound to pay damages, at the rate of three per cent. on the principal, and at the rate of ten per cent., if payable without the United States.

Deeds, Acknowledgments, Etc.—Any deed, contract, power of attorney, or other writing shall be admitted to record as to the person whose name is signed thereto, upon a certificate of his acknowledgment before a justice, notary public, recorder, prothonotary, or clerk of any court within the United States, or commissioner appointed within the same, by the Governor of this State, within or annexed to the same.

Executions.—Upon judgment or decree of any Circuit or Municipal Court may issue within two years after the date thereof, or if none be so issued, the court in which the judgment was rendered, may thereafter and within ten years from date of judgment, upon ten days notice to the party against whom the same is, order an execution to issue thereon, for such sum as remains unpaid, when execution has issued within the two years, others may issue within ten years from return of same, without notice.

Execution in Justice Court may issue within three years from entry of judgment, or date of last execution, or if judgment be renewed from date of such renewal.

An execution becomes a lien upon the personal estate of the debtor, from the time it is delivered to the officer.

Exemptions.—Any husband or parent residing in this state, or the infant children of deceased parents, may hold a homestead of the value of $1,000, and personal property not exceeding $200, to be exempt from force sales; and any mechanic, artisan, or laborer, whether he be a husband, or parent, or not, may hold the working tools of his trade or occupation, exempt from sale or execution.

Such exemption does not effect or impair any claim for purchase money, or any process for collection of taxes, or district or county levies.

Insolvency.—This State has no insolvent laws.

INTEREST.—Legal rate of interest is six per cent. Excess of interest is not recoverable at law. Joint stock companies and municipal corporations may borrow money at higher rates.

JUDGMENTS.—Judgments are a lien upon all the real estate of the debtor, at or after their date; but to secure the lien against a purchaser for valuable consideration without notice, the same must be docketed in the County Clerk's office within ninety days. Judgments bear six per cent. interest from date.

LIMITATION OF ACTIONS.—Ten years on any indemnifying bond, taken under any statue, or upon the bond of an executor, administrator, guardian, curator, committee or public officer.

Twenty years, upon any other contract in writing under seal—executed before the first of April, 1869. Ten years, if executed on or after that date. Ten years upon an award or contract in writing, signed by the party to be charged thereby, or by his agent, but not under seal. Five years upon any other contract, unless it be an action for any article charged in a store account, when it must be brought within three years. An action by one partner against his co-partner, or merchant against merchant, where an action of account would lie, in either of which cases, an action may be brought within five years from cessation of dealings. Revivor, acknowledgment of debt, or promise in writing to pay.

All actions to recover land must be brought within ten years after the time the right shall have first accrued.

MARRIED WOMEN.—Property of wife, acquired at any time, and from any source other than her husband, as her sole and separate property, and the rents, issues and profits thereof, shall be and remain her sole and separate property, as if she were a single woman; and the same shall, in no way, be subject to the control of her husband, or liable for his debts. She may sue and be sued without joining her husband, when the action concerns her separate property; when the action is between herself and husband, and when she is living separate and apart from her husband. When living separate and apart from her husband, she may, in her own name, carry on any trade or business, and the stock and property used in such trade or business, or otherwise, shall be her sole and separate property, and shall not be subject to the control of her husband, nor liable for his debts.

STAY.—Upon judgments in Justice Court, where the judgment, exclusive of interest and costs, does not exceed $50, two months; over $50, and not over $100, four months; over $100, six months.

No stay is allowed upon judgment, upon stay bonds, or other bonds filed in Justice Court, or against constables or justices for official misconduct.

No stay is allowed in higher Courts.

WEST VIRGINIA FORMS.

[Form 1.—ACKNOWLEDGMENTS.]

STATE OF ——, } To-wit.
County of —— }

I, ——, a Commissioner appointed by the Governor of the State of West Virginia for the said State (or territory or district), of ——, (or I, a Justice of the County aforesaid, district or township of ——; or I, ——, Recorder of said County; or I, a Notary of said County; or I, ——, a prothonotary or Clerk of the —— Court of said County) do certify that —— whose name (or names) is (or are) signed to the writing above (or hereto annexed) bearing date on the —— day of ——, has (or have) this day acknowledged the same before me in my said ——. Given under my hand this —— day of —— "or upon a certificate so written or annexed under the official seal of any minister, plenipotentiary, *charge a affaires*, consul-general, consul, deputy consul, vice consul, consular agent, vice consular agent, commercial agent, or vice consul agent, appointed by the government of the United States to any foreign country; or of the proper officer of any court of such country; or of the Mayor or other chief magistrate of any city, town or corporation therein, that the said writing was acknowledged by such person, or proved so to him by two witnesses before any person having such appointment, or before such Court, Mayor or Chief magistrate.

If the acknowledgment be before a Notary without the State, he shall certify under his seal.

[Form 2.—COMMISSIONER'S CERTIFICATE.]

CERTIFICATE OF A MARRIED WOMAN WHO SHALL UNITE WITH HER HUSBAND.

STATE OF ——, } To-wit.
County of ——. }

I, ——, a Commissioner appointed by the Governor of West Virginia for the State (or territory or district) of ——; or I, ——, a Justice for the County aforesaid, and district (or township) of ——; or I, ——, a Notary Public for the County aforesaid; or I, ——, Recorder of said County; or I, ——, prothonotary (or clerk) of the —— Court of said County) do certify that —— the wife of ——, whose names are signed to the writing above (or hereto annexed) bearing date on the —— day of ——, personally appeared before me in the County aforesaid, (or if it be a Commissioner in State, or if it be a Justice in the township (or district) aforesaid, territory or district aforesaid) and being examined by me privily and apart from her husband, and having the said writing fully explained to her, she, the said ——, acknowledged the said writing to be her act, and declared that she had willingly executed the same, and does not wish to retract it.

Given under my hand this —— day of ——.

(Acts of 1882, ch. 149.)

LAWS OF WISCONSIN

RELATIVE TO THE

COLLECTION OF DEBTS, Etc.

..pared expressly for J. A. Graft & Co.'s Legal Directory, by Edward P. Vilas, Attorney and Counselor-at-Law, Madison, Wis.

ARREST.—Defendant may be arrested in a civil action by order of a Judge, or Court Commissioner, at the issuing of a summons, or at any time before judgment, on an affidavit showing that a cause of action exists in an action for the recovery of damages not arising out of contract, where the defendant is a non-resident, or about to remove from the State, or for injury to person, or character; or for seduction or criminal conversation, or for injuring or wrongfully taking, detaining, or converting property, and to recover damages for value of property obtained under false pretenses or tokens; for a fine or penalty, for money received, property embezzled or fraudulently misapplied by a public officer, attorney, solicitor, or counselor; or an officer or agent of a corporation or bank; or by a factor, agent, broker, or any person in a fiduciary capacity; or in an action to recover possession of personal property unjustly detained, where the property, or part of it, has been concealed or disposed of so that it can not be taken by the sheriff. The above does not apply to females, except for a willful injury to person, property, or character.

ASSIGNMENT.—Voluntary assignments for the benefit of creditors can be made under the laws of the State. The assignment is void, unless assignee delivers the bond, provided for by the statute, to the County Judge or a Court Commissioner, before taking upon himself the execution of the trust imposed by the assignment, which bond, together with a copy of the assignment, must be immediately filed by the officer taking the same, in the office of the Clerk of the Circuit Court of the County. The assignment also becomes void if the assignor fails to file in said Clerk's office, within ten days after execution of assignment, an inventory of assets, and list of creditors, verified by his oath, and have affixed a certificate of the assignee, that the same is correct, according to his best knowledge and belief, but no mistake therein shall invalidate assignment or affect the right of any creditor. Within twelve (12) days after execution of assignment, assignee is to give notice by publication and mail, where address is known, requiring creditors to file, within three months, with such assignee, or the Clerk of the Circuit Court, on pain of being debarred a dividend, an affidavit setting forth his name, residence, and post-office address, the nature, consideration, and amount of his debt claimed by him, over and above all off-sets. Creditors must thus prove their claims or be debarred from dividends. Debts to become due may also be proved. Preferences are prohibited, except for wages of laborers, servants, and employees, earned within six months prior to assignment: other preference renders assignment void. Assignee must be resident of State. Debts are only extinguished to the extent of dividends paid thereon.

ATTACHMENTS—May issue against property of debtor, except municipal corporations, either at the time of issuing summons, or at any time before final judgment, in actions on contract, express or implied, or upon judgment, or decree, where the plaintiff, or some one in his behalf, shows by affidavit that the debt exceeds fifty dollars, specifying amount as near as may be, over and above all legal set-offs, and that deponent knows, or has good reason to believe, either:

1. That the defendant has absconded, or is about to abscond, from the State, or is concealed therein to the injury of his creditors; or keeps himself concealed therein with intent to avoid the service of a summons. 2. That he has assigned, conveyed, disposed of, or concealed, or is about to, any of his property, with intent to defraud his creditors. 3. That he has removed, or is about to remove, any of his property out of the State, with like intent. 4. That he fraudulently contracted the debt, or incurred the obligation respecting which the action is brought; or, 5. That he is not a resident of this State; or, 6. That the defendant is a foreign corporation, or if created under the laws of this State, that all the proper officers thereof, on whom to serve the summons, do not exist, are non-residents of the State, or can not be found; or, 7. That the action is brought against the defendant, as principal upon an official bond, to recover money due the State, or some county, or other municipality therein; or that the action is brought against a defendant, as principal, upon a bond or other instrument, given as evidence of indebtedness, for or to secure payment of money embezzled, or misappropriated by the defendant while acting as an officer of the State, or of any county or municipality therein; or an affidavit showing that a cause of action, sounding in tort, exists in favor of the plaintiff against the defendant, named in such writ; that the damages sustained and claimed exceed the sum of fifty dollars, specifying the amount claimed, and the further statement, either: 1. That the defendant is not a resident of this State, or that his residence is unknown, and can not with due diligence be ascertained; or, 2. That the defendant is a foreign corporation.

Attachment may be issued on demand not due, in any case mentioned above, except the 5th, 6th, and 7th: same proceedings had, and like affidavit, except that it must state that the debt is to become due; and the undertaking must be conditioned in three times the amount demanded

Attachment may be traversed by special answer, and plaintiff *must prove* the allegations of the affidavit: proof of *good reason to believe* them true, is insufficient; and on debt not due, if traversed successfully, action will be dismissed with costs against plaintiff.

EXECUTIONS—Upon judgments in Courts of Record may issue at any time within five years from its rendition, and alias execution at any time thereafter within twenty years. But if no execution be issued within the five years, the order of a Judge or Court Commissioner is necessary to authorize it. Personal property must be first exhausted before real estate can be levied on. Executions from Justices' Courts may issue on demand, at any time within five years after judgment.

EXEMPTIONS.—A homestead outside of any city or village, not exceeding forty acres, or instead not exceeding one-fourth of an acre within any city or village; the family bible, family pictures, school books, library, pew in any house of worship, wearing apparel, beds, bedsteads and bedding, stoves, cooking utensils, and all other household furniture, not exceeding two hundred dollars in value, and one firearm not exceeding fifty dollars in value; two cows, ten swine, one yoke of oxen, and one horse or mule; or in lieu thereof, two horses or mules; ten sheep, and wool from same, the necessary food for exempt stock for one year's support; one wagon, cart, or dray; one sleigh, one plow, one drag, and other farming utensils, including tackle for teams, not exceeding $200 in value; provisions and fuel for debtor and family for one year; tools, implements, and stock in trade of any person used for carrying on the business, not exceeding two hundred dollars in value; all articles presented by Congress or Legislature; sewing machines in use and owned by individuals; all inventions from debt of the inventor; the earnings of all married persons having a family dependent upon them for three months next preceding issue of any attachment, execution, garnishment, etc., to the amount of $60, only for each month in which earnings are made; fire engines and their fixtures; moneys arising from insurance of exempt property, including homestead; moneys arising from insurance made for the benefit of married women; printing presses and material to an amount not exceeding fifteen hundred dollars; books, etc., kept for making abstracts of title.

All exemptions are to be selected by the debtor. No personal property is exempt as against any debt for a portion of the purchase money.

GARNISHMENT.—Any creditor may proceed by garnishment against any person (except a municipal corporation) who shall be indebted to, or have any property, either real or personal, in his possession or under his control, belonging to such creditor's debtor at the time of issuing a summons, or at any time before final judgment, in an action founded on contract, express or implied, or upon judgment or decree at any time after issuing execution thereupon, and before same is returnable. In such case, the garnishee debtors are liable for the amount of property in their hands, or the amount of indebtedness due from them to the principal debtor from the time the garnishee summons is served upon them. No judgment can be rendered upon a liability of the garnishee arising by reason of his having drawn, accepted, made, indorsed or guaranteed any promissory note, by reason of money collected by him as an officer, or by reason of any indebtedness depending upon a future contingency.

INSOLVENCY.—An insolvent debtor may be discharged from debt by application to the Circuit Court, by petition setting forth his creditors, their residence, sums due each, cause of the indebtedness, statement of security for each debt, full inventory of his estate, accompanied by affidavits, that he has in no way disposed of, or secreted any of his property. After due notice to creditors and opportunity for them to oppose the discharge (which can be tried by jury) the court may grant the same and order an assignment, and the assignee converts the same into money and disposes of the same, under direction of the Court.

INTEREST.—Parties may contract in writing for ten per cent. per annum, but unless expressly named, the rate will be seven per cent. upon all moneys due and payable with interest, and upon all judgments, except foreclosures, which bear ten per cent. Compound interest is not allowed, unless distinctly agreed upon in writing. Any usurious agreement forfeits the entire interest agreed to be paid, or of any costs in the action.

JUDGMENT.—Judgment of a Court of Record becomes a lien upon all the real estate of the judgment debtor within the county, for a period of ten years from the date of its being docketed in the Clerk's office. Transcript of Justice's judgment may be docketed in the Circuit Court Clerk's office. and is then regarded as Circuit Court judgment, with reference to lien and enforcement. Transcript of judgment of Circuit Court may be docketed in any other County, and becomes lien the same as judgments originally rendered and docketed in that County.

JUSTICE COURT—Has jurisdiction to the amount of two hundred dollars in actions other than actions for libel, slander, malicious prosecution, false imprisonment, debt against decedent's estate, or where title to real estate shall come in question. May take confession of judgment to the amount of three hundred dollars.

LIMITATION OF ACTIONS.—Twenty years, actions on judgments of Courts within the State, and upon sealed instruments, except such given by town, county, city, village, or school district, which are limited to six years.

Ten years, actions on foreign judgments and specialties. Six years, all other contracts, obligations or liabilities, including notes, acceptance, and accounts.

Three years, actions against sheriffs, etc., for liabilities incurred in official capacity; on open mutual accounts, statute begins to run from the date of the last item. Infancy, insanity, imprisonment, extend the period of limitation during the continuance of the disability, provided it be for a period (except in case of infancy) of not more than five years. Actions must be commenced within one year after disability removed. Absence of defendant prevents the statute from running until his return. But payment renews the debt, generally.

NOTES AND BILLS OF EXCHANGE.—Notes signed by person, or by his special or general agent, and payable to order or bearer, and certificate of deposit, issued by persons or corporation, payable to order or bearer, are negotiable as inland bills of exchange, according to the custom of merchants, and days of grace allowed, except as to bills, notes and drafts payable on demand. Acceptance must be signed by acceptor, or by his lawful agent.

PARTNERSHIP.—Limited partnerships may be formed under the laws of the State by publication of the terms of the statute, as provided by statute, and in case of failure to do so the partnership becomes general.

WISCONSIN FORMS.

(Form 1—CERTIFICATE OF ACKNOWLEDGMENT)

STATE OF WISCONSIN,
County of —— } SS,

Personally came before me, a (insert designation of officer) this —— day of —— 188 —, the above (or within) named A. B. and C. B. his wife (or if an officer, adding the name of his office), to me known to be the person who executed the foregoing (or within) instrument, and acknowledged the same.

In witness whereof I have hereunto set my hand and affixed my —— seal, this day and year first above written. ——, (Title).

(Form 2--COMPLAINT AND PROOF OF DEBT).

STATE OF WISCONSIN,
County of —— } SS. IN JUSTICE COURT.
Before —— *Justice of the Peace.*

——
vs. } COMPLAINT.
——

The above named plaintiff —, by —— attorney — complain — of the above named defendant —, and allege that on and between the —— day of ——, A. D. 188 — and the —— day of ——, A. D. 188 — inclusive, the plaintiff — sold and delivered to the defendant —, on account, at —— request, on a credit of —— goods, wares and merchandise at the agreed price of —— dollars, and which were reasonably worth the sum of —— dollars; that the said indebtedness has not been paid, nor any part thereof, —— and that there is now due and owing by the defendant — to the plaintiff —, upon said account, the sum of —— dollars and —— cents, over and above all payments, set-offs and counter claims, with interest thereon from the —— day of ——, A. D. 188 —, the time when said account became due and demand was made; for which sum and interest, and the costs and disbursements of this action, the plaintiff — demand — judgment against the defendant —

——, *Plaintiff — Attorney.*

STATE OF WISCONSIN,
—— County. } SS. ——

being duly sworn, says that he is —— the plaintiff — above named, and that the foregoing complaint is true of his own knowledge.

Subscribed and sworn to before me, this —— day of ——, A. D. 188—

STATE OF WISCONSIN,
County of —— } SS. IN JUSTICE COURT.
Before —— *Justice of the Peace.*

——
vs. } PROOF OF DEBT.
——

STATE OF WISCONSIN,
—— County. } SS. ——

being duly sworn, deposes and says that he is —— the plaintiff — above named;—that on and between the —— day of ——, A. D. 188 —, and the —— day of ——, A. D. 188 — inclusive, the plaintiff — sold and delivered to the defendant —at —— — special instance and request, upon account, goods, wares and merchandise, at and for the agreed price and sum of, and to the amount, and of the value of —— dollars, on a credit of, —— which time — ha— long since fully expired; and that the said indebtedness became due on the —— day of —— A. D. 188—; that the defendant —— indebted to the plaintiff— upon the account alleged in the complaint in the sum of —— dollars; that the annexed account is a correct statement in said sale; and that the said indebtedness has not been paid, nor any part thereof, except the sum of —— which was paid —— and that there is now due and owing upon said sale-- by said defendant —— to said plaintiff — the sum of —— dollars, with interest from ——, and that no set-offs should be allowed.

Subscribed and sworn to before me, this —— day of —— A. D. 188—

[Form 2—ATTACHMENT—AFFIDAVIT].

———— *Plaintiff*, vs. ———— *Defendant*. } ———— COURT, ———— COUNTY,

STATE OF WISCONSIN, County of ———— } ss.

——— being duly sworn, says that he is ——— the above named plaintiff— and makes this affidavit on ——— behalf; that the above named defendant ——— indebted to the said plaintiff — in a sum exceeding fifty dollars, to-wit: in the sum of ———— dollars, and ——— cents, as near as may be, over and above all legal off-sets, and that the same is due upon ———; that this deponent has good reason to believe, and verily does believe ————.

————

Subscribed and sworn to before me, this ——— day of ——— A. D. 188—

[Form 4—UNDERTAKING ON ATTACHMENT].

———— COURT, COUNTY OF ————

———— vs. ———— } UNDERTAKING ON ATTACHMENT.

The above named plaintiff— having applied for a writ of attachment against the property of the above named defendant————.

We ———— of the County of ——— State of Wisconsin, and ———— of the said place, do undertake, pursuant to the statute in such case made and provided, in the sum of two hundred and fifty dollars, that if the said defendant— recover judgment in this action, the above named plaintiff— will pay all costs that may be awarded to the above named defendant— and all damages which the said defendant - may sustain by reason of the said attachment not exceed the sum above mentioned.

————
————

Dated ———— 188 —.

COUNTY OF ———— } ss. [AFFIDVAIT OF SURETY].

One of the subscribers to the foregoing undertaking, being sworn, says that he is a resident and freeholder within this State, and is worth the sum of ——— hundred dollars in property within this State over and above all his debts and liabilities, and exclusive of all property exempt from execution. ————

Subscribed and sworn to by me, this ——— day of ——— 188—

COUNTY OF ———— }ss.

One of the subscribers to the foregoing undertaking, being sworn, says that he is a resident and freeholder within this State, and is worth the sum of ———— hundred dollars in property within this State over and above all his debts and liabilities, and exclusive of all property exempt from execution. ————

Subscribed and sworn to before me, this ——— day of ——— 188—

[Form 5—CHATTEL MORTGAGE].

Know all Men by these Presents, That ———— residing in ———, County of ———, State of Wisconsin, for the purpose of securing the payment of the ———— hereinafter mentioned, and in consideration of one dollar to ———— in hand paid, the receipt of which is hereby acknowledged, do by these presents bargain, sell, assign and set over unto ———— all the following described goods, chattels, and personal property to-wit: said property situated and being now at ———— in the————of————, and County of ———, and State of Wisconsin, and now free and clear from any prior lien or incumbrance, and being in possession of said mortgogor — and to remain in ——— possession until the same shall be taken possession of by said mortgagee as hereinafter provided.

To Have and to Hold the same Forever, upon condition that if said mortgagor — shall pay to said mortgagees the sum of ———— then these presents shall cease and be void. But in case of any default in making such payment, or any part thereof, at the time above agreed on, or in performing any conditions hereof, the said mortgagee ———— hereby authorized and empowered with the aid and assistance of any person or persons, to enter into or upon any place where said mortgaged property may be, and take possession of said mortgaged property and convey it away, and to sell and dispose of the same, at private sale without notice, or at a public sale after giving ——— day's notice of time and place of such sale, in ———— discretion, or so much thereof as may be necessary to satisfy the said debt and interest, and all costs and expenses in taking, keeping and disposing of said property, and to retain the sum out of the proceeds of said sale, rendering the surplus, if any, to said mortgagor —. And in case the said mortgagee — shall at any time deem the said property, or the said debt insecure ——— hereby authorized and empowered to take immediate possession of said mortgaged property, or any part thereof, and to sell and apply the proceeds as above provided

The provisions of this instrument shall extend and apply to the heirs, executors, administrators and assigns of the respective parties.

In Witness Whereof, ——— have hereunto set ——— hand and seal —, this ——— day of ——— A. D., 188 —.

Executed and delivered in the presence of } ———— [SEAL].
———————— ———— [SEAL].

[SCHEDULE REFERRED TO ABOVE].

[Form 6—WARRANTY DEED].

A. B., grantor, of —— County, Wisconsin, hereby conveys and warrants to C. D. grantee of —— County, Wisconsin, for the sum of —— dollars, the following tract of land in —— County, [Here describe the premises].

Witness the hand and seal of said grantor, this —— day of —— 188 —

IN PRESENCE OF } [SEAL].

[Form 7—PROOF OF CLAIM AGAINST ESTATE OF DECEASED].

STATE OF WISCONSIN, }
—— County. } SS.

I —— do solemnly swear that the foregoing —— is true and correct, and that there is justly due and owing to —— from the Estate of —— deceased the sum of $ —— over and above all legal off-sets thereto.

Subscribed and sworn before me, this —— day of —— 188 —

[Form 8—BOND FOR COSTS].

—— COURT, —— COUNTY.

—— *Plaintiff*,
vs.
—— *Defendant*.

Whereas, an order has been made in the above entitled action, requiring the plaintiff — above named to file security for all costs that may be incurred by the defendant — in said action, in the sum of Two Hundred and Fifty Dollars, within twenty days after the service of said order upon said plaintiff —, and staying all proceedings on the part of said plaintiff — in said action until such security be filed:

Now, Therefore, —— of the —— of ——, County of ——, and State of Wisconsin, do undertake that the said plaintiff — will pay, on demand, all costs that may be awarded to the said defendant — in the said action, in any Court not exceeding the sum of Two Hundred and Fifty Dollars.

In Testimony Whereof, the part — above named ha — hereunto set —— hand —— and seal — this —— day of —— A. D. 188 —

IN PRESENCE OF
——
—— } —— [SEAL.]
—— [SEAL.]
—— [SEAL.]

[AFFIDAVIT OF SURETY.]

THE STATE OF WISCONSIN, }
—— County. } SS. ——

being duly sworn, says that he is worth the sum of —— dollars, over and above all his debts and liabilities, in property within the State of Wisconsin, not by law exempt from execution.

Subscribed and sworn to before me, this —— day of —— A. D. 188—

STATE OF WISCONSIN, }
—— County. } SS. ——

being duly sworn, says that he is worth the sum of —— dollars, over and above all his debts and liabilities, in property within the State of Wisconsin, not by law exempt from execution.

Subscribed and sworn to before me this —— day of ——, A. D. 188 —

[Form 9—MORTGAGE].

A. B., mortgagor of —— County, Wisconsin, hereby mortgage to C. D., mortgagee, of —— County, Wisconsin, for the sum of —— dollars, the following tract of land in —— County:

[Here describe the premises].

This mortgage is given to secure the following indebtedness: [here state the amount or amounts of indebtedness, whether on note, bond, or otherwise, time or times when due, rate of interest, by and to whom payable, etc.]

The mortgagor agrees to pay all taxes and assessments on said premises, and the sum of —— dollars attorney's fees in case of foreclosere thereof.

Witness the hand and seal of said mortgagor this, —— day of —— 188 —

—— [SEAL.]
—— [SEAL.]

IN PRESENCE OF
—— }
——

[Form 10—OPENING CLAUSE OF WILL].

I. A. B. of the —— of —— in the County of ——, State of —— being of sound mind and memory, do make, publish and declare this, my last will and testament, hereby revoking all former wills, bequests and devises by me made.

[Form 10*a*—ATTESTATION TO WILL]

Signed, sealed, published and declared by the said A. B. as and for his last will and testament, in the presence of us, who, at his request, in his presence, and in presence of each other have hereunto subscribed our names as attesting witnesses. The words [*state words*] being interlined in [*state where*] and the erasures in [*state where*] being made before singing by the said testator.

[*Names and residence of witnesses*].

LAWS OF WYOMING TERRITORY

RELATIVE TO THE

COLLECTION OF DEBTS, Etc.

Prepared expressly for J. A. Graft & Co.'s Legal Directory, by Potter & Riner, Attorneys and Counsellors at Law, Cheyenne, Wyoming.

ACTIONS.—The old forms of actions (except chancery proceedings) are abolished by the code. Actions commenced in District Court by filing petition, and præcipe; summons issues, returnable on the second Monday after its date. Defendant to answer third Saturday after return day. Actions must be at issue prior to the first day of term, in order to be heard at term.

ATTACHMENTS.—The plaintiff in a civil action for the recovery of money, may have an attachment against the property of the defendant, where the defendant, or one of the defendants is a foreign corporation or a non-resident of the Territory; when the defendant has absconded with intent to defraud his creditors; when he has left the county of his residence to avoid service of summons; when he so conceals himself that summons can not be served upon him; when he is about to remove his property, or a part thereof, out of the jurisdiction of the court, with intent to defraud his creditors; when he is about to convert his property, or a part thereof, into money for the purpose of placing it beyond the reach of his creditors; when he has property or rights of action which he conceals; when he has assigned his property, or a part thereof, with intent to defraud his creditors; or, when he fraudulently contracted the debt, or incurred the obligation for which suit is about to be. or has been brought, and in all cases not exceeding $250, in which the debt is not otherwise secured, and which has not been paid when due, and within ten days thereafter on demand; but an attachment shall not be granted on the ground that the defendant is a foreign corporation or a non-resident of this Territory for any claim other than a debt, or demand arising upon contract, judgment, or decree. Attachment issues upon affidavit and filing of usual undertaking at or after commencement of action. Attachments are allowed in cases when debts are not due in certain cases of fraud.

BONDS FOR COSTS.—Non-resident plaintiffs required to give security for costs, unless paid as they accrue.

COURTS.—Justices' jurisdiction, $100; can try actions for forcible entry and detainer, but can not try cases where title is involved. District Court jurisdiction, unlimited, and have appellate jurisdiction from Justices' Courts. Supreme Court has appellate jurisdiction from District Court in all cases.

ESTATES OF DECEDENTS.—Preferred claims:

1. Funeral and administartion expenses.
2. Expenses of last sickness, wages of servants, and medicines and attendance during last sickness.
3. Judgments rendered against decedent during lifetime.
4. Demands without regard to quality, legally exhibited within six months after first letters granted.

5. All demands thus exhibited within one year after letters granted; claims not exhibited within one year are barred.

Claims, to be legally exhibited, must be served upon representative, stating nature and amount of claim, proved by oath of claimant, to the effect that all credit and off-sets have been given, and that balance is justly due. Claims must be established in Probate Court or any Court of Record having jurisdiction.

EXEMPTIONS.—To a householder, a homestead not exceeding in value $1,500; personal property not exceeding $500 in value; $300 worth of working implements and stock in trade; also the library and implements of a professional man not exceeding $300 in value. Nothing exempt to person about removing from the Territory.

EXECUTION.— No stay in District Court. May be issued any time after judgment. Stay in Justices' Courts, for $25 and not exceeding $50, thirty days; over $50 and not exceeding $10C, sixty days. Bond must be given.

GRACE.—Law merchant governs.

INTEREST.—Legal rate, twelve per cent. Any rate may be agreed upon. No usury laws.

INSOLVENCY.—ASSIGNMENTS.—An insolvent debtor may in good faith execute an assignment of property to one or more assignees in trust for satisfaction of his creditors; but an assignment for the benefit of creditors is void against any creditor of the assignor not assenting thereto, if it give a preference; if it tend to coerce a creditor; if it provide for the payment of a claim known to the assignor to be false or fraudulent; if it reserve any interest in the assigned property; if it make it possible for the assignor to delay the conversion of the assigned property, or if it exempt him from liability for neglect of duty or misconduct.

JUDGMENT LIENS.— A judgment is a lien on the lands and tenements of a judgment debtor from the first day of term at which it is rendered; but judgments by confession, and judgments rendered at the same term at which the action is commenced, bind such lands only from the date of their rendition.

If execution is not sued out within five years from the date of the rendition of judgment, such judgment becomes dormant, and ceases to operate as a lien. The judgment may subsequently be revived, but the lien is not restored, except from the date of revivor.

PROOF OF ACCOUNTS.—Proved in the ordinary way.

PROTEST.—Law merchant governs.

STATUTE OF LIMITATION.—Contract, agreement, or promise, in writing, five pears; not in writing, four years. Debts contracted prior to residence in Territory, are barred after one year's *bona fide* residence here.

TAXES—Due first Monday in September each year. Delinquent after first Monday of November. Lands sold for delinquent taxes by collector, after giving four successive weeks' notice by publication in newspaper published in the county. Redemption within two years by paying purchase money and thirty per cent. being added; also subsequent taxes, with twelve per cent. per annum. Minors, married women, and lunatics, have two years after removal of disability.

WYOMING FORMS.

[Form 1.—ACKNOWLEDGMENT.]

——— OF ———, } ss.
County of ———. }

Be it Remembered, that on this —— day of ——, A. D., 18—, before the undersigned, a (title of officer), within and for the County of —— , and State of ——, personally came ——, who —— personally known to me to be the same person— whose name— —— subscribed to the foregoing instrument of writing, as part— thereto, and acknowledged the same to be —— act and deed for the purposes therein mentioned.

In Testimony Whereof, I have hereunto set my hand and affixed my official seal, at my office in ——, the day and year first above written.

(*Signature and title of officer.*)

[Form 2.—DEED OF TRUST.]

This Deed, Made this —— day of ——, in the year of ——, between ——, (the grantor) of the one part, and —— (the trustee) of the other part; witnesseth: That the said —— (the grantor) doth grant unto the said —— (the trustee) the following property (here describe the property) in trust, to secure (here describe the debts to be secured or the sureties to be indemnified, and insert any special covenants).

Witness the following signatures and seals:

——. [SEAL.]
——. [SEAL.]

[Form 3.—INSTRUCTIONS FOR TAKING DEPOSITIONS.]

The deposition shall be made in the presence of the officer taking the same, and subscribed by the witness; and the officer taking the deposition shall annex thereto a copy of the notice served upon the adverse party, with proof of such service; or if taken upon a special commission the original commission to him issued, and in addition thereto such officer will annex thereto a certificate, showing that the witness was first sworn to testify the truth, the whole truth, and nothing but the truth; that the deposition was reduced to writing by some proper person, (naming him); that the deposition was written and subscribed in the presence of the officer certifying thereto and that the deposition was taken at the time and place specified in the notice.

The deposition so taken and certified shall be sealed up and indorsed with the title of the cause and the name of the officer taking the same; and shall be by him addressed and transmitted to the Clerk of the Court wherein the action or proceeding is pending.

LAWS OF THE PROVINCE OF ONTARIO
RELATIVE TO THE
COLLECTION OF DEBTS, Etc.

Prepared expressly for J. A. Graft & Co's Legal Directory, by Carscallen & Cahill, Barristers &c., Hamilton, Ont.,

ACTIONS.—May be brought in any County, and not necessarily in the County where the defendant lives.

ATTACHMENTS.—If any person resident in Ontario, indebted to any other person absconds from Ontario, with intent to defraud his creditors and is at the time of departing possessed of property etc., he is deemed an absconding debtor and his property may be taken by a writ of attachment for which a Judge's Order must be obtained upon affidavits setting forth the facts, (Rev. Stat. Ontario, Cap. 68.)

Other creditors may share the proceeds of the property seized if they issue their attachments within six months of date, of first writ.

AFFIDAVITS.—If taken in foreign countries should be sworn to before either a Notary Public, a commissioner for Ontario, a Judge of a Court of Record, or the Chief Magistrate of the place and the official seal should be placed on the document.

ARREST.—Imprisonment for debt is abolished except if, on examination before a Judge it is ascertained that the party fraudulently conceals or disposes of his property, or does not disclose full and proper information as to his means &c.

CHATTEL MORTGAGES AND BILLS OF SALE.—All sales and mortgages of personal property, are void as against creditors and subsequent purchasers, or mortgagees, in good faith, for valuable consideration, if not accompanied by an immediate delivery and actual and continual change of possession of the goods mortgaged or sold, unless registered in the office of the Clerk of the County Court of the County where the property is at the time of the execution of the instrument, within five days from the execution thereof, together with an affidavit of the mortgagee or purchaser or his agent as to the bona fides of the mortgage or bill of sale. Within thirty days next preceding the term of one year from the registration of the mortgage, a statement of the mortgagee showing the amount due and his interest in the property mortgaged and an affidavit verifying same and stating that the mortgage is not kept on foot for any fraudulent purpose, must be filed in the Clerk's office, or the mortgage will be void as against creditors and subsequent purchasers or mortgagees in good faith. (Rev. Stat. Ontario, Cap. 119 and 44 vic.)

Assignments and discharges of mortgages may be registered.

CHOSES IN ACTION—Are assignable, but are subject to any defence to which they would have been liable in the hands of the assignor.

EXECUTION.—May issue on judgment, immediately after judgment, unless stayed by the judge at the trial, and is not a lien until placed in the Sheriff's hands and may be issued to several different Counties. Priority between execution creditors is now abolished. All execution creditors rank pro rata for the proceeds of sale.

EXEMPTIONS.—Beds, bedding and wearing apparel of the debtor and his family and a certain quantity of household furniture; provisions to the value of $40, one cow, four sheep, two hogs, and food for thirty days, for same; tools and implements of trade to the value of $60; and fifteen hives of bees, are exempt from seizure under any writ of execution whatever, and the same goods are after the death of the debtor, exempt from the claims of his creditors.

Free grants and homesteads to actual settlers in the districts of Algoma and Nipissing and of certain land between the river Ottawa and the Georgian Bay are also exempt from seizure. (Rev. Stat, Ont., Cap. 66).

FOREIGN JUDGMENTS.—The defendant sued in the Courts of Ontario on a foreign judgment cannot set up as a defence thereto any defence which he set up or might have set up in the original action if he was personally served with process in the said original action, or appeared or pleaded therein.

INSOLVENCY.—The insolvent acts have been repealed except as to cases pending on the 1st, of April, 1880. Debtors, however, may assign to a trustee for the benefit of creditors. The assets in that case should be distributed pro rata without preferrence.

A debtor cannot get a discharge except by consent of creditors.

INTEREST.—Legal rate 6 per cent. Any rate by agreement.

JURISDICTION OF THE COURTS.—Division Courts sits once each month, and has jurisdiction in torts up to $60, debts up to $100, unless acknowledged by signature of defendant, when the Court has jurisdiction up to $200.

County Court sits four times each year and has jurisdiction in all cases for damages up to $200; and in debts liquidated or ascertained by the parties up to $400.

Supreme Court for all matters beyond the jurisdiction of the County Court up to any amount, and sits three times each year in each county town.

The Martitime Court has jurisdiction to any amount and proceedings may be *in rem.*

LIMITATION OF ACTIONS.—Contracts, notes and instruments, not under seal, six years; contracts under seal, including covenants in mortgages, twenty years; on judgments, six years; but may be revived; to recover land, ten years; distress for rent, six years; to recover wild land never in possession of the crown grantee as against person in possession but not claiming under crown grantee, twenty years.

In cases of the plaintiff being under the disability of infancy coverture or lunacy the time runs from the removal of the disability. No greater time is now allowed by reason of the plaintiff's absence from Ontario. The persons under the disability of infancy, lunacy or coverture, or their representatives are allowed five years from the disability or death, notwithstanding the expiry of the period of ten years in which to bring the action, but no action shall be brought except within twenty years next after the right of action approved.

MORTGAGES.—Must be made under seal, by 43 vic. Cap. 42, (Dom. Act) special provision is made for recovery of interest upon money, secured by mortgage in certain cases. There is no redemption after sale under a decree.

A mortgage is discharged by the registration in the land registry office of the county where the land is situated, of a certificate under the hand of the mortgagee, or his assignee, or representative entitled to the money, stating that the mortgage money has been paid.

A mortgage must be registered in order to retain priority.

MARRIED WOMEN.—Real and personal estate exempt from husband's debts, may hold and convey her property as if she was feme sole.

Mechanic Liens.—Every mechanic, machinist, builder, miner, contractor and other person doing work on or furnishing material to be used in constructing any building etc, have a lien to the extent of the owners interest, on the buildings and land for the value of their work or materials, provided that statement, verified by affidavit be filed within one month, in the County Registry Office and proceedings taken to enforce such claims at law within ninety days from time of work completed or material furnished.

Negotiable Investments.—No stamps are required. The law in most respects is the same as the law of England and the United States. Three days of grace are allowed except when payable on demand.

When the last day is a Sunday or legal holiday, the next day succeeding is allowed.

Any rate of interest may be fixed. If no rate fixed, 6 per cent. from date note comes due.

Must be protested when due and parties notified, if not paid, in order to hold endorser liable.

Replevin.—Whenever any personal property has been wrongfully distrained or otherwise wrongfully taken and detained, it may be replevied at the time that the writ is issued upon the plaintiff giving a bond to the Sheriff in treble the value of the property.

Revivor.—By part payment or written acknowledgment.

Security for Costs.—Non-resident plaintiff's may be required to give securfty to the defendant for his costs.

Security may be given either by a bond for $400, executed by two sureties resident in Ontario, or by depositing not less than $200 into Court to abide the event of the suit.

Trust Deeds.—Are not used except for the purpose of effecting family and marriage settlements, or, since the repeal of the insolvent act by debtors for the purpose of paying creditors their just debts rateably.

Witness.—Party interrested may be a witness.

LAWS OF THE PROVINCE OF QUEBEC

RELATIVE TO THE

COLLECTION OF DEBTS, Etc.

Prepared expressly for J. A. Graft & Co.'s Legal Directory, by Andrews, Caron, Andrews & Pentland, Advocates, Quebec, Canada.

Attachment.—Is of various kinds, to facilitate the various remedies of the creditor. In ordinary cases, it takes place as regards movables fifteen days after judgment. After judgment, and before the expiration of the fifteen days, the plaintiff may, on affidavit of the circumstances next hereinafter mentioned, procure the attachment of the debtor's movables. A creditor has also a right, before obtaining judgment, to attach the goods and effects of his debtor, in all cases where as plaintiff he produces an affidavit establishing that the defendant is personally indebted to him in a sum exceeding five dollars, that the defendant absconds, or is immediately about to leave the Province, or is secreting his property, with intent to defraud his creditors, and the plaintiff in particular; or that the defendant is a trader, that he is notoriously insolvent, and has refused to arrange with his creditors, and that in any case the deponent believes that without the benefit of the attachment the plaintiff will lose his debt or sustain damage. A warrant of attachment can be obtained when the claim is not yet due, upon an affidavit of establishing fraud.

EXEMPTIONS—In the sale of movable property of the debtor, the following articles are exempted:

1. Bed, bedding, and bedsteads, in use by himself and his family.
2. The ordinary and necessary wearing apparel of himself and his family.
3. One stove and pipes, one crane and its appendages, one pair of andirons, one set of cooking utensils, one pair of tongs and shovels, one table, six chairs, six knives, six forks, six plates, six tea cups, six saucers, one sugar basin, one milk jug, one tea pot, six spoons, all spinning wheels and weaving looms in domestic use, one ax, one saw, one gun, six traps, such fishing nets and seines, as are in common use, and ten volumes of books.
4. Fuel and food not more than sufficient for thirty days, and not exceeding in value twenty dollars.
5. One cow, four sheep, two hogs, and food therefor for thirty days.
6. Tools and implements, or other chattels ordinarily used in his trade, to the value of thirty dollars.
7. Bees, to the extent of fifteen hives.
8. Nevertheless the things and effects mentioned in paragraphs 4, 5, and 6, are not exempt from seizure and sale when the suit is to recover the price of the purchase, or they have been given in pawn.

The following are also exempt from seizure:

1. Consecrated vessels and things used for religious worship.
2. Alimentary allowance granted by a court.
3. Sums of money or objects given or bequeathed, upon the condition of their being exempt from seizure.
4. Sums of money or pensions given as aliment, even though the donor or testator has not expressly declared that they should be exempt from seizure.
5. Wages and salaries not yet due; certain animals and instruments of agriculture are also exempted by statute passed in the year 1882, viz: two draught horses or oxen, a plough, harrow, working sleigh, tumbril, hay cart, and the harness necessary for farming purposes.

INTEREST.—Interest on judgment debts is fixed at six per cent.; but any rate of interest may be stipulated by consent, except as to banks, which can not stipulate for more than seven per cent.

INSOLVENT LAWS.—The insolvent laws have been repealed, and none now exist.

LEGAL DIRECTORY.

THE ATTORNEYS NAMED HEREIN HAVE BEEN SPECIALLY RECOMMENDED TO US AS BEING PROMPT AND RELIABLE. WE INDORSE THE RECOMMENDATION, AND ANY BUSINESS INTRUSTED TO THEM WILL MEET WITH PROMPT ATTENTION. SHOULD ANY ATTORNEY FAIL TO GIVE PROMPT ATTENTION TO CORRESPONDENCE, COLLECTIONS OR BUSINESS INTRUSTED TO HIS CARE, WE WILL BE THANKFUL TO PATRONS OF THE DIRECTORY TO NOTIFY US PROMPTLY IN ANY SUCH CASE. PARTIES CORRESPONDING WITH ATTORNEYS NAMED IN THE DIRECTORY SHOULD ALWAYS SIGN THEMSELVES "SUBSCRIBERS TO J. A. GRAFT & CO.'S LEGAL DIRECTORY."

PLACES DESIGNATED THUS (*) ARE COUNTY SEATS.

ALABAMA.

POST-OFFICE.	COUNTY.	ATTORNEYS.	POPUL'N.
Abbeville*	Henry	Oates & Cowan	800
Alexander City	Tallapoosa	See Dadeville	800
Andalusia*	Covington	B. H. Lewis	600
Anniston	Calhoun	J. J. Willett	3000
Ashland*	Clay	J. W. McCann	300
Ashville*	St. Clair	See Branchville	600
Athens*	Limestone	W. R. Francis	1200
Auburn	Lee	See Opelika	1200
Bel Green*	Franklin	John T. Ezzell	100
Birmingham*	**Jefferson**	**Wm. M. Bethea**	**18000**
Blountsville*	Blount	L. R. Hanna	500
Branchville	St. Clair	J. H. Vandegrift	200
Brewton	Escambia	James M. Davison	800
Brierfield	Bibb	S. R. Sheppard	1000
Burleson	Franklin	See Bel Green	200
Butler*	Choctaw	W. F. Glover	400
Calera	Shelby	See Columbiana †*Oliver & Oliver.*	500

(†We withdraw our former recommendation.)

Alabama—Continued.

Parties corresponding with Attorneys named in the Directory should ALWAYS sign themselves "Subscribers to J. A. GRAFT & CO.'S LEGAL DIRECTORY." Should any Attorney fail to give prompt attention to correspondence, collections or business intrusted to his care, we will be thankful to patrons of the Directory to notify us promptly in any such case.
Places designated thus (*) are County Seats.

POST-OFFICE.	COUNTY.	ATTORNEYS.	POPUL'N.
Camden*	Wilcox	E. N. Jones	800
Carrollton*	Pickens	M. L. Stansel	800
Centre*	Cherokee	Thomas Mathews	400
Centreville*	Bibb	J. N. Suttle	400
Clanton*	Chilton	See Columbiana	500
Clayton*	Barbour	Thomas & Martin	1500
Collinsville	DeKalb	E. P. Reed	400
Columbia	Henry	D. C. Blackwell	300
Columbiana*	Shelby	J. L. Peters	450
Courtland	Lawrence	Wheeler & Speake	600
Cullman*	Cullman	H. L. Watlington	500
Dadeville*	Tallapoosa	Thomas C. Wynn	500
Daphne*	Baldwin	See Mobile	400
Decatur	Morgan	C. L. Price	1500
Demopolis	Marengo	George G. Lyon	1500
Edwardsville*	Cleburne	J. T. Burton	500
Elba*	Coffee	W. D. Roberts	400
Eufaula	Barbour	Henry D. Clayton, Jr.	5000
Eutaw*	Green	James B. Head	1200
Evergreen*	Conecuh	Stallworth & Burnett	1000
Fayette C. H.*	Fayette	E. P. Jones	400
Florence*	Lauderdale	R. T. Simpson	2000
Fort Payne	De Kalb	See Collinsville	300
Frankfort	Franklin	See Bel Green	300
Gadsden*	Etowah	Denson & Disque †*Benj. F. Pope.*	3500
Gainesville	Sumter	C. L. Winkler	1200
Geneva*	Geneva	C. H. Laney	300
Georgiana	Butler	See Greenville	400
Goodwater	Tallapoosa	See Dadeville	700
Greensboro*	Hale	Coleman & Coleman	1800
Greenville*	Butler	Sam'l J. Bolling	2500
Grove Hill*	Clark	W. D. Dunn, Jr.	400
Guntersville*	Marshall	Hamill & Lusk	1000
Hayneville*	Lowndes	D. J. Little	500
Hillsboro	Lawrence	See Moulton	400
Houston*	Winston	D. C. Vickery	200
Huntsville*	Madison	Betts & Spragins	5000
Jacksonville*	Calhoun	Brothers & Willett	1200
Jasper*	Walker	Appling & McQueen	300

(†We withdraw our former recommendation.)

Alabama—Continued.

Parties corresponding with Attorneys named in the Directory should ALWAYS sign themselves "Subscribers to J. A. GRAFT & CO.'S LEGAL DIRECTORY."
Should any Attorney fail to give prompt attention to correspondence, collections or business intrusted to his care, we will be thankful to patrons of the Directory to notify us promptly in any such case.
Places designated thus (*) are County Seats.

POST-OFFICE.	COUNTY.	ATTORNEYS.	POPUL'N.
La Fayette*	Chambers	J. B. Duke	1400
Landersville	Lawrence	See Moulton	200
Lebanon*	DeKalb	See Collinsville	300
Linden*	Marengo	See Demopolis	300
Livingston*	Sumter	J. J. Altman	800
Marion*	Perry	Kelley & Howze	2800
Meltonsville	Marshall	See Guntersville	100
Mobile*	**Mobile**	**S. P. Gaillard**	**30000**
Monroeville*	Monroe	D. L. Neville	500
Montevallo	Shelby	W. W. Shortridge	600
Montgomery*	**Montgomery**	**Stringfellow & Le Grand**	**25000**
Moulton*	Lawrence	John C. Eyster	500
Mount Hope	Lawrence	See Moulton	200
Opelika*	Lee	B. K. Collier	3500
Oxford	Calhoun	R. B. Kelley	800
Ozark*	Dale	B. F. Cassady	700
Pikeville*	Marion	T. B. Nesmith	200
Pleasant Site	Franklin	See Bel Green	200
Pollard*	Escambia	James M. Davison	500
Prattville*	Autauga	M. A. Smith	1200
Rockford*	Coosa	See Columbiana	300
Russellville	Franklin	See Bel Green	200
Rutledge*	Crenshaw	J. H. Parks	300
Scottsboro*	Jackson	J. H. Gregory	800
Seale*	Russell	James F. Waddel	500
Selma*	Dallas	John C. Reid †*J. S. Diggs.*	10000
Somerville*	Morgan	See Decatur	300
Stevenson	Jackson	See Scottsboro	300
Talladega*	Talladega	John M. Bishop	2500
Troy*	Pike	James B. Cox	4000
Tuscaloosa*	Tuscaloosa	McEachin & McEachin	2000
Tuscumbia*	Colbert	L. B. Cooper	2000
Tuskegee*	Macon	Waddy Thompson	2500
Union Springs*	Bullock	Powell & Cabiness	2000
Uniontown	Perry	George H. Bradfield	1500
Vernon*	Lamar	T. B. Nesmith	500
Wedowee*	Randolph	Smith & Smith	200
Wetumpka*	Elmore	W. P. Gaddis	1200

(†We withdraw our former recommendation.)

ARIZONA TERRITORY.

Parties corresponding with Attorneys named in the Directory should ALWAYS sign themselves "Subscribers to J. A. GRAFT & CO.'S LEGAL DIRECTORY." Should any Attorney fail to give prompt attention to correspondence, collections or business intrusted to his care, we will be thankful to patrons of the Directory to notify us promptly in any such case. Places designated thus (*) are County Seats.

POST-OFFICE.	COUNTY.	ATTORNEYS.	POPUL'N.
Benson	Cochise	Jos. H. Tracy	600
Cerbat	Mobave	See Mineral Park	300
Florence*	Pinal	See Globe	1000
Globe	Pinal	Lemon & McCabe	1000
Mineral Park*	Mohave	Davis & Williams	600
Phœnix*	Maricopa	Tweed, Hancock & Crenshaw	2000
Pinal	Pinal	See Globe	600
Prescott*	Yavapai	John J. Hawkins	2000
Tombstone	Cochise	W. H. Savage	5000
Tucson*	Pima	J. A. Anderson	10000
Yuma*	Yuma	Samuel Purdy	1500

ARKANSAS.

POST-OFFICE.	COUNTY.	ATTORNEYS.	POPUL'N.
Arkadelphia	Clark	J. W. Miller	2000
Arkansas City	Desha	C. H. Harding	800
Augusta*	Woodruff	T. C. Stanley	1200
Batesville*	Independence	Coleman & Yancey	1600
Benton*	Saline	S. H. Whitthorn	600
Bentonville*	Benton	R. W. Ellis	800
Berryville*	Carroll	J. C. Moore	500
Camden*	Ouachita	Thos. W. Hardy	2000
Carrollton	Carroll	See Eureka Springs	400
Centre Point*	Howard	J. E. Borden	400
Clarendon*	Monroe	H. A. Parker	800
Clarksville*	Johnson	J. H. Basham	900
Clinton*	Van Buren	James H. Fraser	300
Conway*	Faulkner	P. H. Prince	1500
Corning	Clay	See Gainesville	400

Arkansas—Continued.

Parties corresponding with Attorneys named in the Directory should ALWAYS sign themselves "Subscribers to J. A. GRAFT & CO.'S LEGAL DIRECTORY."
Should any Attorney fail to give prompt attention to correspondence, collections or business intrusted to his care, we will be thankful to patrons of the Directory to notify us promptly in any such case.
Places designated thus (*) are County Seats.

POST-OFFICE.	COUNTY.	ATTORNEYS.	POPUL'N
Dallas*	Polk	Thomas Wright	200
Danville*	Yell	See Dardanelle	300
Dardanelle	Yell	T. M. Gibson	2000
Des Arc*	Prairie	J. S. Thomas	600
De Witt*	Arkansas	J. A. Gibson	400
Dover*	Pope	See Russellville	400
El Dorado*	Union	See Magnolia	600
Eureka Springs	Carroll	**H. Glitsch** (See card in Appendix, page I.)	**10000**
Evening Shade*	Sharp	S. H. Davidson	300
Fayetteville*	Washington	B. R. Davidson	2000
Forrest City*	St. Francis	John Gatling	1200
Fort Smith	Sebastian	Cooke & Luce	8000
Fulton	Hempstead	See Hope	300
Gainesville*	Greene	J. E. Riddick	300
Greenwood*	Sebastian	See Fort Smith	400
Hamburg*	Ashley	George W. Norman	1500
Hampton*	Calhoun	J. R. Thornton	500
Harrisburg*	Poinsett	E. A. Owen	1200
Harrison*	Boone	Crump & Watkins	1200
Helena*	Phillips	Thweatt & Powell	5000
Hope	Hempstead	B. F. Kennedy	2000
Hot Springs*	Garland	John D. Kimbell	8000
Huntsville*	Madison	R. S. Andrews	400
Jacksonport*	Jackson	See Newport	1200
Jasper*	Newton	See Clarksville	100
Jonesboro*	Craighead	Sam A. Warner, Jr.	300
Lake Village*	Chicot	J. C. Connerly	200
Lewisburg*	Conway	See Morrillton	800
Lewisville*	La Fayette	D. L. King	500
Little Rock*	**Pulaski**	**Dodge & Johnson**	**25000**
Locksburg*	Sevier	Steel & Steel	400
Lonoke*	Lonoke	J. C. & C.W. England	1200
Madison	St. Francis	See Forrest City	200
Magnolia*	Columbia	Charles P. Roberts	2000
Malvern*	Hot Springs	A. Curl	1200
Marianna*	Lee	J. M. Daggett	700
Marion*	Crittenden	R. F. Crittenden	300
Marshall*	Searcy	James L. Muir	300

Arkansas—Continued.

Parties corresponding with Attorneys named in the Directory should ALWAYS sign themselves "Subscribers to J. A. GRAFT & CO.'S LEGAL DIRECTORY." Should any Attorney fail to give prompt attention to correspondence, collections or business intrusted to his care, we will be thankful to patrons of the Directory to notify us promptly in any such case. Places designated thus (*) are County Seats.

POST-OFFICE.	COUNTY.	ATTORNEYS.	POPUL'N
Melbourne*	Izard	R. H. Powell	300
Monticello*	Drew	C. D. Wood	1200
Morrillton	Conway	Carroll Armstrong	1500
Mountain Home*	Baxter	See Evening Shade	300
Mountain View*	Stone	B. F. Williamson	200
Mount Ida*	Montgomery	John A. Watkins	200
Murfreesboro*	Pike	W. B. Thomasson, Jr.	300
Newport	Jackson	M. Mart Stuckey	1500
Osceola*	Mississippi	S. S. Semmes	600
Ozark*	Franklin	Mathes & Berry	1200
Paragould	Greene	See Gainesville	500
Paris*	Logan	Anthony Hall	500
Perryville*	Perry	J. F. Sellers	500
Pine Bluff*	Jefferson	J. M. & J. G. Taylor	6000
Pocahontas*	Randolph	George T. Black	1200
Powhattan*	Lawrence	Baber & Thornburgh	400
Prescott*	Nevada	Smoote & McRae	1500
Princeton*	Dallas	R. T. Fuller	300
Rocky Comfort*	Little River	E. W. Dollarhide	200
Rogers	Benton	See Bentonville	200
Russellville	Pope	R. B. Wilson	1200
Salem*	Fulton	J. C. Claibourn	200
Searcy*	White	J. F. Rives, Jr.	1200
Sheridan*	Grant	T. B. Morton	200
Siloam Springs	Benton	E. D. Fenno	1800
Star City*	Lincoln	J. M. Cunningham	800
Texarkana*	Miller	Todd & Hudgins	5000
Toledo*	Dorsey	W. S. Amis	200
Van Buren*	Crawford	O. P. Brown	2000
Waldron*	Scott	T. N. Sanford	500
Warren*	Bradley	A. C. Jones	300
Washington*	Hempstead	See Hope	1000
Watson's*	Desha	See Arkansas City	500
Wittsburg*	Cross	N. W. Norton	800
Yellville*	Marion	J. F. Wilson	300

CALIFORNIA.

Parties corresponding with Attorneys named in the Directory should ALWAYS sign themselves "Subscribers to J. A. GRAFT & CO.'S LEGAL DIRECTORY." Should any Attorney fail to give prompt attention to correspondence, collections or business intrusted to his care, we will be thankful to patrons of the Directory to notify us promptly in any such case.
Places designated thus (*) are County Seats.

POST-OFFICE.	COUNTY.	ATTORNEYS.	POPUL'N.
Alameda	Alameda	See Oakland	6000
Alturas*	Modoc	F. W. Ewing	300
Anaheim	Los Angeles	See Los Angeles	1000
Auburn*	Placer	J. E. Hale	1200
Bakersfield	Kern	A. C. Maud	1000
Benici	Solano	See Fairfield	2000
Bodie	Mono	O. F. Hakes	3000
Bridgeport*	Mono	W. O. Parker	400
Camptonville	Yuba	J. R. Young	400
Cedarville	Modoc	See Alturas	400
Chico	Butte	F. C. Lusk	5000
Cloverdale	Sonoma	See Santa Rosa	500
Colusa*	Colusa	Richard Bayne	2500
Crescent City*	Del Norte	W. A. Hamilton	800
Dixon	Solano	See Fairfield	1500
Downieville*	Sierra	S. B. Davidson	1000
Dutch Flat	Placer	See Auburn	1000
Eureka*	Humboldt	Frank McGowan	6000
Fairfield*	Solano	W. S. Crocker	700
Folsom City	Sacramento	See Sacramento	2000
Forest City	Sierra	See Downieville	1000
Fort Jones	Siskiyou	See Yreka	500
Fresno City*	Fresno	H. S. Dixon	1500
Gilroy	Santa Clara	See San Jose	3000
Grass Valley	Nevada	C. W. Kitts	600
Gridley	Butte	See Chico	500
Havilah	Kern	See Bakersfield	400
Haywards	Alameda	See Oakland	1500
Healdsburg	Sonoma	Rose & Cochran	1500
Hollister*	San Benito	Briggs & Hawkins	2000
Independence*	Inyo	Reddy & Conklin	1000
Iowa City	Placer	See Auburn	500
Ione	Amador	H. A. Carter	600
Jackson*	Amador	Eagan & Armstrong	1200
Lakeport*	Lake	Woods Crawford	800
Livermore	Alameda	See Oakland	1000

California—Continued.

Parties corresponding with Attorneys named in the Directory should ALWAYS sign themselves "Subscribers to J. A. GRAFT & CO.'S LEGAL DIRECTORY." Should any Attorney fail to give prompt attention to correspondence, collections or business intrusted to his care, we will be thankful to patrons of the Directory to notify us promptly in any such case.
Places designated thus (*) are County Seats.

POST-OFFICE.	COUNTY.	ATTORNEYS	POPUL'N.
Los Angeles*	Los Angeles	Wells, Van Dyke & Lee	30000
Los Gatos	Santa Clara	See San Jose	1000
Mariposa*	Mariposa	L. F. Jones	800
Markleeville*	Alpine	G. E. Lukens	500
Martinez*	Contra Costa	A. H. Griffith	2500
Marysville*	Yuba	E. A. Davis	6000
Mendocino	Mendocino	See Ukiah	800
Merced*	Merced	John K. Law	2000
Michigan Bluff	Placer	See Auburn	600
Modesto*	Stanislaus	George A. Whitby	3000
Napa City*	Napa	Mount, Boke & Co.	5000
Nevada City*	Nevada	Alfred D. Mason	5000
Oakland*	Alameda	Edw. C. Robinson	40000
Oroville*	Butte	John C. Gray	2000
Petaluma	Sonoma	W. B. Haskell	4000
Placerville*	El Dorado	C. F. Irwin	2000
Pomona	Los Angeles	See Los Angeles	500
Quincy*	Plumas	A. T. Nation	1000
Red Bluff*	Tehama	Chapman & Garter	3000
Redding	Shasta	See Shasta	1000
Redwood City*	San Mateo	George W. Fox	2000
Riverside	San Bernardino	See San Bernardino	2000
Sacramento*	Sacramento	I. S. Brown	25000
Salinas*	Monterey	Geil & Morehouse	4000
San Andreas*	Calaveras	J. B. Reddick	1500
San Bernardino*	San Bernardino	John L. Campbell	3500
San Buenaventura*	Ventura	J. Marion Brooks	2000
San Diego*	San Diego	E. W. Hendrick	4000
San Francisco*	**San Francisco**	**Wm. H. H. Hart** Manager Branch Office, No. 130 MONTGOMERY ST. (See card in Appendix, page 1.)	**300000**
San Jose*	Santa Clara	John E. Richards	16000
San Luis Obispo*	San Luis Obispo	J. M. Wilcoxen	3000
San Rafael*	Marin	F. M. Angellotti	4000
Santa Ana	Los Angeles	See Los Angeles	1000
Santa Barbara*	Santa Barbara	E. B. Hall	5000
Santa Clara	Santa Clara	See San Jose	2500

California—Continued.

Parties corresponding with Attorneys named in the Directory should ALWAYS sign themselves "Subscribers to J. A. GRAFT & CO.'S LEGAL DIRECTORY." Should any Attorney fail to give prompt attention to correspondence, collections or business intrusted to his care, we will be thankful to patrons of the Directory to notify us promptly in any such case. Places designated thus (*) are County Seats.

POST-OFFICE.	COUNTY.	ATTORNEYS.	POPUL'N.
Santa Cruz*	Santa Cruz	W. D. Storey	5000
Santa Rosa*	Sonoma	G. A. Johnson	6000
Shasta*	Shasta	A. R. Andrews	2000
Sierra Valley	Sierra	See Downieville	1000
Sonoma	Sonoma	See Santa Rosa	1000
Sonora*	Tuolumne	Street & Street	2000
St. Helena	Napa	See Napa City	1500
Stockton*	San Joaquin	John C. Byers	14000
Suisun City	Solano	See Fairfield	1000
Susanville*	Lassen	E. R. Dodge	1000
Tomales	Marin	See San Rafael	1000
Tulare	Tulare	See Visalia	1000
Ukiah*	Mendocino	James M. Mannon	1500
Vacaville	Solano	See Fairfield	600
Vallejo	Solano	See Fairfield	7000
Visalia*	Tulare	T. E. McNamara	2000
Watsonville	Santa Cruz	See Santa Cruz	2500
Weaverville*	Trinity	C. E. Williams	1500
Wheatland	Yuba	See Marysville	1000
Willow	Colusa	See Colusa	1000
Woodland*	Yolo	C. P. Sprague	3500
Yreka*	Siskiyou	H. B. Warren	2000
Yuba City*	Sutter	S. J. Stabler	1300

COLORADO.

POST-OFFICE.	COUNTY.	ATTORNEYS.	POPUL'N.
Alamosa	Conejos	Eugene Engley	1700
Alma	Park	See Fair Play	1000
Alpine	Chaffee	See Buena Vista	1000
Aspen*	Pitkin	J. M. Downing	800
Black Hawk	Gilpin	See Central City	1500

Colorado—Continued.

Parties corresponding with Attorneys named in the Directory should ALWAYS sign themselves "Subscribers to J. A. GRAFT & CO.'S LEGAL DIRECTORY."
Should any Attorney fail to give prompt attention to correspondence, collections or business intrusted to his care, we will be thankful to patrons of the Directory to notify us promptly in any such case.
Places designated thus (*) are County Seats.

POST-OFFICE.	COUNTY.	ATTORNEYS.	POPUL'N.
Bonanza	Saguache	James M. Denny	1500
Boulder*	Boulder	David Bartlett	3500
Breckenridge*	Summit	Breeze & Breeze	2000
Buena Vista*	Chaffee	John K. Vanatta	2500
Canon City*	Fremont	M. S. Adams	2500
Castle Rock*	Douglas	William Dillon	1500
Central City*	Gilpin	Chase Withrow	3000
Colorado Springs*	El Paso	Ianthus Bentley	6000
Conejos*	Conejos	See Alamosa	1000
Crested Butte	Gunnison	See Gunnison	700
Del Norte*	Rio Grande	Adair Wilson	1500
Delta*	Delta	S. S. Sherman	1000
Denver*	**Arapahoe**	**Harman & Cover** Managers Branch Office, Cass & Graham Block.	**75000**
Durango	La Plata	M. J. McCloskey	2500
Fair Play*	Park	C. A. Wilkin	1000
Fort Collins*	Larimer	Charles H. Marsh	2800
Georgetown*	Clear Creek	A. D. Bullis	3000
Golden*	Jefferson	William A. Dier	3000
Gothic	Gunnison	See Gunnison	800
Grand Junction*	Mesa	James W. Bucklin	800
Greeley*	Weld	James W. McGreery	2000
Gunnison*	Gunnison	Gullett & Karr	2000
Hayden	Routt	Thomas Hooker	300
Hot Sulphur Springs*	Grand	See Boulder	400
Idaho Springs	Clear Creek	See Georgetown	1500
Irwin	Gunnison	See Gunnison	1000
Kiowa*	Elbert	See Castle Rock	500
Kokomo	Summit	See Breckenridge	1500
La Junta	Bent	See Pueblo	500
Lake City*	Hinsdale	Lyman I. Henry	1000
Leadville*	**Lake**	**J. F. Frueauff**	**15000**
Longmont	Boulder	See Boulder	1000
Loveland	Larimer	W. M. Slaughter	1000
Montezuma	Summit	See Breckenridge	500
Montrose*	Montrose	C. W. Blackmer	1000
Ouray*	Ouray	Story & Stevens	1000

Colorado—Continued.

Parties corresponding with Attorneys named in the Directory should ALWAYS sign themselves "Subscribers to J. A. GRAFT & CO.'S LEGAL DIRECTORY."
Should any Attorney fail to give prompt attention to correspondence, collections or business intrusted to his care, we will be thankful to patrons of the Directory to notify us promptly in any such case.
Places designated thus (*) are County Seats.

POST-OFFICE.	COUNTY.	ATTORNEYS.	POPUL'N.
Parrott*	La Plata	See Durango	600
Pitkin	Gunnison	See Gunnison	2000
Poncho Springs	Chaffee	See Buena Vista	300
Pueblo*	Pueblo	Dan. B. Gregg	10000
Rico*	Dolores	Lafe Pence	1000
Rosita*	Custer	Frank P. Warner	1800

HE ATTORNEYS named herein have been
CIALLY RECOMMENDED by TWO or more in-
iduals or firms of their respective
alities.
ATRONS of the Directory can DEPEND
n the reliability of the Attorneys,
feel PERFECTLY SAFE in INTRUSTING
business to them.

CONNECTICUT.

POST-OFFICE.	COUNTY.	ATTORNEYS.	POPUL'N.
Ansonia	New Haven	See New Haven	4000
Birmingham	New Haven	See New Haven	7000
Bridgeport*	Fairfield	Jos. A. Joyce	35000
Bristol	Hartford	Epaphroditus Peck	6000
Brooklyn*	Windham	E. L. Cundall	3000
Canaan	Litchfield	See Litchfield	1500
Chester	Middlesex	See Deep River	2000
Clinton	Middlesex	David L. Peck	2000

Colorado—Continued.

Parties corresponding with Attorneys named in the Directory should ALWAYS sign themselves "Subscribers to J. A. GRAFT & CO.'S LEGAL DIRECTORY." Should any Attorney fail to give prompt attention to correspondence, collections or business intrusted to his care, we will be thankful to patrons of the Directory to notify us promptly in any such case. Places designated thus (*) are County Seats.

POST-OFFICE.	COUNTY.	ATTORNEYS.	POPUL'N.
Bonanza	Saguache	James M. Denny	1500
Boulder*	Boulder	David Bartlett	3500
Breckenridge*	Summit	Breeze & Breeze	2000
Buena Vista*	Chaffee	John K. Vanatta	2500
Canon City*	Fremont	M. S. Adams	2500
Castle Rock*	Douglas	William Dillon	1500
Central City*	Gilpin	Chase Withrow	3000
Colorado Springs*	El Paso	Ianthus Bentley	6000
Conejos*			
C			
D			
D			
D			
D			
F			
F			
G			
G			
G			
G			
G			
G			
Hayden	Routt	Thomas Hooker	300
Hot Sulphur Springs*	Grand	See Boulder	400
Idaho Springs	Clear Creek	See Georgetown	1500
Irwin	Gunnison	See Gunnison	1000
Kiowa*	Elbert	See Castle Rock	500
Kokomo	Summit	See Breckenridge	1500
La Junta	Bent	See Pueblo	500
Lake City*	Hinsdale	Lyman I. Henry	1000
Leadville*	**Lake**	**J. F. Frueauff**	**15000**
Longmont	Boulder	See Boulder	1000
Loveland	Larimer	W. M. Slaughter	1000
Montezuma	Summit	See Breckenridge	500
Montrose*	Montrose	C. W. Blackmer	1000
Ouray*	Ouray	Story & Stevens	1000

Colorado—Continued.

Parties corresponding with Attorneys named in the Directory should ALWAYS sign themselves "Subscribers to J. A. GRAFT & CO.'S LEGAL DIRECTORY."
Should any Attorney fail to give prompt attention to correspondence, collections or business intrusted to his care, we will be thankful to patrons of the Directory to notify us promptly in any such case.
Places designated thus (*) are County Seats.

POST-OFFICE.	COUNTY.	ATTORNEYS.	POPUL'N.
Parrott*	La Plata	See Durango	600
Pitkin	Gunnison	See Gunnison	2000
Poncho Springs	Chaffee	See Buena Vista	300
Pueblo*	Pueblo	Dan. B. Gregg	10000
Rico*	Dolores	Lafe Pence	1000
Rosita*	Custer	Frank P. Warner	1800
Saguache*	Saguache	C. A. Allen	600
Salida	Chaffee	R. K. Hagan	3500
San Luis*	Costilla	See Trinidad	1500
Silver Cliff	Custer	A. J. Rising	2500
Silverton*	San Juan	Gray & Frazier	4000
South Pueblo	Pueblo	See Pueblo	1500
St. Elmo	Chaffee	See Salida	800
Telluride*	San Miguel	W. H. Gabbert	1000
Tin Cup	Gunnison	See Gunnison	500
Tomichi	Gunnison	See Gunnison	500
Trinidad*	Las Animas	O. J. Bates	6000
Villa Grove	Saguache	See Rosita	300
Walsenburg*	Huerfano	R. A. Sullivan	600
West Las Animas*	Bent	See Pueblo	800

CONNECTICUT.

POST-OFFICE.	COUNTY.	ATTORNEYS.	POPUL'N.
Ansonia	New Haven	See New Haven	4000
Birmingham	New Haven	See New Haven	7000
Bridgeport*	Fairfield	Jos. A. Joyce	35000
Bristol	Hartford	Epaphroditus Peck	6000
Brooklyn*	Windham	E. L. Cundall	3000
Canaan	Litchfield	See Litchfield	1500
Chester	Middlesex	See Deep River	2000
Clinton	Middlesex	David L. Peck	2000

Connecticut—Continued.

Parties corresponding with Attorneys named in the Directory should ALWAYS sign themselves "Subscribers to J. A. GRAFT & CO.'S LEGAL DIRECTORY." Should any Attorney fail to give prompt attention to correspondence, collections or business intrusted to his care, we will be thankful to patrons of the Directory to notify us promptly in any such case. Places designated thus (*) are County Seats.

POST-OFFICE.	COUNTY.	ATTORNEYS.	POPUL'N'
Colchester	New London	See Norwich	2500
Collinsville	Hartford	See Hartford	2500
Cromwell	Middlesex	See Middletown	2000
Danbury*	Fairfield	David B. Booth	13000
Danielsonville	Windham	Cundall & Bill	3500
Deep River	Middlesex	W. F. Wilcox	1500
Essex	Middlesex	James Phelps	2500
Falls Village	Litchfield	L. P. Dean	1000
Greenwich	Fairfield	H. W. R. Hoyt	8500
Hartford*	**Hartford**	**George G. Sill**	**50000**
Jewett City	New London	See Norwich	2500
Litchfield*	Litchfield	John T. Hubbard	3500
Meriden	New Haven	O. H. & J. P. Platt	18000
Middletown*	Middlesex	S. L. Warner	12000
Naugatuck	New Haven	See New Haven	5000
New Britain	Hartford	V. B. Chamberlain	15000
New Haven*	**New Haven**	**Wm. A. Wright** Manager Branch Office, 153 Church St. Refers to First National Bank.	**72000**
New London*	New London	Augustus Brandagee	12000
New Milford	Litchfield	See Litchfield	2000
Norwalk	Fairfield	Frank H. Rose	6000
Norwich*	New London	J. J. Desmond	22000
Plainville	Hartford	See Bristol	2000
Portland	Middlesex	D. A. McQuillin	4500
Putnam	Windham	S. H. Seward	6000
Rockville	Tolland	B. H. Bill	7000
Sharon	Litchfield	Willard Baker	2500
Southington	Hartford	M. H. Holcomb	6000
South Norwalk	Fairfield	See Norwalk	10000
Southport	Fairfield	See Bridgeport	4000
Stafford Springs	Tolland	S. E. Fairfield	3000
Stamford	Fairfield	N. R. Hart	10000
Stonington	New London	See Westerly, R. I.	4000

Connecticut—Continued.

Parties corresponding with Attorneys named in the Directory should ALWAYS sign themselves "Subscribers to J. A. GRAFT & CO.'S LEGAL DIRECTORY." Should any Attorney fail to give prompt attention to correspondence, collections or business intrusted to his care, we will be thankful to patrons of the Directory to notify us promptly in any such case.
Places designated thus (*) are County Seats.

POST-OFFICE.	COUNTY.	ATTORNEYS.	POPUL'N.
Suffield	Hartford	See Hartford	4000
Thomaston	Litchfield	A. P. Bradstreet	4000
Thompson	Windham	See Brooklyn	1500
Tolland*	Tolland	E. S. Agard	2000
Torrington	Litchfield	See Litchfield	3000
Wallingford	New Haven	See New Haven	4000
Waterbury	New Haven	Kellogg, Burpee & Kellogg	29000
Westport	Fairfield	See Norwalk	2500
West Winsted	Litchfield	See Winsted	4000
Willimantic	Windham	John M. Hall	8000
Windsor Locks	Hartford	Johnson & Coats	3000
Winsted	Litchfield	Lawrence & Smith	4000

DAKOTA TERRITORY.

POST-OFFICE.	COUNTY.	ATTORNEYS.	POPUL'N.
Aberdeen	Brown	C. N. Harris	2500
Alexandria*	Hanson	R. M. Dott	700
Altoona	Beadle	Mouser and Everitt	1000
Ashton*	Spink	See Redfield	500
Athol	Spink	See Northville	500
Aurora	Brookings	B. J. Kelsey	300
Bathgate	Pembina	See Pembina	200
Big Stone City	Grant	See Millbank	800
		†*Edgar M. Bennett.*	
Bismarck*	Burleigh	Gray & Gray	5000
Blunt	Hughes	Loring E. Gaffy	1200
Bridgewater	McCook	See Sioux Falls	600
Brookings*	Brookings	Mathews & Scobey	1200
Buxton	Traill	See Mayville	400
Caledonia*	Traill	W. F. Ames	500
Canton*	Lincoln	J. W. Taylor.	2000
Carrington*	Foster	A. G. Covell	800
Carthage	Miner	See Howard	300
Casselton	Cass	See Fargo	400

(†We withdraw our former recommendation.)

Dakota—Continued.

Parties corresponding with Attorneys named in the Directory should ALWAYS sign themselves "Subscribers to J. A. GRAFT & CO.'S LEGAL DIRECTORY."
Should any Attorney fail to give prompt attention to correspondence, collections or business intrusted to his care, we will be thankful to patrons of the Directory to notify us promptly in any such case.
Places designated thus (*) are County Seats.

POST-OFFICE.	COUNTY.	ATTORNEYS.	POPUL'N.
Castalia	Charles Mix	See Chamberlain	300
Castlewood*	Hamlin	Webber & Lake	500
Central City	Lawrence	T. E. Harvey	1000
Centreville	Turner	See Parker	300
Chamberlain*	Brule	C. C. Morrow	1200
Clark*	Clark	John E. Bennett	600
Columbia*	Brown	H. A. Tice	700
Cooperstown*	Griggs	Byron Andrus	400
Custer*	Custer	N. P. Cook	500
Dawson	Kidder	Thos. Neill	400
Deadwood*	Lawrence	Moody & Washabaugh	4500
Dell Rapids	Minnehaha	M. R. Kenefick	800
Denver	Kingsbury	See De Smet	800
De Smet*	Kingsbury	A. A. Anderson	1000
Devil's Lake*	Ramsey	Frank W. Wilder	1100
Egan	Moody	G. M. De Groff	400
Elk Point*	Union	A. D. Keller	1000
Elkton	Brookings	See Aurora	400
Ellendale*	Dickey	DeCoster & Flemington	1000
Estelline	Hamlin	See Castlewood	400
Fargo*	Cass	Francis & Francis	10000
Faulkton	Faulk	See Northville	300
Flandrau*	Moody	C. D. Pratt	1000
Frankfort	Spink	See Redfield	400
Frederick	Brown	See Aberdeen	400
Gary*	Deuel	See Watertown	600
Gettysburg	Potter	See Redfield	300
Grafton*	Walsh	C. A. M. Spencer	2500
Grand Forks*	Grand Forks	Merrinan & Hill	5000
Grand View*	Douglas	See Plankinton	300
Groton	Brown	Bowers & Erwin	500
Highmore*	Hyde	L. E. Whitcher	500
Hillsboro.	Traill	Francis & Francis	800
Howard*	Miner	D. D. Holdridge.	800
Hurley	Turner	See Parker	300
Huron*	Beadle	Norton D. Walling	3000
Ipswich	Edmunds	See Roscoe	700
Iroquois	Kingsbury	See De Smet	400
Jamestown*	Stutsman	Roderick Rose	3500
Keystone	Dickey	Horace Gleason	1000

Dakota—Continued.

Parties corresponding with Attorneys named in the Directory should ALWAYS sign themselves "Subscribers to J. A. GRAFT & CO.'S LEGAL DIRECTORY." Should any Attorney fail to give prompt attention to correspondence, collections or business intrusted to his care, we will be thankful to patrons of the Directory to notify us promptly in any such case.
Places designated thus (*) are County Seats.

POST-OFFICE.	COUNTY.	ATTORNEYS.	POPUL'N.
Kimball	Brule	Gabe E. Schwindt	1000
Lake Preston	Kingsbury	George W. Fifield	400
Lakota*	Nelson	Henry D. Fruit	400
La Moure*	La Moure	G. D. Farwell	800
Larimore	Grand Forks	See Grand Forks	500
Lead City	Lawrence	See Deadwood	1200
Le Beau	Walworth	See Aberdeen	500
Lennox	Lincoln	Peter F. Haas	400
Lisbon*	Ransom	Van Pelt & Gammons	1000
Madison*	Lake	F. L. Soper	1200
Mandan*	Morton	Austin N. McGindley	3000
Marion	Turner	See Parker	600
Mayville	Traill	Shanks & Griswold	800
Millbank*	Grant	Sam. S. Lockhart	1800
Miller*	Hand	Manford E. Williams	600
Milltown	Hutchinson	See Olivet	400
Milnor	Sargent	See Wahpeton	400
Minto	Walsh	James Garbutt	600
Mitchell*	Davison	Dillon & Preston	1800
Mt. Vernon	Davison	See Mitchell	700
Northville	Spink	Thomas Sterling	200
Olivet*	Hutchinson	J. N. True	500
Ordway	Brown	Barnes & Luse	500
Oriska	Barnes	See Valley City	300
Parker*	Turner	W. Y. Quigley	900
Pembina*	Pembina	Kneeshaw & Bevans	1500
Pierre*	Hughes	Dell Coy	2100
Plankinton*	Aurora	W. M. Smith	1000
Portland	Traill	See Mayville	500
Rapid City*	Pennington	Mitchell & Benedict	3000
Redfield	Spink	Ferris & Ferris	1800
Ree Heights	Hand	See Miller	400
Roscoe	Edmunds	Edgar Sharpe	200
Salem*	McCook		700
Sanborn	Barnes	Chas. A. Van Warmer	500
Scotland	Bon Homme	A. J. Faulk, Jr.	700
Sheldon	Ransom	See Lisbon	300
Sims	Morton	See Mandan	300

Dakota—Continued.

Parties corresponding with Attorneys named in the Directory should ALWAYS sign themselves "Subscribers to J. A. GRAFT & CO.'S LEGAL DIRECTORY." Should any Attorney fail to give prompt attention to correspondence, collections or business intrusted to his care, we will be thankful to patrons of the Directory to notify us promptly in any such case.
Places designated thus (*) are County Seats.

POST-OFFICE.	COUNTY.	ATTORNEYS.	POPUL'N.
Sioux Falls*	Minnehaha	Coughran & McMartin	6000
Spaulding	Hamlin	See Castlewood	400
Spearfish	Lawrence	W. W. Bradley	300
Springfield	Bon Homme	M. H. Day	300
Steele*	Kidder	See Dawson	300
St. Lawrence	Hand	See Miller	300
St. Thomas	Pembina	See Pembina	200
Sturgis	Lawrence	Charles C. Polk	700
Tower City	Cass	See Fargo	300
Valley City*	Barnes	John W. Scott	1500
Valley Springs	Minnehaha	See Sioux Falls	400
Vermillion*	Clay	John J. Jolley	1500
Volga	Brookings	See Aurora	1000
Wahpeton*	Richland	J. R. Buxton	2000
Watertown*	Codington	J. L. Robinson	3000
Webster*	Day	See Millbank	500
Wessington	Beadle	See Huron	400
Westport	Brown	See Ordway	300
White Lake	Aurora	See Plankinton	500
Wolsey	Beadle	See Huron	300
Woonsocket	Sanborn	F. C. Buten	800
Yankton*	Yankton	S. H. Gruber	4000

DELAWARE.

POST-OFFICE.	COUNTY.	ATTORNEYS.	POPUL'N.
Delaware City	New Castle	See Wilmington	1200
Dover*	Kent	J. Alexander Fulton.	3000
Georgetown*	Sussex	Robert C. White	2000
Middletown	New Castle	See Wilmington	1500
Milford	Kent	James R. Lofland	3000
New Castle	New Castle	See Wilmington	4000

Delaware—Continued.

Parties corresponding with Attorneys named in the Directory should ALWAYS sign themselves "Subscribers to J. A. GRAFT & CO.'S LEGAL DIRECTORY."
Should any attorney fail to give prompt attention to correspondence, collections or business intrusted to his care, we will be thankful to patrons of the Directory to notify us promptly in any such case.
Places designated thus (*) are County Seats.

POST-OFFICE.	COUNTY.	ATTORNEYS.	POPUL'N.
Seaford.	Sussex	E. L. Martin	2000
Smyrna.	Kent	See Dover	3000
Wilmington*	**New Castle**	**Johnston & Hayes** No. 3 E. Eighth St.	**55000**

DISTRICT OF COLUMBIA.

POST-OFFICE.	COUNTY.	ATTORNEYS.	POPUL'N.
Georgetown		See Washington	20000
Washington*		**Milton C. Barnard** Manager Branch Office, No. 472 La. avenue.	**180000**

FLORIDA.

POST-OFFICE.	COUNTY.	ATTORNEYS.	POPUL'N.
Abe's Spring*	Calhoun	See Marianna	200
Apalachicola*	Franklin	See Quincy	1800
Bristol*	Liberty	See Quincy	400
Bronson*	Levy	See Cedar Keys	500
Brooksville*	Hernando	James W. Austin	500
Cedar Keys	Levy	E. J. Lutterloh	1500
Crawfordville*	Wakulla	W. T. Duvall	200
De Land	Volusia	J. D. Broome	500
Enterprise*	Volusia	John W. Price	500
Euchee Anna*	Walton	D. G. McLeod	300

Florida—Continued.

Parties corresponding with Attorneys named in the Directory should ALWAYS sign themselves "Subscribers to J. A. GRAFT & CO.'S LEGAL DIRECTORY." Should any attorney fail to give prompt attention to correspondence, collections or business intrusted to his care, we will be thankful to patrons of the Directory to notify us promptly in any such case.
Places designated thus (*) are County Seats.

POST-OFFICE.	COUNTY.	ATTORNEYS.	POPUL'N.
Fernandina*	Nassau	D. M. Hammond	3000
Gainesville*	Alachua	Hampton & Hampton	4000
Jacksonville*	**Duval**	**Manuel C. Jordan** (See card in Appendix, page 1.)	**18000**
Jasper*	Hamilton	See Live Oak	400
Key West*	Monroe	L. W. Bethel	15000
Lake Butler*	Bradford	See Starke	200
Lake City*	Columbia	A. J. Henry	2000
Leesburgh	Sumter	R. H. Williams	1000
Live Oak*	Suwannee	Joe S. White	1200
Madison*	Madison	H. J. McCall	1200
Marianna*	Jackson	Liddon & Carter	600
Middleburgh	Clay	See Jacksonville	200
Milton*	Santa Rosa	John Chain	1500
Monticello*	Jefferson	W. B. Lamar	1500
New Troy*	La Fayette	See Lake City	200
Ocala*	Marion	McConnell & McConnell	1000
Orlando*	Orange	Harrison & Peeler	2500
Palatka*	Putnam	C. Gillus	2000
Pensacola*	Escambia	**Hays & Eagan** (See card in Appendix, page I.)	**10000**
Perry*	Taylor	See Madison	400
Quincy*	Gadsden	P. B. Stockton	800
Sanderson*	Baker	See Lake City	200
Sanford	Orange	Thomas E. Wilson	1000
Sorrento	Orange	Paxton & Hause	200
Starke	Bradford	Comer L. Peek	800
St. Augustine*	St. John's	See Jacksonville	2500
Tallahassee*	Leon	R. W. Williams	2500
Tampa*	Hillsboro	L. Finley	3000
Vernon*	Washington	See Marianna	200
Volusia	Volusia	See Enterprise	200
Waldo	Alachua	Ned E. Farrell	800

GEORGIA.

Parties corresponding with Attorneys named in the Directory should ALWAYS sign themselves "Subscribers to J. A. GRAFT & CO.'S LEGAL DIRECTORY." Should any Attorney fail to give prompt attention to correspondence, collections or business intrusted to his care, we will be thankful to patrons of the Directory to notify us promptly in any such case.
Places designated thus (*) are County Seats.

POST-OFFICE.	COUNTY.	ATTORNEYS.	POPUL'N.
Abbeville*	Wilcox	See Hawkinsville	200
Acworth	Cobb	See Marietta	800
Albany*	Dougherty	David H. Pope	3500
Alpharetta*	Milton	Thomas L. Lewis	300
Americus*	Sumter	J. C. Mathews	6000
Appling*	Columbia	See Augusta	300
Arlington	Calhoun	See Morgan	200
Athens*	Clarke	H. H. Carlton	8000
Atlanta*	**Fulton**	**Lewis W. Thomas**	**55000**
Augusta*	**Richmond**	**William H. Fleming**	**35000**
Bainbridge*	Decatur	Maston O'Neal	1500
Barnesville	Pike	W. R. Taylor	2000
Baxley*	Appling	G. J. Holton & Son	500
Blackshear*	Pierce	W. R. Phillips	1500
Blairsville*	Union	J. A. Butt	300
Blakely*	Early	E. C. Bower	500
Brunswick*	Glynn	Frank H. Harris	6000
Buchanan*	Haralson	W. J. Head	400
Buena Vista*	Marion	E. W. Miller	1000
Butler*	Taylor	W. S. Wallace & Son	900
Calhoun*	Gordon	W. R. Rankin	800
Camilla*	Mitchell	Isaac A. Bush	1000
Canton*	Cherokee	See Cartersville	500
Carnesville*	Franklin	W. R. Little	300
Carrollton*	Carroll	Cobb & Cobb	1700
Cartersville*	Bartow	A. M. Foute	2500
Cedartown*	Polk	Ivy F. Thompson	1000
Clarkesville*	Habersham	Barrow & Erwin	500
Clayton*	Rabun	J. N. Merritt	500
Cleveland*	White	Underwood & Son	400
Clinton*	Jones	See Macon	400
Colquitt*	Miller	Bush & Bush	300
Columbus*	Muscogee	Porter Ingram	20000
Conyers*	Rockdale	J. N. Glenn	1500
Covington*	Newton	James F. Rogers	2000
Crawfordville*	Taliaferro	See Greensborough	800
Cumming*	Forsyth	H. P. Bell	500
Cusseta*	Chattahoochee	See Columbus	500
Cuthbert*	Randolph	A. Hood, Jr.	3000
Dahlonega*	Lumpkin	W. Boyd	800
Dallas*	Paulding	D. P. Hill	300
Dalton*	Whitfield	W. K. Moore	3000

Georgia—Continued.

Parties corresponding with Attorneys named in the Directory should ALWAYS sign themselves "Subscribers to J. A. GRAFT & CO.'S LEGAL DIRECTORY." Should any Attorney fail to give prompt attention to correspondence, collections or business intrusted to his care, we will be thankful to patrons of the Directory to notify us promptly in any such case.
Places designated thus (*) are County Seats.

POST-OFFICE.	COUNTY.	ATTORNEYS.	POPUL'N.
Danielsville*	Madison	David W. Meadow	300
Darien*	McIntosh	L. E. B. DeLorne	2000
Dawson*	Terrell	J. G. Parks	2000
Dawsonville*	Dawson	H. C. Johnson	300
Decatur*	DeKalb	L. J. Winn	800
Dublin*	Laurens	Thos. B. Felder, Jr.	1000
Eastman*	Dodge	Roberts & Smith	600
Eatonton*	Putnam	Joseph S. Turner	1500
Eden	Effingham	See Savannah	400
Elberton*	Elbert	John P. Shannon †*B. Lee Payne.*	1200
Ellaville*	Schley	W. H. McCrary	300
Fairburn*	Campbell	H. M. Reid	800
Fayetteville*	Fayette	See Newnan	300
Forsyth*	Monroe	O. H. B. Bloodworth.	1500
Fort Gaines*	Clay	J. D. Rambo	1200
Fort Valley	Houston	W. E. Collier	1500
Franklin*	Heard	Frank S. Loftin	500
Gainesville*	Hall	Fletcher M. Johnson.	3200
Georgetown*	Quitman	W. P. Harrison	400
Gibson*	Glascock	See Sparta	300
Greenville*	Meriwether	See Hamilton	600
Greensborough*	Greene	William H. Branch	2000
Griffin*	Spalding	T. R. Mills	5000
Hamilton*	Harris	B. H. Walton	800
Hampton	Henry	E. J. Reagan	800
Hartwell*	Hart	A. G. McCurry	700
Hawkinsville*	Pulaski	Jordan & Watson	2500
Hiawassee*	Towns	W. G. Blackwell	300
Homer*	Banks	P. M. Edwards	200
Homerville*	Clinch	James P. Mattox	500
Isabella*	Worth	W. A. Harris	200
Irwinton*	Wilkinson	James C. Bower	400
Irwinville*	Irwin	See Albany	200
Jackson*	Butts	M. V. McKibben	400
Jasper*	Pickens	W. T. Day	300
Jefferson*	Jackson	Pike & Wardlow	1000
Jeffersonville *	Twiggs	J. D. Jones	200

(† We withdraw our former recommendation.)

Georgia—Continued.

Parties corresponding with Attorneys named in the Directory should ALWAYS sign themselves "Subscribers to J. A. GRAFT & CO.'S LEGAL DIRECTORY." Should any Attorney fail to give prompt attention to correspondence, collections or business intrusted to his care, we will be thankful to patrons of the Directory to notify us promptly in any such case. Places designated thus (*) are County Seats.

POST-OFFICE.	COUNTY.	ATTORNEYS.	POPUL'N.
Jesup	Wayne	S. J. Clark	1000
Jonesboro*	Clayton	W. A. Tigner, Jr.	1200
Knoxville*	Crawford	See Macon	2000
La Fayette*	Walker	George M. Napier	300
La Grange*	Troup	F. M. Longley	3000
Lawrenceville*	Gwinnett	Sam. J. Winn & Son.	700
Leary	Calhoun	See Morgan	300
Leesburgh*	Lee	Kimbrough & Long	500
Lexington*	Oglethorpe	W. G. Johnson	500
Lincolnton*	Lincoln	H. J. Lang	300
Louisville*	Jefferson	Cain & Polhill	800
Lumpkin*	Stewart	J. L. Wimberly	1000
McDonough*	Henry	F. J. Reagan	500
McRae*	Telfair	See Eastman	400
Macon*	**Bibb**	**Lanier & Anderson.**	**30000**
Madison*	Morgan	McHenry & McHenry	2500
Marietta*	Cobb	Frank A. Irwin	3000
Milledgeville*	Baldwin	C. P. Crawford †*J. C. Bell.*	4000
Milner	Pike	Robert A. Holmes	500
Monroe*	Walton	See Social Circle	1200
Montezuma	Macon	R. G. Ozier	1000
Monticello*	Jasper	Fleming Jordan	800
Morgan*	Calhoun	**D. B. Jay** (See card in Appendix, page II.)	**200**
Morganton*	Fannin	James L. Trammell	600
Moultrie*	Colquitt	See Thomasville	200
Mount Vernon*	Montgomery	H. W. Carswell	200
Nashville*	Berrien	Peeples & Son	300
Newnan*	Coweta	McClendon & Freeman	2500
Newton*	Baker	See Morgan	300
Norcross	Gwinnett	See Lawrenceville	800
Oglethorpe*	Macon	F. T. Snead	500
Palmetto	Campbell	H. M. Reid	800
Perry*	Houston	C. C. Duncan	1200
Preston*	Webster	See Americus	300
Quitman*	Brooks	William A. Lane	2000
Reidsville*	Tattnall	H. J. McGee	300

(† We withdraw our former recommendation.)

Georgia—Continued.

Parties corresponding with Attorneys named in the Directory should ALWAYS sign themselves "Subscribers to J. A. GRAFT & CO.'S LEGAL DIRECTORY." Should any Attorney fail to give prompt attention to correspondence, collections or business intrusted to his care, we will be thankful to patrons of the Directory to notify us promptly in any such case. Places designated thus (*) are County Seats.

POST-OFFICE.	COUNTY.	ATTORNEYS.	POPUL'N.
Ringgold*	Catoosa	A. T. Hackett	600
Rome*	Floyd	Dean & Ewing	8000
Sandersville*	Washington	Evans & Evans	2000
Savannah*	**Chatham**	**Wm. Hampton Wade**	**42000**
Shellman	Randolf	See Morgan	300
Social Circle	Walton	James F. Rogers	1200
Sparta*	Hancock	Jordan & Lewis	1000
Springfield*	Effingham	See Savannah	200
Spring Place*	Murray	Trammell Starr	400
Statenville*	Echols	See Valdosta	300
Statesboro*	Bulloch	T. H. Potter	300
St. Mary's*	Camden	See Brunswick	700
Summerville*	Chattooga	W. M. Henry	400
Swainsboro*	Emanuel	Alfred Herrington	600
Sylvania*	Screven	Black & Dell	500
Talbotton*	Talbot	Willis & Mathews	1200
Thomaston*	Upson	J. T. Tisinger	1500
Thomasville*	Thomas	P. J. Franklin	4000
Thomson*	McDuffie	Thomas E. Watson	1000
Toccoa	Habersham	John W. Owen	1000
Trader's Hill*	Charlton	See Brunswick	200
Trenton*	Dade	Jacoway & Son	400
Ty Ty	Worth	Jno. Murrow	1000
Valdosta*	Lowndes	P. B. Whittle	2000
Vienna*	Dooly	J. B. Holmes	700
Walthourville*	Liberty	See Savannah	800
Waresboro	Ware	See Blackshear	400
Warrenton*	Warren	See Sparta	1500
Washington*	Wilkes	M. P. Reese	2000
Watkinsville*	Oconee	B. E. Thrasher	500
Way Cross*	Ware	See Blackshear	300
Waynesboro*	Burke	John J. Jones	1200
West Point	Troup	L. M. Harris	2500
Wrightsville*	Johnson	V. B. Robinson	400
Zebulon*	Pike	See Griffin	500

IDAHO TERRITORY.

Parties corresponding with Attorneys named in the Directory should ALWAYS sign themselves "Subscribers to J. A. GRAFT & CO.'S LEGAL DIRECTORY" Should any Attorney fail to give prompt attention to correspondence, collections or business intrusted to his care, we will be thankful to patrons of the Directory to notify us promptly in any such case. Places designated thus (*) are County Seats.

POST-OFFICE.	COUNTY.	ATTORNEYS.	POPUL'N.
Bellevue	Alturas	See Hailey	400
Blackfoot	Oneida	See Pocatello	500
Boise City*	Ada	Brumback & Lamb	3500
Bonanza City	Custer	See Challis	500
Caldwell	Ada	Chas. H. Reed	1000
Challis*	Custer	Johnson & Onderdonk	500
Eagle	Shoshone	See Lewiston	400
Eagle Rock	Oneida	See Pocatello	500
Hailey*	Alturas	Kingsbury & McGowan	2000
Idaho City*	Boise	C. S. Kingsbury	1500
Ketchum	Alturas	See Hailey	700
Lewiston*	Nez Perces	Jasper Rand	1500
Malad City*	Oneida	See Pocatello	2000
Moscow	Nez Perces	See Lewiston	500
Paris*	Bear Lake	Robert S. Spence	800
Pocatello	Oneida	Crawford & Walsh	300
Rocky Bar	Alturas	See Boise City	600
Salmon City*	Lemhi	H. J. Burleigh	600
Silver City*	Owyhee	See Boise City	1500
Washington	Idaho	See Challis	800
Weiser*	Washington	See Boise City	600

ILLINOIS.

POST-OFFICE.	COUNTY.	ATTORNEYS.	POPUL'N.
Abingdon	Knox	See Galesburg	2200
Adeline	Ogle	See Oregon	400
Albion*	Edwards	W. F. Foster	1100
Aledo*	Mercer	S. D. C. Hays	2000

Illinois—Continued.

Parties corresponding with Attorneys named in the Directory should ALWAYS sign themselves "Subscribers to J. A. GRAFT & CO.'S LEGAL DIRECTORY." Should any Attorney fail to give prompt attention to correspondence, collections or business intrusted to his care, we will be thankful to patrons of the Directory to notify us promptly in any such case. Places designated thus (*) are County Seats.

POST-OFFICE.	COUNTY.	ATTORNEYS.	POPUL'N.
Alexis	Warren	T. R. Squires	600
Altamont	Effingham	See Effingham	1200
Alton	Madison	John F. McGinnis	15000
Altona	Knox	See Galesburg	1200
Amboy	Lee	B. H. Trusdell	2500
Anna	Union	Thomas H. Phillips	2500
Annawan	Henry	See Geneseo	600
Apple River	Jo Daviess	See Galena	1000
Arcola	Douglas	See Tuscola	2000
Arenzville	Cass	See Beardstown	600
Ashland	Cass	S. A. Short	1000
Ashley	Washington	T. E. Crane	1200
Ashton	Lee	See Dixon	1000
Assumption	Christian	See Taylorville	1200
Astoria	Fulton	S. P. Cummings	1600
Athens	Menard	See Petersburg	600
Atkinson	Henry	See Geneseo	800
Atlanta	Logan	See Lincoln	2000
Auburn	Sangamon	See Springfield	1200
Augusta	Hancock	B. P. Hewitt	1500
Aurora	Kane	A. G. McDole	18000
Ava	Jackson	See Carbondale	1000
Avon	Fulton	See Bushnell	1200
Barry	Pike	See Pittsfield	1600
Batavia	Kane	J. O. McClellan	3500
Baylis	Pike	Arthur C. Bentley	700
Beardstown	Cass	Thomas H. Carter	3500
Belleville*	St. Clair	W. J. Underwood	17000
Belvidere*	Boone	Charles T. Spackman	3500
Bement	Piatt	See Monticello	1200
Benton*	Franklin	F. M. Youngblood	900
Blackberry	Kane	See Aurora	800
Blandinsville	McDonough	George S. Fuhr	1500
Bloomington*	McLean	William H. Beaver	20000
Blue Mound	Macon	See Decatur	1000
Bradford	Starke	See Toulon	1000
Braidwood	Will	J. S. Reynolds	8000
Brighton	Macoupin	Samuel D. Goodell	1000
Brimfield	Peoria	See Princeville	1200
Buckley	Iroquois	J. A. Koplin	600
Buda	Bureau	Jesse Emerson	900
Bunker Hill	Macoupin	See Carlinville	1500
Bushnell	McDonough	Solon Banfill	2500
Byron	Ogle	See Oregon	700

Illinois—Continued.

Parties corresponding with Attorneys named in the Directory should ALWAYS sign themselves "Subscribers to J. A. GRAFT & CO.'S LEGAL DIRECTORY." Should any Attorney fail to give prompt attention to correspondence, collections or business intrusted to his care, we will be thankful to patrons of the Directory to notify us promptly in any such case. Places designated thus (*) are County Seats.

POST-OFFICE.	COUNTY.	ATTORNEYS.	POPUL'N.
Cairo*	Alexander	George Fisher	10000
Cambridge*	Henry	Mock & Hand	1800
Camp Point	Adams	See Quincy	1600
Canton	Fulton	Charles J. Main	5000
Capron	Boone	See Belvidere	500
Carbondale	Jackson	B. W. Moore	2500
Carlinville*	Macoupin	Thomas Rinaker	4500
Carlyle*	Clinton	Buxton & White	2500
Carmi*	White	Jasper Partridge	3000
Carrollton*	Greene	James R. Ward	2500
Carthage*	Hancock	Scofield & Scofield	1800
Casey	Clark	See Marshall	1000
Casner	Macon	See Decatur	700
Centralia	Marion	See Salem	4000
Cerro Gordo	Piatt	See Monticello	800
Champaign	Champaign	Thomas J. Smith	7000
Chandlerville	Cass	W. B. Shaw	1000
Charleston*	Coles	Cunningham & Mathes	4500
Chatham	Sangamon	See Springfield	600
Chatsworth	Livingston	George Torrance	1500
Chebanse	Iroquois	Thomas S. Sawyer	1200
Chenoa	McLean	See Bloomington	1200
Chester*	Randolph	Joseph Simpson †*Alexander Hood.*	3000
Chicago*	**Cook**	**Herbert B. Johnson** Manager Branch Office, No. 184 Dearborn street.	**500000**
Chillicothe	Peoria	See Peoria	1200
Chrisman	Edgar	W. E. David	1200
Clayton	Adams	J. L. Staker	1100
Clinton*	De Witt	Oscar E. Harris	3000
Cobden	Union	See Jonesboro	1000
Colchester	McDonough	A. M. Champ	1500
Colfax	McLean	See Bloomington	400
Danvers	McLean	See Bloomington	700
Danville*	Vermillion	Emerson & McFarland	10000
Decatur*	Macon	George Brown	16000
De Kalb	De Kalb	William L. Pond	2000
Delavan	Tazewell		2000
Dixon*	Lee	A. K. Trusdell	4500
Dundee	Kane	See Aurora	1500
Du Quoin	Perry	S. G. Parks	3000
Dwight	Livingston	Chas. L. Romberger	1400

(† We withdraw our former recommendation.)

Illinois—Continued.

Parties corresponding with Attorneys named in the Directory should ALWAYS sign themselves "Subscribers to J. A. GRAFT & CO.'S LEGAL DIRECTORY." Should any Attorney fail to give prompt attention to correspondence, collections or business intrusted to his care, we will be thankful to patrons of the Directory to notify us promptly in any such case. Places designated thus (*) are County Seats.

POST-OFFICE.	COUNTY.	ATTORNEYS.	POPUL'N.
Earlville	La Salle	See Ottawa	1500
East St. Louis	St. Clair	Messick & Rhoads	12000
Edinburg	Christian	See Taylorville	800
Edwardsville*	Madison	G. G. Burnett	3600
Effingham*	Effingham	Henry B. Kepley	4500
Elgin	Kane	Edward C. Lovell	12000
Elizabethtown*	Hardin	John Q. A. Ledbetter.	700
Elmwood	Peoria	Stevens & Clinch	2000
El Paso	Woodford	W. S. Gibson	2000
Elsah	Jersey	See Jerseyville	600
Erie	Whiteside	See Sterling	900
Eureka	Woodford	Briggs & Meek	1500
Evanston	Cook	See Chicago	10000
Evansville	Randolph	**W. M. Schuwerk**	500
Ewing	Franklin	See Benton	400
Fairbury	Livingston	D. L. Murdock	2500
Fairfield*	Wayne	E. C. Kramer	2500
Fairview	Fulton	See Canton	500
Farmer City	De Witt	George W. Herrick	1800
Farmington	Fulton	See Canton	2000
Fieldon	Jersey	See Jerseyville	500
Fisher	Champaign	See Champaign	400
Flanagan	Livingston	See Pontiac	400
Flora	Clay	See Louisville	1600
Forreston	Ogle	See Oregon	1500
Freeport*	Stephenson	P. J. Geib	10000
Fulton	Whiteside	James McCoy	2000
Galena*	Jo Daviess	Jacob Fawcett	7000
Galesburg*	Knox	J. L. Hastings	12000
Galva	Henry	See Toulon	3000
Gardner	Grundy	J. H. Coles	1000
Geneseo	Henry	Charles Dunham	5000
Geneva*	Kane	J. H. Mayborn	1800
Genoa	De Kalb	See Sycamore	700
Gibson City	Ford	S. P. Rady	1300
Gilman	Iroquois	Spencer S. Cone	1500
Girard	Macoupin	G. W. Bowersox	1500
Golconda*	Pope	D. G. Thompson	1500
Grafton	Jersey	See Jerseyville	1000
Grayville	White		2000

Illinois—Continued.

Parties corresponding with Attorneys named in the Directory should ALWAYS sign themselves "Subscribers to J. A. GRAFT & CO.'S LEGAL DIRECTORY." Should any Attorney fail to give prompt attention to correspondence, collections or business intrusted to his care, we will be thankful to patrons of the Directory to notify us promptly in any such case. Places designated thus (*) are County Seats.

POST-OFFICE.	COUNTY.	ATTORNEYS.	POPUL'N.
Greenfield	Greene	G. W. Coonrod	1200
Greenup	Cumberland	See Toledo	800
Greenview	Menard	See Petersburg	600
Greenville*	Bond	Henry Howard	2000
Griggsville	Pike	See Baylis	1800
Hampshire	Kane	Frank Baxter	700
Hardin*	Calhoun	William Keating	500
Harrisburg*	Saline	Parish & Parish	2000
Harvard	McHenry	See Woodstock	2500
Havana*	Mason	O. H. Wright	2500
Hennepin*	Putnam	W. H. Casson	800
Henry	Marshall	Fred. S. Potter	2500
Highland	Madison	Timothy Gruaz	2500
Hillsboro*	Montgomery	A. N. Kingsbury	2000
Hinckley	De Kalb	See De Kalb	600
Homer	Champaign		1100
Hoopeston	Vermillion	Charles P. Huey	1600
Hopedale	Tazewell	See Pekin	500
Hyde Park	Cook	See Chicago	20000
Illiopolis	Sangamon	J. H. Lawrence	1000
Iuka	Marion	See Salem	500
Jacksonville*	Morgan	Julian P. Lippincott.	12000
Jerseyville*	Jersey	Thomas F. Ferns	5500
Joliet*	Will	E. Meers	18000
Jonesboro*	Union	D. W. Karraker	1600
Joy	Mercer	See Keithsburg	300
Kankakee*	Kankakee	Stephen R. Moore	8000
Kansas	Edgar	See Paris	1000
Keithsburg	Mercer	T. W. Bassett	1600
Kewanee	Henry	James K. Blish	3000
Kinmundy	Marion	See Salem	1400
Kirkwood	Warren	See Monmouth	1200
Knoxville	Knox	A. L. Humphrey	2000
Lacon*	Marshall	Shaw & Edwards	2500
La Fayette	Stark	See Toulon	500
La Harpe	Hancock	S. W. King	1200
La Salle	La Salle	Duncan & O'Conor	9000
Lawrenceville*	Lawrence	Philip W. Barnes	800
Lebanon	St. Clair	See Belleville	2500
Lena	Stephenson	See Freeport	2000
Le Roy	McLean	See Bloomington	1500

Illinois—Continued.

Parties corresponding with Attorneys named in the Directory should ALWAYS sign themselves "Subscribers to J. A. GRAFT & CO.'S LEGAL DIRECTORY."
Should any Attorney fail to give prompt attention to correspondence, collections or business intrusted to his care, we will be thankful to patrons of the Directory to notify us promptly in any such case.
Places designated thus (*) are County Seats.

POST-OFFICE.	COUNTY.	ATTORNEYS.	POPUL'N.
Lewistown*	Fulton	Gray & Waggoner	2000
Lexington	McLean	J. M. Weakly	1800
Lincoln*	Logan	John Johnston	8600
Litchfield	Montgomery	See Hillsboro	4500
Lockport	Will	See Joliet	2500
Louisville*	Clay	B. D. Monroe	600
Lovington	Moultrie	W. G. Cochran	800
Mackinaw	Tazewell	George C. Gillan	900
Macomb*	McDonough	Byron Pontious	4000
Macon	Macon	See Decatur	1200
Malta	De Kalb	See De Kalb	800
Manchester	Scott	F. S. Clarkson	500
Mansfield	Piatt	See Monticello	600
Maple Park	Kane	See Aurora	600
Maquon	Knox	See Galesburg	800
Marengo	McHenry	A. B. Coon	1800
Marion*	Williamson	George W. Young	1500
Marissa	St. Clair	See Belleville	900
Maroa	Macon	See Decatur	1000
Marseilles	La Salle	See Ottawa	1500
Marshall*	Clark	H. M. Janney	3000
Mason City	Mason	George W. Ellsbury	2200
Mattoon	Coles	Henley & Rose	7000
McLeansboro*	Hamilton	R. R. Barnett	2500
Mechanicsburg	Sangamon	See Springfield	500
Mendota	La Salle	E. S. Brown	4000
Metamora*	Woodford	W. L. Ellwood	1000
Metropolis*	Massac	Benj. O. Jones	4000
Milan	Rock Island	See Rock Island	2000
Millersburg	Mercer	See Keithsburg	800
Milton	Pike	See Pittsfield	600
Minier	Tazewell	See Pekin	800
Minonk	Woodford	M. L. Newell	2000
Minooka	Grundy	See Morris	800
Moline	Rock Island	See Rock Island	10000
Momence	Kankakee	See Kankakee	1200
Monmouth*	Warren	Porter & Porter	7000
Monticello*	Piatt	David McWilliams	2000
Morris*	Grundy	E. Sanford	3500
Morrison*	Whiteside	F. D. Ramsay	2500
Morrisonville	Christian	See Taylorville	1000
Morton	Tazewell	See Pekin	800
Mound City*	Pulaski	William T. Freeze	2500
Mount Carmel*	Wabash	R. T. Wilkinson	2800
Mount Carroll*	Carroll	Smith & Lee	2500

Illinois—Continued.

Parties corresponding with Attorneys named in the Directory should ALWAYS sign themselves "Subscribers to J. A. GRAFT & CO.'S LEGAL DIRECTORY." Should any Attorney fail to give prompt attention to correspondence, collections or business intrusted to his care, we will be thankful to patrons of the Directory to notify us promptly in any such case.
Places designated thus (*) are County Seats.

POST-OFFICE.	COUNTY.	ATTORNEYS.	POPUL'N.
Mount Morris	Ogle	R. J. Allen	1000
Mount Olive	Macoupin	See Carlinville	1000
Mount Pulaski	Logan	See Lincoln	1500
Mount Sterling*	Brown	J. J. McDonald	2000
Mount Vernon*	Jefferson	A. C. Webb	3000
Moweaqua	Shelby	Felix G. Penn	1000
Murphysboro*	Jackson	Hill & Martin	3000
Naperville	Du Page	Arthur B. Cody	3000
Nashville*	Washington	Thomas S. Le Compte	3000
National Stock Y'ds.	St. Clair	See East St. Louis	1000
Nauvoo	Hancock	George A. Ritter	1600
Neoga	Cumberland	W. W. Whitney	800
Neponset	Bureau	See Princeton	800
Newark	Kendall	John H. Fowler	600
New Berlin	Sangamon	See Springfield	800
New Boston	Mercer	See Keithsburg	800
New Bremen	Cook	See Chicago	1000
Newman	Douglas	See Tuscola	1000
Newton*	Jasper	David Trexler	3000
New Windsor	Mercer	See Keithsburg	800
Nokomis	Montgomery	Stevens & Blue	1500
Normal	McLean	Thomas Slade	2500
Oakland	Coles	J. F. Green	1000
Odell	Livingston	J. H. Funk	1200
Ohio	Bureau	See Princeton	600
Olney*	Richland	John P. Heap	4500
Onarga	Iroquois	A. S. Palmer	1500
Oneida	Knox	See Galesburg	1200
Oquawka*	Henderson	William C. Rice	1200
Oregon*	Ogle	Edward F. Dutcher	2200
Orion	Henry	See Geneseo	800
Oswego	Kendall	A. B. Smith	800
Ottawa*	La Salle	Ben. F. Lincoln	10000
Pana	Christian	J. C. Esseck	4000
Paris*	Edgar	Joseph E. Dyas	5000
Paw Paw	Lee	Chas. F. Preston	1000
Paxton*	Ford	E. C. Gray	2000
Pecatonica	Winnebago	See Rockford	1500
Pekin*	Tazewell	W. A. Tinney	10000
Peoria*	**Peoria**	**G. M. Johnston**	**40000**
Peotone	Will	See Joliet	800

Illinois—Continued.

Parties corresponding with Attorneys named in tne Directory should ALWAYS sign themselves "Subscribers to J. A. GRAFT & CO.'S LEGAL DIRECTORY."
Should any Attorney fail to give prompt attention to correspondence, collections or business intrusted to his care, we will be thankful to patrons of the Directory to notify us promptly in any such case.
Places designated thus (*) are County Seats.

POST-OFFICE.	COUNTY.	ATTORNEYS.	POPUL'N.
Peru	La Salle	See Ottawa	1500
Petersburg*	Menard	S. H. Blane	2500
Philo	Champaign	See Urbana	600
Pinckneyville*	Perry	E. H. Lemon	1500
Piper City	Ford	See Paxton	800
Pittsfield*	Pike	J. S. Irwin	3000
Plano	Kendall	T. J. Beebe	2000
Pleasant Plains	Sangamon	See Springfield	800
Plymouth	Hancock	L. G. Reid	800
Polo	Ogle	Morton D. Swift	2500
Pontiac*	Livingston	R. R. Wallace	3000
Port Byron	Rock Island	See Rock Island	1000
Potomac	Vermillion	See Danville	500
Prairie City	McDonough	Isaac Weaver	1000
Princeton*	Bureau	Henderson & Trimble	4500
Princeville	Peoria	J. H. Hopkins	1200
Prophetstown	Whiteside	John D. Parish	1000
Pullman	Cook	See Chicago	5000
Quincy*	**Adams**	**Carter & Covert**	**35000**
Rankin	Vermillion	See Danville	500
Rantoul	Champaign	See Urbana	1200
Raymond	Montgomery	See Hillsboro	800
Red Bud	Randolph	B. W. Sharp	1500
Richview	Washington	J. B. Pate	700
Roberts	Ford	See Paxton	400
Robinson*	Crawford	E. E. Newlin	1500
Rochelle	Ogle	M. D. Hathaway	2000
Rock Falls	Whiteside	See Sterling	1200
Rockford*	Winnebago	**George M. Clake** (See card in Appendix, page II.)	**20000**
Rock Island*	Rock Island	Medill & Whitehead	15000
Roodhouse	Greene	J. L. Patterson	1400
Roseville	Warren	See Monmouth	1000
Rossville	Vermillion	See Danville	1000
Rushville*	Schuyler	John C. Bagby	2000
Rutland	La Salle	See Streator	700
Salem*	Marion	L. M. Kagy	1700
Sandoval	Marion	See Salem	800
Sandwich	De Kalb	S. B. Stinson	3000
San Jose	Mason	John Corry	500
Savanna	Carroll	D. S. Berry	1000
Saybrook	McLean	See Bloomington	1000
Seaton	Mercer	See Keithsburg	300
Seneca	La Salle	See Ottawa	1200

Illinois—Continued.

Parties corresponding with Attorneys named in the Directory should ALWAYS sign themselves "Subscribers to J. A. GRAFT & CO.'S LEGAL DIRECTORY." Should any Attorney fail to give prompt attention to correspondence, collections or business intrusted to his care, we will be thankful to patrons of the Directory to notify us promptly in any such case.
Places designated thus (*) are County Seats.

POST-OFFICE.	COUNTY.	ATTORNEYS.	POPUL'N.
Shawneetown*	Gallatin	Geo. W. Pillow	2500
Shelbyville*	Shelby	Moulton, Chafee & Headen	3000
Sheldon	Iroquois	S. B. Pool	1200
Somonauk	De Kalb	See Paw Paw	800
Sparta	Randolph	T. F. Alexander	2000
Springfield*	**Sangamon**	**Joseph M. Grout** (See card in Appendix, page II.)	**30000**
Stanford	McLean	See Bloomington	500
Staunton	Macoupin	C. T. Warren	1500
St. Charles	Kane	See Aurora	2000
Sterling	Whiteside	A. A. Wolfersperger	8000
Stewardson	Shelby	See Shelbyville	600
Stillman Valley	Ogle	See Oregon	300
Streator	La Salle	O. Chubbuck	10000
Sullivan*	Moultrie	Mouser & Spitler	1500
Sumner	Lawrence	John W. Stanley	1000
Sycamore*	De Kalb	C. D. Rogers	3000
Table Grove	Fulton	See Canton	600
Taylorville*	Christian	Frank P. Drennan	3000
Tiskilwa	Bureau	J. H. Welsh	1000
Toledo*	Cumberland	Green & Woods	800
Tolono	Champaign	See Urbana	1200
Tonica	La Salle	See La Salle	800
Toulon*	Stark	W. W. Wright	1200
Tremont	Tazewell	See Pekin	400
Tuscola*	Douglas	Thomas D. Minturn	2000
Urbana*	Champaign	Thomas J. Smith	4000
Utica	La Salle	See La Salle	1000
Vandalia*	Fayette	F. M. Guinn	3000
Varna	Marshall	See Lacon	500
Vermont	Fulton	William Mellor	1500
Victoria	Knox	See Galesburg	500
Vienna*	Johnson	T. J. Murray	900
Viola	Mercer	See Aledo	700
Virden	Macoupin	B. Cowen	2000
Virginia*	Cass	J. N. Gridley	2000
Walnut	Bureau	M. Knight	800
Warren	Jo Daviess	See Galena	1800
Warsaw	Hancock	George J. Rogers	3500
Washburn	Woodford	Charles Barnes	700

Illinois—Continued.

Parties corresponding with Attorneys named in the Directory should ALWAYS sign themselves "Subscribers to J. A. GRAFT & CO.'S LEGAL DIRECTORY." Should any Attorney fail to give prompt attention to correspondence, collections or business intrusted to his care, we will be thankful to patrons of the Directory to notify us promptly in any such case.
Places designated thus (*) are County Seats.

POST-OFFICE.	COUNTY.	ATTORNEYS.	POPUL'N.
Washington	Tazewell	George C. Danforth	2000
Wataga	Knox	See Galesburg	1000
Waterloo*	Monroe	Charles Morrison	3000
Watseka*	Iroquois	T. B. Harris	2000
Waukegan*	Lake	Charles Whitney	5000
Waverly	Morgan	See Jacksonville	2000
Wenona	Marshall	John H. Jackson	1100
Wheaton*	Du Page	George W. Brown	1800
White Hall	Greene	Thomas Henshaw	2200
Wilmington	Will	See Joliet	2500
Winchester*	Scott	James Callans	2000
Woodstock*	McHenry	Charles P. Barnes	1600
Wyanet	Bureau	T. G. Brainerd	1000
Wyoming	Stark	Frank Thomas	1800
Xenia	Clay	See Louisville	1000
Yates City	Knox	See Galesburg	1000
Yorkville*	Kendall	B. F. Harrington	800

INDIANA.

POST-OFFICE.	COUNTY.	ATTORNEYS.	POPUL'N.
Albion*	Noble	Fielding Prickett	1200
Alexandria	Madison	Albert C. Carver	1000
Ambia	Benton	John W. Cole	500
Anderson*	Madison	Robinson & Lovett	6000
Angola*	Steuben	Emmet A. Bratton	2000
Attica	Fountain	Charles R. Milford	3000
Auburn*	De Kalb	James E. Rose	2000
Aurora	Dearborn	D. T. Downey	6000
Bedford*	Lawrence	S. D. Luckett	2500
Berne	Adams	See Geneva	500
Bloomfield*	Greene	Axtell & Forbes	1500
Bloomington*	Monroe	John Graham	4000
Bluffton*	Wells	David T. Smith	3500
Boonville*	Warrick	Hatfield & Hazen	1800
Bourbon	Marshall	James H. Porter	1500
Bowling Green	Clay	Walter Bosley	800
Brazil*	Clay	Will P. Blair	3800

Indiana—Continued.

Parties corresponding with Attorneys named in the Directory should ALWAYS sign themselves "Subscribers to J. A. GRAFT & CO.'S LEGAL DIRECTORY." Should any Attorney fail to give prompt attention to correspondence, collections or business intrusted to his care, we will be thankful to patrons of the Directory to notify us promptly in any such case. Places designated thus (*) are County Seats.

POST-OFFICE.	COUNTY.	ATTORNEYS.	POPUL'N.
Bremen	Marshall	See Plymouth	1500
Bringhurst	Carroll	M. Plank, J. P.	300
Brookville*	Franklin	George F. O'Byrne	2500
Brownstown *	Jackson	Applewhite & Applewhite	1200
Bryant	Jay	See Geneva	400
Butler	De Kalb	Oscar L. Young	1800
Cambridge City	Wayne	W. F. Medsker	2800
Camden	Carroll	See Delphi	1000
Cannelton*	Perry	W. S. Lamb	2800
Carbon	Clay	See Brazil	1000
Carthage	Rush	See Rushville	800
Centreville	Wayne	See Cambridge City	1200
Charlestown	Clark	See Jeffersonville	1200
Churubusco	Whitley	W. S. Gandy	1000
Cicero	Hamilton	See Noblesville	800
Clay City	Clay	See Brazil	500
Clinton	Vermillion	M. B. Davis	1200
Colfax	Clinton	See Frankfort	800
Columbia City*	Whitley	J. W. Adair	3000
Columbus*	Bartholomew	Charles S. Baker	6000
Connersville*	Fayette	Murray & McIntosh	4500
Corydon*	Harrison	H. C. Hays	1200
Covington*	Fountain	John B. Martin	2000
Crawfordsville*	Montgomery	Kennedy & Kennedy.	8000
Crown Point*	Lake	John B. Peterson	2000
Danville*	Hendricks	M. W. Hopkins	2500
Decatur*	Adams	France & Merryman.	3000
Delphi*	Carroll	L. G. Beck	2500
Dublin	Wayne	See Cambridge City	500
East Germantown	Wayne	See Cambridge City	500
Edinburg	Johnson	A. C. Deupree	2000
Elkhart	Elkhart	O. T. Chamberlain	7000
Ellettsville	Monroe	See Bloomington	800
Elwood	Madison	See Alexandria	1200
Evansville*	**Vanderburgh**	**Garvin & Cunningham**	**42000**
Fairmount	Grant	See Marion	800
Flora	Carroll	See Delphi	800
Fort Wayne*	**Allen**	**James E. Graham**	**35000**
Fowler*	Benton	Brown & Steward	1500

Indiana—Continued.

Parties corresponding with Attorneys named in the Directory should ALWAYS sign themselves "Subscribers to J. A. GRAFT & CO.'S LEGAL DIRECTORY." Should any attorney fail to give prompt attention to correspondence, collections or business intrusted to his care, we will be thankful to patrons of the Directory to notify us promptly in any such case. Places designated thus (*) are County Seats.

POST-OFFICE.	COUNTY.	ATTORNEYS.	POPUL'N.
Frankfort*	Clinton	John Q. Bayless	5200
Franklin*	Johnson	Oyler & Johnson	4000
Fremont	Steuben	Emory G. Melendy	1000
Garrett	De Kalb	L. Covell	1500
Geneva	Adams	Tharp & Drew	700
Goodland	Newton	See Kentland	1000
Goshen*	Elkhart	Defrees, Vesey & Miller	6000
Gosport	Owen	W. A. Montgomery	1000
Greencastle*	Putnam	George Hathaway	4000
Greenfield*	Hancock	Poulson & McBane	3500
Greensburg*	Decatur	David A. Myers	3500
Hagerstown	Wayne	See Cambridge City	1000
Hartford City*	Blackford	Carroll & Pierce	1600
Hope	Bartholomew		1200
Huntingburg	Dubois	See Jasper	1000
Huntington*	Huntington	James M. Hiltebrand.	6500
Indianapolis*	**Marion**	**George W. Galvin** Manager Branch Office, Nos. 45 and 46 Vance Block.	**100000**
Jasper*	Dubois	B. Buettner	1200
Jeffersonville*	Clark	L. A. Douglass	11000
Jonesboro	Grant	See Marion	1000
Kendallville	Noble	D. H. Kime	3000
Kentland*	Newton	John H. Ash	1200
Knightstown	Henry	See New Castle	2000
Knox*	Starke	Albert I. Gould	1000
Kokomo*	Howard	J. F. Morrison	5500
La Fayette*	**Tippecanoe**	**John F. McHugh**	**25000**
Loogootee	Martin	See Shoals	1000
La Grange*	La Grange	Henry M. Herbert	1500
La Porte*	La Porte	Williams & Crumpacker	8000
Larwill	Whitley	See Columbia City	800
Laurel	Franklin	See Brookville	800
Lawrenceburg*	Dearborn	Charles F. Hayes	5000
Leavenworth*	Crawford	Peckinpaugh & Zenor	1000
Lebanon*	Boone	Charles M. Zion	3500
Liberty*	Union	Thomas D. Evans	2000
Ligonier	Noble	J. A. Linville	2800
Lima	La Grange	See La Grange	800
Linn Grove	Adams	See Geneva	300
Logansport*	Cass	George A. Yopst	15000

Indiana—Continued.

Parties corresponding with Attorneys named in the Directory should ALWAYS sign themselves "Subscribers to J. A. GRAFT & CO.'S LEGAL DIRECTORY." Should any Attorney fail to give prompt attention to correspondence, collections or business intrusted to his care, we will be thankful to patrons of the Directory to notify us promptly in any such case.
Places designated thus (*) are County Seats.

POST-OFFICE.	COUNTY.	ATTORNEYS.	POPUL'N.
Madison*	Jefferson	Walker & Wilson	10000
Marion*	Grant	Van Devanter & Lacey	4500
Martinsville*	Morgan	George W. Grubbs	2500
Metamora	Franklin	See Brookville	400
Michigan City	La Porte	H. B. Tuthill	10000
Middletown	Henry	See New Castle	1000
Milford	Kosciusko	See Warsaw	800
Milton	Wayne	See Cambridge City	800
Mishawaka	St. Joseph	See South Bend	3000
Mitchell	Lawrence	See Bedford	1600
Monticello*	White	W. S. Hartman	1500
Mooresville	Morgan	W. H. Ray	1000
Morristown	Shelby	See Rushville	500
Mount Vernon*	Posey	James W. French	5000
Muncie*	Delaware	Gregory & Silverburg	7500
Nappanee	Elkhart	W. F. Urich	1600
Nashville*	Brown	R. L. Coffey †*George W. Allison.*	500
New Albany*	**Floyd**	**La Follette & Tuley**	**25000**
Newburg	Warrick	See Boonville	1600
New Carlisle	St. Joseph	See South Bend	800
New Castle*	Henry	Hernley & Brown	3000
New Corydon	Jay	See Geneva	300
New Harmony	Posey	See Mount Vernon	1400
Newport*	Vermillion	H. H. Conley	1000
Noblesville*	Hamilton	Frank M. Trissal †*Garver & Pfaff.*	2500
North Manchester	Wabash	See Wabash	1800
North Vernon	Jennings	A. G. Smith	2000
Orland	Steuben	See Angola	600
Osgood	Ripley	See Versailles	800
Oxford	Benton	See Fowler	1200
Paoli*	Orange	John L. Megenity	800
Pendleton	Madison	See Anderson	800
Peru*	Miami	J. T. Cox	8000
Petersburg*	Pike	J. W. Wilson	2000
Pierceton	Kosciusko	John F. Logan	1500
Plainfield	Hendricks	Eli Johnson	1200
Plymouth*	Marshall	B. D. Crawford	3000
Portland*	Jay	Cornelius Corwin	3000
Princeton*	Gibson	Sam'l H. Kidd	3000

(† We withdraw our former recommendation.)

Indiana—Continued.

Parties corresponding with Attorneys named in the Directory should ALWAYS sign themselves "Subscribers to J. A. GRAFT & CO.'S LEGAL DIRECTORY." Should any attorney fail to give prompt attention to correspondence, collections or business intrusted to his care, we will be thankful to patrons of the Directory to notify us promptly in any such case. Places designated thus (*) are County Seats.

POST-OFFICE.	COUNTY.	ATTORNEYS.	POPUL'N.
Remington	Jasper	Harper W. Snyder	1000
Rensselaer*	Jasper	Edwin P. Hammond	1600
Richmond*	Wayne	William H. Ogborn	18000
Ridgeville	Randolph	James H. Williamson	1200
Rising Sun*	Ohio	Rodman L. Davis	2500
Roann	Wabash	See Wabash	500
Roanoke	Huntington	See Huntington	800
Rochester*	Fulton	J. W. Rickel	3200
Rockport*	Spencer	David T. Laird	3500
Rockville*	Parke	Hiram E. Hadley	2500
Rossville	Clinton	See Frankfort	600
Rushville*	Rush	Cambern & Newkirk	4500
Salem*	Washington	Alspaugh & Lawler	1800
Scottsburg*	Scott	C. L. Jewett	600
Seymour	Jackson	See Brownstown	5000
Shelbyville*	Shelby	E. E. Stroup	5000
Shoals*	Martin	Moser & Houghton	1000
South Bend*	**St. Joseph**	**John F. Kirby**	**20000**
South Whitley	Whitley	See Columbia City	600
Spencer*	Owen	William Pickens	1800
Sullivan*	Sullivan	Charles E. Barrett	3000
Tell City	Perry	John T. Patrick	3000
Terre Haute*	**Vigo**	**H. H. Boudinot**	**30000**
Thorntown	Boone	See Lebanon	2000
Tipton*	Tipton	Green & Fippen	2500
Union City	Randolph	John W. Williams	5000
Valparaiso*	Porter	Alvin D. Bartholomew	6000
Vernon*	Jennings	J. N. Hagins	600
Versailles*	Ripley	Charles H. Willson	600
Vevay*	Switzerland	F. M. Griffith	2000
Vincennes*	Knox	John Wilhelm	10000
Wabash*	Wabash	Alex. Hess	4500
Warren	Huntington	See Huntington	800
Warsaw*	Kosciusko	Robert B. Encell	3500
Washington*	Daviess	Francis M. Haynes	5000
Waterloo	De Kalb	J. M. Somers	1600
Waveland	Montgomery	See Crawfordsville	700

Indiana—Continued.

Parties corresponding with Attorneys named in the Directory should ALWAYS sign themselves "Subscribers to J. A. GRAFT & CO.'S LEGAL DIRECTORY." Should any Attorney fail to give prompt attention to correspondence, collections or business intrusted to his care, we will be thankful to patrons of the Directory to notify us promptly in any such case.
Places designated thus (*) are County Seats.

POST-OFFICE.	COUNTY.	ATTORNEYS.	POPUL'N.
Westfield	Hamilton	See Noblesville	500
Williamsport*	Warren	C. V. McAdams	1200
Winamac*	Pulaski	Theo. S. Gorham	2000
Winchester*	Randolph	W. W. Canada	3000
Wolcottville	La Grange	See La Grange	500
Worthington	Greene	H. C. Shaw	1200
Xenia	Miami	See Peru	1000
Zionsville	Boone	C. N. Beamer	1000

INDIAN TERRITORY.

FOR ALL BUSINESS IN THIS TERRITORY, SEND TO

JAMES LAWRENCE, ATTORNEY AT LAW,

WELLINGTON, KANSAS.

IOWA.

POST-OFFICE.	COUNTY.	ATTORNEYS.	POPUL'N.
Ackley	Hardin	Daniel Eiler	2000
Adair	Adair	James M. Moore	500
Adel*	Dallas	D. W. Woodin	1200
Afton*	Union	See Creston	1300
Akron	Plymouth	See Le Mars	600
Albia*	Monroe	Anderson & Anderson	3500
Alden	Hardin	See Eldora	600
Algona*	Kossuth	F. M. Taylor	2000
Allerton	Wayne	E. L. Hart	1200
Allison*	Butler	Craig & Smith	600
Alta	Buena Vista	See Storm Lake	600
Alton	Sioux	See Orange City	600

Iowa—Continued.

Parties corresponding with Attorneys named in the Directory should ALWAYS sign themselves "Subscribers to J. A. GRAFT & CO.'S LEGAL DIRECTORY."
Should any Attorney fail to give prompt attention to correspondence, collections or business intrusted to his care, we will be thankful to patrons of the Directory to notify us promptly in any such case.
Places designated thus (*) are County Seats.

POST-OFFICE.	COUNTY.	ATTORNEYS.	POPUL'N.
Altoona	Polk	See Des Moines	600
Ames	Story	J. L. Stevens	1500
Anamosa*	Jones	John S. Stacy	2500
Angus	Boone	See Boone	700
Anita	Cass	James E. Bruce	1000
Aplington	Butler	See Allison	500
Arcadia	Carroll	See Carroll	600
Atlantic*	Cass	Reynolds & Dolan	5000
Audubon*	Audubon	Holmes, Nash & Phelps	1600
Aurelia	Cherokee	See Cherokee	500
Avoca	Pottawattamie	See Council Bluffs	2000
Bancroft	Kossuth	See Algona	500
Battle Creek	Ida	See Ida Grove	500
Bayard	Guthrie	See Panora	500
Bedford*	Taylor	Charles Thomas	1500
Belle Plaine	Benton	See Vinton	2000
Bellevue	Jackson	J. C. Campbell	2000
Belmond	Wright	Bullard & Packard	900
Beloit	Lyon	See Rock Rapids	400
Bentonsport	Van Buren	Harvey Wilkinson	500
Birmingham	Van Buren	W. S. Allen	800
Blairstown	Benton	See Vinton	800
Blanchard	Page	T. F. Willis	700
Bloomfield*	Davis	S. B. Jones	1600
Bonaparte	Van Buren	See Keosauqua	800
Boone	Boone	E. L. Green	4000
Boonesboro*	Boone	See Boone	1500
Braddyville	Page	See Clarinda	500
Brighton	Washington	Ed. Deeds	1200
Britt	Hancock	J. G. Strong	700
Brooklyn	Poweshiek	John F. Talbott	1300
Brush Creek	Fayette	See West Union	600
Burlington*	**Des Moines**	**Dodge & Dodge**	**30000**
Calliope	Sioux	Isaac N. Deck	1000
Calmar	Winneshiek	See Decorah	800
Cambridge	Story	See Nevada	600
Carroll*	Carroll	Thomas F. Barbee	2500
Carson	Pottawattamie	See Council Blufls	500
Casey	Guthrie	W. D. Kelsey	800
Cedar Falls	Black Hawk	H. C. Hemenway	3500
Cedar Rapids	Linn	Blake & Hormel	15000
Centre Point	Linn	See Cedar Rapids	800

Iowa—Continued.

Parties corresponding with Attorneys named in the Directory should ALWAYS sign themselves "Subscribers to J. A. GRAFT & CO.'S LEGAL DIRECTORY." Should any Attorney fail to give prompt attention to correspondence, collections or business intrusted to his care, we will be thankful to patrons of the Directory to notify us promptly in any such case.
Places designated thus (*) are County Seats.

POST-OFFICE.	COUNTY.	ATTORNEYS.	POPUL'N.
Centerville*	Appanoose	A. J. Baker	3500
Central City	Linn	See Cedar Rapids	300
Chariton*	Lucas	O. A. Bartholomew	3500
Charles City*	Floyd	Boulton & Boulton	3000
Cherokee*	Cherokee	A. R. Molyneux	2000
Clarence	Cedar	Fred. C. James	800
Clarinda*	Page	N. B. Moore	4000
Clarion*	Wright	A. R. Ladd	400
Clarksville	Butler	C. A. L. Rosell	1000
Clearfield	Taylor	See Bedford	400
Clear Lake	Cerro Gordo	Bush & Hurn	1500
Clermont	Fayette	See West Union	700
Clinton*	Clinton	A. P. Barker	10000
Coin	Page	See Clarinda	900
Colfax	Jasper	See Newton	800
Columbus City	Louisa	See Columbus Junction	800
Columbus Junction	Louisa	R. Caldwell	1000
Concord*	Hancock	See Garner	300
Conrad Grove	Grundy	D. C. Kerr	400
Conwa	Taylor	See Bedford	500
Coon Rapids	Carroll	See Carroll	300
Corning*	Adams	Maxwell & Dale	2000
Correctionville	Woodbury	See Sioux City	300
Corydon*	Wayne	Freeland & Miles	1000
Council Bluffs*	**Pottawattamie**	**Jacob Sims**	**30000**
Cresco*	Howard	Reed & Marsh	2500
Creston	Union	John M. Hays	8000
Dakota*	Humboldt	See Humboldt	500
Dallas Centre	Dallas	See Adel	500
Davenport*	**Scott**	**William O. Schmidt**	**25000**
Davis City	Decatur	See Leon	500
Dayton	Webster	See Fort Dodge	400
Decorah*	Winneshiek	Charles P. Brown	3500
Defiance	Shelby	See Harlan	400
Denison*	Crawford	E. K. Burch	2000
Des Moines*	**Polk**	**St. John & Whisenand**	**40000**
De Witt	Clinton	Pascol & Armentrout	1800
Dexter	Dallas	See Adel	1000
Dow City	Crawford	See Denison	600

Iowa—Continued.

Parties corresponding with Attorneys named in the Directory should ALWAYS sign themselves "Subscribers to J. A. GRAFT & CO.'S LEGAL DIRECTORY." Should any Attorney fail to give prompt attention to correspondence, collections or business intrusted to his care, we will be thankful to patrons of the Directory to notify us promptly in any such case.
Places designated thus (*) are County Seats.

POST-OFFICE.	COUNTY.	ATTORNEYS.	POPUL'N.
Dows	Wright	F. M. Williams	500
Dubuque*	**Dubuque**	**Longueville & Lenehan**	**30000**
Dunlap	Harrison	Charles Makenzie	1500
Dyersville	Dubuque	See Dubuque	1000
Dysart	Tama	F. C. Wood	800
Eagle Grove	Wright	C. O. Bailey	1500
Earlham	Madison	See Winterset	400
Earlville	Delaware	See Manchester	500
Early	Sac	See Sac City	300
Eddyville	Wapello	See Ottumwa	1200
Eldora*	Hardin	C. E. Albrook	2000
Elgin	Fayette	See West Union	600
Elkader*	Clayton	W. A. Preston	1000
Elkport	Clayton	See Elkader	400
Elliott	Montgomery	Edward Mills	400
Emerson	Mills	B. P. Griffith	600
Emmetsburg*	Palo Alto	C. E. Cahoon	1800
Essex	Page	See Clarinda	800
Estherville*	Emmet	Ladd & Binford	1000
Exira	Audubon	See Audubon	600
Fairfield*	Jefferson	H. C. Raney	4000
Farragut	Fremont	See Hamburg	600
Fayette	Fayette	W. A. Hoyt	1200
Floyd	Floyd	See Charles City	500
Fonda	Pocahontas	A. B. P. Wood	600
Fontanelle	Adair	John A. Storey	800
Forest City*	Winnebago	Secor Bros. & Law	1200
Fort Dodge*	Webster	Dolliver & More	6000
Fort Madison	Lee	**Thomas S. Espy**	6000
Garden Grove	Decatur	S. H. Amos	700
Garner	Hancock	Brockway & Elder	800
Garrison	Benton	See Vinton	400
Gilman	Marshall	See Marshalltown	700
Gladbrook	Tama	See Toledo	500
Glenwood*	Mills	Shirley Gillilland	2000
Glidden	Carroll	See Carroll	600
Gowrie	Webster	See Fort Dodge	800
Grand Junction	Greene	E. C. Clark	1500
Gravity	Taylor	See Bedford	400

Iowa—Continued.

Parties corresponding with Attorneys named in the Directory should ALWAYS sign themselves "Subscribers to J. A. GRAFT & CO.'S LEGAL DIRECTORY."
Should any Attorney fail to give prompt attention to correspondence, collections or business intrusted to his care, we will be thankful to patrons of the Directory to notify us promptly in any such case.
Places designated thus (*) are County Seats.

POST-OFFICE.	COUNTY.	ATTORNEYS.	POPUL'N.
Greene	Butler	C. M. Greene	900
Greenfield*	Adair	D. W. Church	1200
Grinnell	Poweshiek	Haynes & Lyman	2500
Griswold	Cass	See Atlantic	800
Grundy Centre*	Grundy	Rea & Hayes	1200
Guthrie Centre*	Guthrie	E. W. Weeks	1200
Hamburg	Fremont	Stow & Hammond	2000
Hampton*	Franklin	D. W. Henley	2000
Harlan*	Shelby	D. O. Stuart	2400
Hartley	O'Brien	See Sanborn	800
Hastings	Mills	See Glenwood	600
Hawarden	Sioux	See Orange City	600
Hedrick	Keokuk	J. T. Brooks	500
Holstein	Ida	See Ida Grove	400
Hopkinton	Delaware	See Manchester	800
Hubbard	Hardin	L. O. Lowden	500
Humboldt	Humboldt	C. A. Babcock	1000
Humeston	Wayne	R. C. Poston	1000
Ida Grove*	Ida	L. A. Berry	2000
Imogene	Fremont	O. S. Sexton	300
Independence*	Buchanan	E. M. Thompson	3500
Indianola*	Warren	L. L. Mosher	3000
Iowa City*	Johnson	A. E. Swisher	10000
Iowa Falls	Hardin	S. M. Weaver	1200
Ireton	Sioux	See Orange City	400
Irwin	Shelby	D. T. Quinn	800
Jefferson*	Greene	C. H. Jackson	2000
Jesup	Buchanan	See Independence	1000
Jewell	Hamilton	See Webster City	500
Jolley	Calhoun	See Rockwell City	400
Kellogg	Jasper	Cooper & Cooper	1000
Keokuk	Lee	W. J. Medes	15000
Keosauqua*	Van Buren	Ben. Johnson	1500
Keota	Keokuk	I. Farley	1000
Kingsley	Plymouth	G. A. Garrard	700
Knoxville*	Marion	Johnston & Johnston	3000
Lake City	Calhoun	M. R. McCrary	500
Lake Mills	Winnebago	See Forest City	600
Lansing	Allamakee	L. E. Fellows	2500
Laporte City	Black Hawk	See Waterloo	1800

Iowa—Continued.

Parties corresponding with Attorneys named in the Directory should ALWAYS sign themselves "Subscribers to J. A. GRAFT & CO.'S LEGAL DIRECTORY."
Should any Attorney fail to give prompt attention to correspondence, collections or business intrusted to his care, we will be thankful to patrons of the Directory to notify us promptly in any such case.
Places designated thus (*) are County Seats.

POST-OFFICE.	COUNTY.	ATTORNEYS.	POPUL'N.
Lawler	Chickasaw	W. H. Parker	600
Le Mars*	Plymouth	Townsend M. Zink	5000
Lenox	Taylor	See Bedford	800
Leon*	Decatur	Bullock & Hoffman	2000
Lewis	Cass	See Atlantic	600
Lineville	Wayne	G. Taylor Wright	1000
Lisbon	Linn	P. J. Fisher	1000
Logan*	Harrison	J. W. Barnhart	1200
Lohrville	Calhoun	See Rockwell City	400
Lovilia	Monroe	See Albia	400
Lowden	Cedar	See Tipton	600
Lucas*	Lucas	See Chariton	1200
Lynnville	Jasper	Joseph Arnold	300
Lyons	Clinton	Albert T. Wheeler	5000
Macedonia	Pottawattamie	See Council Bluffs	500
Madrid	Boone	See Boone	400
Magnolia	Harrison	See Logan	400
Malcom	Poweshiek	See Montezuma	600
Malvern	Mills	See Glenwood	1200
Manchester*	Delaware	Satterlee & Summers.	3000
Manning	Carroll	See Carroll	1200
Manson	Calhoun	E. A. Richards	500
Mapleton	Monona	Dudley & French	700
Maquoketa*	Jackson	F. M. Fort	3000
Marble Rock	Floyd	H. H. Davidson	500
Marcus	Cherokee	See Cherokee	300
Marengo*	Iowa	R. H. Kirk	2500
Marion*	Linn	David Smyth	2500
Marshalltown*	Marshall	Kent & Holt	10000
Mason City*	Cerro Gordo	J. H. McConlogue	5000
Maxwell	Story	W. H. Barnes	600
McGregor	Clayton	See Elkader	2200
Mechanicsville	Cedar	A. S. McCartney	1000
Melbourne	Marshall	See Marshalltown	400
Melrose	Monroe	See Albia	400
Menlo	Guthrie	See Guthrie Centre	800
Miles	Jackson	T. W. Darling	300
Milo	Warren	See Indianola	400
Missouri Valley	Harrison	See Logan	2000
Mitchell	Mitchell	See Osage	400
Mitchellville	Polk	G. W. Copley	800
Monroe	Jasper	See Newton	1000
Montezuma*	Poweshiek	John McCandless	1500
Monticello	Jones	B. Stuart	2000
Montour	Tama	See Toledo	600

Iowa—Continued.

Parties corresponding with Attorneys named in the Directory should ALWAYS sign themselves "Subscribers to J. A. GRAFT & CO.'S LEGAL DIRECTORY." Should any Attorney fail to give prompt attention to correspondence, collections or business intrusted to his care, we will be thankful to patrons of the Directory to notify us promptly in any such case. Places designated thus (*) are County Seats.

POST-OFFICE.	COUNTY.	ATTORNEYS.	POPUL'N.
Moravia	Appanoose	See Centerville	400
Morning Sun	Louisa	See Columbus Junction	1000
Morrison	Grundy	See Grundy Centre	400
Moulton	Appanoose	H. L. Marshall	800
Mount Ayr*	Ringgold	Brockett & Bevis	1500
Mount Etna	Adams	See Corning	800
Mount Pleasant*	Henry	Amblers & Campbell	5000
Mount Vernon	Linn	See Cedar Rapids	1200
Muscatine*	Muscatine	J. E. Stevenson	11000
Nashua	Chickasaw	B. A. Billings	2000
Neola	Pottawattamie	See Council Bluffs	500
Nevada*	Story	T. C. McCall	1800
Newell	Buena Vista	See Storm Lake	500
New Hampton*	Chickasaw	J. H. Powers	1500
New Market	Taylor	E. A. Pace	600
New Sharon	Mahaska	Luther Hoffmire	1000
Newton*	Jasper	Cook & Clements	3000
Nora Springs	Floyd	E. S. Wheeler	800
Northwood*	Worth	L. S. Butler	1200
Norway	Benton	T. Jeff. Williams	600
Oakland	Pottawattamie	W. T. Wilcox	800
Odebolt	Sac	Frank J. Long	1200
Oelwein	Fayette	See West Union	500
Ogden	Boone	See Boone	800
Onawa*	Monona	Pendleton Hubbard	1200
Orange City*	Sioux	Finley Burke	1000
Osage*	Mitchell	Clyde & Vanderpoel	2500
Osceola*	Clarke	W. B. Tallman	2500
Oskaloosa*	Mahaska	Gleason & Haskell	7500
Ossian	Winneshiek	M. J. Carter	600
Ottumwa*	Wapello	S. E. Adler	10000
Oxford	Johnson	See Iowa City	700
Oxford Junction	Jones	See Anamosa	500
Panora	Guthrie	Charles W. Hill	1000
Parkersburg	Butler	O. B. Courtright	1000
Pattersonville	Sioux	See Orange City	300
Paulline	O'Brien	See Sheldon	400
Pella	Marion	Bosquet & Earle	3000
Perry	Dallas		3500
Persia	Harrison	A. C. Snyder	1000
Peterson	Clay	C. W. Fillmore	300

Iowa—Continued.

Parties corresponding with Attorneys named in the Directory should ALWAYS sign themselves "Subscribers to J. A. GRAFT & CO.'S LEGAL DIRECTORY." Should any Attorney fail to give prompt attention to correspondence, collections or business intrusted to his care, we will be thankful to patrons of the Directory to notify us promptly in any such case. Places designated thus (*) are County Seats.

POST-OFFICE.	COUNTY.	ATTORNEYS.	POPUL'N.
Pleasantville	Marion	See Knoxville	600
Pocahontas*	Pocahontas	W. D. McEwen	700
Pomeroy	Calhoun	J. A. Gould	400
Postville	Allamakee	F. S. Burling	1000
Prairie City	Jasper	See Newton	1000
Preston	Jackson	A. L. Bartholomew	700
Primghar*	O'Brien	See Sanborn	400
Randolph	Fremont	See Hamburg	1000
Red Oak*	Montgomery	Robert Pritchard	4000
Reinbeck	Grundy	Wm. Riley	700
Richland	Keokuk	T. P. Harris	500
Riverton	Fremont	See Hamburg	600
Rockford	Floyd	E. P. Andrews	1400
Rock Rapids*	Lyon	J. M. Parsons	1200
Rock Valley	Sioux	B. F. McCormack	600
Rockwell City*	Calhoun	Jas. H. Ballagh	600
Rolfe	Pocahontas	See Fonda	300
Ruthven	Palo Alto	See Emmetsburg	400
Sabula	Jackson	J. Hilsinger	1500
Sac City*	Sac	Chas. D. Goldsmith	1500
Salem	Henry	W. S. Withrow	800
Sanborn	O'Brien	Milt. H. Allen	1500
Scranton City	Greene	See Jefferson	500
Seymour	Wayne	John Jamison	1000
Sheffield	Franklin	T. H. Harris	500
Shelby	Shelby	See Harlan	600
Sheldon	O'Brien	Scott M. Ladd	1500
Shell Rock	Butler	G. A. McIntire	1000
Shenandoah	Page	Stockton & Keenan	2500
Sibley*	Osceola	J. T. Barkley	600
Sidney*	Fremont	P. H. Hoop	1000
Sigourney*	Keokuk	Harned & Mohland	2000
Silver City	Mills	See Glenwood	400
Sioux City*	**Woodbury**	**J. P. Blood**	**15000**
Sioux Rapids	Buena Vista	See Storm Lake	500
Sloan	Woodbury	See Sioux City	400
Smithland	Woodbury	See Sioux City	500
South English	Keokuk	See Sigourney	600
Spencer*	Clay	W. S. Bemis	2000
Spirit Lake*	Dickinson	J. W. Cory	400
Springville	Linn	A. F. N. Hambleton	600

Iowa—Continued.

Parties corresponding with Attorneys named in the Directory should ALWAYS sign themselves "Subscribers to J. A. GRAFT & CO.'S LEGAL DIRECTORY." Should any attorney fail to give prompt attention to correspondence, collections or business intrusted to his care, we will be thankful to patrons of the Directory to notify us promptly in any such case. Places designated thus (*) are County Seats.

POST-OFFICE.	COUNTY.	ATTORNEYS.	POPUL'N.
Stanton	Montgomery	See Red Oak	500
State Centre	Marshall	See Marshalltown	1000
Steamboat Rock	Hardin	S. B. Cunningham	800
Storm Lake*	Buena Vista	Sweeley & Slocumb	2500
Story City	Story	See Nevada	500
Strawberry Point	Clayton	See Elkader	1000
Stuart	Guthrie	See Adel	3000
Sumner	Bremer	Josiah Carpenter	500
Sutherland	O'Brien	G. F. Colcord	500
Swan	Marion	See Knoxville	400
Swan Lake*	Emmet	See Estherville	400
Tama City	Tama	See Toledo	1500
Templeton	Carroll	See Carroll	500
Tipton*	Cedar	John N. Neiman	1500
Toledo*	Tama	Struble & Kinne	1500
Traer	Tama	W. H. Bowen	1500
Union	Hardin	J. C. Adams	800
Vail	Crawford	A. A. Leachey	900
Van Horn	Benton	See Vinton	400
Victor	Iowa	J. W. Raffensperger	800
Villisca	Montgomery	A. M. Walters	1500
Vinton*	Benton	Ray Billingsley	3000
Wall Lake	Sac	C. L. Sherwood	500
Walnut	Pottawattamie	A. W. Askwith	1000
Wapello*	Louisa	L. A. Riley	1200
Washington*	Washington	Dewey & Eicher	3500
Waterloo*	Black Hawk	H. H. Bezold	7000
Waucoma	Fayette	See West Union	500
Waukon*	Allamakee	Dayton & Dayton	2000
Waverly*	Bremer	Gibson & Dawson	2500
Webster City*	Hamilton	Martin & Zelie	5000
Weldon	Decatur	R. J. Crichfield	200
West Branch	Cedar	D. E. Mackey	800
West Liberty	Muscatine	See Muscatine	1200
West Side	Crawford	Freeman Knowles	500
West Union*	Fayette	Zeigler & Weed	1500
What Cheer	Keokuk	W. P. McDonald	5000
Whiting	Monona	See Onawa	400
Williamsburgh	Iowa	See Marengo	400
Wilton Junction	Muscatine	See Muscatine	1500
Winfield	Henry	See Mount Pleasant	600

Iowa—Continued.

Parties corresponding with Attorneys named in the Directory should ALWAYS sign themselves "Subscribers to J. A. GRAFT & CO.'S LEGAL DIRECTORY." Should any Attorney fail to give prompt attention to correspondence, collections or business intrusted to his care, we will be thankful to patrons of the Directory to notify us promptly in any such case. Places designated thus (*) are County Seats.

POST-OFFICE.	COUNTY.	ATTORNEYS.	POPUL'N.
Winterset*	Madison	A. W. C. Weeks	3000
Wiota	Cass	See Atlantic	400
Woodbine	Harrison	See Logan	800
Woodward	Dallas	See Adel	400
Wyoming	Jones	W. I. Chamberlain	1200

KANSAS.

POST-OFFICE.	COUNTY.	ATTORNEYS.	POPUL'N.
Abilene*	Dickinson	J. R. Burton	3000
Alma*	Wabaunsee	James Carroll	700
Anthony*	Harper	Grove & Shepard	3000
Arkansas City	Cowley	See Winfield	2500
Atchison*	**Atchison**	**Smith & Solomon**	**16000**
Augusta	Butler	F. L. Jones	2000
Axtell	Marshall	See Marysville	500
Barnes	Washington	See Greenleaf	400
Baxter Springs	Cherokee	See Columbus	1500
Beattie	Marshall	See Frankfort	500
Belle Plaine	Sumner	See Wellington	800
Belleville*	Republic	T. M. Noble	1000
Beloit*	Mitchell	A. W. Hicks	2000
Blue Rapids	Marshall	W. H. H. Freeman	1000
Bull City	Osborne	S. S. Van Sickel	400
Burden	Cowley	See Winfield	400
Burlingame	Osage	William Thompson	1800
Burlington*	Coffey	Henry E. Kelley	2500
Burr Oak	Jewell	See Mankato	600
Burrton	Harvey	See Newton	600
Caldwell	Sumner	M. F. May	2500
Canton	McPherson	See McPherson	600
Carbondale	Osage	See Lyndon	1000
Cawker City	Mitchell	See Beloit	1500
Cedar Vale	Chautauqua	See Sedan	500
Centralia	Nemaha	See Seneca	500
Chanute	Neosho	T. C. Jones	2500

Kansas—Continued.

Parties corresponding with Attorneys named in the Directory should ALWAYS sign themselves "Subscribers to J. A. GRAFT & CO.'S LEGAL DIRECTORY." Should any Attorney fail to give prompt attention to correspondence, collections or business intrusted to his care, we will be thankful to patrons of the Directory to notify us promptly in any such case. Places designated thus (*) are County Seats.

POST-OFFICE.	COUNTY.	ATTORNEYS.	POPUL'N.
Chapman	Dickinson	Swift & Curts	600
Cheney	Sedgwick	See Wichita	400
Cherokee	Crawford	See Girard	700
Cherryvale	Montgomery	C. C. Thompson	3000
Chetopa	Labette	Leroy Neale	1500
Cimarron	Ford	James T. Farris	500
Circleville	Jackson	R. Ousler	500
Clay Centre*	Clay		4500
Clifton	Washington	J. W. Chadwick	1000
Clyde	Cloud	W. D. Hilton	2500
Coffeyville	Montgomery	See Independence	1000
Coldwater*	Comanche	Sisson & McClure	700
Columbus*	Cherokee	J. Railsback	2800
Concordia*	Cloud	Laing & Wrong	3000
Cottonwood Falls*	Chase	Thos. H. Grisham	1000
Council Grove*	Morris	Johnston & Bertram	2000
Defiance	Woodson	See Yates Center	300
Delphos	Ottawa	See Minneapolis	500
Dodge City*	Ford	F. T. M. Wenie	1800
Douglass	Butler	E. H. Hutchins	600
Downs	Osborne	William Mellen	600
Edgerton	Johnson	See Olathe	500
El Dorado*	Butler	E. E. Carr	3500
Elk City	Montgomery	See Independence	500
Elk Falls	Elk	I. B. Alter	700
Ellinwood	Barton	J. D. Ronstadt	800
Ellsworth*	Ellsworth	R. W. Carter	2500
Elmdale	Chase	See Cottonwood Falls	500
Emporia*	Lyon	E. N. Evans	11000
Enterprise	Dickinson	See Abilene	500
Erie*	Neosho	John Hall	1500
Eskridge	Wabaunsee	A. A. Graham	700
Eureka*	Greenwood	Clogston & Fuller	4000
Everest	Brown	See Hiawatha	300
Fall River	Greenwood	L. H. Johnson	700
Florence	Marion	See Marion	1200
Fort Scott*	Bourbon	John H. Crider	8500
Frankfort	Marshall	S. D. McKee	1000
Fredonia*	Wilson	B. M. Short	1500
Galena	Cherokee	George W. Webb	4000
Garden City	Finney	Charles W. Morse	2500
Garnett*	Anderson	A. J. Smith	1500

Kansas—Continued.

Parties corresponding with Attorneys named in the Directory should ALWAYS sign themselves "Subscribers to J. A. GRAFT & CO.'S LEGAL DIRECTORY." Should any Attorney fail to give prompt attention to correspondence, collections or business intrusted to his care, we will be thankful to patrons of the Directory to notify us promptly in any such case. Places designated thus (*) are County Seats.

POST-OFFICE.	COUNTY.	ATTORNEYS.	POPUL'N.
Gaylord	Smith	See Smith Centre	500
Girard*	Crawford	James Brown	2500
Glasco	Cloud	See Concordia	500
Great Bend*	Barton	L. R. Nimocks	2500
Greenleaf	Washington	F. L. Joslyn	1000
Grenola	Elk	See Howard	600
Haddam	Washington	See Hanover	400
Halstead	Harvey	See Newton	600
Hanover	Washington	F. A. Meckel	1000
Harper	Harper	Sam. S. Sisson	4000
Hartford	Lyon	T. B. Nees	700
Havensville	Pottawatomie	See Louisville	400
Hays City*	Ellis	Nathaniel Robbins	5600
Hiawatha*	Brown	Buckles & Newlon	3000
Highland	Doniphan	John P. Johnson	400
Hillsboro	Marion	See Marion	400
Holton*	Jackson	Hoaglin & Crawford	2500
Howard*	Elk	H. S. Douthitt	1500
Humboldt	Allen	A. D. Hubbard	2000
Hunnewell	Sumner	See Wellington	500
Hutchinson*	Reno	R. A. Campbell	3000
Independence*	Montgomery	J. B. Ziegler	4000
Iola*	Allen	A. C. Bogle	1400
Irving	Marshall	Warden & Proctor	600
Iuka*	Pratt	See Pratt	600
Jamestown	Cloud	See Concordia	400
Jewell	Jewell	M. F. Knappenberger	1200
Junction City*	Davis	James McClure	3000
Kenneth	Sheridan	A. D. Urquhart	100
Kingman*	Kingman	Gillett & Raymond	2000
Kinsley*	Edwards	W. H. Robb	1200
Kirwin	Phillips	S. H. Bradley	1500
La Cygne	Linn	J. V. Donaldson	1500
Larned*	Pawnee	P. H. Forbes	1500
Lawrence*	Douglas	Riggs & Nevison	14000
Leavenworth*	**Leavenworth**	**E. N. O. Clough**	**25000**
Lehigh	Marion	See Marion	400
Leon	Butler		
Lincoln*	Lincoln	Ed. F. Coad	1200
Lindsborg	McPherson	See McPherson	700

Kansas—Continued.

Parties corresponding with Attorneys named in the Directory should ALWAYS sign themselves "Subscribers to J. A. GRAFT & CO.'S LEGAL DIRECTORY." Should any Attorney fail to give prompt attention to correspondence, collections or business intrusted to his care, we will be thankful to patrons of the Directory to notify us promptly in any such case.
Places designated thus (*) are County Seats.

POST-OFFICE.	COUNTY.	ATTORNEYS.	POPUL'N.
Linn	Washington	See Greenleaf	400
Logan	Phillips.	H. H. Boyd	500
Longton.	Elk	See Howard	500
Louisburg	Miami	See Paola	800
Louisville	Pottawatomie	R. S. Hick	800
Lyndon*	Osage	John W. Lord	1000
Lyons*	Rice	Lasley & Perry	1500
Manhattan*	Riley	Geo. C. Wilder	2500
Mankato*	Jewell		700
Marion*	Marion	L. F. Keller	1800
Marysville*	Marshall	W. S. Glass	2000
McCune	Crawford	See Girard	400
McPherson*	McPherson	Edgar M. Clark	3000
Medicine Lodge*	Barber	W. H. McCague	1100
Melvern	Osage	See Lyndon	500
Meriden.	Jefferson	See Oskaloosa	500
Millbrook*	Graham	See Stockton	500
Miltonvale	Cloud	See Concordia	400
Minneapolis*	Ottawa	C. W. Stephenson	1200
Mound City*	Linn	See Pleasanton	1000
Mound Valley	Labette	See Oswego	500
Mount Hope	Sedgwick	See Wichita	400
Mulvane	Sumner	E. J. Kuhn	600
Neodesha	Wilson	Wm. H. Cramer	2000
Neosho Falls	Woodson	J. W. Dickson	800
Newton*	Harvey	W. E. Brown	3500
Nickerson	Reno	See Hutchinson	1000
North Topeka	Shawnee	See Topeka	5000
Norton*	Norton	J. R. Hamilton	800
Oberlin*	Decatur	G. Webb Bertram	1200
Olathe*	Johnson	S. D. Scott	3000
Olesburg	Pottawatomie	See Louisville	300
Onaga	Pottawatomie	See Louisville	500
Osage City	Osage	A. M. Hale	4500
Osage Mission	Neosho	See Erie	2000
Osborne*	Osborne	Z. T. Walrond	1000
Oskaloosa*	Jefferson	J. H. Johnson	1200
Oswego*	Labette	Jess Brockway	3700
Ottawa*	Franklin	C. A. Smart	6500
Oxford	Sumner	See Wellington	700
Paola*	Miami	N. W. Wells	3000

Kansas—Continued.

Parties corresponding with Attorneys named in the Directory should ALWAYS sign themselves "Subscribers to J. A. GRAFT & CO.'S LEGAL DIRECTORY."
Should any attorney fail to give prompt attention to correspondence, collections or business intrusted to his care, we will be thankful to patrons of the Directory to notify us promptly in any such case.
Places designated thus (*) are County Seats.

POST-OFFICE.	COUNTY.	ATTORNEYS.	POPUL'N.
Parkersville	Morris	H. S. Day	300
Parsons	Labette	Geo. F. King	10000
Peabody	Marion	J. H. Morse	2000
Phillipsburg	Phillips	G. A. Spaulding	300
Pittsburg	Crawford	Harry R. Thurston	3000
Plainville	Rooks	See Stockton	200
Pleasanton	Linn	J. H. Martin	1500
Pratt	Pratt	R. F. McGrew	400
Quenemo	Osage	See Lyndon	500
Republic	Republic	See Belleville	500
Russell*	Russell	H. C. Hibbard	1000
Sabetha	Nemaha	See Seneca	1000
Salem	Jewell	A. H. Gates	400
Salina*	Saline	J. G. Mohler	5000
Scandia	Republic	See Belleville	800
Scranton	Osage	See Lyndon	1000
Sedan*	Chautauqua	John F. Cheek	1200
Sedgwick	Harvey	See Newton	800
Seneca*	Nemaha	J. P. Taylor	2000
Severance	Doniphan	A. J. Mowry	700
Smith Centre*	Smith	R. M. Pickler	400
Solomon City	Dickinson	James S. Hall	1000
Stafford	Stafford	T. F. Halveson	500
Sterling	Rice	W. P. Fulton	2000
St. John*	Stafford	Weeks & Rose	700
St. Mary's	Pottawatomie	Hagan & Mackay	1000
Stockton*	Rooks	Frank McNulty	1000
Strong	Chase	See Cottonwood Falls.	400
Thayer	Neosho	See Erie	500
Topeka*	**Shawnee**	**Eugene Hagan**	**31000**
Troy*	Doniphan	Thomas W. Heatley.	800
Udall	Cowley	See Winfield	400
Valley Falls	Jefferson	L. A. Myers	1500
Wa Keeney*	Trego	See Hays City	1000
Wallace*	St. John	See Hays City	300
Walnut	Crawford	See Girard	400
Walton	Harvey	See Newton	300
Wamego	Pottawatomie	L. H. Finney	1500

Kansas—Continued.

Parties corresponding with Attorneys named in the Directory should ALWAYS sign themselves "Subscribers to J. A. GRAFT & CO.'S LEGAL DIRECTORY." Should any Attorney fail to give prompt attention to correspondence, collections or business intrusted to his care, we will be thankful to patrons of the Directory to notify us promptly in any such case.
Places designated thus (*) are County Seats.

POST-OFFICE.	COUNTY.	ATTORNEYS.	POPUL'N.
Washington*	Washington	J. T. Hole	1500
Waterville	Marshall	W. W. Smith	1000
Waverly	Coffey	See Burlington	400
Webster	Rooks	See Stockton	200
Wellington*	Sumner	James Lawrence	5000
Westmoreland*	Pottawatomie	See Wamego	500
Wetmore	Nemaha	E. Campfield	600
White Cloud	Doniphan	R. M. Williams	1000
Whiting	Jackson	See Holton	400
Wichita*	Sedgwick	J. M. Balderston	10000
Williamsburg	Franklin	See Ottawa	1200
Willis	Brown	W. J. Cash	400
Wilson	Ellsworth	H. E. Shafer	1000
Windom	McPherson	See McPherson	400
Winfield*	Cowley	McDermott & Johnson	7000
Wyandotte*	Wyandotte	C. H. J. Taylor	13000
Yates Center*	Woodson	M. C. Smith	1500

KENTUCKY.

POST-OFFICE.	COUNTY.	ATTORNEYS.	POPUL'N.
Adairville	Logan	See Russellville	700
Albany*	Clinton	J. M. Bristow	400
Alexandria	Campbell	See Newport	400
Ashland	Boyd	W. C. Ireland	4500
Auburn	Logan	See Russellville	800
Augusta	Bracken	John M. Boude	1800
Barboursville*	Knox	J. N. Brafford	500
Bardstown*	Nelson	J. C. Wickliffe	2500
Beattyville*	Lee	J. M. Beatty	300
Bedford*	Trimble	John T. Bashaw	600
Benton*	Marshall	Gilbert & Reed	400
Blandville*	Ballard	B. S. Bailey	500
Bloomfield	Nelson	See Bardstown	600
Booneville*	Owsley	J. M. Sebastian	300
Bowling Green*	Warren	George R. Gorin	10000
Brandenburg*	Meade	Lewis & Fairleigh	800

Kentucky—Continued.

Parties corresponding with Attorneys named in the Directory should ALWAYS sign themselves "Subscribers to J. A. GRAFT & CO.'S LEGAL DIRECTORY." Should any Attorney fail to give prompt attention to correspondence, collections or business intrusted to his care, we will be thankful to patrons of the Directory to notify us promptly in any such case. Places designated thus (*) are County Seats.

POST-OFFICE.	COUNTY.	ATTORNEYS.	POPUL'N.
Brookville*	Bracken	W. O. Blackerby	400
Brownsville*	Edmonson	L. M. Hazelip	200
Burkesville*	Cumberland	M. O. Allen	600
Burlington*	Boone	A. G. Winston	500
Cadiz*	Trigg	J. E. Kelly	1200
Calhoun*	McLean	Jep. C. Jonson	800
Campbellsville*	Taylor	H. S. Robinson	1000
Campton*	Wolfe	Joseph C. Lykins	300
Carlisle*	Nicholas	Kennedy & Kennedy.	1200
Carrollton*	Carroll	J. A. Donaldson	2000
Caseyville	Union	See Uniontown	600
Catlettsburg*	Boyd	See Ashland	1800
Clinton*	Hickman	Jacob White	800
Cloverport	Breckinridge	J. A. & D. R. Murray	1200
Columbia*	Adair	W. W. Jones	800
Columbus	Hickman	See Clinton	1500
Covington*	**Kenton**	**J. F. & C. H. Fisk**	**35000**
Cynthiana*	Harrison	Swinford & Lafferty	3500
Danville*	Boyle	W. O. Goodloe	3200
Dixon*	Webster	John G. Bailey	800
Eddyville*	Lyon	F. H. Skinner	500
Edmonton*	Metcalfe	J. W. Compton	300
Elizabethtown*	Hardin	Bush & Robertson	2500
Elkton*	Todd	W. L. Reeves	1000
Eminence	Henry	See New Castle	1200
Falmouth*	Pendleton	P. F. Bonar	1200
Flemingsburg*	Fleming	M. M. Teagar	1400
Frankfort*	Franklin	**Frank Chinn** (See card in Appendix, page II.)	**7000**
Franklin*	Simpson	T. M. Goodknight	3000
Frenchburg*	Menifee	See Mount Sterling	400
Fulton	Fulton	B. H. Freeman	2000
Georgetown*	Scott	H. P. Montgomery	2700
Glasgow*	Barren	G. M. Bohannon	2500
Grayson*	Carter	Merritt Magann	600
Greensburg*	Green	D. Hudson	700
Greenup*	Greenup	Roe & Roe	1000
Greenville*	Muhlenburg	M. C. Hay	1500
Hardinsburg*	Breckinridge	Wm. K. Barnes	800

Kentucky—Continued.

Parties corresponding with Attorneys named in ...e Directory should ALWAYS sign themselves "Subscribers to J. A. GRAFT & CO.'S LEGAL DIRECTORY." Should any Attorney fail to give prompt attention to correspondence, collections or business intrusted to his care, we will be thankful to patrons of the Directory to notify us promptly in any such case.
Places designated thus (*) are County Seats.

POST-OFFICE.	COUNTY.	ATTORNEYS.	POPUL'N.
Harlan*	Harlan	See Barboursville	200
Harrodsburg*	Mercer	John W. Hughes	3000
Hartford*	Ohio*	H. D. McHenry & Son	1000
Hawesville*	Hancock	M. A. Mason	1000
Hazard*	Perry	J. C. Eversole	200
Henderson*	Henderson	S. B. & R. D. Vance	8000
Hickman*	Fulton	See Fulton	1600
Hodgensville*	La Rue	Jonn W. Gore	600
Hopkinsville*	Christian	Breathitt & Stites	6000
Horse Cave	Hart		700
Hustonville	Lincoln	See Stanford	500
Independence	Kenton	See Covington	200
Irvine*	Estill	H. C. Lilly	400
Jackson*	Breathitt	See Hazard	200
Jamestown*	Russell	See Somerset	300
La Grange*	Oldham		1000
Lancaster*	Garrard	W. O. Bradley	2500
Lawrenceburg*	Anderson	L. W. McKee	1000
Lebanon*	Marion	H. P. Cooper	3500
Leitchfield*	Grayson	J. S. Wortham	800
Lexington*	**Fayette**	**Watts Parker**	**20000**
Liberty*	Casey	J. B. Stone	400
London*	Laurel	W. R. Ramsey	400
Louisa*	Lawrence	R. T. Burns	500
Louisville*	**Jefferson**	**James G. Givens** Manager Branch Office, Corner Fifth and Court Place.	**160000**
Madisonville*	Hopkins	J. F. Dempsey	2500
Manchester*	Clay	C. B. Lyttle	300
Marion*	Crittenden	S. Hodge	400
Mayfield*	Graves	James T. Webb	3000
Maysville*	Mason	Thomas R. Phister	7000
McKee*	Jackson	See Mount Vernon	200
Midway	Woodford	See Versailles	1200
Millersburg	Bourbon	See Paris	1200
Monticello*	Wayne	J. K. Frazier	400
Morehead*	Rowan	James E. Clark	500
Morganfield*	Union	Jesse S. Taylor	700
Morgantown*	Butler	E. M. Smith	300

Kentucky—Continued.

Parties corresponding with Attorneys named in the Directory should ALWAYS sign themselves "Subscribers to J. A. GRAFT & CO.'S LEGAL DIRECTORY." Should any Attorney fail to give prompt attention to correspondence, collections or business intrusted to his care, we will be thankful to patrons of the Directory to notify us promptly in any such case.
Places designated thus (*) are County Seats.

POST-OFFICE.	COUNTY.	ATTORNEYS.	POPUL'N.
Mount Olivet*	Robertson	W. S. Bayne	600
Mount Sterling*	Montgomery	Wood & Day	3500
Mount Vernon*	Rock Castle	John B. Fish	400
Munfordville*	Hart	George T. Read	400
Murray*	Calloway	G. C. Diuguid	900
New Castle*	Henry	William M. Cravens.	800
New Haven	Nelson	See Bardstown	600
Newport*	**Campbell**	**A. W. Stossmeister**	**24000**
Nicholasville*	Jessamine	Ben. P. Campbell	2500
North Middletown	Bourbon	See Paris	500
Owensboro*	Daviess	Haycraft & Slack	11000
Owenton*	Owen	Montgomery, Lindsay & Botts	1000
Owingsville*	Bath	V. B. Young	1000
Paducah*	McCracken	James W. Eden	12000
Paintsville*	Johnson	J. F. Stewart	400
Paris*	Bourbon	W. M. Purnell	6000
Pikeville*	Pike	J. M. Roberson	400
Pineville*	Bell	M. J. Moss	300
Prestonburg*	Floyd	W. S. Harkins	200
Princeton*	Caldwell	J. R. Hewlett	1600
Richmond*	Madison	Thomas J. Scott	3500
Russellville*	Logan	George S. Hardy	3000
Salyersville*	Magoffin	W. W. Howse	200
Sandy Hook*	Elliott	J. W. Hannah	400
Scottsville*	Allen	A. M. Alexander	500
Sharpsburg	Bath	See Owingsville	400
Shelbyville*	Shelby	L. A. Weakley	2600
Shepherdsville*	Bullitt	F. P. Straus	400
Smithland*	Livingston	John K. Hendrick	800
Smith's Grove	Warren	See Bowling Green	500
Somerset*	Pulaski	James Denton	2500
Springfield*	Washington	Thos. E. Curry	900
Stanford*	Lincoln	W. H. Miller	2000
Stanton*	Powell	J. P. Hill	200
Taylorsville*	Spencer	G. G. Gilbert	700
Tompkinsville*	Monroe	W. S. Maxey	600
Uniontown	Union	See Morganfield	1200

Kentucky—Continued.

Parties corresponding with Attorneys named in the Directory should ALWAYS sign themselves "Subscribers to J. A. GRAFT & CO.'S LEGAL DIRECTORY." Should any Attorney fail to give prompt attention to correspondence, collections or business intrusted to his care, we will be thankful to patrons of the Directory to notify us promptly in any such case. Places designated thus (*) are County Seats.

POST-OFFICE.	COUNTY.	ATTORNEYS.	POPUL'N.
Vanceburg*	Lewis	Parker & Halbert	1300
Versailles*	Woodford	Porter & Wallace	2800
Warfield*	Martin	See Louisa	200
Warsaw*	Gallatin	L. L. Tiller	1000
West Liberty*	Morgan	J. E. Cooper	300
Whitesburg*	Letcher	J. B. Fitzpatrick	300
Williamsburg*	Whitley	R. D. Hill	1500
Williamstown*	Grant	H. Clay White	900
Winchester*	Clark	Jos. T. Tucker	4000

LOUISIANA.

POST-OFFICE.	PARISH.	ATTORNEYS.	POPUL'N.
Abbeville*	Vermillion	W. W. Edwards	500
Alexandria*	Rapides	W. W. Whittington, Jr.	2500
Amite City*	Tangipahoa	Reid & Reid	2500
Bastrop*	Morehouse	Todd & Todd	1200
Baton Rouge*	East Baton Rouge	Knox & Laycock	9000
Bayou Sara*	West Feliciana	H. C. Leake	1200
Bellevue*	Bossier	J. A. Snyder	200
Cameron*	Cameron	See Lake Charles	200
Clinton*	East Feliciana	Thomas A. Moore	1500
Colfax*	Grant	W. L. Richardson	200
Columbia*	Caldwell	George Wear	300
Convent*	St. James	Sims & Poche	700
Coushatta Chute*	Red River	James F. Pierson	800
Covington*	St. Tammany	Joseph A. Reid	900
Delta*	Madison	J. C. Seale	500
Delhi	Richland	H. P. Wells	300
Donaldsonville*	Ascension	G. A. Gondram	3000
Edgard	St. John Baptist	L. De Poorter	1000
Farmersville*	Union	James A. Ramsey	700
Floyd*	West Carroll	See Lake Providence.	300
Franklin*	St. Marys	David Todd	2500

Louisiana—Continued.

Parties corresponding with Attorneys named in the Directory should ALWAYS sign themselves "Subscribers to J. A. GRAFT & CO.'S LEGAL DIRECTORY." Should any attorney fail to give prompt attention to correspondence, collections or business intrusted to his care, we will be thankful to patrons of the Directory to notify us promptly in any such case.
Places designated thus (*) are County Seats.

POST-OFFICE.	PARISH.	ATTORNEYS.	POPUL'N.
Franklinton*	Washington	John Wadsworth	200
Greensburg*	St. Helena	Charles E. Lea	400
Gretna*	Jefferson	John B. Lyman	2500
Harrisonburg*	Catahoula	L. A. Thompson	400
Homer*	Claiborne	Jno. R. Phipps	900
Houma*	Terre Bonne	John B. Winder	1200
La Fayette*	La Fayette	See Opelousas	2000
Lake Charles*	Calcasieu	M. M. Singleton	2500
Lake Providence*	East Carroll	Montgomery & Ransdell	1000
Mansfield*	De Soto	John C. Pugh	1000
Many*	Sabin	James F. Smith	300
Marksville*	Avoyelles	Thorpe, Peterman & Thorpe	700
Minden*	Webster	D. W. Stewart †*James F. Taylor.*	2000
Monroe*	Ouachita	Millsaps & Sholars	3000
Morgan City	St. Marys	See Franklin	2000
Napoleonville*	Assumption	Pugh & Howell	700
Natchitoches*	Natchitoches	McDonald & Tucker.	3000
New Iberia*	Iberia	Merchant & Fontelieu	5000
New Orleans*	**Orleans**	**David Todd** Manager Branch Office, No. 22 Carondelet St.	**240000**
Opelousas*	St. Landry	W. C. Perrault †*Kenneth Baillio.*	2500
Plaquemine*	Iberville	Hebert & Wales	2500
Pointe a la Hache*	Plaquemines	A. Lartigue	500
Pointe Coupee*	Pointe Coupee	A. Provosty	200
Port Allen*	West Baton Rouge	See Baton Rouge	300
Port Vincent*	Livingston	See Baton Rouge	300
Rayne	St. Landry	W. W. Duson	
Rayville*	Richland	H. P. Wells	500
Shreveport*	Caddo	John S. Young	12000

(† We withdraw our former recommendation.)

Louisiana—Continued.

Parties corresponding with Attorneys named in the Directory should ALWAYS sign themselves "Subscribers to J. A. GRAFT & CO.'S LEGAL DIRECTORY." Should any Attorney fail to give prompt attention to correspondence, collections or business intrusted to his care, we will be thankful to patrons of the Directory to notify us promptly in any such case. Places designated thus (*) are County Seats.

POST-OFFICE.	PARISH.	ATTORNEYS.	POPUL'N.
Sparta*	Bienville	B. P. Edwards	300
Springfield	Livingston	See Baton Rouge	300
St. Charles*	St. Charles	See New Orleans	200
St. Francisville*	West Feliciana	See Baton Rouge	1000
St. James	St. James	J. E. Poche	200
St. Joseph*	Tensas	L. V. Reeves	600
St. Martinville*	St. Martin's	Monton & Martin	1500
Thibodeaux*	La Fourche	John Donohue	1800
Vernon*	Jackson	Newton M. Smith	300
Vidalia*	Concordia	G. A. Sawyer	800
Vienna*	Lincoln	Allen Burksdale	400
Washington	St. Landry	See Opelousas	1500
Winnfield*	Winn	See Monroe	500
Winnsboro*	Franklin	C. J. Ellis	500

MAINE.

POST-OFFICE.	COUNTY.	ATTORNEYS.	POPUL'N.
Abbot	Piscataquis	See Dover	1000
Alfred*	York	S. M. Came	1000
Anson	Somerset	See North Anson	1500
Appleton	Knox	F. M. Hawly	1500
Athens	Somerset	J. F. Holman	800
Auburn*	Androscoggin	J. W. Mitchell	10000
Augusta*	Kennebec	H. M. Heath	9000
Bangor*	Penobscot	H. L. Mitchell	18000
Bath*	Sagadahoc	Adams & Combs	8000
Belfast*	Waldo	George E. Johnson	6000
Benton	Kennebec	See Augusta	1500
Berwick	York	See Great Falls, N. H.	2000
Bethel	Oxford	Foster & Herrick	2000
Biddeford	York	W. E. Tibbetts	14000
Booth Bay	Lincoln	George B. Kenniston	3000
Bowdoinham	Sagadahoc	E. J. Millay	1500
Bridgton	Cumberland	See Portland	3000

Maine—Continued.

Parties corresponding with Attorneys named in the Directory should ALWAYS sign themselves "Subscribers to J. A. GRAFT & CO.'S LEGAL DIRECTORY." Should any Attorney fail to give prompt attention to correspondence, collections or business intrusted to his care, we will be thankful to patrons of the Directory to notify us promptly in any such case. Places designated thus (*) are County Seats.

POST-OFFICE.	COUNTY	ATTORNEYS.	POPUL'N.
Brunswick	Cumberland	See Portland	5500
Bucksport	Hancock	O. P. Cunningham	3500
Calais	Washington	M. N. McKusick	7000
Camden	Knox	J. H. Montgomery	5000
Cherryfield	Washington	Milliken & Campbell	1800
Damariscotta	Lincoln	W. H. Hilton	1200
Dexter	Penobscot	See Bangor	2500
Dover*	Piscataquis	J. B. Beaks	1800
Eastport	Washington	S. D. Leavitt	4200
Ellsworth*	Hancock	B. T. Sowle	5500
Fairfield	Somerset	S. S. Chapman	3000
Farmington*	Franklin	S. C. Belcher	3500
Fort Fairfield	Aroostook	See Houlton	800
Freeport	Cumberland	See Portland	2500
Fryeburg	Oxford	D. R. Hastings	2000
Gardiner	Kennebec	Henry Farrington	4500
Gorham	Cumberland	See Portland	3300
Hallowell	Kennebec	See Augusta	3500
Hampden	Penobscot	See Bangor	3700
Houlton*	Aroostook	Ira G. Hersey	3800
Kennebunk	York	See Alfred	3000
Kittery	York	M. A. Safford	3300
Lewiston	Androscoggin	William W. Bolster	22000
Limerick	York	L. S. Moore	1500
Lisbon	Androscoggin	See Auburn	2700
Machias*	Washington	John F. Lynch	2500
Monroe	Waldo	See Belfast	1800
New Castle	Lincoln	Howard E. Hall	2000
Norridgewock	Somerset	John H. Webster	2000
North Anson	Somerset	B. S. Collins	600
North Berwick	York	Nathaniel Hobbs	1200
North Vassalborough	Kennebec	See Augusta	3000
Norway	Oxford	C. F. Whitman	2800
Oakland	Kennebec	See Augusta	1000

Maine—Continued.

Parties corresponding with Attorneys named in the Directory should ALWAYS sign themselves "Subscribers to J. A. GRAFT & CO.'S LEGAL DIRECTORY." Should any Attorney fail to give prompt attention to correspondence, collections or business intrusted to his care, we will be thankful to patrons of the Directory to notify us promptly in any such case.
Places designated thus (*) are County Seats.

POST-OFFICE.	COUNTY.	ATTORNEYS.	POPUL'N.
Old Town	Penobscot	See Bangor	3300
Orono	Penobscot	See Bangor	2300
Paris*	Oxford	G. A. Wilson	3500
Pembroke	Washington	E. K. Smart	2500
Phillips	Franklin	James Morrison, Jr.	1700
Portland*	**Cumberland**	**John C. Cobb**	**36000**
Richmond	Sagadahoc	W. T. Hall	3700
Rockland*	Knox	D. N. Mortland	8000
Rockport	Knox	See Rockland	4500
Saco	York	Fairfield & Emery	6500
Searsport	Waldo	W. T. C. Runnells	3000
Skowhegan*	Somerset	Walton & Walton	4000
South Berwick	York	George C. Yeaton	3200
South Paris	Oxford	George A. Wilson	2000
Springvale	York	See Alfred	2500
Thomaston	Knox	J. H. Hewitt	3000
Waldoboro	Lincoln	S. W. Jackson	4000
Waterford	Oxford	See Paris	5000
Waterville	Kennebec	See Augusta	5000
Wilton	Franklin	See Farmington	2000
Wiscasset*	Lincoln	Henry Ingalls	2000

MARYLAND.

POST-OFFICE.	COUNTY.	ATTORNEYS.	POPUL'N.
Annapolis*	Anne Arundel	Frank H. Stockett, Jr.	6500
Baltimore	(Not embraced in any County.)	**Winfield M. Simpson.** Manager Branch Office, No. 1 St. Paul street. Reference, Howard Bank.	**375000**
Bel Air*	Harford	Harlan & Webster	1000
Berlin	Worcester	See Pocomoke City	1200

Maryland—Continued.

Parties corresponding with Attorneys named in the Directory should ALWAYS sign themselves "Subscribers to J. A. GRAFT & CO.'S LEGAL DIRECTORY." Should any Attorney fail to give prompt attention to correspondence, collections or business intrusted to his care, we will be thankful to patrons of the Directory to notify us promptly in any such case.
Places designated thus (*) are County Seats.

POST-OFFICE.	COUNTY.	ATTORNEYS.	POPUL'N.
Cambridge*	Dorchester	D. M. Henry, Jr.	2500
Centreville*	Queen Anne	P. B. Hopper	1800
Chestertown*	Kent	James A. Pearce	2500
Cumberland*	Allegany	Robert R. Henderson.	11000
Denton*	Caroline	George M. Russum	600
Easton*	Talbot	Albert Lowe	3500
Elkton*	Cecil	Jones & Haines	2000
Ellicott City*	Howard	H. E. Wooten	2500
Emmitsburg	Frederick	See Frederick	1000
Frederick*	Frederick	C. V. S. Levy	9000
Frostburgh	Allegany	Clayton Purnell	2000
Hagerstown*	Washington	Alex. R. Hagner	10000
Havre de Grace	Harford	See Bel Air	3000
Leonardtown*	St. Mary's	Joseph F. Morgan	800
Mechanicstown	Frederick	See Frederick	1000
New Windsor	Carroll	See Westminster	700
Oakland*	Garrett	G. S. Hamill	1200
Pocomoke City	Worcester	Henry M. Voorhees	2000
Port Deposit	Cecil	See Elkton	2500
Port Tobacco*	Charles	John H. Mitchell	400
Prince Frederick*	Calvert	Joseph A. Wilson	300
Princess Anne*	Somerset	Henry Page	1000
Rising Sun	Cecil	See Elkton	500
Rockville*	Montgomery	Alexander Kilgour	800
Salisbury*	Wicomico	Thomas Humphreys.	2800
Sandy Spring	Montgomery	See Rockville	300
Snow Hill*	Worcester	Oliver D. Collins	1500
Taneytown	Carroll	See Westminster	800
Towson*	Baltimore	D. G. McIntosh	2000
Union Bridge	Carroll	See Westminster	800
Uniontown	Carroll	See Westminster	600
Upper Marlboro*	Prince George	Joseph K. Roberts, Jr.	800

Maryland—Continued.

Parties corresponding with Attorneys named in the Directory should ALWAYS sign themselves "Subscribers to J. A. GRAFT & CO.'S LEGAL DIRECTORY." Should any Attorney fail to give prompt attention to correspondence, collections or business intrusted to his care, we will be thankful to patrons of the Directory to notify us promptly in any such case.
Places designated thus (*) are County Seats.

POST-OFFICE.	COUNTY.	ATTORNEYS.	POPUL'N.
Westminster*	Carroll	George M. Pearce	3000
Williamsport	Washington	See Hagerstown	1600
Woodberry	Baltimore	See Baltimore	1000

MASSACHUSETTS.

POST-OFFICE.	COUNTY.	ATTORNEYS.	POPUL'N.
Abington	Plymouth	John F. Simmons	4000
Adams	Berkshire	See North Adams	3000
Amesbury	Essex	Frank C. Whiting	8000
Amherst	Hampshire	Dickinson & Cooper	4000
Andover	Essex	George H. Poor	6000
Arlington	Middlesex	John H. Hardy	5000
Athol	Worcester	George W. Horr	4500
Attleborough	Bristol	George A. Adams	12000
Barnstable*	Barnstable	Smith K. Hopkins	2000
Barre	Worcester	Charles Brimblecom	25000
Beverly	Essex	See Salem	9000
Boston*	**Suffolk**	**Sam'l W. Clifford, Jr.** Manager Branch Office, No. 23 Court St. Rooms 91 and 92.	365000
Braintree	Norfolk	Asa French	4000
Bridgewater	Plymouth	See Plymouth	4000
Brighton	Suffolk	See Boston	4000
Brockton	Plymouth	Elliot L. Packard	15000
Brookfield	Worcester	See Worcester	3000
Brookline	Norfolk	C. A. Williams	8000
Cambridge*	Middlesex	C. J. McIntire	50000
Cambridgeport	Middlesex	See Cambridge	5000
Canton	Norfolk	Thomas E. Grover	4500
Chelsea	Suffolk	J. L. O'Neill	25000
Chicopee	Hampden	See Springfield	12000
Clinton	Worcester	John W. Corcoran	8000
Concord	Middlesex	John S. Keyes	3500
Danvers	Essex	E. L. Hill	7000
Dedham*	Norfolk	Hill & Mackintosh	7000

Massachusetts—Continued.

Parties corresponding with Attorneys named in the Directory should ALWAYS sign themselves "Subscribers to J. A. GRAFT & CO.'S LEGAL DIRECTORY." Should any Attorney fail to give prompt attention to correspondence, collections or business intrusted to his care, we will be thankful to patrons of the Directory to notify us promptly in any such case. Places designated thus (*) are County Seats.

POST-OFFICE.	COUNTY.	ATTORNEYS.	POPUL'N.
East Bridgewater	Plymouth	See Plymouth	3000
East Cambridge	Middlesex	See Cambridge	10000
Easthampton	Hampshire	See Northampton	12000
Edgartown*	Dukes	J. T. Pease	2000
Fairhaven	Bristol	See New Bedford	1500
Fall River	Bristol	Braley & Swift	50000
Fitchburgh*	Worcester	J. H. McMahon	14000
Florence	Hampshire	See Northampton	1000
Foxborough	Norfolk	Robert W. Carpenter	3000
Framingham	Middlesex	Frederick M. Esty	6000
Franklin	Norfolk	George W. Wiggin	4000
Gardner	Worcester	Charles D. Burrage	8000
Georgetown	Essex	W. A. Butler	2500
Gloucester	Essex	W. W. French	20000
Grafton	Worcester	D. B. Hubbard	5000
Great Barrington	Berkshire	Dewey & Wright	3000
Greenfield*	Franklin	F. C. Griswold	4000
Harwich	Barnstable	H. P. Harriman	2500
Haverhill	Essex	J. Otis Wardwell	21000
Haydenville	Hampshire	See Northampton	2500
Hingham	Plymouth	See Plymouth	4500
Holliston	Middlesex	J. H. Ladd	3000
Holyoke	Hampden	Porter Underwood	30000
Hopkinton	Middlesex	L. H. Wakefield	4000
Hudson	Middlesex	James T. Joslin	4000
Hyde Park	Norfolk	Edmund Davis	8000
Ipswich	Essex	Charles A. Sayward	4000
Lancaster	Worcester	Daniel H. Bemis	2500
Lawrence*	Essex	Sherman & Bell	40000
Lee	Berkshire	See Pittsfield	4000
Leicester	Worcester	Henry O. Smith	3000
Leominster	Worcester	See Gardner	6000
Lexington	Middlesex	E. A. Scott	3000
Lowell*	**Middlesex**	**John J. Pickman**	**65000**
Lynn	**Essex**	**T. F. Bartlett**	**40000**
Malden	Middlesex	George D. Ayers	15000
Marblehead	Essex	See Lynn	10000
Marlborough	Middlesex	Edw. F. Johnson	10000
Medford	Middlesex	B. F. Hayes	8000

Massachusetts—Continued.

Parties corresponding with Attorneys named in the Directory should ALWAYS sign themselves "Subscribers to J. A. GRAFT & CO.'S LEGAL DIRECTORY." Should any Attorney fail to give prompt attention to correspondence, collections or business intrusted to his care, we will be thankful to patrons of the Directory to notify us promptly in any such case. Places designated thus (*) are County Seats.

POST-OFFICE.	COUNTY.	ATTORNEYS.	POPUL'N.
Medway	Norfolk	C. H. Deans	4000
Merrimac	Essex	Thomas H. Hoyt	2500
Methuen	Essex	Wm. M. Rogers	4500
Middleborough	Plymouth	See Plymouth	5000
Milford	Worcester	See Worcester	10000
Millbury	Worcester	See Worcester	5000
Monson	Hampden	See Springfield	4000
Nantucket*	Nantucket	Allen Coffin	4000
Natick	Middlesex	Charles Q. Tirrell	8000
New Bedford*	Bristol	Alex. M. Goodspeed	28000
Newburyport*	Essex	Charles C. Dame	14000
Newton	Middlesex	E. H. Pierce	17000
North Adams	Berkshire	George P. Lawrence	13000
Northampton*	Hampshire	John B. O'Donnell	14000
North Attleborough	Bristol	Joseph E. Pond, Jr.	8000
North Brookfield	Worcester	See Worcester	4500
North Easton	Bristol	John O'Connell	1500
Orange	Franklin	See Greenfield	3000
Oxford	Worcester	See Worcester	3000
Palmer	Hampden	Charles L. Gardner	8000
Peabody	Essex	Frank E. Farnham	10000
Pittsfield*	Berkshire	John C. Crosby	16000
Plymouth*	Plymouth	Arthur Lord	8000
Provincetown	Barnstable	See Barnstable	4500
Quincy	Norfolk	Sigourney Butler	10000
Randolph	Norfolk		4000
Reading	Middlesex	Solon Bancroft	3300
Rockport	Essex	See Salem	4000
Salem*	Essex	William H. Gove	30000
Salisbury	Essex	Frank C. Whiting	5000
Shelburne Falls	Franklin	Henry M. Puffer	1600
Southbridge	Worcester	A. J. Bartholomew	6500
South Framingham	Middlesex	George W. Travis	5500
South Weymouth	Norfolk	See Weymouth	4000
Spencer	Worcester	A. W. Curtis	8000
Springfield*	**Hampden**	**E. P. & H. A. Bartholomew**	**40000**
Stockbridge	Berkshire	H. J. Dunham	2500
Stoneham	Middlesex	W. B. Stevens	4500

Massachusetts—Continued.

Parties corresponding with Attorneys named in the Directory should ALWAYS sign themselves "Subscribers to J. A. GRAFT & CO.'S LEGAL DIRECTORY."
Should any Attorney fail to give prompt attention to correspondence, collections or business intrusted to his care, we will be thankful to patrons of the Directory to notify us promptly in any such case.
Places designated thus (*) are County Seats.

POST-OFFICE.	COUNTY.	ATTORNEYS.	POPUL'N.
Taunton*	Bristol	Lawrens N. Francis	22000
Townsend	Middlesex	F. A. Worcester	2000
Turner's Falls	Franklin	See Greenfield	2000
Uxbridge	Worcester	George W. Hobbs	3500
Wakefield	Middlesex	Samuel K. Hamilton	5500
Waltham	Middlesex	C. F. Stone	12000
Ware	Hampshire	H. C. Davis	5000
Wareham	Plymouth	See Plymouth	3000
Watertown	Middlesex	J. J. Sullivan	6000
Webster	Worcester	Denfield & Hill	6000
Wellfleet	Barnstable	H. P. Harriman	2500
Westborough	Worcester	W. T. Forbes	5500
Westfield	Hampden	H. W. Ashley	10000
West Stockbridge	Berkshire	W. C. Spaulding	2200
Weymouth	Norfolk	N. H. Pratt	10000
Whitinsville	Worcester	See Uxbridge	2200
Williamsburg	Hampshire	See Northampton	2500
Winchendon	Worcester	Frank B. Spalter	4000
Winchester	Middlesex	George S. Littlefield	6000
Woburn	Middlesex	John W. Johnson	12000
Worcester*	**Worcester**	**C. F. Stevens**	**50000**
Wrentham	Norfolk	Samuel Warner	2700

MICHIGAN.

POST-OFFICE.	COUNTY.	ATTORNEYS.	POPUL'N.
Ada	Kent	See Grand Rapids	600
Addison	Lenawee	See Adrian	400
Adrian*	Lenawee	George W. Ayers	12000
Albion	Calhoun	See Marshall	3000
Allegan*	Allegan	Wm. W. Warner	4500
Allen	Hillsdale	See Hillsdale	600
Alma	Gratiot	Francis Palmer	800
Almont	Lapeer	See Lapeer	1000
Alpena*	Alpena	Clayberg & Sleator	10000
Ann Arbor*	Washtenaw	E. S. Crawford	10000

Michigan—Continued.

Parties corresponding with Attorneys named in the Directory should ALWAYS sign themselves "Subscribers to J. A. GRAFT & CO.'S LEGAL DIRECTORY."
Should any Attorney fail to give prompt attention to correspondence, collections or business intrusted to his care, we will be thankful to patrons of the Directory to notify us promptly in any such case.
Places designated thus (*) are County Seats.

POST-OFFICE.	COUNTY.	ATTORNEYS.	POPUL'N.
Athens	Calhoun	See Marshall	700
Au Sable	Iosco	See Tawas City	1500
Bad Axe*	Huron	George A. Maywood	800
Baldwin*	Lake	F. E. Withey	600
Bancroft	Shiawassee	E. A. Warren	600
Bangor	Van Buren	See Paw Paw	1300
Battle Creek	Calhoun	Loran A. Palmer	10000
Bay City*	Bay	George W. Mann	30000
Belding	Ionia	See Ionia	600
Bellevue	Eaton	See Charlotte	800
Benton Harbor	Berrien	See Niles	1500
Benzonia*	Benzie	See Frankfort	400
Berrien Springs*	Berrien	See Niles	1000
Big Rapids*	Mecosta	M. Brown	6000
Blissfield	Lenawee	Oscar F. Sheldon	1500
Boyne Falls	Charlevoix	See Kalkaska	400
Brighton	Livingston	See Howell	1800
Brockway Centre	St. Clair	See Port Huron	500
Bronson	Branch	See Coldwater	1000
Brooklyn	Jackson	See Jackson	600
Buchanan	Berrien	A. A. Worthington	2500
Burr Oak	St. Joseph	A. M. Graham	1000
Cadillac*	Wexford	Dunham & Thorp	4000
Calumet	Houghton	John B. Curtis	8500
Caro*	Tuscola	H. H. Markham	2500
Carson City	Montcalm	George P. Stone	1000
Cass City	Tuscola	See Caro	500
Cassopolis*	Cass	H. D. Smith	1000
Cedar Springs	Kent	See Grand Rapids	1500
Centreville*	St. Joseph	William Sadler	1000
Charlevoix*	Charlevoix	J. M. Clark	1200
Charlotte*	Eaton	Henry F. Pennington	4000
Cheboygan*	Cheboygan	George W. Bell	3000
Chelsea	Washtenaw	See Ann Arbor	1800
Chesaning	Saginaw	See Saginaw	1000
Clare	Clare	C. W. Perry	800
Clarkston	Oakland	See Pontiac	500
Clayton	Lenawee	See Adrian	600
Clinton	Lenawee	J. E. McCollum	1000
Coldwater*	Branch	John S. Evans	5000
Colon	St. Joseph	See Centreville	600
Concord	Jackson	See Jackson	800
Constantine	St. Joseph	Elmer D. Smith	1500
Coopersville	Ottawa	See Grand Haven	800

Michigan—Continued.

Parties corresponding with Attorneys named in the Directory should ALWAYS sign themselves "Subscribers to J. A. GRAFT & CO.'S LEGAL DIRECTORY." Should any Attorney fail to give prompt attention to correspondence, collections or business intrusted to his care, we will be thankful to patrons of the Directory to notify us promptly in any such case. Places designated thus (*) are County Seats.

POST-OFFICE.	COUNTY.	ATTORNEYS.	POPUL'N.
Corunna*	Shiawassee	James M. Goodell	1500
Croswell	Sanilac	See Lexington	600
Dearborn	Wayne	See Detroit	600
Decatur	Van Buren	See Paw Paw	1600
Detroit*	**Wayne**	**Paine & Lodge** Managers Branch Office, No. 28 Campau Building.	**180000**
Dexter	Washtenaw	See Ann Arbor	1200
Douglas	Allegan	See Allegan	700
Dowagiac	Cass	See Cassopolis	2500
Dundee	Monroe	S. C. Randall	1000
Eagle River*	Keweenaw	See Houghton	400
East Saginaw	Saginaw	Wisner & Draper	30000
East Tawas	Iosco	See Tawas City	1200
Eaton Rapids	Eaton	Corbin & Cobb	2800
Edmore	Montcalm	See Stanton	800
Escanaba*	Delta	John Power	5000
Evart	Osceola	See Reed City	1500
Farwell	Clare	See Harrison	700
Fentonville	Genesee	See Flint	2500
Flint*	Genesee	Long & Gold	10000
Flushing	Genesee	See Flint	700
Fowlerville	Livingston	See Howell	1200
Frankfort	Benzie	D. B. Butler	1500
Fremont	Newaygo	Ed. E. Edwards	1500
Galesburgh	Kalamazoo	See Kalamazoo	1000
Gaylord*	Otsego	A. D. Marshall	1000
Goodrich	Genesee	See Flint	800
Grand Haven*	Ottawa	R. W. Duncan	6000
Grand Ledge	Eaton	See Charlotte	1600
Grand Rapids*	**Kent**	**Stone & Hyde**	**50000**
Grass Lake	Jackson	See Jackson	800
Greenville	Montcalm	W. E. Hoyt	3500
Hancock	Houghton	See Houghton	3000
Hanover	Jackson	See Jackson	500
Harbor Springs*	Emmet	See Petoskey	1000
Harrison*	Clare	William H. Brown	500
Harrisville*	Alcona	W. E. Depew	700
Hart*	Oceana	C. A. Gurney	1000
Hartford	Van Buren	Lincoln H. Titus	1200

Michigan—Continued.

Parties corresponding with Attorneys named in the Directory should ALWAYS sign themselves "Subscribers to J. A. GRAFT & CO.'S LEGAL DIRECTORY." Should any Attorney fail to give prompt attention to correspondence, collections or business intrusted to his care, we will be thankful to patrons of the Directory to notify us promptly in any such case. Places designated thus (*) are County Seats.

POST-OFFICE.	COUNTY.	ATTORNEYS.	POPUL'N.
Hastings*	Barry	William B. Sweezey	2800
Hersey*	Osceola	J. B. Judkins	800
Hesperia	Newaygo	William Tiffany	900
Hillsdale*	Hillsdale	Edwin J. March	4000
Holland	Ottawa	Gerrit J. Diekema	3500
Holly	Oakland	Patterson & Collier	2500
Homer	Calhoun		1200
Houghton*	Houghton	T. M. Brady	3000
Howard City	Montcalm	See Stanton	1200
Howell*	Livingston	Edward G. Ambler	2500
Hubbardston	Ionia		600
Hudson	Lenawee	J. C. Sawyer	2700
Imlay City	Lapeer	See Lapeer	1200
Ionia*	Ionia	F. D. M. Davis	6000
Iron Mountain	Menominee	See Menominee	300
Iron River	Marquette	See Marquette	300
Ishpeming	Marquette	George W. Hayden	6500
Ithica*	Gratiot	E. H. Ashley	1600
Jackson*	Jackson	Melville McGee	20000
Jonesville	Hillsdale	D. W. C. Merriam	1600
Kalamazoo*	Kalamazoo	E. A. Crane	16000
Kalkaska*	Kalkaska	Perkins & Ellis	1000
Laingsburgh	Shiawassee	See Owosso	900
Lakeview	Montcalm	See Stanton	700
L'Anse*	Baraga	See Houghton	1200
Lansing	Ingham	Olds & Robson	10000
Lapeer*	Lapeer	Frank Millis	3200
Leslie	Ingham	F. C. Woodworth	1500
Lexington	Sanilac	Wilford Macklem	1000
Lowell	Kent	M. H. Walker	1800
Ludington*	Mason	M. D. Seeley	6000
Lyons	Ionia	See Ionia	800
Mackinac	Mackinac	See St. Ignace	800
Manchester	Washtenaw	Hewett & Freeman	1200
Manistee*	Manistee	John H. Grant	11000
Maple Rapids	Clinton	See St. John's	800
Marcellus	Cass	W. J. Sampson	800
Marine City	St. Clair	See Port Huron	1800
Marlette	Sanilac	See Peck	600
Marquette*	Marquette	Ball & Hanscom	7000

Michigan—Continued.

Parties corresponding with Attorneys named in the Directory should ALWAYS sign themselves "Subscribers to J. A. GRAFT & CO.'S LEGAL DIRECTORY." Should any Attorney fail to give prompt attention to correspondence, collections or business intrusted to his care, we will be thankful to patrons of the Directory to notify us promptly in any such case.
Places designated thus (*) are County Seats.

POST-OFFICE.	COUNTY.	ATTORNEYS.	POPUL'N.
Marshall*	Calhoun	Frank A. Vernor	4800
Mason*	Ingham	Huntington & Henderson	2000
Mecosta	Mecosta	See Big Rapids	400
Mendon	St. Joseph	G. P. Doan	1200
Menominee*	Menominee	Sawyer & Waite	5500
Middleville	Barry	M. F. Jordan	900
Midland City*	Midland	Gordon & Fales	2500
Milford	Oakland	See Rochester	1400
Minden City	Sanilac	See Lexington	300
Monroe*	Monroe	H. Shaw Noble	5000
Montague	Muskegon	See Muskegon	1400
Morenci	Lenawee	See Adrian	1300
Mount Clemens*	Macomb	Martin Crocker	5000
Mount Pleasant*	Isabella	Brown & Seaton	1500
Muir	Ionia	Zophar Simpson, J. P.	800
Muskegon*	Muskegon	Henry H. Holt	18000
Nashville	Barry	W. S. Powers	1200
Negaunee	Marquette	J. Q. Adams	4000
Newaygo*	Newaygo	Daniel E. Soper	1200
Niles	Berrien	Worth Landon	5000
North Adams	Hillsdale	See Hillsdale	600
North Branch	Lapeer	V. S. Miller	600
Northport*	Leelenaw	See Charlevoix	500
Northville	Wayne	See Detroit	1000
Olivet	Eaton	See Charlotte	700
Ontonagon*	Ontonagon	C. M. Howell	900
Otsego	Allegan	See Allegan	1200
Ovid	Clinton	See St. John's	1700
Owosso	Shiawassee	Jerome E. Turner	4000
Oxford	Oakland	See Pontiac	1000
Palmyra	Lenawee	See Adrian	500
Paw Paw*	Van Buren	Crane & Breck	2000
Peck	Sanilac	H. O. Babcock	800
Pentwater	Oceana	William E. Ambler	1500
Petoskey	Emmet	E. C. Barnum	2500
Pewamo	Ionia	See Ionia	500
Pinckney	Livingston	See Howell	600
Plainwell	Allegan	E. J. Anderson	1500
Plymouth	Wayne	See Detroit	1100
Pontiac*	Oakland	Henry M. Look	5000
Port Austin	Huron	See Bad Axe	1000

Michigan—Continued.

Parties corresponding with Attorneys named in the Directory should ALWAYS sign themselves "Subscribers to J. A. GRAFT & CO.'S LEGAL DIRECTORY." Should any Attorney fail to give prompt attention to correspondence, collections or business intrusted to his care, we will be thankful to patrons of the Directory to notify us promptly in any such case. Places designated thus (*) are County Seats.

POST-OFFICE.	COUNTY.	ATTORNEYS.	POPUL'N.
Port Huron*	St. Clair	Stevenson & Phillips.	10000
Portland	Ionia	Clarence Cole	2000
Port Sanilac	Sanilac	See Peck	700
Quincy	Branch	Ezra Berry	1300
Reading	Hillsdale	See Hillsdale	1000
Reed City	Osceola	W. E. Bellows	2500
Richmond	Macomb	O. S. Burgess	1000
Rochester	Oakland	Henry M. Look	1100
Rockford	Kent	Charles G. Hyde	1000
Rogers City*	Presque Isle	See Alpena	500
Romeo	Macomb	J. L. Starkweather	2000
Roscommon*	Roscommon	George L. Alexander.	400
Saginaw*	Saginaw	William E. Crane	12000
Sand Beach	Huron	See Bad Axe	700
Sandusky*	Sanilac	See Lexington	300
Saranac	Ionia	See Ionia	1000
Sault de St. Marie*	Chippewa	W. B. Cady	3300
Schoolcraft	Kalamazoo	See Kalamazoo	1100
Shelby	Oceana	See Hart	600
Sheridan	Montcalm	James Newton	800
Sherman	Wexford	See Cadillac	1200
Sherwood	Branch	See Coldwater	400
South Haven	Van Buren	J. H. Johnson	2000
South Lyon	Oakland	See Pontiac	600
Sparta Centre	Kent	See Grand Rapids	800
Stanton*	Montcalm	Frank A. Miller	1800
Stephenson	Menominee	H. J. Woessner	500
St. Charles	Saginaw	See Saginaw	800
St. Clair	St. Clair	See Port Huron	2500
St. Ignace*	Mackinac	James McNamara	2000
St. John's*	Clinton	H. & H. E. Walbridge	2500
St. Joseph	Berrien	N. A. Hamilton	3000
St. Louis	Gratiot	Newell Leonard	3000
Stockbridge	Ingham	W. B. Gildart	300
Sturgis	St. Joseph	D. E. Thomas	2500
Tawas City*	Iosco	E. E. Williams	1000
Tecumseh	Lenawee	See Adrian	2300
Tekonsha	Calhoun	See Homer	800
Three Oaks	Berrien	See Niles	600
Three Rivers	St. Joseph	David Knox, Jr.	2600
Traverse City*	Grand Traverse	Pratt, Hatch & Davis	2000

Michigan—Continued.

Parties corresponding with Attorneys named in the Directory should ALWAYS sign themselves "Subscribers to J. A. GRAFT & CO.'S LEGAL DIRECTORY." Should any Attorney fail to give prompt attention to correspondence, collections or business intrusted to his care, we will be thankful to patrons of the Directory to notify us promptly in any such case.
Places designated thus (*) are County Seats.

POST-OFFICE.	COUNTY.	ATTORNEYS.	POPUL'N.
Union City	Branch	M. A. Merrifield	2000
Unionville	Tuscola	Dozier & Dozier	500
Vandalia	Cass	Joseph L. Sturr	800
Vassar	Tuscola	Henry S. Hadsall	2000
Vernon	Shiawassee	See Corunna	700
Vicksburg	Kalamazoo	Tyrrell Rayner, Jr.	1000
Wayne	Wayne	See Detroit	1800
West Bay City	Bay	See Bay City	7000
West Branch*	Ogemaw	D. P. Markey	500
Westwood	Kalkaska	See Kalkaska	500
Whitehall	Muskegon	See Muskegon	2000
White Pigeon	St. Joseph	S. N. Gurney	1500
Williamstown	Ingham.	E. D. Lewis	1200
Wyandotte	Wayne	See Detroit	3500
Ypsilanti	Washtenaw	Edward P. Allen	6500
Zeeland	Ottawa	See Grand Haven	600

MINNESOTA.

POST-OFFICE.	COUNTY.	ATTORNEYS.	POPUL'N.
Ada*	Norman	H. H. Phelps	1000
Adrian	Nobles	See Worthington	400
Aitkin*	Aitkin	M. P. Hayne	400
Albert Lea*	Freeborn	A. G. Wedge	2500
Alexandria*	Douglas	Nelson, Reynolds & Treat	2000
Anoka*	Anoka	H. S. Lord	3000
Appleton	Swift	A. D. Countryman	500
Ashby	Grant	See Fergus Falls	300
Atwater	Kandiyohi	Samuel Porter	500
Austin*	Mower	Richardson & Day	3500
Avoca	Murray	T. O'Leary	200
Battle Lake	Otter Tail	See Fergus Falls	400
Beaver Bay*	Lake	See Duluth	400

Minnesota—Continued.

Parties corresponding with Attorneys named in the Directory should ALWAYS sign themselves "Subscribers to J. A. GRAFT & CO.'S LEGAL DIRECTORY." Should any Attorney fail to give prompt attention to correspondence, collections or business intrusted to his care, we will be thankful to patrons of the Directory to notify us promptly in any such case.
Places designated thus (*) are County Seats

POST-OFFICE.	COUNTY.	ATTORNEYS.	POPUL'N.
Beaver Falls*	Renville	S. R. Miller	400
Belle Plaine	Scott	R. A. Irwin	1000
Benson*	Swift	S. H. Hudson	700
Bird Island	Renville	J. F. Fowler	500
Blooming Prairie	Steele	See Owatonna	600
Blue Earth City*	Faribault	B. F. Goodrich	1500
Brainerd*	Crow Wing	Holland & McClenahan	10000
Breckenridge*	Wilkin	C. F. Falley	600
Brown's Valley*	Traverse	John S. Noble	800
Brownton	McLeod	See Glencoe	500
Buffalo*	Wright	J. H. Wendell	600
Byron	Olmstead	See Rochester	400
Caledonia*	Houston	P. J. & E. H. Smalley	1200
Cambridge*	Isanti	H. F. Barker	700
Canby	Yellow Medicine	John P. Arnott	700
Cannon Falls	Goodhue	See Red Wing	500
Carver	Carver	Frank Warner	800
Chaska*	Carver	W. C. Odell	1300
Chatfield	Fillmore	Kingsley & Shepherd	1500
Crookston*	Polk	John McLean	4500
Currie*	Murray	Henry C. Grass	500
Deer Creek	Otter Tail	See Fergus Falls	500
Delano	Wright	See Buffalo	1000
Detroit City*	Becker	S. J. Offord	900
Dodge Centre	Dodge	C. H. Benton	1000
Dover Centre	Olmstead	See Rochester	300
Duluth*	St. Louis	Herman E. Long	20000
Edgerton	Pipe Stone	See Pipe Stone	400
Elk River*	Sherburne	H. M. Atkins	900
Evansville	Douglas	See Alexandria	400
Eyota	Olmstead	See Rochester	600
Fairmont*	Martin	A. L. Ward	1000
Faribault*	Rice	M. H. Keeley	6000
Farmington	Dakota	W. A. Gray	800
Fergus Falls*	Otter Tail	R. H. Marden	4000
Fisher	Polk	See Crookston	300
Gaylord	Sibley	Horace Soper	300
Glencoe*	McLeod	James C. Edson	1500
Glenwood*	Pope	T. T. Ofsthun	600
Graceville	Big Stone	See Ortonville	300

Minnesota—Continued.

Parties corresponding with Attorneys named in the Directory should ALWAYS sign themselves "Subscribers to J. A. GRAFT & CO.'S LEGAL DIRECTORY." Should any attorney fail to give prompt attention to correspondence, collections or business intrusted to his care, we will be thankful to patrons of the Directory to notify us promptly in any such case.
Places designated thus (*) are County Seats.

POST-OFFICE.	COUNTY.	ATTORNEYS.	POPUL'N.
Grand Meadow	Mower	See Austin	600
Granite Falls*	Yellow Medicine	Martin Rathbone	1000
Hastings*	Dakota	W. DeW. Pringle	4500
Henderson*	Sibley	S. O. Kipp	1000
Herman	Grant	C. M. Stevens	500
Howard	Wright	T. R. Briggs	600
Hutchinson	McLeod	G. M. Nelson	800
Jackson*	Jackson	T. J. Knox	1200
Janesville	Waseca	S. D. Crump	1300
Jordan	Scott	McClelland & Bragg	1200
Kasson	Dodge	R. A. Moses	1200
Kerkhoven	Swift	See Benson	300
Lac-qui-parle*	Lac-qui-parle	Kris. O. Jerde	400
Lake Benton*	Lincoln	John L. Cass	400
Lake City	Wabasha	H. D. Stocker	3000
Lake Park	Becker	O. L. Larson	300
Lamberton	Redwood	M. M. Madigan	400
Lanesboro	Fillmore	B. A. Man	1000
Le Roy	Mower	J. F. Trask	1200
Le Sueur	Le Sueur	D. D. Williams	1600
Le Sueur Centre*	Le Sueur	See Le Sueur	300
Litchfield*	Meeker	Frank P. Olney	2000
Little Falls*	Morrison	Storey & Worthington	2000
Long Prairie*	Todd	L. M. Davis	500
Luverne*	Rock	E. H. Canfield	1500
Madelia	Watonwan	F. L. Jones	900
Mankato*	Blue Earth	T. W. Hammond	9000
Mantorville*	Dodge	George A. Norton	800
Mapleton	Blue Earth	See Mankato	500
Marshall*	Lyon	Drew Bros. & Carpenter	1200
Minneapolis*	**Hennepin**	**Abbott & Stratton** Managers Branch Office, No. 300 Nicollet Avenue.	**140000**
Minneiska	Wabasha	A. Z. Putnam	500
Minneota	Lyon	See Marshall	400
Montevideo*	Chippewa	Budd & Moyer	1000
Monticello	Wright	James C. Tarbox	700
Moorhead*	Clay	Burnham, Mills & Tillotson	4500
Morris*	Stevens	Stephen C. Murphy	1500

Minnesota—Continued.

Parties corresponding with Attorneys named in the Directory should ALWAYS sign themselves, "Subscribers to J. A. GRAFT & CO.'S LEGAL DIRECTORY." Should any Attorney fail to give prompt attention to correspondence, collections or business intrusted to his care, we will be thankful to patrons of the Directory to notify us promptly in any such case.
Places designated thus (*) are County Seats.

POST-OFFICE.	COUNTY.	ATTORNEYS.	POPUL'N.
New Prague	Scott	See Shakopee	400
New Ulm*	Brown	Joseph A. Eckstein	3500
Northern Pacific Junction	Carlton	Hawkins & Oldenbury	1200
Northfield	Rice	Perkins & Whipple	3500
Norwood	Carver	John Stahel	600
Ortonville*	Big Stone	T. M. Grant	1000
Osakis	Douglas	H. Green	500
Owatonna*	Steele	Burlingame & Crandall	3500
Pelican Rapids	Otter Tail	See Fergus Falls	300
Pine City*	Pine	See Cambridge	500
Pipe Stone*	Pipe Stone	Burt Newport	1000
Plainview	Wabasha	John F. Pope	1000
Preston*	Fillmore	Gray & Thompson	1200
Princeton*	Mille Lacs	J. T. Brady	1000
Red Wing*	Goodhue	Henry Johns	7500
Redwood Falls*	Redwood	M. E. Powell	1200
Rochester*	Olmsted	Henry C. Butler	5500
Rush City	Chisago	J. D. Markham	800
Rushford	Fillmore	See Lanesboro	1300
Sauk Centre	Stearns	Storey & Foster	1500
Sauk Rapids*	Benton	Wood & Clark	800
Shakopee*	Scott	H. J. Peck	2500
Sleepy Eye	Brown	G. W. Somerville	1000
Spring Valley	Fillmore	See Lanesboro	1500
St. Charles	Winona	See Winona	1500
St. Cloud*	Stearns	A. C. Robertson	5000
St. Hilaire	Polk	See Crookston	400
Stillwater*	Washington	E. D. Buffington	15000
St. James*	Watonwan	J. W. Seager	600
St. Paul*	**Ramsey**	**David Sanford, Jr.** No. 349 Wabasha St.	**118000**
St. Peter*	Nicollet	G. S. Ives	3800
St. Vincent	Kittson	R. R. Redenberg	1000
Taylor's Falls	Chisago	See Rush City	1200
Thomson*	Carlton	See Northern Pacific Junction	500
Tracy	Lyon	F. S. Brown	500

Minnesota—Continued.

Parties corresponding with Attorneys named in the Directory should ALWAYS sign themselves "Subscribers to J. A. GRAFT & CO.'S LEGAL DIRECTORY." Should any Attorney fail to give prompt attention to correspondence, collections or business intrusted to his care, we will be thankful to patrons of the Directory to notify us promptly in any such case. Places designated thus (*) are County Seats.

POST-OFFICE.	COUNTY.	ATTORNEYS.	POPUL'N.
Verndale	Wadena	Law & Bullard	500
Villard	Pope	See Glenwood	300
Wabasha*	Wabasha	John Stewart	2500
Waconia	Carver	See Chaska	500
Wadena*	Wadena	A. G. Broker	600
Warren*	Marshall	A. Grindeland	1000
Waseca*	Waseca	Washburn & Maddox	3000
Waterville	Le Sueur	M. R. Everett	800
Wells	Faribault	J. E. Greene	800
Willmar*	Kandiyohi	B. F. Jenness	1200
Windom*	Cottonwood	A. D. Perkins	600
Winnebago City	Faribault	A. C. Dunn	1200
Winona*	Winona	D. E. Vance	17000
Woodstock	Pipe Stone	See Pipe Stone	300
Worthington*	Nobles	L. M. Lange	1500
Wykoff	Fillmore	See Lanesboro	500
Zumbrota	Goodhue	John C. English	1000

MISSISSIPPI.

POST-OFFICE.	COUNTY.	ATTORNEYS.	POPUL'N.
Aberdeen*	Monroe	James B. Dowd	4000
Ackerman	Choctaw	See Chester	500
Ashland*	Benton	J N. McDonald	400
Augusta*	Perry	John J. Bradford	500
Austin*	Tunica	J. B. Perkins	800
Batesville	Panola	James Stone	800
Biloxi	Harrison	See Pass Christian	1500
Booneville*	Prentiss	C. R. Lacy	900
Brandon*	Rankin	W. A. White	1000
Brookhaven*	Lincoln	R. H. Thompson	2400
Canton*	Madison	William S. Murphy	2900
Carrollton*	Carroll	Helm & Somerville	700

Mississippi—Continued.

Parties corresponding with Attorneys named in the Directory should ALWAYS sign themselves "Subscribers to J. A. GRAFT & CO.'S LEGAL DIRECTORY." Should any Attorney fail to give prompt attention to correspondence, collections or business intrusted to his care, we will be thankful to patrons of the Directory to notify us promptly in any such case.
Places designated thus (*) are County Seats.

POST-OFFICE.	COUNTY.	ATTORNEYS.	POPUL'N.
Carthage*	Leake	Joseph D. Eads	500
Charleston*	Tallahatchie	Bailey & Bailey	700
Chester*	Choctaw	White & Barron	400
Clarksdale	Coahoma	See Friar's Point	300
Coffeeville*	Yalobusha	J. T. Blount	800
Columbia*	Marion	T. S. Ford	300
Columbus*	Lowndes	Humphries & Sykes	6000
Corinth*	Alcorn	G. C. Chandler	3000
Crystal Springs	Copiah	See Hazlehurst	1200
Decatur*	Newton	See Meridian	200
De Kalb*	Kemper	J. H. Currie	300
Duncansby	Issaquena	A. J. Wilkinson	1000
Durant	Holmes	R. A. Anderson	800
Ellisville*	Jones	N. C. Hill	300
Enterprise	Clarke	A. F. McGee	1500
Fayette*	Jefferson	Torley & Truly	700
Forest*	Scott	Huddleston & Nichols	800
Friar's Point*	Coahoma	D. A. Scott	1000
Fulton*	Itawamba	James L. Herbert	300
Greenville*	Washington	Rucks & Jayne	2700
Greenwood*	Le Flore	A. McC. Kimbrough	400
Grenada*	Grenada	W. H. Fitz-Gerald	2500
Hattiesburg	Perry	See Augusta	100
Hazlehurst*	Copiah	Joe Purser	2000
Hernando*	De Soto	A. M. Lauderdale	800
Hickory	Newton	J. M. Gage	500
Holly Springs*	Marshall	James C. Totten	4000
Houston*	Chickasaw	Martin & Bates	600
Indianola*	Sun Flower	E. A. Gibson	300
Iuka*	Tishomingo	Chandler & Chandler	1000
Jackson	Hinds	H. R. Ware	6000
Johnsonville	Sun Flower	J. H. Baker	100
Jonestown	Coahoma	See Friar's Point	300
Kosciusko*	Attala	Butt & Butt	1800
Leakesville*	Greene	See Augusta	100
Lexington*	Holmes	W. W. Hoskins	1000

Mississippi—Continued.

Parties corresponding with Attorneys named in the Directory should ALWAYS sign themselves "Subscribers to J. A. GRAFT & CO.'S LEGAL DIRECTORY." Should any Attorney fail to give prompt attention to correspondence, collections or business intrusted to his care, we will be thankful to patrons of the Directory to notify us promptly in any such case.
Places designated thus (*) are County Seats.

POST-OFFICE.	COUNTY.	ATTORNEYS.	POPUL'N.
Liberty*	Amite	George F. Webb	800
Louisville*	Winston	William Price	800
Macomb	Pike	See Meadville	2200
Macon*	Noxubee	**W. F. Eiland** (See card in Appendix, page III.)	2500
Magnolia*	Pike	See Meadville	700
Mayersville*	Issaquena	See Rolling Fork	400
Meadville*	Franklin	Guice & Bridges	300
Meridian*	Lauderdale	W. C. Forsee	8000
Mississippi City*	Harrison	See Pass Christian	300
Monticello*	Lawrence	A. E. Weathersby	400
Natchez*	Adams	**James G. Leach** (See card in Appendix, page III.)	10000
New Albany*	Union	J. L. Young	500
Newport	Attala	See Koskiusko	200
Newton	Newton	See Meridian	400
Okolona	Chickasaw	W. H. Kimbrough	3000
Oxford*	La Fayette	Jno. H. Kimmons	2000
Pass Christian	Harrison	Lewis H. Champlin	2000
Paulding*	Jasper	T. J. Hardy †*J. A. Robinson.*	400
Philadelphia*	Neshoba	R. E. Holmes	100
Pittsboro*	Calhoun	Thomas P. Gibbs	300
Pontotoc*	Pontotoc	Oliver C. Carr	500
Port Gibson*	Claiborne	E. S. Drake	1600
Quitman*	Clarke	T. A. Wood	600
Raleigh*	Smith	E. Currie	300
Raymond*	Hinds	See Jackson	1000
Ripley*	Tippah	See Holly Springs	1000
Rolling Fork*	Sharkey	McLaurin & McLaurin	500
Rosedale*	Bolivar	**O. G. McGuire** (See card in Appendix, page III.)	100
Sardis*	Panola	Miller & Rainwater	1200
Scranton*	Jackson	J. C. Heidelburg	1200
Senatobia*	Tate	Shands & Johnson	1500
Starkville*	Oktibbeha	Thos. J. Wood	2000
Summit	Pike	See Meadville	2000

(† We withdraw our former recommendation.)

Mississippi—Continued.

Parties corresponding with Attorneys named in the Directory should ALWAYS sign themselves "Subscribers to J. A. GRAFT & CO.'S LEGAL DIRECTORY." Should any Attorney fail to give prompt attention to correspondence, collections or business intrusted to his care, we will be thankful to patrons of the Directory to notify us promptly in any such case.
Places designated thus (*) are County Seats.

POST-OFFICE.	COUNTY.	ATTORNEYS.	POPUL'N.
Tupelo*	Lee	See Verona	1200
Verona	Lee	A. J. Russell	800
Vicksburg*	**Warren**	**Catchings & Dabney.**	**15000**
Walthall*	Webster	J. E. Clark	200
Water Valley	Yalobusha	A. B. Fly, Sen.	4000
Waynesboro*	Wayne	D. M. Taylor	200
Wesson	Copiah	See Hazlehurst	2000
West Point*	Clay	Beall & Herndon	3000
Westville*	Simpson	See Hazlehurst	1400
Williamsburg*	Covington	See Monticello	200
Winona*	Montgomery	R. F. Holloway	2000
Woodville*	Wilkinson	W. P. S. Ventress	1000
Yazoo City*	Yazoo	Williams, Thornton & Williams	3000

MISSOURI.

POST-OFFICE.	COUNTY.	ATTORNEYS.	POPUL'N.
Adrian	Bates	See Butler	500
Albany*	Gentry	T. M. Humphrey	2000
Alexandria	Clarke	N. T. Cherry	1000
Alton*	Oregon	M. B. Clark †*W. J. Williams.*	400
Appleton City	St. Clair	Harry W. Grantley	2000
Arrow Rock	Saline	See Slater	1000
Ash Grove	Greene	See Springfield	600
Ashland	Boone	See Columbia	500
Aullville	La Fayette	See Higginsville	400
Barnard	Nodaway	See Maryville	600
Belton	Cass	See Pleasant Hill	800
Bethany*	Harrison	W. H. Skinner	1800
Bismarck	St. Francois	See Farmington †*D. L. Rivers.*	500
Blackburn	Saline	See Marshall	400
Bloomfield*	Stoddard	Henry H. Bedford	500

(†We withdraw our former recommendation.)

Missouri—Continued.

Parties corresponding with Attorneys named in the Directory should ALWAYS sign themselves "Subscribers to J. A. GRAFT & CO.'S LEGAL DIRECTORY." Should any Attorney fail to give prompt attention to correspondence, collections or business intrusted to his care, we will be thankful to patrons of the Directory to notify us promptly in any such case.
Places designated thus (*) are County Seats.

POST-OFFICE.	COUNTY.	ATTORNEYS.	POPUL'N.
Blue Springs	Jackson	See Independence	700
Bolckow	Andrew	See Savannah	500
Bolivar*	Polk	C. L. Allen	1500
Boonville*	Cooper	Walker & Johnston	3900
Bowling Green*	Pike	Champ Clark	2500
Breckenridge	Caldwell	See Hamilton	1000
Brookfield	Linn	George W. Bailey	3500
Browning	Linn	R. M. Tunnell	800
Brownsville	Saline	V. C. Yantis	1500
Brunswick	Chariton	Charles Hammond	2500
Buffalo*	Dallas	W. P. Porter	1000
Burlington Junction	Nodaway	See Maryville	800
Butler*	Bates	DeArmond & Smith	3500
Cainesville	Harrison	See Bethany	400
Calhoun	Henry	See Clinton	700
California*	Moniteau	Moore & Williams	1700
Cameron	Clinton	William Henry	3000
Canton	Lewis	David Wagner	3000
Cape Girardeau	Cape Girardeau	J. B. Dennis	5000
Carrollton*	Carroll	J W. Sebree	3000
Carthage*	Jasper	McReynolds & Halliburton	7000
Caruthersville	Pemiscot	F. D. Roberts	400
Cassville*	Barry	A. H. Wear	600
Centralia	Boone	H. S. Booth	1800
Centreville*	Reynolds	See Ironton	200
Charleston*	Mississippi	Hatcher & Russell	1800
Chillicothe*	Livingston	C. H. Munsur	4500
Clarence	Shelby	C. S. Brown	700
Clarksville	Pike	See Bowling Green	1600
Clinton*	Henry	E. A. Gracey	3500
Columbia*	Boone	C. B. Sebastian	4000
Commerce	Scott	J. H. Moore	600
Concordia	La Fayette	See Higginsville	1200
Corder	La Fayette	See Higginsville	300
Craig	Holt	See Oregon	700
Cunningham	Chariton	See Keytesville	500
Cuba	Crawford	Ellis G. Evans	500
Danville*	Montgomery	E. M. Hughes	500
De Soto	Jefferson	Joseph T. Tatum	3000
De Witt	Carroll	See Carrollton	700
Doniphan*	Ripley	Thomas A. Jenkins	600
Eagleville	Harrison	David Jodon	500
East Lynne	Cass	D. M. Beers	500

Missouri—Continued.

Parties corresponding with Attorneys named in the Directory should ALWAYS sign themselves "Subscribers to J. A. GRAFT & CO.'S LEGAL DIRECTORY." Should any Attorney fail to give prompt attention to correspondence, collections or business intrusted to his care, we will be thankful to patrons of the Directory to notify us promptly in any such case.
Places designated thus (*) are County Seats.

POST-OFFICE.	COUNTY.	ATTORNEYS.	POPUL'N.
Edgerton	Platte	See Platte City	300
Edina*	Knox	W. C. Hollister	1800
Eminence*	Shannon	L. L. Munsell	300
Emporia	Daviess	See Gallatin	300
Excelsior Springs	Clay	William E. Fowler	1500
Fairfax	Atchison	See Rockport	500
Farmingon*	St. Francois	F. M. Carter	1200
Fayette*	Howard	A. J. Herndon	1500
Forest City	Holt	See Oregon	600
Forsyth*	Taney	R. V. Burns	300
Fredericktown*	Madison	Cahoon & Cahoon	2500
Fulton*	Callaway	I. W. Boulware	2800
Gainesville*	Ozark	G. E. McClendon	300
Galena*	Stone	See Forsyth	200
Gallatin*	Daviess	Gillihan & Brosius	1800
Gayoso*	Pemiscot	George W. Carleton	200
Glasgow	Howard	Russell W. Caples	2500
Glenwood	Schuyler	John B. Glaze	900
Golden City	Barton	Seaver & Breeden	1200
Gower	Clinton	See Plattsburg	300
Grant City*	Worth	A. D. Austin. †*J. L. Downing.*	1500
Greenfield*	Dade	L. W. Shafer	1000
Greenville*	Wayne	E. P. Settle	250
Green Ridge	Pittus	Jas. S. Ream	1000
Hale City	Carroll	Geo. F. Davis	1000
Hamilton	Caldwell	S. M. Young	1300
Hannibal	Marion	R. E. Anderson. †*E. W. Southworth.*	16000
Harrisonville*	Cass	J. H. Kyle	2700
Hartville*	Wright	See Marshfield	600
Hermann*	Gasconade	E. M. Clark	1500
Hermitage*	Hickory	F. Marion Wilson	250
Higginsville	La Fayette	E. F. Keyton	2500
Hillsboro*	Jefferson	W. H. H. Thomas	400
Holden	Johnson	J. P. Orr	2500
Hopkins	Nodaway	See Maryville	1100
Houston*	Texas	V. M. Hines	300
Humansville	Polk	See Bolivar	500
Huntsville*	Randolph	Thomas B. Reed	2000
Independence*	Jackson	Charles S. Crysler	3300
Ironton*	Iron	Barnard Zwart	800

(† We withdraw our former recommendation.)

Missouri—Continued.

Parties corresponding with Attorneys named in the Directory should ALWAYS sign themselves "Subscribers to J. A. GRAFT & CO.'S LEGAL DIRECTORY." Should any Attorney fail to give prompt attention to correspondence, collections or business intrusted to his care, we will be thankful to patrons of the Directory to notify us promptly in any such case.
Places designated thus (*) are County Seats.

POST-OFFICE.	COUNTY.	ATTORNEYS.	POPUL'N.
Jackson*	Cape Girardeau	See Cape Girardeau	800
Jamesport	Daviess	Samuel W. Buzard	1000
Jefferson City*	Cole	J. C. Fisher	5000
Jericho	Cedar	See Stockton	300
Joplin	Jasper	Galen Spencer	8000
Kahoka*	Clarke	W. H. Robinson	1200
Kansas City	**Jackson**	**Crosby, Rusk & Craig** Managers Branch Office, No. 523 Delaware st.	**120000**
Kearney	Clay	See Liberty	700
Kennett*	Dunklin	See Gayoso	300
Keytesville*	Chariton	J. C. Wallace	1000
King City	Gentry	See Albany	300
Kingston*	Caldwell	David D. Temple	700
Kirksville*	Adair	P. F. Greenwood	8000
Knob Noster	Johnson	See Warrensburg	1200
La Belle	Lewis	Minter & Dowell	500
Laddonia	Audrain	See Mexico	300
La Grange	Lewis	See Canton	1500
Lamar*	Barton	Burr & Harkless	3000
Lamonte	Pettis	See Sedalia	500
Lancaster*	Schuyler	Higbee & Rally	900
La Plata	Macon	See Macon City	700
Lathrop	Clinton	See Cameron	1000
Lawson	Ray	See Richmond	400
Lebanon*	Laclede	W. J. Wallace	2000
Lee's Summit	Jackson	See Independence	800
Lexington*	La Fayette	Walker & Phetzing	5000
Liberty*	Clay	D. C. Allen	2000
Linn*	Osage	Samuel Mosby	400
Linn Creek*	Camden	Alex. A. Russell	200
Linneus*	Linn	H. K. West	1000
Lockwood	Dade	See Greenfield	300
Louisiana	Pike	John W. Matson	4500
Macon City*	Macon	B. E. Guthrie	4000
Maitland	Holt	See Oregon	300
Malta Bend	Saline	See Slater	600
Marble Hill*	Bollinger	George E. Conrad	500
Marshall*	Saline	H. M. Harvey	5000
Marshfield*	Webster	Samuel Dickey	1600
Martinsburg	Audrain	See Mexico	400
Maryville*	Nodaway	Ira K. Alderman	4500

Missouri—Continued.

Parties corresponding with Attorneys named in the Directory should ALWAYS sign themselves "Subscribers to J. A. GRAFT & CO.'S LEGAL DIRECTORY."
Should any Attorney fail to give prompt attention to correspondence, collections or business intrusted to his care, we will be thankful to patrons of the Directory to notify us promptly in any such case.
Places designated thus (*) are County Seats.

POST-OFFICE.	COUNTY.	ATTORNEYS.	POPUL'N.
Maysville*	De Kalb	Brown & Putnam	700
Mayview	La Fayette	See Higginsville	400
McFall	Gentry	See Albany	300
Meadville	Linn	See Brookfield	600
Memphis*	Scotland	John C. Moore	1700
Mexico*	Audrain	W. B. McIntire	5000
Miami	Saline	See Slater	1000
Milan*	Sullivan	George W. Butler	1700
Missouri City	Clay	L. B. Sublett	800
Moberly	Randolph	Martin & Hardin	9000
Monroe City	Monroe	See Paris	1000
Montgomery City	Montgomery	James D. Barnett	1600
Monticello*	Lewis	James T. Lloyd	500
Montrose	Henry	See Clinton	600
Mound City	Holt	See Oregon	800
Mount Vernon*	Lawrence	See Pierce City	600
Neosho*	Newton	Robert W. Jones	2000
Nevada*	Vernon	M. T. January	5000
New London*	Ralls	See Hannibal	700
New Madrid*	New Madrid	Hawkins & Hawkins	900
Norborne	Carroll	See Carrollton	700
Oak Grove	Jackson	See Independence	300
Odessa	La Fayette	See Higginsville	600
Oregon*	Holt	Irvine & Irvine	300
Osborn	De Kalb	See Maysville	600
Osceola*	St. Clair	W. P. Sheldon	700
Ozark*	Christian	J. J. Gideon	500
Palmyra*	Marion	H. J. Drummond	2700
Paris*	Monroe	Thomas P. Bashaw	1500
Parkville	Platte	F. M. McDonald	600
Pattonsburg	Daviess	See Gallatin	500
Perryville*	Perry	Killin & Killin	800
Piedmont	Wayne	J. N. Morrison	800
Pierce City	Lawrence	F. C. Johnston	2200
Pilot Grove	Cooper	See Boonville	300
Pilot Knob	Iron	See Ironton	1500
Pineville*	McDonald	J. C. Lamson	400
Platte City*	Platte	S. C. Woodson	700
Plattsburg*	Clinton	Roland Hughes	1800
Pleasant Hill	Cass	Henry Cordell	3000
Poplar Bluff*	Butler	I. M. Davidson	1500
Potosi*	Washington	See Bismarck	1000
Princeton*	Mercer	Hyde Norton	1400

Missouri—Continued.

**Parties corresponding with Attorneys named in the Directory should ALWAYS sign themselves. "Subscribers to J. A. GRAFT & CO.'S LEGAL DIRECTORY."
Should any Attorney fail to give prompt attention to correspondence, collections or business intrusted to his care, we will be thankful to patrons of the Directory to notify us promptly in any such case.
Places designated thus (*) are County Seats.**

POST-OFFICE.	COUNTY.	ATTORNEYS.	POPUL'N.
Rich Hill	Bates	Templeton & Denton.	5000
Richmond*	Ray	George A. Stone	1500
Rocheport	Boone	See Columbia	1000
Rockport*	Atchison	J. M. Osborn	1500
Rolla*	Phelps	L. T. Parker	1700
Salem*	Dent	L. Judson	2000
Salisbury	Chariton	W. S. Stockwell	1000
Sarcoxie	Jasper	See Carthage	500
Savannah*	Andrew	W. W. Caldwell	1000
Schell City	Vernon	F. Childs	1000
Sedalia*	Pettis	Gilmer Gilbreath	18000
Seneca	Newton	R. S. Rutledge	700
Shelbina	Shelby	W. O. F. Jewett	1500
Shelbyville*	Shelby	P. B. Dunn	1500
Sheldon	Vernon	See Nevada	300
Skidmore	Nodaway	See Maryville	200
Slater	Saline	John W. Quisenberry	2500
Springfield*	Greene	T. J. Murray	20000
Stanberry	Gentry	Shoemaker & Williams	3000
St. Charles*	St. Charles	W. A. Alexander	6000
Steelville*	Crawford	B F. Russell	600
Stewartsville	De Kalb	H. S. Buck	700
St. Genevieve*	St. Genevieve	C. C. Rozier	1800
St. Joseph*	**Buchanan**	**Crosby, Rusk & Craig**	**53000**
St. Louis	(Not embraced in any County.)	**Mills & Flitcraft** Managers Branch Office, No. 204 N. Third St. (See card in Appendix, page III.)	**500000**
Stockton*	Cedar	Clement Hall	600
Sturgeon	Boone	See Columbia	800
Thayer	Oregon	Harris & Miley	800
Tarkio	Atchison	See Rockport	500
Tipton	Moniteau	See California	1000
Trenton*	Grundy	George Hall	4000
Troy*	Lincoln	Norton & Dryden	1000
Tuscumbia*	Miller	See Linn Creek	300
Union*	Franklin	John H. Pugh	600
Unionville*	Putnam	Bonfoey & Sumner	1200
Van Buren*	Carter	See Eminence	200
Vandalia	Audrain	See Mexico	700

Missouri—Continued.

Parties corresponding with Attorneys named in the Directory should ALWAYS sign themselves "Subscribers to J. A. GRAFT & CO.'S LEGAL DIRECTORY." Should any Attorney fail to give prompt attention to correspondence, collections or business intrusted to his care, we will be thankful to patrons of the Directory to notify us promptly in any such case.
Places designated thus (*) are County Seats.

POST-OFFICE.	COUNTY.	ATTORNEYS.	POPUL'N.
Versailles*	Morgan	See California	800
Vienna*	Maries	See Linn	600
Warrensburg*	Johnson	Samuel P. Sparks	6000
Warrenton*	Warren	See Troy	800
Warsaw*	Benton	R. W. Campbell	1000
Washington	Franklin	Chas. F. Gallenkamp	4000
Waverly	La Fayette	See Higginsville	1200
Waynesville*	Pulaski	See Lebanon	100
Webb City	Jasper	See Carthage	1800
Wellsville	Montgomery	Barker & Shackleford	1000
Wentzville	St. Charles	Charles J. Walker	600
Westboro	Atchison	See Rockport	300
Weston	Platte	James W. Coburn	1500
West Plains*	Howell	H. D. Green	800
Windsor	Henry	F. L. Baird	1800
Wright City	Warren	J. V. Hayes	800

MONTANA TERRITORY.

POST-OFFICE.	COUNTY.	ATTORNEYS.	POPUL'N.
Anaconda	Deer Lodge	See Deer Lodge	200
Bannack City	Beaver Head	See Dillon	500
Billings*	Yellowstone	See Bozeman	500
Bozeman*	Gallatin	J. J. Davis	1000
Butte City*	Silver Bow	Francis L. Burton	20000
Deer Lodge*	Deer Lodge	W. Napton	1200
Diamond City	Meagher	See Helena	1200
Dillon*	Beaver Head	Robert B. Smith	500
Fort Benton*	Choteau	John J. Donnelly	2000
Glendale	Beaver Head	See Dillon	1000
Glendive	Dawson	J. F. Malony	1500
Helena*	Lewis & Clarke	Rudolf Von Tobel, Jr.	9000
Livingston	Gallatin	See Bozeman	400

Montana Territory—Continued.

Parties corresponding with Attorneys named in the Directory should ALWAYS sign themselves "Subscribers to J. A. GRAFT & CO.'S LEGAL DIRECTORY." Should any Attorney fail to give prompt attention to correspondence, collections or business intrusted to his care, we will be thankful to patrons of the Directory to notify us promptly in any such case.
Places designated thus (*) are County Seats.

POST-OFFICE.	COUNTY.	ATTORNEYS.	POPUL'N.
Miles City*	Custer	C. R. Middleton	2000
Missoula*	Missoula	Stephens & Beckford.	1500
Radersburgh*	Jefferson	See Helena	600
Thompson Falls	Missoula	See Missoula	300
Virginia City*	Madison	Henry N. Blake	1200
White Sulphur Sp'gs*	Meagher	See Helena	500

NEBRASKA.

POST-OFFICE.	COUNTY.	ATTORNEYS.	POPUL'N.
Ainsworth*	Brown	See Stuart	1000
Albion*	Boone	S. R. Anstine	700
Alexandria	Thayer	George W. Clawson	800
Alma*	Harlan	John Dawson	1000
Arapahoe	Furnas	Morlan & Wright	500
Arlington	Washington	See Blair	500
Ashland	Saunders	See Wahoo	1200
Atkinson	Holt	See O'Neill City	300
Aurora*	Hamilton	E. J. Hainer	1200
Avoca	Cass	See Weeping Water	300
Bancroft	Cuming	See Emerson	300
Battie Creek	Madison	See Madison	400
Bazile Mills	Knox	See Creighton	300
Beatrice*	Gage	Hardy & McCandless.	6500
Beaver City*	Furnas	James P. Lindsey	400
Bellwood	Butler	See David City	300
Belvidere	Thayer	H. E. Garzee	400
Bennet	Lancaster	H. D. Rhea	1000
Blair*	Washington	W. H. Eller	1800
Bloomington*	Franklin	George W. Sheppard	800
Blue Hill	Webster	See Red Cloud	500
Blue Springs	Gage	W. W. Wright	1500

Nebraska—Continued.

Parties corresponding with Attorneys named in the Directory should ALWAYS sign themselves "Subscribers to J. A. GRAFT & CO.'S LEGAL DIRECTORY." Should any Attorney fail to give prompt attention to correspondence, collections or business intrusted to his care, we will be thankful to patrons of the Directory to notify us promptly in any such case. Places designated thus (*) are County Seats.

POST-OFFICE.	COUNTY.	ATTORNEYS.	POPUL'N.
Bradshaw	York	C. M. Failing	1000
Broken Bow	Custer	S. A. Holcomb	300
Brownville*	Nemaha	Broady & Cecil	1800
Burchard	Pawnee	See Pawnee City	600
Burnett	Madison	See Madison	300
Cambridge	Furnas	See Beaver City	300
Carleton	Thayer	See Belvidere	300
Cedar Rapids	Boone	See Albion	300
Central City*	Merrick	J. W. Sparks	1000
Chadron	Dawes	Alfred Bartow	1800
Chester	Thayer	See Hubbell	500
Clarks	Merrick	John McLean	300
Clay Center*	Clay	See Edgar	600
Columbus*	Platte	Speice & North	3000
Cortland	Gage	A. B. McNickle	600
Crab Orchard	Johnson	See Tecumseh	300
Craig	Burt	See Tekamah	200
Creighton	Knox	Elias Underwood	200
Crete	Saline	B. F. Cochran	2500
Culbertson	Hitchcock	M. M. House	500
Dakota*	Dakota	H. D. Rogers	400
Davenport	Thayer	See Edgar	500
David City*	Butler	McLoud & Clingman	1500
Decatur	Burt	W. E. Drury	600
De Witt	Saline	See Wilber	500
Dorchester	Saline	John Panter	600
Edgar	Clay	S. W. Christy	1200
Elk Creek	Johnson	See Tecumseh	500
Emerson	Dixon	Feauto & McCarthy	500
Endicott	Jefferson	See Fairbury	300
Ewing	Holt	See O'Neill City	300
Exeter	Fillmore	F. M. Shirley	600
Fairbury*	Jefferson	W. H. Snell	1500
Fairfield	Clay	J. L. Epperson	800
Fairmont	Fillmore	Will R. Gaylord	1000
Falls City*	Richardson	Aug. Schoenheit	3000
Firth	Lancaster	See Lincoln	400
Fort Niobrara	Cherry	See Stuart	300
Franklin	Franklin	See Bloomington	300
Fremont*	Dodge	George L. Loomis	6000
Friend	Saline	Joshua Palmer	1300
Fullerton*	Nance	George D. Meiklejohn	500
Geneva*	Fillmore	John D. Carson	800
Genoa	Nance	See Fullerton	300

Nebraska—Continued.

Parties corresponding with Attorneys named in the Directory should ALWAYS sign themselves "Subscribers to J. A. GRAFT & CO.'S LEGAL DIRECTORY." Should any Attorney fail to give prompt attention to correspondence, collections or business intrusted to his care, we will be thankful to patrons of the Directory to notify us promptly in any such case.
Places designated thus (*) are County Seats.

POST-OFFICE.	COUNTY.	ATTORNEYS.	POPUL'N.
Gibbon	Buffalo	See Kearney	300
Gordon	Sioux	W. H. Westover	700
Grafton	Fillmore	See Geneva	500
Grand Island*	Hall	H. E. Clifford	6000
Greenwood	Cass	Thomas O. Moon	800
Guide Rock	Webster	See Red Cloud	300
Hampton	Hamilton	John H. Lincoln	300
Hardy	Nuckolls	See Superior	300
Hartington	Cedar	A. M. Gooding	600
Harvard	Clay	Leslie G. Hurd	1200
Hastings*	Adams	J. L. Finley	8000
Hebron*	Thayer	J. F. Gates	1200
Holdrege	Phelps	G. Norberg	1100
Hooper	Dodge	George B. Parsons	300
Hubbell	Thayer	S. F. Vinton	500
Humboldt	Richardson	E. A. Tucker	1300
Humphrey	Platte	See Columbus	300
Indianola*	Red Willow	R. H. Criswell	500
Juniata	Adams	See Hastings	500
Kearney*	Buffalo	Savidge & Nevius	5000
Kenesaw	Adams	See Hastings	400
La Porte*	Wayne	See Wayne	400
Liberty	Gage	N. T. Gadd	600
Lincoln*	**Lancaster**	**Foxworthy & Son**	**21000**
Long Pine	Brown	See Stuart	300
Louisville	Cass	See Plattsmouth	500
Loup City*	Sherman	Aaron Wall	400
Lowell	Kearney	See Kearney	300
Lyons	Burt	See Tekamah	300
Madison*	Madison	H. D. Kelly	1000
Marquette	Hamilton	See Aurora	200
McCook	Red Willow	J. E. Cochran	800
Milford	Seward	C. H. Hamlin	500
Minden*	Kearney	Joel Hull	1400
Nebraska City*	Otoe	F. T. Ransom	7000
Neligh	Antelope	Howard W. Zink	1200
Nelson*	Nuckolls	W. A. Bergstresser	400
Niobrara*	Knox	Solomon Draper	200

Nebraska—Continued.

Parties corresponding with Attorneys named in the Directory should ALWAYS sign themselves "Subscribers to J. A. GRAFT & CO.'s LEGAL DIRECTORY."
Should any Attorney fail to give prompt attention to correspondence, collections or business intrusted to his care, we will be thankful to patrons of the Directory to notify us promptly in any such case.
Places designated thus (*) are County Seats.

POST-OFFICE.	COUNTY.	ATTORNEYS.	POPUL'N.
Norfolk	Madison	N. A. Rainbolt	1500
North Bend	Dodge	Harry Claire	1000
North Loup	Valley	See Ord	500
North Platte*	Lincoln	William Neville	2600
Oakdale*	Antelope	B. F. Admire	700
Oakland	Burt	See Tekamah	500
Odell	Gage	See Wymore	500
Ogallala*	Keith	See North Platte	200
Omaha*	**Douglas**	**Henry D. Estabrook** Manager Branch Office, No. 508 S. Fifteenth St.	**65000**
O'Neill City*	Holt	M. P. Kinkaid	600
Ord*	Valley	E. J. Clements	800
Orleans	Harlan	Lewis H. Kent	400
Osceola*	Polk	T. H. Utterback	1000
Oxford	Furnas	L. L. Feltham	400
Palmyra	Otoe	See Nebraska City	300
Papillion*	Sarpy	George A. Nagney	300
Pawnee City*	Pawnee	A. S. Story	1800
Phelps*	Phelps	Rhea & Rhea	200
Pierce*	Pierce	E. P. Holmes	500
Plattsmouth*	Cass	Frank H. Wilson	6000
Pleasant Hill	Saline	See Dorchester	300
Plum Creek*	Dawson	W. D. Kelsey	1500
Ponca*	Dixon	Barnes Bros	1200
Red Cloud*	Webster	G. R. Chaney	2000
Republican City	Harlan	E. D. Crawford	500
Reynolds	Jefferson	See Fairbury	200
Rising City	Butler	See David City	300
Riverton	Franklin	A. J. Benjamin	200
Salem	Richardson	See Falls City	200
Sargent	Custer	See Broken Bow	300
Saronville	Clay	See Sutton	300
Schuyler*	Colfax	T. B. Crewitt	2000
Scotia*	Greeley	Scott Sprecher	400
Scribner	Dodge	See Fremont	500
Seward*	Seward	Norval Bros	2500
Shelton	Buffalo	See Kearney	300
Sidney*	Cheyenne	George W. Heist	1000
Springfield	Sarpy	See Papillion	200
Stanton*	Stanton	John A. Ehrhardt	700

Nebraska—Continued.

Parties corresponding with Attorneys named in the Directory should ALWAYS sign themselves "Subscribers to J. A. GRAFT & CO.'S LEGAL DIRECTORY."
Should any Attorney fail to give prompt attention to correspondence, collections or business intrusted to his care, we will be thankful to patrons of the Directory to notify us promptly in any such case.
Places designated thus (*) are County Seats.

POST-OFFICE.	COUNTY.	ATTORNEYS.	POPUL'N.
St. Edward	Boone	See Albion	300
Stella	Richardson	See Falls City	200
Sterling	Johnson	E. J. Moore	500
St. Helena*	Cedar	Thomas Edwards	300
St. Paul*	Howard	Thompson McNabb	800
Stromsburg	Polk	John D. Haskell	1100
Stuart	Holt	Henry H. Grimes	500
Superior	Nuckolls	J. W. Clements	1200
Sutton	Clay	George W. Bemis	1500
Syracuse	Otoe	See Nebraska City	500
Table Rock	Pawnee	Will L. Scism	800
Talmage	Otoe	See Nebraska City	400
Tecumseh*	Johnson	Osgood & Harris	1500
Tekamah*	Burt	M. W. Lee	1500
Ulysses	Butler	See David City	700
Utica	Seward	John Davies	800
Valentine*	Cherry	See Stuart	300
Valparaiso	Saunders	J. K. Van Demark	300
Wahoo*	Saunders	E. S. Merritt	2500
Wakefield	Dixon	E. W. Drake	500
Wayne	Wayne	A. A. Welch	1000
Weeping Water	Cass	Jno. W. Clark	1000
Western	Saline	See Wilber	300
West Point*	Cuming	R. F. Stevenson	800
West Union	Custer	See Broken Bow	300
Wilber*	Saline	J. H. Grimm	1200
Wisner	Cuming	See West Point	600
Wood River	Hall	See Grand Island	300
Wymore	Gage	Phil. E. Winter	2000
York*	York	France & Harlan	3000

NEVADA.

POST-OFFICE.	COUNTY.	ATTORNEYS.	POPUL'N.
Aurora*	Esmeralda	A. W. Crocker	600
Austin*	Lander	Henry Mayenbaum	2000

Nevada—Continued.

Parties corresponding with Attorneys named in the Directory should ALWAYS sign themselves "Subscribers to J. A. GRAFT & CO.'S LEGAL DIRECTORY."
Should any Attorney fail to give prompt attention to correspondence, collections or business intrusted to his care, we will be thankful to patrons of the Directory to notify us promptly in any such case.
Places designated thus (*) are County Seats.

POST-OFFICE.	COUNTY.	ATTORNEYS.	POPUL'N.
Belmont*	Nye	A. H. Stocker	500
Carson City*	Ormsby	Trenmor Coffin	5000
Dayton*	Lyon	See Carson City	600
Elko*	Elko	Rand & Dorsey	1000
Eureka*	Eureka	Benjamin Sanders	3000
Genoa*	Douglas	D. W. Virgin	500
Gold Hill	Storey	See Virginia City	3000
Hamilton*	White Pine	Wilson & Truce	1000
Paradise	Humboldt	R. G. Wheeler	500
Pioche*	Lincoln	Bishop & Sabin	800
Reno*	Washoe	John Bowman	3000
Ruby Hill	Eureka	See Eureka	2000
Stillwater*	Churchill	Lemuel Allen	500
Virginia City*	Storey	W. E. F. Deal	10000
Wadsworth	Washoe	See Reno	800
Winnemucca*	Humboldt	O. R. Leonard	1000

NEW HAMPSHIRE.

POST-OFFICE.	COUNTY.	ATTORNEYS.	POPUL'N.
Alton	Belknap	John W. Currier	600
Amherst	Hillsborough	See Manchester	1000
Andover	Merrimack	See Concord	1500
Bath	Grafton	E. Woods	1000
Bristol	Grafton	Fling & Chase	1400
Canaan	Grafton	See Bristol	1000
Charlestown	Sullivan	See Claremont	1200

New Hampshire—Continued.

Parties corresponding with Attorneys named in the Directory should ALWAYS sign themselves "Subscribers to J. A. GRAFT & CO.'S LEGAL DIRECTORY." Should any Attorney fail to give prompt attention to correspondence, collections or business intrusted to his care, we will be thankful to patrons of the Directory to notify us promptly in any such case. Places designated thus (*) are County Seats.

POST-OFFICE.	COUNTY.	ATTORNEYS.	POPUL'N.
Claremont	Sullivan	Herman Holt	4000
Colebrook*	Coos	James I. Parsons	1600
Concord*	Merrimack	L. S. Morrill	15000
Danbury	Merrimack	See Concord	800
Dover*	Strafford	W. F. Mason	12000
East Jaffrey	Cheshire	Jesse B. Twiss	1300
Exeter*	Rockingham	Marston & Eastman	2000
Farmington	Strafford	George N. Eastman	2000
Fishersville	Merrimack	See Concord	2800
Fitzwilliam	Cheshire	See Keene	1200
Francestown	Hillsborough	See Manchester	800
Franklin Falls	Merrimack	Edward G. Leach	3500
Gorham	Coos	Alfred R. Evans	1800
Great Falls	Strafford	Burleigh & Russell	6000
Hanover	Grafton	See Plymouth	2000
Haverhill*	Grafton	Wm. F. Westgate	1200
Hillsborough Bridge	Hillsborough	See Nashua	1500
Keene*	Cheshire	E. P. Dole	7000
Laconia*	Belknap	E. P. Jewell	2800
Lake Village	Belknap	Samuel C. Clark	2500
Lancaster*	Coos	Haywood & Haywood	2500
Lebanon	Grafton	Spring & Spring	2500
Littleton	Grafton	Bingham & Aldrich	2000
Manchester	**Hillsborough**	**N. H. Wilson** Manager Branch Office For Upper New England States.	**40000**
Meredith Village	Belknap	See Laconia	1200
Milford	Hillsborough	See Manchester	2000
Nashua*	Hillsborough	Charles W. Hoitt	15000
New Market	Rockingham	Irving T. George	2500
Newport*	Sullivan	Albert S. Wait	2000
Orford	Grafton	See Plymouth	1200
Ossipee*	Carroll	See Wolfborough	1000
Peterborough	Hillsborough	See Nashua	2200
Pittsfield	Merrimack	See Concord	1500
Plymouth*	Grafton	Burleigh & Adams	1500
Portsmouth	Rockingham	Calvin Page	10000

New Hampshire—Continued.

Parties corresponding with Attorneys named in the Directory should ALWAYS sign themselves "Subscribers to J. A. GRAFT & CO.'S LEGAL DIRECTORY." Should any Attorney fail to give prompt attention to correspondence, collections or business intrusted to his care, we will be thankful to patrons of the Directory to notify us promptly in any such case. Places designated thus (*) are County Seats.

POST-OFFICE.	COUNTY.	ATTORNEYS.	POPUL'N.
Rochester	Strafford	Worcester & Gaffney	6000
Salmon Falls	Strafford	See Great Falls	1500
Sandwich	Carroll	See Wolfborough	1200
Suncook	Merrimack	See Concord	3500
Tilton	Belknap	See Laconia	1200
Walpole	Cheshire	J. G. Bellows	2000
Wilton	Hillsborough	See Manchester	1500
Winchester	Cheshire	E. M. Forbes	2000
Wolfborough	Carroll	E. C. Banfield	1500

NEW JERSEY.

POST-OFFICE.	COUNTY.	ATTORNEYS.	POPUL'N.
Asbury Park	Monmouth	David Harvey, Jr.	3000
Atlantic City	Atlantic	Thompson & Endicott	10000
Belvidere*	Warren	J. G. Shipman & Son.	3000
Bloomfield	Essex	See Newark	6000
Bloomsbury	Hunterdon	See Frenchtown	1000
Bordentown	Burlington	See Mount Holly	6000
Boundbrook	Somerset	See Somerville	1200
Bridgeton*	Cumberland	James R. Hoagland	10000
Burlington	Burlington	Howard Flanders	8000
Camden*	**Camden**	**Herbert A. Drake**	**50000**
Cape May	Cape May	John B. Huffman	2500
Cape May C. H.*	Cape May	Herbert W. Edmunds	2000
Clinton	Hunterdon	See Frenchtown	1000
Cranbury	Middlesex	See New Brunswick	1000
Deckertown	Sussex	L. J. Martin	1200
Dover	Morris	See Morristown	3000
Eatontown	Monmouth	James Steen	1500
Elizabeth*	Union	Robert E. Chetwood	28000

New Jersey—Continued.

Parties corresponding with Attorneys named in the Directory should ALWAYS sign themselves "Subscribers to J. A. GRAFT & CO.'S LEGAL DIRECTORY." Should any Attorney fail to give prompt attention to correspondence, collections or business intrusted to his care, we will be thankful to patrons of the Directory to notify us promptly in any such case.
Places designated thus (*) are County Seats.

POST-OFFICE.	COUNTY.	ATTORNEYS.	POPUL'N.
Flemington*	Hunterdon	E. R. Bullock	2500
Freehold*	Monmouth	Vredenburgh & Parker	3000
Frenchtown	Hunterdon	William T. Srope	1200
Gloucester City	Camden	See Camden	6000
Hackensack*	Bergen	William M. Johnson.	5000
Hackettstown	Warren	Augustus H. Dellicker	3000
Hightstown	Mercer	See Trenton	1800
Hoboken	Hudson	See Jersey City	30000
Jamesburgh	Middlesex	See New Bruswick	800
Jersey City*	**Hudson**	**Cornelius S. See** No. 54 Montgomery St.	**150000**
Key Port	Monmouth	See Freehold	3000
Lambertville	Hunterdon	Walter F. Hayhurst	4500
Long Branch	Monmouth	See Red Bank	5000
Madison	Morris	See Morristown	2000
Manasquan	Monmouth	See Red Bank	1500
Matawan	Monmouth	See Red Bank	2000
May's Landing*	Atlantic	See Atlantic City	1000
Medford	Burlington	See Mount Holly	1000
Millville	Cumberland	George B. Ogden	8000
Morristown*	Morris	Augustus W. Cutler	7000
Mount Holly*	Burlington	Walter A. Barrows	5000
Newark*	**Essex**	**John W. Taylor** No. 757 Broad street.	**137000**
New Brunswick*	Middlesex	J. H. Van Cleef	18000
Newton*	Sussex	David B. Hetzel	3000
Ocean Beach	Monmouth	See Asbury Park	500
Ocean Grove	Monmouth	See Asbury Park	500
Orange	Essex	J. W. & J. K. Field	13000
Paterson*	**Passaic**	**John F. Kerr**	**60000**
Perth Amboy	Middlesex	John W. Beekman	4000
Phillipsburg	Warren	William M. Davis	9000
Plainfield	Union	Joseph B. Coward	12000
Princeton	Mercer	See Trenton	4000
Rahway	Union	Vail & Ward	7000
Raritan	Somerset	See Somerville	2000

New Jersey—Continued.

Parties corresponding with Attorneys named in the Directory should ALWAYS sign themselves "Subscribers to J. A. GRAFT & CO.'S LEGAL DIRECTORY." Should any Attorney fail to give prompt attention to correspondence, collections or business intrusted to his care, we will be thankful to patrons of the Directory to notify us promptly in any such case.
Places designated thus (*) are County Seats.

POST-OFFICE.	COUNTY.	ATTORNEYS.	POPUL'N.
Red Bank	Monmouth	D. W. Willguss	4000
Salem*	Salem	M. P. Grey	6000
Somerville*	Somerset	Bartine & Griggs	3500
Stanhope	Sussex	See Newton	1500
Swedesborough	Gloucester	See Woodbury	1000
Tom's River*	Ocean	I. W. Carmichael	2000
Trenton*	Mercer	John A. Steen	30000
Vincentown	Burlington	See Mount Holly	1000
Vineland	Cumberland	Willis T. Virgil	5000
Washington	Warren	Daniel Vliet	3000
Woodbury*	Gloucester	Belmont Perry	2500
Woodstown	Salem	Enoch S. Fogg	2000

NEW MEXICO TERRITORY.

-OFFICE.	COUNTY.	ATTORNEYS.	POPUL'N.
Albuquerque	Bernalillo	Stone & Stone	4000
Cimarron	Colfax	See Springer	500
Deming	Grant	See Silver City	500
Fernandez de Taos*	Taos	See Santa Fe	2000
Georgetown	Grant	See Silver City	800
Hillsboro*	Sierra	See Silver City	500
Kingston	Sierra	H. W. Elliott	1400
Las Cruces	Dona Ana	S. B. Newcomb	2000
Las Vegas*	San Miguel	Lee & Fort	9000
Lincoln*	Lincoln	George T. Beall, Jr.	1000
Los Lunas*	Valencia	See Albuquerque	1000

New Mexico—Continued.

Parties corresponding with Attorneys named in the Directory should ALWAYS sign themselves "Subscribers to J. A. GRAFT & CO.'S LEGAL DIRECTORY." Should any attorney fail to give prompt attention to correspondence, collections or business intrusted to his care, we will be thankful to patrons of the Directory to notify us promptly in any such case. Places designated thus (*) are County Seats.

POST-OFFICE.	COUNTY.	ATTORNEYS.	POPUL'N.
Mora*	Mora	See Las Vegas	1000
Raton	Colfax	See Springer	2000
Santa Fe*	Santa Fe	W. B. Sloan	7000
Silver City*	Grant	Elliott, Pickett & Elliott	2500
Socorro*	Socorro	Chilion Riley	3000
Springer*	Colfax	William C. Wrigley	500
Taos	Taos	See Santa Fe	600
Tome	Valencia	See Albuquerque	500
Wagon Mound	Mora	Fernando Nolan	300
White Oaks	Lincoln	John Y. Hewitt	300

NEW YORK.

POST-OFFICE.	COUNTY.	ATTORNEYS.	POPUL'N.
Adams	Jefferson	E. F. Ramsdell	2000
Addison	Steuben	See Bath	2200
Akron	Erie	See Buffalo	1200
Albany*	**Albany**	**Buel C. Andrews** No. 14 North Pearl street.	**100000**
Albion*	Orleans	E W. Taylor	5000
Amenia	Dutchess	See Poughkeepsie	900
Amsterdam	Montgomery	Charles S. Nisbet	12000
Andes	Delaware	See Delhi	600
Andover	Allegany	B. C. Brundage	900
Angelica	Allegany	John S. Gillies	1400
Arcade	Wyoming	See Warsaw	1000
Argyle*	Washington	See Salem	500
Athens	Greene	See Catskill	2200
Attica	Wyoming	See Warsaw	3000
Auburn*	Cayuga	Harold E. Hills	28000
Aurora	Cayuga	See Auburn	500
Avon	Livingston	E. A. Nash	2500
Babylon	Suffolk	See Greenport	2200
Bainbridge	Chenango	C. C. Williams	1500
Baldwinsville	Onondaga	James R. Shea	2200
Ballston*	Saratoga	George L. Lewis	4000
Batavia*	Genesee	Tarbox & Sherwin	5000

New York—Continued.

Parties corresponding with Attorneys named in the Directory should ALWAYS sign themselves "Subscribers to J. A. GRAFT & CO.'S LEGAL DIRECTORY."
Should any Attorney fail to give prompt attention to correspondence, collections or business intrusted to his care, we will be thankful to patrons of the Directory to notify us promptly in any such case.
Places designated thus (*) are County Seats.

POST-OFFICE.	COUNTY.	ATTORNEYS.	POPUL'N.
Bath	Steuben	McMaster & Parkhurst	3000
Belmont*	Allegany	See Angelica	1500
Binghamton*	Broome	Wm. M. Crosby, Jr.	22000
Boonville	Oneida	L. W. Fiske	1800
Brewster	Putnam	A. J. Miller	2500
Brockport	Monroe	See Rochester	2500
Brookfield	Madison	D. B. Stillman	800
Brooklyn*	**Kings**	**George W. Pinckney** No. 26 Court St.	**650000**
Buffalo*	**Erie**	**Hawkins & Gibbs** Managers Branch Office, No. 276 Main St.	**225000**
Cambridge	Washington	See Salem	2000
Camden	Oneida	Alpha F. Orr	2000
Camillus	Onondaga	See Syracuse	1000
Canajoharie	Montgomery	Cook & Barnes	2500
Canandaigua*	Ontario	J. P. Faurot	5800
Canastota	Madison	G. A. Forbes	2000
Candor	Tioga	See Owego	1200
Canisteo	Steuben	Eli Soule	2500
Canton*	St. Lawrence	William H. Sawyer	3000
Carmel*	Putnam	Clayton Ryder	1200
Carthage	Jefferson	F. T. Evans	3000
Castile	Wyoming	See Warsaw	1200
Castleton	Rensselaer	See Troy	1200
Catskill*	Greene	Halleck & Jennings	8000
Cazenovia	Madison	E. N. Wilson	2000
Champlain	Clinton	William H. Dunn	2000
Chatham	Columbia	J. A. Mills	2000
Cherry Valley	Otsego	William Burch	1000
Chester	Orange	See Newburgh	2000
Chestertown	Warren	Adam Armstrong, Jr.	500
Chittenango	Madison	Kellogg & Baker	1000
Clayton	Jefferson	H. E. Morse	1500
Clinton	Oneida	A. W. Mills	2000
Clyde	Wayne	Vandenberg & Saxton	3500
Cobleskill	Schoharie	See Schoharie	2000
Coeymans	Albany	See Albany	1000
Cohoes	Albany	See Albany	22000
Cold Spring	Putnam	S. B. Nelson	2200
Constableville	Lewis	See Lowville	1500
Cooperstown*	Otsego	Walter H. Bunn	2800
Corning*	Steuben	A. S. Kendall	6000
Cornwall	Orange	See Newburgh	2500
Cortland*	Cortland	Jerome Squires	6500

New York—Continued.

Parties corresponding with Attorneys named in the Directory should ALWAYS sign themselves "Subscribers to J. A. GRAFT & CO.'S LEGAL DIRECTORY."
Should any Attorney fail to give prompt attention to correspondence, collections or business intrusted to his care, we will be thankful to patrons of the Directory to notify us promptly in any such case.
Places designated thus (*) are County Seats.

POST-OFFICE.	COUNTY.	ATTORNEYS.	POPUL'N.
Coxsackie	Greene	See Catskill	2000
Cuba	Allegany	S. C. Swift	2500
Dansville	Livingston	Falkner & Bissell	4000
Delhi*	Delaware	W. H. Johnson	1800
Deposit	Broome	See Binghamton	1800
De Ruyter	Madison	See Oneida	800
Dryden	Tompkins	Geo. E. Monroe	800
Dundee	Yates	L. M. Hair	1200
Dunkirk	Chautauqua	Charles D. Murray	8000
East Randolph	Cattaraugus	See Little Valley	1000
Elizatbethtown*	Essex	Richard L. Hand	1200
Ellenville	Ulster	G. G. & J. B. Keeler	3000
Ellicottsville	Cattaraugus	George M. Rider	1200
Elmira*	Chemung	Edgar Denton	25000
Fairport	Monroe	See Rochester	2200
Fayetteville	Onondaga	See Syracuse	2000
Fishkill	Dutchess	See Poughkeepsie	5000
Flushing	Queens	Benj. W. Downing	10000
Fonda*	Montgomery	See Amsterdam	1200
Fort Edward	Washington	Robert O. Bascon	3500
Fort Plain	Montgomery	See Amsterdam	2600
Frankfort	Herkimer	See Little Falls	1500
Franklin	Delaware	R. T. Johnson	1000
Franklinville	Cattaraugus	See Little Valley	1000
Fredonia	Chautauqua	See Jamestown	3000
Friendship	Allegany	See Angelica	1500
Fulton	Oswego	F. D. VanWagenen	5000
Geneseo*	Livingston	Abbott & Abbott	2200
Geneva	Ontario	George L. Bachman	8000
Glen's Falls	Warren	Isaac Mott	8000
Gloversville	Fulton	N. H. Annibal	7000
Goshen*	Orange	See Newburgh	2600
Gouverneur	St. Lawrence	See Canton	2200
Gowanda	Cattaraugus	See Salamanca	2100
Granville	Washington	F. W. Betts	1000
Greene	Chenango	See Norwich	1000
Greenport	Suffolk	Benj. H. Reeve	3000
Greenwich	Washington	James White	2000
Groton	Tompkins	See Ithaca	1200
Hamburgh	Erie	See Buffalo	1200
Hamilton	Madison	D. G. Wellington	2000

New York—Continued.

Parties corresponding with Attorneys named in the Directory should ALWAYS sign themselves "Subscribers to J. A. GRAFT & CO.'S LEGAL DIRECTORY." Should any Attorney fail to give prompt attention to correspondence, collections or business intrusted to his care, we will be thankful to patrons of the Directory to notify us promptly in any such case. Places designated thus (*) are County Seats.

POST-OFFICE.	COUNTY.	ATTORNEYS.	POPUL'N.
Havana	Schuyler	See Watkins	1500
Haverstraw	Rockland	Irving Brown	4500
Hempstead	Queens	J. S. Snedeker	1500
Herkimer*	Herkimer	Steele & Prescott	3000
Holley	Orleans	See Albion	1200
Homer	Cortland	Franklin Pierce	2500
Hornellsville	Steuben	Irving Paine	10000
Horseheads	Chemung	See Elmira	2300
Hudson*	Columbia	Andrews & Edwards.	9000
Huntington	Suffolk	See Greenport	3000
Ilion	Herkimer	See Little Falls	4000
Ithaca*	Tompkins	A. A. Hungerford	10000
Jamaica*	Queens	Henry A. Monfort	4000
Jamestown	Chautauqua	Bootey, Fowler & Weeks	11000
Johnstown*	Fulton	Carroll & Fraser	7000
Jordan	Onondaga	See Syracuse	1600
Keeseville	Essex	See Elizabethtown	2500
Kinderhook	Columbia	Gerrit S. Collier	2000
Kingston*	Ulster	W. N. Gill	20000
Lake George*	Warren	See Glen's Falls	500
Lansingburgh	Rensselaer	See Troy	8000
Lenox	Madison	See Morrisville	1000
Le Roy	Genesee	W. H. Smith	2000
Liberty	Sullivan	Bruce Winner	800
Lima	Livingston	George W. Atwell, Jr.	2000
Limestone	Cattaraugus	See Salamanca	1000
Little Falls	Herkimer	Mills, Palmer & Morgan	7000
Little Valley*	Cattaraugus	Charles Z. Lincoln	800
Livonia	Livingston	See Geneseo	800
Lockport*	Niagara	Joshua Gaskill	18000
Lowville*	Lewis	Henry E. Turner	1200
Lyons*	Wayne	C. G. Blaine	5000
Malone*	Franklin	Cantwell, Badger & Cantwell	5000
Marathon	Cortland	W. C. Crombie	1200
Marion	Wayne	H. R. Taber	500
Mayville*	Chautauqua	See Jamestown	1200
Medina	Orleans	Stanley E. Filkins	4000
Mexico	Oswego	J. A. Johnson	2000

New York—Continued.

Parties corresponding with Attorneys named in the Directory should ALWAYS sign themselves "Subscribers to J. A. GRAFT & CO.'S LEGAL DIRECTORY." Should any Attorney fail to give prompt attention to correspondence, collections or business intrusted to his care, we will be thankful to patrons of the Directory to notify us promptly in any such case. Places designated thus (*) are County Seats.

POST-OFFICE.	COUNTY.	ATTORNEYS.	POPUL'N.
Middleburgh	Schoharie	W. E. Thorne	1200
Middletown	Orange	Charles G. Dill	9000
Mohawk	Herkimer	See Little Falls	1600
Montgomery	Orange	See Newburgh	1200
Monticello*	Sullivan	Timothy F. Bush	1200
Moravia	Cayuga	See Auburn	1800
Morrisville*	Madison	J. E. Smith	1200
Mount Morris	Livingston	J. M. Hastings	2000
Mount Vernon	Westchester	C. H. Ostrander	5000
Naples	Ontario	See Canandaigua	2000
Newark	Wayne	E. K. Burnham	2600
New Berlin	Chenango	See Norwich	1500
New Brighton	Richmond	See Port Richmond	12000
Newburgh*	Orange	A. S. Cassedy	20000
New Paltz	Ulster	See Kingston	800
New Rochelle	Westchester	Banks & Henderson	5000
New York*	**New York**	**J. A. Graft & CO.** MANAGERS EASTERN OFFICE OF THE LEGAL REPORTING AND COLLECTION AGENCY. **Henry Melville Walker, Resident Attorney,** 319 Broadway, Room 10. (See card in Appendix, page IV.)	**1300000**
Niagara Falls	Niagara	Henry C. Tucker	7000
Norwich*	Chenango	W. B. Leach	6000
Norwood	St. Lawrence	See Canton	1500
Nunda	Livingston	F. C. Olney	1500
Nyack	Rockland	Seth B. Cole	4500
Ogdensburgh	St. Lawrence	Foote & Kellogg	10000
Olean	Cattaraugus	W. H. Nourse	6000
Oneida	Madison	Edwin J. Brown	4500
Oneonta	Otsego	See Cooperstown	3200
Oswego*	Oswego	H. C. Benedict	26000
Ovid*	Seneca	F. C. Allen	1000
Owego*	Tioga	Oscar B. Glezen	10000
Oxford	Chenango	James W. Glover	1500
Palmyra	Wayne	H. R. Durfee	3000
Panama	Chautauqua	See Jamestown	1000
Patchogue	Suffolk	See Greenport	2500
Pawling	Dutchess	See Poughkeepsie	800
Pearsall's	Queens	See Flushing	2000
Peekskill	Westchester	J. W. Crumb	7000
Penn Yan*	Yates	John T. Knox	5000
Perry	Wyoming	See Warsaw	1500

New York—Continued.

Parties corresponding with Attorneys named in the Directory should ALWAYS sign themselves "Subscribers to J. A. GRAFT & CO.'S LEGAL DIRECTORY." Should any Attorney fail to give prompt attention to correspondence, collections or business intrusted to his care, we will be thankful to patrons of the Directory to notify us promptly in any such case.
Places designated thus (*) are County Seats.

POST-OFFICE.	COUNTY.	ATTORNEYS.	POPUL'N.
Phelps	Ontario	See Canandaigua	1600
Phœnix	Oswego	See Oswego	1800
Plattsburgh*	Clinton	Wm. H. Mellor	6000
Port Byron	Cayuga	See Auburn	1500
Port Chester	Westchester	See White Plains	3500
Port Henry	Essex	William H. Carr	2000
Port Jervis	Orange	O. P. Howell	9000
Port Richmond	Richmond	John Croak	4000
Potsdam	St. Lawrence	C. E. Sanford	3000
Poughkeepsie*	Dutchess	John H. Millard	23000
Pulaski	Oswego	J. W. Shea	1800
Randolph	Cattaraugus	J. E. Weeden	1500
Red Creek	Wayne	J. B. Decker	1000
Rhinebeck	Dutchess	A. Lee Wager	1800
Riverhead*	Suffolk	See Greenport	2200
Rochester*	**Monroe**	**James S. Garlock** No. 14 Wilder Block.	**120000**
Rome	Oneida	Benj. B. Kenyon.	15000
Rondout	Ulster	W. N. Gill	10000
Roslyn	Queens	See Flushing	1200
Rushford	Allegany	See Angelica	800
Sag Harbor	Suffolk	See Greenport	2200
Salamanca	Cattaraugus	V. C. Reynolds †*J. J. Inman.*	3500
Salem	Washington	James Gibson	1800
Sandy Hill	Washington	See Salem	2500
Saratoga Springs	Saratoga	Willard J. Miner	14000
Saugerties	Ulster	Egbert Whitaker	4000
Schenectady*	Schenectady	J. A. De Remer	15000
Schoharie*	Schoharie	Krum & Grant	1600
Schuylersville	Saratoga	See Saratoga Springs.	1800
Seneca Falls	Seneca	Charles A. Hawley	6000
Sherburne	Chenango	See Norwich	1500
Sing Sing	Westchester	Smith Lent	7000
Skaneateles	Onondaga	See Syracuse	2000
Sodus	Wayne	See Lyons	1000
Springville	Erie	See Buffalo	1600
South Dayton	Cattaraugus	W. D. Phelps	1300
Syracuse*	**Onondaga**	**Kellogg & Wells**	**75000**
Tarrytown	Westchester	George C. Andrews	4000
Tonawanda	Erie	F. L. Clark	6000

(† We withdraw our former recommendation.)

New York—Continued.

Parties corresponding with Attorneys named in the Directory should ALWAYS sign themselves "Subscribers to J. A. GRAFT & CO.'S LEGAL DIRECTORY." Should any Attorney fail to give prompt attention to correspondence, collections or business intrusted to his care, we will be thankful to patrons of the Directory to notify us promptly in any such case. Places designated thus (*) are County Seats.

POST-OFFICE.	COUNTY.	ATTORNEYS.	POPUL'N.
Troy*	**Rensselaer**	**John P. Curley**	**60000**
Trumansburgh	Tompkins	See Ithaca	1600
Union Springs	Cayuga	R. F. Hoff	1600
Utica*	**Oneida**	**J. D. F. Stone**	**40000**
Walden	Orange	See Newburgh	2000
Walton	Delaware	S. H. Fancher	1600
Warsaw*	Wyoming	Augustus Harrington	3500
Warwick	Orange	John J. Beattie	1600
Waterford	Saratoga	See Saratoga Springs	2500
Waterloo*	Seneca	Charles E. Opdyke, Jr.	4000
Watertown*	Jefferson	W. F. Porter	12000
Waterville	Oneida	E. H. Lamb	2000
Watkins*	Schuyler	Charles M. Woodward	3500
Waverly	Tioga	See Owego	3000
Weedsport	Cayuga	C. M. Elliott	2000
Wellsville	Allegany	F. H. Church †*J. C. Sullivan.*	3000
Westfield	Chautauqua	See Jamestown	2000
West Troy	Albany	John H. Gleason	14000
West Winfield	Herkimer	Charles D. Thomas	1500
Whitehall	Washington	J. S. Potter	4200
White Plains*	Westchester	A. Jackson Hyatt	4700
Whitestone	Queens	See Flushing	3000
Wolcott	Wayne	William Roe	2000
Yonkers	Westchester	See White Plains	20000

NORTH CAROLINA.

POST-OFFICE.	COUNTY.	ATTORNEYS.	POPUL'N.
Albemarle*	Stanly	S. J. Pemberton	300
Ashborough*	Randolph	James T. Crocker	500
Asheville*	Buncombe	Wm. R. Whitson †*Natt Atkinson.*	5000
Bakersville*	Mitchell	Jacob W. Bowman	1200

(†We withdraw our former recommendation.)

North Carolina—Continued.

Parties corresponding with Attorneys named in the Directory should ALWAYS sign themselves "Subscribers to J. A. GRAFT & CO.'S LEGAL DIRECTORY." Should any Attorney fail to give prompt attention to correspondence, collections or business intrusted to his care, we will be thankful to patrons of the Directory to notify us promptly in any such case. Places designated thus (*) are County Seats.

POST-OFFICE.	COUNTY.	ATTORNEYS.	POPUL'N.
Beaufort*	Carteret	See New Berne	500
Boone*	Watauga	L. L. Green	200
Brevard*	Transylvania	W. A. Gost	300
Burgaw*	Pender	John T. Bland	400
Burnsville*	Yancey	See Marion	300
Camden C. H.*	Camden	S. E. Overby	1000
Carthage*	Moore	J. A. Worthy	700
Charleston*	Swain	See Webster	300
Charlotte*	Mecklenburgh	W. W. Flemming	10000
Clinton*	Sampson	J. L. Stewart	1000
Columbia*	Tyrrell	R. P. Felton	400
Columbus*	Polk	See Hendersonville	300
Concord*	Cabarrus	H. S. Puryear	1300
Currituck C. H.*	Currituck	See Elizabeth City	200
Dallas*	Gaston	George F. Bason	500
Danbury*	Stokes	A. H. Joyce	200
Dobson*	Surry	See Danbury	200
Durham*	Durham	Manning & Manning.	6000
Edenton*	Chowan	W. J. Leary, Jr	1500
Elizabeth City*	Pasquotank	J. W. Albertson & Son	3000
Elizabethtown*	Bladen	C. C. Lyon	400
Enfield	Halifax	See Halifax	1200
Fayetteville*	Cumberland	George M. Rose	6000
Franklin*	Macon		300
Gatesville*	Gates	L. L. Smith	300
Goldsborough*	Wayne	Jos. E. Robinson	5000
Graham*	Alamance	E. S. Parker	500
Greensborough*	Guilford		2100
Greenville*	Pitt	L. V. Morril	2200
Halifax*	Halifax	Robert O. Burton, Jr.	500
Hayesville*	Clay	See Webster	200
Henderson*	Vance	H. T. Watkins	2800
Hendersonville*	Henderson	Thos. J. Rickman	900
Hertford*	Perquimans	T. G. Skinner	900
Hickory	Catawba	D. H. Tuttle	1500
Hillsborough*	Orange	A. W. Graham	1000
Jackson*	Northampton	Peebles & Gay	300
Jacksonville*	Onslow	See Richlands	100

North Carolina—Continued.

Parties corresponding with Attorneys named in the Directory should ALWAYS sign themselves "Subscribers to J. A. GRAFT & CO.'S LEGAL DIRECTORY." Should any Attorney fail to give prompt attention to correspondence, collections or business intrusted to his care, we will be thankful to patrons of the Directory to notify us promptly in any such case.
Places designated thus (*) are County Seats.

POST-OFFICE.	COUNTY.	ATTORNEYS.	POPUL'N.
Jefferson*	Ashe	J. W. Todd	200
Jonesborough	Moore	See Carthage	500
Kenansville*	Duplin	See Goldsborough	400
Kinston*	Lenoir	See New Berne	1500
Lake Landing	Hyde	N. Beckwith	200
Lenoir*	Caldwell	G. N. Folk	400
Lexington*	Davidson	F. C. Robbins	700
Lillington*	Harnett	See Raleigh	200
Lincolnton*	Lincoln	B. C. Cobb	1000
Louisburg*	Franklin	E. W. Timberlake	1000
Lumberton*	Robeson	Thomas A. McNeill	800
Manteo*	Dare	See Columbia	300
Marion*	McDowell	E. T. Greenlee	500
Marshall*	Madison	See Asheville	300
Milton	Caswell	See Roxborough	800
Mocksville*	Davie	John M. Clement	1000
Monroe*	Union	J. Reese Blair	2500
Morganton*	Burke	J. G. Bynum	1000
Murfreesborough	Hertford	See Winton	1000
Murphy*	Cherokee	James W. Cooper	200
New Berne*	Craven	O. H. Guion †*L. J. Moore.*	7600
Newton*	Catawba	See Lincolnton	700
Oxford*	Granville	Robert W. Winston	2000
Pittsborough*	Chatham	Manning & Womack	500
Plymouth*	Washington	Charles Latham	2000
Raleigh*	Wake	Gray & Stamps	14000
Reidsville	Rockingham	See Wentworth	1500
Richlands	Onslow	Frank Thompson, Jr.	100
Robbinsville*	Graham	See Webster	300
Rockingham*	Richmond	Chas. W. Tillett	1600
Rocky Mount	Edgecombe	See Tarborough	600
Roxborough*	Person	J. S. Merritt	800
Rutherfordton *	Rutherford	L. F. Churchill	1500
Salem	Forsyth	See Winston	1800
Salisbury*	Rowan	J. S. Henderson	3000
Shelby*	Cleveland	R. McBrayer	1200

(† We withdraw our former recommendation.)

North Carolina—Continued.

Parties corresponding with Attorneys named in the Directory should ALWAYS sign themselves "Subscribers to J. A. GRAFT & CO.'S LEGAL DIRECTORY." Should any Attorney fail to give prompt attention to correspondence, collections or business intrusted to his care, we will be thankful to patrons of the Directory to notify us promptly in any such case. Places designated thus (*) are County Seats.

POST-OFFICE.	COUNTY.	ATTORNEYS.	POPUL'N.
Smithfield*	Johnston	N. R. Richardson †*J. T. Langston.*	600
Smithville*	Brunswick	See Wilmington	1200
Snow Hill*	Greene	G. M. Lindsay	500
Sparta*	Alleghany	See Jefferson	300
Statesville*	Iredell	Harry Burke	3000
Stonewall*	Pamlico	See New Berne	300
Swan Quarter*	Hyde	See Lake Landing	200
Tarborough*	Edgecombe	H. L. Staton, Jr.	2500
Taylorsville*	Alexander	See Statesville	200
Trenton*	Jones	See New Berne	400
Troy*	Montgomery	J. M. Brown	200
Wadesborough*	Anson	John D. Pemberton	1500
Warrenton*	Warren	W. A. Montgomery	1200
Washington*	Beaufort	W. B. Rodman & Son	3500
Waynesville*	Haywood	See Webster	300
Webster*	Jackson	Walter E. Moore	200
Wentworth*	Rockingham	Boyd & Reid	300
Whiteville*	Columbus	McDaniel & Shulken.	300
Wilkesborough*	Wilkes	Isaac C. Wellborn	300
Williamston*	Martin	J. E. Moore	600
Wilmington*	**New Hanover**	**Jas. Taylor Elliott**	**20000**
Wilson*	Wilson	John E. Woodward	2000
Windsor*	Bertie	D. C. Winston	500
Winston*	Forsyth	R. B. Kerner	6000
Winton*	Hertford	George Cowper	300
Yadkinville*	Yadkin	R. C. Puryear	200
Yanceyville*	Caswell	See Roxborough	500

(† We withdraw our former recommendation.)

OHIO.

Parties corresponding with Attorneys named in the Directory should ALWAYS sign themselves "Subscribers to J. A. GRAFT & CO.'S LEGAL DIRECTORY." Should any Attorney fail to give prompt attention to correspondence, collections or business intrusted to his care, we will be thankful to patrons of the Directory to notify us promptly in any such case. Places designated thus (*) are County Seats.

POST-OFFICE.	COUNTY.	ATTORNEYS.	POPUL'N.
Ada	Hardin	B. A. Holland	2000
Akron*	**Summit**	**John H. Campbell**	**30000**
Alliance	Stark	O. B. Hoover	6000
Antwerp	Paulding	See Paulding	1500
Arcanum	Darke	See Greenville	1000
Ashland*	Ashland	Smith & Smith	4000
Ashley	Delaware	See Delaware	800
Ashtabula	Ashtabula	R. W. Calvin	7000
Athens*	Athens	Emmett Tompkins	2500
Attica	Seneca	See Tiffin	800
Bainbridge	Ross	See Chillicothe	1000
Barnesville	Belmont		3000
Batavia*	Clermont	R. J. Bancroft	1400
Batesville	Noble	See Caldwell	600
Bellaire	Belmont	J. B. Smith	10000
Bellefontaine*	Logan	E. J. Howenstine	4500
Bellevue	Huron	J. B. Miller	2500
Bellville	Richland	A. H. Redding	1100
Berea	Cuyahoga	See Cleveland	1800
Berlin Heights	Erie	See Sandusky	600
Beverly	Washington	See Marietta	1000
Blanchester	Clinton	See Wilmington	1000
Bluffton	Allen	G. W. Murray	1500
Bowling Green*	Wood	Guy C. Nearing	2200
Bridgeport	Belmont	See Bellaire	2500
Bryan*	Williams	Charles A. Bowersox	3000
Buckeye City	Knox	J. R. Tilton	300
Bucyrus*	Crawford	Teel & Bennett	5000
Burton	Geauga	See Cleveland	600
Butler	Richland	See Mansfield	600
Cadiz*	Harrison	Walter G. Shotwell	2000
Caldwell*	Noble	William C. Okey	1000
Caledonia	Marion	See Marion	800
Cambridge*	Guernsey	Robert T. Scott	4000
Camden	Preble	See Eaton	1000
Canal Dover	Tuscarawas	John A. Hostetler	2500
Canal Fulton	Stark	See Massillon	1300
Canfield	Mahoning	See Youngstown	800
Canton*	Stark	J. Whiting, Jr.	20000
Cardington	Morrow	R. F. Bartlett	1500
Carey	Wyandot	See Upper Sandusky	1500
Carrollton*	Carroll	A. P. Mortland	1500
Celina*	Mercer	J. D. Johnson	2500

Ohio—Continued.

Parties corresponding with Attorneys named in the Directory should ALWAYS sign themselves "Subscribers to J. A. GRAFT & CO.'S LEGAL DIRECTORY." Should any Attorney fail to give prompt attention to correspondence, collections or business intrusted to his care, we will be thankful to patrons of the Directory to notify us promptly in any such case. Places designated thus (*) are County Seats.

POST-OFFICE.	COUNTY.	ATTORNEYS.	POPUL'N.
Centreburgh	Knox	See Mount Vernon	500
Chagrin Falls	Cuyahoga	See Cleveland	1500
Chardon*	Geauga	W. H. Osborne	1500
Chillicothe*	Ross	J. B. McLaughlin	12000
Cincinnati*	**Hamilton**	**J. A. Graft & Co.** MANAGERS WESTERN OFFICE OF THE LEGAL REPORTING AND COLLECTION AGENCY. **David Davis, Resident Attorney,** Rooms 73, 74 and 75 Johnston Building, S. W. Cor. 5th and Walnut Sts.	**325000**
Circleville*	Pickaway	Smith & Morris	7000
Cleveland*	**Cuyahoga**	**M. M. Hobart** Manager Branch Office, No. 14 Blackstone Building.	**190000**
Clyde	Sandusky	James Hunt	3000
Columbiana	Columbiana	John G. Beatty	1400
Columbus*	**Franklin**	**B. F. Martz** 29½ N. High St. (Room 6)	**60000**
Columbus Grove	Putnam	See Ottawa	1500
Conneaut	Ashtabula	Allen M. Cox	1500
Corning	Perry	A. H. Ward	1000
Coshocton*	Coshocton	Thomas E. Willis	3500
Covington	Miami	See Piqua	1500
Crestline	Crawford	See Galion	3500
Creston	Wayne	See Wooster	500
Cuyahoga Falls	Summit	See Akron	2500
Danville	Knox	See Buckeye City	500
Dayton*	**Montgomery**	**Horace McDermont** Room 1, Callahan Block.	**40000**
Defiance*	Defiance	William Carter	7000
De Graff	Logan	H. Wheeler	1200
Delaware*	Delaware	O. F. Parker	10000
Delphos	Allen	Emerson Priddy	5000
Delta	Fulton	See Wauseon	1000
Deshler	Henry	See Napoleon	1000
Doylestown	Wayne	See Wooster	1500
Dresden	Muskingum	See Zanesville	1500
Dunkirk	Hardin	See Kenton	1500
East Liverpool	Columbiana	H. R. Hill	6000
East Palestine	Columbiana	See Columbiana	1500
Eaton*	Preble	John V. Campbell	3500
Edgerton	Williams	See Bryan	1000

Ohio—Continued.

Parties corresponding with Attorneys named in the Directory should ALWAYS sign themselves "Subscribers to J. A. GRAFT & CO.'S LEGAL DIRECTORY." Should any Attorney fail to give prompt attention to correspondence, collections or business intrusted to his care, we will be thankful to patrons of the Directory to notify us promptly in any such case.
Places designated thus (*) are County Seats.

POST-OFFICE.	COUNTY.	ATTORNEYS.	POPUL'N.
Elmore	Ottawa	T. J. Sadler	1200
Elyria*	Lorain	P. H. Boynton	5500
Fayette	Fulton	See Wauseon	700
Felicity	Clermont	See Batavia	1200
Findlay*	Hancock	Theo. Totten	5500
Flushing	Belmont	See St. Clairsville	500
Forest	Hardin	H.V. & B.W. Waltermire	1500
Fort Recovery	Mercer	See Celina	1200
Fostoria	Seneca	George A. Knight	5500
Frankfort	Ross	See Chillicothe	800
Franklin	Warren	J. D. Miller	4000
Fredericktown	Knox	See Mount Vernon	1000
Fremont*	Sandusky	J. T. Garver	9000
Galion	Crawford	H. C. Carhart	7000
Gallipolis*	Gallia	Hampton & Summers	6000
Garrettsville	Portage	R. S. Webb	1000
Geneva	Ashtabula	See Ashtabula	2000
Genoa	Ottawa	See Elmore	1000
Georgetown*	Brown	W. J. Thompson	1500
Germantown	Montgomery	Adam Frank	1800
Girard	Trumbull	See Warren	1500
Granville	Licking	See Newark	1300
Greenfield	Highland	William P. Hughey	2200
Green Spring	Seneca	C. S. Burton	1200
Greenville*	Darke	Judy & Irwin	5000
Greenwich	Huron	See Norwalk	800
Hamilton*	Butler	John C. Slayback	15000
Harmar	Washington	See Marietta	1800
Harrison	Hamilton	James A. Graft	2500
Hicksville	Defiance	Thompson & Forlow	2000
Hillsboro*	Highland	Olin J. Ross	4000
Holgate	Henry	See Napoleon	800
Hubbard	Trumbull	See Youngstown	1800
Hudson	Summit	See Akron	2000
Huron	Erie	See Sandusky	1300
Ironton*	Lawrence	Lot Davis	13000
Jackson*	Jackson	C. A. Atkinson	4000
Jamestown	Greene	See Xenia	1000
Jefferson*	Ashtabula	Trask & Cadwell	2000
Jeffersonville	Fayette	See Washington C. H.	500

Ohio—Continued.

Parties corresponding with Attorneys named in the Directory should ALWAYS sign themselves "Subscribers to J. A. GRAFT & CO.'S LEGAL DIRECTORY." Should any Attorney fail to give prompt attention to correspondence, collections or business intrusted to his care, we will be thankful to patrons of the Directory to notify us promptly in any such case.
Places designated thus (*) are County Seats.

POST-OFFICE.	COUNTY.	ATTORNEYS.	POPUL'N.
Johnstown	Licking	See Newark	500
Kent	Portage	C. B. Newton	4500
Kenton*	Hardin	I. N. Everett	4800
Killbuck	Holmes	C. C. Thompson	300

E ATTORNEYS named herein have been IALLY RECOMMENDED by TWO or more induals or firms of their respective lities.
TRONS of the Directory can DEPEND the reliability of the Attorneys, feel PERFECTLY SAFE in INTRUSTING business to them.

POST-OFFICE.	COUNTY.	ATTORNEYS.	POPUL'N.
Lucas	Richland	See Mansfield	[illegible]
Lynchburg	Highland	See Hillsboro	800
Madison	Lake	See Painesville	1000
Malta	Morgan	See McConnelsville	800
Manchester	Adams	Henry Collings	1600
Mansfield*	Richland	Cummings & McBride	12000
Marietta*	Washington	Samuel S. Knowles	10000
Marion*	Marion	McNeal & Wolford †*John J. Williams.*	5000
Martin's Ferry	Belmont	See Bellaire	4000
Martinsville	Clinton	J. M. Townsend	300
Marysville*	Union	E. E. Cole	3000
Massillon	Stark	R. W. McCaughey	9000
McArthur*	Vinton	William J. Rannells	1200
McClure	Henry	See Napoleon	400
McConnelsville*	Morgan	William B. Crew	2000
Mechanicsburg	Champaign	See Urbana	1700
Medina*	Medina	George Hayden	1300
Miamisburg	Montgomery	Amos K. Clay	2200
Middleport	Meigs	See Pomeroy	4000

(† We withdraw our former recommendation.)

Ohio—Continued.

Parties corresponding with Attorneys named in the Directory should ALWAYS sign themselves "Subscribers to J. A. GRAFT & CO.'S LEGAL DIRECTORY." Should any Attorney fail to give prompt attention to correspondence, collections or business intrusted to his care, we will be thankful to patrons of the Directory to notify us promptly in any such case. Places designated thus (*) are County Seats.

POST-OFFICE.	COUNTY.	ATTORNEYS.	POPUL'N.
Elmore	Ottawa	T. J. Sadler	1200
Elyria*	Lorain	P. H. Boynton	5500
Fayette	Fulton	See Wauseon	700
Felicity	Clermont	See Batavia	1200
F			
F			
F			
F			
F			
F			
F			
F			
F			
G			
G			
G			
G			
G			
G			
G			
G			
Granville	Licking	See Newark	1300
Greenfield	Highland	William P. Hughey	2200
Green Spring	Seneca	C. S. Burton	1200
Greenville*	Darke	Judy & Irwin	5000
Greenwich	Huron	See Norwalk	800
Hamilton*	Butler	John C. Slayback	15000
Harmar	Washington	See Marietta	1800
Harrison	Hamilton	James A. Graft	2500
Hicksville	Defiance	Thompson & Forlow	2000
Hillsboro*	Highland	Olin J. Ross	4000
Holgate	Henry	See Napoleon	800
Hubbard	Trumbull	See Youngstown	1800
Hudson	Summit	See Akron	2000
Huron	Erie	See Sandusky	1300
Ironton*	Lawrence	Lot Davis	13000
Jackson*	Jackson	C. A. Atkinson	4000
Jamestown	Greene	See Xenia	1000
Jefferson*	Ashtabula	Trask & Cadwell	2000
Jeffersonville	Fayette	See Washington C. H.	500

Ohio—Continued.

Parties corresponding with Attorneys named in the Directory should ALWAYS sign themselves "Subscribers to J. A. GRAFT & CO.'S LEGAL DIRECTORY." Should any Attorney fail to give prompt attention to correspondence, collections or business intrusted to his care, we will be thankful to patrons of the Directory to notify us promptly in any such case. Places designated thus (*) are County Seats.

POST-OFFICE.	COUNTY.	ATTORNEYS.	POPUL'N.
Johnstown	Licking	See Newark	500
Kent	Portage	C. B. Newton	4500
Kenton*	Hardin	I. N. Everett	4800
Killbuck	Holmes	C. C. Thompson	300
Kingston	Ross	See Chillicothe	600
Kinsman	Trumbull	See Warren	400
Kossuth	Auglaize	George Haller	500
Lancaster*	Fairfield	A. R. Eversole	7000
Lebanon*	Warren	James N. Bell	3000
Leesburg	Highland	See Hillsboro	700
Leetonia	Columbiana	See Columbiana	2500
Leipsic	Putnam	J. Werner	1500
Liberty	Trumbull	See Youngstown	2500
Liberty Center	Henry	See Napoleon	600
Lima*	Allen	James L. Price	10000
Lodi	Medina	See Medina	600
Logan*	Hocking	Carl H. Buerhaus	3000
London*	Madison	F. Webster	4500
Lorain	Lorain	See Elyria	1800
Loudonville	Ashland	David Quick	2000
Louisville	Stark	See Canton	1300
Lucas	Richland	See Mansfield	500
Lynchburg	Highland	See Hillsboro	800
Madison	Lake	See Painesville	1000
Malta	Morgan	See McConnelsville	800
Manchester	Adams	Henry Collings	1600
Mansfield*	Richland	Cummings & McBride	12000
Marietta*	Washington	Samuel S. Knowles	10000
Marion*	Marion	McNeal & Wolford †*John J. Williams.*	5000
Martin's Ferry	Belmont	See Bellaire	4000
Martinsville	Clinton	J. M. Townsend	300
Marysville*	Union	E. E. Cole	3000
Massillon	Stark	R. W. McCaughey	9000
McArthur*	Vinton	William J. Rannells	1200
McClure	Henry	See Napoleon	400
McConnelsville*	Morgan	William B. Crew	2000
Mechanicsburg	Champaign	See Urbana	1700
Medina*	Medina	George Hayden	1800
Miamisburg	Montgomery	Amos K. Clay	2200
Middleport	Meigs	See Pomeroy	4000

(† We withdraw our former recommendation.)

Ohio—Continued.

Parties corresponding with Attorneys named in the Directory should ALWAYS sign themselves "Subscribers to J. A. GRAFT & CO.'S LEGAL DIRECTORY." Should any Attorney fail to give prompt attention to correspondence, collections or business intrusted to his care, we will be thankful to patrons of the Directory to notify us promptly in any such case.
Places designated thus (*) are County Seats.

POST-OFFICE.	COUNTY.	ATTORNEYS.	POPUL'N.
Middletown	Butler	W. H. Todhunter	5000
Milan	Erie	Darwin Fay, J. P.	1200
Milford Centre	Union	See Marysville	500
Millersburg*	Holmes	E. J. Duer	1700
Minerva	Stark	See Canton	700
Monroeville	Huron	See Norwalk	1500
Montpelier	Williams	See Bryan	600
Morrow	Warren	J. D. Wallace	1200
Moscow	Clermont	See Batavia	700
Mount Gilead*	Morrow	Dalrymple & Powell	1500
Mount Pleasant	Jefferson	See Steubenville	800
Mount Sterling	Madison	See London	600
Mount Vernon*	Knox	D. C. Montgomery & Mendenhall	7000
Napoleon*	Henry	Martin Knupp	3500
Nelsonville	Athens	See Athens	3000
Nevada	Wyandot	See Upper Sandusky.	1200
Newark*	Licking	Frank G. Warden	12000
New Athens	Harrison	See Cadiz	500
New Baltimore	Stark	See Canton	400
New Bremen	Auglaize	F. H. L. Nieter	1800
New Carlisle	Clarke	See Springfield	1000
New Comerstown	Tuscarawas	See New Philadelphia	1200
New Lexington*	Perry	Tussing & Donaldson.	1500
New Lisbon*	Columbiana	William J. Jordan	2500
New London	Huron	See Wellington	1200
New Madison	Darke	See Greenville	800
New Paris	Preble	John A. Moore	1000
New Philadelphia*	Tuscarawas	Buchanan & DeGreif.	5000
New Richmond	Clermont	Frank Davis	2800
New Straitsville	Perry	W. E. Allen	3000
New Vienna	Clinton	W. H. West	900
New Washington	Crawford	See Bucyrus	800
Niles	Trumbull	See Warren	4000
North Amherst	Lorain	See Elyria	1800
North Lewisburg	Champaign	See Urbana	1000
Norwalk*	Huron	C. B. Stickney	8000
Oberlin	Lorain	W. B. Bedortha	4000
Orrville	Wayne	S. N. Coe	1600
Orwell	Ashtabula	E. L. Gibbs	1000
Ostrander	Delaware	See Delaware	500
Ottawa*	Putnam	Wm. C. G. Krauss	2000
Oxford	Butler	See Hamilton	2500
Painesville*	Lake	S. B. Amidon	4000

Ohio—Continued.

Parties corresponding with Attorneys named in the Directory should ALWAYS sign themselves "Subscribers to J. A. GRAFT & CO.'S LEGAL DIRECTORY." Should any Attorney fail to give prompt attention to correspondence, collections or business intrusted to his care, we will be thankful to patrons of the Directory to notify us promptly in any such case. Places designated thus (*) are County Seats.

POST-OFFICE.	COUNTY.	ATTORNEYS.	POPUL'N.
Paulding*	Paulding	J. B. Brodnix	2000
Perrysburg	Wood	D. K. Hollenbeck	2000
Piqua	Miami	John M. McDonald	9000
Pitt	Wyandot	See Upper Sandusky	400
Plain City	Madison	See London	1000
Plymouth	Richland	See Mansfield	1300
Poland	Mahoning	See Youngstown	600
Pomeroy*	Meigs	Guthrie & Giles	6000
Port Clinton*	Ottawa	J. H. & H. B. Magruder	1800
Portsmouth*	Scioto	Dever & Livingston	12000
Prospect	Marion	S. W. Van Winkle	1500
Quaker City	Guernsey	See Cambridge	700
Ravenna*	Portage	O. P. Sperra	5000
Richwood	Union	P. R. Kerr	1500
Ripley	Brown	W. D. Young	3000
Rock Creek	Ashtabula	See Ashtabula	800
Rushsylvania	Logan	See Bellefontaine	600
Sabina	Clinton	See Wilmington	900
Salem	Columbiana	J. C. Boone	4000
Salineville	Columbiana	See Wellsville	2500
Sandusky*	Erie	H. & L. H. Goodwin	18000
Scio	Harrison	See Cadiz	700
Seville	Medina	See Medina	700
Shelby	Richland	See Mansfield	2000
Shiloh	Richland	See Mansfield	800
Shreve	Wayne	Lorenzo D. Cornell	1200
Sidney*	Shelby	John E. McCullough	5000
Smithfield	Jefferson	See Steubenville	700
Somerton	Belmont	See St. Clairsville	400
South Charleston	Clarke	A. Bradford	1200
South Toledo	Lucas	See Toledo	2000
Spencerville	Allen	See Lima	800
Springfield*	**Clarke**	**J. Warren Keifer**	**25000**
St. Clairsville*	Belmont	A. H. & W. Mitchell	1400
Steubenville*	Jefferson	R. G. Richards	15000
St. Mary's	Auglaize	Charles F. Bullock	1900
St. Paris	Champaign	Charles E. Buroker	1500
Sunbury	Delaware	See Delaware	500
Thurman	Gallia	See Gallipolis	500

Ohio—Continued.

Parties corresponding with Attorneys named in the Directory should ALWAYS sign themselves "Subscribers to J. A. GRAFT & CO.'S LEGAL DIRECTORY." Should any Attorney fail to give prompt attention to correspondence, collections or business intrusted to his care, we will be thankful to patrons of the Directory to notify us promptly in any such case. Places designated thus (*) are County Seats.

POST-OFFICE.	COUNTY.	ATTORNEYS.	POPUL'N.
Tiffin*	Seneca	James Pillars	10000
Tippecanoe City	Miami	See Troy	2000
Toledo*	**Lucas**	**J. C. Rike** Manager Branch Office, No. 2 Anderson Block.	**60000**
Troy*	Miami	A. F. Broomhall	4500
Uhrichsville	Tuscarawas	T. D. Healea	3000
Upper Sandusky*	Wyandot	W. F. Pool	3500
Urbana*	Champaign	McKenzie & Bryan	7000
Utica	Licking		1000
Van Wert*	Van Wert	Hathaway Kemper	5000
Versailles	Darke	See Greenville	1400
Wadsworth	Medina	See Medina	1500
Wapakoneta*	Auglaize	Layton & Stueve	3000
Warren*	Trumbull	L. F. Hunter	5000
Washington C. H.*	Fayette	J. H. Patton	5000
Wauseon*	Fulton	H. H. & T. F. Ham	2000
Waverly*	Pike	John W. Higgins	1700
Waynesville	Warren	See Lebanon	1000
Wellington	Lorain	J. H. Dickson	3000
Wellsville	Columbiana	Thomas H. Silver	5000
Wellston	Jackson	E. B. Bingham	3000
Westerville	Franklin	See Columbus	1500
West Jefferson	Madison	See London	800
West Liberty	Logan	See Bellefontaine	900
West Milton	Miami	See Troy	800
Weston	Wood	See Bowling Green †*C. F. Lewis.*	1000
West Salem	Wayne	See Wooster	1000
West Union*	Adams	Bayless & Scott †*D. W. Thomas.*	1000
Wharton	Wyandot	See Upper Sandusky	500
White House	Lucas	See Toledo	700
Willoughby	Lake	See Painesville	1200
Willshire	Van Wert	J. F. Shaffner	700
Wilmington*	Clinton	Melville Hayes	3000
Wilmot	Stark	See Massillon	600
Winchester	Adams	T. C. Downey	700
Woodsfield*	Monroe	Hunter & Mallory	1000
Woodstock	Champaign	See Urbana	500
Wooster*	Wayne	Alfred J. Thomas	7000

(†We withdraw our former recommendation.)

Ohio—Continued.

Parties corresponding with Attorneys named in the Directory should ALWAYS sign themselves "Subscribers to J. A. GRAFT & CO.'S LEGAL DIRECTORY." Should any Attorney fail to give prompt attention to correspondence, collections or business intrusted to his care, we will be thankful to patrons of the Directory to notify us promptly in any such case.
Places designated thus (*) are County Seats.

POST-OFFICE.	COUNTY.	ATTORNEYS.	POPUL'N.
Xenia*	Greene	C. L. Maxwell	8000
Yellow Springs	Greene	See Xenia	1600
Youngstown*	**Mahoning**	**George C. Hatch**	**30000**
Zanesville*	**Muskingum**	**H. S. Moody**	**20000**

OREGON.

POST-OFFICE.	COUNTY.	ATTORNEYS.	POPUL'N.
Albany*	Linn	Flinn & Chamberlain	2000
Ashland	Jackson	See Jacksonville	1000
Astoria*	Clatsop	C. J. Curtis	6000
Baker City*	Baker	Sterns, Israel & Manvill	3000
Canyon City*	Grant	E. A. Brackett	500
Corvallis*	Benton	W. S. McFadden	1700
Dallas*	Polk	C. A. Johns	1200
East Portland	Multnomah	See Portland	3000
Ellensburg*	Curry	See Roseburg	500
Empire City*	Coos	S. H. Hazard	500
Eugene City*	Lane	George S. Washburn	2000
Hillsborough*	Washington	T. B. Hanley	800
Jacksonville*	Jackson	B. F. Dowell	1500
Kerby*	Josephine	See Jacksonville	400
La Fayette*	Yam Hill	H. Hurley	400
La Grande	Union	See Pendleton	500
Lakeview*	Lake	Charles A. Cogswell	400
Lebanon	Linn	See Albany	300

Oregon—Continued.

Parties corresponding with Attorneys named in the Directory should ALWAYS sign themselves "Subscribers to J. A. GRAFT & CO.'S LEGAL DIRECTORY." Should any Attorney fail to give prompt attention to correspondence, collections or business intrusted to his care, we will be thankful to patrons of the Directory to notify us promptly in any such case.
Places designated thus (*) are County Seats.

POST-OFFICE.	COUNTY.	ATTORNEYS.	POPUL'N.
McMinnville	Yam Hill	J. L. Story	800
Oakland	Douglas	See Roseburg	500
Oregon City*	Clackamas	See Portland	1500
Pendleton*	Umatilla	H. J. Bean	2500
Portland*	**Multnomah**	**B. F. Dowell**	**30000**
Roseburg*	Douglas	Willis & Jones	1000
Salem*	Marion	**Seth R. Hammer** (See card in Appendix, page IV.)	5000
Silverton	Marion	See Salem	300
St. Helen*	Columbia	See Portland	300
The Dalles*	Wasco	W. S. Myers	2500
Tillamook*	Tillamook	J. L. Story	200
Union*	Union	See Pendleton	500

PENNSYLVANIA.

POST-OFFICE.	COUNTY.	ATTORNEYS.	POPUL'N.
Allegheny City	**Allegheny**	**James W. Collins**	**80000**
Allentown*	Lehigh	James S. Biery	2000
Altoona	**Blair**	**J. S. Leisenring**	**25000**
Ashland	Schuylkill	William A. Marr	6000
Athens	Bradford	See Towanda	1700
Beaver*	Beaver	Joseph Ledlie	1500
Beaver Falls	Beaver	Roger Cope	9000
Bedford*	Bedford	John H. Jordan	2500
Bellefonte*	Centre	Adam Hoy	5000
Berwick	Columbia	See Bloomsburg	2100
Bethlehem	Northampton	J. B. Kemerer	5500
Blairsville	Indiana	See Indiana	1300

Pennsylvania—Continued.

Parties corresponding with Attorneys named in the Directory should ALWAYS sign themselves "Subscribers to J. A. GRAFT & CO.'S LEGAL DIRECTORY." Should any Attorney fail to give prompt attention to correspondence, collections or business intrusted to his care, we will be thankful to patrons of the Directory to notify us promptly in any such case.
Places designated thus (*) are County Seats.

POST-OFFICE.	COUNTY.	ATTORNEYS.	POPUL'N.
Bloomsburg*	Columbia	H. V. White	4000
Boyertown	Berks	Calvin F. Emes	1200
Braddock	Allegheny	See Pittsburgh	3500
Bradford	McKean	McSweeney & Byles	10000
Bristol	Bucks	A. Weir Gilkeson	6000
Brookville*	Jefferson	John M. Van Vliet	2500
Brownsville	Fayette	See Uniontown	1500
Butler*	Butler	A. M. Cornelius	5200
Canton	Bradford	E. J. Cleveland	1800
Carbondale	Lackawanna	J. E. Burr	8000
Carlisle*	Cumberland	Henderson & Hayes	7000
Carrolltown	Cambria	See Ebensburg	700
Catasauqua	Lehigh	R. Clay Hammersly	3200
Catawissa	Columbia	W. H. Rhawn	2000
Chambersburg	Franklin	W. Rush. Gillan	8000
Chester	Delaware	Orlando Harvey	15000
Clarion*	Clarion	Wilson, Jenks & Reed	1500
Clearfield*	Clearfield	Singleton Bell	2000
Coatesville	Chester	See West Chester	3000
Cochranton	Crawford	See Meadville	1000
Columbia	Lancaster	William B. Given	10000
Connellsville	Fayette	See Uniontown	4000
Conshohocken	Montgomery	See Norristown	4500
Corry	Erie	S. B. Brooks	7000
Coudersport*	Potter	Larrabee & Lewis	1000
Curwensville	Clearfield	Roland D. Swoope	1200
Danville*	Montour	E. H. Baldy & Son	9000
Downington	Chester	See West Chester	1600
Doylestown*	Bucks	Louis B. Thompson	2500
Du Bois	Clearfield	Truman Ames	6000
Dushore	Sullivan	John H. Cronin	500
Easton*	Northampton	J. R. Serfass	13000
Ebensburg*	Cambria	A. V. Barker	1500
Edinborough	Erie	See Erie	1000
Emporium*	Cameron	Newton & Green	1500
Erie*	**Erie**	**F. F. Marshall**	**35000**
Everett	Bedford	See Bedford	1300
Franklin*	Venango	W. W. Dale	6000
Freeport	Armstrong	See Kittanning	2000
Gettysburg*	Adams	Edward J. Cox	3100

Pennsylvania—Continued.

Parties corresponding with Attorneys named in the Directory should ALWAYS sign themselves "Subscribers to J. A. GRAFT & CO.'S LEGAL DIRECTORY."
Should any Attorney fail to give prompt attention to correspondence, collections or business intrusted to his care, we will be thankful to patrons of the Directory to notify us promptly in any such case.
Places designated thus (*) are County Seats.

POST-OFFICE.	COUNTY.	ATTORNEYS.	POPUL'N.
Girard	Erie	See Erie	700
Greencastle	Franklin	B. F. Winger	2000
Greensburg*	Westmoreland	W. H. Klingensmith.	5000
Greenville	Mercer	William Maxwell	4000
Hanover	York	See York	2300
Harrisburg*	**Dauphin**	**Robt. Snodgrass**	**35000**
Hazleton	Luzerne	Philip V. Weaver	7000
Hellertown	Northampton	See Easton	900
Hollidaysburg*	Blair	M. A. Young	5000
Honesdale*	Wayne	W. H. Lee	5000
Huntingdon*	Huntingdon	Jere B. Rex	5000
Houtzdale	Clearfield	Geo. W. Zeigler	5000
Indiana*	Indiana	Thomas Sutton	3000
Jamestown	Mercer	See Greenville	1000
Jersey Shore	Lycoming	See Williamsport	1500
Johnstown	Cambria	D. McLaughlin	9000
Kittanning*	Armstrong	H. L. Golden	4000
Kutztown	Berks	See Reading	1300
Lancaster*	**Lancaster**	**Thomas Whitson**	**26000**
Laporte*	Sullivan	E. P. Ingham	300
Latrobe	Westmoreland	See Greensburg	2000
Lebanon*	Lebanon	Grant Weidman	11000
Leechburg	Armstrong	See Kittanning	1200
Lewisburg*	Union	Dill & Beale	3500
Lewistown*	Mifflin	H. J. Walters	3500
Lititz	Lancaster	See Lancaster	1200
Littlestown	Adams	J. H. Le Fevre	1000
Lock Haven*	Clinton	**Jesse Merrill** (See card in Appendix, page IV.)	7000
Lykens	Dauphin	J. C. Durbin	2200
Mahanoy City	Schuylkill	James F. Grady	8000
Marietta	Lancaster	D. B. Case	3000
Mauch Chunk*	Carbon	Craig & Loose	5500
McConnellsburg*	Fulton	E. H. Cunningham	600
McKeesport	Allegheny	Robert M. Horner	14000
Meadville*	Crawford	Lewis Walker	9000
Mechanicsburg	Cumberland	See Carlisle	4000
Media*	Delaware	J. M. Broomall & Son	2000
Mercer*	Mercer	John W. Bell	2500

Pennsylvania—Continued.

Parties corresponding with Attorneys named in the Directory should ALWAYS sign themselves "Subscribers to J. A. GRAFT & CO.'S LEGAL DIRECTORY." Should any attorney fail to give prompt attention to correspondence, collections or business intrusted to his care, we will be thankful to patrons of the Directory to notify us promptly in any such case.
Places designated thus (*) are County Seats.

POST-OFFICE.	COUNTY.	ATTORNEYS.	POPUL'N.
Mercersburg	Franklin	See Chambersburg	1200
Meyersdale	Somerset	See Somerset	1500
Middleburg*	Snyder	T. J. Smith	500
Middletown	Dauphin	See Harrisburg	3500
Mifflinburg	Union	See Lewisburg	1200
Mifflintown*	Juniata	Louis E. Atkinson	2000
Milford*	Pike	J. H. Van Etten	1000
Millersburg	Dauphin	Simon S. Bowman	1500
Millerstown	Butler	See Butler	1500
Milton	Northumberland	Samuel T. Swartz	5000
Minersville	Schuylkill	See Pottsville	3500
Monongahela City	Washington	See Washington	3500
Montrose*	Susquehanna	G. G. Watrous	1800
Mount Carmel	Northumberland	W. B. Faust	4000
Mount Joy	Lancaster	See Lancaster	2200
Mount Pleasant	Westmoreland	See Greensburg	1200
Muncy	Lycoming	See Williamsport	1300
Nanticoke	Luzerne	D. J. M. Loop	6000
New Bloomfield*	Perry	McIntire & Stewart	800
New Brighton	Beaver	Gilbert L. Eberhart	5000
New Castle*	Lawrence	W. T. Burns	12000
New Milford	Susquehanna	See Montrose	1000
Newport	Perry	See New Bloomfield	2000
Newtown	Bucks	George A. Jenks	1400
Newville	Cumberland	See Carlisle	2000
Norristown*	Montgomery	Wm. F. Dannehower	15000
North East	Erie	See Erie	2000
Oil City	Venango	William McNair	10000
Osceola Mills	Clearfield	See Philipsburgh	1500
Oxford	Chester	W. T. Fulton	1800
Parker's Landing	Armstrong	See Kittanning	2000
Petrolia	Butler	See Butler	2000
Philadelphia*	**Philadelphia**	**Angelo T Freedley** Manager Branch Office, No. 710 Walnut St.	**1000000**
Philipsburgh	Centre	G. H. Lichtenthaler	4000
Phœnixville	Chester	H. H. Gilkeson	7000
Pittsburgh*	**Allegheny**	**James W. Collins** Manager Branch Office, No. 94 Diamond street.	**170000**
Pittston	Luzerne	F. H. Nichols	8000
Pleasantville	Venango	C. W. Benedict	900

Pennsylvania—Continued.

Parties corresponding with Attorneys named in the Directory should ALWAYS sign themselves "Subscribers to J. A. GRAFT & CO.'S LEGAL DIRECTORY." Should any Attorney fail to give prompt attention to correspondence, collections or business intrusted to his care, we will be thankful to patrons of the Directory to notify us promptly in any such case. Places designated thus (*) are County Seats.

POST-OFFICE.	COUNTY.	ATTORNEYS.	POPUL'N.
Plymouth	Luzerne	See Wilkes Barre	6000
Pottstown	Montgomery	M. D. Evans	6500
Pottsville*	Schuylkill	John W. Ryon	16000
Punxsutawney	Jefferson	John E. Calderwood.	1200
Quakertown	Bucks	See Bethlehem	1800
Reading*	**Berks**	**Adam B. Rieser** No. 526½ Washington St.	**55000**
Reynoldsville	Jefferson	M. M. Davis	1800
Ridgway*	Elk	Charles B. Earley	2000
Rochester	Beaver	See New Brighton	2500
Saltsburgh	Indiana	See Indiana	1000
Scranton*	**Lackawanna**	**Willard & Warren**	**68000**
Selin's Grove	Snyder	Horace Alleman	1500
Shamokin	Northumberland	Addison G. Marr	12000
Sharon	Mercer	John H. Elliott	7000
Sharpsburg	Allegheny	See Pittsburgh	3500
Sharpsville	Mercer	See Mercer	2000
Shenandoah	Schuylkill	See Mahanoy City	10000
Shippensburgh	Cumberland	A. G. Miller	2500
Smethport*	McKean	Sterrett & Rose	1000
Somerset*	Somerset	Henry F. Schell	1500
South Bethlehem	Northampton	John Kline	6000
St. Mary's	Elk	Harry Alvan Hall	2500
St. Petersburg	Clarion	See Clarion	1200
Stroudsburg*	Monroe	J. B. Storm	2000
Sunbury*	Northumberland	Lewis Dewart	4500
Susquehanna	Susquehanna	See Montrose	3500
Tamaqua	Schuylkill	C. F. Shindel	6000
Tidioute	Warren	See Warren	1300
Tionesta*	Forest	Miles W. Tate	600
Titusville	Crawford	Sherman & Grumbine	10000
Towanda*	Bradford	E. J. Angle	4000
Troy	Bradford	Rockwell & McCollom	1400
Tunkhannock*	Wyoming	Wm. M. Piatt & Sons	1500
Tyrone	Blair	W. L. Hicks	3000
Union City	Erie	J. W. Sproul	3000
Uniontown*	Fayette	Hutchinson & Wakefield	6000
Warren*	Warren	Allen & Higgins	5000

Pennsylvania—Continued.

Parties corresponding with Attorneys named in the Directory should ALWAYS sign themselves "Subscribers to J. A. GRAFT & CO.'S LEGAL DIRECTORY."
Should any Attorney fail to give prompt attention to correspondence, collections or business intrusted to his care, we will be thankful to patrons of the Directory to notify us promptly in any such case.
Places designated thus (*) are County Seats.

POST-OFFICE.	COUNTY.	ATTORNEYS.	POPUL'N.
Washington*	Washington	W. F. Wright	5500
Waynesborough	Franklin	See Chambersburg	2200
Waynesburgh*	Greene	James E. Sayers	2500
Wellsborough*	Tioga	Hugh Young	3000
West Chester*	Chester	Chas. H. Pennypacker	7000
West Middlesex	Mercer	See Sharon	1000
Wilkes Barre*	**Luzerne**	**D. L. O'Neill**	**25000**
Williamsport*	**Lycoming**	**Thomas W. Lloyd**	**20000**
York*	**York**	**George E. Neff**	**20000**

RHODE ISLAND.

POST-OFFICE.	COUNTY.	ATTORNEYS.	POPUL'N.
Anthony	Kent	Eugene F. Warner	1500
Ashaway	Washington	See Westerly	1000
Bristol*	Bristol	Henry Wingate Hayes	7000
Centreville	Kent	See East Greenwich	2000
Cumberland	Providence	See Providence	1000
East Greenwich*	Kent	S. W. K. Allen	2000
Greenville	Providente	See Providence	1200
Hope Valley	Washington	See Westerly	1500
Kingston*	Washington	E. C. Clark	1500
Newport*	Newport	Samuel R. Honey	16000
North Scituate	Providence	See Providence	1200
Pascoag	Providence	See Providence	1500
Pawtucket	Providence	See Providence	20000
Phenix	Kent	Ira O. Seaman	1500

Rhode Island—Continued.

Parties corresponding with Attorneys named in the Directory should ALWAYS sign themselves "Subscribers to J. A. GRAFT & CO.'S LEGAL DIRECTORY." Should any Attorney fail to give prompt attention to correspondence, collections or business intrusted to his care, we will be thankful to patrons of the Directory to notify us promptly in any such case.
Places designated thus (*) are County Seats.

POST-OFFICE.	COUNTY.	ATTORNEYS.	POPUL'N.
Providence*	**Providence**	**John M. Brennan**	**120000**
Slatersville	Providence	See Providence	1000
Wakefield	Washington	See Kingston	1000
Warren	Bristol	George L. Cooke, Jr.	5000
Warwick	Kent	See East Greenwich	1200
Westerly	Washington	Thomas H. Peabody	4000
Wickford	Washington	See Westerly	1000
Woonsocket	Providence	Edwin Aldrich	18000

SOUTH CAROLINA.

POST-OFFICE.	COUNTY.	ATTORNEYS.	POPUL'N.
Abbeville C. H.*	Abbeville	Samuel C. Cason	1500
Aiken*	Aiken	Claude E. Sawyer	2000
Anderson C. H.*	Anderson	B. F. Whitner	2000
Bamberg	Barnwell	Skinner & Williams	1000
Barnwell C. H.*	Barnwell	Joseph W. Blanton	800
Batesburg	Lexington	See Lexington C. H.	600
Beaufort*	Beaufort	W. J. Verdier	3500
Bennettsville*	Marlborough	D. D. McCall	700
Blackville	Barnwell	W. R. Kelly	1000
Camden*	Kershaw	Kennedy & Nelson	2500
Charleston*	**Charleston**	**Smythe & Lee** Managers Branch Office, No. 5 Broad St. (See card in Appendix, page V.)	**55000**
Cheraw	Chesterfield	Newton & McQueen	1100
Chester C. H.*	Chester	S. P. Hamilton	2500
Chesterfield C. H.*	Chesterfield	See Cheraw	400
Columbia*	Richland	Clark & Muller	10000
Conway*	Horry	Walsh & Scarborough	700
Darlington C. H.*	Darlington	Dargan & Dargan	1200

South Carolina—Continued.

Parties corresponding with Attorneys named in the Directory should ALWAYS sign themselves "Subscribers to J. A. GRAFT & CO.'S LEGAL DIRECTORY." Should any Attorney fail to give prompt attention to correspondence, collections or business intrusted to his care, we will be thankful to patrons of the Directory to notify us promptly in any such case. Places designated thus (*) are County Seats.

POST-OFFICE.	COUNTY.	ATTORNEYS.	POPUL'N.
Edgefield C. H.*	Edgefield	Arthur S. Tompkins.	900
Florence	Darlington	W. A. Brunson	2500
Gaffney City	Spartanburgh	James E. Webster	800
Georgetown*	Georgetown	Richard Dozier	3000
Grahamville	Beaufort	See Beaufort	400
Graniteville	Aiken	See Aiken	2000
Greenville C. H.*	Greenville	Isaac M. Bryan	10000
Hampton C. H.*	Hampton	Warren & Warren	400
Kingstree*	Williamsburg	B. Pressley Barron	400
Lancaster C. H.*	Lancaster	Moore & Moore	2000
Laurens C. H.*	Laurens	Todd & Martin	1200
Lexington C. H.*	Lexington	Metze & Mullen	500
Manning*	Clarendon	B. Pressley Barron	1000
Marion C. H.*	Marion	Sellers & Sellers	1500
Newberry C. H.*	Newberry	George S. Mower	2800
Orangeburg C. H.*	Orangeburg	Malcolm I. Browning	2000
Pickens C. H.*	Pickens	Child & Boggs †*Charles E. Robinson.*	300
Ridgeway	Fairfield	See Winnsborough	400
Rock Hill	York	See Yorkville	1000
Spartanburg C.H.*	Spartanburg	S. T. McCravy	4500
Sumter C. H.*	Sumter	T. B. Fraser, Jr	2000
Union*	Union	S. S. Stokes	2000
Walhalla*	Oconee	S. P. Dendy	1000
Walterborough *	Colleton	Howell & Murphy	900
Winnsborough*	Fairfield	Douglass & McCants.	2000
Yorkville*	York	C. E. Spencer	1500

(† We withdraw our former recommendation.)

TENNESSEE.

Parties corresponding with Attorneys named in the Directory should ALWAYS sign themselves "Subscribers to J. A. GRAFT & CO.'S LEGAL DIRECTORY." Should any Attorney fail to give prompt attention to correspondence, collections or business intrusted to his care, we will be thankful to patrons of the Directory to notify us promptly in any such case. Places designated thus (*) are County Seats.

POST-OFFICE.	COUNTY.	ATTORNEYS.	POPUL'N.
Alamo*	Crockett	Buchanan & Spence	500
Alexandria	De Kalb	W. B. Stokes	1500
Ashland*	Cheatham	S. D. Power	300
Athens*	McMinn	W. S. Henderson	1500
Bartlett	Shelby	W. F. Hamner	400
Bell's Depot	Crockett	See Alamo	700
Benton*	Polk	J. C. Williamson	400
Blountville*	Sullivan	See Bristol	500
Bolivar*	Hardeman	Wood & McNeal	1200
Bristol*	Sullivan	Charles R. Vance	2500
Brownsville*	Haywood	Bond & Rutledge	3000
Camden*	Benton	J. E. Jones	400
Carthage*	Smith	Turner & Fisher	500
Celina*	Clay	John H. McMillan	300
Centreville*	Hickman	O. A. Nixon	400
Charleston	Bradley	A. B. Porter	500
Charlotte*	Dickson	Hardin Leech	500
Chattanooga*	**Hamilton**	**H. M. Wiltse**	**25000**
Clarksville*	Montgomery	A. S. Major	5000
Cleveland*	Bradley	J. H. Gant	2700
Clinton*	Anderson	W. R. Hicks	500
Columbia*	Maury	E. H. Hatcher	5000
Cookville*	Putnam	Walton Smith	500
Covington*	Tipton	N. W. Baptist	1200
Crossville*	Cumberland	See Sparta	200
Dandridge*	Jefferson	Alexander Hynds	600
Decatur*	Meigs	V. C. Allen	200
Decaturville*	Decatur	J. M. Porterfield	300
Decherd	Franklin	See Winchester	1200
Dover*	Stewart	Nathan Brandon	500
Dresden*	Weakley	John McGlothlin	800
Dunlap*	Sequatchie	See Chattanooga	400
Dyersburg*	Dyer	S. R. Latta	1200
Edgefield	Davidson	See Nashville	6000
Elizabethton*	Carter	John C. Smith	600
Erin*	Houston	W. C. Shelton	800
Erwin*	Unicoi	See Jonesborough	200
Fayetteville*	Lincoln	J. H. Holman & Wright	2500
Franklin*	Williamson	Thomas & House	2000

Tennessee—Continued.

Parties corresponding with Attorneys named in the Directory should ALWAYS sign themselves "Subscribers to J. A. GRAFT & CO.'S LEGAL DIRECTORY." Should any Attorney fail to give prompt attention to correspondence, collections or business intrusted to his care, we will be thankful to patrons of the Directory to notify us promptly in any such case. Places designated thus (*) are County Seats.

POST-OFFICE.	COUNTY.	ATTORNEYS.	POPUL'N.
Gadsden	Crockett	See Alamo	800
Gainesborough*	Jackson	W. W. Draper	400
Gallatin*	Sumner	Wm. C. Dismukes	3000
Greeneville*	Greene	J. F. Hale	2500
Greenfield	Weakley	See Dresden	500
Hartsville*	Trousdale	A. F. Burnley	800
Helenwood	Scott	J. C. Parker	300
Humboldt	Gibson	See Trenton	2000
Huntingdon*	Carroll	Murray & Hawkins	1400
Huntsville*	Scott	See Helenwood	300
Jacksborough*	Campbell	John Jennings	400
Jackson*	Madison	Bullock & Anderson	7000
Jamestown*	Fentress	S. V. Bowden	100
Jasper*	Marion	Foster V. Brown	1000
Jenks	Roane	See Kingston	300
Johnson City	Washington	See Jonesborough	1000
Jonesborough*	Washington	A. J. Brown	1200
Kingston*	Roane	W. H. Dietz	1000
Knoxville*	**Knox**	**Ingersoll & Cocke**	**30000**
La Fayette*	Macon	M. N. Alexander	500
Lawrenceburg*	Lawrence	S. A. Carroll, Jr.	800
Lebanon*	Wilson	J. T. Lane	3000
Lewisburg*	Marshall	C. A. Armstrong	800
Lexington*	Henderson	John M. Taylor	500
Linden*	Perry	James K. Sloan	300
Livingston*	Overton	James W. Wright	400
Loudon*	Loudon	Henry A. Chambers	1200
Lynchburg*	Moore	W. D. L. Record	500
Madisonville*	Monroe	J. E. H. McCroskey	500
Manchester*	Coffee	P. C. Isbell	700
Martin	Weakley	See Dresden	1300
Maryville*	Blount	Will A. McTeer	2000
Maynardville*	Union	J. W. Branson	200
McMinnville*	Warren	Wm. T. Murray	200
Memphis*	**Shelby**	**Frazer & Boyle** No. 1 Madison street.	**65000**
Milan	Gibson	See Trenton	1800
Morristown*	Hamblen	J. T. Essary	2500
Mountain City*	Johnson	R. R. Butler	500
Murfreesborough*	Rutherford	P. P. Mason	4000
Nashville*	**Davidson**	**Eben T. Fleming** No. 64½ N. Cherry street.	**60000**
Newberg*	Lewis	J. M. Fain	200
Newport*	Cocke	McSween & Son	400

Tennessee—Continued.

Parties corresponding with Attorneys named in the Directory should ALWAYS sign themselves "Subscribers to J. A. GRAFT & CO.'S LEGAL DIRECTORY." Should any Attorney fail to give prompt attention to correspondence, collections or business intrusted to his care, we will be thankful to patrons of the Directory to notify us promptly in any such case. Places designated thus (*) are County Seats.

POST-OFFICE.	COUNTY.	ATTORNEYS.	POPUL'N.
Ooltewah*	James	See Chattanooga	400
Palmetto	Bedford	See Shelbyville	500
Paris*	Henry	F. M. Thompson	2000
Pikeville*	Bledsoe	R. B. Schoolfield	200
Pulaski*	Giles	Jones, Son & Ewing	2500
Purdy*	McNairy	D. Hiram Bain	400
Ripley*	Lauderdale	Thomas Steele	1000
Rockwood	Roane	See Kingston	1200
Rogersville*	Hawkins	Hugh S. Kyle	1000
Rutledge*	Grainger	J. N. Goldman	500
Savannah*	Hardin	Will J. Watson	1000
Sevierville*	Sevier	W. R. Turner	300
Sewanee	Franklin	See Winchester	1500
Sharon	Weakley	See Dresden	400
Shelbyville*	Bedford	Barclay M. Tillman	3000
Smithville*	De Kalb	R. E. Robinson	1000
Sneedville*	Hancock	William B. Davis	200
Somerville*	Fayette	H. C. Moorman	1000
Sparta*	White	T. J. Bradford	700
Spencer*	Van Buren	A. J. McElroy	300
Springfield*	Robertson	John W. Judd	2000
Sweet Water	Monroe	Frank P. Dickey	800
Taylorsville *	Johnson	R. R. Butler	400
Tazewell*	Claiborne	E. A. Hurst	500
Tiptonville*	Lake	See Dyersburg	1000
Tracy City	Grundy	J. K. P. Pearson	2000
Trenton*	Gibson	John R. Walker	2000
Troy*	Obion	Charles Wright, Jr.	400
Tullahoma	Coffee	J. G. Aydelott	1200
Union City	Obion	Felix W. Moore	4000
Wartburg*	Morgan	See Kingston	200
Wartrace	Bedford	See Shelbyville	500
Washington*	Rhea	See Kingston	300
Waverly*	Humphreys	Daniel B. Johnston	800
Waynesborough*	Wayne	J. F. Montague	400
Winchester*	Franklin	Estill & Whitaker	1200
Woodbury*	Cannon	J. H. Cummings	500

TEXAS.

Parties corresponding with Attorneys named in the Directory should ALWAYS sign themselves "Subscribers to J. A. GRAFT & CO.'S LEGAL DIRECTORY." Should any Attorney fail to give prompt attention to correspondence, collections or business intrusted to his care, we will be thankful to patrons of the Directory to notify us promptly in any such case. Places designated thus (*) are County Seats.

POST-OFFICE.	COUNTY.	ATTORNEYS.	POPUL'N.
Abilene	Taylor	Thomas M. Willis	5000
Albany*	Shackelford	William G. Webb	2000
Alvarado	Johnson	Andrew King	2000
Anderson*	Grimes	Alex. F. Brigance	500
Athens*	Henderson	M. E. Richardson	1000
		†*J. E. Grigsby.*	
Atlanta	Cass	W. O. Henderson	2000
Austin*	**Travis**	**Sheeks & Sheeks**	**20000**
Baird	Callahan	Otis Bowyer	900
Bandera*	Bandera	Hugh C. Duffy	500
Bastrop*	Bastrop	R. A. Brooks	1000
Beaumont*	Jefferson	O'Brien & Johns	4000
Beeville*	Bee	John C. Bleasley	600
Bellville*	Austin	M. M. Kenney	600
Belton*	Bell	D. L. Russell	5000
Ben Ficklin*	Tom Green	See San Angelo	500
Blanco*	Blanco	W. W. Burnett	400
Boerne*	Kendall	W. V. Henderson	500
Bonham*	Fannin	Charles D. Grace	4000
Boston*	Bowie	See Texarkana	500
Bowie	Montague	Kerr & Thomas	3000
Brackettville*	Kinney	J. F. Robinson	1200
Brady*	McCulloch	Walter Anderson	400
Brazoria*	Brazoria	W. Stephen Bittel	1100
Breckenridge*	Stephens	William Veale & Son	1000
Bremond	Robertson	See Franklin	1200
Brenham*	Washington	O. L. Eddins.	5000
Brownsville*	Cameron	Mason, Miller & Carr	6000
Brownwood*	Brown	R. P. Conner	1500
Bryan*	Brazos	J. D. Thomas	4000
Burkeville	Newton	See Newton	300
Burnet*	Burnet	A. R. Johnson	2000
Caldwell*	Burleson	Thomas R. Batte	1500
Calvert	Robertson	J. W. McNutt	3000
Cameron*	Milan	Hefley & Wallace	1500
Canton*	Van Zandt	T. R. Yantis	500
Carrizo*	Zapata	James Downing	400
Carthage*	Panola	Thomas E. Boren	400
Cason	Morris	See Daingerfield	400
Castroville*	Medina	See San Antonio	1000
Center*	Shelby	J. S. Stephenson	300

(† We withdraw our former recommendation.)

Texas—Continued.

Parties corresponding with Attorneys named in the Directory should ALWAYS sign themselves "Subscribers to J. A. GRAFT & CO.'S LEGAL DIRECTORY." Should any Attorney fail to give prompt attention to correspondence, collections or business intrusted to his care, we will be thankful to patrons of the Directory to notify us promptly in any such case.
Places designated thus (*) are County Seats.

POST-OFFICE.	COUNTY.	ATTORNEYS.	POPUL'N.
Centreville*	Leon	W. M. Johnston	300
Chapel Hill	Washington	See Brenham	800
Cisco	Eastland	J. E. Luse	800
Clarksville*	Red River	Taylor & Chambers	2500
Cleburne*	Johnson	W. J. Ewing	3500
Clinton*	De Witt	See Cuero	300
Cold Spring*	San Jacinto	Lea & McKellar	300
Coleman*	Coleman	J. O. Woodward	1000
Colorado*	Mitchell	Ball & Burney	6000
Columbia	Brazoria	See Brazoria	1000
Columbus*	Colorado	Logue & McCormick	3000
Comanche*	Comanche	E. L. Shropshire	1500
Cooper*	Delta	See Sulphur Springs	400
Corpus Christi*	Nueces	Welsh & Givens	4000
Corsicana*	Navarro	Harris & Lee	6500
Cresco	Palo Pinto	See Palo Pinto	400
Crockett*	Houston	Cooper & Son	1000
Cuero	De Witt	A. B. Davidson	2500
Daingerfield*	Morris	R. D. Hart	800
Dallas*	**Dallas**	**R. H. West** No. 513 Elm street.	**24000**
Decatur*	Wise	McGee & Gose	2500
Del Rio*	Val Verde	Hinde & Quickenstedt	2000
Denison	Grayson	Decker & Harris	11000
Denton*	Denton	G. W. Gann	2200
Dublin	Erath	See Stephenville	500
Eagle Pass*	Maverick	Winchester Kelso	2000
Eastland*	Eastland	J. H. Davenport	1000
Ednaville	Jackson		500
El Paso	El Paso	John Bailey	4000
Emory*	Rains	H. W. Martin	1000
Ennis	Ellis	See Waxahachie	2000
Fairfield*	Freestone	Bell & Bell	500
Flatonia	Fayette	F. A. Hess	1000
Floresville*	Wilson	B. F Ballard	500
Fort Concho	Tom Green	See San Angelo	800
Fort Davis*	Presidio	A. V. D. Old	1200
Fort Worth*	**Tarrant**	**Oliver S. Kennedy**	**23000**
Franklin*	Robertson	Thos. N. Graham	1000
Fredericksburg*	Gillespie	A. O. Cooley	1500
Frio Town*	Frio	See Pearsall	200
Gainesville*	Cooke	W. T. Roberts	7000

Texas—Continued.

Parties corresponding with Attorneys named in the Directory should ALWAYS sign themselves "Subscribers to J. A. GRAFT & CO.'S LEGAL DIRECTORY." Should any Attorney fail to give prompt attention to correspondence, collections or business intrusted to his care, we will be thankful to patrons of the Directory to notify us promptly in any such case.
Places designated thus (*) are County Seats.

POST-OFFICE.	COUNTY.	ATTORNEYS.	POPUL'N.
Galveston*	**Galveston**	**Mann & Baker**	**35000**
Gatesville*	Coryell	Vardiman & Atkinson	2000
Gavett	Morris	See Daingerfield	300
Georgetown*	Williamson	Makemson & Price	1800
Giddings*	Lee	John F. Crowe	1200
Gilmer*	Upshur	L. J. Camp, Jr.	600
Goliad*	Goliad	J. Payne	1500
Gonzales*	Gonzales	Wm. M. Atkinson	2000
Graham*	Young	C. W. Johnson	800
Granbury*	Hood	Cooper & Estes	800
Greenville*	Hunt	Upthegrove & Hefner.	1500
Groesbeck*	Limestone	See Mexia	600
Hallettsville*	Lavaca	Green & Green	800
Hamilton*	Hamilton	G. R. Freeman	400
Hardin*	Hardin	P. A. Work	200
Hearne	Robertson	John P. Burt	1600
Helena*	Karnes	Frank R. Graves	300
Hemphill*	Sabine	J. A. Whittlesey	300
Hempstead*	Waller	W. J. Pool	2000
Henderson*	Rusk	J. H. Jones	1800
Henrietta*	Clay	R. D. Melborne	2000
Hidalgo*	Hidalgo	J. C. Scott	500
Hillsboro*	Hill	J. M. Johnson	2500
Homer*	Angelina	James D. Gann	500
Honey Grove	Fannin	See Bonham	1000
Houston*	**Harris**	**Geo. Goldthwaite**	**30000**
Hubbard City*	Hill	See Hillsboro	1500
Huntsville*	Walker	McKinney & Leigh	2000
Indianola*	Calhoun	Celestin Villeneuve	800
Industry	Austin	See Bellville	800
Itasca	Hill	See Hillsboro	1000
Jacksboro*	Jack	Taylor & Somervell	1000
Jasper*	Jasper	H. C. Howell	500
Jefferson*	Marion	Todd & Eldridge	3200
Jewett	Leon	J. J. Dotson	600
Kaufman*	Kaufman	Grubbs & Morrow	600
Kerrville*	Kerr	Garrett & Walker	500
Kosse	Limestone	See Mexia	800
La Grange*	Fayette	Timmons & Brown	1800
Lampasas*	Lampasas	Alex. McFarland	4000
Laredo*	Webb	Pierce & Randell	6000

Texas—Continued.

Parties corresponding with Attorneys named in the Directory should ALWAYS sign themselves "Subscribers to J. A. GRAFT & CO.'S LEGAL DIRECTORY." Should any Attorney fail to give prompt attention to correspondence, collections or business intrusted to his care, we will be thankful to patrons of the Directory to notify us promptly in any such case. Places designated thus (*) are County Seats.

POST-OFFICE.	COUNTY.	ATTORNEYS.	POPUL'N.
Liberty*	Liberty	S. R. Perryman	600
Linden*	Cass	O'Neal & Son	500
Livingston*	Polk	James E. Hill	200
Llano*	Llano	James Flack	1000
Lockhart*	Caldwell		1000
Longview*	Gregg	McCord & Campbell	2000
Luling	Caldwell		2000
Madisonville*	Madison	J. F. Randolph	300
Marlin*	Falls	W. A. Patrick	1500
Marshall*	Harrison	Arthur H. Cooper	7000
Mason*	Mason	H. M. Holmes	800
Matagorda*	Matagorda	D. E. E. Braman	600
McGregor	McLennan	See Waco	300
McKinney*	Collin	John S. Jenkins	3500
Menardville*	Menard	See San Saba	100
Meridian*	Bosque	Herbert Fielder	500
Mexia	Limestone	Thomas J. Gibson	2000
Mineola	Wood	W. M. Giles	1800
Mobeetie*	Wheeler	**W. H. Grigsby** (See card in Appendix, page V.)	300
Montague*	Montague	W. J. Sparks	500
Montgomery*	Montgomery	J. E. McComb	600
Moody	McLennan	See Waco	200
Morgan	Bosque	See Waco	600
Mount Pleasant*	Titus	T. J. Colquitt	1200
Nacogdoches*	Nacogdoches	Tom R. Jennings	1500
Navasota	Grimes	See Anderson	1800
New Braunfels*	Comal	J. D. Quinn	2000
Newton*	Newton	George F. Poole	200
Oakville*	Live Oak	J. C. Cade	300
Orange*	Orange	Walter J. Wingate	2500
Overton	Rusk	C. C. Leverett	500
Palestine*	Anderson	Thos. B. Greenwood	3000
Palo Pinto*	Palo Pinto	C. W. Massie	500
Paris*	Lamar	B. F. Fuller	5000
Pearsall	Frio	H. Maney & Son	2200
Pecos	Reeves	See Fort Davis	300
Pennington*	Trinity	Robb & Stephenson	500
Pilot Point	Denton	See Denton	1000
Pittsburg*	Camp	Blocker & Conly	1500
Plano	Collin	See McKinney	800
Pleasanton*	Atascosa	See Pearsall	500

Texas—Continued.

Parties corresponding with Attorneys named in the Directory should ALWAYS sign themselves "Subscribers to J. A. GRAFT & CO.'S LEGAL DIRECTORY." Should any Attorney fail to give prompt attention to correspondence, collections or business intrusted to his care, we will be thankful to patrons of the Directory to notify us promptly in any such case. Places designated thus (*) are County Seats.

POST-OFFICE.	COUNTY.	ATTORNEYS.	POPUL'N.
Quitman*	Wood	A. J. Angle	500
Refugio*	Refugio	See Victoria	500
Richmond*	Fort Bend	Peareson & McCamly.	2000
Rio Grande City*	Starr	Horatio L. King	3500
Rockdale	Milam	See Cameron	1500
Rockport*	Aransas	George W. Fulton	600
Rockwall*	Rockwall	Wade & Goss	400
Round Rock	Williamson	See Taylor	1000
Runnels*	Runnels	G. W. Perryman	400
Rusk*	Cherokee	Guinn & Gregg	1000
San Angelo	Tom Green	Charles A. Dailey	2500
San Antonio*	**Bexar**	**Breneman & Bergström**	**30000**
San Augustine*	San Augustine	Rufus Price	700
San Diego*	Duval	J. Williamson Moses.	2200
San Marcos*	Hays	Fisher & Rose	1600
San Patricio*	San Patricio	P. H. O'Callaghan	400
San Saba*	San Saba	Yoe & Harris	1000
Schulenburg	Fayette	Neill L. McKinnon	1000
Seguin*	Guadalupe	W. E. Goodrich	2000
Seymour*	Baylor	Carter Taylor	1000
Sherman*	Grayson	Brown & Gunter	10000
Stephenville*	Erath	C. J. Shapard	1200
St. Mary's	Refugio	See Victoria	400
Strawn	Palo Pinto	See Palo Pinto	800
Sulphur Springs*	Hopkins		4000
Sweet Water*	Nolan	Cowan & Posey	1500
Taylor	Williamson	John Threadgill	1500
Temple	Bell	See Belton	700
Terrell	Kaufman	J. O. Terrell	2800
Texana*	Jackson	See Ednaville	200
Texarkana	Bowie	Todd & Hudgins	5000
Thornton	Limestone	See Mexia	500
Trinity	Trinity	Samuel T. Robb	200
Tyler*	Smith	George M. Johnson	7000
Uvalde*	Uvalde	Baker, Archer & Clark	1500
Vernon*	Wilbarger	Thompson & McGhee.	500
Victoria*	Victoria	Glass & Callender	2500
Waco*	**McLennan**	**Rogers & Harris** (See card in Appendix, page VI.)	**15000**

Texas—Continued.

Parties corresponding with Attorneys named in the Directory should ALWAYS sign themselves "Subscribers to J. A. GRAFT & CO.'S LEGAL DIRECTORY." Should any Attorney fail to give prompt attention to correspondence, collections or business intrusted to his care, we will be thankful to patrons of the Directory to notify us promptly in any such case.
Places designated thus (*) are County Seats.

POST-OFFICE.	COUNTY.	ATTORNEYS.	POPUL'N.
Wallisville*	Chambers		300
Waxahachie*	Ellis	Bascom McDaniel	3000
Weatherford*	Parker	J. M. Richards	4000
Weimar	Colorado	See Columbus	1000
Wharton*	Wharton	W. J. Croom	400
Whitney	Hill	See Hillsboro	800
Wichita Falls	Wichita	Robert E. Huff	500
Will's Point	Van Zandt	C. B. Kilgore	1000
Woodville*	Tyler	Stephen P. West	500
Ysleta*	El Paso	See El Paso	2500

UTAH TERRITORY.

POST-OFFICE.	COUNTY.	ATTORNEYS.	POPUL'N.
Beaver*	Beaver	John W. Christian	2500
Box Elder*	Box Elder	See Ogden City	2500
Corinne	Box Elder	See Ogden City	1000
Frisco	Beaver	R. S. Anderson	1000
Logan*	Cache	Hammond & Maughan	4000
Manti*	San Pete	William K. Reid	2000
Morgan*	Morgan	See Ogden City	800
Ogden City*	Weber	R. K. Williams	10000
Park City	Summit	See Salt Lake City	2000
Parowan*	Iron	John W. Brown	1500
Providence	Cache	See Logan	800
Provo City*	Utah	Sutherland & Son	4000
Randolph*	Rich	See Logan	400
Richfield*	Sevier	W. G. Baker	1500
Salt Lake City*	**Salt Lake**	**U. J. Wenner**	**30000**

Utah Territory—Continued.

Parties corresponding with Attorneys named in the Directory should ALWAYS sign themselves "Subscribers to J. A. GRAFT & CO.'S LEGAL DIRECTORY." Should any Attorney fail to give prompt attention to correspondence, collections or business intrusted to his care, we will be thankful to patrons of the Directory to notify us promptly in any such case.
Places designated thus (*) are County Seats.

POST-OFFICE.	COUNTY.	ATTORNEYS.	POPUL'N.
Spring City	San Pete	Jacob Johnson	1000
St. George*	Washington	See Parowan	1500
Tooele*	Tooele	H. S. Gowans	1200

VERMONT.

POST-OFFICE.	COUNTY.	ATTORNEYS.	POPUL'N.
Alburgh	Grand Isle	J. P. Ladd	1800
Bakersfield	Franklin	H. R. Start	1000
Barre	Washington	W. A. & O. B. Boyce	1200
Barton	Orleans	John L. Carr	1000
Bellows Falls	Windham	J. D. Bridgman	3000
Bennington*	Bennington	E. L. Sibley	4000
Bethel	Windsor	See Springfield	800
Bradford	Orange	John B. Peckett, Jr.	1600
Brandon	Rutland	Ormsbee & Briggs	3500
Brattleborough	Windham	Martin & Eddy	5000
Bristol	Addison	See Middlebury	1500
Burlington*	Chittenden	David J. Foster	13000
Cambridge	Lamoille	See Hyde Park	500
Castleton	Rutland	Bromley & Clark	1000
Chelsea*	Orange	C. S. Emery	1000
Chester	Windsor	Hugh Henry	1000
Danville	Caledonia	See St. Johnsbury	2200
Derby	Orleans	See Newport	2200
Eden	Lamoille	See Hyde Park	1200
Elmore	Lamoille	See Hyde Park	900
Essex Junction	Chittenden	See Burlington	1000
Fair Haven	Rutland	George M. Fuller	2500
Guildhall*	Essex	See St. Johnsbury	500
Hartford	Windsor	See Springfield	1500

Vermont—Continued.

Parties corresponding with Attorneys named in the Directory should ALWAYS sign themselves "Subscribers to J. A. GRAFT & CO.'S LEGAL DIRECTORY." Should any Attorney fail to give prompt attention to correspondence, collections or business intrusted to his care, we will be thankful to patrons of the Directory to notify us promptly in any such case. Places designated thus (*) are County Seats.

POST-OFFICE.	COUNTY.	ATTORNEYS.	POPUL'N.
Highgate	Franklin	See St. Albans	800
Hinesburg	Chittenden	See Burlington	1800
Hyde Park*	Lamoille	**Edward B. Sawyer** (See card in Appendix, page V.)	1800
Irasburg*	Orleans	L. H. Thompson	500
Island Pond	Essex	T. M. Mansur	800
Jamaica	Windham	E. L. Waterman	700
Johnson	Lamoille	See Hyde Park	800
Ludlow	Windsor	W. H. Walker	1800
Lyndon	Caledonia	Cahoon & Hoffman	1000
Manchester	Bennington	Miner & Fenn	1200
Middlebury*	Addison	Lyman E. Knapp	3000
Milton	Chittenden	See Burlington	2000
Montpelier*	Washington	T. J. Deavitt	3200
Morrisville	Lamoille	See Hyde Park	1200
Newfane*	Windham	See Brattleborough	400
Newport	Orleans	J. L. Edwards	1200
North Bennington	Bennington	See Bennington	800
Northfield	Washington	Frank Plumley	3000
North Hero*	Grand Isle	See St. Albans	800
Norwich	Windsor	See Springfield	1000
Proctorsville	Windsor	See Springfield	800
Richford	Franklin	E. H. Powell	1200
Royalton	Windsor	See Springfield	400
Rutland*	Rutland	Charles L. Howe	15000
Sheldon	Franklin	C. P. Hogan	1500
Springfield	Windsor	A. M. Allbe	2500
St. Albans*	Franklin	Wilson & Hall	7000
St. Johnsbury*	Caledonia	Belden & Ide	5000
Stowe	Lamoille	See Hyde Park	1600
Vergennes	Addison	George W. Grandey	2000
Wallingford	Rutland	See Rutland	1000
Waterbury	Washington	P. Dillingham & Son	1000
Waterville	Lamoille	See Hyde Park	800
Wells River	Orange	See Chelsea	800
West Randolph	Orange	See Chelsea	1200
Wilmington	Windham	O. E. Butterfield	800
Windsor	Windsor	Gilbert A. Davis	2200
Wolcott	Lamoille	See Hyde Park	1500
Woodstock*	Windsor	W. E. Johnson	1800

VIRGINIA.

Parties corresponding with Attorneys named in the Directory should ALWAYS sign themselves "Subscribers to J. A. GRAFT & CO.'S LEGAL DIRECTORY." Should any Attorney fail to give prompt attention to correspondence, collections or business intrusted to his care, we will be thankful to patrons of the Directory to notify us promptly in any such case. Places designated thus (*) are County Seats.

POST-OFFICE.	COUNTY.	ATTORNEYS.	POPUL'N.
Abbott	Craig	**John A. I. Lee** (See card in Appendix, page V.)	500
Abingdon*	Washington	See Bristol Tenn.	2000
Accomack C. H.*	Accomack	Gunter & Blackstone.	500
Alexandria*	Alexandria	Francis L. Smith	16000
Amelia C. H.*	Amelia	T. K. Weisiger	400
Amherst C. H.*	Amherst	Josiah R. Ellis	900
Appomattox C. H.*	Appomattox	See Pamplin City	200
Ashland	Hanover	W. J. Leake	1000
Aylett's	King William	W. R. Aylett	200
Berryville*	Clarke	McDonald & Moore	1500
Blacks and Whites	Nottoway	G. S. Wing	200
Blacksburgh	Montgomery	Charles H. Miller	1000
Bland C. H.*	Bland	See Wytheville	300
Bowling Green*	Caroline	J. M. Hudgin	500
Boydton*	Mecklenburgh	Finch & Atkins	1500
Brentsville*	Prince William	C. E. Nicol	300
Bridgewater	Rockingham	See Harrisonburgh	500
Buckingham C. H.*	Buckingham	William M. Cabell	700
Charles City C. H.*	Charles City	Isaac H. Christian	300
Charlottesville*	Albemarle	Micajah Woods	5000
Chatham*	Pittsylvania		1000
Christiansburgh*	Montgomery	James C. Taylor	1000
Clarksville	Mecklenburgh	Wood & Wood	800
Covington*	Alleghany	Robert L. Parrish	600
Culpeper *	Culpeper	Hill & Jeffries	1700
Cumberland C. H.*	Cumberland	William Lancaster	200
Danville	Pittsylvania	Thomas Hamlin	10000
Dinwiddie C. H.*	Dinwiddie	See Petersburgh	200
Eastville*	Northampton	E. J. Spady	300
Estillville*	Scott	A. C. D. Manes	300
Fairfax C. H.*	Fairfax	D. M. Chichester	500
Farmville*	Prince Edward	J. M. Crute	2300
Fincastle*	Botetourt	J. H. H. Figgat	800
Floyd C. H.*	Floyd	B. S. Pedigo	400
Franklin	Southampton	See Jerusalem	700
Fredericksburgh	Spottsylvania	Marye & Fitzhugh	5000
Front Royal*	Warren	H. H. Downing	1200
Gloucester C. H.*	Gloucester	B. F. Bland	100
Goochland C. H.*	Goochland	W. D. Leake	200

Virginia—Continued.

Parties corresponding with Attorneys named in the Directory should ALWAYS sign themselves "Subscribers to J. A. GRAFT & CO.'S LEGAL DIRECTORY." Should any Attorney fail to give prompt attention to correspondence, collections or business intrusted to his care, we will be thankful to patrons of the Directory to notify us promptly in any such case.
Places designated thus (*) are County Seats.

POST-OFFICE.	COUNTY.	ATTORNEYS.	POPUL'N.
Gordonsville	Orange	P. P. Barbour	1200
Grundy*	Buchanan	Alex. Beavers	200
Halifax C. H.*	Halifax	N. T. Green	400
Hampton*	Elizabeth City	Thomas Tabb	2600
Hanover C. H.*	Hanover	See Ashland	200
Harrisonburgh*	Rockingham	Charles D. Harrison	3000
Heathsville*	Northumberland	Lloyd T. Smith	500
Hicksford*	Greenville	Reese & Tredway	500
Hillsville*	Carroll	Norman Hale	500
Independence*	Grayson	A. M. Davis	500
Isle of Wight C. H.*	Isle of Wight	See Smithfield	200
Jerusalem*	Southampton	Wm. J. Sebrell	200
Jonesville*	Lee	Richmond & Orr	500
King George C. H.*	King George	J. J. Mason	100
King William C.H.*	King William	See Aylett's	100
Lancaster C. H.*	Lancaster	W. W. Walker	100
Lawrenceville*	Brunswick	R. Turnbull	250
Lebanon*	Russell	Henry A. Routh	300
Leesburgh*	Loudoun	J. B. McCabe	2000
Lexington*	Rockbridge	S. H. Letcher	3000
Liberty*	Bedford	Burks & Burks	2500
Little Plymouth	King and Queen	...	200
Louisa C. H.*	Louisa	W. E. Bibb	500
Lovingston*	Nelson	R. H. Cabell	1700
Lunenburgh C. H.*	Lunenburgh	John Jackson	200
Luray*	Page	**Walton & Bro.** (See card in Appendix, page VI.)	1200
Lynchburgh	**Campbell**	**James E. Edmunds**	**27000**
Madison C. H.*	Madison	F. H. Hill	800
Manchester	Chesterfield	Charles Page	6000
Marion*	Smyth	G. W. Richardson	1200
Martinsville*	Henry	S. A. Anderson	400
Matthews*	Matthews	John B. Donovan	400
Monterey*	Highland	Charles P. Jones	200
Montrose*	Westmoreland	Charles C. Baker	300
Mount Jackson	Shenandoah	L. Triplett, Jr.	700
Newbern*	Pulaski	J. B. Baskerville	400
New Castle*	Craig	John A. I. Lee	300

Virginia—Continued.

Parties corresponding with Attorneys named in the Directory should ALWAYS sign themselves "Subscribers to J. A. GRAFT & CO.'S LEGAL DIRECTORY." Should any Attorney fail to give prompt attention to correspondence, collections or business intrusted to his care, we will be thankful to patrons of the Directory to notify us promptly in any such case. Places designated thus (*) are County Seats.

POST-OFFICE.	COUNTY.	ATTORNEYS.	POPUL'N.
New Kent C. H.*	New Kent	See Richmond	100
New Market	Shenandoah	See Woodstock	800
Norfolk*	**Norfolk**	**Whitehurst & Hughes.**	**30000**
Nottoway C. H.*	Nottoway	W. H. Mann	200
Orange C. H.*	Orange	T. P. Wallace	700
Palmyra*	Fluvanna	W. B. Pettit	200
Pamplin City	Appomattox	W. C. Franklin	200
Pearisburgh*	Giles	T. L. Henritze	500
Petersburgh	**Dinwiddie**	**R. T. Wilson**	**23000**
Pittsylvania	Pittsylvania	B. B. Munford	1000
Portsmouth	Norfolk	V. O. Cassell & Son	17000
Powhatan C. H.*	Powhatan	Willis J. Dance	200
Prince George C. H.*	Prince George	See Petersburgh	200
Princess Anne C. H.*	Princess Anne	See Norfolk	300
Richmond*	**Henrico**	**John Hunter, Jr.**	**75000**
Roanoke	Roanoke	R. H. Woodrum	5000
Rocky Mount*	Franklin	George E. Dennis	400
Salem*	Roanoke	L. C. Hansbrough	2000
Saluda*	Middlesex	Robert McCandlish	200
Scottsville	Albermarle	F. C. Moon	800
Smithfield	Isle of Wight	G. R. Atkinson	1000
Smithville*	Charlotte	M. M. Martin	350
South Boston	Halifax	See Halifax C. H	500
Spottsylvania C. H.*	Spottsylvania	See Fredericksburg	200
Stafford C. H.*	Stafford	See Fredericksburg	100
Standardsville*	Greene	Henry Mayes	500
Staunton*	Augusta	Craig & Paul	10000
Stuart*	Patrick	P. Bouldin, Jr	200
Suffolk*	Nansemond	Wilber J. Kilby	2500
Surry C. H.*	Surry	See Smithfield	200
Sussex C. H.*	Sussex	R. T. Wilson	100
Tappahannock*	Essex	T. R. B. Wright	800
Tazewell C. H.*	Tazewell	A. J. & S. D. May	800
Warm Springs*	Bath	R. L. Parrish	400
Warrenton*	Fauquier	Grenville Gaines	1800
Warsaw*	Richmond	John D. Garland	200
Warwick C. H.*	Warwick	M. D. Wright	2000

Virginia—Continued.

Parties corresponding with Attorneys named in the Directory should ALWAYS sign themselves "Subscribers to J. A. GRAFT & CO.'S LEGAL DIRECTORY." Should any Attorney fail to give prompt attention to correspondence, collections or business intrusted to his care, we will be thankful to patrons of the Directory to notify us promptly in any such case.
Places designated thus (*) are County Seats.

POST-OFFICE.	COUNTY.	ATTORNEYS.	POPUL'N.
Washington*	Rappahannock	See Luray	300
West Point	King William	Thomas P. Bagby	900
Williamsburgh*	James City	B. D. Peachey	1500
Winchester*	Frederick	W. Roy Stephenson	5000
Windsor Station	Isle of Wight	See Smithfield †*W. S. Holland.*	400
Wise C. H.*	Wise	E. M. Fulton	300
Woodstock*	Shenandoah	Walton & Walton	1000
Wytheville*	Wythe	William L. Yost	3000
Yorktown*	York	See Warwick C. H.	400

WASHINGTON TERRITORY.

POST-OFFICE.	COUNTY.	ATTORNEYS.	POPUL'N.
Cascades*	Skamania	See Vancouver	200
Cathlamet*	Wahkiakum	See Astoria, Oregon	300
Chehalis	Lewis	See Olympia	500
Cheney	Spokane	M. G. Barney	1500
Colfax*	Whitman	Jacob Hoover	500
Colville	Stevens	Samuel Douglas	500
Dayton*	Columbia	J. K. Rutherford	1500
Ellensburgh	Kittitass	See Yakima	200
Friday Harbor*	San Juan	See Port Townsend	200
Goldendale*	Klikitat	Hiram Dustin	800
Montesano*	Chehalis	See Olympia	500
Oakland*	Mason	See Olympia	200
Olympia*	Thurston	M. A. Root	3000
Pomeroy*	Garfield	S. G. Cosgrove	600
Port Madison*	Kitsap	See Seattle	300
Port Townsend*	Jefferson	D. W. Smith	2000
Seattle*	King	Howard H. Lewis	10000
Snohomish*	Snohomish	S. H. Piles	400

(†We withdraw our former recommendation.)

Washington Territory—Continued.

Parties corresponding with Attorneys named in the Directory should ALWAYS sign themselves "Subscribers to J. A. GRAFT & CO.'S LEGAL DIRECTORY." Should any Attorney fail to give prompt attention to correspondence, collections or business intrusted to his care, we will be thankful to patrons of the Directory to notify us promptly in any such case. Places designated thus (*) are County Seats.

POST-OFFICE.	COUNTY.	ATTORNEYS.	POPUL'N.
Spokane Falls*	Spokane	Strobach & Munter	2800
Sprague	Lincoln		1000
Steilacoom City	Pierce	See Tacoma	300
Tacoma*	Pierce	Harry H. Sharp	7000
Vancouver*	Clarke	A. O. Marsh	2000
Walla Walla*	Walla Walla	T. J. Anders	4000
Whatcom*	Whatcom	W. H. Harris	1500
Yakima*	Yakima	J. B. Beavis	300

WEST VIRGINIA.

POST-OFFICE.	COUNTY.	ATTORNEYS.	POPUL'N.
Barboursville*	Cabell	See Huntington	500
Berkeley Springs*	Morgan	J. Rufus Smith	800
Beverly*	Randolph	Edward T. Jones	500
Braxton C. H.*	Braxton	E. S. Bland	400
Buckhannon*	Upshur	A. M. Poundstone	1200
Ceredo	Wayne	Taylor Vinson	600
Charleston*	Kanawha	W. S. Laidley	7500
Charlestown*	Jefferson	Lucas & Bedinger	2300
Clarksburgh*	Harrison	John Bassel	1800
Clay C. H.*	Clay	James A. Frame	200
Elizabeth*	Wirt	William Beard	500
Fairmont*	Marion	Howard N. Ogden	1500
Fairview*	Hancock	J. G. Marshall	600
Fayetteville*	Fayette	M. Van Pelt	300
Fort Gay	Wayne	See Ceredo	200
Franklin*	Pendleton	George A. Blackmore	400
Glenville*	Gilmer	Kidd & Hays	400
Grafton*	Taylor	See Fairmont	4000

West Virginia—Continued.

Parties corresponding with Attorneys named in the Directory should ALWAYS sign themselves "Subscribers to J. A. GRAFT & CO.'S LEGAL DIRECTORY." Should any Attorney fail to give prompt attention to correspondence, collections or business intrusted to his care, we will be thankful to patrons of the Directory to notify us promptly in any such case.
Places designated thus (*) are County Seats.

POST-OFFICE.	COUNTY.	ATTORNEYS.	POPUL'N.
Grantsville*	Calhoun	Linn & Hamilton	200
Guyandotte	Cabell	See Huntington	1200
Hamlin*	Lincoln	C. W. Campbell	300
Harper's Ferry	Jefferson	James D. Butt	1000
Hinton*	Summers	Adams & Miller	2500
Huntersville*	Pocahontas	H. S. Rucker	300
Huntington	Cabell	Thomas L. Michie	7000
Jackson C. H.*	Jackson	Warren Miller	800
Keyser*	Mineral	George E. Price	2000
Kingwood*	Preston	Robert W. Monroe	400
Lewisburg*	Greenbrier	Arbuckle & McPherson	1200
Logan C. H.*	Logan	J. S. Miller	200
Madison*	Boone	See Logan C. H.	100
Mannington	Marion	See Fairmont	1000
Martinsburgh*	Berkeley	Faulkner & Ingles	6500
Middlebourne*	Tyler	G. D. Smith	400
Moorefield*	Hardy	H. S. Carr	800
Morgantown*	Monongalia	See Fairmont	1200
Moundsville*	Marshall	D. B. Evans	2000
New Martinsville*	Wetzel	George H. Umstead	1700
Nicholas C. H.*	Nicholas	J. D. Alderson	200
Oceana*	Wyoming	See Logan C. H.	400
Parkersburgh*	Wood	R. Heber Smith	10000
Peeryville*	McDowell	W. P. Payne	200
Petersburgh*	Grant	Dyer & Pugh	400
Philippi*	Barbour	D. W. Gall	500
Piedmont	Mineral	See Keyser	2000
Point Pleasant*	Mason	**James B. Menager** (See card in Appendix, page VI.)	1200
Princeton*	Mercer	A. W. Reynolds	600
Pruntytown	Taylor	See Grafton	500
Raleigh C. H.*	Raleigh	J. W. McCreery	300
Ravenswood	Jackson	N. C. Prickett	800
Ritchie C. H.*	Ritchie	H. C. Showalter	400
Romney*	Hampshire	Robt. W. Dailey, Jr.	600

West Virginia—Continued.

Parties corresponding with Attorneys named in the Directory should ALWAYS sign themselves "Subscribers to J. A. GRAFT & CO.'S LEGAL DIRECTORY." Should any attorney fail to give prompt attention to correspondence, collections or business intrusted to his care, we will be thankful to patrons of the Directory to notify us promptly in any such case. Places designated thus (*) are County Seats.

POST-OFFICE.	COUNTY.	ATTORNEYS.	POPUL'N.
Shepherdstown	Jefferson	G. M. Beltzhoover	1600
Sistersville	Tyler	John H. McCoy	600
Spencer*	Roane	Pendleton & Green	500
St. George*	Tucker	W. B. Maxwell	300
St. Mary's*	Pleasants	J. L. Richardson	400
Union*	Monroe	Hereford & Hereford.	700
Wayne C. H.*	Wayne	See Ceredo	200
Webster C. H.*	Webster	J. A. Thompson	200
Wellsburgh*	Brooke	J. B. Somerville	2000
Weston*	Lewis	George C. Cole	1500
West Union*	Doddridge	C. J. Stewart	500
Wheeling*	**Ohio**	**Robt. White**	**33000**
Winfield*	Putnam	J. T. Boyer	400

WISCONSIN.

POST-OFFICE.	COUNTY.	ATTORNEYS.	POPUL'N.
Ahnapee	Kewaunee	J. R. McDonald	1200
Alma*	Buffalo	Robert Lees	1500
Antigo*	Langlade	Latta & Trever	2500
Appleton*	Outagamie	Samuel Baird	10000
Arcadia	Trempealeau	Higbee & Comstock	900
Arena	Iowa	See Dodgeville	500
Ashland*	Ashland	Tomkins & Merrill	3000
Augusta	Eau Claire	See Eau Claire	1300
Baldwin	St. Croix	Henry Anderson	900
Baraboo*	Sauk	J. P. Wilson	4500
Barron*	Barron	See Rice Lake	500
Bayfield*	Bayfield	A. M. Warden	1200
Beaver Dam	Dodge	Lander & Lander	4000
Beloit	Rock	J. B. Dow	6000
Berlin	Green Lake	M. L. Kimball	4000
Black River Falls*	Jackson	C. M. Olson	1800
Bloomer	Chippewa	C. D. Tillinghast	700

Wisconsin—Continued.

Parties corresponding with Attorneys named in the Directory should ALWAYS sign themselves "Subscribers to J. A. GRAFT & CO.'S LEGAL DIRECTORY."
Should any Attorney fail to give prompt attention to correspondence, collections or business intrusted to his care, we will be thankful to patrons of the Directory to notify us promptly in any such case.
Places designated thus (*) are County Seats.

POST-OFFICE.	COUNTY.	ATTORNEYS.	POPUL'N.
Bloomington	Grant	See Lancaster	600
Boscobel	Grant	Wilson & Provis	1800
Brodhead	Green	See Monroe	1600
Burlington	Racine	Merton & Kearney	1800
Cambria	Columbia	See Portage	800
Chilton*	Calumet	John E. McMullen	1500
Chippewa Falls*	Chippewa	R. Sleight	7000
Clinton	Rock	See Beloit	1200
Clintonville	Waupaca	F. M. Guernsey	1500
Colby	Clark	R. B. Salter	500
Columbus	Columbia	A. G. Cook	2000
Cumberland	Barron	See Rice Lake	500
Darlington*	La Fayette	Marshall & Conly	1800
Dartford*	Green Lake	A. E. Dunlap	500
Delavan	Walworth	A. S. Spooner	2000
De Pere	Brown	See Green Bay	2200
Dodgeville*	Iowa	Aldro Jenks	2000
Dorchester	Clark	See Colby	400
Durand*	Pepin	H. E. Houghton	1000
Eau Claire*	**Eau Claire**	**Doolittle, Gunnison & Doolittle**	**20000**
Edgerton	Rock	See Janesville	1000
Elkhorn*	Walworth	J. B. Wheeler	1400
Ellsworth*	Pierce	J. W. Hancock	1000
Elroy	Juneau	B. C. Smith	1200
Evansville	Rock	See Janesville	1200
Fair Play	Grant	See Boscobel	700
Fennimore	Grant	See Boscobel	500
Fifield	Price	See Phillips	400
Florence*	Florence	W. H. Clark, Jr.	500
Fond du Lac*	**Fond du Lac**	**C. S. Matteson**	**13000**
Fort Atkinson	Jefferson	Rogers & Craig	2500
Fort Howard	Brown	See Green Bay	3500
Fountain City	Buffalo	August Finkelnburg	1200
Fox Lake	Dodge	W. N. Hamilton	2000
Friendship*	Adams	S. W. Pierce	600
Galesville*	Trempealeau	E. W. Freeman	700
Grand Rapids*	Wood	George L. Williams	3000
Grantsburg*	Burnett	E. M. Wilson	200
Green Bay*	Brown	Warren J. Lander	9000

Wisconsin—Continued.

Parties corresponding with Attorneys named in the Directory should ALWAYS sign themselves "Subscribers to J. A. GRAFT & CO.'S LEGAL DIRECTORY." Should any Attorney fail to give prompt attention to correspondence, collections or business intrusted to his care, we will be thankful to patrons of the Directory to notify us promptly in any such case.
Places designated thus (*) are County Seats.

POST-OFFICE.	COUNTY.	ATTORNEYS.	POPUL'N.
Hammond	St. Croix	See Hudson	500
Hartford	Washington	See West Bend	1500
Hayward*	Sawyer	See Shell Lake	400
Horicon	Dodge	J. B. Hays	1500
Hudson*	St. Croix	McDonald & Smith	3000
Janesville*	Rock	J. B. Doe, Jr. †*A. Hyatt Smith.*	12000
Jefferson*	Jefferson	W. H. Porter.	2200
Juda	Green	See Monroe	400
Juneau*	Dodge	E. C. Lewis	600
Kaukauna	Outagamie	G. H. Dawson	1000
Kenosha*	Kenosha	James Cavanaugh	5500
Kewaunee*	Kewaunee	Sedgwick & Biron	1500
Kilbourn City	Columbia	See Portage	1200
Kingston	Green Lake	W. M. Chapel	600
La Crosse*	**La Crosse**	**J. H. Alex. Ginder**	**20000**
Lake Geneva	Walworth	See Elkhorn	2000
Lake Mills	Jefferson	See Jefferson	1000
Lancaster*	Grant	Bushnell & Watkins.	1500
Linden	Iowa	See Dodgeville	800
Madison*	**Dane**	**Edward P. Vilas**	**13000**
Manitowoc*	Manitowoc	G. G. Sedgwick	8000
Marinette*	Marinette	Edmund C. Lane	8500
Marshfield	Wood	Frank A. Cady	2000
Mauston*	Juneau	Windsor & Veeder	1500
Mazo Manie	Dane	See Madison	1500
Medford*	Taylor	Adams & Schweppe	2000
Menasha	Winnebago	P. V. Lawson, Jr.	3600
Menomonee*	Dunn	George Shafer	4200
Merrill*	Lincoln	Almon A. Helms	4000
Merrillon	Jackson	See Black River Falls	1300
Milton	Rock	See Janesville	800
Milton Junction	Rock	See Janesville	600
Milwaukee*	**Milwaukee**	**Adolf Herdegen** Manager Branch Office, No. 102 Wisconsin st.	**150000**
Mineral Point	Iowa	J. M. Smith	3300
Monroe*	Green	Colin W. Wright	4000
Montello*	Marquette	S. A. Pease	800

(† We withdraw our former recommendation.)

Wisconsin—Continued.

Parties corresponding with Attorneys named in the Directory should ALWAYS sign themselves "Subscribers to J. A. GRAFT & CO.'S LEGAL DIRECTORY." Should any Attorney fail to give prompt attention to correspondence, collections or business intrusted to his care, we will be thankful to patrons of the Directory to notify us promptly in any such case. Places designated thus (*) are County Seats.

POST-OFFICE.	COUNTY.	ATTORNEYS.	POPUL'N
Montfort	Grant	See Lancaster	600
Mosinee	Marathon	See Wausau	500
Necedah	Juneau	See New Lisbon	1800
Neenah	Winnebago	George W. Todd	4500
Neillsville*	Clark	R. F. Kountz	3000
New Lisbon	Juneau	J. J. Hughes	1300
New London	Waupaca	L. S. Porter	2500
New Richmond	St. Croix	Harry H. Smith	1200
Oconomowoc	Waukesha	Hurlbut & Robinson	2500
Oconto*	Oconto	H. H. Woodmansee	4800
Omro	Winnebago	See Oshkosh	1800
Osceola Mills*	Polk	Jermain Post	800
Oshkosh*	**Winnebago**	**H. I. Weed** † *W. H. Casey.*	**23000**
Peshtigo	Marinette	See Marinette	3000
Phillips*	Price	Willis Hand	500
Plainfield	Waushara	Thomas H. Walker	500
Platteville	Grant	Carter & Cleary	3000
Plymouth	Sheboygan	M. C. Mead	1300
Portage*	Columbia	James B. Taylor	5000
Port Washington*	Ozaukee	See Milwaukee	1600
Prairie du Chien*	Crawford	Thomas & Fuller	3200
Prescott	Pierce	J. S. White	1200
Racine*	**Racine**	**A. Cary Judd**	**25000**
Reedsburg	Sauk	Lusk & Perry	1800
Rice Lake	Barron	Fred. B. Kinsley	1400
Richland Centre*	Richland	Miner & Berryman	1800
Ripon	Fond du Lac	H. E. Giese	3600
River Falls	Pierce	See Hudson	1800
Sauk City	Sauk	J. S. Tripp	1200
Sharon	Walworth	See Elkhorn	1000
Shawano*	Shawano	Joseph Maurer	1100
Sheboygan*	Sheboygan	Seaman & Williams	8000
Sheboygan Falls	Sheboygan	J. H. James	1500
Shell Lake*	Washburn	L. H. Mead	1200
Shullsburg	La Fayette	P. B. Sampson	1800
Sparta*	Monroe	Tyler & Dickinson	3000
Spencer	Marathon	See Colby	800
Stevens' Point*	Portage	B. B. Park & Bro	7500
Stoughton	Dane	See Madison	1500
Sturgeon Bay*	Door	L. M. Sherman	1900

(† We withdraw our former recommendation.)

Wisconsin—Continued.

Parties corresponding with Attorneys named in the Directory should ALWAYS sign themselves "Subscribers to J. A. GRAFT & CO.'S LEGAL DIRECTORY." Should any Attorney fail to give prompt attention to correspondence, collections or business intrusted to his care, we will be thankful to patrons of the Directory to notify us promptly in any such case. Places designated thus (*) are County Seats.

POST-OFFICE.	COUNTY.	ATTORNEYS.	POPUL'N.
Superior*	Douglas	Champ Green	3000
Tomah	Monroe	George Graham	1500
Trempealeau	Trempealeau	J. C. Button	1000
Unity	Clark	See Colby	400
Viroqua*	Vernon	H. C. Forsyth	1000
Watertown	Jefferson	F. B Tuttle	8000
Waukesha*	Waukesha	M. S. Griswold	3500
Waupaca*	Waupaca	Charles Churchill	2500
Waupun	Fond du Lac	J. A. Kelley	2500
Wausau*	Marathon	Silverthorn, Hurley & Ryan	9000
Wautoma*	Waushara	R. L. D. Potter	800
West Bend*	Washington	Miller, Pors & Pors	1500
Weyauwega	Waupaca	See Waupaca	1000
Whitehall*	Trempealeau	S. S. Miller	1000
White Water	Walworth	James G. Kestol	4500
Winneconne	Winnebago	See Oshkosh	1200
Wonewoc	Juneau	Andrew Carter	1000

WYOMING TERRITORY.

POST-OFFICE.	COUNTY.	ATTORNEYS.	POPUL'N.
Buffalo*	Johnson	Charles H. Burritt	800
Carbon	Carbon	See Rawlins	1500
Cheyenne*	Laramie	C. N. Potter	7500
Evanston*	Uintah	C. M. White	1700
Fort Fred Steele	Carbon	See Rawlins	400
Green River City*	Sweetwater	A. B. Conaway	500
Lander	Sweetwater	See Green River City	300
Laramie City*	Albany	J. P. Caldwell	3000
Rawlins*	Carbon	Z. T. Brown	1500
South Pass City	Sweetwater	See Green River City	200

CANADA.

Parties corresponding with Attorneys named in the Directory should ALWAYS sign themselves "Subscribers to J. A. GRAFT & CO.'S LEGAL DIRECTORY." Should any Attorney fail to give prompt attention to correspondence, collections or business intrusted to his care, we will be thankful to patrons of the Directory to notify us promptly in any such case.

Manitoba.

POST-OFFICE.	COUNTY	ATTORNEYS.	POPUL'N.
Winnepeg	**Selkirk**	**Daniel Carey**	**25000**

New Brunswick.

POST-OFFICE.	COUNTY.	ATTORNEYS.	POPUL'N.
Chatham	Northumberland	See New Castle	4000
Fredricton	York	Wetmore & Winslow	7000
Moncton	Westmoreland	See Sackville	5000
New Castle	Northumberland	M. Adams	4000
Sackville	Westmoreland	Thos. A. Kinnear	5000
St. Andrews	Charlotte	Benj. R. Stevenson	3000
St. John	**St. John**	**Seely & McMillan**	**27000**
St. Stephen	Charlotte	See St. Andrews	3000
Woodstock	Carleton	Fisher & Connell	3000

Newfoundland.

POST-OFFICE.	COUNTY.	ATTORNEYS.	POPUL'N.
St. John's	**St. John's**	**John H. Boone**	**22000**

Nova Scotia.

Parties corresponding with Attorneys named in the Directory should ALWAYS sign themselves "Subscribers to J. A. GRAFT & CO.'S LEGAL DIRECTORY." Should any Attorney fail to give prompt attention to correspondence, collections or business intrusted to his care, we will be thankful to patrons of the Directory to notify us promptly in any such case.

POST-OFFICE.	COUNTY.	ATTORNEYS.	POPUL'N.
Amherst	Cumberland	Townsend & Dickey	3000
Annapolis	Annapolis	J. M. Owen	1500
Antigonish	Antigonish	McIsaac, Macgilloray & Chisholm	1000
Bridgewater	Lunenburg	W. H. Owen	1000
Digby	Digby	T. C. Shreve, Q. C.	1500
Guysborough	Guysborough	See New Glasgow	2000
Halifax	**Halifax**	**J. N. & T. Ritchie**	**36000**
Liverpool	Queens	J. N. S. Marshall	3000
New Glasgow	Pictou	J. H. Sinclair	3000
North Sidney	Cape Breton	See Pictou	1500
Pictou	Pictou	G. H. Elliott	3500
Shelburne	Shelburne	White & Blanchard	2200
Truro	Colchester	Geo. Campbell	2500
Windsor	Hants	W. M. Christie	3000
Yarmouth	Yarmouth	Pelton & Clements	6000

Ontario.

POST-OFFICE.	COUNTY.	ATTORNEYS.	POPUL'N.
Alexandria	Glengary	E. H. Tiffany	1000
Alliston	Simcoe	T. W. Howard	1000
Almonte	Lanark	Macdonald & Dowdall	2800
Amherstburg	Essex	See Windsor	2000
Arnprior	Renfrew	Richard Dulmage	2200
Ayr	Waterloo	See Galt	1400
Barrie	Simcoe	Lount & Lount	5000
Belleville	Hastings	E. Guss Porter	12000
Berlin	Waterloo	Miller & Betzer	4000

Ontario—Continued.

Parties corresponding with Attorneys named in the Directory should ALWAYS sign themselves "Subscribers to J. A. GRAFT & CO.'S LEGAL DIRECTORY." Should any Attorney fail to give prompt attention to correspondence, collections or business intrusted to his care, we will be thankful to patrons of the Directory to notify us promptly in any such case.

POST-OFFICE.	COUNTY.	ATTORNEYS.	POPUL'N
Bowmanville	Durham	J. K. Gilbraith	3500
Bracebridge	Muskoka	See Barrie	2200
Brampton	Peel	Morphy & Fleming	3000
Brantford	Brant	Wilson & Smyth	10000
Brighton	Northumberland	See Cobourg	2000
Brockville	Leeds	Fraser & Reynolds	8000
Cannington	North Ontario	C. C. Keller	1000
Cayuga	Haldimand	Henderson & Snider.	1000
Chatham	Kent	Robinson, Wilson, Rankin & Bell	10000
Cobourg	Northumberland	W. R. Riddell	6000
Collingwood	Simcoe	Moberly & Gamon	5000
Cornwall	Stormont	Maclennan & Liddell.	6000
Deseronto	Hastings	See Napanee	2000
Dresden	Kent	See Chatham	2000
Essex Center	Essex	See Windsor	500
Galt	Waterloo	Ball & Ball	6000
Goderich	Huron	Seager & Lewis	4500
Guelph	Wellington	Clarke & Canniff	10000
Hamilton	**Wentworth**	**Carscallen & Cahill**	**40000**
Ingersoll	Oxford	J. F. McDonald	4500
Kincardine	Bruce	W. C. Loscombe	3000
Kingston	Frontenac	E. H. Smythe	15000
Lindsay	Victoria	John A. Barron	5000
Listowell	Perth	See Stratford	2600
London	**Middlesex**	**John Taylor**	**30000**
L Original	Prescott	John Butterfield	1000
Milton	Halton	D. McGibbon	1500
Morrisburg	Dundas	F. Tyrrell	2000
Mount Forest	Wellington	M. O. Macgregor	2500
Napanee	Lennox	D. H. Preston	3600
Oakville	Halton	See Milton	1700
Oshawa	Ontario	McGee & Jones	1000

Ontario—Continued.

Parties corresponding with Attorneys named in the Directory should ALWAYS sign themselves "Subscribers to J. A. GRAFT & CO.'S LEGAL DIRECTORY." Should any Attorney fail to give prompt attention to correspondence, collections or business intrusted to his care, we will be thankful to patrons of the Directory to notify us promptly in any such case.

POST-OFFICE.	COUNTY.	ATTORNEYS.	POPUL'N.
Ottawa	**Carleton**	**George McLaurin** No. 19 Elgin street. (See card in Appendix, page VI.)	**30000**
Owen Sound	Grey	W. R. Armstrong	4700
Pembroke	Renfrew	Deacon & Deacon	3000
Perth	Lanark	F. A. Hall	3000
Peterborough	Peterborough	W. A. Stratton	7000
Picton	Prince Edward	Geo. O. Alcorn	4000
Port Hope	Durham	H. A. Ward	5500
Prescott	Grenville	F. J. French	3000
Sandwich	Essex	See Windsor	1200
Simcoe	Norfolk	G. Bruce Jackson	2700
St. Catharines	Lincoln	Albert G. Brown	10000
St. Marys	Perth	Smith & White	4000
Stratford	Perth	G. W. Lawrence & Son.	8000
St. Thomas	Elgin	MacDougall & Robertson	13000
Toronto	**York**	**John Leys** Manager Branch Office, No. 18 Court street.	**120000**
Trenton	Hastings	Forbes & Hilton †*A. L. MacLellan.*	3000
Walkerton	Bruce	A. B. Klein	2500
Walkerville	Essex	See Windsor	200
Welland	Welland	See St. Catharines	2800
Whitby	Ontario	J. K. Gordon	3500
Windsor	Essex	J. H. Wilkinson	8500
Woodstock	Oxford	Bird & Martin	5000

Prince Edward Island.

POST-OFFICE.	COUNTY.	ATTORNEYS.	POPUL'N.
Charlottetown	Queens	McLean & Martin	12000
Souris	Kings	See Charlottetown	1000
Summerside	Prince	McLeod, Morson & McQuarrie	3000

(† We withdraw our former recommendation.)

Quebec.

Parties corresponding with Attorneys named in the Directory should ALWAYS sign themselves "Subscribers to J. A. GRAFT & CO.'S LEGAL DIRECTORY." Should any Attorney fail to give prompt attention to correspondence, collections or business intrusted to his care, we will be thankful to patrons of the Directory to notify us promptly in any such case.

POST-OFFICE.	COUNTY.	ATTORNEYS.	POPUL'N.
Arthabaskaville	Arthabaska.	See Quebec	1000
Aylmer	Ottawa	Thomas P. Foran	2000
Beauharnois	Beauharnois	L. A. Seers	2000
Granby	Shefford	See Waterloo	1200
Hull	Ottawa	Henry A. Goyette	7000
Joliette	Joliette	L. A. McConville	3500
Montmagny	Montmagny	P. Aug. Choquette	1800
Montreal	**Hochelaga**	**Lacoste, Globensky, Bisaillon & Brosseau**	**200000**
Nelsonville	Brome & Missisquoi	See Waterloo	1000
Quebec	**Quebec**	**Andrews, Caron, Andrews & Pentland**	**75000**
Rock Island	Stanstead	H. M. Hovey	1000
Sherbrooke	Sherbrooke	Ives, Brown & French	7000
Sorel	Richelieu	C. J. C. Wurtele.	6000
St. Andrews	Argenteuil	J. A. N. McKay	1200
St. Hyacinthe	St. Hyacinthe	R. E. Fontaine	5500
St. Johns	St. Johns	Paradis & Chasse	5000
St. Scholastique	Two Mountains	Provost & Mathieu	1000
Three Rivers	Three Rivers	P. N. Martel	10000
Waterloo	Shefford	D. Darby	1800

English Probate Practice a Specialty.

TO OBTAIN COPIES OF WILLS.

The fee to search for a will, if date of testator's death is given within two years, is $25. If that can not be done, the fee is $3 for each year searched after two years. Copies of wills obtained in England, Scotland and Ireland. Copies of wills, 50 cents a folio extra. We have correspondents in every large city in England, Ireland and Scotland.

Prepared expressly for J. A. Graft & Co.'s Legal Directory, by Henry Melville Walker, of New York, late Solicitor of Her Majesty's High Court of Justice, England and Ireland.

NOTE.—In cases where there are two or more deponents to one affidavit, *each* must be named in the jurat, except that if the affidavit of all the deponents is taken at one time by the same officer, it is sufficient to state that it was sworn by both (or all) of the "above named" deponents; and so, also, where two or more of several parties execute a deed, their names must be specified in the attestation clause. In wills, the testator must always be referred to either by name or as "the said testator" in the attestation clause; indeed, the double reference is often adopted.

FORMS OF JURATS.

CHANCERY AND COMMON LAW DIVISIONS.

FOR ONE DEPONENT.

Sworn at the Royal Courts of Justice this —— day of ——, 188—, before me,
—— ——,
Class Clerk in the Filing and Record Department. (Central Office.)

FOR TWO DEPONENTS.

Sworn by both the deponents, A. B. and C. D., at, etc. (as above).
If there be more than two deponents sworn at the same time, they must each be named in the jurat.

WHEN SWORN IN COUNTRY.

Sworn at Portsmouth, in the County of Hants, this —— day of ——, 18—, before me,
C. F.,
A Commissioner to administer oaths in the Supreme Court of Judicature in England.

WHERE DEPONENT IS A MARKSMAN.

At the end of the jurat, and before signing it, add these words: "This affidavit having been first read over by me [or *in my presence*] to the above named A. B., who seemed perfectly to understand the same, and who made —— mark thereto in my presence."
Before me, ——.

WHERE DEPONENT IS BLIND.

Sworn by the deponent, A. B., at —, this day of —, the witness to the mark [or signature] of the said deponent having been first sworn that he had truly, distinctly, and audibly read over the contents of this affidavit to the said deponent, he being blind, and that he saw him make his mark [or sign his name] thereto. (See above Hand-book, page 35, as to witness), etc. Before me, ——.

These forms can be used in bankruptcy proceedings also.

DIVORCE AND MATRIMONIAL CAUSES.

Sworn in Her Majesty's High Court of Justice, at Westminster Hall, in the County of Middlesex, this — day of —, 18—. Before me, ——.

By 21 and 22 Vic., c. 108, s. 12, Registrars, Surrogates, Commissioners for taking oaths in the Court of Chancery, and "all other persons now or hereafter authorized to administer oaths under 20 and 21 Vic., c. 77, or under this Act," shall have power to administer oaths under 20 and 21 Vic., c. 85 (the Divorce and Matrimonial Causes Act) —. But see Sec. 82 of Judicature Act, 1873.

ATTESTATIONS.

TO A WILL.

Signed and acknowledged by the said A. B., the testator, as and for his last will and testament, in the joint presence of us, who, before leaving his presence, or the presence of each other, have hereunto subscribed our names as witnesses.

WHERE TESTATOR IS A MARKSMAN.

Signed by the said A. B., the testator (by his making his mark thereto, he having declared to us that the above will had been read over to him by Mr. C. F., of Portsmouth, solicitor, and that he had a perfect knowledge of its contents), etc., etc.

TO DEEDS.

Signed, sealed, and delivered by the within named [or said, or above named] A. B., in the presence of —, etc.

Signature is usually not essential to a deed, to render the same operative; the act of sealing is so, however.

ATTESTATION TO A WARRANT OF ATTORNEY.

Signed, sealed, and delivered by the above named A. B., in my presence; and I declare myself to be solicitor for the said A. B., and that I subscribe my name as such solicitor.

C. F.,
Solicitor for the said A. B.

TABLE
OF
DISTRIBUTION OF INTESTATES' ESTATES

Under 3 & 4 Wm. IV., c. 106; 22 & 23 Car. II., c. 10; 29 Car. II., c. 30; and 1 Jac. II., c. 17.

Customs of London and York and other places are now abolished, so far as they affect *personal* property of persons dying after 31st December, 1856 (19 and 20 Vic., c. 94); but the customs of Gavelkind and Borough English still affect *real* property in certain localities, the former principally in County Kent.

The following is a short table showing how property is distributed in cases where the owner dies entitled in his own right, without having made a will or settlement; the fourth column also shows what persons would be entitled to letters of administration entitling them to the right of receiving and distributing the personal estate.

N. B.—In each instance it is supposed there are no nearer relations than those named.

If a person die leaving	*LAND—Real Property (except leaseholds) would descend*	*MONEY—Personal Property (including leaseholds) would be divided*	*Persons entitled to administration*
Wife and no relations	One-third to wife for life, rest to the Crown if the deceased had the legal estate (copyholds to the lord of the manor (*Note A*)	Half to wife, rest to the Crown	Wife
Wife and father......	One-third to wife for life, rest to father if the deceased had acquired the fee by purchase and not by descent (*Note A*)	Equally	Wife
Wife and mother....	One-third to wife for life, rest to mother in default of any heirs on father's side (*Note A*)	Equally (*Keilway v. Keilway*, 2 *P. Wms.* 344)	Wife
Wife, father, brothers and sisters	One-third to wife for life, rest to father if the deceased had acquired the fee by purchase and not by descent (*Note A*)	Equally between wife and father	Wife
Wife, mother, brothers and sisters, whether by whole or half blood	One-third to wife for life, rest to eldest brother, by whole blood (*Note A*)	Half to wife, rest equally divided between mother, brothers and sisters	Wife
Wife, mother, nephews and nieces (children of deceased brother)	One-third to wife for life, rest to nephew (eldest son of brother) or nieces (daughters of deceased brother if he left no son (*Note A*)	Half to wife, one-fourth to mother, rest between nephews and nieces (*Stanley v. Stanley*, 1 *Atk.*)	Wife

If a person die leaving	*LAND — Real Property (except leaseholds) would descend*	*MONEY — Personal Property (including leaseholds) would be divided*	*Persons entitled to administration*
Wife, brothers and sisters	One-third to wife for life, rest to eldest brother (*Note A*)	Half to wife, rest equally to brothers and sisters	Wife
Wife, sons and daughters (*Note C*)	One-third to wife for life, rest to eldest son (*Note A*)	One-third to wife, rest equally among sons and daughters	Wife
Wife and daughter (*Note C*)	One-third to wife for life, rest to daughter (*Note A*)	One-third to wife, rest to daughter	Wife
Wife and daughters (*Note C*)	One-third to wife for life, rest equally between daughters (*Note A*)	One-third to wife, rest equally between daughters	Wife
Wife and grandchildren (sons of deceased son)	One-third to wife for life, rest to eldest grandchild (*Note A*)	One-third to wife, rest equally between grandchildren	Wife
Husband (where there has been issue born alive capable of inheriting the realty)	All for life, afterwards to heir at law (*Note B*)	All (*Note E*)..........	Husband
Husband (where there has not been issue born alive capable of inheriting the realty)	To heir at law.......	All to husband (*Note E*)	Husband
Husband, sons and daughters	All to husband for life, afterwards to eldest son (*Note B*)	All to husband (*Note E*)	Husband
Husband and child (son or daughter)	All to husband for life, afterwards to child (*Note B*)	All to husband (*Note E*)	Husband
Husband and daughters	All to husband for life, afterwards to daughters equally (*Note B*)	All to husband (*Note E*)	Husband
Husband and grandchildren (daughters of deceased son or daughter)	All to husband for life, afterwards to grandchildren equally (*Note B*)	All to husband (*Note E*)	Husband
Sons and daughters, whether by one or more wife or wives, and whether or not posthumous	All to eldest son....	Equally divided (*Wallis v. Hodson.* 2 *Atk.* 117)	Either son or daughter, or any number not exceeding three of either or both
One child, either son or daughter	All..................	All..................	Child
Daughters...........	Equally divided.....	Equally divided.....	Either or any number of them not exceeding three
Younger son and grandchild (son or daughter of eldest son)	All to grandchild....	Equally divided.....	Younger son

If a person die leaving	*LAND—Real Property (except leaseholds) would descend*	*MONEY—Personal Property (including leaseholds) would be divided*	*Persons entitled to administration*
Eldest son, sons and daughters, and grandchildren	All to eldest son.....	Equally divided (but grandchildren only take deceased parent's share equally between them)	To any son or daughter, or any number not exceeding three of either or both
Daughters and grandchild (son or daughter of deceased son)	All to grandchild....	Equally..............	To any daughter, or any number of them not exceeding three
Daughters and granddaughters (children of deceased son)	All to granddaughters	Equally (but granddaughters only take their father's share between them)	To any daughter, or any number of them not exceeding three
Daughters and grandchildren (sons and daughters of deceased daughter)	Equally between daughters and eldest son of deceased daughter	Equally (but grandchildren only take their parent's share equally between them)	To any daughter, or any number of them not exceeding three
Grandchildren (sons and daughters of two sons and daughter)	All to grandson, eldest son of eldest son	Equally (*per capita, i.e.*, in their own right) (*Walsh v. Walsh*, 1 *Eq. Cas. Abr.* 249 *pl.* 7—*S. C. Prec. Chan.* 74)	To any grandchild, or any number of them not exceeding three
Grandchildren (daughters of a son and sons of a daughter)	All to granddaughters equally	Equally *per capita*...	To any grandchild or any number of them not exceeding three
Grandchildren (sons and daughters of a daughter, and daughters of another daughter)	Half to eldest son of one daughter, and half equally between daughters of other daughter	Equally *per capita*...	To any grandchild or any number of them not exceeding three
Deceased son's widow and child (*Bridge v. Abbott*, 3 *Bro. C. C.* 226)	All to child..........	All to child..........	Child
Grandchild and great-grandchild, elder branch	Great-grandchild	Equally..............	Grandchild
Father and mother and brothers and sister	All to father.........	All to father.........	Father
Mother and brothers and sisters	All to eldest brother	Equally..............	Mother
Mother and sister...	All to sister..........	Equally..............	Mother
Mother only.........	All (in default of any heirs on father's side)	All....................	Mother
Sisters and nephews and nieces (children of deceased brother)	All to nephew (eldest son of deceased brother)	Equally, but nephews and nieces take *per stirpes* (*i.e.* their deceased parent's share)	To one or more of the sisters, not exceeding three

If a person die leaving	*LAND — Real Property (except leaseholds) would descend*	*MONEY— Personal Property (including leaseholds) would be divided*	*Persons entitled to administration*
Sisters and nieces (children of deceased brother)	All to nieces equally	Equally, but nieces take *per stirpes*	To one or more of the sisters, not exceeding three
Sisters and nephews and nieces (children of deceased sister)	Equally between sisters and nephew (eldest son of deceased sister)	Equally, but nephews and nieces take *per stirpes*	To one or more of the sisters, not exceeding three
Sisters and nieces (children of deceased sister)	Equally, but nieces take *per stirpes*	Equally, but nieces take *per stirpes*	To one or more of the sisters, not exceeding three
Brother or sister of whole blood, and brother or sister of half blood on father's side, and brother or sister of half blood on mother's side	All to brother or sister of whole blood	Equally..............	Either or both
Brother or sister of the half blood on father's side, and distant cousin on father's side	All to half-brother or sister	All to half-brother or sister	Brother or sister of half blood
Brother or sister of the half blood on mother's side, and distant cousin on father's side	All to distant cousin on father's side	All to half-brother or sister	Brother or sister of half blood
Brothers and sisters and grandfather or grandmother	All to eldest brother	Equally between brothers and sisters (*Evelyn v. Evelyn*, 3 *Atk.* 762)	To one or more of brothers and sisters, not exceeding three
Nephews and nieces by deceased brother, and nephews and nieces by deceased sister	All to eldest nephew (son of deceased brother)	Equally *per capita* (*i.e.* shared equally without reference to the number of each family)	To either of the nephews or nieces, or any number of one or both not exceeding three
Niece by deceased brother, and nephews and nieces by deceased sister	All to niece (daughter of deceased brother)	Equally *per capita*...	To either of the nephews or nieces, or any number of one or both not exceeding three
Nieces by deceased brother, and nephews and nieces by deceased sister	All to nieces (daughters of deceased brother)	Equally *per capita*...	To either of the nephews or nieces, or any number of one or both not exceeding three
Nephews and nieces by one deceased sister, and nieces by another deceased sister	Half to eldest nephew by one deceased sister, and half equally between nieces by other deceased sister	Equally *per capita*...	To either of the nephews or nieces, or any number of one or both not exceeding three

If a person die leaving	*LAND—Real Property (except leaseholds) would descend*	*MONEY—Personal Property (including leaseholds) would be divided*	*Persons entitled to administration*
Nephew (son of deceased sister) and great niece (granddaughter of deceased brother)	Great niece..........	Nephew (*Pett v. Pett*, 1 Salk. 250)	Nephew
Niece (brother or sister's daughter) and great nephew (eldest brother's grandson)	All to great nephew, eldest brother's grandson	All to niece, brother's or sister's daughter	Niece
Father's father or mother, and mother's father or mother	All to father's father or mother	Equally (*Moor v. Badham, cited in Blackborough v. Davis, P. Wms.* 53)	To either or both
Grandfather, great-grandfather, uncle and aunt on father's side, and grand father, uncle and aunt on mother's side	All to grandfather on father's side	Equally between two grandfathers	To either or both grandfathers
Grandfather on mother's side, and uncle or aunt on father's side	All to uncle or aunt	All to grandfather...	Grandfather
Grandmother, uncle or aunt (all on same side)	All to uncle or aunt	All to grandmother (*Mentney v. Petty, Prec. Chan.* 593)	Grandmother
Grandmother on father's side, and uncle or aunt on mother's side	All to grandmother	All to grandmother (*Mentney v. Petty, Prec. Chan.* 593)	Grandmother
Great-grandfather, uncles and aunts on father's side	All to eldest uncle	Equally *per capita* (*Loyd v. Tench*, 2 *Ves. Sen.* 215)	To either or any number not exceeding three of either or both
Uncles and aunts on mother's side, and nephews (sons of deceased sister) and nieces (daughters of a deceased brother)	Equally between nieces, daughters of brothers	Equally *per capita*..	To either or any number not exceeding three of either or both
Uncles and aunts on father's side, and uncles and aunts on mother's side	All to eldest uncle on father's side	Equally among them	To either or any number not exceeding three of either or both
Aunts on father's side, and uncles or aunts on mother's side	All equally to aunts on father's side	Equally among them	To either or any number not exceeding three of either or both
Cousins.............	The eldest son of the deceased father's eldest brother (or according to heirship, as the case may be)	Equally *per capita*..	To either or any number not exceeding three of either or both

If a person die leaving	*LAND — Real Property (except leaseholds) would descend*	*MONEY — Personal Property (including leaseholds) would be divided*	*Persons entitled to administration*
Uncle on mother's side, and cousin (son of another uncle on father's side)	All to cousin........	All to uncle.........	Uncle
No relations.........	All to the Crown (copyholds would go to the Lord of the Manor)	All to the Crown...	To the Crown, or to a redictor, should he apply

Note A.—The wife is only entitled to the third of the gross rental of the real estate for life as her dower, but in most cases this is barred, rather as a matter of form by lawyers than for any other reason, and she then takes no interest in the real estate.

Note B.—This only applies to real estate in possession; the husband would take no benefit from his wife's reversionary interests in real estate.

Note C.—Children who have had advances from the *father* in the lifetime are to bring them into account.

Note D.—The above table to successions to real property does not extend to the decease of any person dying before 1st January, 1834, nor to Gravelkind lands in Kent and other places, nor to land held subject to Borough English custom, nor to Copyholds, nor to Estates Tail.

Note E.—The husband is entitled by canon law right, and not under the Statute of Distributions. He would, therefore, be excluded from taking any share of his wife's effects if given by any deed or will to "her next of kin" at her decease.—Milne v. Gilbert, L. J. vol. 23, N. S. Chy. 828.

NOTE.

We will also furnish, for $5 each, the title of any English Act from William I. to the present time, giving the part or parts of England to which each Act applies—for instances:

Wills, Amd. Law of, 7 W. 4 & 1 Vict., ch. 26; Act amd. 15 & 16 Vict., ch. 24; also amd. 24 and 25 Vict., ch. 114, 121.

Intestate Personal Estate, governed by 39 & 40 Vict., ch. 18.

SOLICITORS OF THE SUPREME COURT OF JUDICATURE.

ENGLAND.

London. Middlesex County.

Field, Roscoe & Co., 36 Lincoln's Inn Falls.
Arnold & Co., 60 Carey St., Lincoln's Inn.
Needham, F., 10 New Inn, Strand,

	POST-TOWN.	COUNTY.
Davies, John F.	Aberavor	Glamorganshire.
Challenor & Son	Abingdon	Berkshire.
Ford, Loyd & Bartlett	Abingdon	Berkshire.
New, Herbert	Alcester	Warwickshire.
Firth, H. M.	Ashburton	Devonshire.
Childs, R. W., & Brother	Ashburton	Devonshire.
Marshall, W.	Ashton-under-Tyne	Lancaster.
Day, F. G.	Bunbury	Oxfordshire.
Field, Roscoe & Co.	Bunbury	Oxfordshire.
Cumberland, John	Bath	Somersetshire.
Barton, Smith & Pinscut	Birmingham	Warwickshire.
Taylor, Jeffery & Little	Bradford	Yorkshire.
Veale, E. W.	Bristol	Bristol.
Christmas, J. S.	Cambridge	Cambridgeshire.
Wightwick, W. N.	Canterbury	Kent.
Ince, Francis	Cardiff	Glamorganshire.
Harris, G. H.	Exeter	Devonshire.
Whitcombe & Gardom	Gloucester	Gloucestershire.
Rollet, A.	Hull	Hull.
Hepherd, W. H.	Leek	Staffordshire.
Atkinson, J. W.	Leeds	Yorkshire.
Gill & Archer	Liverpool	Lancashire.
Dismore, T. G.	Liverpool	Lancashire.
Atkinson, Saunders & Co.	Manchester	Lancashire.
Barker, J. W.	New-Castle-upon-Tyne	Northumberland.
Lawrence, E.	Newport	Monmouthshire.
Fosters, Burroughes & Robberds	Norwich	Norwich.
Taylor, H. R.	Oxford	Oxfordshire.
Ashington, H.	Sheffield	Yorkshire.
Everett, J. E.	Stafford	Staffordshire.
Draper, J. H.	Stockton-on-Tees	Durham.
Evans, D	Towyn	Merwuthshire Wales
Dale, R. A.	Walsall	Staffordshire.
Prior, J.	Wolverhampton	Staffordshire.
Leeman, G.	York	Yorkshire.

IRELAND.

J. L. & W. Scallan, 17 Bachelor Wall, Dublin.
Dickson, Alex, 17 Chichester St., Belfast.
Babington, D. R..........Londonderry.
Babington, Thomas.......Cork.
Smyth, James...........Drogheda.
Moore, Wm. H. D.........Lurgan.
Rogers, William R........Dundalk, Galway.

SCOTLAND.

Marwick, D............. Glasgow.
Smith, Doig & Lawse .....Edinborough.
Gordon, William..........Aberdeen.

WEST INDIES.

Burke, S. Constantine.....Kingston....... ....Jamaica.
Hendrick, Thomas.... .Kingston...............Jamaica.

AUSTRALIA.

Mann, Hon. Charles.......Adelaide...... ....South Australia.
Southerland, R. A........Victoria.

NATAL.

Gallwey, M. H............Natal ....Africa.

NEW ZEALAND.

Reid, W. S., Solicitor General, Auckland.

W. F. EILAND,

Attorney at Law,

MACON, MISS.

JAMES G. LEACH,

Attorney at Law and Solicitor in Chancery,

NATCHEZ, MISS.

Practices in the Courts at Natchez, Miss., and Vidalia, La., and in the Supreme Courts of both States.

O. G. McGUIRE,

Attorney at Law,

ROSEDALE, BOLIVAR CO., MISSISSIPPI.

ATTORNEY FOR COUNTY TREASURER.

REFERENCE: Any of Court Officers.

H. E. MILLS. P. R. FLITCRAFT.

MILLS & FLITCRAFT,

Attorneys and Counselors at Law,

509 CLIVE STREET, ST. LOUIS, MO.

Commercial Law and Collections a Specialty. Practice in all the State and Federal Courts.

REFERENCES: St. Louis—St. Louis National Bank; Provident Savings Bank; Hon. W. H. Stone, President St. Louis Hot Pressed Nut and Bolt Mfg. Co.; Morris, Butt & Co.; Winning, Hagey & Co.; M. J. Murphy Furnishing Goods Co.; Southern Barbed Wire Co.; Kendall Bayle Cracker Co. Cincinnati—J. A. Graft & Co.; Van Antwerp, Bragg & Co.; Procter & Gamble. Chicago—First National Bank; Walkup, Fisher & Co.; Campbell Printing Press and Mfg. Co. Pittsburgh—D. F. Agnew & Co. Philadelphia—Fleisher Bros.; Blumenthal Bros. & Co. New York—Kidder, Peabody & Co.; Devlin & Co.; Hammerslough Bros; A. D. Napier & Co.; Robert K. Davies & Co.; Morrison & Hutchinson; Campbell Printing Press and Mfg. Co. Boston—Edward Russell & Co. General Reference—R. G. Dun & Co., at their various offices.

ROBT. H. ROGERS. A. M. HARRIS.

ROGERS & HARRIS,

ATTORNEYS AT LAW,

NO. 423 AUSTIN AVENUE,

Notaries Public. WACO, TEXAS.

M. L. WALTON. S. A. WALTON.

WALTON & BRO.

ATTORNEYS AT LAW,

LURAY, VIRGINIA.

M. L. Walton practices in the Court of Appeals, U. S. District Court, and Courts of Shenandoah County.

Collection of Claims a specialty. Best of references furnished on application.

JAMES B. MENAGER,

ATTORNEY AT LAW,

POINT PLEASANT, WEST VIRGINIA,

Prosecuting Attorney.

REFERENCE:

President of the Merchants National Bank, Point Pleasant.

GEO. McLAURIN, B. A., LL. B.

BARRISTER, ETC.

Prompt attention to all collections in Ottawa District,

OFFICE, 19 ELGIN STREET,

OTTAWA, ONTARIO, CANADA.

www.ingramcontent.com/pod-product-compliance
Lightning Source LLC
Chambersburg PA
CBHW030909270326
41929CB00008B/624